Cornell University Library

Garrett Biblical Institute
In exchange

The date shows when this volume was taken.
To renew this book copy the call No. and give to the librarian.

HOME USE RULES

All Books subject to Recall

All borrowers must register in the library to borrow books for home use.

All books must be returned at end of college year for inspection and repairs.

Limited books must be returned within the four week limit and not renewed.

Students must return all books before leaving town. Officers should arrange for the return of books wanted during their absence from town.

Volumes of periodicals and of pamphlets are held in the library as much as possible. For special purposes they are given out for a limited time.

Borrowers should not use their library privileges for the benefit of other persons.

Books of special value and gift books, when the giver wishes it, are not allowed to circulate.

Readers are asked to report all cases of books marked or mutilated.

Do not deface books by marks and writing.

Cornell University Library
BX8481.B8 S22

Old Sands Street Methodist Episcopal Chu

3 1924 029 471 459

olin

CAPT. THOMAS WEBB.
Pioneer Methodist Preacher in Brooklyn.

OLD SANDS STREET

METHODIST EPISCOPAL CHURCH,

OF

BROOKLYN, N. Y.

AN ILLUSTRATED CENTENNIAL RECORD,

HISTORICAL AND BIOGRAPHICAL.

BY

THE REV EDWIN WARRINER,

Corresponding Secretary of the New York East Conference Historical Society.

WITH AN INTRODUCTION

BY

THE REV. ALBERT S. HUNT, D. D.

NEW YORK:
PUBLISHED FOR THE AUTHOR BY
PHILLIPS & HUNT, 805 BROADWAY.
1885.

Copyright 1885, by
REV. EDWIN WARRINER,
NEW YORK.

PREFACE.

There is much in the history of every church, and in the life-story of each individual Christian to illustrate and magnify the grace of God. A short time before that eloquent minister of Jesus Christ, Thomas Sewall, rose in rapture to the upper skies," he said to a friend: "I reckon that most of the literature of heaven will be the storied illustration of divine wisdom and goodness in the experience of poor, saved sinners. O my God! on those bright shelves of marvels, far down and obscure, yet there may a little tract be found, entitled, 'How it pleased God through Jesus Christ, his Son, to save soul of Thomas Sewall.'"

While it is neither possible nor needful that there should be in this world such impartial, unerring, and all-comprehending records as heaven will disclose, when "we shall know even as also we are known," yet in my opinion, we might and should possess a carefully prepared history of the work of the people of God in each particular locality, and at least a brief record of the lives of the ministers and members of every church. This desirable work I have accomplished in the case of one of the older and more prominent societies of our Methodism. The history of Old Sands Street Church for about one hundred years, including a roll of all the ministers, officers, etc., is condensed into nine brief chapters, so that the far greater part of this work is biographical. About four score and ten pastors and presiding elders, most of whom are deceased, have by appointment of the authorities ministered to this church. To the carefully written biographies of these preachers I have added as complete an account as I could give of the nineteen hundred members whose names are found in the books. A friend, referring to the large number of memorials of eminent men here grouped about the history of one local church, with characteristic humor remarked, "It seems like hanging a very heavy weight on a very small nail."

It will require but a brief paragraph to explain how this work came to be written. Having undertaken some years since to prepare a history of Methodism in Suffolk County, N. Y., I found that it would be well-nigh impossible to make a satisfactory history of the church within that small territory, which in the earlier days formed only a part of a large and well defined circuit, namely the whole of Long Island. I then formed the purpose to prepare a Cyclopedia of Long Island Methodism, containing an account of every circuit and of every local church, (including sketches of the founders and prominent members,) also of every pastor and presiding elder—a work as yet incomplete, but on which a large amount of labor has been bestowed. Searching for facts on the west end of Long Island, especially concerning Brooklyn Methodism, I had soon accumulated so much material appertaining to the mother of Brooklyn Methodist churches, that I was almost compelled to make a separate volume, entitled *Old Sands Street Church*. The prospect of the speedy abandonment of the original site so long and so successfully held by Methodism in Brooklyn, gave additional interest to the subject. The official board and many friends of the church and of the pastors expressed their hearty approval of my purpose, and this encouragement held me to my task when its accomplishment seemed almost impossible.

To one engaged in such researches it becomes painfully apparent that many noble ministers and laymen have passed away, of whose services the church has preserved no suitable memorial. On the other hand, after attempting to "count the dust of Jacob, or number the fourth part of Israel" within even a small territory, one just begins to realize how truly "the world itself could not contain the books," if memoirs of all the saints were recorded.

It is not an easy task to prepare memorials of persons long since dead, about whom little or no timely record has been made. Dr. Abel Stevens writes thus concerning this kind of literary labor: "The private correspondence, the collection of documents, the harmonization of conflicting statements, the grouping of events, lacking often the most essential connecting links, the portraiture of characters historically important, but almost totally obscured in undeserved oblivion, present embarrassments which may well constrain the writer to throw down his pen in despair."

A very few of the prominent ministers, whose life history is here given, turned aside from the right way. To have exhibited only the better side of their lives and characters, would have been to write romance, and not history or biography; therefore, the two or three who fell, are set forth as admonitory beacons. In this I follow the example of the chief historians of our Church, who record the backslidings of good and eminent men, and their lapse into crime.

I have written, and here inserted, scores of memorials of the deceased wives of the preachers. This has cost a great deal of personal inquiry and correspondence, since comparatively little note has been made of them in the annals of our Church.

In another direction my toil has been rewarded, namely, the diligent research concerning the posterity of the preachers, and the early members of old Sands Street Church, whereby I have been able to illustrate one important truth concerning the righteous, that " his seed is blessed." It may prove not a little instructive to observe how much stronger in some families of Methodist preachers and laymen, than in others, is the attachment to our own denomination, and to study the reasons for that difference.

It has been my aim to be accurate as to facts, names, dates, etc.; but the mass of details is so great, and the chances for mistakes are so many, that it cannot, by any means, be supposed that I have avoided all errors. No known source of information has been neglected. I have made use of all the available books containing the data required, besides innumerable newspapers, magazines, inscriptions on gravestones, manuscript journals, letters from hundreds of correspondents, and testimonies of hundreds of old people, many of whom have fallen asleep since my interview with them. In the foot-notes and in the body of the work I have given due credit to a large number of authorities.

The portraits and other illustrations, to the number of eighty-six, have been obtained through much trouble and expense, but they certainly add greatly to the value of the work. Of the eighty-nine pastors and presiding elders, twenty-five died leaving no likenesses, at least none that can now be found. Portraits of twelve others are omitted, contrary to my earnest desire and solicitation. Upward of eighty interesting autograph signatures are herein reproduced. A few of those desired I have been unable to find.

It is scarcely necessary to refer to the literary character of this work. The aim has been to put on record certain valuable facts in as direct and concise a form as possible, even at the sacrifice of an elegant and graceful style.

The researching and the writing have been a labor of love, and with a consciousness of having attempted to perform a real service for the Methodist Episcopal Church, I now submit to the reader this imperfect fruit of my labor, in the hope that the reminiscences I have preserved will fill the mind of many an aged Christian with bright pictures of the past, and wake the

"Echoes that start
When memory plays an old tune on the heart."

I trust, also, that these pages will serve as a source of instruction and inspiration to the middle-aged and the young, as they are hereby reminded how "other men labored," and we have "entered into their labors." And not a little satisfaction is afforded by the hope that, possibly, future writers concerning Methodism, will find in this volume a permanent record of valuable facts that would otherwise have been forever lost in oblivion.

E. WARRINER.

CLINTON, CONN., *February*, 1885.

ILLUSTRATIONS.

		PAGE
1.	Thomas Webb....................................Frontispiece.	
2.	Woolman Hickson Preaching his First Sermon in Brooklyn—opposite	6
3.	A Portion of Sands-street church-yard........................	11
4.	Brooklyn in 1798...	12
5.	Old White Church...	16
6.	Kirk's Printing-office ....opposite	18
7.	Old Sands-street Church...................................... "	27
8.	Sunday-school Certificate of Admission.......................	28
9.	Parsonage and Sunday-school Building on High-street..........	29
10.	Sands-street Church—Interior View...........................	40
11.	Rev. Freeborn Garrettson..........................opposite	69
12.	Rev. Henry Willis.. "	76
13.	Rev. Thomas Morrell.. "	79
14.	Rev. William Phœbus... "	91
15.	Rev. Aaron Hunt.. "	100
16.	Rev. Ezekiel Cooper.. "	123
17.	Rev. George Roberts.. "	133
18.	Rev. William Thacher... "	156
19.	Rev. Samuel Merwin... "	164
20.	Rev. Elijah Woolsey.. "	179
21.	Rev. Daniel Ostrander.. "	187
22.	Rev. Reuben Hubbard.. "	192
23.	Rev. Lewis Pease...	197
24.	Rev. William Ross.................................opposite	206
25.	Rev. Nathan Bangs, D.D....................................... "	211
26.	Rev. Alexander M'Caine.......................................	216
27.	Rev. Peter P. Sandford, D.D.......................opposite	225
28.	Rev. Henry Chase, A.M.. "	229
29.	Rev. Laban Clark, D.D.. "	232
30.	Rev. Stephen L. Stillman.....................................	244
31.	Rev. Samuel Luckey, D.D...........................opposite	247
32.	Rev. Seymour Landon.. "	252
33.	Rev. Noah Levings, D.D....................................... "	258
34.	Rev. James Covel, Jr., A.M................................... "	263
35.	Rev. John C. Green...	268
36.	Rev. Charles W. Carpenter....................................	271
37.	Rev. John C. Tackaberry...........................opposite	275
38.	Rev. John Kennaday, D.D...................................... "	279
39.	Rev. John Luckey...	283
40.	Rev. Bartholomew Creagh ....opposite	288

			PAGE
41.	Rev. William H. Norris	opposite	296
42.	Rev. Fitch Reed, D.D.		300
43.	Rev. Stephen Martindale	opposite	304
44.	Rev John J. Matthias	"	319
45.	Rev. John B. Merwin, D.D.	"	325
46.	Rev. John W. B. Wood	"	328
47.	Rev. Henry J. Fox, D.D	"	331
48.	Rev. Levi S. Weed, D.D	"	334
49.	Rev. Buel Goodsell	"	339
50.	Rev. Wilbur F. Watkins, D.D.	"	344
51.	Rev. Bernard H. Nadal, D.D	"	351
52.	Rev. Daniel Curry, D.D., LL.D.	"	357
53.	Rev. Charles Fletcher	"	360
54.	Rev. Benjamin Pillsbury, D.D.	"	365
55.	Rev. Bishop Edward G. Andrews, D.D., LL.D.	"	369
56.	Rev. Edwin E. Griswold, D.D.	"	373
57.	Rev. Thomas G. Osborn, A.M	"	389
58.	Rev. Freeman P. Tower, A.M.	"	394
59.	Rev. George Taylor	"	397
60.	Rev. John S. Breckinridge, A.M	"	401
61.	Rev. Ichabod Simmons, A.M	"	405
62.	Memorial of Jacob Brown		416
63.	Rev. Daniel De Vinne	opposite	424
64.	Hon. John Dikeman		430
65.	John Garrison		437
66.	John E. Hanford		440
67.	Joseph Wesley Harper	opposite	441
68.	Memorial of J. Wesley Harper		443
69.	Joseph Herbert		446
70.	Aaron Kingsland		451
71.	Rev. Robert M. Lockwood	opposite	456
72.	Rev. William M'Allister	"	459
73.	Andrew Mercein		463
74.	Susanna Moser		467
75.	Joseph Moser		468
76.	Hon. Moses F. Odell	opposite	470
77.	Memorial of M. F. Odell		471
78.	Mary Powers		475
79.	William I. Preston	opposite	476
80.	Rev. Elnathan Raymond	"	479
81.	Rev. Marvin Richardson, D.D.		483
82.	Thomas Sands		488
83.	Rev. Nicholas Snethen		492
84.	Robert Snow		496
85.	Memorial of the Summerfields		507
86.	George J. Vining		526

CONTENTS.

INTRODUCTION, ... Pages 1-4

BOOK I.
HISTORICAL RECORD.

CHAPTER I.

A RECORD OF TEN YEARS; 1787—1796.

A Pioneer Church—Capt. Webb and the First Methodist Sermon—Woolman Hickson—Sermon in the Street—Peter Cannon's Cooper-shop—Class formed—Date decisively Ascertained—Thomas Foster, First Presiding Elder—John Dickins—Brooklyn an Outpost of New York Station—Henry Willis, Elder—Freeborn Garrettson joins Dickins in New York—Thomas Morrell, Elder, with Garrettson—Robert Cloud, John Merrick and William Phœbus in New York and Brooklyn—J. B. Matthias visits Brooklyn—David Kendall appointed to Long Island in 1790—Reinforced by Wm. Phœbus and Aaron Hunt—Jacob Brush, Presiding Elder—Brooklyn becomes a part of Long Island Circuit—Small Class—Services in Private Dwellings—Benj. Abbott and his Colleague on Long Island—Brooklyn Sinners crying for Mercy—Accessions—Few Foot-prints remain—The Record on High—Other Pastors; Brush, Ragan, Boyd, Totten and Strebeck—Nicholas Snethen, a Class Leader in Brooklyn—Church Incorporated—First Trustees—First Church Edifice—Sermon by Bishop Asbury—Ezekiel Cooper and Lawrence M'Combs, New Preachers in New York and Brooklyn—George Roberts, Presiding Elder—Brooklyn a Station—First Stationed Preacher—Thirty-five Members—Gradual Growth 5—11

CHAPTER II.

A RECORD OF TEN YEARS; 1797—1806.

A French Artist and his Picture of Brooklyn—Sylvester Hutchinson, Presiding Elder—Andrew Nichols and the Oldest Church Register—List of Members to the Year 1800—Hannah Stryker—First Death—Richard Everitt—Cyrus Stebbins—David Buck—Peter Jayne—Ezekiel Canfield—Church Edifice Enlarged—People Forsaken by a Pastor—Wm. Thacher, Presiding Elder—Samuel Merwin—Preachers' Boarding Place—James Harper—Price of Board—Samuel Thomas—Pastor's House Rent—Joseph Moser, Sexton—His Duties—Salary—Church-yard—Precious Dust—Another Boarding Place—John Garrison—Oliver Sykes . . . . 12—14

CHAPTER III.

A RECORD OF TEN YEARS; 1807-1816

Joseph Crawford—Elijah Woolsey—John Wilson—Death of Mrs. Woolsey—Interesting Marriage Record—Slavery in Brooklyn—Daniel Ostrander—Debt Cancelled—Parsonage Lot Given—Parsonage built—Andrew Mercein, Thomas Kirk and Gerge Smith, Building Committee—Reuben Hubbard—Ebenezer Washburn—Another Pastor leaves his Flock—Amusing Comment—The Station supplied—Thomas Drummond—Old Church, Dimensions—Negroes in the Gallery—The Building moved—New Church Edifice—Remembered as the "Old White Church"—Wm. Thacher's Labors—Asbury in the New Church—Lewis Pease stationed in Brookyn—Health fails—Thomas Drummond, (a second time) Pastor—Samuel Merwin returned—Nathan Emery and Joseph Crawford, Pastors—The Sexton instructed—Candle-light—Boys looked after—Catechism

viii   *Contents.*

taught by Thomas Drummond—List of Learners—Thomas Sands proposes the Establishment of a Sunday-school—Kirk's Printing-office—DeVinne's School-room—Robert Snow, Andrew Mercein, Joseph Herbert, Daniel DeVinne and John G. Murphy, Founders of the Sunday-school—Printed Address—Methodism takes the lead—DeVinne's Description of the School—Children saved from the Street—Wild Boys—Brooklyn Sunday-school Union—Methodists among the First Officers—Union Sunday-school—Held in a District-school Building—Methodist Teachers—James Engles—Richard Cornwell and Wife—John Dikeman and wife—James Herbert. . . . . . . 15—19

CHAPTER IV.

A RECORD OF TEN YEARS; 1817—1820.

Presiding Elders and Pastors—Union Sunday-school—Lack of Teachers—Opposition from Church Members—The School suspended—Resumed after three Years—New Sunday-school Building—Happy New Year—Swarms from the Old Hive—Methodists left alone—Prosperity—Increase of Colored Members—Separate Place of Worship—Still under the Supervision of Sands-street Pastors—"African Asbury Methodist Episcopal Church"—Secession of the Colored People—Quarterly Conference Action—Subsequent Increase of Colored Methodists in Brooklyn—Alexander M'Caine resigns—Henry Chase succeeds him—Lewis Pease's Ministry—Revivals—Camp-meeting at Musketo Cove—Large Increase—Yellow Hook—Class formed—Germ of Bay Ridge Methodism—Original Members—Wm. Ross' Second Term—York-street Church organized—Death of Wm. Ross—M. B. Bull, Supply—Burial of John Summerfield—Thomas Burch and S. L. Stillman, Pastors—Class formed in Red Hook Lane—Gratifying Increase of Members. . . . . 20—23

CHAPTER V.

A RECORD OF TWENTY YEARS; 1827-1846.

S. Luckey, S. L. Stillman and S. Landon, Pastors—Young Men's Missionary Society—Ann Eliza Luckey—Marsden VanCott—Anniversary—S. L. Stillman—Dr. Reese—D. Ostrander, Presiding Elder—N. Levings' and J. Covel's Ministry—Hempstead Harbor Camp-meeting—Revival—Sailors converted—"Grog stopped"—Another Refreshing—John N. Maffit—Committee on Delinquents—J. C. Green, C. W. Carpenter, J. Tackabury, Pastors—Washington-street Church and Parsonage erected—A Circuit with three Churches—Thomas Burch's Second Term—John Kennady—First Annual Conference in Sands-street Church—John Luckey—Property divided—Churches separate—Bartholomew Creagh—Salary $600.00—Church Extension contemplated—Liberal Offer declined—No Steeples allowed—W. H. Norris' First Pastoral Term—Fitch Reed—Another Session of the N. Y. Conference in Sands-street Church—Stephen Martindale, Presiding Elder—Peter C. Oakley—First Board of Stewards—L. M. Vincent's Ministry—Revival—Old White Church demolished—Regretted by the Older Members—New Brick Church Dedication—Sermons by Chas. Pitman, Nathan Bangs, Noah Levings and David Reese—Vote against petitioning for a Favorite Minister—J. J Matthias, Presiding Elder—H. F. Pease, Pastor—N. Bangs, Pastor with J. C. Tackaberry—New Parsonage. 24—28

CHAPTER VI.

A RECORD OF TEN YEARS, 1847-1856.

J. B. Merwin and Dr. Bangs, Pastors—W. H. Norris Pastor a Second Term—Church and Parsonage burned and rebuilt—Building Committee—Sunday School and Class Rooms—Juvenile Missionary Society—Constitution—First Officers—Missionary Festival—Wesley Harper speaks—Ole Bull—Class Names adopted. 29-31

CHAPTER VII.

A RECORD OF TWENTY-EIGHT YEARS; 1857-1884.

Statistics—Large Benevolent Collections—Chaplain M'Cabe—Pastors of this Period—List of Presiding Elders—Holding the Fort—Interesting Anniversaries—Grand Missionary Jubilee—Model Way of Giving—L. S. Weed and D. Terry—Another Festival—Decorations—Musical Instruments—Old Fire Bucket—Henry Ward Beecher's Address—Almost a Century—Ever Young and Vigorous—Growth of the City—East River Bridge—Offer of $125,000 declined—What will become of the Church Organization?—Proposed Combination of Churches not accomplished—The Old Grave Yard—Outlook for Time—Outlook for Eternity—The Itinerant System Illustrated—Ten Thousand Sermons—Hallowed Memories—Unwritten History. 32-40

Contents. ix

CHAPTER VIII.
RECORD OF MINISTERIAL APPOINTMENTS AND STATISTICS.

1. A Chronological List of Presiding Elders—2. A Chronological List of Pastors, with the Numbers reported, including Probationers, at the Close of their Respective Terms. 41-44

CHAPTER IX.
A RECORD OF OFFICIAL MEMBERS, ETC.

1. Local Preachers—2. Licensed Exhorters—3. Class Leaders—4. Trustees—5. Stewards—6. First Male Sunday School Superintendents—7. Second Male Superintendents—8. Third Male Superintendents—9. Fourth Male Superintendents—First Female Superintendents—11. Second Female Sup'ts—12. Secretaries—13. Treasurers—14. Librarians—15. Organists—16. Male Teachers:-Intermediate and Senior Departments—17. Female Teachers:-Intermediate and Senior Departments—18. Sup'ts and Teachers of the Infant Department—19. Officers of the Juvenile Missionary Society—20. Sextons. 45-58

BOOK II.
BIOGRAPHICAL RECORD OF MINISTERS.

I.
WOOLMAN HICKSON.

Founder of Brooklyn Methodism—Early History Unknown—Pastoral Record—Faithful Ministry—Rhoda Laws' Conversion—Thomas Haskins' Testimony—Hickson in New York and Brooklyn—Jesse Lee's and Dr. Wakeley's Account of his Last Hours—Tenderly cared for—Lamented—Uncertainty concerning the Location of his Grave—Neither Portrait nor Signature. 59-62

II.
THOMAS FOSTER.

Elder in Hickson's Time—Birth—Pastoral Record—Heroic Service—Primitive Notions—Fringes not allowed—Thomas Smith's Tribute—Useful Local Preacher—Death—Grave—His Wife—Of Methodist Stock—Sleeps beside Him. 63-64

III.
JOHN DICKINS.

Hickson's Colleague—Native of London—College Training—Joins the Methodist Church in Virginia—Conference Record—Asbury's Comment—Makes the First Move toward the Establishment of a Methodist Educational Institution in America—First to approve of the Organization of American Methodism—Author of the Name of the Denomination—J. B. Matthias hears Him—"My Thundering John Dickins"—Book Steward and Pastor—Two Men's Work—Founder of the Great "Book Concern"—Rapturous Death—Last Resting Place—Noble Traits—Eminent Attainments—First Methodist Pastor's Wife in this Region—A Protracted and Beautiful Life—Children of John and Elizabeth Dickins. 65-68

IV.
FREEBORN GARRETTSON.

His Eminent Rank—Native of Maryland—Methodist Influence—Converted on Horseback—Emancipates his Slaves—Alarmed to find Himself a Preacher—Ezekiel Cooper hears him—Long Connection with Brooklyn—Persecutions and Labors—Herald of the Christmas Conference—Wesley's Choice for Bishop—General Conference Record—His New York District—Compeer of Lee in New England—Perils and Accidents—Honorable and Happy Marriage—"Traveler's Rest"—Asbury's Friendship—Last Sermon—Last Words Triumphant—Memorial Stone—Character and Work—Mrs. Garrettson—Pioneer Methodist in Rhinebeck—Beautiful Life and Character—Miss Mary Garrettson—Brilliant Intellect—Incidents—Loving Zeal for God. 69-75

V.
HENRY WILLIS.

Presiding Elder and Pastor in Brooklyn—A Saint Indeed—Birth and Early Ministry—Ministerial Record—Soul on Fire—Frail Body—Self-support—Letter to Freeborn Garrettson—Receives William Thacher into the Church—Lorenzo Dow's Marriage—Ordained by Asbury—Portrait—Canonicals—Triumphant Death—Burial—Asbury's Love for Willis—The Bishop Blesses his Children—Mrs. Willis—Daughter of an Eminent Layman—Rare Intelligence and Piety—Outlives Husband and Children—Death and Burial—Portrait Preserved. 76-78

VI.
THOMAS MORRELL.

Native of New York—Parentage—Brave Revolutionary Officer—Honorable Wounds—Conversion—Successful Failure in Preaching—Appointments—Builds and Dedicates Forsyth-street Church—Morrell and Dickins hold an Official Interview with Washington—Travels with Asbury—"Help Yourselves to Tea"—Answer to William Hammett—Asbury's Comment—A "Solemn" Wedding—Unique Personal Appearance—Buried in a Vault—His Wives—Rev. T. A. Morrell, his Son. 79-83

VII.
ROBERT CLOUD.

Birth—Converted in a Soldier's Uniform—Pastoral Appointments—First Location on Record—Travels extensively—Why so little Known?—The Reason Suggested—His Fall—Reinstated—Labors in the West—President of a State Bible Society—Adheres to the Methodist Episcopal Church—Peaceful Death—His Grave—A Positive Character—His Likeness Lost—Mrs. Cloud—Six Children—Dr. Caleb Wesley Cloud. 84-88

VIII.
JOHN MERRICK.

Place of Birth Unknown—Probably a Revolutionary Soldier—Pastoral Record—Rev. J. P. Fort's Discovery—Merrick's Great Public Power—Peter Vannest's Recollections—Asbury's Prediction—Merrick's Death—His Bones Discovered—Memorial Tablet. . 89-90

IX.
WILLIAM PHŒBUS.

Pre-eminently a Brooklyn Preacher—Birth—Conference Appointments—Member of the Christmas Conference—General Conference Delegate—How he matched Benj. Abbott—Marriage and Location—Physician and Editor—Death—Burial Place—Character Unique—Ability Highly Appreciated. 91-95

X.
JACOB BRUSH.

First Native Presiding Elder for Long Island—His Appointments in the Ministry—Victim of the Yellow Fever—Early Death—Unfulfilled Marriage Engagement—His Grave—Aaron Hunt's Marriage—Brush's Signature—A Bright and Shining Light. . . . 96-98

XI.
DAVID KENDALL.

Little Known of him—Work in Brooklyn Interrupted—Six Years in the Active Ministry—Laid Aside—Record on High. 99

XII.
AARON HUNT.

Birth—Boyhood—A Happy Convert—Leads in Family Prayer—Hears Benj. Abbott—Appointed Class-leader—First Sermon—Sent to Long Island—Conference Record—Little Farm—Small Salary—Location—Introduces Methodism into Danbury, Conn.-"According to Discipline"—"Breaks up New Ground"—The People wonder—Originates the Motion to adopt the Two Years' Rule—Introduces the Custom of inviting Penitents to the Altar—Wife dies—Second Marriage—Stilwellite Secession—An Old Connecticut Law—Mr. Hunt contends for Methodist Preachers' Rights—He wins—His Last Days—Closing Hours—Position and Character—Place of Burial—His Three Wives and his Children. 100-108

XIII.
BENJAMIN ABBOTT.

A Most "Memorable" Man—Unpromising Youth—Rescued from the Depths of Sin—Family Blessed—Begins to Preach—"Hell Neck"—Persecution—Great Power attends his Words—Joins Conference—Appointments—Not a Learned Man—"Thundergust Sermon"—Happy Death—Ostrander's Memorial—Mrs. Abbott—David, their Son. 109-114

XIV.
JOHN RAGAN.

An Irishman—Joins Conference in America—Appointments—Traces of him in New Brunswick—Greatly Useful on his Last Charge—Death by Yellow Fever—Grave—An Honorable Tribute by his Brethren. 115-116

XV.
JAMES BOYD.

On Long Island Circuit in 1792—Brief Record—Marriage in Nova Scotia—Withdrawal from the Church—Returns to the United States—Efforts to Trace him Further as yet Unsuccessful. 117

XVI.
JOSEPH TOTTEN.

Dedicates the Original Sand-street Church—First Stationed Preacher—Birth—Conversion—One of the Founders of Staten Island Methodism—His Marriage—Itinerant Record—General Conference Delegate—Old Rule concerning Quarterage for Preachers' Children adopted on his Motion—Last Sermon on Staten Island—Selects a Burial Place—Sudden Death—Burial—Character—Personal Appearance—His Wife—His Descendants. 118-120

XVII.
GEORGE STREBECK.

One of Asbury's "Promising Young Men"—Brief Itinerant Career—Becomes a Lutheran Minister—Then an Episcopalian—Remarkably Popular for a Time—Founder of Zion Protestant Episcopal Church, New York City—He and his Friends establish St. Stephen's Church—No Permanent Success—Comments of Dr. Wakeley—Remarks of the Rev. J. H. Price—Goes South—No Further Definite Traces of him. . . . 121-122

XVIII.
EZEKIEL COOPER.

Native of Maryland—Hears Freeborn Garrettson—A Lasting Impression—Sixty-two Years in the Itinerancy—Seven Times General Conference Delegate—Long Island his First Circuit—Founder of Several Prosperous Societies—Pastor in Brooklyn—Leads C. W. Carpenter to Christ—Abel Stevens' Account of Ezekiel Cooper—Great Learning and Eloquence—Powerful Debater—Another Izaac Walton—Business Talent—Book Agent—Private Fortune—Legacy—Oldest Methodist Preacher in America—Peaceful Departure—Funeral—Burial—Portrait. 123-127

XIX.
LAWRENCE M'COMBS.

A Native of Delaware—Converted in Youth—Conference Record—Early Ministerial Su cess—Location—Peaceful Death—Final Resting Place—Opinions of Kennaday, Sco Clark, and Others—Characteristic Letter—Personal Appearance—Brief Account of l Two Wives. 128–1

XX.
GEORGE ROBERTS.

Of English Parentage—Graduates from the Chimney Corner—Poor Clothes for a Preacher Marriage—Wife's Early Death—Conference Record—Pioneer in New England—Labc and Privations—Receives Lorenzo Dow into the Church—Second Marriage—His Locati explained—Physician and Local Elder—Rapturous Death—Resting Place in Mt. Oliv Cemetery—Dr. Stevens' Eulogy—Mrs. Susannah Roberts—Asbury's Affectionate Tribu —Beautiful Life and Death—Dr. George C. M. Roberts and other Children. . 133–1

XXI.
SYLVESTER HUTCHINSON.

A Family of Preachers—Native of New Jersey—Born Again—Record as a Conferen Preacher—Voice like a Trumpet-blast—Thrilling Pictures of Pioneer Work—Person Appearance—Various Accounts of his Trouble with Asbury—Land Agency—Marriage Assists in founding the A. M. E. Zion Church—Joins the Methodist Protestant Chur —Unaccomplished Purpose to return to his Former Church Home—Death and Burial Wife and Children. 138–1

XXII.
ANDREW NICHOLS.

Author of the Oldest Known Record of the Members of Sands-street Church—List of l Appointments—Pastor in New York—A Soul Winner—Wakeley's Interesting Story—L cated—More ought to be Known concerning Andrew Nichols. 142–1

XXIII.
CYRUS STEBBINS.

Birth—Pastoral Record—In his Youth a Pungent and Powerful Preacher—Not Satisfi with Methodist Doctrines and Usages—Becomes an Episcopalian Clergyman—Commen by Dr. Abel Stevens, Lorenzo Dow, and Others—Honors Received—Twice Married—Pe sonal Appearance—Death and Burial. 144–1

XXIV.
DAVID BUCK.

Birth and Conversion—Itinerant Record—Marriage and Location—Asbury holds forth his Paper Mill—A Shining Light on Long Island—Elijah Hebard's Testimony—Buck Missionary Zeal—Happy Death—Burial Place—Mrs. Buck—Friend of the Itinerants—H Grave in Searingtown. 147–1

XXV.
PETER JAYNE.

Born in Marblehead, Mass.—Reared under Methodist Influences—Converted Young—Ear Itinerant Labors—Marriage—Thanksgiving Sermon—Lays the Corner-stone of Old Bror field-st. Church in Boston—His Early Death mourned by the Church—Buried in Bostc —Personal Description—Dr. Stevens' Tribute—Mrs. Jayne and the Children. . 150–1

XXVI.
EZEKIEL CANFIELD.

Eulogized by Stevens—Native of Connecticut—Conversion—Conference Record—Marriage Some Traces of his Work—Last Days Triumphant—Death, Funeral, and Burial—A Go Record—Mrs. Canfield. 154–1

XXVII.
WILLIAM THACHER.

Born of Congregational Parents in Connecticut—Learns the Tailor's Trade—Converted Among Methodists in Baltimore—Returns to New England—Jesse Lee Introduces him to the New York Methodists—His Marriage—Wife Converted—Pioneer Methodists in New Haven—Long Ministerial Career—Poor Outfit and Poor Salary—Four Preachers from the Converts on One Circuit—The First Camp-meeting East of the Hudson and the First on Long Island held under his Direction—Wife dies—Second Marriage—Enterprising Church Builder—Old White Church—"Chops a Yoke in Two"—Fights Many Battles—Champion Opponent of Abolition—Centennial Sermon—Death and Burial—Personal Description—A Veteran Teetotaler—A Pointed, Practical Preacher—Some Account of his Wives and his Children. 156–163

XXVIII.
SAMUEL MERWIN.

Of English Ancestry—A Native of Durham, Conn.—Fell from the Piety of his Childhood—Restored Through Methodist Influence—Conference Appointments—Some Events of his Ministry—Death and Burial—A Truly Great Preacher—Exceedingly Popular—Interesting Testimonies by Asbury, Reed, Bangs, Luckey, Osborn, and Stevens—Widow of Peter Jayne—Married Mr. Merwin—Survived him Eight Years—Their Children.   164–168

XXIX.
SAMUEL THOMAS.

Scanty Records Concerning his Early Life—A Methodist in New Jersey—Conference Appointments—Revival in Brooklyn—Most Valuable Fruits—Honorable Tribute in Conference Minutes—His Removal to Ohio—Peaceful Death—Burial Place—Family almost Forgotten. 169–170

XXX.
OLIVER SYKES.

Birth and Boyhood—Unusual Serious Impressions—Calvinistic Instructions—Conversion—Call to Preach—Dejection—Joins Conference—Appointments—Early Promise—Physical Infirmities—Happy Death—His Grave in Stratford—Eccentricities—Bequest to the China Mission—Quotation from his Journal. 171–174

XXXI.
JOSEPH CRAWFORD.

His Nativity—Conference Record—Great Success in Vermont—Laban Clark's Spiritual Father—A True Evangelist—His Relation to Bishop Asbury—Affecting Farewell—Mrs. P. P. Sandford's Testimony—Incidents—Sudden Close of his Ministry—Rev. Cyrus Prindle's Letter—Mr. Crawford's Last Years in Sandusky, O.—His Death and Burial Place—Personal Description—Rev. A. D. Knapp's Letter. 175–178

XXXII.
ELIJAH WOOLSEY.

Birth—Religious Training—Methodist Preachers—Conversion—Enters the Ministry—Conference Record—Pioneer Work in Canada—Unconquerable Zeal—Hardships—Romantic Experiences—Wife dies in Brooklyn—General Conference Record—"The Supernumerary"—Last Days—Burial Place—Personal Appearance—Some Elements in his Character—First Wife's Grave in Sands-street Church-yard—Second Wife—Dr. Finch's Letter. 179–183

XXXIII.
JOHN WILSON.

Native of England—Trained in Piety—A Methodist from his Youth—Emigrates to America—A Local Preacher there—Conference Record—Marriage—Scholarship—Holiness his Theme—Conference Secretary—Asthmatic Affection—Grave in Forsyth-street Church-yard. 184–186

xiv   *Contents.*

XXXIV.
DANIEL OSTRANDER.

Rugged Ancestry—Early Conversion—Conference Appointments—Pioneer in New Engla —Remarkable General Conference Record—Unbroken Health—Marriage—Calls out M vin Richardson—Portraiture by Gilder—Semi-Centennial Sermon—From Sixteen to S(enty-two in the Service of the Church—Death and Burial—Marked Characteristics—Cl Discernment—An Incident—Mrs. Ostrander's Interesting Character and History—I scendants of Daniel and Mary Ostrander.   187–

XXXV.
REUBEN HUBBARD.

English Ancestry—Born in Massachusetts—Early Connection with Methodism—Epitome his Ministerial Services in Two Churches—Member of One General Conference—Glim₁ of his Early Ministry—A Letter—Leaves the Methodists—Becomes a Hard-working E₁ copalian Itinerant—Dr. A. B. Carter's Eulogy—A Well-merited Tribute—Death and I rial of Mr. Hubbard—His Wife and Children.   192–

XXXVI.
THOMAS DRUMMOND.

Much of his History Unknown—Pastoral Record—The Children's Spiritual Instructo: Charged with Crime and Expelled.   1

XXXVII.
LEWIS PEASE.

Born of Pious Parents—A Thoughtful Youth—Calvinistic Notions—A Happy Deliverance Itinerant Record—A Frail Body—Great Revivalist—Unparalleled Success in Sands-str(—Bereavement—Consumption—Happy Death—Burial—Dr. Wakeley's Description Lewis Pease—Twice Married—His Widow marries Rev. James Erwin—Memorial by I Reddy. 197–₂

XXXVIII.
NATHAN EMERY.

Birth and Ancestry—In his Boyhood One of the Founders of Methodism in Maine— Youthful Preacher—Itinerant Record—Ebenezer Washburn's Testimony—Marriage—F Name Associated with the Establishment of Sunday-schools in Brooklyn—David Holn Converted under his Ministry—His Life in the West—Passes safely through Deatl River—His Grave—His Wife and Daughter—J. B. Finley's Testimony.   201–₂

XXXIX.
WILLIAM ROSS.

Twice Pastor of Sands-street Church—Birth and Education—Flees from a Ball-room to se Christ—Erects a Family Altar—Enters the Itinerancy—Appointments—War of 181₂ Driven out of Canada—Delicate Health—Receives Rev. S. Landon into the Church—G(eral Conference Record—A Popular Preacher—Joyful Premonitions—Triumphant De₂ —Buried in Sands-street Church-yard—The Body Removed—Wife and Children.   206–₂

XL.
NATHAN BANGS.

A Son of Connecticut—Farmer Boy in New York State—School-teacher—Teacher and S₁ veyor in Canada—Converted Among the Pioneer Methodists—Adopts Methodist Custo —Enters the Itinerancy—Ministerial Record—Heroic Service and Hard Fare—A Less concerning Impressions—A Sister who could Exhort—Marriage—Heman Bangs—Lo Horseback Ride—Vast and Varied Labors—General Conference Record—His Relation Our Great Publishing, Missionary, and Educational Institutions—Marked Elements Character—Death—Funeral—Burial Place—Brief Family Record.   .   .   .   211–₂

XLI.
ALEXANDER M'CAINE.

Born and reared in Ireland—Intended for the Ministry of the Established Church—Becomes a Methodist—Soon afterward a Pastor in the United States—Ministerial Record—Twice Located—The Cause—His Daughter's Recollections of Sands-street Church—Coke and Asbury—General Conference Record—Leading Agitator and Author among the Reformers—List of his Works—Account of his Death and Burial—Portraiture of his Character—The Two Wives and Five Children of Mr. M'Caine.   .   .   216–224

XLII.
PETER P. SANDFORD.

From a Reputable Family—Inclined to Preach when but a Very Young Lad—Conversion—Ministerial Record—Dr. Noah Levings One of his Spiritual Children—Leading General Conference Delegate—Marked Ability—Authorship—Honorary Degree—Triumph in Death—Grave—His Two Wives and his Thirteen Children.   .   .   .   225–228

XLIII.
HENRY CHASE.

Of Quaker Parentage—Ambitious and Diligent in his Studies—Conversion—Ministerial Appointments—Pre-eminently the Sailor's Friend—Marries Ten Thousand Couples—His Recognized Scholarship—Fine Personal Appearance—Death and Burial—Wife and Children.   229–231

XLIV.
LABAN CLARK.

Birth and Childhood—Disposed to Think for himself concerning Calvinism—Attracted to Methodism—Calls it the "Old Bible Way"—Joseph Crawford leads him to Christ—Becomes at once a Pioneer Worker—Associate of Martin Ruter—Itinerant Record—Dr. N. Levings Converted under his Ministry—A Founder of the Missionary Society and of Wesleyan University—Semi-centennial Sermon—Honorary Degree—His Long Life comes to a Close—Burial Place—Characterized in Stevens' History and New York Conference Minutes—Two Wives and a Daughter.   232–236

XLV.
MITCHELL B. BULL.

An Irishman—Converted Young—Emigrates to New York—Ministerial Record—Pastor of Sands-street Church as a Supply—His Valuable Memoranda—Great Industry—Health fails—Locates—Prospers in Business—A Faithful Steward—Diligent as a Local Preacher—Inclined to Second Adventism in 1843—Personal Description—Death—Burial—Manuscript Sermons—His Three Wives.   237–239

XLVI.
THOMAS BURCH.

Native of Ireland—Parents Members of the Established Church—Converted through the Labors of Gideon Ouseley—Soon afterward a Class Leader and Local Preacher in America—Encouraged by Henry Boehm—Conference Record—Sent to Canada at a Critical Time—General Conference Record—Last Sermon—Death and Burial—Samuel Luckey's Tribute—Dr. Bangs' Description—Wife and Children.   240–243

XLVII.
STEPHEN L. STILLMAN.

Born of Seventh-Day Baptists in Connecticut—Joins the Baptists in Childhood—Later becomes a Methodist—Conference Record—Laborious Circuits—Great Revival in Albany—Death—Burial Place—Eulogized in Conference Memorial—Two Wives and Five Children of Mr. Stillman.   244–246

xvi   *Contents.*

XLVIII.
SAMUEL LUCKEY.

Birth and Early Christian Experience—Conference Record—Pioneer Labors in Canada—Incidents—Great Revival in Troy—Honorary Degrees—Civil Promotion—Three Times Delegate to General Conference—Author of Several Books—Remarkable Activity in Old Age—His Death described—His Grave—Fine Tribute by the Minutes of his Conference—Three Wives and Seven Children. 247–251

XLIX.
SEYMOUR LANDON.

Reared Under Methodist Influence—Incidents of his Boyhood—A Solemn Question—Brought to Christ under the Ministry of William Ross—Enlightened on Calvinism but not Converted to the Doctrine—Persuaded to forego a College Training—Conference Record—Death and Burial—His Character sketched by Dr. G. L. Taylor—Total Abstinence Movement—Abolition—Stern Fidelity to Principle—Victorious at Last—An Appropriate Testimonial—Mrs. Landon—Their Children. 252–257

L.
NOAH LEVINGS.

His New England Home—Removes to Troy, N. Y.—An Apprentice—Laban Clark aids the Poor Blacksmith Boy—Samuel Luckey discovers Rare Promise in him—An Affecting Scene—Conference Appointments—Incidents of his Ministry in Brooklyn—Revival in Schenectady—Honorary Degree—Thrice a Member of General Conference—Literary Remains—Fair Haven Church—A Wonderful Sermon—Bishop Clark's Estimate of Dr. Levings—Personal Description—Dies away from Home—Final Resting Place—Wife and Children. 258–262

LI.
JAMES COVEL, JR.

Son of a Methodist Minister—His Early Conversion—A Young Preacher—Pastoral Record—Preaching with his Coat off—A "Boy Team"—"Not Convinced"—Three Days' Meeting in Brooklyn—Tobias Spicer's Testimony—Revival in Troy—Scholastic Attainments—Literary Works—Personal Appearance—Death—Funeral—Burial—Mrs. Covel—Her Children's Beautiful Tribute to her Memory. 263–267

LII.
JOHN C. GREEN.

Native of New York city—Son of a Physician—Pastoral Record—Charged with Intemperance—Acquitted—Trouble concerning Maffit—Withdrawal—Pastor of a Congregational Methodist Church—Green *versus* Pierce—Mr. Green Vindicated—Not a Teetotaler—Death and Burial Place—Wife, her Birth, Death, and Burial—List of the Children. 268–270

LIII.
CHARLES W. CARPENTER.

Son of a Pioneer Methodist—Native of New York—Converted in Sands-street Church—Tells his own Story—Columbia College—First License—Ministerial Record—In Business in the South—Sag Harbor—Conference Record—General Conference—Death and Burial—Encomiums by Judge Dikeman and Dr. Luckey—Mrs. Carpenter—The Children. 271–274

LIV.
JOHN C. TACKABERRY.

Born in Ireland—Methodist Parentage—His Brother a Preacher—Residence in Quebec—Conversion—License and Ordination—Conference Appointments—Visits Europe—Perils—Thrilling Experience—An Uncongenial Colleague—W. H. Dikeman's Testimony—"Walking Concordance"—Failing Health—Death and Burial—Family. . . . 275–278

LV.
JOHN KENNADAY.

Born in New York—His Father an Irish Catholic—Conversion—Heman Bangs his Spiritual Father—First Love-feast Testimony—The "Silvery Voice"—Begins to Preach—Appointments—Remarkable Labors—Marriage—Twenty-two Years in Five Churches—Sudden Death—Tribute by Bishop Janes—Manship's Testimony—Great Skill as a Spiritual Helper and Instructor—Mrs. Kennaday—Her Admirable Character—Recent Death—List of the Children. 279–282

LVI.
JOHN LUCKEY.

Brother of Samuel—Ancestry—Pious Mother—Early Conversion—License to Exhort—List of Appointments—Organized the Flushing Circuit—Married to Miss Rutherford—Southold Circuit—Wonderful Work among the Poor and the Prisoners—C. C. North's Record—Western Home—Luckey's Chapel—Visited by an Old Friend—Last Farewell—Public and Family Worship—Closing Scenes—Buried in Sing Sing—Mrs. Luckey and the Children. 283–287

LVII.
BARTHOLOMEW CREAGH.

Birth—Ancestry—Trained and Confirmed in the Church of England—Methodist Meetings—Complete Consecration at Sixteen—Ambitious Worldly Plans—All Renounced for the Gospel—Thorough Preparation—Emigrates to America—Enters the Itinerancy—Saintly Character—Dr. Prime's Tribute—Social Qualities—A Lover of Nature—Beautiful Letter to his Daughter—Incident at Wildercliffe—Miss Garrettson and Mrs. Olin—Personal Influence—General Conference—Leads the Delegation—Dr. Bushnell's Friendship—Effect of Bishop Hedding's Death—Mr. Creagh's Triumphant Departure—Testimonies of Eminent Ministers—Mrs. Creagh—A Quiet and Useful Life—"Palace Beautiful"—Bereavement—"Grand Step beyond the Stars." 288–295

LVIII.
WILLIAM H. NORRIS.

Two Successful Terms in Sands-street Church—A Worthy Ancestry—Converted Young—Ministerial Record—Several Re-appointments to Important Stations—Continuous Revivals—Dr. F. Bottome's Portraiture of his Character—Dr. Curry's Statement—A Useful Missionary—His Services in Demand—Literary Work—Great Affliction—Death and Burial—The Family. 296–299

LIX.
FITCH REED.

Born in Amenia, N. Y.—A Convert under Marvin Richardson's Ministry—Abandons Medical Studies for the Ministry—A Distinct and Emphatic Call—Appointments—A Frail Young Man—Interesting and Amusing Reminiscences—A Hard Circuit, a Subject for Thanksgiving—A Gospel Pioneer in Canada—Marriage—General Conference Record—Honorary Degree—Blessed Experience in Old Age—Death—Burial Place—His Family—A Fitting Memorial adopted by his Conference. 300–303

LX.
STEPHEN MARTINDALE.

Son of a Methodist Local Preacher—Orphan Boy—Itinerant Record—A Scanty Support—Revivals—Father Taylor and Poston—General Conference Record—Long and Active Ministry—Happy Death—Funeral—Burial Place—Admirable Characteristics—How he made Methodists of his Children—Mrs. Martindale—A Remarkable Woman—Pleasing Testimonials—The Children—A Gratifying Record. 304–310

LXI.
PETER C. OAKLEY.

Of Good English Stock—Born in New York—Savingly Impressed by a Printed Sermon—His Father's Sudden Death—Apprenticed to Harper & Brothers—Joined Old John-street Church—Student in Wesleyan Seminary—Ministerial Record—Fifty Years of Uninter-

xviii *Contents.*

rupted Work—No Murmuring—Twice Married—Reminiscences of Old Sands-street Church—A Tranquil Old Age—A Remnant of the Family Left—Brief Memorial of his First Wife. 311-313

LXII.
LEONARD M. VINCENT.

Early Home by the Hudson—His Father dies—Experience of a "Farmer Boy"—Bitter Repentance—Precious Fruit of Faithful Cross-bearing—Reluctant to Preach—His First Sermon—Last Call to Some of the Hearers—Conference Record—Successful Pastorate in Brooklyn—Incidents—Brief Note concerning his Family. 314-318

LXIII.
JOHN J. MATTHIAS.

Son of a Noble Methodist Preacher—Learns the Printer's Trade—Called of God to the Ministry—Successive Stations—Appointment to Africa—Chaplain to Seamen—On the Retired List—Death and Burial—Eulogistic Testimonies—Extract from one of his Sermons—His Two Wives—His Son. 319-322

LXIV.
HART F. PEASE.

Born of Congregational Parents—Converted in Youth—Engaged in Business—Seminary and College—Enters the Ministry—List of Appointments—An Honored Pastor and Presiding Elder—Brief Notice of his Family. 323-324

LXV.
JOHN B. MERWIN.

Son of the eminent Samuel Merwin—Taught by Ruter, Bascom, and Durbin, of Augusta College—Conference Record—Honorary Degree—General Conference Delegate—A Remarkable Ride—A Truly Honorable Life Record. 325-327

LXVI.
JOHN W. B. WOOD.

Well Born—Methodist Ancestry—Studies Interrupted—Years Spent on the Ocean—A Loud Call—An Honest Answer—Converted at a Camp-Meeting—Conference Record—Revivals —Brief Characterization—Wife and Children. 328-330

LXVII.
HENRY J. FOX.

Of Wesleyan Parentage—Native of England—Joins a Small Sect of Methodists—Afterward becomes a Wesleyan Methodist—A Preacher among them—Welcomed in New York—Ministerial Appointments—His Scholarship Recognized and Honored—Services during the War—Experience in the South—Successful Lecturer and Author—Useful Preacher and Pastor—Brief Note concerning his Family. 331-333

LXVIII.
LEVI S. WEED.

Birth—Conversion—An Evangelist from the First—Theological Studies—Literary Course—Mistaken Counsel concerning a College Training—Conference Record—Sands-street Church—Pleasant Facts and Opinions—Personal Appearance—Well-earned Popularity—Missionary Sermon—General Conference—Honorary Title—Marriage and Bereavement—Some Account of his Family. 334-338

LXIX.
BUEL GOODSELL.

Presiding Elder of Long Island District—A Good Record—Birth—Early Conversion—Conference Appointments—General Conference Record—Marriage—Bereavement—Brief Glance at his Character and Work—His First Wife—Her Triumphant Death—Mr. Goodsell's Widow—His Children. 339-341

LXX.
JOHN MILEY.

German Ancestry—Native of Ohio—Only Survivor of his Father's Family—Boyhood—Taste for Reading—College Course—Conversion—Ministerial Record—General Conference—Degrees—Eminent as a Preacher, Pastor, Theological Professor and Author—Wife Deceased—The Children. 342-343

LXXI.
WILBUR F. WATKINS.

Native of Baltimore—Early Call to the Ministry—Seminary and College—An Itinerant of the Primitive Type—Epitome of his Ministerial Life--Two Years in a Theological School—Brief Pastoral Supply in Sands-street Church—Revival--Marriage--Popular and Useful Preacher—Becomes an Episcopalian—Reasons for the Change—Mr. Tibbals' Sketch—Large and Wealthy Parishes—Remarkable Gifts—Mrs. Watkins—The Children. 344-347

LXXII.
JOHN B. HAGANY.

Birth and Training—Restless under Discipline—A Runaway—His Conversion—Ministerial Record—Duplicate Appointments—Transfers—His Conference Memorial—Dr. Crooks' Estimate of his Eloquence and Learning—Fletcher Harper's Guests—Dr. Hagany's Sudden Death—Funeral—Grave—Mrs. Hagany—The Daughters. 348-450

LXXIII.
BERNARD H. NADAL.

Father born in France, of Catholic Parents—Mother a Methodist—Maryland his Native State—An Apprentice—Converted—Saddle-making and Studying Combined—Conference Record—Marriage—Pastor and Student at the Same Time--His Graduation—Honorary Degrees—Patriotism—Drew Seminary—Death and Burial—Glowing Testimonials by Dr. Punshon, Bishop Foster, Dr. Buttz, and others—An Interesting Family. . . 351-356

LXXIV.
DANIEL CURRY.

Ancestors—Birth—Youthful Occupations—Early Christian Life—Graduation—Professorship—Conference Record—Marriage—Titles—General Conference Record—Remarkably Sustained Prominence in the Church—Bibliographical Record—A Veteran Editor—Dr. Buckley's Statement—The Family. 357-359

LXXV.
CHARLES FLETCHER.

Of English Birth—A Bright Boy—Small Advantages—Early Conversion—Youthful Preacher—Trained in the Factory—Begins Life in America—Foster's Interesting Account—Conference Record—Locates—Conscience not at Rest—Re-enters the Itinerancy to stay—Elements of Strength—Plainville Camp-Meeting—Dr. Buckley's Estimate—Did he Write his Sermons?—Sickness and Death—Greenwood—His Wife—Niece of Samuel Marsden—Admirer and Valuable Assistant of her Husband—Homesick for Heaven—Rest at Last—Their Two Sons. 360-364

LXXVI.
BENJAMIN PILSBURY.

Review of his Term as Presiding Elder of Long Island—Birth and Ancestry—Small Advantages well Improved—Wesleyan University—Difficulties overcome—Honorable Rank in his Class—Conversion—Early Success in Holding Meetings—Theological Course—Ministerial Record—Events of his Ministry—General Conference Record—Honorary Degree—Some Account of his Family. 365-368

LXXVII.
EDWARD G. ANDREWS.

Of New England Stock—Methodist Parentage—Dr. Buckley's Notice of the Bishop's Mother—Edward One of Eleven Children—A Christian Family—A Young Student at Cazenovia

—Wesleyan University—Early Christian Work—School Teacher—Ministerial Record—Voice fails—Some Years in Charge of Literary Institutions—Honorary Degrees—Missionary Sermon—Other Addresses—Sands-street Church Records—Valuable member of the New York East Conference—General Conference Delegate—Bishop—Personal Description—Family. 369-372

LXXVIII.
EDWIN E. GRISWOLD.

Birth—Family Connections—Childhood—Conversion—"Comfortable Assurance"—A Young Class Leader—A Studious Boy—Marriage—Call to Preach—Mr. Hubbell's Account—Conference Record—Four General Conferences—Leads his Delegation—Degree of D.D.—Death and Burial—Marked Excellences—His Memory Cherished—His First Wife—Her Patient Suffering—Happy Death—Dr. Griswold's Widow and Children. . . . 373-377

LXXIX.
ALBERT H. WYATT.

Son of a Methodist Preacher—Sketch of William Wyatt—Grandson of Reuben Reynolds—Birth—Conversion—First License to Preach—Chaplain in the Army—College Course—Conference Record—Two Deceased Wives—Third Marriage—Excellent Fruits—The Ministry of Affliction. 378-380

LXXX.
GILBERT DE LA MATYR.

Son of an Aged Local Elder—Five Preachers in the Family—Early Conversion—Conference Record—Army Chaplain—Drawn into Politics—Member of Congress—Eloquent Lecturer—Some Characteristics—His Two Wives Deceased. 381-383

LXXXI.
GEORGE F. KETTELL.

Patriotic and Pious Ancestry—Native of Boston—Student in Germany—Apprentice in Connecticut—A Brilliant and Attractive Lad—Old Methodist Meeting-House—Kettell's Conversion—Dr. Hunt's Account of It—Steady Progress—Marriage—Preacher's License—Pastoral Record—Deserved Promotion—Loss of an Eye—United States Consul—Degree of D.D.—Sudden Death—Funeral—Impressive Services—Encomiums—"Christian Advocate"—Conference Memorial—Dr. Kettell's First Wife—His Widow. . . 384-388

LXXXII.
THOMAS G. OSBORN.

Ancestry—Methodist Parents—Notable Gifts and Services—Methodism in Riverhead, L. I.—Birthplace of T. G. Osborn—Franklin Academy—Wesleyan University—College Honors—A Law Student—Ministerial Record—Great Success in Southampton, New York, and Other Places—Impaired Health—Personal Description—Mrs. Osborn—Surviving Children—Three Wives in their Graves—Children Deceased. 389-393

LXXXIII.
FREEMAN P. TOWER.

Genealogy—Birth—Student and Teacher—Early Conversion—College Course—Ministerial Record—Sinners Converted—Church-Building Enterprises in Connecticut, California and Oregon—Willamette University—Financial Agency—Success—E. O. Haven Professorship—The Bishop's Funeral—Brief Portraiture of Mr. Tower—Mrs. Tower—Their Children. 394-396

LXXXIV.
GEORGE TAYLOR.

Native of England—Methodist Parentage—Childhood Piety—Classical Instruction—Theological School—Local Preacher in England—His Church Home in New York—Ministerial Appointments—Marriage—Family—Brief Description—General Conference Delegate 397-398

Contents. xxi

LXXXV.
ALBERT S. GRAVES.

Born of Methodist Parents—Converted in Youth—Was Graduated at Wesleyan University—Ministerial Record—A Testimonial—Conference Secretary—General Conference Delegate—Principal of a Seminary—Presiding Elder—Personal Appearance—First Wife Deceased—Present Wife and Children. 399

LXXXVI.
LINDSAY PARKER.

Native of Dublin—Methodist Parents—Converted Young—Attended a Wesleyan Methodist School—Dr. Robert Crook his Teacher—Some Time in a Lawyer's Office—Four Years in the Irish Conference—Epitome of his Ministry in his Native Land and in America—Marriage—Pulpit Talent—Social Qualities—An Episcopal Clergyman—Reason for Leaving the Methodist Episcopal Church. 400

LXXXVII.
JOHN S. BRECKINRIDGE.

Son of a Methodist Minister—A Noble Mother—Young Breckinridge's Conversion—An Interesting Story—Thorough Preparation for his Chosen Life-Work—God's Blessing on his Ministry—European Tour—Lectures—Sermon on " Eternal Punishment "—Patriotic Service—Published Articles—Personal Description—Wife and Children. . . 401-404

LXXXVIII.
ICHABOD SIMMONS.

Native of Massachusetts—Father a Universalist—Mother not a Church Member—Conversion—First License to Preach—Cabinet Maker—Student at Newbury, Concord, Northfield, and Middletown—Pastor at the Same Time—Ministerial Record—Singleness of Purpose—Baptism of the Spirit—European Tour—Successful and Beloved—Wife and Daughters. 405-406

LXXXIX.
LEWIS R. STREETER.

Closes the Succession to Date—Son of a Methodist Local Preacher—Native of England—Of a Large Family—Converted at Nine Years of Age—Sent to School—A Local Preacher in England—Begins to Itinerate in Indiana—A Course of Theological Study—Conference Record—Marriage—Highly Esteemed. 407

BOOK III.
ALPHABETICAL AND BIOGRAPHICAL RECORD OF MEMBERS.

PRELIMINARY. 408
ABBREVIATIONS. 409
RECORD OF MEMBERS. 409-520

INTRODUCTION.

Here is the carefully written story of Christian work inaugurated a hundred years ago in a quiet village, now grown to be the third city of the land. The aim and merits of the volume are so readily discerned, that it needs no introduction, yet I am glad of an opportunity to declare that I feel myself strongly attracted by this and other efforts to preserve the record of the struggles and victories of the founders of Methodism. The author of the work deserves hearty thanks for his conscientious, careful and successful efforts to rescue from oblivion so many of the original materials out of which in due time the philosophy of Methodist history must be constructed.

It cannot have escaped the notice of those who are even partially familiar with the best Christian writers of recent years, that their allusions to Methodism are for the most part, discriminative and kind. If the doctrines or the polity of the denomination are criticised, the spirit of the criticism is dignified and respectful. Since Thomas Chalmers pronounced the oft-repeated encomium, many pleasant things have been spoken concerning Methodism; but neither his "Christianity in Earnest," nor any other word which has fallen under my eye, seems so rich and so hearty as that which was spoken by Alexander Vinet, the Swiss divine who has been styled the Pascal of the Reformed Church. "Methodism," he says, "the object of our earnest respect, is only Christianity trying to be consistent. Here, after all, lies its glory and its crown." We surely must not accept this tribute in the spirit of self-complacency and pride, or we shall prove that it was unmerited; but, on the other hand, we should be untrue to the God of our fathers, if, when thoughtful men of other branches of the Church of Christ find so much to attract them in Methodist doctrines and usages, we should hold these doctrines and usages with indifference, or even with formal affection. It has been asked whether the period has not been reached when positive modifications should be made in our denominational polity. The question is very broad, and of great moment, and it deserves careful consideration. It will be well for us to move prayerfully, seeking light not only from the most discreet and experienced men of our own communion, but also from thoughtful minds of other branches of the Church. Before we abandon or materially modify our own methods, we should ascertain the recognized wants of other denominations. These convictions have been most impressively awakened of late by some fervid paragraphs I have met in the writings of Dale of Birmingham, the gifted successor of John Angell James; in which, without mentioning, and probably without a thought of Methodism, he waxes earnest in his advocacy of measures which are thoroughly Methodistic. In an address on "The Communion of Saints," delivered before the Congregational Union of England and Wales, he says: "I ask you to consider whether in addition to our present services it would not be well to institute services of altogether a different type, in which a free interchange of religious thought might be encouraged. We know too little of the perplexities and troubles by which the souls of our brethren are saddened; the perplexities might be relieved, and the troubles lightened, if they had opportunity to speak of them frankly. The discoveries of God's love which are made to the individual Christian, are not all intended merely to perfect the peace and confirm the strength of the soul that receives them; they belong, not to the individual merely, but to the Church. We shall never fulfill God's idea of our relationship to each other, until every man that enters the Church feels that he has come into the 'household of faith'—a household in which no heart need suffer alone, and in which the joy of one member is the joy of all." This celebrated divine, in speaking thus, proves clearly that he is looking for a Methodist class meeting. It is equally clear that he approves of a lay ministry, since we hear him declare in an address on "The Holy Spirit in relation to the Ministry, the Worship and the Work of the Church:" "I long to see a great army of preachers rising up among the people themselves—preachers who shall be familiar, as the wealthy cannot be, with their sorrows, their hardships, their pleasures, the passions by which they are stirred, the hopes by which they are animated, their skepticism and their faith; and who shall speak to them, in their own tongue, of the infinite love of God, revealed to mankind through Christ Jesus our Lord. And what reason can be alleged why Christian merchants, manufacturers, professional men and tradesmen are not more frequently called to the pastorate? * * * It is one of the evil traditions which we have received from ecclesiastical communities founded on principles which are altogether different from our own, that no man can become a minister, and yet abide in the same calling in which he was called."

Such sentiments from such a source, I submit are worthy of our most careful consideration. At a time when some among us are speaking of the "class meeting" and of the "local ministry" in terms of indifference, if not of disparagement, we find one of the most profound, sagacious and polished men of our times, declaring that the Independent Churches of Great Britain are in pressing need of the help which only the most informal social service and the lay ministry can supply. The Methodist Episcopal Church approaches the close of its first century. While devoutly thankful for the triumphs of the past, may we have grace to cherish, in all coming time, the usages which have been so largely instrumental in making our fathers joyous and strong.

The honored and devout worthies of "Old Sands Street" who have passed away, have left us a priceless legacy. They were an honored part of a great multitude who revered the perfections of the infinite God, and were grateful for His numberless mercies; who repented of sin after a godly way, and trusted in Christ like little children; and whose emotions of reverence, and gratitude, and penitence and trust found expression in fervent prayers, and in heart-felt songs of contrition or of gladness. If our second century shall prove as it ought, to be better than the first, it will be because nothing artificial or perfunctory shall be allowed to displace the simple service of song, the informal prayers, the direct and searching appeals to the conscience, and the patient efforts to win souls, which have characterized the genuine followers of Wesley always and everywhere. Above all may we in our day cherish, as our fathers cherished, the unwavering conviction that the Infinite Father is so near to us, one by one, that each for the asking, may have grace to take up the jubilant cry of the Psalmist, "The Lord liveth, and blessed be my Rock."

ALBERT S. HUNT.

Old Sands Street Church.

BOOK I
HISTORICAL RECORD.

CHAPTER I.

A RECORD OF TEN YEARS; 1787—1796.

THE "Mother Church" of Brooklyn Methodism outranks in age all other ecclesiastical organizations save two, in "The City of Churches." As early as 1768, Capt. Thomas Webb preached in Brooklyn,[1] which was then a rural hamlet, less populous than Jamaica or Newtown, where he likewise preached, and laid the foundations of Methodism on Long Island. There were people in Brooklyn who occasionally heard Thomas Webb in the sail-loft in New York,[2] and it was probably in the house of some friend by whom he had been invited, that he held forth the word of life in this suburban neighborhood. In the frontispiece of this work, he is represented as he appeared when preaching, and in fancy we may very easily group about him his little Brooklyn congregation.

There is no history or tradition of other Methodist preachers in Brooklyn until after the Revolution. In two or three other places on Long Island, where Methodism had taken root, it barely survived the demoralizing effect of the war, and the number of members on the island, reported in 1784, was only twenty-four.

Rev. Woolman Hickson, while stationed in New York, came over to Brooklyn, and preached in the open air, upon a table, in New-street, afterward named Sands-street, near

---

[1] Methodist Quarterly Review, 1831, p. 260.
[2] Stiles' History of Brooklyn, vol. iii, p. 700.

the site of the present Sands-street Church. A motley group appears in the picture, such as would naturally assemble in a rural neighborhood for an out-door service conducted by an old-time Methodist preacher. The antique dress, the low-roofed houses, the old scow ferry-boat, and the unoccupied hills of Manhattan Island remind us strongly of a hundred years ago.

The result of Woolman Hickson's holy raid beyond the outposts of his station in New York comprises the theme of this book, and doubtless furnished a theme for celestial anthems. The effect of his preaching was such as to make him welcome to return; for, upon his offering to visit the neighhood again if a place could be found for a meeting, a friend named Peter Cannon proposed to open his cooper-shop near the ferry, and make it as comfortable as possible for the congregation. The best authorities[3] say that soon after this time Woolman Hickson formed a class, the first organized in Brooklyn. These events transpired in 1787, and from that time we trace the history of Brooklyn Methodism.[4]

---

[3] Noah Levings in Meth. Quar. Rev., 1831, p. 260. Wakeley and Stevens follow him.

[4] In regard to this date discordant statements have been made, whereby some confusion has arisen. In 1831, on the authority of the then "living remnant of the first class," the Rev. Dr. Noah Levings wrote: "This class must have been formed *about* the year 1785 or 1786,"—*Meth. Quarterly*, 1831, p. 260. Stiles, following him, gives the same dates in his History of Brooklyn. The Rev. J. L. Gilder, in an article in *The Christian Advocate*, Feb. 29, 1882, shows from the record of appointments in the Conference Minutes, that Mr. Hickson's fields of labor 1782-1786 were far distant from Brooklyn, and forthwith arrives at the following conclusion; "If the first class was formed in 1785 or 1786, then it could not have been formed by Woolman Hickson. . . . If Woolman Hickson, as is claimed and conceded, organized the first class, the origin of Methodism in Brooklyn dates back as far as 1781 or the early part of 1782." A communication by the present writer appeared in the same paper, March 19, proving from the early trustees' record of the John-street church in New York—the "old book" quoted by Wakeley in *Lost Chapters*, p. 315—that Hickson was pastor in New York in 1787, and reference was made to Wakeley and Stevens to confirm the statement that during that year he formed a class in Brooklyn. In a later article this statement of the historians was summarily set aside by Mr. Gilder as "obviously a *non sequitur* and wholly inferential," notwithstanding the foregoing testimony by Dr. Levings, taken from the lips of the earliest members, that the class was formed "*about* 1786" and notwithstanding the unquestioned fact that Hickson was stationed within a mile of Brooklyn in 1787, while he is not known to have been within scores of miles of that place at any other time. Wakeley and Stevens decided upon evidence quite conclusive, that Hickson organized the class in 1787; their critic decides without evidence, that before Mr. Hickson began his ministry in Maryland, that is, previous to 1782, he must have been in Brooklyn and established Methodism there.

Woolman Hickson Preaching His First Sermon in Brooklyn, 1787.

Historical Record.

Thomas Foster was presiding elder in this region that year. John Dickins was colleague of Woolman Hickson in New York, and doubtless rejoiced with him in the addition of this little Brooklyn company to their pastoral charge. The Memoir of Garrettson informs us that he came from the South, and labored a few months in New York previous to the Conference of 1788, during which time he must have been considered one of the pastors of this society. Henry Willis was appointed elder in 1788. The New York preacher having charge of Brooklyn, was John Dickins. Dr. Levings says, "Brooklyn continued to be visited occasionally by the preachers stationed in New York, and by the local preachers residing there." At first this place was unquestionably an outpost of New York station.

In 1789, F. Garrettson and T. Morrell were assigned to the eldership in the New York District. Robert Cloud, John Merrick and Wm. Phœbus were the New York preachers. At the same time Phœbus was in charge of Long Island circuit with John Lee, junior colleague. Lee's Journal proves (see note 4) that during the part of the year covered by his

---

He bases his belief that Hickson would not be likely to form a class in Brooklyn in 1787, on the fact that "he was in impaired health." But ill health could not quench the zeal of such an evangelist. He died in the harness.

Mr. Gilder assumes that because of its geographical location, Brooklyn must have belonged to the *Long Island charge* from the beginning, and asks, "What call had Woolman Hickson within the bounds of another circuit?" Dr. Levings furnishes the following reply: "From this time [about 1786,] Brooklyn continued to be visited occasionally by the preachers stationed in New York, and by the local preachers residing there. At this time also, the whole of Long Island was but one circuit, and but one preacher was appointed to it. At what particular time Brooklyn became one of the regular appointments on this circuit we cannot say."

The "Life of John Lee" contains a full account of his labors as the colleague of Wm. Phœbus on L. I. circuit in 1789, and we trace him from Comac to Searingtown, Rockaway, Newtown, and many other places, but search in vain for the slightest mention of Brooklyn. The reason is that Brooklyn was cared for by New York city preachers. Aaron Hunt's MS. Journal states that in the Conference year 1790 he preached regularly in private houses in Brooklyn, as one of the Long Island circuit preachers. Previous to that date there is no evidence that Brooklyn was supplied by Long Island pastors. Hence the supposed unknown date of its first becoming a part of L. I. circuit is 1790. This little society was remote from all others on Long Island, Newtown being the nearest, while it was easy of access to the New York preachers, and for two years or more they seem to have had charge of Methodism here. This arrangement was so natural and convenient that some years later (1794) Brooklyn was taken from Long Island circuit, and attached to New York. From the foregoing facts we do not hesitate to name 1787 as the date when Methodism in Brooklyn took organic form.

term, Brooklyn was not connected with Long Island circuit, hence we infer that this year also, the pastors of the Brooklyn society were the preachers stationed in New York. J. B. Matthias had joined the John-street Church, and, by permission of the preachers, was already on the wing, going about and holding meetings. His memoir says he visited Brooklyn, and quotes his own words: "Many a happy time have I had with that small society."

In 1790 Brooklyn was taken into Long Island circuit. David Kendall stands on the Minutes as the preacher for Long Island, but it appears that Wm. Phœbus, though appointed to New Rochelle, came to the Long Island circuit, and, Kendall being sick, he was reinforced by a young local preacher, Aaron Hunt, appointed to travel as a supply. The presiding elder was Jacob Brush, who seems to have taken the place of Thomas Morrell appointed to that post.[5] Aaron Hunt writes concerning this field in the conference year 1790: "This circuit extended from Brooklyn, (where we had a small class and preached in a private house), over every considerable part of the island."[6]

In 1791 Benjamin Abbott joined Wm. Phœbus on the Long Island circuit, and began his year's work in the little hamlet of Brooklyn. He writes:

I received my appointment to Long Island, and accordingly took my station. The next day I preached to a small congregation with life and power. The Lord attended the word with success. Some young ladies were cut to the heart, and one gentleman cried out for mercy, and before meeting ended he found peace and joined the society. Next day I went to Newtown.[7]

It is manifest that Brooklyn is here meant though not named, because there were at that time only the Newtown and Brooklyn societies on this end of the island. He says further:

I then returned and went to the place where I began my circuit. Here, while I rode this time round the circuit, four or five were added. Next day I went to Newtown.[8]

These few incidents, with the appointments in the Conference Minutes, furnish all the information we have concerning the labors of Methodist preachers in Brooklyn during seven years beginning with the date of the apostolic preach-

---

[5] Compare Conf. Min., 1790, and Stevens' Memorials of Methodism, p. 120.
[6] Unpublished Journals. [7] Life of Abbott, p. 179. [8] *Ibid.*, p. 184.

ing by Woolman Hickson in the cooper-shop and in the street. So quickly do the waves of time wash away the footprints of men! But we know who the preachers were, and it is enough to know that their faithful words and deeds are recorded in God's book.

Long Island circuit continued to be manned by two preachers, and Brooklyn remained an appointment on its western boundary until the conference of 1794. During this time those earnest servants of God, Jacob Brush, John Ragan, James Boyd, Joseph Totten and George Strebeck, opened the word of life to the little companies of Methodist worshippers assembled in such places as they could find before the church was built. Totten and Strebeck labored alternately a month in Brooklyn and a month in other parts of the island. By this arrangement they were enabled to supply Brooklyn constantly with preaching and other pastoral attentions.[9]

In the absence of any known source of information, it is impossible to record the name of any person as having certainly been a member of this church previous to 1793. At that time John Garrison joined the only Methodist class in Brooklyn, and Nicholas Snethen was his class-leader.[10] Wakeley's statement, repeated by Stevens, that Nicholas Snethen was appointed class-leader by Woolman Hickson is an error, because Mr. Hickson died in 1788, and Mr. Snethen first professed faith among the Episcopalians in 1789, and joined the Methodists in 1791.[11]

The church was incorporated in 1794 under the title, "First Methodist Episcopal Church in the town of Brooklyn, Kings County, Nassau Island."[12]

At a meeting held May 19 of that year, at the house of Peter Cannon, the following persons were elected the first board of trustees—John Garrison, Thomas VanPelt, Burdett Stryker, Stephen Hendrickson, Richard Everit and Isaac

---

[9] Levings in Meth. Quar. Review, 1831, p. 260.   [10] *Ibid.*, p. 261.

[11] Compare Sprague's Annals, Wakeley's Lost Chapters, p. 312, Stevens' History M. E. Church, vol. ii, p. 110, and vol. iii, p. 260. See sketch of Snethen in Book III.

[12] The act of 1693, changing the name of Long Island to Nassau Island, it is said, has never been repealed, but has become obsolete by disuse. Stiles' Hist. of Brooklyn, vol. i, p. 205.

Moser. They purchased from Joshua and Comfort Sands a lot fronting on New (afterward Sands) Street, and commenced the erection of a house of worship.[13] The corner stone was laid by the Rev. Wm. Phœbus, at that time stationed in Brooklyn as a supernumerary; and a sermon was subsequently preached on the foundation by the Rev. David Buck, a young man about entering upon his itinerant labors—from Isa. xxviii, 16; "Behold I lay in Zion for a foundation a stone," etc.

The Rev. Joseph Totten of Long Island circuit preached on the occasion of the dedicatory service, Sunday, June 1, 1794, taking his text in Exodus xx, 24: "In all places where I record my name," etc.

On a Sunday morning in the following October, Bishop Asbury preached here; and again in 1796, he writes:

> I went over to Brooklyn where we have a small society. I had very few hearers except those who came from the city. I administered the sacrament and we had some life. We then returned to the city, where I preached to about 1,600 people, some of whom were wicked and wild enough. . . . O when will the Lord appear as in ancient times?[14]

The old church books contain records of Bishop Asbury's visits.

The first pastors after the church was built were Ezekiel Cooper and Lawrence M'Combs of "New York and Brooklyn" charge, with Wm. Phœbus, Jacob Brush and David Kendall, supernumerary preachers.

In 1795, George Roberts was presiding elder, and Brooklyn became for the first time, a separate station, Joseph Totten, pastor. He left thirty-nine members at the close of the year, having found thirty-five at the beginning.

The next year, 1796, Freeborn Garrettson was presiding elder for a third term, and Wm. Phœbus was a third time appointed to preach the Gospel in Brooklyn. A gain of eleven members was reported at the close of the year.

---

[13] This was more than ten years previous to the erection of the first St. Ann's church. See Stiles' Hist. of Brooklyn, vol. ii, p. 108.

[14] Asbury's Journal, Ed. 1852, vol. ii, pp. 243, 310.

A PORTION OF THE OLD SANDS STREET CHURCHYARD. 1882.

BROOKLYN IN 1798–(As seen from the north.)
Showing the Original Sands Street M. E. Church.

CHAPTER II.

A RECORD OF TEN YEARS; 1797—1806.

TILES' History of Brooklyn contains a wood-cut, from which the above is copied. The original sketch was accurately made by a French artist four years after the first Methodist church was built. It is a view from the New York side of the East River, about opposite Navy Yard Point. In the distance, on the right, are New York Bay and Bergen Point; nearer, Governor's Island, the East River, and the old Brooklyn ferry-house; and in the center, partly hidden by the sail of the sloop, is probably shown the original Sands-street church, built in 1794.

In the year 1797, the second year of Wm. Phœbus' third term as pastor, Sylvester Hutchinson being presiding elder, the membership increased from fifty to eighty-one. The earliest known register of members was made at the close of the Conference year 1798, (Andrew Nichols, pastor,) and from the records beginning at that time. we copy the names of all who are known to have been members of Sands-street Church, up to the close of the eighteenth century.[1]

---

[1] For memorials of nearly all the founders of this church, see Book III.

WHITE MEMBERS.

Thomas Van Pelt, trustee, and Sarah his wife; John Garrison, leader and trustee, and Mary his wife; Burdett Stryker, trustee, and Hannah his wife; Richard Everit, trustee, and Sarah his wife; Isaac Moser, leader and trustee, and Susannah his wife; James DeGraw, leader and trustee, John Hastings, and Deborah his wife; Joseph Moser, Margaret Moser, Ida Moser, Jeremiah Smith, Hannah Smith, Caleb Shreeve, Meliscent Shreeve, James Herbert, Joseph Webb, John Leaneigh, Samuel Engle, Sarah Engle, John DeVosnell, Joseph Herbert, John Harris, John Cornelison, William Foster, John Trim, John Schnell, Anna Schnell, Mary Powers, Jemima Kissam, Sarah Hillear, Catharine Johnson, Rebecca Lynch, Anna Sutliff, Mary Denton, Elizabeth Rote, Sally Howzy, Leanah Smith (afterward Lany Valentine), Anna Day, Betsey Dale, Leah Connor, Eleanor Ward, Rachel Cannon, Lany Acker, Eleanor Ferguson.

COLORED MEMBERS.

Abraham Anthony, Susannah Anthony, Peter Anthony, Wm. Thompson, Hannah Thompson, Thos. Hartley, Harvey Anderson, Thomas Bristol, Caty Jackson, Dinah Benson, Susannah Thomas, Adam Francis, Bethany Stewart, Mary Dolph, Frances, John Grace, Isaac Minix, Thomas Peterson, Philip Leonard, Cornelius Anderson, Caty Anderson, Titus, Nanny, Sarah, John Graw, Nelly.

It will be observed that some of the black people in those days had no surnames, and the names they were called by would hardly distinguish them from dogs and horses; but even such names, we cannot doubt, are written in the Book of Life.

On a stone in the church-yard is inscribed the name of Hannah Stryker, who departed this life in 1787. If tradition be true, she joined the original class, and was the first of the Brooklyn Methodists to gain a crown of immortality. Richard Everit, a trustee, died in 1798, and his is the earliest obituary record in the old church books.

Cyrus Stebbins and David Buck complete the list of pastors, to the close of the eighteenth century. There had been a decrease in membership for a year or two, and at the Conference of 1800, the number of members reported was only fifty-four. In three years thereafter, under the administration of David Buck, Peter Jayne and Ezekiel Canfield, the number had reached the former maximum, seventy-three.

In 1804, while Cyrus Stebbins was pastor a second term, the church building was enlarged. He withdrew from the denomination in December of that year, and Ezekiel Cooper, the book agent, supplied the vacancy until conference. Wm. Thacher was then presiding elder. Mr. Cooper continued as the stationed preacher from the June conference, 1805, but the old record states that Samuel Merwin occupied the station the last quarter, from February till the conference in May, 1806.

These preachers boarded with James Harper, the grandfather of the celebrated Harper Brothers, the price of board being fixed by the trustees at $3.25, or twenty-six York shillings per week.

The next name on the list of preachers is that of Samuel Thomas, associate pastor with Ezekiel Cooper in 1806. The trustees agreed to pay his house-rent, and the sum to be paid was $160.00 per annum. During the same year it was

Resolved: That there shall be a new set of steps erected at the front door of the church, and seats in the altar all round from the altar door, also that of a dark night, when there is a public meeting, the sexton shall light the lamp at the church door.

Joseph Moser was sexton on an annual stipend of £7 and grave digger's perquisites. Previous to this time the Methodists had begun to use the church-yard as a burying-ground, and the trustees adopted a resolution that none but regular attendants upon divine service in this church, should have the privilege of interment there; and furthermore, that "no person guilty of suicide could be buried in this ground under any pretence or condition."

Here was originally interred the sacred dust of Summerfield and Ross, and many of the early Brooklyn Methodists. There many of them remain, and the visitor may read upon the mossy tomb-stones their names and modest epitaphs.

In the trustees' record, January, 1807, there is a minute, stating that Ezekiel Cooper had left Brooklyn for the South, and that Oliver Sykes came to board at John Garrison's on the 21st of January. Sykes was junior pastor with S. Thomas.

CHAPTER III.

A RECORD OF TEN YEARS; 1807—1816.

At the conference of 1807 Joseph Crawford was appointed to the New York District; Elijah Woolsey and John Wilson were stationed in Brooklyn. These pastors found two hundred and twenty-five members, and left two hundred and fifty-three. During this conference year preachers and people mourned the death of a pastor's wife, Mrs. Electa Woolsey. The following curious record may be seen in the old church book:

Jacob and Susan, joined together in marriage, October 12, 1807, by me, **Elijah Woolsey**—Consent of George Bennett, owner

Many of the most respectable people of Brooklyn held slaves at that period, and the institution did not come to an end until about 1825. After a pastoral term of one year, Messrs. Woolsey and Wilson were succeeded by Daniel Ostrander.

In 1808, Joshua Sands, an Episcopalian, canceled a debt of one hundred dollars, the amount due him for land on which the church was built, and in the following year he gave the society a lot for a parsonage, on High-street adjoining the church property. Andrew Mercein, Thomas Kirk and George Smith were the parsonage building committee, appointed in January, 1809. During the next conference year, the pastor, Rev. Reuben Hubbard, withdrew from the Methodists, and we find this amusing note in one of the church records:

Cyrus Stebbins left the Methodist connection, and joined the Church of England. He is stationed in Schenectady, and was formerly stationed in Brooklyn. Little Reuben Hubert left our connection, and joined *the Church*. He was formerly a Methodist preacher, stationed in Brooklyn. *Poor things!*

Rev. Thomas Drummond, of the Philadelphia Conference, was appointed to fill the unexpired term of Mr. Hubbard. The length of the church edifice having been increased previous to 1810, it was now sixty feet long and thirty feet wide, with end gallery for the Africans.[1] The congregation having increased beyond the capacity of the church, the pastor offered a resolution which was adopted Sept. 10, 1810, to build a new church edifice. George Smith, one of the official members, purchased the old structure, and it was moved to the Jamaica turnpike, (Fulton Street), opposite High Street, and devoted to various purposes. In one part Judge Garrison held court, and in another the leaders met their classes. The pastor, Wm. Thacher, labored with remarkable energy. He states that the brethren were inclined to increase the size of the original building, fearing to incur the expense of a new edifice. He writes:

> The challenge was given by the preacher, "Put me in command, and I will show you that it is easier to raise $3,000 to build than $1,400 for enlargement." The result was a house 70 by 42 feet, with galleries and furniture, at a cost of $4,200. Subscriptions, $3,300; sale of old church $260; raised at dedication $220; in all $3,780. This increased the church debt $420, but resulted in the enlargement of the congregation, the conversion and addition of souls to the church, and an improvement of the finances.[2]

OLD WHITE CHURCH.

This new edifice was provided with seats for more than twelve hundred persons. It is remembered as the "Old White Church." Bishop Asbury preached in the building,

---

[1] Thacher's MS. Autobiography.   [2] MS. Autobiography.

Sunday, May 17, 1812, and described it as an "elegant house."[3]

At the expiration of the conference year 1811, an incident occurred which is thus narrated by Mr. Thacher:

> It was at a love-feast, and I spoke in the following terms: "Brethren, I now close my labors as your preacher. You have paid me all my claims, and that I may not be suspected of any sinister design, I tell you that I ask no favors for myself; but I speak in the interest of my successors. You are in the habit of paying $350 for the support of a married preacher. New York pays $500 for the same purpose. They know that the whole of this is needed to support a family, and let me tell you that no man has paid so much to support your preacher as Wm. Thacher. I ask you to give more in the future to the support of your preachers. As to myself I have no claims on you."
>
> The meeting was dismissed, the trustees remained in the house and voted four hundred dollars for the next preacher, and then surprised me with a gift of sixty dollars.

The remaining pastors during this decade were Lewis Pease whose health failed, Thomas Drummond a second term, Nathan Emery and Joseph Crawford. The old trustees' record contains the following resolution adopted in the year 1815:

> Resolved, that the sexton be instructed to have the church open and the candles lighted at least a quarter of an hour before meeting begins, and to see that the boys make no disturbance.

Thomas Drummond has the honorable distinction of having formed the first class of children in Sands-street church (so far as the record shows) for instruction in the catechism. We here transcribe the complete roll of this class of juvenile learners, and should the reader chance to recognize the names of now aged parents or friends he will be pleased to find this recorded testimony to the fact that they in their childhood were taught the knowledge of God.

A Register of the Children that learn the Methodist Catechism, Brooklyn, March 1, 1814. By me, THOMAS DRUMMOND.

Thomas Garrison, Cornelia Garrison, George Smith, Sarah Smith, Samuel Moser, Pelmiah Duryea, Fannie Duryea, Nancy Hoey, Mary Fowler, Amelia Jackson, Hiram Richardson, Henry Moore, Ann Tunstill, Sarah Smith, Eliza Ann DeGraw, Maria DeGraw, Elizabeth Cann, Mary Ann Pray, Nancy Valentine, Eliza Herbert, Mary Herbert, Lucinda Vail, Hannah Bennett, Ebenezer Bennett, James Herbert, Benjamin Richardson, Hannah Snell, Eleanor Cozine, Mary Thomas, Mary Ann Higbie, Lenah Ann Wiliams, Deborah Smith Hasings.

---

[3] Asbury's Journal, Ed. 1852, vol. iii, p. 386.

This was a pioneer work among the children, and was exactly two years in advance of the first Sunday-school movement in Brooklyn.

On the 11th of February, 1816, while Nathan Emery was pastor, at a meeting of the quarterly conference, Thomas Sands, a local preacher in this church,—subsequently a large shipping merchant, and mayor of Liverpool, England—proposed to establish a Sunday-school in the village of Brooklyn. The following is a copy of the record:

Brother Sands proposed setting up a Sunday-school. The conference agreed to give him their aid.

The school was accordingly organized—the first Sunday-school in Brooklyn,—and the credit of the suggestion belongs without doubt to Mr. Sands, although it is not known that he was actually engaged in forming or conducting the school. The children were brought together on the Sabbath in a building known as Thomas Kirk's printing office, a long, narrow framed edifice on Adams-street, between Sands-street and High-street, in an apartment then occupied as a school-room by Daniel DeVinne. They entered the door shown on the right of the picture, and their room was close by on the left. The building still remains, and Mr. DeVinne remained with us until 1883, an esteemed minister of Christ.

The recognized founders of this school were Robert Snow, superintendent, and his assistants, Andrew Mercein, Joseph Herbert, and Daniel DeVinne. To these should be added Thomas Sands who first proposed the enterprise, John G Murphy and Joseph G. Harrison whose signatures were appended to the first printed statement or address to the people of the village concerning the Sunday-school, in March, 1816.[4]

This address did not represent the school as professedly denominational, but requested parents and guardians to express their wishes as to what catechism they would have their children study, and promised that they should be taken to such church services as their parents might choose; nevertheless it is a fact that all the men prominently connected with this pioneer Sunday-school enterprise, including the

---

[4] See Stiles' Hist. of Brooklyn, vol. ii, p. 19.

Kirk's Printing Office, Birth place, (in 1816), of the original Brooklyn Sunday School; as it appeared in 1881.

occupants of the building where the school was held, were members of Sands-street church. Rev. Mr. DeVinne writes:

Ninety-seven names were received at the first meeting, although only half that number were present. The children were mostly of poor parents, and not more than one half of them knew their letters. There was a good deal of aristocratic spirit in those days, and few well-to-do people would allow their children to attend the same school with the poor ones.[5]

The founders of this school stated in their address that it was "under the management of four superintendents, a standing committee of seven, and a number of [volunteer] teachers male and female;" that the design of the institution was to gather "poor children from the most destructive of all places to the morals of youth—the street—on the Sabbath day," and to "combine religious and moral instruction with ordinary learning." The historian of Brooklyn says:

In those early days, the gatherings of boys in and about the rope walks then so numerous in Brooklyn, and the card playing, profanity and other vices which they then indulged in, had become a most serious nuisance to the better part of the community.

Thus the quiet and comfort of the village, as well as the personal benefit the children might receive, incited the founders of the school to their noble work. These zealous and benevolent men, rising above sectarian motives, and hoping to induce many to co-operate with them, joined in a call published in *The Star*, March 27, 1816, for a public meeting, which "Christians of every denomination, all advocates of decency and order, and all friends of * * * religion," were invited to attend for the purpose of organizing a village Sunday-school Union, the object of the society to be the establishment of a Union Sunday-school. The result was the organization of the "Brooklyn Sunday School Union Society" on the 8th of April, 1816, and among those who signed the first code of rules were the following members of Sands-street church: A. Mercein, vice-president of S. S. Union, Thomas Sands, treasurer, John G. Pray, Robert Snow. The Sunday-school in Kirk's building thereby became a union school, and was removed to the school-house of District No. 1, on the corner of Concord and Adams streets. James Engles,

---

[5] Semi-centennial Sermon.

CHAPTER IV.

A RECORD OF TEN YEARS; 1817—1826.

HE presiding elders during this period were Samuel Merwin, Nathan Bangs, Peter P Sandford, and Laban Clark; and the pastors were Joseph Crawford, William Ross, Alexander M'Caine, Henry Chase, (supply), Lewis Pease, Mitchel B. Bull, (supply), Thomas Burch and Stephen L. Stillman. The Sunday-school, so hopefully begun, was destined to suffer a temporary defeat. A lack of teachers, and a strenuous opposition on the part of some of the church members who regarded teaching in the Sunday-school as a desecration of the Lord's day, resulted in the suspension of the school for a period of about three years. In the mean time, the Episcopalians organized a Sunday-school in Brooklyn, and certain members of the Baptist Churches in New York proposed coming over to the village and organizing another. The Sunday-school veterans of Brooklyn could not stand idly by, and see people from abroad superceding them in this good work; and, in 1821, the Union Sunday-school was resumed in the District school building, where it had formerly been held.

As the school increased in numbers, its original accommodations became too restricted, and the first Sunday-school building was erected in Prospect-street, near Adams. It was built by Robert Snow, James Engles, Joseph Moser and Robert Nichols, "with beams and timbers from Mr. Snow's old potash store in New York," and made large enough to contain all the Sunday-school children in Brooklyn. The first of January was always signalized as *Happy New Year*, and the Sunday-school room was made a *happy place* by the distribution of cakes and apples, and the dispensing of "shoes, stockings, flannel garments, etc., which had been solicited from the wealthier citizens." *Christmas* was not at that time as now in this country, pre-eminently the children's holiday. From this building after the Sunday-school session, the children were accustomed to repair to those places of worship which their parents attended, or to return to their homes. In a few years, each of the churches becoming sufficiently established to maintain its own Sunday-school, the children of the other denominations gradually withdrew, leaving the Methodists to conduct the Sunday-school on Prospect-street, "where under the supervision of Messrs. Snow, Mercein, Herbert, Moser and others, it flourished exceedingly."[1] One of the most devoted and useful laborers in this school was Abraham Vanderveer, who, though a member of the Reformed Dutch Church, was thoroughly and permanently identified with the Methodists in their Sunday-school work. The building on Prospect-street continued to be the rallying place for the Sunday-school until a Sunday-school building was erected near the parsonage on High-street in the rear of the church.

The colored members, having become quite numerous, desired a separate place of worship, and, about 1817, being assisted by the members of the church generally, they succeeded in erecting a small meeting-house on High-street, between Bridge and Pearl. They were, however, under the pastoral care of the stationed preacher of Sands-street church. The church register, April 22, 1818, Joseph Crawford pastor, contains a record of the "African Asbury Methodist Episcopal Church," seventy-four members. The leaders were Thomas Bristol, Israel Jemison, Benjamin Croger,[2] Peter Croger, Samuel Anderson.

In the year 1820, while Alexander M'Caine was pastor, the colored members seceded in a body, only six remaining in the old church. At this date the reasons for their departure may not be fully known. It has in a summary and general way been attributed to a spirit of insubordination to the Discipline.[3] The following are the only records of official action concerning them:

---

[1] Stiles' Hist. of Brooklyn, vol. ii, p. 29.
[2] Benjamin and Peter Croger afterward joined the N. Y. Conf., A. M. E. Church. The former died in 1853.
[3] N. Levings in Meth. Quar. Review, 1831, p. 265.

October 15, 1819. Motion made and carried that the colored people of the Methodist Church in Brooklyn be requested to pay ten dollars per quarter for services rendered by Brother M'Caine, in taking care of aforesaid Church.

Feb. 17, 1820. It was suggested that from present appearances the colored people are about to separate from the charge. It was asked if it would not be advisable in such an event to set apart some seats in the house for the use of those who wish to remain among us. It was decided in the affirmative.[4]

Two years previous to their entire separation they numbered seventy-four members. Since that time several other Methodist churches have been organized among the colored people of Brooklyn. Alexander M'Caine resigned his charge soon after this secession took place, and Henry Chase was appointed a supply for the remainder of the year.

In 1821, Lewis Pease having been appointed a second time to Brooklyn, this church was visited with a revival. It began at a camp-meeting at Musketo Cove,[5] and another refreshing was enjoyed by this same people and pastor immediately after the Musketo Cove camp-meeting in the following year,—a meeting of great interest and power, and largely attended by the Brooklyn people.[6] The membership increased under Mr. Pease's ministry from 216 to 401.

During the Conference year 1822, a little society was organized at Yellow Hook.[7] This class, originally connected with the Brooklyn Methodists, afterward became the Bay Ridge M. E. Church. The following persons were the first members of this class: Daniel Field, leader; Adrian Bogart, Phœbe, his wife; Getty Bogart, Ellen Gold, Henry Stillwell, Anna Stillwell, Polly Bailey, Peter Bogart, Peggy Spingsteel and Anna Spingsteel. Soon were added Walter VanPelt, Winant Bogart, John DeGroff, Margaret Vanier, Elizabeth VanPelt, James VanPelt, Edward Williams, Eliza Ferman and others.[8]

At the close of Mr. Pease's successful pastorate, William Ross, a former pastor and very much esteemed, was returned to the charge. Soon after his arrival, in 1823, a considerable number of members colonized and formed the York-street church, but this new society continued for twelve years under the same pastoral supervision as the mother church.

---

[4] Quar. Conf. Record. [5] Meth. Magazine, 1822, p. 69.
[6] Meth. Magazine; 1823, p. 117, also Bangs' Hist. of the M. E. Church.
[7] Meth. Magazine, 1823, p. 118. [8] For biographical notices see Book III.

Except in the sad case of Woolman Hickson, the founder of this church, the Sands-street people had never been called to lament the death of a pastor in the midst of his useful labors among them. Now they were to pass through that mournful experience. In his youthful prime, the eloquent and popular William Ross was called from labor to reward, and when he was buried a large concourse of broken-hearted people watered his grave with their tears. The long and solemn procession, composed of nearly all the people of the village, formed at the parsonage on High-street. The bier, covered with a pall, was borne on the shoulders of four men; the choir, consisting of more than twenty chosen singers, led by Richard Cornwell, marched near the ministers at the head of the procession, and as they passed from the parsonage around the corner into Fulton-street, they sang to the tune "China" in sweet yet mournful harmony, one of our solemn and appropriate hymns.

The church records show that Mitchell B. Bull, as a supply, filled Mr. Ross' unexpired term. In the following year the "seraphic Summerfield," as the time of his departure drew near, expressed a desire to be buried by the side of his beloved friend, William Ross, in the old Sands-street churchyard, and for many years, till their subsequent removal, the mortal forms of those two holy men reposed together there.

The conference of 1825 sent Thomas Burch to take charge of Brooklyn Methodism, and S. L. Stillman was appointed his colleague in 1826. That year a class was formed in Red Hook Lane, consisting of the following persons: Christopher Rutherford, leader; Joseph Baggott, John Baggott, Mary Goldsmith, Phœbe Langdon, Lucretia (or Lucinda) Moser, Samuel Shepherd, Leonora Baggott (1828). This class was sustained for a number of years, and was led by the following persons; 1826 C. Rutherford, 1828 Joseph Moser, 1830 Isaac Moser, 1831 James Sweeney. In 1826 the eloquent Bascom preached in this church. On that same Sabbath George Smith, one of the pillars of the church, passed peacefully away.[9] During this decade, notwithstanding the secession of the colored people, the membership increased from 271 to 436.

---

[9] So states Burdet Stryker, of Brooklyn.

CHAPTER V.
A RECORD OF TWENTY YEARS; 1827-1846.

AMUEL LUCKEY followed Thomas Burch as preacher in charge of the Brooklyn circuit. In 1827 S. L. Stillman was his colleague; in 1828 Seymour Landon. The statistics show a steady increase in the membership. The Sabbath-school was especially prosperous. It was mentioned by Laban Clark in the New York Advocate in January, 1828, as the best conducted Sunday-school he had seen.

While Samuel Luckey was preacher in charge, the Young Men's Missionary Society of Brooklyn, auxilliary to the parent Missionary Society, was organized. The author has no knowledge of the length of time it continued to flourish. Young people of both sexes were among its supporters. The pastor's daughter, Miss Ann Eliza Luckey, is said to have suggested the formation of the society. One of the original members writes; "She was so earnest that my five brothers, my sister and I all joined. Marsden Van Cott took an active part in organizing the society."[1] The junior preacher, S. L. Stillman, was president, and the first anniversary was held March 19, 1828, in the York-street church. The chairman, after speaking of the insufficiency of worldly charity and benevolence, said:

<blockquote>The gospel alone can strike at the root of human misery. When once the gospel panacea has diffused its healing virtues through the souls of men, the mighty cure is wrought, the fountain head of the muddy stream of moral pollution is dried up, and its turbid waters cease to flow. *** Hence, though it may be expedient to lend occasional aid to those minor institutions, it should never be forgotten that to assist the gospel in its operation is the only effectu-</blockquote>

---

[1] Letter to the author by the widow of the Rev. John Luckey. Her father was the Rev. Christopher Rutherford, a local preacher in Sands-street church.

al way to restrain the course of vice, instruct the ignorant, lift up the humble poor, release the abject slave, and illuminate, and civilize, and evangelize, and save a ruined world.[2]

D. M. Reese, M .D. of New York also addressed the meeting.

Daniel Ostrander succeeded Laban Clark as presiding elder in 1828. A notable revival in the Sands-street church followed the Hempstead Harbor camp-meeting in 1829, the first year of the pastoral term of Noah Levings and James Covel, Jr. It commenced among the sailors of the U. S. navy in Brooklyn. A band of Methodists including several exhorters held service on shipboard. They were doubtless burning with zeal on their return from the camp-meeting. Thirty-five of the sailors joined class, and a goodly number gave in their names to the lieutenant to have their "grog stopped." Many were baptized on board the war ship.

During the following year J. N. Maffitt and D. Ostrander aided in extra meetings, and the altar was thronged with the penitents. It may cast a shade of reproof over the lax discipline of our day to call attention to the fact that the church records of those times were often marked by the word *expelled*. Here, likewise, is a suggestive record:

Simon Richardson, John Smith and Adam Seabury were appointed a standing committee for one month to try delinquents,——Dec., 1830.

A change of pastors brought John C. Green and C. W. Carpenter to this charge in 1831, and they were re-inforced by J. C. Tackaberry in 1832, after the formation of a new colony from the mother church. The Washington-street church and parsonage were erected in 1831, at a cost of about $24,000.[3] For about four years Sands-street and Washington-street churches constituted one charge, being undivided in their financial interests, and under the same pastoral supervision.

Thomas Burch was appointed a second time to this charge in 1833 and 1834. His colleagues on the circuit were John Kennaday and John Luckey. There were four churches under their watch-care, including New Utrecht, and the membership numbered more than a thousand.

The New York Conference for the first time held its session in Sands-street church in 1835. This year it was deemed

---

[2] Christian Advocate and Journal, 1828.

[3] J. W. Harper in Trustees' Record, 1843. They were finished in 1832.

expedient to make a division of the church property. Pastors were appointed to the three churches severally, separate boards of trustees were elected, each church assuming a portion of the debt,[4] and obtaining sole possession of the property which it occupied. Of the burial grounds on Concord-street and at Wallabout, each church held an undivided third.[5] For about three years, however, the several boards of trustees met in joint session. A committee was appointed by the joint board of trustees in 1836, consisting of one from each church, to ascertain if ground suitable for a meeting-house could be obtained in the neighborhood of the residences of Christopher Hempstead and Mrs. Mary Powers, [not far from Hanson Place,] and upon what terms and conditions, and to report. The committee did nothing; but "a plot of ground, with building stones and a part of the necessary fixtures for a house of worship, was offered as a donation by James E. Underhill through Mr. Ingles. This offer was declined by the board on account of the situation being *too far from the settled part of the city*, and because Mr. Underhill required that *the church should have a steeple.*"[6]

Bartholomew Creagh was the first to have pastoral charge in Sands-street after the division, and his allowance was $600 a year. In 1837 W. H. Norris succeeded Mr. Creagh. During his two years term the membership increased from 402 to 667. Fitch Reed was his successor for one year. The annual conference of 1839 was held in the Sands-street church. In 1840 Long Island was set off as a presiding elder's district, in charge of Stephen Martindale. P. C. Oakley was appointed pastor of this church, and under his administration in 1841, the first regular board of stewards was elected.[7]

In 1843, L. M. Vincent pastor, the membership was largely increased by a revival. It was at this time decided to demolish the church building, and erect in its place a new and larger structure, the "old white church" being insufficient to

---

[4] The entire indebtedness after Washington-street church was built, was $18,500. Sands-street became responsible for $5,500, York-street for $3,000 and Washington-street for $10,000.

[5] Trustees Record, Washington-street church.   [6] Trustees Record, 1836.

[7] Joseph Wesley Harper's statement in Trustees' Record Book, 1843.

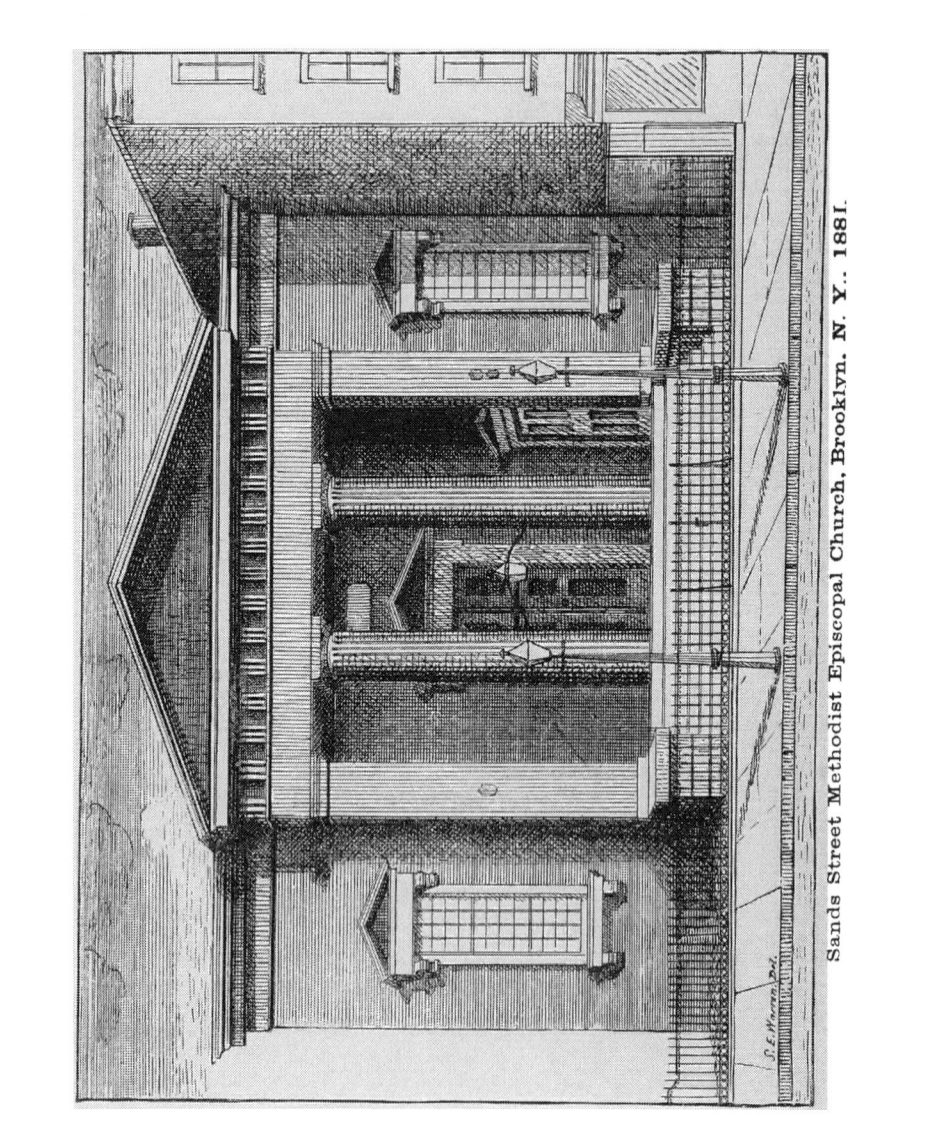

Sands Street Methodist Episcopal Church, Brooklyn, N. Y., 1881.

accommodate the crowds attending upon Mr. Vincent's ministry. With intense emotion did the congregation, especially the older people, assemble for the last time in the doomed building, and listen to "the tearing down sermon" by the pastor. The senior members regarded the dear old church with an almost superstitious veneration. It had stood wellnigh forty years. From its high pulpit they had heard scores of honored ministers proclaim the word of life. Asbury and Dow and Summerfield and Bascom, and many pastors of the church, scarcely less eloquent or renowned, had preached there; and at its altars they had worshipped with the Garrisons, Harpers, Kirks, Mosers and Merceins. The demolition of the church was effected notwithstanding this profound regret, and on the 15th of January, 1844, a new brick church was dedicated. The preachers on that occasion we e Chas. Pitman and Nathan Bangs. On the following Sabba h Noah Levings and David M. Reese occupied the pulpit, and a subscription was taken, amounting to $1,400.[8] The building was of Grecian architecture, eighty feet in length, and sixty feet in width. While the builders were at work on this edifice, the congregation worshipped in a hall on the corner of Fulton and Nassau streets. At the expiration of Mr. Vincent's first year in May, 1843, a resolution was adopted by the quarterly conference—nine against eight—condemning the practice of petitioning for particular preachers. In 1844 John J. Matthias was appointed to the district, and Hart F Pease to the station. Nathan Bangs was stationed here in 1846 with John C. Tackaberry. A parsonage was built that year. The entire outlay for buildings amounted by this time to $18,000, of which the church owed $10,000.

The Sunday-school was conducted during these years with marked thoroughness and efficiency. On the following page is an exact copy of the certificate of membership presented to each scholar, the names and dates being inserted with a pen. Many of these certificates have been preserved.

In 1843 Moses F. Odell and Miss Esther Hollis, (now the widow of the Rev. William M'Allister,) organized the infant class with ten scholars.

---

[8] Christian Advocate.

SUNDAY-SCHOOL CERTIFICATE OF ADMISSION.

The Children walking in Wisdom's way.

.... having complied with the rules of admission to .... attached to the .... Sunday-school, is this day enrolled as a member thereof, and is henceforth entitled to all its privileges. May God guide and keep .... and bless the instruction .... may here receive, to the everlasting good of .... soul.

18......

.... *Superintendent,*

Roll Book, No

Class,

Teacher,

PARSONAGE AND SUNDAY SCHOOL BUILDING ON HIGH-ST.

CHAPTER VI.

A RECORD OF TEN YEARS; 1847–1856.

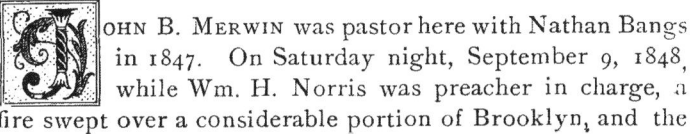

JOHN B. MERWIN was pastor here with Nathan Bangs in 1847. On Saturday night, September 9, 1848, while Wm. H. Norris was preacher in charge, a fire swept over a considerable portion of Brooklyn, and the new church and parsonage were burned—insurance only about $1,200. Fortunately the walls of the church were found to be perfectly safe for rebuilding, and without waste of time this enterprising people, encouraged by their zealous pastor, proceeded to repair their loss. While doing this, they erected a building in the rear of the church, fronting on High-street, containing Sunday-school rooms and a lecture room, and connected with the main building by a department for class rooms, eighteen by sixty feet, and two stories high. The building committee consisted of David Coope, Warren Richmond, Nathaniel Bonnell, Jacob Brown, and John J. Studwell. This church was dedicated March 25, 1849, a discourse being delivered by Dr. Stephen Olin. The Rev. T. W. Chadwick says that Dr. Olin's glorious sermon gave him a grand conception of the dignity of being a Christian.

The Sunday-school continued its career of prosperity. After the removal of its veteran founders, Robert Snow and Joseph Herbert, the leadership fell into the hands of men equally well qualified to superintend its affairs.

The following quotation from the minutes of a teachers' meeting of the Sands-street Sunday-school, held May 3, 1847, is a brief account of the origin of a remarkably successful Sunday-school missionary society:

On motion it was

Resolved, That a Juvenile Missionary Society be formed in this school; and that the officers of such society consist of a president, a vice-president, a secretary and a treasurer.

The meeting, on motion, proceeded to the election of said officers. Charles H. Fellows was elected president, Joshua I. Gascoigne, vice-president; Gilbert H. Read, secretary; Egbert Acker, treasurer. On motion it was

Resolved, That each teacher select a scholar in his or her class, whose duty it shall be to collect funds in such class, and pay them to the treasurer.

An infant-class missionary society had previously been organized, and, as already narrated, a young men's missionary society was in operation some twenty years antecedent to this date; but this was the beginning of the only *permanent* missionary organization connected with this church. The aggregate amount of money raised and paid into the general missionary treasury by this society is more than $50,000. It has also appropriated considerable sums to local missionary effort. A constitution was adopted July 19, 1847. Wm. Cartwright was made second vice-president; and the following persons were chosen the first board of managers: Ira Perego, Jr., James Cheetham, Horace N. Harrison, Benj. Haff, James Bogart, Wm. Marvin, Elisabeth E. Haff, Belinda Vanderveer, Josephine Curtis, Jane Vining, Mary Wadsworth, Harriet Oakley. A little later it was ordered that the last Sabbath in each month be set apart for missionary purposes. The first Sunday-school missionary festival was held in the Sunday-school room, December 25, 1849. The secretary made the following minute:

Brothers Kirk, Murphy, North and others addressed the meeting. Fifty dollars was collected. Thomas Kirk, Charles C. North, J. N. Judson, Wm. A. Walker and —— Camp of Eighteenth-street, New York, were made life members of the Juvenile Missionary Society. The school then had a treat of good things, and the remainder was taken to the poor school at F—.

One of the "others" among the speakers to whom the secretary refers, was J. Wesley Harper. This was to him a double celebration, for he was born on Christmas day. So deeply moved was he that he asked Sup't Odell to allow him to say a word. It was an unheard-of thing for him to address the children, and they listened with profound attention.

On Christmas day, 1854, certain features then quite novel, were introduced into the missionary celebration. It was a new departure, of which the following account is given:

The school was organized into fifty different societies, each having its own name and motto, and they collected about $680. The exercises in the church consisted of singing and addresses, and receiving the collections from the different societies [or classes]. After the school returned to the school-room, Superintendent Odell gave the classes baskets and boxes of good things. Ole Bull was present, and dedicated a new violin to the school, in return for which he was made a life member of the Juvenile Missionary Society.

It can hardly fail to awaken pleasant recollections in the minds of many who were present on those occasions, to find here recorded the names of some of the classes. A few will serve as specimens: "Old Sands-street, the Homestead;" "Lenders to the Lord;" "Father Snow Society;" "Stockholders in the never-failing Bank;" "Mrs. Ann Wilkins Society;" "Missionary Life and Trust Company." The mottoes, in most cases, were beautiful and appropriate passages of Scripture.

Events of ordinary interest which occurred during this comparatively recent period, need not be recorded here. The church flourished as in former years. The names of the eminent and worthy pastors during this decade,—Bangs, Merwin, Norris, Wood, Fox, Weed and Miley,—are in themselves unquestioned evidence that the spiritual interests of the church were ably and faithfully administered.

CHAPTER VII.

A RECORD OF TWENTY-EIGHT YEARS; 1857-1884.

THE published statistics of Methodism previous to 1857, consisted solely of the number of names on the class books. Since that date more complete tabulated statistical reports have been printed; and from these has been compiled a summary of statistics of old Sands-street Church for the last quarter of a century. The number of deaths reported, 1857 to 1883, inclusive, is 124; (The church records, incomplete as they are, contain the names of more than two hundred persons who have fallen asleep in Jesus, while in fellowship with this church, since 1798.) Baptized since 1856—adults, 119, children, 247. Besides making liberal provision for the support of pastors, presiding elders, bishops and worn-out conference preachers—for repairs, supplies and other miscellaneous objects, this church has contributed since the statistics have been published, the following amounts, in round numbers:— to the Tract Society, $700; to the Sunday School Union, $700; to the American Bible Society, $3,000; to the Board of Education, $350; to the Freedmen's Aid Society, $400; to the Woman's Foreign Missionary Society, $700; to the Board of Church Extension, $900; to the parent Missionary Society, $53,000; to various other missionary institutions, about $7,000; the whole being an average annual contribution of $2,500 for the last twenty-seven years. The collection for Church Extension reported in 1882, was the largest for that cause ever made by this church;—Chaplain M'Cabe had been there. The pastor, J. S. Breckinridge, conducted the services on Children's Day, 1882, and the amount then contributed for the cause of education surpassed all previous collections for that object. The names of the pastors during this latest period are as follows:—John Miley, John B. Hagany, B. H. Nadal, L. S. Weed, Charles Fletcher, E. G. Andrews, A. H.

Wyatt, G. De La Matyr, G. F. Kettell, F. P. Tower, George Taylor, Lindsay Parker, J. S. Breckinridge, L. R. Streeter; presiding elders, Buel Goodsell, Wm. H. Norris, John Kennaday, Daniel Curry, Benjamin Pillsbury, E. E. Griswold, T. G. Osborn, Charles Fletcher, A. S. Graves, G. F. Kettell, I. Simmons.

No portion of the history of this church is more remarkable, all things considered, than the record of the last few years. While some, if not most of the churches in "Old Brooklyn" struggled for existence, the old mother church maintained much of the vigor and the uniform prosperity of earlier days. Of necessity or of choice, from time to time many of the Sands-street people transferred their membership to other churches, but not a few resolved to stay and "hold the fort." Undismayed by the prospect of a speedy removal, they strove to improve the latest opportunities, and make the last days of Sands-street Methodism worthy of the past.

The class leaders and the Sunday-school workers emulated the zeal and enterprise of the fathers. The anniversaries were never more interesting. The Rev. Dr. Weed was present at the Christmas missionary festival, 1881. Having written a beautiful description of the decoration, and the arrangement of the children, he adds:

The Revs. D. Terry, A. S. Graves, J. E. Cookman, G. P. Mains, Lindsay Parker, and many of the well-known laymen of Brooklyn were in the congregation and on the platform. For nearly thirty consecutive years the Rev. David Terry, of the parent Missionary Society has been present at this Christmas festival, and opened the exercises with prayer. It was a great joy to many of his old friends to greet him once more. He was called upon to offer the opening prayer by Mr. S. S. Utter, the teacher of the infant class, who, assisting the superintendent of the school, Mr. Wm. I. Preston, presided with admirable tact over the services of the morning.

The call of the classes was intensified in interest by the splendid chorus singing by the entire school of the verse motto of the class called.

The motto of the young gents of the infant class is "The Young Guard;" that of the little misses, "Spring Flowers." A little fellow of four or five years, dressed in uniform, represented the boys; and a little girl of about the same age, was a symbol of spring flowers. They brought in from the class two hundred dollars.

To pastors and superintendents generally it may, we think, be a matter of very serious thought whether this way may not be the "better way." The whole effort and enthusiasm of the congregation, Church and Sunday-school are concentrated upon this one day of the year for collecting and reporting missionary money. All are interested, and all are represented by their gifts — parents, children, grandchildren, all are there. Even little babes are brought up in their fathers' or mothers' arms, with gifts in their little hands for the mission cause. * * * Without any large gifts from wealth, in a congregation and in the midst of a population representing what has come to be called the great middle class of society, Sands-street Church, through its Sunday-school, has for many years collected on this festival day for the missionary work what it collected on the day just passed, Dec. 26, 1881, namely, $2,000.[1]

Brothers Weed and Terry supposed this to be the last Christmas missionary festival in Sands-street; it was, indeed, *their* last; ere many months had gone, they were both translated to the Church above.

The Christian Advocate published the following additional notice of the work of the society during that year:

The thirty-fifth anniversary of the Sunday-school Missionary Society of Sands-street Methodist Episcopal Church, the Rev. J. S. Breckinridge, pastor, was held April 6. The annual report, presented by D. B. Phillips, the secretary, showed that $2,200 had been collected during the year, $100 of which was appropriated to the Howard Mission in New York, $150 to the Five Points Mission, in the same city, and $1,800 to the Parent Society of the Methodist Episcopal Church. A very interesting address was given on the occasion by the Rev. Gideon Draper, D. D., on mission work in Sweden, and the pastor stated that the first conference held in Sweden was presided over by Bishop Andrews, a former pastor of Sands-street.

The most memorable of all the annual missionary festivals was held Dec. 25, 1882. A large and beautiful painting of the "Old White Church" had been made from memory and was suspended on the wall in the rear of the pulpit. A star of blazing gas jets was seen above the painting, and on either side were appropriate emblems.

A profusion of North Carolina hanging moss and floral baskets adorned the front of the galleries, and near the organ a cluster of Sunday-school banners was displayed. Portraits of Robert Snow and Joseph Herbert were suspended in front of the gallery facing the pulpit, and between them hung the beautiful banners of the infant class. On elevated benches, behind the pulpit, reaching to the gal-

---

[1] Christian Advocate, Jan. 12, 1882.

Historical Record.

leries, the children of the infant class were seated,—a lovely sight to behold. The Sunday-school occupied the front seats in the body of the church. The house was crowded to its utmost capacity, for the general belief that this would be their last opportunity to attend such a meeting in the old Sabbath home, had drawn thither a host of the former members and friends of the school. A. B. Thorn officiated as leader of the singing, in which teachers and scholars joined. Even David himself would have been satisfied with the number and variety of musical instruments accompanying their voices—organ, cornet, piano, piccolo and bells. Among the distinguished visitors were Henry Ward Beecher and his assistant, Mr. Halliday; ex-mayor Howell, ex-mayor Booth, ex-mayor Hunter, Edward Rowe and ex-alderman Whiting. Sam S. Utter presided. At 10:30 A. M. the exercises were opened with an appropriate song:

> Ring out, O bells! right merrily,
> For Christmas time is here!

In place of the assistant secretary at the mission rooms, David Terry—absent for the first time in thirty years—John Parker, one of the Brooklyn pastors, offered prayer. The missionary offerings were then made in the usual manner. Some one had brought the old fire bucket which formerly belonged to "Poppy" Snow, and laid it on the platform. In this were deposited the offerings of the infant class, amounting to $250.

Mr. Beecher on being introduced, was greeted with applause. The Brooklyn Daily Eagle gave the following report of his address:

He said, as he remembered them the New England Congregationalists used to be big bugs. The Methodists had a hard time to get a hold in New England. They were not grand. When he went to Indiana, he found that things were reversed. There, said Mr. Beecher, the Methodists were on the top, and we were nowhere. The public sentiment of that State was in the hands of the Methodists. On the whole they were a nice sort of folks, and I came to have a warm heart for them. They had the good sense to go out among the common people, and they had a habit of exhibiting their feelings. I was a Presbyterian then, and I think very well of the Presbyterians. Their wells are deep, however, and they never run over. The water is good, but we have to pump for it. The Methodists are like springs—they need no pumping;

their wells flow over. When I came to Brooklyn, it was my good fortune to fall into the society of the members of this very church, among whom was Brother Odell, whose school at that time was considered the best in Brooklyn. I afterward gave some members to you, and that bound me to you; and some came to my prayer-meeting from this church. Brother Loper, who thought a man couldn't go to Heaven who wore a mustache or a goatee, used to come round; therefore it seems to me for various reasons, you could have gone farther and fared worse than having me speak to you. [Applause.] The warm-heartedness and fiery spirit of this church were always noticeable, and I would like to see some of this spirit to-day. You are going to leave this place that is consecrated. ... It is your purpose, I believe, to join forces and erect a great memorial church some where on the heights. I am sorry for it, and would recall to your minds in this connection the fable of the snail and the lobster shell. Beware of the devil of respectability; and don't be afraid to be common. My fear is that you will attempt to make a big, magnificent, popular church; my prayer is that God may defeat you. When you go, if you have any spare members, send them over to me, and I will take care of them. [Loud applause.]

One of the children stepped forward at the close of this address, and presented to Mr. Beecher a beautiful candy basket. Then followed an interesting scene; a score or more of the very youngest of the visitors,—some of them grandchildren and great-grandchildren of the early members of the school—came forward to "Grandpa" Utter with their offerings. From this source $441 was realized; and in a few minutes $250 more was subscribed, making the entire contribution $2,000. After singing and brief addresses, the festival was pleasantly and appropriately closed with the distribution of Christmas gifts to the children.

The pastor, J. S. Breckinridge said in his farewell sermon, in April, 1883:

Since I have been pastor, the church has contributed three thousand dollars annually to missionary purposes. The church is vigorously alive, and it has a grand future before it. It is stronger to-day than when I came, the membership having increased twenty per cent. The bridge is approaching completion, and soon the church will be removed. If you remain this side of Fulton-street, you will do well; if you go on the heights, you will do better. That part of the city needs a Methodist church. With no debt, a good leader, and one hundred and fifty thousand dollars in your treasury, you can storm and capture Brooklyn as Gen. Wolfe did the Heights of Abraham, at Quebec.

Sam. S. Utter presided at the Christmas exercises in 1883. The decorations were attractive and the attendance large, many of the old-time Sands-street people rallying as usual.

In the center of the large platform, improvised for the occasion, stood a very tall Christmas tree, laden with the gifts of Santa Claus, and perched upon it were two white turtle doves indicating the peace which Christmas tide betokens. Beneath was represented the manger in which Christ was born, to which was added the shepherd scene, and the Star of the East pending overhead—the whole furnishing a very impressive picture. * * * Mr. Utter said that some of the children present represented the sixth generation of worshippers at this church. The sum collected was about $2,200. The Rev. L. R. Streeter, the pastor, then made a short address, depicting vividly the birth of Christ and the circumstances surrounding it, the work he had accomplished, and the lesson to be derived from it. The exercises closed with the distribution of Christmas gifts.[2]

The Christmas of 1884 was duly celebrated, and the total missionary offerings amounted to nearly $1,600. The Rev. Dr. J. M. Reid, missionary secretary, made the principal address.[3]

It became evident as early as 1870 that the days of old Sands-street church were numbered. The prosperous growth of Brooklyn, to which the churches have in a large degree contributed, compels some of them to recede from their original location. The East River bridge with its increasing tide of traffic and travel must render this ancient stronghold of Methodism untenable for religious services. The site has been and will be desired for secular purposes. The bridge company made a liberal offer, ($125,000,) for the church property, but the trustees declined to sell at that price.

The outlook is uncertain. At this hour none can predict in what form, if at all, the church organization will survive. A proposition strongly urged, particularly in 1882, by many leading ministers and laymen, to unite Sands-street and Pacific-street churches in the formation of a new organization on the "Heights," did not commend itself to some of the more influential members of Sands-street church. Attempts to consolidate other Methodist Churches in "Old" Brooklyn

---

[2] "Brooklyn Eagle," December 26, 1883.

[3] In the time of pastor Vincent, John M. Reid, then a young man, often preached in the Sands-street church. He says: "I went over there one night and preached, and most marvelous manifestations appeared. We invited seekers forward and the altar was filled. We cleared a row of seats and they were filled; another, and they were filled, and at last we concluded that the whole house was an altar of seeking. Thereupon followed a great revival, during which I labored as often as my strength would permit. I was at that time principal of the Mechanics' Institute School in New York city and a local preacher."

met with similar defeat. Dr. Buckley wrote in *The Christian Advocate:*

<blockquote>
All the efforts at consolidation in connection with the five churches—the York-street, the Sands-street, the Washington-street, the Johnson-street, and the Pacific-street—have failed. Yet it is obvious to all that they do not comprise materials for more than two strong charches. Many Methodists have been discouraged by the state of things and have joined other congregations. It is certain that decay and death await some of these churches, and the valuable properties which they have in trust will be eaten up in a few years. The history of the debates already had shows that no difficulties except those which arise from a want of broad views, and which have no higher source than prejudice, are in the way. It now looks as though, through mismanagement or want of management, Methodism in those parts of Brooklyn will continue to diminish, and that much of the property will be consumed.
</blockquote>

There are some who seem to cling with fondness to those sacred memories and associations which could not be transferred to any other place of worship, but it should be borne in mind that a removal of the church will not of necessity involve the abandonment of the name and memory of Sands-street Methodism. One writer makes this suggestion:

<blockquote>
Imitating other churches on the "Heights," this new Methodist church might establish and maintain a mission Sunday-school not far from the present site of Sands-street church, and thus continue its noble work among the children, under changed, though perhaps more favorable conditions. The Mayflower mission, sustained by the Plymouth church, and other missions, cared for by the Henry-street Presbyterian, and St. Ann's Episcopal, and Pierrepont-street Baptist, and other churches on the Heights, are successful. There is no reason why the Brooklyn Heights Methodist Episcopal church might not work as successfully a Sands-street mission, and thus worthily perpetuate the name and memory of the mother church of Brooklyn Methodism.[4]
</blockquote>

Right alongside the multitudes as they surge up and down the great thoroughfare are the pious dead who were laid to rest beneath the shadow of the "old white church." The widening stream of traffic and travel will soon disturb their repose. The old church-yard which holds the sacred dust of James Harper, Andrew Mercein, Thomas Carpenter, John Garrison, Robert Snow, and other equally devoted men, with their godly wives, must soon totally disappear. It is hoped that the friends of old Sands-street church will see that all possible pains are taken to identify the graves of these Methodist worthies, and to re-bury their bones with tender care.

---

[4] B., in The Christian Advocate.

The simplicity and the strength of Methodism have in many respects been exemplified in the history of this church. Without tower or bell, without pompous ritual or gorgeous architecture; without sensational devices of any description, this old church has kept time to the march of Methodism. There has been no rebellion against the appointed pastor, no disparagement of the class meetings, no departure from the old methods, no abandonment of the old principles.

This church has maintained a prosperous career throughout one of the brightest of the sixty centuries of the world's history, but in the brightening glory of the coming years, she will continue to live in the ever widening results of her faithful service, and the increasing usefulness of her children —the many prosperous churches in Brooklyn, which are properly classed among the descendents of the old mother church.

To the praise of our itinerant system, it should be made known that during almost a century this church, in the days of her feebleness and the days of her strength, was never deprived of regular pastoral oversight and the stated ministrations of the Gospel. More than eighty ministers have held the relation of pastor to the Sands-street Church, three fourths of whom have gone to their reward on high, and hundreds of others have occasionally proclaimed the Gospel of salvation in this sacred place. Could a record be made of the sermons preached on Sabbath days and during revival services upon this watch-tower of Methodism, the number would scarcely fall below ten thousand. And these efforts have not been in vain. The word has not returned void. When the Lord writeth up his people it shall be said, This and that man was born there.

Besides the hundreds who have died while in fellowship with this people, other hundreds have transferred their membership to churches near or distant, and thence to the church triumphant. Multitudes of grateful Christians in this world and in the world above, remember the Sands-street altars as Jacob remembered Bethel and Peniel. They can never dissociate from the memory of their best experience upon earth, the old Sabbath home where they enjoyed the

SANDS STREET CHURCH, ERECTED 1848—INTERIOR VIEW

communion of saints — the foretastes of a blessed heavenly fellowship

It is pleasing and instructive to review so much as can be recorded of the history of a church organization for a hundred years; but the most vital and interesting portion of the history of any church must forever remain unwritten. No pen can record the unknown personal experience, the secret heart-struggles, and the unobserved deeds of charity and faith which constitute the real life-work of the followers of Christ. For a history of our life and its vast results, we await the day when the books shall be opened. Who will say that we may not yet find in Heaven's library, some bright volume, entitled " The True History of the Redeemed Company that came up from the Sands Street Church ? "

CHAPTER VIII.

RECORD OF MINISTERIAL APPOINTMENTS AND STATISTICS.

I. A Chronological List of Presiding Elders.

Conference Years.[1]	PRESIDING ELDERS.	Districts.[2]
1787	Thomas Foster	
1788	Henry Willis	
1789	F. Garrettson and Thomas Morrell	
1790	Thomas Morrell,[3]	
1791	Robert Cloud	
1792–1793	Jacob Brush	
1794	Freeborn Garrettson	
1795	George Roberts	
1796	Freeborn Garrettson	
1797	S. Hutchinson and F. Garrettson	
1798–1799	Sylvester Hutchinson	
1800–1803	Freeborn Garrettson	New York.
1804–1806	William Thacher	" "
1807–1810	Joseph Crawford	" "
1811–1814	F. Garrettson	" "
1815–1818	Samuel Merwin	" "
1819	Nathan Bangs	" "
1820–1823	Peter P. Sandford	" "
1824–1827	Laban Clark	" "
1828–1831	Daniel Ostrander	" "
1832–1835	Samuel Merwin	" "
1836–1839	Daniel Ostrander	" "
1840–1843	Stephen Martindale	Long Island.
1844–1847	John J. Matthias	" "
1848–1850	Laban Clark	" "
1851–1854	Seymour Landon	" "
1855–1858	Buel Goodsell	" "
1859–1862	William H. Norris	" "

[1] Formerly these began sometimes as late as October, but recently in May or April.

[2] At first the Districts were large, and no names were given to them until the year 1800.

[3] Aaron Hunt's statement that Jacob Brush was presiding elder of the New York District that year is probably a mistake. See memorials of Jacob Brush and Aaron Hunt in Book II.

Old Sands Street Church.

Conference Years.	PRESIDING ELDERS.	Districts.
1863 . .	John Kennaday,[4] W. H. Norris	Long Island.
1864–1867	Dan'l Curry,[5] Benj. Pilsbury. . .	L. I. South.
1868–1871	Edwin E. Griswold	" "
1872–1875	Thomas G. Osborn,[6] Chas. Fletcher	" "
1876–1879	Albert S. Graves	Brooklyn.
1880–1882	George F. Kettell	"
1883 . .	Ichabod Simmons	"

II. A Chronological List of Pastors, with the Numbers reported, including Probationers, at the Close of their Respective Terms.

Conference Years.	PASTORS.	No. of Members. and Prob.
1787 . .	Woolman Hickson, John Dickins, Freeborn Garrettson	.Unknown.[7]
1788 . .	Henry Willis, (elder,) J. Dickins . .	"
1789 . .	Robert Cloud, John Merrick, William Phœbus	"
1790 . .	David Kendall, Wm. Phœbus, Aaron Hunt, J. Brush	"
1791 . .	Wm. Phœbus, Benj. Abbott . . .	"
1792 . .	John Ragan, James Boyd . .	"
1793 . .	Joseph Totten, George Strebeck . .	"
1794 . .	Ezekiel Cooper, Lawrence M'Combs; also, Wm. Phœbus, David Kendall, supernumerary preachers[8] . . .	35
1795 . .	Joseph Totten[9]	39
1796–1797	William Phœbus[10]	81
1798 . .	Andrew Nichols	73
1799 . .	Cyrus Stebbins	54

[4] Died Nov. 14, 1863.

[5] Elected Editor of the Christian Advocate, in May, 1864.

[6] Resigned after a few months on account of ill health.

[7] Included in the membership of New York station. 1787–1789, and of L. I. circuit, 1790–1793.

[8] All appointed to New York and Brooklyn circuit. M'Combs was to change every three months with Sylvester Hutchinson of New Rochelle cir., and Robert Hutchinson of Long Island circuit.

[9] First stationed preacher. Appointed for six months. It is presumed he remained a full year.

[10] Practically a stationed preacher; for although Brooklyn was connected these two years and for some time afterward, by a system of exchanges, with L. I. cir., and so represented in the printed lists of appointments, Brooklyn was really a separate station, as shown by the financial record of the L. I. Quarterly Conference Minutes.

Historical Record.

Conference Years.	PASTORS.	No. of Members and Prob.
1800–1801	David Buck	71
1802	Peter Jayne	71
1803	Ezekiel Canfield	73
1804	Cyrus Stebbins, Ezekiel Cooper[11]	74
1805	Ezekiel Cooper, Samuel Merwin[12]	136
1806	Ezekiel Cooper, Samuel Thomas, Oliver Sykes.	225
1807	Elijah Woolsey, John Wilson	253
1808	Daniel Ostrander	245
1809	Reuben Hubbard, T. Drummond[13]	255
1810–1011	William Thacher[14]	210
1812–1813	Lewis Pease, T. Drummond[15]	239
1814	Samuel Merwin	198
1815	Nathan Emery	231
1816–1817	Joseph Crawford	271
1818	William Ross	320
1819–1820	Alex. M'Caine, Henry Chase[16]	216
1821–1822	Lewis Pease	401
1823–1824	W. Ross, M. B. Bull,[17] (two ch's.)	414
1825	Thomas Burch, (two churches.)	424
1826	T. Burch, S. L. Stillman, (two ch's)	436
1827	S. Luckey, S. L Stillman, (two ch's)	454
1828	S. Luckey, S. Landon, (two ch's)	508
1829–1830	N. Levings, J. Covel, Jr., (two ch's)	663
1831	John C. Green, C. W. Carpenter, (three churches.)	986
1832	J. C. Green, C. W. Carpenter, J. C. Tackaberry, (three churches.).	971
1833–1834	T. Burch, J. Kennaday, J. Luckey, (four ch's, including New Utrecht.)	1037

---

[11] Stebbins left the station, and the old church book states that Ezekiel Cooper was pastor half the year.

[12] Mr. Merwin was pastor during the last quarter.

[13] Records,—Hubbard went to the Episcopalians. Drummond was appointed to supply the place.

[14] He was to exchange every month with Francis Ward. They exchanged only once.

[15] Mr. Pease's health failed in June, 1813, and Mr. Drummond was in charge the last part of the year.

[16] Mr. M'Caine left the charge in February, 1821, and Mr. Chase was pastor till Conference. A large number of the colored members seceded.

[17] Mr. Ross died during the second year of his term, and the church records indicate that Mr. Bull was in charge after his death.

Old Sands Street Church.

Conference Years.	PASTORS.	No. of Members and Prob.
1835–1836	B. Creagh, (Sands-st. Church only)	402
1837–1838	Wm. H. Norris	667
1839	Fitch Reed	606
1840–1841	Peter C. Oakley	521
1842–1843	Leonard M. Vincent	677
1844–1845	Hart F. Pease	604
1846	N. Bangs, J. C. Tackaberry	612
1847	N. Bangs, J. B. Merwin	564
1848–1849	Wm. H. Norris	557
1850–1851	John W. B. Wood	500
1852–1853	Henry J. Fox, M. B. Bull, sup'y, 1853	601
1854–1855	Levi S. Weed, M. B. Bull, sup'y	470
1856–1857	John Miley, B. Bull, sup'y	601
1858	W. F. Watkins (supply,)[18] J. B. Hagany	539
1859	John B. Hagany	587
1860–1861	Bernard H. Nadal[19]	606
1862–1863	Levi S. Weed	605
1864–1866	Charles Fletcher	600
1867	Edward G. Andrews	599
1868	A. H. Wyatt, (supply),[20] G. DeLaMatyr	590
1869	Gilbert DeLaMatyr	595
1870–1871	George F. Kettell	514
1872–1873	Freeman P. Tower[21]	476
1874–1876	George Taylor	476
1877–1879	Lindsay Parker	539
1880–1882	John S. Breckinridge	555
1883–1884	Lewis R. Streeter	

[18] Mr. Watkins was in charge during the few weeks intervening between the sessions of the New York East and New York Conferences.

[19] Dr. George R. Crooks stands in the Minutes as one of the pastors of this station in 1861 and 1862, but the appointment was merely nominal.

[20] Mr. Wyatt had charge after conference until Mr. DeLaMatyr arrived in June. H. B. Elkins received in 1868 a nominal appointment to this church.

[21] Charles Fletcher was nominally assigned to this church with F. P. Tower for a short time in 1872.

CHAPTER IX.

A RECORD OF OFFICIAL MEMBERS.
(CHRONOLOGICAL)

TO WHICH IS ADDED A LIST OF TEACHERS, ETC., IN THE SUNDAY SCHOOL.

The Dates indicate when the several Officers were first named as such in the Records.

I. Local Preachers.

1808	Marvin Richardson		John Brice
1809	Ithiel Smead	1835	Charles C. Leigh
"	Linden	1836	John Collett
1811	Wm. Blagborne		Samuel Bedell
"	John Brower	1839	Walker Booth
1815	Chas. W. Carpenter	"	Chas. S. Macreading
"	Wm. Dawson	1840	John A. Edmonds
"	Thomas Sands	1841	George Hollis
	John Dalton	1843	Wm. McAllister
1817	James Ambler	1844	John Rossell
1818	Anthony E. Nichols	1845	Wm. Stevens
"	Artemas Stebbins	"	Nathaniel Ruggles
"	John Nickerson	1846	D. I. Reed
1822	Wm. Summerfield	1847	Wm. S. Finch
"	Christopher Rutherford	"	John Redfield
1823	Jonathan Lyon	1849	John Cottier
"	Elnathan Raymond	"	Robert Ibbotson
1824	Oliver V. Amerman	"	James Clayton
1827	John Dikeman	"	Francis Bottome
"	Wm. Mundell	"	Thomas H. Burch
"	Joseph Baggott	1852	Thomas Noden
"	Wm. Ducker	1853	Joshua L. Burrows
1830	Fred. D. McFarlan		Chas. J. Fox Julius
1833	Charles Pomeroy	1854	Thos. Stephenson
"	Wm. Smith	1856	David Tuthill
"	John B. Merwin	"	John Bull
"	Chas. Stearns	"	David G. Stratton

46   *Old Sands Street Church.*

1860 Benj. W. Bond
"   Thomas N. Laine
1861 Robert Owen Jones
"   Robert Robson
1862 John G. Fay
"   John Jeffrey

1863 Thomas Owen
1864 B. F. B. Leach
1866 Robert M. Moore
"   John W. Banta
1869 C. W. Drake
1872 Alfred F. Farnell

II. Licensed Exhorters.

1811 John Brower
1814 Peter Conger, (colored)
"   James Titus, (colored)
1822 Wm. Burnett
"   Daniel Field
1826 Wm. Ducker
1831 Wm. N. Searles
1834 Chas. C. Leigh

1834 John C. Melvin
"   Fred. R.. Anderson
1836 David Allen
1842 John H. Ackerman
"   Sidney E. Brewer
1843 Wm. M'Allister
1846 Thos. J. Humphrey
1867 George Leavens

III. Class Leaders.

1793 Nicholas Snethen
1798 John Garrison
"   Isaac Moser
"   James DeGraw
1804 Ithiel Smead
1806 Joseph Moser
"   George Smith
"   John Brower
"   James Herbert
"   Joseph Herbert
1807 Thomas Kirk
"   Simon Richardson
1808 Wm. Foster
"   Andrew Mercein
"   John Cooper
"   Isaac DeVoe
"   John C. Bennett
"   Jeremiah Wells
"   Jacob Brown
1819 Benj. Cook
"   Abraham Bennett
1822 Daniel Field
1823 Adrian Bogart
1824 Elnathan Raymond
1825 Christopher Hempstead
1826 Richard Smith
"   Chauncey Carter
"   Christopher Rutherford

     John Smith
1827 Henry R. Piercey
     Jacob Garrison
     Adam Seabury
     John G. Murphy
     Benj. R. Prince
1829 Thomas Frazier
"   John Dikeman
     Christopher Stibbs
     John Brice
     Walter Blair
1830 Samuel H. Moser
"   Peter C. Bell
     Linus K. Henshaw
     Richard VanVoorhis
1831 James N. Hyde
"   James Sweeney
"   Ebenezer Latimer
"   Augustus Rolph
     Warren Richmond
1832 David Coope
"   John G. Pray
"   D. T. Tarbell
"   Samuel Husted
1833 Geo. R. Booth
"   Ebenezer T. Web
"   Chas. Stearns
"   Wm. Ducker

Historical Record. 47

1833	John T. Tarbull		Andrew D. Gale
1835	Thomas Thorp		John Rossell
"	Aaron Kimball	1850	Dr. Dillon S. Landon
"	Thomas M'Coy	"	Wm. Edsell
"	Carman A. Simonson	1852	Ira Perego, Sen.
"	Benj. Handley		Israel Willersdorf
"	Daniel T. Wells		Melville Kelsey
"	Sidney E. Brewer		David O'Neill
"	Joseph (or Sam'l) Dykes		Ira Perego, Jr.
	Moses Bedell		Watson Sanford
	Lorenzo Stansbury	1853	Conklin S. Gabel
1837	John C. Melvin	"	John G. Fay
"	Jos. Wesley Harper		Aaron Kingsland
"	Fred. R. Anderson		Daniel D. Whitney
1838	Rob't M'Chesney		Martin Fanning
"	Nathaniel Bonnell	1856	John M. Bradstreet
"	Ellis Parcell	"	James L. Romer
"	James B. Gascoigne	1859	Robert M. Lockwood
1840	Wm. D. Odell	1862	Wm. Foster, 2nd
1842	John H. Ackerman	"	John Jeffrey
"	——— Holly	"	Daniel A. Cooke
"	Chas C. Leigh		Robert J. Powell
"	Dr J. W Corson		Walter L. Bennett
"	Solon C. Foster		R. Shapton
1843	Robert W. Peck	1866	Harvey Hubbell
"	Samuel Hurlburt	"	Geo. Leavens
"	Samuel B. Tuthill	"	Wm. I. Preston
"	Wm. M'Donald	"	John M. Espenscheid
"	Jacob M. Gray	"	Samuel P. Kittle
"	John Benjamin	"	C. B. Hobart
"	Samuel Utter	1867	Wm. Parker
	Nelson Morris	"	Walter Lock
	Wm. Stevens	1868	Fred. G. Reast
	Thos. W. Chadwick		D. K. Elmendorf
	Moses F. Odell		S. U. F. Odell
1846	Wm. Cartwright		Richard Bunce
"	Stephen R. Frazier		Chas. L. Pitts
"	Wm. Wall		Edgar M'Donald
"	Orrin Swift		Willis M'Donald
"	James DeGray		Miss Jane Vanderveer
	John E. Hanford		Augustus T. Gurlitz
	Richard Lawrence	1880	James D. Robertson
1848	Thomas H. Burch	1881	Alfred Dredge
	John Cottier	1883	George S. Richards

IV. Trustees.

1794	John Garrison	1794	Burdet Stryker
"	Thomas VanPelt	"	Stephen Hendrickson

1794 Richard Everitt
 "   Isaac Moser
 "   James De Graw
     James Herbert
     John Cornelison
1800 James Harper
1807 Thomas Kirk
     George Smith
     Wm. Henry
     Andrew Mercein
1812 Robert Snow
1819 Isaac Devoe
     John G. Pray
     Samuel T. Anderson
1823 Joseph Herbert
     Isaac Nostrand
1824 John G. Murphy
 "   Jacob Brown
 "   Richard Van Voorhis
1825 Isaac Searles
 "   Jeremiah Wells
     Samuel Harper
     Joseph Moser
     Nathaniel Bonnell
     Joseph Wesley Harper
     Wm. Foster
1833 Thomas Frazier
 "   John Smith
 "   Chr'opher M. Hempstead
     John Dikeman
1834 David Coope
 "   Samuel H. Moser
     Wm. M'Donald
1850 John J. Studwell
 "   George J. Vining
1855 Tapping Reeve
1856 Ira Perego, Sen.
1860 Harvey Hubbell
1862 Abia B. Thorn
 "   John Cottier
1864 Daniel D. Whitney
1866 Crawford C. Smith
1868 Wm. I. Preston
 "   Aaron Kingsland
1870 John J. Barnier
1879 Fred G. Reast.

V. Stewards.

1833 Jacob Brown
     Samuel H. Moser
     David Coope
1841 Joseph Wesley Harper
 "   Noah Silleck
 "   Richard Cadmus
 "   Nathaniel Bonnell
1843 Crawford C. Smith
1844 Samuel Hurlburt
1847 John J. Studwell
     John Cottier
1856 S. U. F. Odell
1857 James B. Gascoigne
1859 Ira Perego
1866 Daniel D. Whitney
1868 Joshua I. Gascoigne
1868 John J. Barnier
1869 Sam S. Utter
1870 Henry G. Fay
     David Stanley
     John M. Espenscheid
1873 Augustus T. Gurlitz
1875 Lowery Somerville
 "   David S. Quimby, Jr.
 "   Erastus Hyde
1877 James M'William
 "   Egbert Acker
 "   Philip Waters
1881 Wm. R. Hegeman
 "   James D. Robertson
1882 Daniel B. Phillips

VI. First Male Sunday School Superintendents.

1816 Robert Snow
1833 Joseph Herbert
1861 Moses F. Odell[1]
1866 Ira Perego

[1] Odell was practically First Superintendent earlier, Herbert in his old age holding the first place nominally, as a merited honor.

Historical Record.

1867 Samuel U. F. Odell
1875 Sam S. Utter
1876 William I. Preston
1877 Henry G. Fay
1882 John M. Espenscheid

VII. Second Male Sunday School Superintendents.

1816 Joseph Herbert[2]
1833 Orrin Swift
1842 Charles C. Leigh
1848 Moses F. Odell
1862 John Cottier
1865 Samuel U. F. Odell
1867 Sam S. Utter
1876 John J. Barnier
1877 John M. Espenscheid

VIII. Third Male Sunday School Superintendents.

Chauncey Carter
Orrin Swift
1834 David Coope
1836 Thomas Thorp
1841 John Bryant
1847 William M'Donald
1847 John Cottier
1848 James De Gray
1853 John G. Fay
1862 Ira Perego
1864 S. U. F. Odell
1865 Robert M. Lockwood

IX. Fourth Male Sunday School Superintendents.

Orrin Swift
1833 Newall Bond

X. First Female Sunday School Superintendents

1821 Sarah Swim
1853 Mary Ann M'Gee
1868 S. Virginia Cutter
1870 Elizabeth Vanderveer
1871 Ella Folger

XI. Second Female Sunday School Superintendents.

1847 Mary Ann M'Gee
1853 Lavinia M. Thorn[3]
1857 S. Virginia Cutter
1868 Elizabeth Vanderveer
1870 Ella Folger

XII. Sunday School Secretaries.

James E. Underhill
James Hall
1833 Joshua Marsden VanCott
1834 Isaac H. Herbert
1836 Albert Carpenter
1838 Valentine Carman
" Thomas W. Chadwick
Moses F. Odell
1847 Thomas H. Burch
1848 James Cheetham
1854 Joshua I. Gascoigne
" Richard F. Vanderveer
" John E. Fay
1862 Daniel B. Phillips
1869 David S. Quimby, Jr.
1878 Edwin W. Dorlon
1881 H. H Guhrauer

---

[2] He was one of the founders of the school at that time, and probably ranked next to Robert Snow,

[3] Married Joshua I. Gascoigne.

50   *Old Sands Street Church.*

XIII. Sunday School Treasurers.

1853 David O'Neill   1880 John L. Utter
1869 Egbert Acker   1881 Sam S. Utter

XIV. Sunday School Librarians.

1837 Thomas W. Chadwick   1864 Edgar M'Donald
1838 Benj. M. Stilwell   "   E. A. Smith
"   Job G. Habberton   "   W. S. Weeks
"   James C. Akins   1867 J. R. Burnett
1841 Sidney C. Herbert   1869 C. C. Smith, Jr.
1842 Edwin Beers   1870 Joseph Carson
1847 John G. Smith   "   Edward M'Gill
"   Chas. H. Stilwell   1872 Chas. E. Hyde
"   Washington Wadsworth   "   A. J Powell
"   Joshua I. Gascoigne   1873 Joseph A. Archer
"   Wm. A. Walker   "   Fred. A. Nast
1850 G. Snowden Dey   1874 Gerald Whitney
1851 Joseph Richards   "   John L. Utter
1852 Richard M'Donald   1877 Wm. H. Aitkin
1855 Abia B. Thorn   "   Britton C. Thorn
"   David O'Neill   1878 Geo. B. Weaver
"   Wm. Walker   "   John E. Nast
1856 Edward Hoagland   "   Wm. J. Rusher
1857 John E. Fay   1879 H. H. Guhrauer
1858 Henry G. Fay   "   Wm. N. Coler, Jr.
"   Joshua Trippett   "   J. P. Simonson
1859 John W. Haskins   1881 Wm. J. Reast
1859 Chas. J. Ashley   "   John Carrougher
1860 Lucien Warner   1882 Wm. H. Creshull
1862 Clarence Stanley   1883 Clarence White
"   Joseph A. Hoyt

XV. Sunday School Organists.

1875 A. J. Powell   1881 Thos. L. Doyle
1878 H. H. Nast   1882 Wm. Neidlinger

XVI. Male Sunday School Teachers:—Intermediate and Senior Departments.

1816 Robert Snow   1816 Richard Cornwell
"   Joseph Herbert   Samuel Hall
"   Daniel DeVinne   Enoch Jacobs
"   Andrew Mercein   Sidney Herbert
"   John Dikeman   David Coope
"   James Engles   Calvin Knowlton
"   Abraham Vanderveer   Alfred Bush
"   John G. Murphy   John S. Wright

John Wright
John T. Stibbs
John Bryant
Benj. Payne
J. Marsden Van Cott
Daniel Stanley
Jeremiah Mundell
Samuel S. Powell
John B. Brewster
John Carhart
John A. Swim
John Webb
Newall Bond
Isaac A. Swaim
Chas. C. Leigh
Wm. Bennett
Martin Mandeville
William Smith
Isaac Tillottson
Wm. S. Burnett
1833 Hamilton Reeve
" Isaac H. Herbert
" Daniel T. Wells
" Benj. Vail
" Thomas W. Chadwick
" George W. Williams
" William Rushmore
" Hosea Clark
1834 William S. Osborn
" Frederick Stevenson
" Samuel Bragaw
" Theron Burnett
" John Balderson
" William O. Stibbs
1835 Richard Thomas
" Albert Carpenter
" James Lovejoy
" John Baldwin
" Cornelius Garrison
" Henry Lane
" Edward Bishop
" Daniel Downs
" Andrew Pinkney
" Edward Morehouse
" Richard Ducker
1836 George Hollis
" George Slaughter
" Edwin C. Estes

1836 Chester Bedell
" Wm. Bowmen
" Valentine Carman
" Asaph M. Youngs
" Isaac Carhart
" Jesse Gilbert
" Peter P. Haff
" John Van Ness
1837 Henry Mallery
" Job G. Habberton
" Peter W. La Roza
" Wm. Clinton
" Wm. S. Habberton
" Richard Cadmus
" Benjamin Handley
" Homer Wiltse
" George Heneger
" Isaac Selover
1839 John H. Benjamin
" James C. Akin
" Ephraim J. Whitlock
" Benj. M. Stilwell
" Alfred Dykes
" George W. Copeland
" William E. Cornell
" Edwin Beers
" Joseph Adams
" Edmund Morehouse
1840 Charles H. Stilwell
1841 John G. Smith
" Wm. M'Allister
" John B. Sandford
" Joseph Harrison
" Charles D. Wadsworth
" Washington Wadsworth
1842 Stephen R. Frazier
" William H. Drew
" Richard Buggy
" Thomas H. Burch
Charles H. Fellows
Horace Harrison
Moses F. Odell
Oliver C. Lincoln
William Edmonds
Thomas Reed
Edward Sandford
Egbert Acker
William J. Bogart

W. C. Marvin
John Wiggins
Joseph Way
John W. Valentine
William Walsh
Orrin Swift
James DeGray
Ira Perego, Jr.
Benjamin A. Haff
Samuel Utter
Watson Sandford
Ira Sturgis
John Moore
Cornelius Moore
James Bogart
Edward Allen
1847 Sam S. Utter
" Alexander Alexander
" James Cheetham
Gilbert Reed
Dillon Stevens Landon
Edward Thomas
Robert Turner
1848 Benjamin Bennett
" William S. Finch
" Charles T. Wales
" George W. Valentine
1849 Gilbert S. Dye
" John Davis
" Harlow Fenn
" Jacob Weck
" John W. Corson
" John Albro
" Robert Young
" Charles S. Norton
1850 Julius R. Pomeroy
" William Irvine
" Henry G. Howell
" Frederick Hart
" Sidney Smith
" Charles J. Oliver
" Henry Broad
" Henry D. Gould
" Benjamin Moore
1851 William E. Shelden
" William M. Ketchell
" Thomas W. Armstrong
" John J. Gentry

1851 F. G. DeVictor
" John D. Burtnett
" F. Asbury Johnson
" David O'Neill
" John Badger
1852 Thomas Wright
" Robert Brown
" George A. Williams
" Henry B. Keane
" Henry Deane
1853 Charles E. Davis.
" John G. Fay
" Augustus C. Wessell
" George S. Benjamin
" Samuel W. Bliss
1854 James F. Greenwood
" James B. Gascoigne
" James B. Craig
" John B. Tuthill
" William Ringwood
" Alfred P. Reynolds
" Frank A. Gale
" John W. Haskins
" John M. Sawyer
" William Parker
" David Tuthill
" G. Sawyer
" Joseph A. Armfield
" Lemuel Burrows
1855 Benjamin Cornwell
" Benjamin Bryer
" John Randolph Martin
" Bethuel Rogers
" Charles Shaw
" David A. Cooke
" James M. Bradstreet
" W. Sales
" Edward Hoagland
" Robert M. Lockwood
1857 Henry G. Fay
" Alfred Perego
" Charles Nordhoff
" Edward Torbitt
" James L. Romer
" Benjamin Bond
" David Stanley
" Thomas Markley
" A. T. VanWyck

1858 Edward P. Bellows
" Henry Duren
" John O. Hoyt
" Henry J. Cutbill
" John E. Fay
" Andrew Merwin
" Francis Dunn
" Z. Clayton
" Sam'l U. F. Odell
" John Cottier
" James Clayton
" Abia B. Thorn
" John Bentley
" George Vernam
1860 Thomas Tilley
" Charles A. Righter
" Robert L. Tilton
" Charles B. Hobart
1861 Thomas G. Peckham
1862 Thomas P. Waldron
" Charles Wood
" Remington Vernam
1864 Peter Backman
" Robert M. Moore
" James Darling
" James E. Bloomer
" John Parker
" Lewis N. Haskins
" Clarence Stanley
" Richard F. Vanderveer
1865 Charles A. Barnard
1866 David S. Quimby, Jr.
" Ebenezer Bell
" S. J. Hammond
" Willis M'Donald
" William I. Preston
" John Jeffrey
1867 William A. Knowles
" Theodore Sutherland
" J. Frank Dillont
" George E. Henderson
1868 William J. Tate
" Lewis N. Smith
" Samuel P. Kittle
" Augustus T. Gurlitz
" John M. Espenscheid
" Fred. A. Nast

1868 Edgar M'Donald
" John J. Barnier
1869 Henry L. Stiles
" P. T. Horton
1870 E. P. Alvord
1872 Erastus Hyde
" Thomas Wintringham
" Nathaniel F. Elkin
" J. B. Sutton
" James M'William
" Daniel B. Phillips
1873 J. S. Seaman
" Jason Moore
" John Reed
1874 John B. Weaver
1875 L. B. Strong ;
" Edwin W. Dorlon
" Richard Bunce
1876 William E. Lowe
" Britton C. Thorn
" J. DeBaun
" S. J. Strong
" W. H. Soden
" Lowery Somerville
1877 William R. Hegeman
1878 George A. Smith
" John Walhizer
" Frank Whiteley
" Jewell F. Harris
" LaGrange Browne
" Thomas L. Geehr
1879 William A. Heydecker
" Philip Brooks
" Andrews Preston
" W. R. Wengorovius
" Longworth Parker
1880 Richard A. Brown
" Orris Thayer
1881 George S. Richards
1882 Herbert E. James
" H. C. Wood
1883 J. W. Robinson
" Richard Moore
" Charles S. Downs
" George A. Smith
" P. J. Gruman

XVII. Female Sunday School Teachers:—Intermediate and Senior Departments.[4]

1816 Susan Remsen
married John Dikeman
" Mrs. Richard Cornwell
1822 Ida DeGraw
" Huldah Frazier
married Samuel S. Powell
" Elizabeth Rogers
married Ira C. Buckelew
" Ann Noon
" Julia A. Herbert
married Orrin Swift
" Mary Garrison
married ——— Washburn
" Ellen Mayor
married ——— Wallace
" Eliza Wright
married Barzillai Russell
" Magdalen Storms
" Ann Wright
married Edward Rowe
1829 Cecelia Stansbury
married Daniel Stanley
Jane Silleck
married Henry Case
Ann Silleck
married John Emmons
Betsey C. Griswold
married Warren Richmond
Mrs. Welch
Elisabeth F. Vanderveer
Sarah Bumford
Jane Ann Lewis
Elisabeth Leonard
Margaret M'Donald
married Rev. F. Bottome
Mrs E. Davis
Sarah Ann Holland
Mrs. Sarah E. Crook
Phœbe A. Gascoigne
Eliza Todd
Phœbe A. Morrell
Mrs. Robert M'Chesney
Maria H. Hewett
Mrs. John Wright
Abby Fowler

Sarah De Gray
married Thomas Reed
Ruthella Smith
Mrs. Emily Buddin
Alice Ostram
Mary Ann M'Gee
1847 Mrs. Andrew Mercein
" Justine Curtis
married Edwin Butler
" Amelia M. Haff
married John J. Welsh
" Sarah Stilwell
married ——— Bradstreet
" Henrietta Kingsland
" Elisabeth E. Haff
married Egbert Acker
" Mary Whitlock
married James Lent
" Sarah E. Smith
" Rebecca Bangs
" Margaret Perego
" Julia Newton
" Amanda Munson
" Harriet E. Frisby
married James Gillen
" Mary Ann Mundell
" Sarah A. Fowler
married ——— DeMott
" Martha M. Oakley
" S. Lucinda Beers
" Mrs. Samuel Utter
" Isabella Mundell
married ——— Nattrass
" Emeline Stringham
married Alex. M'Kay
" Henrietta C. Sperry
married Rev. R. S. Maclay
" Alice Appleyard
" Cornelia Smith
" Mrs. Emily Barndollar
" Eliza A. Ward
" Sarah A. Hewett
married Henry Funnell
" Sarah Silleck
1849 Charlotte Mallory

---

[4] Some of the early teachers are probably omitted on account of the absence of records.

1849 Isabella Lane
" Mrs. Ann Eliza Crook
" Eliza Bertschi
" Charlotte Lawton
" Mary Augusta Bonnell
married Joseph Way
" Caroline M. Tryon
" Jane Rowland
" Sarah A. Small
1850 Susan Elizabeth Mount
" Lydia Bedell
" Harriet Eliza White
" Mary E. Keeler
" Wilhelmina Hertel
" Joanna Zimmerman
" Alma L. Powell
" Sarah Gertrude Watson
" Cordelia Johnstone
" Mrs. Maria Dunham
" Mary Wright
" Angeline Tuthill
" Mrs. Jane Hollis
" Elizabeth Hadden
1851 Emma Tuthill
married Samuel W. Tubbs
" Christiana Beatty
" Elizabeth W. Goodsell
" Elizabeth Powell
married A. B. Thorn
" Lavinia Thorn
married Joshua I. Gascoigne
" Emma A. Watson
married ―――― Duryea
" Louisa Gildersleeve
1852 Sarah Matilda Kelsey
" Caroline Elizabeth Swift
married Abram Inslee
" Sarah Jane M'Keon
married William Smith
" Susan Wright
1853 Harriet A. Peck
married Dr. Baker
" Mrs. F. W. Murray
" Mrs. Virginia Cutter
" Margaret Stryker
married Fred. G. Reast
" Annie Herbert
" Hannah Chadwick
" Belinda Skippon
married Thos. J. Humphreys
" Mrs. Phœbe Claxton
" Josephine Potter
" Adaline P. Harper
married ―――― Vernam; afterward Henry Vanderveer.
" Adaline Goodfellow
1854 Cornelia Wiggins
" Mrs. Moses F. Odell
" Mrs. Mary T. Burns
married Henry G. Fay
" Eliza Jane Wright
1855 Fanny Baker
married Joseph Richards
" Mrs. John W. Haskins
" Mrs. A. Wessell
" Mrs. Caroline Chappelle
" Mary A. Lightburn
" Julia E. Knapp
" Mrs. L. Canton
" Theresa Beatty
" Mrs. Cilley
1856 Anna Hinton
" Carrie M'Donald
married Rev. T. H. Pearne
" Cornelia Anderson
" Kate Tompkins
married ―――― Beekman
1857 Mrs. Cath'n H. Scudder
" Julia B. Ruggles
" Caroline Torbitt
" Mary Trippett
1858 Emma Clayton
" Mary M. M'Cormick
" Mary E. Beatty
married ―――― Simmons
" Carrie A. Wright
" Mrs. G. W. Napier
" Miss S. Strong
" Mrs. Sarah Jane Utter
" Mrs. J. O. Hoyt
1859 Miss J. Clayton
" Jennie M'Donald
married Robert M. Moore
" Georgia Bentley
" Amanda Drummond
" Mary Bentley
" Miss J. Goodmanson
" Mrs. Thomas Tilley
1862 Mrs. Rebecca Hull

Old Sands Street Church.

1862	Harriet Farley	1872	Lizzie M. Olliffe
	married ―― Avila		married Sidney Smith
"	Mrs. David Hobart	"	Miss E. A. Seabury
"	Annie O. Gray	"	Mary H. Price
	married Theo. W. Sheriden	"	Rebecca M. Nadal
1863	Eliza L. M'Gee	"	Maria M. Hyde
"	Mrs. S. U. F. Odell	1873	Mrs. Jean M'Cloud
"	Elizabeth Landon	"	Eleanor E. Seivwright
"	Emma Baylis	1874	Mrs. Rev. Geo. Taylor
"	Sarah Hines	1875	Libbie M. Wells
"	Mary A. Burrows	"	Mrs. J. C. Drew
1864	Miss C. J. Stewart	"	Jennie L. Taylor
"	Mrs. Elizabeth Quimby	"	Susie A. Allen
"	Ella Folger	1876	Phœbe A. Allen
"	Mrs. S. E. Chamberlain	"	Susie Taylor
"	Miss M. E. Hatfield	"	Josie Taylor
"	Mrs. Emily Darrow	"	Mrs. E. H. Landon
"	Mrs. Eliza Mott	1877	Mrs. Wm. R. Hegeman
"	Mary E. M'Donald	"	M. Addie Guhrauer
	married Wm. J. Tate	"	Mrs. J. T. Stratton
"	Josephine Crane	"	Rhoda Clark
"	Mrs. Georgie Douglas	"	Mrs. Geo. A. Smith
1865	Annie Mumford	"	Mary I. Pritchard
"	Isobel B. Embree		married Jason Moore
1866	Mary G. Smith	"	Ada L. Buell
"	Emily Luckey	1879	Bella Peck
"	Julia Cutter	"	Mary J. Murray
"	Mary H. Wilkinson		married C. C. Luckey
	married ―― Wilhelm	"	Addie L. Heckler
"	Julia E. Gable	"	Emma C. Muldoon
1867	Amy Landon	"	Emma J. Allen
	married A. T. Gurlitz	"	Louise C. Clayton
"	Elizabeth Shaw	"	Alice Johnston
"	Miss M. E. Thompson	"	Mrs. O. C. Cobb
"	Mary J. Tate	"	M. Ethel Green
"	Miss E. M'Kinley	"	Martha L. Nast
"	Mrs. Charlotte S. Weller	"	Mrs. William I. Preston
"	Mrs. Rev. E. G. Andrews	1880	Emma S. Miller
1868	Matilda M. Wallace	"	Emily A. Goodwin
1869	Lizzie M'Kay	"	Georgia Clancey
"	Miss E. M. Olliffe	"	Mattie Malcolm
"	Mrs. A. E. Van Zandt	"	Mrs. Rebecca Winner
"	Mrs. Sarah Creshull	"	J. W. M'Ardle
"	Fannie Moore	1882	Mattie J. Brown
"	Jennie A. Price	"	Lizzie Bunce
1870	Emma L. Hyde	"	Miss A. C. Wengorovius
"	Maria E. Ducker	"	Lizzie M. Carpenter
"	Mrs. Edgar M'Donald	"	Mrs. P. J. Gruman
"	Mrs. D. K. Ducker		

1883 Mrs. Geo. R. Harrison   1883 Sophy Stratton
" Mrs. Sarah Cottrel   " Fannie Bunce
" Mrs. M. J. Luckey

XVIII. Superintendents and Teachers of the Infant Department of the Sunday School.

1843 Moses F. Odell
" Esther Hollis
    married Rev. Wm. M'Allister
" Mary M'Allister
1847 William Cartwright
1848 John E. Hanford
" Lucy Vining
" Hannah Chadwick
1850 Betsey C. Griswold
    married Warren Richmond
" William Edsall
1854 Lavinia M. Thorn
    married Joshua I. Gascoigne
1855 David A. Cooke
1857 Mary E. Cooke
1862 Mrs. Egbert Acker

1867 Mary H. Price
1868 Mrs. Harriet Taws
    married W. Slade
1870 Julia E. Gable
" Mrs. Rev. G. F. Kettell
1872 Sam S. Utter
" J. Allen
" Mrs. Wm. I. Preston
1874 Mary H. Reast
    married ——— Slater
1875 William I. Preston
" Mary E. Phillips
    married Gerald Whitney
1880 Ella Valentine
1881 Mrs. M. E. Pearsall
1882 Minnie Estabrook

XIX. Officers of the Sunday School Missionary Society.

PRESIDENTS—1847–'49, Charles H. Fellows; '50–'53, Watson Sanford; '54, Wm. Edsall; '55, David O'Neill; '56, John G. Fay; '58–'62, Rob't M. Lockwood; '64, S. U. F. Odell; '65–'68 M. F. Odell; '69 and '77, A. B. Thorn; '70–'73 and '80–'83, Sam S. Utter; '74–'75, Henry G. Fay; '76, D. B. Phillips; '78–'79, D. D. Whitney.

VICE PRESIDENTS—1847, Joshua I. Gascoigne, Wm. Cartwright; '50, Joseph Way; '51–'53, Wm. Edsall; '54, Watson Sanford; '55–'56, Richard F. Vanderveer; '58–'61, James L. Romer; '62–'68 and '76, A. B. Thorn; '69, and '78–'79, Sam S. Utter; '70–'71, S. U. F. Odell; '72–'73, Henry G. Fay; '74–'75, D. S. Quimby, Jr.; '80–'83, D. D. Whitney.

SECRETARIES—1847, Gilbert H. Read, S. S. Utter; '48, S. S. Utter; '49, H. N. Harrison; '50, Chas. G. Norton; '51–'52, Ira Perego, Jr., Sidney Smith; '53, Sidney Smith; '54–'56, Joshua I. Gascoigne; '58–'59, Abia B. Thorn; '60–'61, James L. Romer; '62, David Stanley; '64–'68, '72–'75, '77–'83, D. B. Phillips; '69–'71, Edgar M'Donald; '76, D. S. Quimby, Jr.

TREASURERS—1847–,52, Egbert Acker; '53, David O'Neill; 54–'56; Edward Allen; '58–'59; J. M. Bradstreet; '60–'61; A. B. Thorn; '62–'68, Sam. S. Utter; '69–'76, and '78–,83, J. J. Barnier; '77, F. G. Reast.

XX. Sextons.

Joseph Moser, Abraham Bennett, Aaron Kimball, James Gillen, Conklin L. Gable, David Stewart, Hewlett G. Allen.

Susanna Moser and Mary Garrison used often to light the candles.

BOOK II.

BIOGRAPHICAL RECORD OF MINISTERS.

Chronologically Arranged according to the Dates[1] of the earliest Connection of the several Ministers with this Church as Presiding Elders or Pastors; and accompanied by brief Memorial Sketches of the deceased Wives of the Preachers.

I.

WOOLMAN HICKSON.

LIKE the ancient "Prophet of Fire," the REV. WOOLMAN HICKSON, whose name leads the list of Brooklyn Methodist preachers, suddenly strides into view as an anointed messenger of the Most High. The Church seems to have inherited no history of his birth or early life. Beginning six years prior to his death, we trace him as follows by his

PASTORAL RECORD: 1782, Somerset cir., Md., with F. Garrettson and J. Magary; removed during the year to East Jersey cir., where John Tunnell and Joseph Everett had been appointed[2]; 1783, West Jersey cir., with J. Magary; 1784, Orange cir.; 1785, Georgetown cir.; 1786, Baltimore cir., with Adam Cloud; 1787, (ordained elder)–his name does not appear on the record of appointments, but he labored in **New York** and **Brooklyn** with John Dickins and Freeborn Garrettson.

In the absence of a complete history of this faithful minister's work, we are thankful for such a glimpse of his character and his soul-saving labors as we have in the following incident, recorded by Lednum. It transpired in Worcester Co., Md., within the bounds of Somerset circuit, his first charge, in 1782.

---

[1] The dates in the lists of successive appointments do not represent calendar years, but conference years, beginning with the adjournment of the annual gatherings of itinerant ministers.

[2] Atkinson—New Jersey Methodism, p. 305.

One of tne appointments was at Robin Davis', near Indiantown, not far from the residence of a gentleman named Elijah Laws, a vestryman of the Church of England, as it was styled at that time. This man gave the Methodist preachers a hearing, bnt he declared them to be deceivers and refused to hear them again. He had a daughter Rhoda, then in her twelfth year, who had been taught, in accordance with the views that church people generally held at that time, that dancing and other worldly amusements were quite innocent and proper diversions. Rhoda visited a widow lady of her acquaintance, with whom she went for the first time to hear a Methodist preacher. The minister they heard was Woolman Hickson.

After the sermon in which he condemned dancing, and warned his hearers against the awful consequences of all kinds of worldliness and irreligion, as the historian says,

Brother Hickson read the General Rules, and requested all who wished to join him to follow him upstairs. Robin Davis, his brother, their wives, the widow woman and Rhoda Laws followed him. The preacher spoke to each. Rhoda was asked if she would have her name enrolled. A question was raised as to the propriety of consulting her father first. Mr. Davis replied that her father was a man of moderation, and would use no violence toward his daughter. Before the preacher wrote her name he lifted up his eyes, hands and soul to God, and prayed that her name might be written in heaven and never erased. She returned home, fearing to tell her father what had taken place. Early next morning her brother Elijah, who was settled in the neighborhood, was seen riding with great speed to his father's house. He hastily threw the reins of the bridle over the horse's head on the pales, saying, "What do you think? Yesterday Rhoda joined that new preacher, and now she must give up gay dress, dancing and worldly amusement. She is ruined, and she cannot be got away." The father listened to the tale, and after a moment replied, "Well, if the Methodists disown people for dancing, they will soon be clear of Rhoda, as she will dance the first opportunity she has."

In a short time a ball was gotten up at this man's house, in which she was urged to join. When her father chided her for reading the Bible instead of engaging in the amusement, her honest, loving answer brought tears to his eyes. Mr. Lednum adds;

"Soon the father and mother became Methodists, and her brother Elijah, who was panic-stricken when he heard of what he supposed was her ruin, if not the ruin of the whole family, was made class-leader over his father, his mother and his sister Rhoda."[3]

The writer of the above had the account from the lips of this same Rhoda, after she had spent sixty-eight years of devoted service in the Methodist Episcopal Church.

---

[3] Rise of Methodism, pp. 342–344.

The Rev. Thomas Haskins, who traveled Chester circuit in 1783, thus refers in his manuscript journal to this faithful minister, then laboring on West Jersey circuit.

September 23, 1783. Stayed in town for Brother Asbury's coming; but he was detained. Brother Hickson preached from I Samuel, ii, 30, a useful discourse. He made me blush with shame to hear how far he excelled me in grace and gifts.

Jesse Lee states that "his labors were mostly in the country, a small distance from New York, and on the east side of the North River. He then returned to the city of New York, and died, and was buried in the city."[4] Wakeley records the plaintive tale of his sufferings, and the kind attention of the New York brethren, who "nursed him when sick, and buried him when dead." They provided a nurse, Ann Wheeler by name, and paid her £4 6s. They also paid his funeral expenses, 16 shillings.[5] At so small a cost there could have been no pomp or ceremony attending his burial. He evidently desired none. When his ministerial brethren assembled in conference after his death, they paused to weep and to pay a brief but glowing tribute to the memory of his "genius" and his "upright life;" then they grasped his fallen sword and mantle, and marched on to increasing triumphs.

There is probably no authoritative record concerning the exact place of his burial, and it seems both strange and sad that the children of those who wept over his grave should have forgotten the place of his rest. It may with reason be presumed that he was buried under the old John-st. church. Wakeley states by authority that "vaults were built very early under Wesley Chapel in which to bury the dead. Mr. Lupton's vault was there, and Philip Embury fixed the door of it in 1770."[6] Robert Duncan placed certain valuables belonging to the Methodists in those vaults for safe-keeping during the war.[7] Mr. Lupton's body was placed in his vault in 1796, and removed twenty-one years later. Wakeley says:

In 1817, when the old church edifice was torn down to erect upon the site a new and beautiful church, they disinterred the dead. It was necessary, as they

---

[4] History of the Methodists 1. 138.
[5] See "Lost Chapters," pp. 313, 314.   [6] Ibid., p. 130.
[7] Ibid., p. 330.

were about to erect a larger edifice. Some of the bones were gathered together and buried under one end of the church, and the others were interred in burying-grounds.[8]

Robert Duncan and perhaps others of the early Methodists were buried in Trinity church-yard;[9] but it seems probable that an esteemed pastor, dying far from his relatives, (if he had any,) and buried by the trustees, would be laid to rest in a Methodist vault or grave. Such considerations, doubtless, led to the statement in the memorial record in the New York Conference minutes, that Woolman Hickson's ashes lie beneath the old John-street church.

The introduction of Methodism into Brooklyn, an account of which has been given in a former part of this work, will be forever considered the distinguishing honor of Woolman Hickson. Should the father of old Sands-street Church repose in an unmarked tomb, and should the place of the church itself know it no more, yet we are well assured that the soul of Woolman Hickson lives, and his work will never die.

---

[8] "Lost Chapters," p. 330.

[9] Ibid., p. 434. Dr. Wakeley in "Lost Chapters," p. 124, erroneously locates the grave of Barbara Heck in Trinity church-yard. See "Women of Methodism," pp. 199–205.

II.

Thomas Foster

HE "elder" in charge of the district including Brooklyn at the time of the establishment of Methodism there by Woolman Hickson, was the REV. THOMAS FOSTER. He was born in Queen Anne County, Maryland,[1] October 1, 1757. When about twenty-three years of age he began his itinerant labors, and thenceforth received from the conference the following

APPOINTMENTS: 1780, Frederick circuit, Md., with Wm. Watters; 1781, Pittsylvania cir., Va., with James Mallory; 1782; Roanoke cir.; with James Martin; 1783, Sussex cir., with Thos. S. Chew; 1784, Mecklenberg cir., with Reuben Ellis; 1785, (ordained deacon and elder,) presiding elder in Va.; 1786, presiding elder, Eastern Shore of Md.; **1787, presiding elder for all the territory north of Philadelphia;** 1788, Talbot cir., Md., with John Jarrell and Lenox Martin; 1789, Fells Point; 1790, Northampton cir., with George Pickering; 1791, Dover cir., Del., with Evan Rogers; 1792, located.

The above is an outline record of eleven years of most "heroic service." Rev. John Lednum, who knew him personally, affirmed that "no minister was more esteemed on account of sound talent and a holy life."

A pastor stationed in the neighborhood in which Foster spent his last years, after making inquiries of his few remaining contemporaries, wrote as follows:

He was a plain Methodist preacher of the olden type. Every body regarded him with the greatest respect. He boldly condemned the fashions; when some of the sisters bought shawls with fringes, and wore them to church, he told them they must cut the fringes off, and the commands were complied with. The fringes were cut off and the shawls hemmed.[2]

---

[1] Lednum—"Rise of Methodism," p. 305. Stevens' statement that he was a native of Virginia, would seem to be an unauthorized and unintentional deviation from Lednum, whom he quotes as his sole authority in respect to Foster. See Hist. M. E. Church, vol. II, p. 83.

[2] Letter from the Rev. J. E. Kidney to the author.

In 1848 one of the veteran preachers paid a grateful tribute to the memory of Mr. Foster, who encouraged him in his early ministerial work. He says:

> To be bid God speed by such a saint, such a truly apostolic man as Thomas Foster, was like hearing a voice from Heaven. Blessed was the young preacher in those days, who was favored with his advice and counsel.[3]

During the last twenty-six years of his life he continued a local preacher, "a light and ornament to the church." He resided on a little farm in Dorchester, Md., near Washington Methodist Episcopal Church, then known as "Foster's Meeting House," and was secretary of the board of trustees in that church for many years. From the neatly written minutes of the trustee meetings his signature was obtained. No one has been found who could give a description of his personal appearance; and it is believed that no likeness of him was ever made.

It is stated that Mr. Asbury esteemed Thomas Foster very highly, and sojourned in his hospitable cottage when on a tour through the Peninsula. Lednum recollected having heard him preach and lead class in the Washington Chapel, in 1814. About two years later he listened to the last sermon ever heard from his lips, from Eccl. iii, 16: "And moreover, I saw under the sun a place of judgment, that wickedness was there; and a place of righteousness, that iniquity was there." The wickedness of courts, royal, civil and ecclesiastical; and the iniquity practiced at places of worship was the theme of his discourse.

He died "much lamented," on the 10th of November, 1816, aged fifty-nine years. The Rev. William Prettyman preached his funeral sermon. A plain marble slab marks the place of his interment in the family burial ground on the farm upon which he lived, a few hundred yards from the church. It has been proposed to remove his remains to the churchyard, and erect a monument over them.

NANCY, his wife, a daughter of Jacob Wright, who was one of the founders of the Washington Methodist Episcopal Church, sleeps by his side, but her grave is without a memorial. They left no children.

---

[3] Experience and Ministerial Labors of Rev. Thomas Smith, p. 23.

III.

Jn. Dickins

OOLMAN HICKSON'S colleague in New York and Brooklyn, the REV. JOHN DICKINS, was born in London in 1746,[1] and educated at Eton College. He united with the Methodists in Virginia[2] at the age of twenty-seven. Three years later he joined the Conference, and the following is a record of his

APPOINTMENTS: 1777, North Carolina cir., with John King, Le Roy Cole and Edward Pride; 1778, Brunswick cir. Va., with E. Pride; 1779, Roanoke cir., with Henry Willis; 1780, ditto with Henry Ogburn; 1781-1782, a local preacher, continuing his ministerial labors in Virginia and North Carolina;[3] 1783, York city, with Samuel Spragg; 1784, remaining in New York; 1785, Bertie cir., Va., with David Jefferson; 1786, (ordained deacon,[4]) New York city a second time; **1787**, (ord. elder,) remaining in **New York**, in charge of the **Brooklyn** class, with Woolman Hickson and F. Garrettson;[5] **1788**, still in **New York** and **Brooklyn**, with Henry Willis, "elder;" 1789-1796, Sup't. of the Printing and Book business in Philadelphia; 1797, not named in Conf. Min.

Bishop Asbury met him in Virginia, in 1780, and wrote thus concerning him:

Brother Dickins spoke on charity very sensibly, but his voice is gone. He reasons too much; is a man of . . great skill in learning, . . yet prays and walks close with God. He is a gloomy countryman of mine, and very diffident of himself.[6]

At this time "Dickins framed a subscription for a Seminary on the plan of Wesley's Kingswood school, the first project of a literary institution among American Methodists. It

---

[1] See Conf. Minutes, 1798, p. 79.   [2] Lee's History of the Methodists.
[3] From Lee's History of the Methodists, p. 253, and Wakeley's Lost Chapters, p. 293, we learn that although Mr. Dickens located, he labored incessantly as pastor and book-steward. He was practically a conference preacher.
[4] Asbury's Journal, Ed. 1852, Vol. i, p. 518, and Conf. Minutes, 1786.
[5] See "Lost Chapters," pp. 310, 321.   [6] Asbury's Journal, Vol. i, p. 377.

It resulted in Cokesbury College."[7] He was the first married preacher in John-street, New York.[8] While stationed in that city, Mr. Dickins had the honor of being "the first Methodist preacher to receive Coke, and approve his scheme of the organization of the denomination."[9] He is said to be the author of the name "Methodist Episcopal Church," adopted by the Christmas Conference, of which he was a member.[10]

While he was stationed in New York, in 1788, J. B. Matthias attended his ministry, and he was probably the first Methodist preacher that Matthias ever heard. He writes concerning him: "He was a plain-dressed man, and preached with all his might;" and he seems, although unconverted, to have become attached to him, for he thus describes the change of preachers at the ensuing conference: "They took away my thundering John Dickins, and gave us Robert Cloud and Thomas Morrell."

When John Dickins entered upon his work as book steward, he was required to do two men's work, being at the same time pastor in Philadelphia. The seven years of his service in the Book Concern constituted the formative period of the publishing interests of the denomination, and their subsequent magnificent growth is largely due to his fidelity, ability, and enterprise in that department. The following statement is a tribute to his industry:

During the four years immediately preceding his death he issued about 114,000 books and pamphlets, taking charge of every thing pertaining to the work.[11]

He died of yellow fever in Philadelphia, September 27, 1798, aged fifty-two years. When dying he clasped his hands, while tears of rapture coursed down his cheeks, and shouted, "Glory to Jesus! My soul now enjoys such sweet communion with him that I would not give it for all the world. Love him! Trust him! Praise him!" Rev. Ezekiel Cooper preached his funeral sermon, which was published.[12] His remains were first deposited in the cemetery of St. George's, in Crown-street, Philadelphia.[13] They were afterward placed

---

[7] Stevens—Hist. M. E. Church, vol. ii, p. 41.   [8] "Lost Chapters," p. 299.
[9] Stevens—Hist. M. E. Church, vol. ii, p. 41.
[10] Meth. Quar. Rev., 1832, p. 98.   [11] Funeral sermon by Ezekiel Cooper.
[12] Noticed by Lednum and Sprague.   [13] Lednum, p. 198.

in the old Methodist burial ground in Baltimore, but were some years later removed with the remains of his widow, at the expense of the Baltimore preachers, to the Mount Olivet Cemetery near that city, where many of the heroes of Methodism sleep.[14] His death brought a greater sense of loss to the church than that of any other preacher up to that time.[15] Asbury said on hearing of his death:

He was in person and affection another Thomas White to me. * * * I feared death would divide us soon.[16]

He still further testifies:

For piety, probity, profitable preaching, holy living, Christian education of his children, secret closet prayer, I doubt whether his superior is to be found either in Europe or America.[17]

As a public man he was eminent among the chieftains of early Methodism; and few, if any, excelled him in classic scholarship. He "was in literature, logic, zeal and devotion, a Paul among the preachers."[18]

His wife, before their marriage, was MISS ELIZABETH YANCEY. She resided near Halifax, N. C. When in 1783 the question was asked for the first time in conference, "How many preachers' wives [in the entire connection] are to be provided for?" the answer was, "Eleven;" and among them was named "Sister Dickins." Four years later the following was published in the Minutes:

Question 18. Are not many of our preachers and people dissatisfied with the salaries allowed our married preachers who have children? They are. Therefore, for the future, no married preacher shall demand more than £48, P. C.

Mrs. Dickins was the pioneer preacher's wife in this region, and the first to occupy the John-street parsonage. Few if any of her successors have filled the station of minister's wife more honorably. She wrote affectionately concerning her husband and the transport of his dying hour. Lednum says:

She survived her husband until 1835, when she ended her days in Baltimore,

---

[14] Letter of Rev. Dr. James H. Brown to the author.
[15] Lee's History of the Methodists, p. 254.
[16] See Lednum, p. 198.   [17] Quotations in Sprague's Annals.
[18] Lednum, p. 201.

at the house of her son in law, Dr. Samuel Baker. She had been a Methodist for more than fifty years, and was seventy years old at the time of her death.[19]

One of John Dickins' daughters died of yellow fever the day before his death; another maiden daughter lived with her sister, Mrs. Dr. Baker.

John Dickins had a son, *Asbury Dickins*, who was well and honorably known in our day. The following extract is from a first-class authority:

Asbury Dickins, born July 29, 1780, was in 1801 associated with Joseph Dennie in founding the "Port Folio" at Philadelphia. He was first clerk in the United States treasury department from 1816 to 1833, and in the state department from 1833 to 1836, when he was elected secretary of the United States senate, which office he held till July 16, 1861. While in the treasury and state departments he was often acting secretary, and wrote many important state papers. He died in Washington, October 23, 1861.[20]

---

[19] Rise of Methodism, p. 198.   [20] American Cyclopædia.

Rev. FREEBORN GARRETTSON.

IV.
FREEBORN GARRETTSON.

AMONG the early Methodist preachers in Brooklyn, none has reached a higher rank in history than the REV. FREEBORN GARRETTSON.

He left his charge on the Peninsula and came North to spend the latter part of the Conference year 1787 in New York, as the associate of Dickins and Hickson, both of whom were in feeble health,[1] and it may be presumed that he applied himself to carrying forward in Brooklyn the work which Hickson had begun. Two years later he succeeded Henry Willis in taking charge of the district.which included Long Island. He was the first to bear the full title of "Presiding Elder," but his predecessors, "Elders," filled the same office, attending the quarterly conferences, superintending the preachers, and administering the sacraments.

Freeborn Garrettson was born in Maryland, August 15, 1752, and was born again in 1775, when twenty-three years of age. He appears to have been a moral young man, and outwardly religious. A word spoken to him personally by a Methodist exhorter filled his conscience with alarm. He tried to quiet his fears by living a "respectable" life, and "serving God in a quiet manner," but when he listened to the searching appeals of Asbury and Shadford and Daniel Ruff, his "foundations would shake." He was converted on horseback, while returning from a Methodist meeting through a lonely wood. "I threw," he says, "the reins of my bridle on my horse's neck. and putting my hands together, I cried out, 'Lord, I submit!' *** My soul was so exceedingly happy that I seemed as if I wanted to

---

[1] Wakeley—"Lost Chapters," p. 321.

take wings and fly away to Heaven.'"[2] That very day he established a family altar; and shortly after, "while standing in the midst of his slaves, with a hymn book in his hand, beginning their family worship, he pronounced his servants free."[3]

He commenced holding meetings and exhorting his neighbors from house to house. He accompanied Martin Rodda on his circuit, and so suddenly and unexpectedly did he find himself a preacher, that he was "alarmed," and "mounted his horse to escape fifty miles to his home." But he did not diminish his evangelistic labors. Presently (1775,) "Daniel Ruff called him out to a circuit. He went, never to turn back."[4]

It was in the midst of these earliest itinerant labors, that he yielded to a sudden impression, and preached that memorable sermon to the soldiers, by which the youthful Ezekiel Cooper was led to Christ. His ministerial career, thus begun, covers the long period from 1775 to 1827. He never superannuated. The following are his

CONFERENCE APPOINTMENTS: 1776, Frederick cir., Md., with M. Rodda; 1777, Brunswick cir., Va., with Wm. Watters and John Tunnell; 1778, Kent cir., on the Peninsula, with Joseph Hartley, John Littlejohn, and John Cooper; 1779, State of Delaware cir., with Francis Asbury, Caleb B. Pedicord, Lewis Alfrey, M. Debruler; 1780, Baltimore cir., Md., with Daniel Ruff, and Joshua Dudley, 1781, Sussex cir., Va., with James Morris; 1782, Somerset cir. Md., with James Magary; 1783, Talbot cir., with John Mayor; 1784, ditto, with William Thomas; 1785, (ordained deacon and elder,) Shelburne, Nova Scotia; 1786, associate "elder" in Nova Scotia with James O. Cromwell; 1787, "elder" of a district on the Md. Peninsula, and a few months previous to the conference in October, 1788, in New York with John Dickins and Woolman Hickson; 1788, elder, Hudson River and Lake Champlain Dist.; **1789**, **New York Dist.,—Long Island** to Lake Champlain; 1790-1792,, Hudson River Dist.; 1793, elder, Philadelphia Dist., and pastor Philadelphia station;[5] **1794**, **New York Dist.**; 1795, "elder" Western Mass. and Eastern New York; **1796-1797**, New London, Pittsfield and **New York Dist.**, with Sylvester Hutchinson, associate; 1798, Albany Dist.; 1799, New Jersey Dist.; **1800–1803, New York Dist.**; 1804, Rhinebeck; 1805, New York, with N. Sne-

---

[2] Bangs' Life of Garrettson, p. 37.
[3] Stevens' Hist. M. E. Church, vol. i, p. 354.   [4] Ibid., vol. i, p. 355.
[5] At the end of six months he was to exchange places with Thomas Morrell of New York, but this arrangement seems not to have been carried out on account of the failure Mr. Morrell's health. See "Lost Chapters," by Wakeley, p. 578.

then, A. Hunt, John Wilson; 1806, do., with T. Bishop, S. Crowell, John Wilson; 1807, conference missionary; 1808, Rhinebeck again; 1809-1810, missionary; 1811-1814, **New York Dist.** again; 1815, no station; 1816, missionary; 1817, sup'y, Bridgeport, Ct., with A. Hunt; 1818-1820, sup'y, without appointment; 1821-1827, conference missionary.

Wakeley says that while in New York, previous to the conference of 1788, he "occasionally made an excursion on Long Island;"[6] and it is not improbable that he was one of the first to repeat the gospel call that Woolman Hickson had sounded on the slopes of Brooklyn. The record of appointments shows that he was once pastor and twelve years presiding elder over the Sands-street church.

The labors and trials of his early ministry were almost unparalleled even in his day. He preached twice, thrice, and even four times a day in Maryland. On one occasion he was nearly killed by the blow of an assailant, but continued preaching, "his face bruised, scarred, and bedewed with tears." Once a ruffian attempted to drown the voice of the preacher by beating a drum. A great fire was made in the fireplace of the room where he was preaching in a very warm day, and the author of the mischief stalked through the house ringing a bell. While preaching at another time he was siezed by a mob and thrust into prison; but in the midst of all this opposition, his triumph was wonderful. Mobs were terrified, and their ringleaders converted. He won the respect and affection of the masses, and people often walked twelve miles to hear him preach; and before many years that whole region—eastern Maryland and Delaware—had been conquered for Methodism.

It was a notable period in the life of Garrettson, when he spent six weeks in traveling twelve hundred miles to warn out the preachers to attend the Christmas conference in 1784, when the Methodist Episcopal Church was formally organized. At this conference he was ordained by Bishop Coke, and volunteered for Nova Scotia, where his success was so great that Wesley desired that he might be appointed bishop for the British Provinces. Dr. Bangs says the reason why the conference did not accede to Mr. Wesley's request was probably the unwillingness of the preachers in the states "to

---

[6] "Lost Chapters," p. 321.

have him entirely separated from them.'"[7] Coke wrote to Garrettson in letters that have never been published,[8] not that he had been requested, but that he had been *"ordered"* by Wesley to ordain Mr. Garrettson bishop; and the exact truth may be that the conference began to think it best to do as they pleased, and not as Mr. Wesley "ordered." Freeborn Garrettson was a member of every general conference from 1804 to 1824. The story of his pioneer movements on the Hudson River District (1788) with his little band of ardent young men, reads like a romance, and Coke at the next conference triumphantly records:

> He has not only carried our work in New York state as high as Lake Champlain, but has raised congregations in most of the states of New England, and also in the little state of Vermont within about a hundred miles of Montreal.

Garrettson shares with Jesse Lee the honor of planting Methodism in the New England states. These old friends met on the highway near Boston, and such an affectionate greeting is rarely witnessed in this world.

In 1789 a severe accident befell him in Sharon, Conn. He was thrown down by his horse and lay unconscious for some time. His shoulder was dislocated and his body very much bruised. He says:

> I knew not who I was nor where I was. After lying for a considerable time, I made an atempt to lay my head on my hat for a pillow. I saw the two first letters of my name upon my hat, and immediately I knew myself and cried out, "Is this poor Carrettson?"

But that same day he borrowed a carriage and rode on; and without any cessation continued his travels and his preaching, his body racked with pain, but his "mind sweetly calm and happy."[9]

In the year 1793 Freeborn Garrettson, then forty-one years of age, was married to Miss Catharine Livingston, daughter of Robert R. Livingston of Clermont, and sister of Chancellor Robert R. Livingston, Washington's friend. The ceremony was performed by Peter Moriarty in the First Methodist Episcopal Church in Rhinebeck, and on the same

---

[7] Life of Garrettson, p. 166.

[8] Extracts from these letters were read by Rev. Dr. A. S. Hunt in his centenary sermon before the New York East Conference, 1884.

[9] Bangs' Life of Garrettson, p. 180.

occasion they all partook of the Lord's supper.[10] Through his wife, as one of the heirs of the property belonging to the Livingston Manor, Mr. Garrettson came into possession of the Rhinebeck estate. The Garrettson mansion was Bunyan's "Palace Beautiful," and for many a weary itinerant it was a refuge, a hospital, a sanctuary and a home. Asbury admired its "beautiful land and water prospect," and named it "Traveler's Rest."[11] Here the pioneer bishop spent many an hour in communion with his life-long and intimate friend. They were not always of one mind; Garrettson differed with him in his views of the general superintendency, holding the opinion that instead of having the whole continent under one general superintendency, it would have been better if it had been divided among several, each superintendent being responsible to the general conference for his own particular district.[12] Many of the early Methodists believed that but for these views of church government, he would have been made a bishop.

Mr. Garrettson preached his last sermon in Duane-street church, New York, on "Growing in Grace." In the same city soon after this, quite unexpectedly he fell asleep, Sept. 26, 1827, in the seventy-sixth year of his age. He died with devout and rapturous praise upon his lips. His last sentence was, "Holy, holy, holy, Lord God Almighty! Hallelujah! Hallelujah!" William Phœbus, Nathan Bangs, and Thomas Burch preached powerful sermons on the character and memory of this great and good man. The prominent traits of his character were sincerity, zeal, liberality, equinimity of temper and unconquerable perseverence. His integrity was never questioned.

He was one of the the founders of the Missionary Society of the Methodist Episcopal Church, and a valuable friend and supporter of other benevolent institutions. As a preacher he was sometimes eloquent, and his sermons were always instructive and practical. A tombstone, appropriately inscribed, marks the place of his rest in Rhinebeck, N. Y.

---

[10] Bangs' Life of Garrettson, p. 208.
[11] Asbury's Journal, vol. ii, p. 462, and vol. iii, p. 77.
[12] Life of Garrettson, p. 205.

His wife, CATHARINE, only two months his junior, survived him twenty-two years, and died at the age of ninety-six. The Rev. Dr. A. S. Hunt, who is familiar with her genealogy, states that she was a lineal descendent from the distinguished Covenanter, John Livingston, of Scotland. Simpson's Cyclopedia says:

She was a daughter of Judge Robert R. Livingston, who inherited a large estate on the Livingston Manor on the Hudson River. Her mother was the daughter of Col. Beekman, who was governor of what is now the state of Delaware, under a commission from Sweden. Her brother, Robert R. Livingston, was one of the committee who framed the Declaration of Independence, and was first chancellor of the state of New York, and administered the oath to Washington, when first inaugurated President. He was also Secretary of Foreign Affairs, and Minister to France. She had six sisters,—women of more than ordinary talent, three of whom married generals famous in the history of their country. Their house was a center of deep patriotic interest, where public movements were noted and discussed, and no small sacrifices were made.

In the year 1789, two years after her conversion, with one other person she formed a Methodist class at Rhinebeck. That one other was a poor, ignorant laborer. When her friends in great distress and chagrin inquired why, if she must be a Methodist, she had not joined a class with some respectable persons in it, she replied that she had joined *that* class in order that it might have one respectable person. A class meeting was held at her house several years, usually conducted by the pastor. In her last class meeting she said she wished "to know more of God," and soon that wish was gratified. As she neared the gates of death her soul was exultant. She exclaimed, "He is coming!" and raised her hands and looked upward after she could speak no more. Dr. Stephen Olin preached her funeral sermon. Two other well-known ministers, John Seys and J. N. Shaffer, took part in the services; and the Rev. L. W. Peck wrote for The Christian Advocate an obituary containing some of the facts above mentioned. In a work entitled "Our Excellent Women," (page 31) it is said:

To the last her fine intellect was preserved, and she knew little of the infirmities which usually accompany extreme age. Her eye had lost none of its brightness, her form was erect, and her step elastic.

The visitor will find her grave beside that of her husband. Tablets with epitaphs to the memory of both were placed in the church at Rhinebeck.[18] Dr. Stevens' "Women of Methodism" contains a beautiful sketch of Mrs. Garrettson.

Miss Mary, only daughter of Freeborn and Catharine Garrettson, the author once met at a session of the New York East Conference. The writer of a memorial sketch has this paragraph concerning her youth:

Related to a large number of prominent families, and accustomed to visit or be visited by them, her reminiscences of early life—or many of them—are worthy of permanent record. In company with Mrs. Col. Wm. Few, she visited the notorious infidel, Thomas Paine, as he lay on his death-bed at the house of Madame Bonneville, and graphically described the conversation between him and the kind Christian lady who strove to lead him to the great Physician. On all subjects but religion he conversed freely; on that he maintained a sullen, unbroken silence.[13]

After visiting her in company with Dr. Pope, Dr. Rigg of London wrote:

She is eighty-two years old, and a woman of remarkable ability and culture, of various and extended reading, as well as of great benevolence. So bright a woman of her age it has not been my lot to meet.

Before her death she became blind as Milton, but continued to be quite as busy. She organized a sewing society for the aid of our missionary work among the women of Utah. In her zeal to attend that society which met on an inclement day, she took cold and returned home to die. She is the author of the beautiful epitaphs of her father and mother in the Rhinebeck church.

She bequeathed her entire estate to the church. Wildercliffe, as the old homestead has for many years been called, passed by purchase into the hands of a relative.

---

[13] Rev. R. Wheatley, D. D., in The Christian Advocate.

V.

HENRY WILLIS.

THE REV. HENRY WILLIS was presiding elder and pastor during the last year of John Dickins' term (1788), and doubtless often preached in Brooklyn. He shines forth as one of the brilliant stars in the galaxy of early Methodist preachers. His memory has much of the same fragrance as that of Summerfield. His contemporaries, Quinn, Ware, Garrettson and Asbury, vie with each other in admiring the greatness and rejoicing in the usefulness of this saintly minister of the Lord Jesus Christ

Mr. Willis was a native of Brunswick County, Virginia. We are without further knowledge of him until we find him, in 1778, remaining on trial in the itinerant ranks, which fact indicates that he had previously been appointed to a circuit. From the old Minutes we gather the following

MINISTERIAL RECORD: 1778, Pittsylvania cir., Va., with Wm. Gill and John Major; 1779, Roanoke cir. with John Dickins; 1780, Mecklenburgh cir. with Moses Park; 1781, Talbot cir. with Jeremiah Lambert; 1782, Dorchester cir. with Samuel Rowe; 1783, New Hope, N. C.; 1784, Holsten, Tenn.; 1785, (ordained deacon and elder) presiding elder in the Holsten region; 1786, Charleston, S. C., with Isaac Smith; 1787, appointed to New York with John Dickins, but no traces of him are seen; he was probably called to another field — (See sketch of Woolman Hickson); **1788, elder for New York and Long Island,** with two Conference preachers and probably several local preachers under him; 1789, associate presidng elder with Lemuel Green in Delaware, Pennsylvania and Ohio; 1790, local preacher in Baltimore; 1791-1792, Philadelphia, with John Dickins the book agent; 1793, ditto with F. Garrettson, Thomas Morrell and John Dickins; 1794-1795, a "located" elder, or what is since known as supernumerary without an appointment; 1796, Old Town; also Baltimore Town with Wm. Jessop, Andrew Nichols and John Hagerty; 1797, Baltimore city with John Harper and Nelson Reed; 1798, ditto with John Harper and Thos. Lyell; 1799, ditto with Thos. Morrell and L. Mansfield; 1800, Frederick cir. with Thos. Lucas, Jos. Stone and Jonathan Forrest; 1801, ditto with Joseph Stone and Noah Fiddler; 1802, ditto with Curtis Williams,

Henry Willis

From Roberts' "Centenary Album."

Fielder Parker and J. Forrest, sup'y; 1803, Fredericktown, sup'y, with Jonathan Forrest; 1804. Frederick cir. again, with R. R. Roberts and James Lucas, sup'y; 1805, sup'y, without appointment; 1806, sup'y, Frederick cir., with H. Jefferson, F. Parker and John Watson; 1807, sup'y, without appointment.

The foregoing record shows how extensively he traveled, and how frequently he was compelled to retire from the effective ranks, returning to the front again and again, with a soul full of fire and zeal. He was the first man ordained deacon and elder by Bishop Asbury after the Christmas Conference in 1884, having in his absence been elected to orders by that conference.[1] He received William Thacher into the church in Baltimore in 1790.[2] It is quite probable that he was the "Brother Willis" who solemnized the marriage of Lorenzo and Peggy Dow in 1805.[3]

Endowed by nature with rare gifts, respectably educated, and imbued with much of the spirit of Christ, he performed heroic service for the church while sinking slowly to the grave with pulmonary consumption. James Quinn, who knew Henry Willis in the Redstone valley, thus describes him:

He was six feet in stature, slender, well read, an eloquent man, mighty in the Scriptures, and a most profound and powerful reasoner.[4]

During the last years of his life, although stationed at Fredericksburgh as a supernumerary preacher, he was most of the time, in fact, a retired minister, settled with his family on a farm of five hundred acres, at Pipe Creek, within the bounds of that circuit. In 1801 the Baltimore Conference held its session in his parlor. When not able to perform full ministerial work, he would accept no pay from the church.[5] He was one of the dearest friends of Asbury. The good bishop "kissed and encircled in his arms the orphan children of his departed friend, Henry Willis, and blessed them in the name of the Lord."[6]

Mr. Willis died in the early part of the year 1808, "with triumphant faith in Christ," at his home in Pipe Creek, Frederick County, Md., in the immediate vicinity of the

---

[1] Lednum, "Rise of Methodism," p. 224.
[2] Wm. Jewett, in The Christian Advocate.   [3] See Dow's Journal.
[4] Quoted in M'Clintock and Strong's Cyclopedia.
[5] Minutes of Conferences, 1808, p. 157.   [6] Bœhm's Reminiscences, p. 189.

place where Strawbridge introduced Methodism into Maryland. A low brick monument, without inscription marks the spot where his sacred dust reposes, not far from the house in which he lived. It is near the Wakefield station, on the Western Maryland Railroad.

The following brief extract from a letter by Henry Willis to Freeborn Garrettson, dated New York, November 11, 1788, breathes the sweet spirit of this saintly man.

> I received your letter by Thomas, and I really rejoice to hear that the Lord is with you. I hope you will lay the foundation of much good this year. * * * Who can commemorate the gracious acts of divine merit, or proportion unto God the praise that is his due? * * * Thoughts are not sufficiently quick to trace the footsteps of [divine] goodness; they are more than the soul is able to recount. * * * The day and the night are full of God, and all the way that I go he is round about it. I trust he will give me a heart to love him more and more.[7]

ANN, wife of Henry Willis, was the daughter of an eminent layman, Jesse Hollingsworth, of Baltimore,—a woman of intelligence and of a sweet Christian spirit. The venerable Joshua Warfield, of Sam's Creek, Maryland, wrote as follows:

> The wife and children of Henry Willis I remember very well, and frequently visited the family when I was growing up to manhood, in company with my sisters. Some years after, the place was sold, and Mrs. Willis bought a farm on Sam's Creek, adjoining my father's, and lived there several years, and finally removed to Baltimore and died there.[8]

She survived her husband thirty-four years, and outlived all her children. Their names were *Henry*, *William*, *Jesse*, *Mary Yellott*, *Jeremiah*, and *Francis Asbury*. On the sixteenth of February, 1842, at the age of seventy-three, "she bade earth adieu, and, passing peacefully the shades of death, leaning on the Savior's arm, entered triumphantly the city out of sight."[9] Her remains are sleeping in the old burial ground that belonged to the Methodists, in the rear of Greenmount Cemetery in Baltimore, and the place is marked by a tombtone.[10] Her portrait, with that of her husband, has been preserved by the Baltimore Conference Historical Society.

---

[7] Copied from the original, in possession of the Rev. Dr. A. S. Hunt.
[8] Letter to the author.   [9] Extract from inscription on her tombstone.
[10] Roberts' Centenary Album, p. 55.

VI.
Thomas Morrell

THE REV. THOMAS MORRELL was born in New York city, November 22, 1747. He was a school-mate and life-long friend of Lindley Murray, the grammarian. His mother was converted through the labors of Philip Embury, and joined the first Methodist class in America. The family afterward moved to Elizabethtown, New Jersey.[1]

The eventful history of Thomas Morrell previous to his conversion is thus narrated by the Rev. Dr. S. R. Dunn, of New Jersey:

At the outbreak of the Revolutionary war, and on receiving the news of the battles of Concord and Lexington, he formed a company of volunteers and joined the patriot army.[2] He was severely wounded in the battle of Long Island, in which three thousand patriots lost their lives. His own company, being in advance of the main army, was nearly cut to pieces. Lying wounded on the field of battle, and only escaping the brutal fury of the British soldiery by feigning himself dead, Washington permitted six soldiers to carry him on a hurdle to New York, and thence to his father's house in Elizabethtown. From thence, as Lord Cornwallis approached, he was removed to New Providence, to the house of Rev. Jonathan Elmer, where he finally recovered. He received,

---

[1] The father was a resident of Newtown, L. I., before going to New York. See Sprague's Annals.

[2] For the name and number of his military company, see sketch of the Rev. John Merrick in this book.

while there, a commission as major of the Fourth New Jersey Regiment of the Continental army. Accepting the appointment, he was out in active service nearly the whole year 1777. He was in the battle of Brandywine, where, guarding the passage of Chadsford, his regiment suffered severely, and finally gave way under the furious charge of Kuyphausen. It was in this battle that Lafayette was wounded in the leg, from which he never fully recovered. Major Morrell was also in the battle of Germantown. His health, after this hotly contested battle, which was so honorable to the army of Washington, was so feeble that he retired from the army amid the regrets of Washington and his fellow patriots. He returned to Elizabethtown, and re-engaged with his father in mercantile pursuits.[3]

When about thirty-eight years of age, he was brought to repentence by the powerful preaching of the Rev. John Haggerty. In three months thereafter he was induced by this earnest preacher to abandon his lucrative business and devote himself to the ministry of the word. One of his early efforts has been styled a "successful failure." So completely had he failed in his own estimation that he concluded he was not called of God to preach, and determined to proceed no farther in that direction. The sequel is thus narrated by the Rev. John Atkinson:

Early the ensuing morning while at breakfast at his uncle's, there was a knock at the door. A lady entered desiring to see the preacher of the previous evening. In a few moments another came, and then an old man upon the same errand, all of whom had been awakened under the sermon deemed by him a failure. He of course recalled his purpose to preach no more, and was encouraged to go forward.[4]

Here follows the list of his

APPOINTMENTS: 1786, supply on Newark cir., N. J., (including Staten Island, N. Y.,) with Robert Cloud; 1787, (traveling connection,) Elizabethtown cir., with R. Cloud; 1788, ordained deacon, Trenton cir., with J. Johnson; **1789**, ordained elder, associate **presiding elder**, with F. Garrettson, **New York** Dist., also New York city and Brooklyn, with Robert Cloud, John Merrick, Wm. Phœbus, and last part of the conference year, Jacob Brush;[5] **1790, presiding elder, New York Dist,**; 1791, New York city, with R. Whatcoat and J. Mann; Traveled with Asbury, and preached in Charleston, S. C., several months previous to the session of the New York Conference, 1792; 1792, New York again, with Lemuel Green and Geo. Strebeck; 1793, ditto, six months, with Daniel Smith and Evan Rogers;[6] 1794, Philadelphia, Pa.; 1795, no appointment on account of ill health; 1796-1797, local; 1798,

---

[3] Year Book of Churches in New Jersey, 1881.
[4] Memorials of New Jersey Methodism.
[5] "Lost Chapters," p. 368. [6] Ibid., p. 395.

Record of Ministers.

Elizabethtown, N. J., with James Tolleson and S. Thomas; 1799, (Baltimore Conference,) Baltimore cir., Md., with L. Mansfield and H. Willis; 1800, Baltimore and Fell's Point, with Geo. Roberts, Philip Bruce and N. Snethen; 1801, New York city, with John M'Claskey, D. Ostrander and M. Coate; 1802, ditto, with Thomas F. Sargent and John Wilson; 1803, ditto, with Michael Coate, Ralph Williston and John Wilson; 1804, (Phila. Conf.,) Elizabethtown, N. J., with B. Iliff and S. Budd; 1805, no appointment; 1806–1824, local; 1825-1826, (Phila. Conf.,) sup'y, Elizabethtown, N. J., with T. B. Sargent; 1827–1828, ditto, with Daniel Parish; 1830–1831, ditto, with E. S. Janes; 1832, ditto, with William A. Wilmer; 1833, ditto with E. L. Janes; 1834, ditto, with Wm. H. Gilder; 1835-1836, ditto, with James Buckley; 1837, (N. J. Conf.,) sup'y, Elizabethtown, with J. A. Raybold; 1838, ditto, with I. N. Felch.

His appointment to New York in 1789 is not mentioned in the Minutes. In his unpublished journal, however, he states that he was so appointed with Robert Cloud, who was with him all the year, and John Merrick, who was with him four months. During a part of that year he was engaged by order of the conference in building the old Forsyth-street church. In less than six months from the date of his commission he preached the dedicatory sermon. It was at the

he would have replied better."[10] The verdict of history is, however, that the bishop had good reason to be satisfied. That strong defense of Methodism added to its author's already acquired fame as a leading man in the denomination.

Mr. Morrell was twice married. Bishop Asbury officiated at both nuptial ceremonies. Concerning the former the bishop on the day of the marriage wrote:

Wonders will never cease. Nothing could serve but I must marry Thomas Morrell to a young woman. Such a solitary wedding, I suppose, has been but seldom seen. Behold Father Morrell, fifty-five, Father Whatcoat, sixty-five, Francis Asbury, fifty-seven, and the ceremony performed solemnly at the solemn hour of ten at night.[11]

Soon after his location in 1796, his good old mother died. Although his ministerial record shows that he was supernumerary many years, he preached during much of the time as frequently as when he was numbered among the effective preachers. He lived to be past ninety, and was held in great honor. When in his eighty-ninth year, he was invited to dedicate the second Forsyth-street church in New York, but was too feeble to comply. The following—the only paragraph from his writings which our space will permit us to quote—gives a pleasing view of his experience in the calm sunset of his life.

Through the tender mercy of God I have lived to see the beginning of another year, being now ninety years, one month, and nine days old—a longer period than any of our family have lived. I have many things to be thankful for—my life prolonged to so advanced an age, having the faculties of mind in perfect exercise, my health tolerably good, sleep sound, appetite good, my wife in health, my children all religious and in health, my son successful as a preacher, my soul devoted to God, and plenty of temporal things. Would to God I was more thankful, more holy, more heavenly-minded. This morning I have devoted my soul and body to God; and though I am unable to preach as formerly, yet I am endeavoring by grace to walk with God.[12]

He died in triumph, August 9, 1838, in Elizabethtown, N. J. He said in his last moments: "I am going to glory; I have gotten the victory; all is well!" Throughout the length and breadth of the land, the church which had increased from twelve members when his mother joined, to upwards of sixty

---

[10] Asbury's Journal, edition 1852, vol. ii, p. 154.
[11] Asbury's Journal, vol. iii, p. 67.
[12] Stevens—Hist. M. E. Church, vol. iii, p. 148.

thousand at the time of his death, heard with deep emotion the tidings of his departure. He had been a contemporary and friend of Washington and La Fayette, of Wesley, and Coke, and Asbury, and had given a long life of pure and noble devotion to the country and the church.

He is described as "a man of thoroughly defined habits and character," "an early riser, scrupulously temperate and frugal, and punctual to preciseness." One who knew him well, says:

He was always occupied with something; and hence to the very last he was cheerful. He carried with him down to extreme old age, the freshness, bouyancy, and energy of youthful feeling, and the entire capability of attending to all his business with the utmost punctuality and accuracy. * * * His appearance was unique and striking. He was rather short in stature, but strongly built; his neck was short, his head not large, his eye bright and blue, his lips thin, and his whole appearance indicative of more than ordinary firmness. He always wore a covering on his head like a smoking cap, from which his hair fell gracefully on his neck. He wore a long frock coat buttoned to the chin, and without the least ostentation was a man of the old school.[13]

VII.

Robert Cloud,

THE REV. ROBERT CLOUD was stationed in New York soon after the formation of the little sóciety in Brooklyn, and while it was yet under the care of New York city preachers. Soon afterward he was in charge of Brooklyn as presiding elder.

He was born in Brandywine Hundred, New Castle County, Delaware, August 21, 1755. One who knew him intimately wrote as follows in an obituary notice:

· When about twenty-one years of age, through the instrumentality of the Rev. Mr. Webster,[1] of Harford County, Md., he embraced the religion of the Lord Jesus Christ, and united with the Methodist Episcopal Church. The writer has often heard him relate the circumstance of his conversion, in a Methodist class-room, habited in the uniform of a soldier of the Revolution, which, however, he soon exchanged for the uniform of a Methodist preacher.[2]

This fact makes him conspicuous, for notably few are the heroes of early Methodism with whom Robert Cloud must share the honor of having been a soldier in the Revolution. And had he been the only man to enter the itinerant ranks from out the

" Heaven-born band,
Who fought and bled in Freedom's cause,"

It would have imparted no brighter lustre to his name than now gilds it as accompanied on the roll of honor by the names of such renowned soldier-preachers as Thomas Morrell, Thomas Ware, John Merrick, and Robert Hutchinson.

His obituary further states that he commenced his min-

---

[1] This was the Rev. Richard Webster who joined the Methodists in 1768, and faithfully served the Church as an itinerant and local preacher, till his death at the age of eighty-five, in the year 1824. *Lednum*.

[2] Baltimore Visitor, 1833.

isterial labors in 1777, and suffered his full share of the privations incident to the itineracy of that early day. From various sources we have compiled the following brief

MINISTERIAL RECORD: 1777, local preacher; 1778, (traveling connection,) appointment not known,[3] 1779-1784, located; 1785, (re-admitted to conf.) Trenton cir., N. J., with John M'Claskey and Jacob Brush; 1786, Newark; 1787, ordained deacon,—Elizbethtown cir., with Thomas Morrell; 1788, Long Island cir.; **1789**, ordained elder,—**New York and Brooklyn**, with John Merrick, Wm. Phœbus, Thomas Morrell, and Jacob Brush;[4] 1790, New York, with Wm. Jessop; **1791, presiding elder, New York Dist.**—L. I. to Newburgh; 1792, presiding elder, Wyoming to Staten Island; 1793, Chester, Penn., six months, and Wilmington, Del., six months; 1794-1796, "under a location;" 1767-1808, probably most of the time a located preacher; 1809, (Western Conf.) missionary; 1810, Knox, Ind.; 1811, Delaware, Ohio, 1812, Deer Creek, with Chas, Waddle; 1813-1832, located.

His location in 1779 is the first on record in the history of the itineracy in America. The reader will observe that he returned to the conference in 1785, located again in 1794, was again re-admitted to the traveling connection in 1809, and located a third time in 1813. His first location occurred

iam Jessop? The only explanation of his passing into comparative obscurity that can be given, is his temporary departure from God, his lapse into immorality.[5]

He sought forgiveness and regained the favor of God; and in the west, whither he removed, his downfall appears not to have been remembered against him.[6] The author of his obituary describes his zealous labors in the itineracy, and then adds:

Nor did his exertions cease when compelled by ill health and family concerns to locate; far, very far from it. Every hour that could be spared was employed in carrying the glad tidings of salvation to those who were destitute. Societies were formed, houses built and then handed over to the itinerant brethren, while he went in pursuit of more lost sheep. Yes, "the wilderness" cf Ohio "heard his voice and did rejoice." In Kentucky, also, where he ended his days, so long as he was able, although in his seventy-eighth year, did he preach the unsearchable riches of Christ.

A "Report of the Independent Kentucky Bible Society

---

[5] The Rev. Geo. W. Lybrand writes: "It is painful—the blot on Mr. Cloud's name. He was overtaken by adultery, and his fall is proved by testimony from four sources:

(1.) Memoir of Jesse Lee, p. 242:—'Saturday Oct. 6, 1798. On to Wm. Howell's at North East, and put up with him. I was greatly pained at hearing of the apostacy of R—— C——, an old minister, dismally fallen.' 'Sun., Oct. 7. We staid at North East, and at 11 o'clock Mr. Asbury preached on Heb. xii, 15-17. He gave us a good discourse, and I exhorted. There was some stir among the hearers.'

(2.) Asbury's Journal, vol. ii, p. 329:—The bishop was with Lee. His journal indicates trouble. 'Maryland. On Saturday [October 6, 1798,] we rode six miles to North East. My bruised side pained me much; my spirits were sad. Dark clouds imposed over Methodism here.' 'Sunday, Oct. 7. I preached in the North East church on Heb. xii, 15-17. The substance of my sermon was, 1. A caution against failing to obtain the repenting, converting, persevering, sanctifying grace of God. 2. How some bad principles, persons and practices were like wormwood, gall and poison to society. 3. How small the gain—how great the loss of peace. 4. That some might apostatize beyond the possibility of being restored, and weep hopeless and unavailing tears, etc.'

(3.) Methodism in New Jersey, by Rev. John Atkinson, p. 351:—'Robert Cloud * * * is said to have been an excellent preacher, but he unfortunately departed from the narrow path. * * * Rev. Thomas Morrell received a letter from Mr. Cloud, in which he stated that he was restored to the church, and intended to remain within its enclosure till his death.

(4.) I traveled (1860 and 1861) Newark circuit—one of the points Cherry Hill, Cecil County, Md. An aged member, a mother in Israel, knew all about his fall, his restoration in the revival of 1799, his preaching again, going west in 1800, and she heard his farewell sermon. I have no doubt that he was fully restored."—Letter to the author.

[6] It remained unknown to some of his nearest friends. One of them writes: "My grandfather never left the Methodist Episcopal Church, nor did he ever 'depart from the narrow path.' I lived with him from my earliest recollection till his death in 1833, and never heard of such a thing. A more consistent man I never met with, I think."—Letter to the author.

for 1819," printed that year in *The Weekly Recorder*, a religious journal published in Chillicothe, Ohio, and signed "Robert Cloud, President, J. W. Palmer, Secretary," indicates great energy and enterprise on the part of the officers, and bears testimony to the activity of Mr. Cloud in those days. His published obituary adds:

> It is but just to say that in the latter part of his life he became dissatisfied with the form of government in the Methodist Episcopal Church, and although he continued in connection with it, he often lamented its departure from primitive Methodism, and manifested much concern for the Methodist Protestant Church. But let all his friends know, let the church of Christ know that he died in the full assurance of faith. He retained his senses to the last, and left this for a better world without a struggle or a groan.

His death occurred at the residence of his son, in Lexington, Ky., on the 5th of June, 1833, in the seventy-eighth year of his age. The place of his rest is marked by a head-stone in Dr. Cloud's family ground in the city where he died.

Mr. Cloud was a man of decided convictions and never failed to make known his opposition to those things which

a consistent life, and died in the faith four years after the death of her husband.

Robert and Rachel Cloud were the parents of five sons and one daughter. Their names were *Jesse, Caleb, Wesley, Enoch, Robert, Israel,* and *Mary*. The extreme difficulty of maintaining so large a family on the pittance which the Methodist preacher in those days received, is sufficient to account for the frequent repetition of the words "under a location" in the pastoral record of Mr. Cloud.

Of the six children the *Rev. Dr. Caleb W. Cloud* seems to have been the most noted. He entered the Methodist itinerancy in 1804, and his appointments were in Ohio, Mississippi, Tennessee, and Kentucky. He possessed, and possibly inherited from his father, a restless disposition. He located while in Kentucky, in 1811, and entered upon the practice of medicine in Lexington. In 1820 he withdrew from the Methodist Episcopal Church, and established in Lexington an independent Methodist church, which never gained much influence, and gradually dwindled away. On good authority it is stated that " Dr. Cloud was somewhat addicted to drink in those days;"[12] and that after he had become blind he returned to the (by that time) Methodist Episcopal Church, South, and "died in peace" May 14, 1850.[13]

---

[12] Letter of Hiram Shaw, Esq., to the author.
[13] See Redford's "Methodism in Kentucky," vol. ii, p. 56.

VIII.
JOHN MERRICK.

WHEN the Rev. JOHN MERRICK was pastor in New York and Brooklyn he was known throughout the land as an eloquent and popular champion of the doctrines and usages of Methodism. If his name is now an unfamiliar one in the church, it is because he located, and no memorial of his life and character appeared in the Conference Minutes. It is cause for profound regret that only a mere fragment of the history of this man can now be obtained.

He was born in the year 1759. The place of his nativity is not known. The following communication from the Rev. Jacob P. Fort establishes the strong probability that this John Merrick was a soldier in the Revolution. He says:

I had the curiosity to turn to the Record of Names of Officers and Privates

Merrick began to preach as an itinerant in 1786. The published Minutes furnish us with his

PASTORAL RECORD: 1786, Somerset cir., Md., with James Riggin; 1787, Kent cir., with Ira Ellis; 1788, ordained deacon,—Trenton cir., N. J., with Thomas Morrell and Jethro Johnson; **1789, New York, including Brooklyn,** four months—Robert Cloud and Wm. Phœbus were to follow him, each for the same length of time; 1790, ordained elder,—Burlington cir., N. J, with James Bell; 1791–1794, presiding elder—district including nearly all of New Jersey; 1795, ditto, with the addition of portions of Pa. and Del. and Canada; 1796, no appointment named; 1797, located.

There is no evidence that John Merrick ever married. Wakeley heard those who knew affirm that Merrick was a remarkably eloquent preacher. There are persons now living who remember often hearing the fathers speak of his wonderful power in the pulpit. He has been likened to Charles Pitman in the style and force of his oratory.

Few men, even in his day, ever traveled so large a presiding elder's district as his, reaching from the Delaware Bay to the northern shore of Lake Ontario. We are indebted to the Rev. J. P. Fort for the following facts in relation to this extraordinary man:

Peter Vannest, who was presiding elder a few years after him on part of the same district, frequently related that at the conference, when he asked for a location, Bishop Asbury gave him a peculiar but significant look, and then replied, with great impressiveness: "John Merrick, if you locate you will either backslide or die before one year." This language, said Vannest, startled the conference. He did not backslide, but he died before the year closed. He died of fever near Hornerstown and was buried in the rear or east end, close up to the building of the old Methodist Episcopal church, New Mills, (now Pemberton,) N. J.

The church at New Mills was erected in 1775; rebuilt in 1833. While the workmen were digging for the basement, a few of the bones of Merrick's body that remained were reached. They were carefully collected by the writer, a deeper grave on the same spot was digged, and they were laid away again, thirty-five years after their first interment. On an old-formed marble tablet in the rear of the new church, Pemberton, N. J, is the following epitaph:

IN MEMORY OF
THE REV. JOHN MERRICK,
WHO DIED JULY 30, 1798,
AGED 39 YEARS.

Ye who survey with anxious eye
This tomb where Merrick's ashes lie;
His worth through various life attend,
His virtues learn, and mourn his end.[2]

---

[2] The Christian Advocate, New York, Aug. 12, 1880.

The same writer adds, in a letter to the author:

My father, the Rev. Andrew Fort, born February 18, 1787, was in his twelfth year when Merrick died, and he remembered his funeral. The procession, he said, reached over a mile, and the excitement among the people was intense. The whole country for miles around was aroused, and everybody seemed to be there. This I remember hearing forty years ago.

Diligent search has been made in vain for additional information; also for a copy of his portrait and autograph signature.

Contemporary with the subject of this sketch was another Methodist preacher of the same name, in New England, who married a sister of the Rev. Enoch Mudge, but the two should not be confounded.

IX.

WILLIAM PHŒBUS.

THE REV. DR. WILLIAM PHŒBUS labored in Brooklyn and vicinity for a longer period than most of the early itinerants, and for many years throughout this region, his name was a household word.

He was born August 4, 1754, in Somerset Co., Md., where his ancestors settled in 1675. The Phœbus family was originally attached to the Church of England.[1]

The Conference Minutes say; "Of his early days little is known, nor is the period of his conversion ascertained." When he joined conference, he had reached his twenty-ninth year. The story of his extended ministerial life is briefly set forth in the following

PASTORAL RECORD: 1783, Frederick cir., Md., with J. Pigman; 1784, East Jersey cir., with S. Dudley; 1785, West Jersey cir., with Thos. Ware and Robt. Sparks; 1786, not named in the appointments; 1787, (ordained deacon,) Redstone cir., Pa. and Va., with J. Wilson and E. Phelps; 1788, Rockingham cir., Va., with James Riggin; **1789, New York city and Brooklyn**, with Robert Cloud and John Merrick—each four months, and Jacob Brush several months,[2]—also, Long Island cir., with John Lee; **1790**, ordained elder, appointed to New Rochelle cir., with M. Swaim and Jacob Brush, but continued to preach on **Long Island** with D. Kendall and A. Hunt;[3] **1791, L. I. cir.,** with B. Abbott; 1792-1793, local; **1794**, supernumerary, **New York and Brooklyn** with Ezekiel Cooper, L. M'Combs, J. Brush, sup'y, and D. Kendall, sup'y; 1795, no appointment; **1796-1797, Brooklyn** station, exchanging systematically with the Long Island preachers; 1798-1805, local; 1806-1807, New York Conf., Albany; 1808, South Carolina Conf., Charleston, with John M'Veau; 1809, New York Conf., Long Island cir., with Francis Ward and Henry Redstone; 1810, Troy;[4] 1811, New York, with N Bangs, Laban Clark, Wm. Blagborne, Jas. M. Smith, P. P. Sandford; 1812, ditto, with Joseph Crawford, Laban Clark, Phineas Cook; 1813, New Rochelle cir., with W.

---

[1] Rev. Geo .A. Phœbus, D. D.—Letter to the author.
[2] "Lost Chapters," p. 367.   [3] See sketch of Aaron Hunt in this book.
[4] Here he found no prospect of an adequate support, and he left the charge by the consent of the presiding elder.

REV. WILLIAM PHŒBUS.

Thacher and O. Sykes; 1814, New York, with S. Cochran, N. Emery, M. Richardson, T. Drummond, and Wm. Blagborne; 1815, ditto, with Wm. Thacher, E. Washburn, M. Richardson, and A. Scholefield; 1816, Albany; 1817, Jamaica cir., L. I., with John M. Smith; 1818, New York, "Zion and Asbury;" 1819-1820, missionary; 1821, sup'y without appointment; 1822, Schenectady, N. Y.; 1823, no station; 1824-1831, superannuated.

From the foregoing record it appears that he was frequently re-appointed to the same circuit or station. As an associate of Dickins, Ware, Asbury, Garrettson, and others in the Christmas Conference of 1784, he was one of the men who organized the Methodist Episcopal Church. He represented the South Carolina Conference in the General Conference of 1808, and was a member of the "Committee of Fourteen" appointed to devise and report a plan for a Delegated General Conference. He was elected a delegate to the New York Conference in 1812 and 1816.

When on the Long Island circuit, in 1791, as colleague of Benjamin Abbott, the worldly people in Rockaway expressed their notion of the difference between the two men by saying that "Abbott raised the devil, but Phœbus laid him again."[5] It was during this year that he was married to a Miss Anderson, and the next year he thought himself justified in locating in order "to provide for himself and his household."[6] He maintained a successful practice in New York as a physician when not actively engaged in ministerial work. While supernumerary, in 1794, he laid the corner-stone of the original Sands-street church, in Brooklyn. Shortly after this (1796,) he began to edit *The Experienced Christian's Magazine.* One of the most important of his literary works was a *Life of Bishop Whatcoat.* He preached frequently in New York during the years of his location.

Dr. Phœbus departed this life in peace November 3, 1831, in the seventy-seventh year of his age. His remains were deposited in a burial ground in First-street, New York,[7] but were removed about the year 1855 to the "Asbury Removal Grounds" in Cypress Hills Cemetery, L. I. His grave is marked by a head-stone. The memorial adopted by his Conference says:

He was a man of great integrity, uniformly pious, deeply learned in the Scriptures, and a sound, experimental, and practical preacher.[8]

---

[5] Life of Abbott, p. 187.   [6] Bangs' Hist. M. E. Church, vol. iv, p. 128.
[7] Wakeley—"Lost Chapters," p. 327.
[8] Minutes of Conferences, 1832, p. 162.

The character of his discourses may be inferred from the following description of a sermon preached by him at a camp-meeting in Cow Harbor, L. I., in 1817. The account was given by the Rev. Dr. Fitch Reed, nearly fifty years after the event:

At this meeting Dr. Phœbus preached a sermon which at this distance I remember with greater distinctness and particularity than almost any sermon I ever heard. His theme was suggested by the account of Mary anointing the feet of Jesus, as narrated in the twelfth chapter of John. His propositions were: *The Act of a Women ; The Censure of a Traitor ; The Decision of a Judge.* The woman symbolized the Church in acts of piety for the honor and spread of the gospel ; Judas was the representative of all who either openly or covertly oppose the Church ; and the reply of Jesus sets forth the true estimate both of the Church and its opposers, and of the ultimate finding and open decision of the infinite Judge in the great day. The illustrations and application of this sermon were of thrilling interest, and produced a most decided effect.[9]

Although an able preacher, he was not especially popular with the masses, and alluding to the habit of those who left the church when they saw him in the pulpit, and started off to hear their favorite preacher, he said, in a pleasant way, that "when he preached there was generally *a moving time.*"[10] On one occasion he preached in the place of Summerfield, who was sick. When asked how he could supply the place of so popular a man he dryly and pleasantly remarked : " Don't you see that the Summer-fields cannot flourish without the rays of Phœbus?"[11]

During the session of the New York Conference of 1823, Dr. Phœbus preached the sermon on the occasion of the ordination of elders on Sunday afternoon, from the words of our Lord, "I am the door." George Coles, who heard the sermon, writes :

I thought his preaching was too metaphysical to be remembered ; but in the course of his sermon he showed the importance of personal piety in a minister in a very striking and solemn manner.[12]

William Phœbus belongs to that noted company of eccentric but truly godly Methodist preachers, whose singular words and ways can never be forgotten. He was sociable or taciturn, as his moods might chance to be. He had great veneration for antiquity, and perhaps paid undue deference to the views and opinions of the old divines. He was not favorable to the office of

---

[9] "Reminiscences," in the Northern Christian Advocate, 1863.
[10] " Lost Chapters," p. 328.
[11] Ibid., p. 329.
[12] " My First Seven Years in America," p. 263.

presiding elder in the Methodist Episcopal Church.[13] The following portraiture is copied from the writings of an intimate friend:

> Dr. Phœbus had acquired a large stock of useful information, but lacked that systematic arrangement of knowledge which we expect in a mind that has had an early and classical training. * * * He had great independence of mind, * * * great contempt for every thing designed merely for show, * * * and a deep insight into human nature. He was much given to enigmatical expression, which the mass of his hearers did not comprehend. * * * His character was, on the whole, one of varied excellence and uncommon power, while yet he appeared like a different man under the exhibition of its different qualities. Dr. Phœbus was of medium height, compactly built, and had a countenance decidedly intellectual, and expressive of great sincerity.[14]

The accompanying portrait will aid the reader in forming an estimate of the sturdy nobleness of this great and good man.

Concerning his wife and children, almost nothing has been definitely ascertained. ANN PHŒBUS, (probably his wife,) and *Abdiel Asbury Phœbus*, (presumably his son,) are buried in the same grave with him. One of his brothers was grandfather of the Rev. George A. Phœbus, D.D., of the Wilmington Conference.

---

[13] Bangs' Hist. M. E. Church, vol. iv., p. 128.
[14] Dr. N. Bangs in Sprague's Annals, vol. vii, p. 88.

X.

Jacob Brush.

UST before the Brooklyn society was annexed to the Long Island circuit, the REV. JACOB BRUSH, having come from Delaware, was employed as a preacher in New York, and he doubtless assumed his share of the pastoral charge in Brooklyn. Two years later he had supervision of the district. He was the first, and until 1872, the only native of Long Island assigned to the presiding elder's office in that section.

In what part of Long Island he was born has not been definitely ascertained.[1] Very little is known concerning him previous to the appearance of his name in the Conference Minutes We trace him from year to year by the following

APPOINTMENTS: 1785,[2] Trenton cir., N. J., with Robert Cloud and John M'Claskey; 1786, West Jersey cir., with John Simmons and J. Lurton; 1787, Dover cir., Del., with A. Hutchinson; 1788, ordained deacon, Northampton cir., Md., with L. Ross; 1789, Dover and Duck Creek cir., Del. and Pa. A part of the winter and spring previous to the N. Y. Conf. of 1790, he was in New England, with Jesse Lee, George Roberts and Daniel Smith;[3] and the same year he labored some time in New York and probably Brooklyn, with Thos. Morrell and Rob't Cloud;[4] 1790, October, New Rochelle cir.,N. Y.[5]

---

[1] The Rev. Z. Davenport, who knew some of his relatives, said to the author that he was well-nigh assured that the birth place of Mr. Brush was in the vicinity of Merrick, L. I.

[2] Stevens (Hist. M. E. Church, vol. ii, p. 436,) makes the date 1783; doubtless a typographical error.

[3] Stevens—Hist. M. E. Church, vol. ii, p. 435.

[4] "Lost Chapters," pp. 367, 368.

[5] Aaron Hunt, quoted by Stevens, (History M. E. Church, vol. iii, p. 221,) gives the impression that Mr. Brush was presiding elder of New York District *at this time.* He was Hunt's pastor in 1790, and his presiding elder in 1792.

Record of Ministers.

with M. Swaim, and the Minutes say Wm. Phœbus, but Phœbus was, some part at least of that year, on Long Island cir.; 1791, returned to New Rochelle cir., with T. Everard and T. Lovelle; **1792, presiding elder for L. I.** and other parts of N. Y. and Western Conn., a district embracing nearly the same territory now included in the N. Y. East Conf.; **1793, "elder"** of a district embracing parts of N. J. and N. Y., including **Long Island**;[6] **1794,** sup'y, New York and **Brooklyn,** with E. Cooper, L. M'Combs, W Phœbus, sup'y, and D. Kendall, sup'y.

His coming north was like the advent of an angel from heaven. He found Thomas Morrell and the other New York preachers worn out in revival work, and taking his place by their side as a fellow-laborer, saw four hundred added to the roll of the converts in eight weeks. He then passed on with George Roberts and Daniel Smith to re-enforce Jesse Lee at Dantown in New England. "No one knows," says Lee, "but God and myself what comfort and joy I felt at their arrival." That was genuine pioneer work. Brush was the only ordained elder among the four preachers, and the members in New England were not more than two for each preacher. He soon returned to New York.

Through his influence Aaron Hunt was led to enter the ministry. In recording this fact, Stevens, by a *lapsus pennæ*, erroneously quotes Aaron Hunt as saying that Jacob Brush was an "old man."[7]

In his thirty-fourth year he fell a victim to the yellow fever, in the city of New York, on the 24th of September, 1795. In his conference memorial his brethren state that he died in peace; that when the power of speech was gone he indicated by a pressure of the hand that all was well. They also record their apprecation of him as "an active man of God, a great friend to order and union."[8]

Wakeley says he was engaged to be married to an amiable young woman, a daughter of a Methodist preacher, but death prevented their union.[9] His remains were laid to rest in the burial ground in the rear of the Forsyth-street church, New York, where his tombstone may be found. Lines of no great

---

[6] Stevens errs in saying that this district was wholly in New York. Compare Hist. M. E. Church, vol. ii, p. 437, and Conf. Minutes, 1793, p. 51.

[7] Compare Stevens' Hist. M. E. Church, vol. iii, p. 221, and "Lost Chapters," p. 369. See, also, Conf. Minutes, 1796, p. 66.

[8] Minutes, 1796, p. 66.

[9] "Lost Chapters," p. 369.

literary merit, but expressive of the general and profound sorrow occasioned by his death, were published a few months after the event.[10]

Jacob Brush was a burning and a shining light in the church. When compelled, by a chronic inflammation of the throat, to take a supernumerary relation, he had traveled eight years successively. Few men in his or any generation were more constantly or successfully devoted to the work of the Christian ministry.

The Rev. W. D. Thompson, of the New York East Conference, has in his possession a valuable memento of this pioneer preacher—a copy of Lord King's " Plain Account of the Constitution of the Christian Church in the First Three Centuries." It was owned by Mr. Brush and contains his signature. The volume was presented to Mr. Thompson by the late Rev. Z. Davenport.

---

[10] ".Experienced Christian's Magazine," Wm. Phœbus, editor, 1796, p. 89. See the same in " Lost Chapters," p. 370.

XI.
DAVID KENDALL.

AMONG the pastors of the Sands-street church there is perhaps not another whose history so completely eludes the search of the biographer, as that of the REV. DAVID KENDALL. Personal correspondence and inquiries published in The Christian Advocate and in Zion's Herald have failed to call forth the least word of testimony concerning this good and useful minister of Christ.

In 1790, he succeeded John Lee as the colleague of Wm. Phœbus on Long Island. His name alone is set down for Long Island circuit in the printed Conference Minutes; but from Aaron Hunt's journal we infer that Phœbus was assigned to the circuit with Kendall. Hunt was there also during Kendall's sickness. From the Minutes we obtain a chronological list of his

APPOINTMENTS: 1788, New City cir., N. Y., with S. Q. Talbot; 1789, Lake Champlain cir., with Wm. Losee; **1790**, ordained deacon—**Long Island cir.**, with Wm. Phœbus, and A. Hunt; 1791, Saratoga cir.; 1792, Pittsfield cir., Mass., with R. Dillon and J. Rexford; 1793, ordained elder,—Greenwich cir., R. I., with E. Mudge; **1794**, sup'y, New York and **Brooklyn**, with E. Cooper, L. M'Combs, W. Phœbus and J. Brush; 1795, "located through weakness," etc.

Stevens, writing concerning him and Losee, and the Champlain circuit in 1789,—then the northernmost outpost of Methodism on the continent—says:

Their journeys brought them within sight of Canada. The circuit seems not, however, to have been successful, for in 1790 it was abandoned.[1]

It can but be inferred from the important character of his appointments that he was a man of respectable talent and good standing in the connection, yet most of his history has passed into oblivion. His work abides in the hearts and lives, as well as in the thoughts of many who never heard his name.

> Though they may forget the singer,
> They will not forget the song.

---
[1] Hist. M. E. Church, vol. ii, p. 392.

XII.

AARON HUNT.

THE REV. AARON HUNT was born in East Chester, Westchester County, N. Y., March 28, 1768. The war of the Revolution transpired during his boyhood, and he was shocked by the "scenes of horror and suffering" which he witnessed. Although surrounded in youth by wicked associates, he was preserved, to a large extent, from their corrupting influence. When seventeen years of age he took up his residence in New York city, and attended the Protestant Episcopal Church.

After two years had elapsed, while passing old John Street Church one evening, in company with a fellow clerk, their attention was arrested by the earnest tones of the preacher. They went in and heard a part of the sermon. His comrade reviled, but *he* was favorably impressed, and continuing to attend the services, he was, on the 18th of March, 1789, while in his twenty-first year, brought to a saving knowledge of Christ. He wrote in his journal the following vivid account of his conversion:

> While my heart sank within me, I ventured out of self and all self-dependence. Heaven seemed to stoop and pity the sinner in distress. My burden was removed, and all was light; I clasped my hands, and walked, and said, "Glory, glory to God!"

He immediately began to lead others to Christ. His burning zeal constrained him to establish family prayer in the home of an older brother with whom he was boarding. The cross was very great. He took a candle and started for his room, but replaced it, saying, "May I pray?" When he rose from his knees after an earnest prayer, his sister-in-law sneeringly said, "Aaron has been to the Methodist meetings, and wants to show us how well he has learned to pray." But his

REV. AARON HUNT, 1st.

brother in penitence accompanied him to the meetings, and was converted. Thenceforward Moses and Aaron were united heart and hand in the service of Christ. About this time, in a prayer-meeting, he first met Benjamin Abbott. When he heard that wonderful man give out and sing the hymn,

"Refining fire, go through my heart,"

he and nearly all others present were seized with "an awful trembling," and he "agonized for a clean heart." Having returned from New York to his native town, he was soon made leader of a class. With his conversion came a conscious call to the ministry. He preached his first sermon near his home, on the New Rochelle circuit in 1790, from Rom. xiii, 12: "The night is far spent," etc.; and in the latter part of the same conference year, (January, 1791,) encouraged by his friend and pastor, Jacob Brush,[1] he went to serve as a supply on Long Island circuit, which then included Brooklyn, and extended eastward to the farthest outposts of Methodism in Suffolk county. He was young and inexperienced, but in his journal he writes:

As I went round the circuit, I found the people not only willing to bear with my weakness, but apparently glad to hear me. I saw fruits of my endeavors, and enjoyed many gracious seasons.

Thus began an extended and useful ministry, which is briefly sketched in the following

PASTORAL RECORD: 1790, last part of this conference year, **supply on L. I. cir.**, N. Y., with W. Phœbus and D. Kendall; 1791, (joined the itinerancy,) Fairfield cir., Conn., with N. B. Mills; 1792, Middletown cir., with R. Swain; 1793, ordained deacon—Fairfield cir., with J. Coleman; 1794-1799, local; 1800, (N. Y. Conf., re-admitted,) ordained elder,—Litchfield cir., Conn., with E. Batchelor; 1801, no appointment, by request; 1803, New London cir., with M. Coate; 1804, New Rochelle cir., with Wm. Thacher; 1805-1806, New York city cir., with F. Garrettson, N. Snethen, and John Wilson; 1806, ditto, with T. Bishop, S. Crowell, F. Garrettson, and John Wilson; 1807, Litchfield cir., Conn., with J. Lyon; 1808-1810, presiding elder, Rhinebeck Dist.; 1811, Redding cir., Conn., with O. Sykes and J. Reynolds; 1812, Middletown cir., with A. Scholefield; 1813, Redding cir., with H. Eames; 1814, Croton cir., N. Y., with Eben Smith; 1815, ditto, with E. Canfield; 1816, Stamford cir., Conn., with Theod. Clark; 1817, Bridgeport cir., with F

---

[1] See Stevens' Hist. M. E. Church, vol. iii, p. 221, where Hunt is quoted as saying that Jacob Brush was his presiding elder. I find no other evidence that Brush had charge of the district that year, or that he was presiding elder until 1792.

Garrettson—sup'y.; 1818, Courtlandt cir., N. Y., with B. Northrop; 1819, New York, with S. Merwin, Laban Clark, B. Hibbard, T. Spicer, and N. Morris; 1820, ditto, with J. Soule, B. Hibbard, T. Spicer, and E. Hebard; 1821, Redding cir., Conn,, with Laban Clark; 1822, ditto, with S. Cochran; 1823, sup'y, Danbury cir.; 1824, Redding and Bridgeport cir., with M. Richardson, H. Humphreys, and F. W. Sizer; 1826, sup'y, ditto, with M. Richardson, H. Humphreys, and O. Sykes, sup'y; 1827–1839, sup'y, Amenia cir., N. Y.,—his colleagues were Wm. Jewett, J. C. Bontecou, A. S. Hill, F. Reed, Lorin Clark, S. Cochran, F. Donnelly, S. U. Fisher, E. Washburn, R. Wymond, D. G. Sutton, D. Holmes, J. P. Ellsworth, G. L. Fuller, B. Silleck, D. Keeler, and W. K. Stopford; 1840–1857, superannuated.

This record covers the long period of sixty-eight years, but shows that he was on the effective list less than half of that time. A small farm in Redding, Conn., having fallen to him by inheritance, it became, for the most part, the permanent home of his family; but during each of the twenty-seven years when he was appointed to a charge, he devoted himself faithfully to his ministerial work, submitting ofttimes to long and trying absence from home—his receipts sometimes not exceeding twenty dollars a year.

His location in 1794 was not intended to be permanent. He preached statedly on the Sabbath, and sometimes during the week, and when his health and his business permitted him to resume regular pastoral work, he declined favorable opportunities to enter the ministry of another denomination, and returned to the itinerant ranks. Right nobly he endured the hardships and fought the battles that fell to the lot of the pioneer Methodist preacher.

In 1792 he preached the first Methodist sermon in Danbury, Conn. The meeting was held in the court-house. No one spoke to him, and he put up at a tavern, at his own expense. That was a common experience. But he soon saw a society organized there, and a little chapel erected, toward which he contributed one hundred dollars, taking the deed in his own name, and conveying the property to the trustees, "according to the Discipline." The watch-word of his ministry appears to have been, "According to Discipline!"

During the following year, while on the Middletown circuit, he was sent forward to plant the standard of our denomination where no Methodist preacher's voice had been heard. His journal says:

In May, 1793, my presiding elder directed me to go across the Connecticut River, and "break up new ground," as he expressed it. This was very trying, but to obey them that had the rule over me was my determination. I again renewed my covenant with the Lord and set forward, and traveled through the counties of New London and Windham, making a small excursion into the State of Massachusetts. An itinerant preacher was a new thing in those lands. Some inquired whether I was sent by the president, or by Congress, or by what authority.

In 1793 he was married to Miss Eunice Sanford. She died in 1805, leaving him sorely bereaved.

Mr. Hunt was the originator of the motion to adopt the two-years rule in the itinerancy—a law enacted by the General Conference in 1804. It is well known that previous to that date there was no specified limit to the pastoral term. It was not uncommon to change preachers even oftener than every year, while some remained longer than two or three years. Concerning the circumstances which led to the adoption of the two-years rule Mr. Hunt writes as follows:

Soon after the commencement of the present century, two or three cases occurred that gave the bishop great annoyance. Some preachers, finding themselves in pleasant stations, and by the aid of self-constituted committees—believing, of course, that they could do better in the place than any one else— objected to removal, while the more pious part of the society would have preferred a change; but the officious committee prevailed.[2]

One case to which he specifically alludes was that of the Rev. Cyrus Stebbins. He had been pastor of Albany City station four years, (1800-1803,) many of the leading members having wished him to remain, while many of the more humble desired a change. Asbury felt that it would be for the general good to remove him, but, finding that he could not do so without causing a rupture, he was greatly perplexed as to what course to pursue. He spoke to his son, Aaron, as he always called him, concerning this case, and what followed is thus narrated by Mr. Hunt:

In conversation with the bishop, I suggested the two-years rule, to which he pleasantly replied: "So, then, you would restrict the appointing power?" "Nay, sir," was the reply, "we would aid its execution, for in the present case it seems to be deficient." His laconic reply of "So, so," encouraged me, at the ensuing General Conference of 1804, to present the resolution signed by myself, and seconded by the Rev. Joseph Totten, of the Philadelphia Conference. When it was read by the secretary, one observed that such a rule would limit the Episcopacy; another, that it would tacitly station for two years. Of course it was laid on the table. It was talked over out of doors, and scanned in all its bearings by the firesides, and when called up again [by George Dougherty,] it passed after some discussion by a very general vote.

---

[2] The Christian Advocate and Journal, March 6, 1851.

During his first term as preacher in charge of New York city circuit, he introduced the custom of inviting penitents in our churches to come forward and kneel at the altar. His own written statement of the matter is as follows:

In September, 1806, I appointed a prayer-meeting, particularly for those who had been at the camp-meeting [at Cow Harbor, L. I.] Many attended in the church in Second-street, [better known as Forsyth-street church.] It was a time of great power. Many wept, and cried aloud for mercy. Soon the cry of mourners became general throughout the church, and many prayers were put up in their behalf. It was in this revival needful to regulate our prayer-meetings by calling the mourners to the altar, and inviting the praying brethren into the altar.

It is stated by those who were personally acquainted with Methodist usages in those days that penitent persons were expected to kneel down in whatever part of the house they happened to be. The Christians present would then gather around them and pray. Thus several little prayer-meetings were held at the same time in various parts of the congregation. Mr. Hunt, as preacher in charge, was not willing that this disorderly custom should any longer prevail. About that time he received a letter from his friend and former colleague, the Rev. Nicholas Snethen, describing the custom which had just been adopted at the camp-meetings in the South, of inclosing a space in front of the stand, called an altar, where mourners and those who were considered capable of instructing them and praying with them, were invited to meet apart from the great congregation. After much consideration and prayer, he determined upon adopting a similar course in the church, and at the "second camp-meeting prayer-meeting" he invited all who were seeking the Saviour to come forward and kneel at the altar, but not one person complied with the request. The three preachers met the next day in consultation, Mr. Hunt assigned as his reason for proposing to introduce the altar service, that the confusion of previous meetings would thereby be avoided, and the name, residence, and spiritual condition of each convert and seeker could be ascertained, making it possible to watch over them more successfully. Truman Bishop, one of the colleagues, concurred, but Seth Crowell, the other preacher, put in a stern remonstrance, and in the evening took a back seat to watch the result of what he considered an interference with God's order, and a steadying of the ark. But the penitents, having reflected on the propriety of gathering about the altar, pressed forward as soon as the invitation was given, filling the entire kneeling place about the altar rail, and several of the front seats. Many of these rejoiced in the pardon of their sins, and Mr. Crowell, witnessing the happy result, discontinued his opposition, and joined zealously in the work.

From this experiment the custom soon came to be generally adopted in the Methodist revival services throughout the land. In later years Mr. Hunt expressed concern lest the usage might degenerate into a form in which some might trust rather than in the Saviour, and of which others might take advantage in hypocrisy to impose upon the Church.

Aaron Hunt was at first very strongly opposed to the presiding elder's office, but his experience in his large district convinced him of the necessity of some sort of supervision. His appointment to the district was much against his desire. He says:

> Bishop Asbury knew well my objections to the office of presiding elder. At our Annual Conference in Amenia, in 1808, all things progressed pleasantly to the reading of the appointments, when my name was reserved to the last. Then came out, "Aaron Hunt for Rhinebeck District." Instantly I rose to my feet requesting to be heard. The reply was, "No time to be heard now —let us pray;" and such a prayer as Asbury only could offer, followed by a score of loud "amens," almost stunned me. I was somewhat offended at the strange movement, but Asbury came along, and said, "Come, Aaron, I am going home with you." This in some degree softened my feelings, and led me to conclude that perhaps he had some reasons for making the appointment that I did not see.

The trouble among New York Methodists, resulting in the Stilwell secession, occurred during his administration. A circumstantial history of these events, written by Mr. Hunt, appeared in "The Christian Advocate and Journal," and the following extracts will enable the reader to form an estimate of his rigid adherence to the Discipline of the Church. He writes:

> I was stationed in New York in 1819 and 1820, with the care of all our societies, then in the circuit form, consisting of six or seven churches. Our people had been in a state of turmoil for several years, which had for its pretext the erection of the second John-street church, but, in fact, arose from a disposition in some " to have the pre-eminence." My predecessor in charge [Dr. Bangs] had labored in vain to restore harmony. Having been previously in the station, I had some knowledge of persons and circumstances, and felt it a heavy trial to enter on so important a charge. Looking for divine direction, with the Bible and Discipline in my hand, I determined to follow peace with all men.

By bringing some of the estranged parties together in the conducting of revival meetings, he succeeded in allaying the ill feeling to a large extent; but how the strife was renewed and continued is narrated as follows :

Previous to the annual election of trustees, some restless spirits began to electioneer. By this course the Stilwellites (or up-town party) succeeded in getting a majority in the board of trustees.

The board of trustees claimed the *legal* right to receive and control the moneys collected for the preachers. It had been customary in New York for the trustees to do all the business, but the new board refused to provide for the preachers, yet they proposed to receive the class money from the leaders, and when they paid it over to the stewards, who might be appointed, to take their receipts, and the amount the stewards would receive would depend on whether they would comply with that condition. Having obtained the opinion of high legal authority that this claim of the trustees was not valid, Mr. Hunt had a board of stewards appointed, and called "a general leaders' meeting." He says:

When convened, about seventy were present; and after singing and prayer we proceeded to read the Discipline—stewards' duties and leaders' duties, observing that, *as Methodists*, both preachers and people were under obligation to adhere to these rules. One leader said he did not care what the Discipline said—he would go according to law, for that was his plea. I said, "Brother, please give me your class-book." He gave it up. This gave a check to some of the warm heads. Brother Soule, [afterward bishop,] my right hand colleague, remarked, "That is right."

Mr. Hunt and those who were with him perseveringly resisted the claim of the trustees to receipts for money paid over to the stewards, declaring the stewards to be amenable to the Quarterly Conference and not to the trustees. Hunt's journal thus informs us what followed :

The morning after the general leaders' meeting, two of the trustees, a number of leaders, and private members to the number of thirty called on me for certificates of dismission from the Church. Under the circumstances I did not think it proper to give them certificates, but as they persisted in leaving, we wrote on the records against their names, "withdrawn." They poured upon us a torrent of misrepresentation and falsehood, making every effort to draw off all they could, and finally they succeeded in obtaining about two hundred members and one hundred probationers. To me these were days and years of no ordinary toil and anxiety, which often deprived me of sleep, and wore upon my health. At the ensuing Annual Conference we [meaning himself and colleagues] suggested the propriety of a committee to investigate our proceedings; but it was refused, the conference being satisfied with our course.

In contending for their rights the early Methodist preachers found a brave champion in Aaron Hunt. George Roberts, when presiding elder, had been fined one hundred dollars by a court held in Middletown, for solemnizing a marriage ceremony in the State of Connecticut, but that did not frighten Mr. Hunt into employing the parish minister at his own wedding. He invited his presiding elder, Jacob Brush, to officiate, and when the elder hesitated on account of the law, he assured him that if he were brought to account, he would meet all the charges, and pay all fines and costs. Subsequently, when legal proceedings for the same offense had been instituted against one of the preachers, Mr. Hunt appeared on his behalf, and made the law appear so odious that the suits were withdrawn.

He represented his brethren in General Conference in 1804, 1812, and 1816. About 1828 he sold his property in Redding, and purchased a small farm in the town of Sharon, Conn., near Amenia Union, N. Y. There he resided until his removal to Leedsville, N. Y., a few years before his death. He spent his last winter with his son, Zalmon S. Hunt, in Sharon. As death approached, his mind was clear, and he was often favored with seasons of great tenderness and rapture. He passed away on the 25th of April, 1858, past ninety years of age, and was buried in the ground which he had given for a Methodist cemetery, in Sharon, Conn. His grave is marked by a marble slab, appropriately inscribed.

For many years Aaron Hunt was recognized as "the patriarch of the New York Conference." In their published memorial its members say:

He was strongly attached to the Discipline of the Church, and watched with jealous anxiety any deviation from the old ways, but always indorsed those new measures that seemed likely to increase the spirituality and strength of the Church. He was plain and neat in appearance, and prompt in the discharge of his ministerial duties.

EUNICE SANFORD, sister of the Rev. Aaron Sanford, Sen., was the first wife of Aaron Hunt. Their union was happy, but not long—from their marriage, in 1793, to her death, on the 6th of February, 1805, she lived well and died in peace, commending her husband and her four little children to our heavenly Father's care. A head-stone marks her grave in Redding, Conn., where she had spent most of her life.

HANNAH SANFORD, daughter of the elder Aaron Sanford, and sister to Hawley Sanford, was married to Aaron Hunt about two years after the death of his first wife. She was possessed of a very sweet Christian spirit, and chiefly through her instruction and example all the children were converted in youth, and joined the Methodist Episcopal Church. She was in feeble health many years, and died September 18, 1831, aged forty eight years. Her body is buried beside her husband's.

NANCY THOMPSON, a native of Goshen, Conn., whose parents were among the earliest converts to Methodism in New England, became the third wife of Aaron Hunt, in 1832, and in his "age and feebleness extreme" her kind hands ministered to his wants. Her writings concerning him evince a remarkable affection and veneration for her husband. She was a superior woman—intelligent, pious, very zealous in Sunday-school work, a pioneer in the organization of "infant classes" in New England, a contributor to the columns of the Sunday School Advocate and other periodicals. The tract entitled "Procrastination; or, an Echo from the Voice of the Dying," is from her pen. After the death of her husband she removed to Michigan, and subsequently to Leavenworth, Kansas, where, at the residence of her nephew, she died in great peace, September 8, 1867, aged seventy-eight years. She was actively engaged in organizing and conducting an infant class a few months previous to her death. Her remains were deposited near those of her sister, in the town of Schoolcraft, near Kalamazoo, Mich. The Rev. Dr. A. S. Hunt wrote a fitting memorial of her, which was published in The Christian Advocate.

Children of Aaron Hunt by first marriage: *Zalmon*, died young; *Joseph*, father of Andrew and Albert S. Hunt, Methodist preachers; *Aaron*, more than forty years a member of the New York Conference; *Phoebe*, who married the Rev. A. S. Hill; *William*, who left no children. Children by second marriage: *Sarah Ann*, single; *Electa*, married George W. Ingraham, of Amenia, N. Y.; *Zalmon*, who resides at Amenia Union.

XIII.

BENJAMIN ABBOTT.

AMONG "the most memorable men of early Methodism" was the REV. BENJAMIN ABBOTT His father and two brothers were natives of Long Island, but he was born in Pennsylvania, in 1732. This was years before Lee, or Garrettson, or Morrell, or (so far as known) any other native American Methodist preacher was born. His parents' names were Benjamin and Hannah. They died when he was quite young, and he "grew up in great wickedness, drinking, fighting, swearing and gambling."

In his thirty-second year he dreamed an awful dream about hell, and from that time till he was forty years of age, he was troubled at intervals on account of his sins. He was then living in New Jersey. His wife was a Presbyterian, but unconverted, and when they heard the gospel from the lips of Abraham Whitworth, a Methodist preacher,[1] they were brought into the light and united with the Methodists. Six of their children followed their example, and David, one of the sons, became an itinerant minister.[2]

Soon after his conversion he began to preach at Hell Neck and other God-forsaken places, and gathered around him his astonished comrades who had been the witnesses of his bloody fights and foul profanity.

He met with great opposition from the enemies of the truth. At Trenton a false alarm of fire was given to draw the people away from his meeting. He was surrounded by

---

[1] This man departed from the faith, and became a soldier in the British army, and was probably killed in battle. See Stevens' Hist. M. E. Church, vol. i, p. 203.

[2] Life of Abbott, p. 110.

mobs, but he awed them by his courage, and preached in their presence with wondrous liberty and power, and many vile sinners were awakened and saved.

He contended earnestly for the doctrines and usages of the Methodists, and complained that in one place "the Baptist preacher, who afterward turned Universalist and then deist, stole away nine of our sheep, and ran them into the mill-pond."[3]

He was a flaming evangelist, going from place to place throughout that portion of New Jersey, seeking the salvation of souls. In 1788, during the last of the sixteen years of his irregular but efficient labors as a local preacher, he met with a severe affliction in the death of his faithful wife. The next year he joined conference, and the following is his

ITINERANT RECORD: 1789, Dutchess cir., N. Y., with S. Q. Talbot; 1790, ordained deacon,—Newburgh cir., with Joseph Lovell: **1791, Long Island cir.**, with Wm. Phœbus; 1792, Salem cir., N. J., with David Bartine; 1793, ordained elder;—1793-1794, Cecil cir., Md., with Fred. Curp; part of this time, as his manuscripts show, he was on Kent cir.;[4] 1795, health failed—not named in the Minutes.

His labors on Long Island, as well as on other circuits, are quite fully narrated in his published memoirs. They are almost without a parallel in "the rough energy, saintly devotion, and apostolic zeal" they display. Fearless, earnest, magnetic, he thrilled his audiences with rapture or terror, exercising an almost superhuman power on large congregations of various degrees of culture, and he possessed this power in the absence of the ordinary amount of learning which the humbler class of ministers had acquired. One of his contemporaries writes:

On a certain occasion, when exhorting before one of the bishops, among other expressions, he spoke of the "Seatic" ocean. The bishop, in much kindness, told him that he should have called it the Atlantic ocean, and corrected other blunders, and requested him to be more accurate in his language; all of which he took in good part, and expressed much gratitude to the bishop, together with a determination to follow up his counsel. But now for the sequel. The next day he was set to preach before the bishop; he resolved to have his discourse as nice as possible, but he felt cramped and embarrassed, and saw that no interest was excited. At length he came to a pause and exclaimed: "If all the bishops on earth, and all the devils in hell were here, I must preach like Ben. Abbott." He then made a new start, and went

---

[3] Life, p. 66.   [4] Ibid., p. 219.

ahead with his usual style and energy, which was followed with a great move in the assembly and a shout of victory.[5]

Dr. Fitch Reed states that Abbott committed an amusing blunder once in preaching from the text, "Thou art an austere man."

He read it "oyster man," and so went on in his preaching to compare the Lord in the work of converting sinners to a man catching oysters with what were known as oyster tongs, describing the well-known process with much precision, and making the application as he went along.[6]

He probably spoke of the "oyster man," raking in the natural oyster beds, as gathering where he had not strewn, and we may imagine how the preacher could use this fact to teach his hearers that, while God never brought men into sin, he can and does lift them up out of it.

His own account of a love-feast in New York, about the time he was appointed to Long Island, shows that his brethren were sometimes not a little tried with his loud and boisterous manner. He writes:

We went into the city of New York, and the next day conference was opened. We went on very lovingly in the affairs of the Church from day to day, until it came to the appointment of the love-feast; then it was brought on the carpet by Bro. R. Cloud concerning the love-feast at our last conference. He said that I hallooed, and bawled, and cried "Fire! fire!" Brother G. [probably Garrettson] got up and seconded him, and opposed the work with all the powers he had. Brother J. Lee said he was happy in the love-feast. The bishop said he did not want to hear them halloo, and shout, and bawl, but he wanted to hear them speak their experience.[7]

He adds, that when the love-feast came to be held, though there were several hundred present, the meeting was "dead," and the preachers, "in discoursing together, acknowledged that they had been wrong in what they had done and said on the subject."

"Abbott's thunder-gust sermon" was, perhaps, the most memorable discourse he ever preached. It was on a funeral occasion at the Kent meeting-house, Md., in the midst of the most awful thunder-storm ever known in that country. "The people crowded in, up stairs and down, to screen themselves from the

---

[5] Autobiography of Dan Young, p. 216.
[6] "Reminiscences" in Northern Christian Advocate, 1863.
[7] Life of Abbott, p. 177.

storm," and while the lightning glared, and the thunder crashed, and the windows rattled, he set forth the terrors of the judgment; and while the people quaked, and cried, and fell as dead men, he continued to preach, answering now and then to the voice of the storm—"My God, thunder on outside, while I thunder inside!" "Many were convinced and many converted on that great day."[8] To the day of their death those who heard him did not cease to tell of the terrifying power which attended his words, when he made "the flesh quiver on their trembling bones."[9]

The following incident is related by the Rev. Isaac L. Hunt, of the Northern New York Conference, whose parents were well acquainted with Benjamin Abbott. About the time that Mr. Abbott preached on the Dutchess circuit, some of the opponents of Methodist doctrines sent word to the preacher about the time of beginning the service in a school-house, that they would like to hear him preach from the text, "Jacob have I loved, and Esau have I hated." The Calvinists were out in force, intent on witnessing the embarrassment and discomfiture of the poor, ignorant itinerant. No allusion to the matter escaped the lips of the preacher until he knelt in prayer; then he told the Lord of this peculiar difficulty of his position, and prayed for help. "Help, Lord, help!" he cried. "Send the *power*, POWER, POWER!" he repeated, with thrilling, terrifying earnestness. "Send down the POWER, Lord! Let the *power* fall! *Power*, POWER, POWER!" The deacons and elders began to tremble, and so did all who sympathized with them in their attempt to entangle the preacher; and before the prayer was over they had all fled from the house, to escape that awful power which they felt that Abbott's wonderful prayer was bringing down upon them. The result was that when he rose to preach he felt quite relieved, because those who wanted a sermon from the Jacob-and-Esau text were not there.

Though a man of great physical strength, he wore himself out in the service of God. His last year on earth was one of extreme suffering. He was graciously sustained, however, and died in triumph, clapping his hands, and exclaiming: "I see heaven sweetly opened before me! Glory! glory! glory!"[10]

---

[8] See Stevens' Hist. M. E. Church, vol. i, p 402.
[9] Elegy in Phœbus' Magazine, 1796, p. 317.   [10] Life of Abbott, p. 274.

His funeral sermon was preached, in accordance with his request, by the eloquent John M'Claskey, who is said to have been his son in the Gospel.[11] His doctor's bill and funeral expenses, amounting to £9 7s. 6d., were paid from the preachers' fund.[12]

In the year 1831 the Rev. Dr. Noah Levings and Judge Garrison, of Brooklyn, visited his grave in the Walnut-street Methodist church-yard of Salem, N. J., where, up to that time, he had slept without a memorial. Only one man, an old negro, could point out the grave with certainty.[13] Dr. Levings assisted in erecting upon the spot a suitable monument, bearing the following inscription, prepared by Daniel Ostrander:

Sacred to the memory of Benjamin Abbott, 23 years a member, 16 years a local preacher, and 7 years a traveling preacher in the M. E. Church. He died Aug. 14, 1796, aged 64 years. A holy, zealous, and useful man of God. O happy exit, etc. *Erected by J. Garrison, Esq., and others, of Brooklyn, Kings County, N. Y.*

Mr. Abbott was one of the founders of Methodism in Salem, and for some time a resident of the place, hence it is fitting that his mortal remains should repose there.

Search has been made in vain for likeness and autograph signature of this remarkable man. Mr. Ward, trustee of the original church in Salem, owned an old-style profile likeness of Benjamin Abbott. His son writes:

Since my father's death my mother has moved, and she thinks the likeness of the good old man must have been lost or mislaid. She and my sister both remember the likeness, and describe it as a very well-cut silhouette, which was prized as gold by my father.

I recently visited my father's grave, in the old South-street church-yard, the same burial ground in which rest the ashes of those honored ministers, Abbott, Ware, Crane, and Newell. Ware was Abbott's intimate friend and co-laborer in the cause of the Master, and the other two remembered him well, and had heard him preach several times. I have heard James Newell and Moses Crane again and again speak of "Daddy Abbott." They described him as a man of great size and strength, with a voice like the roar of a lion.[14]

His wife was a Presbyterian and "a praying woman" at the time of his conversion, but, as he tells us, "knew nothing about experimental religion." She favored family prayer, but chided

---

[11] "Lost Chapters," p. 509.   [12] Minutes of Conferences, 1797, p. 71.
[13] Levings, in The Christian Advocate and Journal.
[14] John W. Ward, M.D., letter to the author.

him for exhorting his neighbors so constantly; but the time soon came when she, too, was thoroughly converted. Pardon and peace came to her heart at a meeting led by Philip Gatch. Her husband was overjoyed. He says:

It was the happiest day we had ever seen together. "Now," said she, "I am willing to be a Methodist, too;" from that time we went on hand and hand, helping and building each other up in the Lord, * * * and in the course of about three months after my wife's conversion we had six children converted to God.

One of the six, *David Abbott*, began to preach as an itinerant in 1781, locating in 1784. He traveled again in 1793 and 1794. It was at his home, in Upper Alloways Creek, N. J., that his father died. A few months later Bishop Asbury mentioned him as a merchant in Crosswicks, in the same State. He remained faithful till his death. His son, David, was living about 1859 at Old Chester, Pa., walking in the steps of his father and grandfather.[15]

---

[15] Lednum—Rise of Methodism, p. 326.

XIV.

JOHN RAGAN.

SOON after the close of the Revolutionary war the Rev. JOHN RAGAN came from Ireland, his native land, to the United States. He joined the Methodist itinerant ministry before the close of the conference year 1789. After that year he received the following

APPOINTMENTS: 1790, Montgomery cir., Md., with George Hagerty; 1791, ordained deacon,—. . John, N. B.; **1792, Long Island cir.**, with James Boyd; 1793, ordained elder,—Elizabethtown cir., N. J., with Wm. Rainor; 1794, named among the elders—no appointment; 1795, Trenton cir., N. J. with Joshua Taylor; 1796, Bethel cir., with Anthony Turck.

T. Watson Smith mentions him as one of the volunteer missionaries to Nova Scotia in 1791, with William Jessop, John Cooper, Wm. Early, Benj. Fisler and James Boyd,—all from the States. "Ragan remained at Halifax to attend to the work there."[1]

In the absence of records of his time, we find at this late day no trace of his ministry in Brooklyn. Raybold, one of our Methodist historians, wrote in 1849 concerning John Ragan as follows:

His labors and sufferings on the Bethel circuit, together with his success in winning souls to Christ, cannot be forgotten even at this day. We ourselves have found some of his living children.*** His colleague was Anthony Turck, a good preacher, but stern, unconciliating and severe in his preaching. Ragan, on the other hand, was all love, sweetness, kindness and mildness, and crowds followed him from one appointment to another on the circuit.

After one of his sermons, about a dozen young men, being deeply convicted of sin, followed Mr. Ragan from the meeting-house to the place where he dined, but were afraid to go in and speak to him as they longed to do. As he sat down to dinner he saw through the open door the company of young people. Mr. Raybold says:

---

[1] See Methodism in Eastern British America, pp. 218, 219.

He stopped eating, and inquired what they sought. None could answer. He arose, went out to them, and seeing tears on many faces, and the solemn countenances of all, invited them to come in. The table was set aside; and there was no more dinner eaten for many hours. These hours were devoted to exhortation, prayer, and praise; and the result was that many of these young people were then and there truly converted to God.[2]

He was attacked with the yellow fever while on a visit to Philadelphia in August, 1797, and died soon after his return to the Bethel circuit, the scene of his pastoral labors. A recent pastor writes from the old Bethel circuit:

He was buried in the church-yard of the Bethel M. E. Church at Hurffville, Washington township, Gloucester county, N. J. His grave is marked by a plain, gray, marble slab, with the following inscription:

IN MEMORY OF

REV. JOHN RAGAN,

Who departed this Life
September 11, 1797.
Aged 45 years.

*He has gone from all afflictions here
To reign in joys eternal there.*

He reposes about eight feet north of the church, and a fir-tree grows near his grave.[3]

His memoir in the Minutes incorrectly states that he was between thirty-five and forty years of age at the time of his decease. The conference put on record the testimony that he was "conscientious" and "upright," remarkably studious, and well versed in history; and, notwithstanding he was characterized by "great solitude of mind, and was subject to depression of spirits, * * * his labors were greatly blessed." "We believe," said his brethren, "that he is now numbered among the spirits made perfect, in possession of uninterrupted pleasures above."[4]

There is no evidence that he ever married. Neither portrait nor autograph signature has been found.

---

[2] "Methodism in West Jersey," pp. 72, 73.
[3] Rev. J. T. Price, letter to the author.
[4] Minutes of Conferences, 1797, p. 73.

XV.
JAMES BOYD.

ONG ISLAND circuit, which included Brooklyn, was manned by two preachers in 1792. One of these was the REV. JAMES BOYD. The following is his ITINERANT RECORD: 1791, Anapolis cir., Nova Scotia; **1792, Long Island cir.**, N. Y., with John Ragan; 1793, ordained deacon,—no appointment named, probably Nova Scotia; 1794, Nova Scotia, with William Jessop, Isaac Lunsford, Daniel Fidler, Benj. Wilson, James Mann, John Mann and Richard Stockett; 1795, reported withdrawn.

Besides the above which is gleaned from the Conference Minutes, the following is the only undoubted reference to his man which the author has been able to find:

Boyd, who withdrew from the ministry, did not by that act surprise his brethren, who had stood in doubt of him. In 1796 he caused some confusion in Sheffield by an attempt to obtain the pastorate of the Congregational church in that place; though sustained in his application by a number of persons connected with the congregation, he failed in his effort, and two years later returned to the United States. Previous to his withdrawal from the itinerancy he had married, and marriage at that day, when ministerial allowances were exceedingly small and extremely uncertain, frequently involved early retirement from the active ranks. "So it is," wrote Jessop in reference to Boyd's withdrawal, to a brother whom he suspected of matrimonial intentions; "the devil tells us, when about to marry, that it will not hinder our traveling, but in the end, to our sorrow, we find him a liar. Wherefore, if we want to travel, the best way is to live single."[1]

At this point James Boyd vanishes from our view.[2]

Thomas Boyd, "a native of Europe," joined conference the same year with James Boyd, and died in 1794.[3] Whether or not they were of the same family is unknown.

---

[1] T. Watson Smith—Methodism in Eastern British America, p. 309.

[2] Another James Boyd, an eminent Methodist preacher in North Carolina and Virginia from 1804 to 1836, was at first thought to be the same man, but an extended correspondence with his friends has assured us to the contrary.
In the Yale College library is a collection of "Narratives of Missions," (Congregational,) which gives a brief history of one James Boyd, missionary in that part of Ohio formerly known as New Connecticut. He was ordained pastor of the churches in Warren and Newton in 1809, and retained the position till his death, March 3, 1813. The report mentions "his afflicted family," and discourses upon his character and work in terms of highest commendation. His identity with the subject of this sketch is possible, but has not been established.

[3] Minutes of Conferences, 1795, p. 60.

XVI.

Joseph Totten

HE REV. JOSEPH TOTTEN was born in the town of Hempstead, Queens County, N. Y., Feb. 4, 1759. In the same township, within seven years, were born Albert Van Nostrand, Joseph Totten and probably Jacob Brush, who were to become prominent among the pioneer Methodist preachers in their native island home. We learn from his published memoir that previous to his conversion

> He was restrained from prevailing vice, and lived what was called a moral life, but when he heard the Methodist preachers he was deeply convinced of sin, and after a painful struggle he obtained a sense of pardoning mercy, and immediately united with the Methodist Episcopal Church. He soon became conspicuous as an exhorter and leader, and was made useful to many in his neighborhood.[1]

At what age he became a Christian is not known to the author, nor whether it was previous to his removal to Staten Island. A relative, E. J. Totten, of Tottenville, who was personally acquainted with the Rev. Joseph Totten, writes:

> There were three brothers here, owning farms near each other; Gilbert, (my grandfather,) Silas and Joseph Totten. Joseph married Miss Mary Androvett."[2]

The inscription on Joseph Totten's tombstone at Woodrow states that "he was among the first members of the Methodist Episcopal Church on this island." It was probably from his farm on Staten Island, that, "satisfied of his call to the work of the ministry, he entered the traveling connection in 1792," when thirty-three years of age. He received appointments from the conference for twenty-seven consecutive years, and the following is his

ITINERANT RECORD: 1792, Elizabethtown cir., N. J., with John Clark; 1793, Long Island cir., with George Strebeck; 1794, ordained dea-

---
[1] Conference Minutes, 1819, p. 325.
[2] Letter to the author.

:on, Freehold cir., N. J., with J. Robinson; **1795, Brooklyn,** "six months," probably twelve; 1796, ordained elder, New Rochelle and Croton cir., with David Brown and Ezekiel Canfield ; 1797, Long Island cir., with A. Nichols, —— Donnovan, and E. M'Lane ; the Minutes add *Brooklyn*, but he only exchanged at intervals with Wm. Phœbus, the Brooklyn pastor;[3] 1798, New Rochelle cir., with John Clark ; 1799, Dutchess cir., with Roger Searle ; 1800–1802, (Philadelphia Conf.,) Elizabethtown cir., N. J., with J. Justice and Wm. Mills ; 1803, Burlington cir., with J. Osborn ; 1804, Trenton cir., with Geo. Woolley ; 1805, Gloucester cir., with Wm. Bishop ; 1806, Philadelphia, with James Smith, M. Coate, and T. Everard ; 1807–1810, presiding elder, Jersey Dist.; 1811, New Brunswick ; 1812, New Brunswick and Trenton cir., with Wm. Mills; 1813, Bergen cir., with Joseph Bennett ; 1814, Freehold cir., with Wm. Smith ; 1815, Essex and Staten Island cir., with J. Robertson and D. Moore ; 1816. ditto, with J. Potts and D. Moore ; 1817, Sussex and Hamburgh cir., with Jos. Osborn ; 1818, Philadelphia, St. John's church.

He appears in the record of the General Conference of 1800 as the author of the following important rule:

Brother Totten moved that every child of a traveling preacher shall receive sixteen dollars until the age of seven years, and from seven to fourteen years, fourteen dollars. Agreed to.[4]

He was an active member of General Conference, also, in 1804, 1808, and 1816. His memoir says:

After receiving his last appointment at the Philadelphia Conference, [in 1818,] he returned to his family on Staten Island, and on May 10, preached in the meeting-house at Westfield, [Woodrow,] from 1 Cor. ii, 2 : "For I determined not to know any thing among you save Jesus Christ and him crucified." After the services he descended from the pulpit, and walked with his wife into the burying ground, and marked out a spot, saying, "There I wish to be buried," as though he apprehended his end was nigh.[5]

On the following Sabbath he preached three times in Philadelphia. He preached again with great power on Tuesday evening, and retired feeling perfectly well. In the morning he complained of being ill, but walked out into the yard. Presently the barking of a dog attracted the attention of a lady, and she discovered him lying on the ground. "He was brought into the house, but expired in a few moments without uttering a word." Thus Joseph Totten passed away on May 20, 1818, aged fifty-nine years. A mound was made over him on the spot he had

---

[3] Quarterly Conference Record of the Long Island circuit.
[4] Journal of General Conference, vol. i, p. 37.
[5] Conference Minutes, 1819, p. 325.

selected, and there, in the church-yard at Woodrow, he awaits the resurrection of the just.

Joseph Totten was a noble specimen of the early race of Methodist preachers. His brethren of the conference, in the memoir from which we have already quoted, admiringly commended his ministerial faithfulness, and described him as "a man of piety, zeal, and courage, fearing no faces, and sparing no crimes."

It is to be regretted that no portrait of Joseph Totten exists. E. J. Totten, now well-nigh eighty years of age, has distinct recollections of his great uncle, Joseph Totten. He writes:

I frequently heard him and my father, who was the son of Gilbert Totten, debate on political matters, and become sometimes quite excited; and I well recollect his personal appearance, and his voice in particular. He was rather short, stout, robust, with a strong voice, and quite commanding presence.[6]

MARY, wife of Joseph Totten, survived him nearly ten years. She died January 8, 1828, and was buried beside her husband. Their graves are marked by head-stones, appropriately inscribed.

John C. Totten, the printer, whose name is on the title-page of many an old Methodist book, was a relative—a nephew, it is presumed. He married *Letitia*, a daughter of Joseph Totten.[7]

E. J. Totten writes from his personal recollection concerning two sons and three daughters of Joseph and Mary Totten. The sons were named *Mark* (he thinks) and *Asbury*. Asbury left a son, whose son is now living, and has a family of children to perpetuate the name, and, it is hoped, the virtues of their ancestor. Two of the daughters' husbands were John C. Totten and John Pray. Mr. Pray and his wife were highly esteemed members of the Methodist Episcopal Church on Staten Island. The third daughter married in New York.

---

[6] Letter to the author.   [7] Letter from E. J. Totten.

XVII.

George Strebeck

SBURY wrote that several "promising" young men had joined the traveling connection on trial in 1792. Among these was the Rev. George Strebeck. He remained but a short time among the itinerant preachers, as will be seen by the following

MINISTERIAL RECORD: 1792, *Methodist*, New York cir., with T. Morrell and L. Green; 1793, Long Island cir., with Joseph Totten; 1794, name disappears;—Wakely says he withdrew, but he seems never to have joined the conference in full connection; 1797–1804, *Lutheran*, pastor of a church located, first in Pearl-street, New York, afterward in Mott-street, which under his administration went over to the Episcopalians,—from his day until now it has been styled the Zion Episcopal Church of New York;[1] 1804, *Episcopalian*, ordained deacon by Bishop Moore, July 18, 1804, officiating in Bedford, N. Y., and vicinity; 1805, called to Grace Church, Jamaica, L. I., for six months; 1805–1808, rector St. Stephen's Church, New York; 1809–1811, residing in New York—had an honorary seat in the convention; 1814, name not on clergy list.[2]

While in charge of the Lutheran congregation in New York, "Mr. Strebeck was a very zealous, popular preacher, and crowds attended his ministry."[3] A local historian in the Protestant Episcopal Church writes as follows:

Mr. Strebeck was the minister of a Lutheran church in Mott-street, New York city. He and the mass of the congregation conformed to the Church. Soon after this a disaffection sprang up towards him in the congregation. It was too serious to be resisted, and his friends retired from Zion Church, and together with others proposed the erection of this church, [St. Stephen's,] as an act of kindness to him.[4]

He further states that at a meeting in the spring of 1805, a commitee was appointed consisting of the Rev. George Strebeck, Cornelius Schuyler and Isaac Emmons to take the necessary measures to become under the law a

---

[1] See Wakeley's "Lost Chapters," pp. 386, 387. The dates are taken from an old record of Zion Church.

[2] See "Lost Chapters," and Journals of Conventions in Diocese of New York.

[3] Wakeley.

[4] Rev. Joseph H. Price—Historical Sketch of St. Stephen's Church, New York.

religious society, and that arrangements were soon afterward made for the purchase of lots for a church on the corner of First and Bullock streets. He also records the following:

> On April 22, 1805, the Rev. Mr. Strebeck was invited to the rectorship, and being present at the meeting, accepted. * * * April 25, 1809, the Rev. Mr. Strebeck, in an unexpected and informal manner, resigned the rectorship, having occupied it about four years. I have nothing to say concerning the efficiency or inefficiency of Mr. Strebeck's ministry in this church. If inefficient, then it must be acknowledged that the compensation for his service, small and uncertain in its payment, was a fair offset to his deficiency, and I think our better way is to let the poor man rest, and believe that the most ungrateful task any man can undertake is to sow the seed from which others are to reap the fruit. There are more martyrs in the church militant than are honored in the church calendar.

In 1806 Mr. Strebeck gave the following report to the convention

> The congregation is increasing, and those who are regular members of it appear generally to be attached to the doctrines and worship of the Protestant Episcopal Church. To me it is peculiarly gratifying that they join with fervor in the responses of the service. One hundred families holding pews; sixty communicants.

Dr. Wakeley, who had no patience with those who turned aside from the Methodist ministry to other churches, says:

> His children had been baptized, but he repudiated their former baptism, and they were rebaptized in the Protestant Episcopal Church. * * * I have watched the course of Mr. Strebeck, as of others who have left us. Instead of being pastor of a large church, with splendid parsonage and a great salary, he was pastor of a little country church, where he had very dry fodder; and, as discretion is the better part of valor, he retired from his pulpit duties and pastoral labors, to keep a boarding school for boys.[5]

The same authority states that he left New York after a short time, and went South, and died in Charleston or Savannah. Mrs. James S. Carpenter, of Glen Cove, L. I., said to the author that he married her cousin, Jerusha Mott. Diligent effort to obtain further information concerning George Strebeck has been without avail.

---

[5] "Lost Chapters," pp. 387, 388.

Rev. EZEKIEL COOPER.

XVIII.
EZEKIEL COOPER.

BROOKLYN never rejoiced in a Methodist pastor of greater talent and popularity than the REV. EZEKIEL COOPER. He was born in Caroline Co., Md., February, 22, 1763, and died Sunday, February 21, 1847, having just completed his eighty-fourth year. He had spent sixty two years in the ministry.

His step-father, Nathan Downs, was an officer in the Revolutionary army.[1] Freeborn Garrettson came into the neighborhood in 1776 and proposed to preach. The soldiers were drawn up in front of the house, and formed into a hollow square, while Garrettson stood in the center and addressed them. The preacher noticed among the most thoughtful and respectful listeners, a boy standing, and leaning upon the gate. That boy was Ezekiel Cooper; and that sermon seems to have made a profound impression upon him and decided his future course. Before he became of age, he commenced preaching under Francis Asbury, and a year or two later he entered the itinerant ranks, and rendered the most distinguished service to the church in the following

APPOINTMENTS: 1785, Long Island cir.; 1786, East Jersey cir., wih John M'Claskey; 1787, Trenton cir., with Nath'l B. Mills; 1788, ordained deacon,—Baltimore, Md., with Francis Spry; 1789, ordained elder,—Anapolis; 1790, ditto; 1791, Alexandria, Va.; 1792, no appointment named: 1793, presiding elder, Boston District; **1794,** (New York Conf.) **New York and Brooklyn,** with L. M'Combs, Wm. Phœbus, sup'y, J. Brush, sup'y, and D. Kendall, sup'y; 1795, Phila., with John M'Claskey; 1796, ditto with Wilson Lee; 1797-1798, Wilmington, Del. Appointed book agent in 1798, *vice* John Dickins, deceased.[2] 1799-1804, editor and general book agent. (From 1802, in the Phila. Conf.) **1804,** last part, **Brooklyn,** in place of C. Stebbins, resigned; **1805,** (New York Conf.) still in **Brooklyn**—Sam'l Merwin was there the last quarter; **1806, ditto,** with Samuel Thomas and Oliver Sykes;[3] 1807, New York

---

[1] Lednum—Rise of Methodism; Introduction, p. xix.
[2] Simpson's Cyclopædia.   [3] See sketch of O. Sykes in this book.

cir., with T. Bishop, F. Ward, P. Peck, and S. Thomas; 1808, ditto, with W. Thacher, J. Wilson, F. Ward, L. Andrus, and P. Peck; 1809, Wilmington, Del.; 1810–1811, "missionary;" 1812, Baltimore city, with A. Schinn, J. Smith, and J. Fry; 1813–1819, located; 1820, (Phila. Conf.,) Philadelphia, St. George's, with James Smith, Sen., and James Smith "of Baltimore;" 1821, sup'y, same church, with James Smith and Thomas Miller; 1822, New Castle, Del.; 1823–1824, sup'y, without appointment; 1825, sup'y, presiding elder, West Jersey Dist.; 1826, sup'y, Philadelphia, St. George's, with S. Merwin, L. Prettyman and R. Lutton; 1827, conf. missionary; 1828–1834, sup'y, conf. miss'y; 1835–1836, sup'y, without appointment; 1837, sup'y, Philadelphia, St. George's with Charles Pitman; 1838, ditto, with Jos. Lybrand; 1839–1840, ditto, with R. Gerry; 1841–1842, ditto, with J. B. Hagany; 1843, ditto, with E. L. Janes; 1844–1845, sup'y, without appointment; 1846, superannuated.

He was seven times a member of General Conference, representing the Philadelphia Conference first in 1804, and the last time in 1832. He was superannuated less than one out of the threescore years of his ministry.

Ezekiel Cooper was the first of the large number of Methodist preachers who began their itinerant ministry on Long Island. His field in 1785 included the whole of the island, but there was no Methodism in Brooklyn, and the place was not until five years later included in that circuit. The only Methodist societies that Cooper found on Long Island were at Newtown and Comac. Philip Cox had wrought nobly as a pioneer, and established several preaching appointments. It is also probable that the number of members increased, (he made no report,) but he did not, so far as is known, form any new classes. At the close of Ezekiel Cooper's year on the island, he reported 154 members, having organized societies at Rockaway, Searingtown, Hempstead South, and Musketo Cove, (now Glen Cove.)

Among those who were brought to Christ through his faithful ministry in Brooklyn was a lad fourteen years of age, named Charles Wesley Carpenter. He became one of the pastors of the Sands-street Church, and a St. John among them all.

The greatest historian of American Methodism says of Ezekiel Cooper:

His personal appearance embodied the finest ideal of age, intelligence, and tranquillity. His frame was tall and slight, his locks white with years, his forehead high and prominent, and his features expressive of reflection and serenity. A wen had been enlarging on his neck from childhood, but without detracting from the peculiarly elevated and characteristic expression of his face. He was considered by his associates a living encyclopedia in respect not only to theology, but most other departments of knowledge, and his large and accurate information was only surpassed by the soundness of his judgment.[4]

The following extract from his correspondence will serve to illustrate his practical wisdom and common-sense, as well as his ability to express his thoughts with clearness and precision. Mrs. Catherine Garrettson had written him a letter which called for his judgment as to the importance to be attached to certain remarkable " dreams and visions," the details of which are not known to us. He replied:

As to the cause of the dreams and visions of Miss K——, I have but little that I wish to say upon that subject. Time will show and make manifest better and more fully than any other commentary. I agree, "It is our business to investigate truth and support the cause of God, whatever we may suffer in its defense;" but we are not bound to support, or to believe, that which is not supported by rational evidence drawn from credible and competent sources, either human or divine, and more especially when it clashes with established rules and principles in nature, fact, or revelation, by which we are to test truth and detect error in our investigations. A person may "be sincere," and yet labor under great delusions of imagination. "Marvelous and momentous things, times and events" may be imagined from the fanciful effervescence and effusions of a lively, inventive, and heated imagination, which cannot stand the test of calm, deliberate investigation. We may, in such cases, admit great error of judgment, without impeaching the moral intention.[5]

In the pulpit he gained a position among the "brightest lights" and "ablest orators" of his day. Says a writer in The (New York) Methodist:[6]

At times an irresistible pathos accompanied his preaching, and in the forest worship audiences of ten thousand would be so enchanted by his discourses that the most profound attention, interest, and solemnity prevailed. In public debate he possessed powers almost unequaled, and he seldom advocated a measure that did not prevail.

The Rev. Dr. John Kennaday says, in an appreciative criticism:

His ability as a preacher and debater excelled his ability as an author. In discussion his name was Mercurius, because he was the chief speaker.[7]

He published a "Funeral Sermon" on the Rev. John Dickins, and the "Substance of a Funeral Sermon on the Rev. Francis

---

[4] Stevens' Hist. M. E. Church, vol. iii, p. 132.
[5] Unpublished letter, dated Philadelphia, February 3, 1821.
[6] June 16, 1866.
[7] Sprague's Annals.

Asbury." The latter was a 32mo volume of 320 pages.[8] Previous to its publication he said, in a letter to Freeborn Garrettson:

> Did you ever write down the substance of your discourse on the death of Bishop Asbury? I have written mine, agreeably to the request of the conference, but I have never given it up, nor submitted it to the inspection of the committee, nor to any other person. It is rolled up among my papers. I don't know but I may yet consent to let it be published. I am undetermined at present ; sundry considerations influence me to keep it back for a while. I wish to do what may be right and most prudent in the case.[9]

In the same letter he wrote :

> I cannot labor constantly, but occasionally I stand forth to bear my testimony. I am pressed rather too much at times for my strength and health. Could I do the work of three strong men, I have sufficient calls and invitations to fill up all the time. If I venture to preach twice in one day, which sometimes I do, it hurts me. I am going down hill. Oh that we both may make a safe and happy close of life and labor in the Lord's good time !

This reads like the language of an old warrior on the eve of his discharge, but it was written thirty years before his work on earth was done.

Like most men of mark, he had his peculiarities. An authority already quoted writes :

> He was known as a great angler ; like Izaac Walton he carried his fishing-tackle with him, and was ever ready to give a reason for his recreation. Bishop Scott says that his walking-cane was arranged for a fishing-rod, and he always had on hand a Scripture argument to prove that fishing was an apostolic practice. On one occasion, when he returned from an excursion without catching any thing, a preacher was much disposed to laugh at his poor success. "Never mind," said the reverend old angler, "although I have caught nothing, while watching my line I have finished the outline of one or two sermons." So his time had not been idly spent.[10]

Some peculiarity of his disposition may be supposed to account for his continuing in "a state of single blessedness." He possessed rare business talent. Under his management the capital stock of the "Book Concern" advanced in six years from almost nothing to $45,000, and at his death his personal estate was valued at $50,000. He was frugal to a fault, but at the

---

[8] See M'Clintock and Strong's Cyclopædia.
[9] Unpublished letter, dated Burlington, N. J., October 24, 1817.
[10] Stevens' Hist. M. E. Church, vol. iii, p. 134 ; quoted from The Methodist.

me time " liberal to the poor." Simpson's Cyclopædia states
at he made a bequest for the benefit of the poor in the St.
George's church, Philadelphia. It is said, however, that, in
consequence of an imperfect codicil, the portion of his estate
which was designed for benevolent objects "failed of its good
mission." A note in The Christian Advocate states that he
bequeathed an octavo Bible to every child named after him.
However, Ezekiel Coopers do not seem to be a numerous race.
He attained the age of eighty-four years lacking one day.
His sickness was neither long nor very painful. Calmly, peacefully, and sometimes exultingly, with hallelujahs on his lips, he
waited for the chariot to come, and at length, on the 21st of
February, 1847, the hero of a hundred battles, the oldest member of a Methodist conference then in America,[11] was translated
to the highest heavens. His intimate and venerable friend,
Nathan Bangs, preached his funeral sermon in the St. George's
church, Philadelphia, in front of which, near the grave of Lawrence M'Combs, his remains were interred.

His portrait in oil has been preserved in the Methodist building in New York, of which the accompanying engraving is a
very excellent copy. His fore-finger hides the large wen on his
cheek. So Alexander the Great, while the artist painted his portrait, covered an imperfection in his face.

---

[11] Stevens' Hist. M. E. Church, vol. iii, p. 130.

XIX.

THE REV. LAWRENCE M'COMBS[1] was pastor of the Brooklyn charge one year—1794. This was his second appointment, and he was twenty-five years of age, having already given promise of the commanding eminence he was destined to attain in the Church.

He was born of wealthy parents,[2] in Kent County, Del., March 11, 1769. At a very early period, as his memorial in the Conference Minutes affirms, he obtained remission of sins. There appears to be no further record concerning him until 1792, the date of his admission on trial into the traveling ministry. His history subsequent to this time is epitomized in the following

MINISTERIAL RECORD: 1792 Newburgh cir., N. Y., with S. Fowler; 1793 ditto with S. Weeks; 1794 (ordained deacon[3]) **New York** and **Brooklyn** with Ezekiel Cooper: (supernumeraries, Wm. Phœbus, J. Brush and D. Kendall); 1795 New London cir., New England, with G. Thompson; 1796 (ordained elder) Middletown cir.; 1797–1798 Tolland cir.; 1799 New London a 2nd term, with A. Wood; 1800 Philadelphia; 1801 Balt. Conf., Baltimore, with George Roberts; 1802 Baltimore city and Fell's Point, with J. Wells and S. Coate; 1803 Fell's Point; 1804 Baltimore cir., with N. B. Mills; 1805 among the elders, but no appointment named; 1806–1814 a local preacher; 1815 Philadelphia Conf., Smyrna cir., Del., with John Collins; 1816 ditto with S. P. Levis; 1817 Queen Ann's cir., Md., with Thomas Ware; 1818 Kent cir., Md., with W. Ryder; 1819–1822 P. E. Jersey District; 1823 Essex and Staten Island with I. W.nner; 1824–1825 Philadelphia, St. John's; 1826 Wilmington, Del.; 1827–1828 P. E. Jersey Dist. 2nd term; 1829–1832 Chesapeake Dist.; 1833 South Phila. Dist.; 1834 sup'y at Philadelphia, St. Paul's Church, with Wm. Urie; 1835–1836 superannuated.

---

[1] Incorrectly spelled M'Coombs in his conference obituary and in the index to Stevens' Hist. M. E. Church.

[2] Rev. E. De Pew in M'Clintock and Strong.

[3] His name, though on the roll of those received into full connection, is, it would seem, inadvertently omitted from the list of deacons.

No one, so far as known, is able to furnish reminiscences of his ministerial labors in Brooklyn. It is well known, however, that he "performed an unprecedented amount of labor, and left the impress of his energetic character wherever he went."[4] It is related that on his first circuit

This intrepid young man urged his way over mountains and through valleys, stirring the community wherever he came with hymn and sermon, until the wilderness and solitary places were made glad. His popularity became almost unbounded, and from the very commencement of his ministry crowds attended his appointments. There were few church edifices, and his preaching during the milder season was chiefly in the fields.[5]

Of his services on the New London circuit, after leaving New York and Brooklyn, Stevens says:

The tireless Lawrence M'Combs succeeding in fortifying the yet feeble societies of that large circuit, and in planting several new ones.[6]

He was a member of every General Conference from 1804 to 1832, excepting the two held in 1808 and 1812, while he was a located preacher. He distinguished himself in 1812 as a volunteer to defend the village of Havre de Grace. During his period of location, 1806 to 1814, he is said to have preached frequently and with unabated zeal in the vicinity of his residence on the Eastern Shore of Maryland, near the head of the Chesapeake Bay. His record shows that he held a superannuated relation but a little more than a year, and his memoir says, mournfully, that during that time he was "agonized in body, enfeebled in mind, and nearly deprived of speech;" yet he suffered all without a murmur. In Paul's language, about being with Christ, he expressed the steadfast hope of his heart, and those were the last words that fell from his lips.[7] Thus peacefully he departed this life at his residence in Philadelphia, on the 11th of June, 1836, aged sixty-seven years.

He was laid to rest in the old St. George's church-yard, and a memorial tablet on the wall of the church commemorates appropriately his greatness and his usefulness.[8]

In an admirable portraiture of his character, one of his intimate friends says of him:

---

[4] M'Clintock and Strong. [5] Rev. Dr. J. Kennaday in Sprague's Annals.
[6] Hist. M. E. Church, vol. iv, p. 61.
[7] Minutes of Conference, 1837, p. 492.
[8] Letter of John Whiteman to the author.

No hostility could intimidate him in the course of duty, nor could any provocation betray him into petulance or resentment. His perceptions were quick and clear, and his judgment sober and impartial. He had a fine imagination, which, being restrained and regulated by his admirable taste, gave beauty and warmth to all his pictures.[9]

Another, who knew him well, says:

He spoke in the pulpit with a fluency and power almost unsurpassed. A Frenchman after hearing him preach exclaimed: "That man's tongue is hung in the middle, and goes at both ends." The foreigner was converted and became a Methodist preacher.[10]

Bishop Scott, who accords to M'Combs a natural geniality and cheerfulness of spirit, adds the following qualifying statement:

There was a tendency in the latter part of his life to melancholy and impatience. * * * As a preacher he had great power over the masses. He dealt much in controversy, but was not a close thinker, and his style was diffuse and even wordy.[11]

It is presumed by one of his biographers,[12] from the favorable conditions of his early life, that he was distinguished for culture. It is true, that he held a high place as an orator, and was honored in the councils of the Church; he was a member of the General Conference Committee on Education in 1828. These facts, however, do not establish his reputation for a high grade of scholarship. Like most of his contemporaries, he is not known to have published any sermons or other literary composition. The following extracts from a letter[13] written by him will aid the reader to form an estimate, not only of the spirit of the man, but of his style also:

BALTIMORE, *March* 17, 1802.

Dear Brother: I received your letter, which was the first intimation that you were in the Province of Maine. Since I left the New England States I have had but a superficial knowledge of the state and stations of the preachers. But I perceive that they are still upon the circulating plan, and I hope they are still getting and doing good.

The work of the Lord in this part and south of us is very prosperous. We

---

[9] Rev. Dr. J. Kennaday in Sprague's Annals, vol. vii, p. 211.
[10] Laban Clark, in Sprague.   [11] Sprague's Annals.
[12] E. De Pew, in M'Clintock and Strong.
[13] The original is in the library of the New England Methodist Historical Society. Many of the words are misspelled.

have some of the most powerful conversions in the public congregations that you ever beheld. The work is so general that from the aged down to the children they can speak good in the name of the Lord. South of us the Methodists, Baptists, and Presbyterians have so far united as to hold their public and private meetings together, and the work is going on with a most astonishing rapidity. And to the westward of us, in the wilderness, they continue, according to the most recent accounts, to meet in the woods—from 75 to 20,000 persons at one place—have their wagons at the distance from 50 to 100 miles, and strike their tents, and there continue from one to five, six, or seven days, preaching, singing, and praying. And from 100 to 500 have professed to find peace at one of those meetings. The work astonishes even the most pious—it is so great as to the numbers converted, and the effect it hath upon their lives. The work is now spreading in Georgia, North and South Carolina, and Virginia, Kentucky, and Tennessee. I hope the flame will continue until it reaches the Province of Maine. I don't feel any doubt but God will continue his work, and will spread it far and wide, if the people will receive it. But I know it would be rejected by some in New England, though others might rejoice in it. What would the people think and say if they were to see from 100 to 500 people of all descriptions fall down upon the ground and call for mercy?

Ah! brother, this is serious and solemn work. We have in this city the last year hundreds converted to God. The work is of the above kind. It is enough to melt the heart of stone, comparatively speaking, to see and hear hundreds of souls call at the same time for God to have mercy on them.

Myself and child are well, and hope these will find you in health and peace. I am, etc.,

L. M'COMBS.

REV. EPAPHRAS KIBBY, Monmouth.

Dr. Kennaday thus further describes him:

His personal appearance was very imposing. In stature he was full six feet in height, with a finely developed form, though not corpulent; the breadth of his chest indicated the prodigious strength which enabled him to perform his almost gigantic labors. The general expression of his countenance betokened intelligence, gentleness, and energy; while his full, frank face was illumined by his ever-kindling eye. His voice was full, clear, and of great flexibility, sweeping from the lowest to the highest tone, and modulated in the most delicate manner, in beautiful harmony with his subject. In preaching in the field, which was his favorite arena, I used to think he was quite an approach to Whitefield. Such was his known power at camp-meetings, that the announcement that he was to be present on such an occasion would draw a multitude of people from great distances.[14]

Another says:

As he warmed in speaking he had a singular habit of elevating, I think, his right shoulder by sudden jerks. He wore his hair combed smoothly back,

---

[14] Sprague's Annals.

and being long, it fell somewhat upon his shoulders. His countenance was of an open and benevolent expression. His whole appearance was attractive and impressive, suggesting repose of mind, sympathy, self-possession, and authority.[16]

It is a matter of regret that no likeness of Lawrence M'Combs can be found.

His first wife was a native of Port Royal county, Va.,—a Christian from her childhood. Dr. Kennaday wrote of her as a lady of most discreet and amiable deportment. She died, in great peace, in Wilmington, Del., April 17, 1832. By this marriage he had one daughter, a lovely girl, who survived her mother but a few months. An old Methodist writes on the authority of the Rev. A. Atwood, that both mother and daughter are buried in Wilmington, Del., in the grounds of the Asbury Methodist Episcopal church.[16] The pastor of that church, in 1881, wrote as follows:

I have inquired and searched diligently in reference to the persons about whom you inquire. The first wife of Lawrence M'Combs *is not* buried in the grounds of Asbury M. E. church. His daughter is, but there is no stone, that I can find, to mark her resting-place.[17]

On the 4th of April, 1833, Mr. M'Combs was married to MRS. SARAH ANDREWS, of Philadelphia,[18] whose " fortitude and kindness contributed much to the comfort of his declining years." [19]

---

[15] Bishop Scott, in Sprague.
[16] John Whiteman, of Philadelphia, letter to the author.
[17] Rev. Charles Hill, letter to the author.
[18] Notice in The Christian Advocate and Journal.
[19] Kennaday.

George Roberts

REV. GEORGE ROBERTS, M. D.
From "Centenary Album," by Roberts, Baltimore, 1866.

XX.

GEORGE ROBERTS.

THE REV. GEORGE ROBERTS, M. D. was born about 1766, of English parents, probably after their immigration to the neighborhood of Easton, Pa. During his boyhood he worked on his father's farm. He was studious, and often sat in the chimney corner, reading by the light of the fire such books as he could find. Candles were an expensive luxury which his parents could not afford. His Christian life began on the 29th of April, 1783, when he was seventeen years of age. After his father's death he managed the little farm for his mother, who was a gentle, amiable woman, a member of the Church of England, as was also his sister, Mrs. Rue.

His son relates that "his first efforts at preaching were made when he was about nineteen years of age. His youth and unpretending appearance led many to go out and hear him," and he preached with acceptability, notwithstanding "his homely dress and old woolen hat, with its crown kept in place by stitches of white country thread here and there appearing."[1] He served the Church four years as a local preacher.

In his twenty-third year he married a lady of the Eastern Shore, whose name is unknown. She was a woman of great excellence, but survived her marriage only a few months.[2] Soon after her death, "in the fall of 1789,"[3] he entered upon his itinerant labors, which covered a period of sixteen years, as indicated in the following

---

[1] Roberts' Centenary Album, p. 93.   [2] Sprague's Annals.
[3] His letter to Bishop Asbury, quoted in Centenary Album, p. 97. Stevens' Hist. M. E. Church, Vol. ii, p. 439, says "1790." but see Conf. Minutes, 1790, p. 36, where he is reported as "remaining on trial."

CONFERENCE RECORD: 1789, appointment not known; 1790,[4] Annamessex cir., Md., with J. Wyatt; the same year he went to New England with Jacob Brush and Daniel Smith, to re-enforce Jesse Lee; 1791, ordained deacon—Middlefield cir., Ct., with John Allen; 1792, Hartford cir., with Hope Hull and F. Aldridge; 1793, ordained elder—New London cir., with R. Swain and F. Aldridge; 1794, elder, his district including about the entire western half of New England; **1795,** in charge of a **district including Long Island,** and reaching to Pittsfield, Mass.; 1796, New York city, with Andrew Nichols; 1797, ditto, with J. Wells and W. Beauchamp; 1798, ditto, with Joshua Wells and Cyrus Stebbins; 1799, Baltimore Conf., Annapolis, Md.; 1800, Baltimore and Fell's Point, with T. Morrell, P. Bruce, and N. Snethen; 1801, ditto, with L. M'Combs; 1802, (Phila. Conf.,) Philadelphia, with J. M'Claskey, and W. P. Chandler, sup'y; 1803, ditto, with Solomon Sharp, and T. F. Sargent; 1804, (Balt. Conf.,) Baltimore, Md., with J. Bloodgood, and T. F. Sargent; 1805, ditto, with T. F. Sargent and Alex. M'Caine; 1806, local elder in Baltimore.

Stevens graphically describes the arrival of Roberts and his colleagues, Jacob Brush and Daniel Smith, at Dantown, in New England, in 1790, and the joy of Jesse Lee, as he saw them riding up, and welcomed them with the benediction, "Blessed is he that cometh in the name of the Lord."[5] It would require volumes to record his labors and privations in the Eastern States. His son wrote to Dr. Stevens:

> I once heard my father say that during the whole period of his labors in New England he never received over forty dollars per annum from any source. He never had more than one suit of clothes at a time. On one occasion Bishop Asbury punched his saddle-bags with his cane and said, "Brother Roberts, where are your clothes?" His reply was, "On my back, sir." He accompanied the bishop, piloting him through New England, in his first visit to that portion of our country.[6]

While preaching in New England he received Lorenzo Dow into the Church.[7] On the 16th of August, 1797, about eight years after the death of his first wife, he was united in marriage to a daughter of Samuel LePage, of New York. That same year, June 29, he laid the corner-stone of the old Duane-street church. Bishop Asbury made an exception in his case, and allowed him to continue three years in that city. He was embarrassed by the example, and wrote to Thomas Morrell, under date of June 10, 1790:

---

[4] About this time he was in Talbot, Md., and adjoining counties. See Stevens' Hist. M. E. Church, vol. ii, p. 439.

[5] Hist. M. E. Church, vol. ii, p. 435.

[6] Ibid., vol. ii, pp. 440, 441. "Lost Chapters," p, 501.

Feeling the great, the exceeding great want of preachers, I wished to keep one another year, *George Roberts*. He hath stayed an unwarrantable time in New York. He cannot be supported upon any station but Baltimore.[8]

Mr. Roberts was a member of the General Conference in 1804. Dr. Wakeley errs in assigning ill health as the reason for his locating in 1806.[9] His son, Dr. George C. M. Roberts, states that he attended two courses of medical lectures while preaching in Philadelphia, and while stationed in Baltimore was licensed to practice medicine; but that he abstained from doing so until he ceased to be an itinerant preacher. The change in his occupation is thus explained:

> The manner of his locating, or what led to it, was somewhat peculiar, and is not generally known. He attended conference in 1806, having no intention of locating at that time until the day before the conference closed. On this occasion he was seated at the table, when Bishop Asbury wrote him a short note, stating the great difficulty he had in stationing him, on account of the size of his family, and his unwillingness to send him to any place where their comfort would be jeopardized in the least, and asked him what he could do under the circumstances. My father replied that he did not wish, in the slightest degree, to embarrass the bishop or trammel the work; that when the Church was unable to support him, he would ask a local relation. When the appointments were announced by the bishop, his name appeared as having located, thus taking by surprise his numerous friends, who had not known before of the circumstances.[10]

From that time until his death he sustained an honorable place as physician and local elder in the city of Baltimore. He died December 2, 1827, aged sixty-two years, translated from a death-bed scene of physical anguish and spiritual triumph, "never, perhaps, surpassed in the history of man." One who heard his shouts of rapture, says:

> A night or two previous to his dissolution, I urged him to spare himself, and offered, as a reason for it, the possibility of his disturbing the neighbors. He immediately replied: "Be quiet, my son? No, no! If I had the voice of an angel, I would rouse the inhabitants of Baltimore for the purpose of telling the joys of redeeming love. Victory! victory!" "Victory through the blood of the Lamb," was the last sentence that ever trembled on his dying lips.[11]

His friends laid him to rest in Mt. Olivet cemetery, a few feet from the grave of Bishop Asbury.

---

[8] See The Christian Advocate, May 1, 1884.
[9] See "Lost Chapters," p. 509.   [10] Centenary Album, p. 95.
[11] Dr. G. C. M. Roberts; letter to Dr. Abel Stevens.

The accompanying portrait, copied from the one drawn by Ruckle, is said to be an excellent likeness, though made from recollections of him after his death. Abel Stevens gives a clear portraiture of George Roberts in the following words:

> The person of Dr. Roberts was large and athletic, his manners exceedingly dignified, and in social life, relieved by a subdued cheerfulness. To his dignity, which well befitted his noble person, was added, in the pulpit, a most impressive power of persuasion. His sermons were systematic and digested, and in their application often overwhelming. Wherever he went, his presence at once commanded respect. The infidel and the scorner grew serious, or shrunk from before him, in either the public congregation or the conversational circle. A reckless skeptic once attempted with the air of a champion to engage him in a difficult discussion in presence of a company of friends. Roberts heard him for several minutes without uttering a word, but as he advanced in his scornful criticisms, the listening preacher's countenance and whole bearing assumed an expression of solemn scrutiny, which struck the by-standers with awe and made the skeptic quail. When he had concluded, Roberts placed his hand on the infidel's breast, and with a look of irresistible power, exclaimed, "Sir, the conscience which God has placed within you refutes and confounds you." The rebuked scoffer trembled and fled from his presence. This fact illustrates, better than could pages of remark, the character of this mighty man of God.[12]

Of the first wife of George Roberts only the facts already stated are known. His second wife, SUSANNAH MORRELL LE-PAGE, was born in Albany, N. Y. She removed with her parents to New York city, and there, while a child, she found converting grace, and joined the Methodist Episcopal Church, of which she continued a faithful and honored member for seventy-six years. She was an intimate friend of Bishop Asbury, whom she frequently entertained at her house, and for whom she performed many kind offices. On one occasion, after she had washed his feet, the venerable bishop said, "Susan, many daughters have done virtuously, but thou excellest them all." The graces of the Spirit were harmoniously and beautifully developed in her character and life. Her intellect, at the advanced age of eighty, remained unimpaired. She departed this life, at the residence of her son, the late Rev. Dr. Geo. C. M. Roberts, in Baltimore, in the month of November, 1869. Her obituary says:

> As she approached the margin of the river her spiritual sky brightened. She was anxious to depart. Bidding loved ones adieu, she leaned on the

---

[12] Hist. M. E. Church, vol. ii, p. 441.

Record of Members. 137

bosom of the Lord, and in the same room, and on the same bed where her sainted husband expired, forty-two years before, calmly fell asleep.[13]

George and Susannah Roberts were the parents of eleven children.[14] Four of their sons were physicians. The author had the honor of the acquaintance of one of them, the Rev. Dr. George C. M. Roberts. He was every way worthy of his noble parents, very closely resembling his father in person and character. " The oldest daughter, Emily Roberts, married Dr. Isaac Hulse, U. S. N., and died and was buried at sea, between Pensacola and New York. Her little girl was taken to her grandmother's, and under the sweet influence of that home, developed unusual talent. She is the Mrs. George Hulse M'Leod, whose graceful pen and sweet voice have rendered efficient aid to the cause of temperance. The only remaining child of Dr. George Roberts is Mrs. Hough, of Virginia."[15] One of the daughters married the Rev. Henry Slicer in 1827, and died in 1873.[16]

---

[13] Rev. W. H. Chapman, in The Christian Advocate.
[14] Sprague's Annals.
[15] Miss Fidelia M. Creagh, letter to the author.
[16] The Christian Advocate, Aug. 5, 1875.

XXI.

Sylvester Hutchinson

HE REV. SYLVESTER HUTCHINSON was the third of four brothers, all of whom became Methodist preachers. Three of the four were itinerants. Asbury was a friend to this family, and mentions in his journal the grandmother of these brothers, Ann Hutchinson, who died nearly 102 years of age.

Sylvester Hutchinson was born in the town of Milford, N. J., April 20, 1765. At the age of twenty-one he was convicted of sin, and sought forgiveness through Jesus Christ. His experience was peculiar, but of a character more common in his day than now. It is related that he saw an appearance "at the head of his bed, which he believed to be the figure of Christ. This at once satisfied him, and he no more doubted."[1]

Two or three years later he began his career as an itinerant preacher, which is briefly rcorded in the following list of

APPOINTMENTS: 1789, Salem, N. J., with Simeon Pile and Jethro Johnson; 1790, ordained deacon,—Chester, Penn., with John Cooper; 1791, Fells Point, Md.; 1792, Wilmington, Del.; 1793, ordained elder,—Croton cir., N. Y., with Jacob Egbert; 1794, Croton and New Rochelle cir., with P. Moriarty and D. Dennis—to change every three months with L. M'Combs of **New York and Brooklyn**; 1795, Long Island cir., six months; 1796–1797, associate elder with F. Garrettson in a district including **Long Island**, New York city, and the state of Conn.; 1798–1799, in charge of a presiding elder's district including **Long Island** and most of the territory between the Hudson and Connecticut rivers; 1800, New York, with John M'Claskey and John Lee; 1801, traveling with Bishop Whatcoat; 1802, named as an elder,—no appointment; 1803, presiding elder, Pittsfield District; 1804, on the list of elders,—no appointment named; 1805, not named at all; 1806, a local preacher.

We have no record or tradition of his preaching in Sandsstreet church, but have occasional glimpses of him while trav-

---

[1] Atkinson—Memorials of Methodism in New Jersey, p. 425.

eling the large district in which Brooklyn was included. He signed, as presiding elder, Daniel Webb's first license to preach, on the recommendation of a quarterly conference held in Norwich, Conn., New London circuit, June 16, 1798.[2]

Father Boehm knew and remembered this earnest itinerant and wrote of him as a "thundering preacher."[3] Clark, in his "Life of Hedding," makes honorable mention of Sylvester Hutchinson, as presiding elder on the Pittsfield district in 1799, and characterizes him as a man of burning zeal and indomitable energy. He says:

> Mounted upon his favorite horse, he would ride through the entire district once in three months, visiting each circuit, and invariably filling his numerous appointments. His voice rang like a trumpet-blast.

While on this district he penetrated into the far north. Raybold draws a vivid picture of the pioneer preacher lost in a dense Canadian forest in the dead of winter, and providentially rescued from the greedy wolves at two o'clock at night, nearly dead from cold and hunger, having traveled all day without food.[4] Such incidents illustrate the wonderful zeal and energy of this man of God. It is known that he often rode fifty or sixty miles per day, and preached twice, when his receipts were only thirty dollars a year.

Dr. Wakeley describes him as a small, spare man, with a very intelligent countenance, an able minister, a son of thunder, and at times exceedingly "rough." He tells us that when preaching

> He would sometimes begin in a low tone of voice, and then raise it to the highest pitch, till he screamed, and then it was rather disagreeable.[5]

The statement by the same authority, that Mr. Hutchinson's location was occasioned by mental suffering produced by the breaking up of a matrimonial engagement, and that his subsequent history shows the danger of locating, has elicited the following comment:

> It is impossible to get all the facts at this late day which would give a true history of his location. The widow and son, however, recollect distinctly

---

[2] The original copy of this certificate of license is now in the archives of the New England Methodist Historical Society.
[3] Boehm's Reminiscences, p. 25.
[4] See "Methodism in West Jersey," pp. 19-21.
[5] "Lost Chapters," p. 532.

having heard him say over and over again that Mr. Asbury was to blame for his leaving the Church. He said he was in the good graces of Mr. Asbury until the difficulty occurred about his marriage: that he was to marry a young lady belonging to an influential family, and the friends, especially one brother, made such desperate opposition, that the engagement was broken off the day the wedding was to have taken place; that Mr. Asbury reprimanded him severely for not marrying the girl at all hazards, as he was engaged to her; that both of them being of good metal, they had a warm time; that Sylvester came home on a visit, and that Mr. Asbury had his name left off the Minutes.[6]

According to a further statement by his son,

He remonstrated with Mr. Asbury for having done it, and offered to continue in the ministry. Mr. Asbury finally offered him a circuit, but it was one in which he was not acceptable to the people. There was also another preacher, who was not very acceptable where he had been sent, and Mr. H. and he proposed to Mr. Asbury that they should be changed. But this was refused, and turning to Mr. H., he said, "Go there, or go home;" to which Mr. H. answered, "Then I must go home;" and thus ended his connection with the M. E. Church.[7]

He went West and entered into a land agency; he also became a book publisher in Trenton, N. J.[8] On the 10th of May, 1808, he was married to Miss Phœbe Phillips.

He was one of the three preachers who ordained the first elders in the African Methodist Episcopal Zion Church, in 1822.[9] It is doubtful if he was regularly connected with any Church at that time. He at length became one of the ministers of the Methodist Protestant Church, but that denomination was not organized until a score of years after he parted with Asbury. Atkinson states that the last station he filled was the Kensington Methodist Protestant Church, in Philadelphia. Mr. Beegle adds:

Before he died his wife asked him if he had not better come back to the old Church. He expressed himself perfectly willing, but his death occurring soon after, it was never consummated.

The same writer strongly repels any intimation which may be contained in Dr. Wakeley's book, that Mr. Hutchinson was not good and true to the last. At the age of seventy years, on the 11th of November, 1840, Sylvester Hutchinson finished his earthly life. A tombstone marks the place where his

---

[6] Rev. H. B. Beegle in Atkinson's "New Jersey Methodism," p. 425.
[7] See Atkinson's "Memorials." [8] Wakeley—"Lost Chapters," p. 531.
[9] Rush—Rise of the African Methodist Episcopal Church, p. 78.

remains are buried in the cemetery in the borough of Hightstown, N. J.

His wife, PHŒBE HUTCHINSON, was born January 19, 1782, and died about 1865, in the eighty-fourth year of her age. She is buried in Hightstown, N. J. From Atkinson's " Memorials " we learn that she was a very estimable woman.[10] Four sons and three daughters were born to Sylvester and Phœbe Hutchinson. Their names were *John K.*, *Aaron*, *Isaac*, *Elizabeth*, *Cornelia*, *Armenia* and *Daniel P.*, all of whom lived to maturity. One of these seven children, *John K. Hutchinson*, of New Brunswick, N. J., was the only survivor, January 3, 1882, when he wrote the above statement concerning the family. His children—a son and two daughters—and the son and daughter of his sister, *Cornelia*, are the only grandchildren of Sylvester and Phœbe Hutchinson.

---

[10] Her son, John K. Hutchinson, in a letter to the author, states that Mr. Lednum is manifestly mistaken in saying that Sylvester Hutchinson married Sarah Deveau, of New Rochelle, N. Y. See " Rise of Methodism," p. 103.

XXII.

Andrew Nichols

HE REV. ANDREW NICHOLS was a Methodist pastor in Brooklyn in 1798. During his administration the oldest known list of members was written in a substantial book procured for the purpose. From that book his signature was taken.

It is probably too late to rescue from oblivion the material for a full sketch of his life. Of his history either before or after the ten years of his itinerant ministry nothing seems to be known. The following is his

PASTORAL RECORD: 1791, Baltimore cir., Md., with J. Lurton; 1792, Harford cir., with J. Lurton; 1793, Prince George's cir.; 1794, ordained deacon,—Fairfax cir., Va., with Elijah Sparks; 1795, ordained elder,—Winchester cir., Va., with T. Lucas; 1796, New York, with George Roberts; 1797, Long Island, Comac and Southold cir.;[1] **1798, Brooklyn**; 1799, Lynn and Marblehead, Mass., 1800, Merrimac; 1801, located.

Such a list of appointments speaks well for his ability and standing as a preacher. Aside from this record, perhaps the only direct testimony that has come down to us is the following by Dr. J. B. Wakeley:

Mr. Nichols was an excellent man, and a good pastor and preacher. I have heard the old Methodists speak highly of him. He resided in the parsonage at Second-street, (now Forsyth- street.) They were going to hold a love-feast in the church one evening, and two lads wished to go in. In those days the Methodists were very careful who were admitted to them. The doors were closed, and none were admitted unless they had a ticket of membership or a permit from the preacher. Peter Parks was then sexton. The boys concluded if they volunteered to help him bring water and attend to making the fires, he would admit them into love-feast. Neither of them had ever attended such a meeting. He sent them to Mr. Nichols for a permit, for he could admit none without. They went to Mr. Nichols, and he treated them very kindly, and gave

---

[1] Brooklyn is added in the Minutes, but the Quarterly Conference records of the Long Island circuit indicate that Brooklyn was separate, and under the charge of Wm. Phœbus.

them permits. The love-feasts in those days were meetings of great power. One of the boys was deaf and dumb. He was all attention as the people, one after another, gave in their testimony; he watched the motion of their lips, and saw the expression of joy in their countenances; and, though he could not hear one word, it had a powerful effect, and was the means of his awakening and conversion to God. He was as happy as a king. They might have sung, with great propriety:

> " Hear him, ye deaf; his praise, ye dumb,
> Your loosened tongues employ." [2]

The companion of the little deaf-mute was led by him to the Saviour; both immediately joined the Church; and both lived sixty years or more afterward, to thank God for that love-feast, and to tell the story of Mr. Nichols' kindness to the boys. If there is any other written or printed reference to him, it is not known to the author.[3] Several Methodist historical societies have been established within the territory in which he labored as a preacher, and it is to be sincerely hoped that the Church will yet come into possession of further information concerning the life and death of this excellent minister of Jesus Christ.

---

[2] "Lost Chapters," p. 485.

[3] "Zion's Herald," January 4, 1824, refers to an address by Andrew Nichols, Esq., before the Essex Agricultural Society. If this were proved to be the same Andrew Nichols, (which is doubtful,) it might furnish a clew for the ascertaining of additional facts concerning him.

XXIII.

Cyrus Stebbins

HE REV. CYRUS STEBBINS, D. D. was the son of Phineas and Anna Stebbins. He was born in Wilbraham, Mass., Oct. 30, 1772, and joined Conference at New London, in July, 1795, before he was twenty-three years of age. His entire ministry, first among the Methodists, and then in the Protestant Episcopal Church, may be epitomized in the following

PASTORAL RECORD: 1795, Warren cir., R. I., with Zadok Priest; 1796, ordained deacon,—Readfield cir., Me., with J. Broadhead; 1797, Pittsfield cir., Mass., with E. Stevens; 1798, ordained elder,—New York city, with Joshua Wells and George Roberts; **1799, Brooklyn;**[1] 1800–1803, Albany city;[2] **1804,** (N. York Conf.,) **Brooklyn**; 1805, reported "withdrawn;" 1805–1818, rector of St. George's Church, Schenectady, N. Y.; 1819–1831, rector of Christ Church, Hudson; 1832–1841, rector of Grace Church, Waterford.

He was deservedly popular in the early days of his itinerant ministry. Dr. Abel Stevens says:

He was a pungent and powerful preacher; some of his sermons are still often recalled in conversation by our older ministers in New England, one of them particularly, preached under the trees of the old homestead of Pickering on the text: "Those mine enemies which would not that I should reign over them, bring hither and slay them before me." The whole assembly stood appalled at the declaration of divine wrath against all ungodliness; trembling spread throughout their midst, and many went home to call on God and prepare for his coming retribution. Had he remained in the itinerancy, his peculiar talents would have secured for him an extended influence and usefulness, but on leaving it, he entered the Protestant Episcopal Church, where he lingered through many years of comparative uselessness, and died in obscurity.[3]

---

[1] The Conference Minutes say "Brooklyn and Long Island, with James Campbell and John Wilson," but the quarterly conference records show that the charges were practically separate.

[2] Strange as it may appear to us now, Albany and the Mohawk and Black River regions were in 1802–1803, included in the Philadelphia Conference. After 1803 they became a part of the New York conference.

[3] Memorials of Methodism, 1st series, p. 339.

As we have already observed in our sketch of Aaron Hunt, Mr. Stebbins caused Bishop Asbury no little anxiety on account of the difficulty of removing him from Albany city station, which, indeed, the bishop could not or did not do until the close of a four-years term, when the adoption of the two-years limit by the General Conference made his removal necessary and practicable. We here discover, as in almost every other instance in which he appears to our view, a want of the genuine spirit of Methodism. In the few references to him by the historians of the denomination, they invariably speak of his lack of harmony with our prominent peculiarities, and the consistency of his course in withdrawing from us. William Thacher makes the following note of the doings of the New York Conference in 1804:

On the sixth day of our session the subject of sanctification was called up, and Stebbins, its enemy, came on with his objections.[4]

Lorenzo Dow, as we could readily believe from our knowledge of the two men, found no admirer of his eccentricities in Cyrus Stebbins. He says:

June, 1804. Cyrus Stebbins objected to my preaching where he was stationed, [Albany,] though the trustees were mostly friendly. He withdrew from the connection soon after, which showed what spirit he was of. *August*, 1804. When I arrived in Albany the preaching-house doors, which had been shut in Stebbins' time, were now open.[5]

During his first term in Brooklyn (1799) the membership diminished; but his return, four years later, and the enlargement of the church building during that term, would indicate prosperity.

The Rev. George Coles, who was pastor of the Methodist Episcopal church in Hudson, N. Y., in 1822, without any definite knowledge of Mr. Stebbins' antecedents, makes a very charitable mention of him as the rector of the Protestant Episcopal Church in that place, who had formerly been a Methodist preacher.[6] While in Hudson he received the honorary title of D.D. from Trinity College, of Hartford, Bishop Brownell then being president, and a personal friend.[7]

---

[4] Manuscript autobiography.
[5] Dow's Journal, old edition, pp. 176, 178.
[6] See "My First Seven Years in America," p. 249.
[7] Letter of G. N. Stebbins to the author.

The following statement, by the Rev. Frank L. Wilson, is important:

I learn from reliable sources that, notwithstanding he was regarded by his congregation in Hudson as a very able preacher, his resignation was requested on account of his habits of drinking. He was married twice. His last marriage proved unhappy, which is believed to account for his intemperate habits.[8] He is remembered as a man inclined to portliness, short, broad-shouldered, and remarkably social. He had two sons and one daughter. One son, Cyrus Stebbins, a noted and talented lawyer, fell a victim to drink, and died in New York. The daughter married a Roman Catholic and became a convert to that faith. The other son, George N., is connected with the Washington Life Insurance Company in New York city.[9]

Dr. Stebbins died in Waterford, N. Y., February 8, 1841, in the sixty-ninth year of his age. Bishop B. T. Onderdonk, in reporting his death at the Annual Convention, said:

He closed the life of a devout Christian, a faithful minister of Jesus, and a divine of more than ordinary ability, by a truly Christian death, the approach of which, by a lingering and painful disease, was met as the spirit and armor supplied by Christ can alone enable the Christian to meet the king of terrors.[10]

The above somewhat but not greatly modifies Dr. Abel Stevens' statement that, "after entering the Protestant Episcopal Church, he lingered through many years of comparative uselessness, and died in obscurity." This statement was made in view of the remarkably bright promise of his earlier years. His remains were buried in the St. George's church-yard, Schenectady, N. Y.

---

[8] It may be that in later years he obtained the mastery over this besetment.
[9] Letter to the author.
[10] Journals of Conventions, N. Y. State, 1841, p. 59.

XXIV.

D. Buck

We have already made note of a sermon preached by the Rev. DAVID BUCK in 1794, on the foundation of the original Sands-street church before the building was completed. He afterward spent two of the nine years of his itinerant ministry as pastor of this church.

He was born in the town of Freehold, Monmouth Co., N. J., Sept. 12, 1771. "His father's name was Ephraim Buck, and both he and his wife were devoted Methodists, as well as ardent patriots in the Revolution. So decided were they in favor of American independence, and so confident of its final success, that all the gold and silver money they had was exchanged for continental money in bills, put into jars and buried in the cellar."[1]

"When David Buck was about eighteen years of age, he embraced the Lord Jesus by faith."[2] At the age of twenty-three he began to travel his first circuit as a conference preacher.

ITINERANT RECORD: 1794, (New York Conf.) Delaware cir., N. Y., with R. Dillon; 1795, Newburgh cir., with M. Swaim; 1796, ord. deacon,—Long Island cir.; 1797, Redding cir., Conn., with A. Jocelyn; 1798, elected to elder's orders, but not ordained on account of the sickness and absence of Bishop Asbury,[3]—no appointment named; 1799, ordained elder,—Albany city; **1800–1801, Brooklyn**; 1802, Long Island cir., with J. Fennegan and Sylvester Foster, 1803; local.

The author has frequently heard his name mentioned by aged residents of Southold, L. I., whose fathers and mothers were converted under his ministry. Having taken a wife, and his health being infirm, he felt obliged to locate, but abated not in the least degree his zeal in his Master's work.

---

[1] Letter of Rev. Valentine Buck to the author.
[2] Rev. Elijah Hebard in Methodist Magazine, 1823, p. 279.   [3] Ibid.

He settled in Hempstead Harbor, (now Roslyn,) and, in company with his father-in-law, William Valentine, and his brother-in-law, he purchased the paper-mill property, including the "old mill" in which Bishop Asbury preached, and which served as a preaching-place for many years.

His son, the Rev. Valentine Buck, himself now a veteran in the New York Conference, writes:

My father's house was, from my earliest recollection, the stopping-place of all the Methodist preachers on the Jamaica circuit, and of all others who chanced to be passing through the place. As a local preacher he was in labors abundant, preaching not only at Roslyn, but also at Searingtown, Herrick's, Glen Cove, Hempstead, Jamaica, and various other places; and his labors were always gratuitous.[4]

After twenty years' residence and ministry among the people, his popularity had not waned; and, as one of his brethren writes,

Few preachers could collect larger congregations of attentive and willing hearers. He was a powerful preacher. At quarterly meetings and camp-meetings, wherever he spoke, he was heard with interest and delight. God was with him, and the sacred unction usually attended his word, and hundreds on this island have reason to thank God that they ever heard him proclaim the message of salvation.[5]

The old Jamaica circuit quarterly conference record book bears testimony to the fidelity and ability with which for many years he discharged the duties of recording steward.

In the year 1822, three years after the establishment of the Methodist Missionary Society, he wrote to the Corresponding Secretary, announcing the formation of an auxiliary society on the Jamaica circuit, of which he was one of the officers. The following extract reveals the character and spirit of the man:

This institution is, it is true, in its infancy, and its funds but small; but our expectations are large. The interest already excited in the hearts of our brethren gives us reason to hope that this infant society will arrive to manhood, and become a powerful auxiliary to the parent institution. Dear brother, * * * if I possessed the energy and activity I did in 1793, when I first entered the traveling connection, I would hasten with cheerfulness to the heathen and savage tribes, to preach unto them a risen Saviour. That system of doctrine and discipline so zealously enforced by our venerable predecessors in the ministry must ultimately prevail. The prospect brightens! The fields are white; and although age and infirmities confine me to a more

---

[4] Letter to the author.
[5] Hebard in "Methodist Magazine."

circumscribed field of action, yet I rejoice that God is raising up young men in every section of our country who are able to take the field, and who will, I hope, transmit to posterity the unsullied doctrines of the Gospel so successfully taught by Wesley and his immediate successors in the ministry. Hallelujah! The Lord God omnipotent reigneth!

DAVID BUCK, *Secretary*.[6]

His old complaint, the gravel, aggravated by a violent cold, was the cause of his death. His suffering was extreme, but he endured uncomplainingly, expressing concern lest he should exhibit impatience, and at the same time giving utterance to his unwavering faith in God, and sweet hopes of everlasting rest. The author of his obituary records the words he uttered concerning his departure to his wife, his niece, Ruth Searing, and his son Valentine; and then adds:

When spoken to afterward by Sister Starkins, he said: "My conscience is pure; there is nothing that I have cause to fear or dread." These were his last words, and about one o'clock on Friday morning, May 2, 1823, his immortal spirit fled, we have reason to believe, to the mansions of the just.[7]

He was fifty-one years of age.[8] He sleeps in one of the oldest Methodist burial-grounds on Long Island, close beside the little Searingtown church, in which he preached the Gospel as long ago as 1796.

NANCY VALENTINE was married to Mr. Buck about the time of the close of his itinerant labors, hence she never shared them with him; but she was a valued friend of the itinerants for many years, and gladly ministered to their wants, making her home a cheerful and comfortable retreat for them always. She survived her husband twenty-four years, and died at the residence of her brother-in-law, Cornelius Westlake, in Newtown, (now Brooklyn,) November 9, 1847, in the seventy-ninth year of her age. She was buried beside her husband.

---

[6] "Methodist Magazine," 1822, p. 120.

[7] Hebard.

[8] If copied correctly, the inscription on his tombstone says he had attained his fifty-fifth year.

XXV.

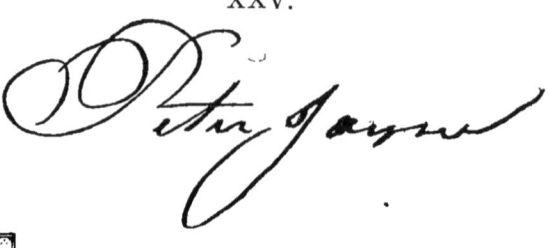

Peter Jayne

AFTER five years of itinerant labors, divided between the states of Maine, Mass., Conn. and New York, the REV. PETER JAYNE was appointed to Brooklyn,—the successor of David Buck. He had traveled the Long Island circuit the previous year, and as the Minutes indicate, occasionally exchanged with the Brooklyn pastor. The signature is from the trustees' record book of Sands-street, and was written in 1802.

He was born in Marblehead, Mass., March 16, 1778.[1] Peter Jayne, his father, was a school teacher in Marblehead for many years, and attended the Congregational church. His mother's name was Dorothy. The elder Peter Jayne died in 1784, when the son was but six years of age, as we learn from the town records of Marblehead.[2] Six years subsequently the widow was married to Joshua Prentice.

An upper room was fitted up for Methodist meetings in their house, where it is believed the first Methodist society in Marblehead was organized. The name of Dorothy Prentice stands first on the list of seven females who formed the original class.

Jesse Lee writes in his journal:

October 28, 1794: We proceeded to Marblehead to quarterly meeting. We held love-feast in Brother Prentice's house, and a few people spoke with life and freedom. The company was melted to tears. I was pleased to find them so much engaged in religion. Afterward we held watch-night; I preached and brother Ketcham exhorted.

---

[1] Town Records.
[2] These facts were gathered from the records by the Rev. Joseph Candlin.
[3] Candlin's Historic Sketch.

It was probably in one of these meetings that Peter Jayne, a youth of sixteen years, first made a confession of Christ. He was "licensed" by the quarterly conference of Lynn,[4] and when about eighteen years of age began to travel a circuit.[5] The following is his published

ITINERANT RECORD: 1797, (New York Conf.,) Middletown cir., Conn., with M. Coate; 1798, ordained deacon—Pleasant River, Me.; 1799, Granville cir., Mass. and Conn., with E. Batchelor; 1800, ordained elder—Dutchess cir., N. Y., with W. Thacher; 1801, Long Island cir., with Billy Hibbard;[6] **1802, Brooklyn;** 1803-1804, (N. E. Conf.,) Lynn, Mass.; 1805-1806, Boston, with Reuben Hubbard and Samuel Merwin.

Contrary to the custom of the itinerants of those times, he was married during the first or second year of his ministry. While stationed in Lynn he preached and published a discourse, entitled "*The Substance of a Sermon preached at Lynn, in the Methodist Episcopal Church, on the First Day of December,* 1803, *being the Day of Publick Thanksgiving for the Commonwealth of Massachusetts: and now made publick at the request of several of the hearers and others. By P. Jayne, Minister of said Church. Salem.*" *Printed by William Carlton,* 1803.[7] In the preface he says:

You will discover from the contents [of this discourse,] no doubt, that I am not entirely destitute of national pride, if such it may be termed, to feel peculiar attachment to the country that has brought us forth. * * * I hope no one will feel disposed to censure my attachment to the present administration, (when it is remembered that I am a member of a Church that has long been looked upon with an eye of contempt,) inasmuch as the administration which at present exists knows no one denomination more than another, or in preference to another. Here we all are equal, and have the vast field of action before us, and stand or fall according to our character in the religious world. Do we wish for pre-eminence? We must obtain it by our virtue and piety.

The sermon is founded upon Psalm cxlvii, 20: "He hath not dealt so with any nation. Praise ye the Lord." His patriotic pride is plainly expressed in the following sentences:

---

[4] Quarterly Conference record. A score or more of preachers were sent out by that church. See Memorial Sermon by Rev. Dr. Chas. Adams, 1841.

[5] Minutes of Conferences, 1807, p. 146.

[6] While the Minutes indicate that Brooklyn was included in his charge in 1801, the quarterly conference records of both charges show that he received his support entirely from the L. I. circuit, and although, perhaps, exchanging at times with the Brooklyn preacher, he was not considered pastor of that church until 1802.

[7] A pamphlet of 13 pp., in the library of the New England Methodist Historical Society, Boston.

We are all blessed with liberty, free from anarchy; a freedom not only to dispose of the labors of our hands as we please, but also to worship God according to the disposition of our minds. Free in body, free in mind, we are not necessitated to sacrifice our conscience or our interest to the caprice of a landlord who is adding field to field till there is no place for the poor to dwell but at his covetous disposal. * * * We are a nation of kings; the authority is vested in us all, generally speaking, according to our capacity and merit. No one presumes to govern us, or claim an exclusive right over us, upon the principle that his father hath left us to him as an estate. We are not subject, therefore, to be governed by an idiot, or an infant of days, or what in its nature is far more impious, and in its consequences far more pernicious to society, by corrupt courtiers. Will any raise themselves to posts of honor and dignity amongst us? They must graduate by their wisdom and merit; then they must have an eye upon their conduct, lest the same authority that invested them with power should divest them of it. So that, strictly speaking, while they rule they are our servants. Honorable station, to both rule and serve a nation of kings.

In thankfulness for spiritual blessings, he adds:

While the spirit, the pacific spirit of grace, has prevailed the past year in the accession of thousands of perishing sinners who have witnessed to the power of God to save in the Southern States, the windows of heaven have not been altogether closed to us in the Northern, especially in this commonwealth; so that, while the South is giving up, the North reverberates, and will no longer keep back. Surely America will become a mountain of holiness, a dwelling-place of peace with truth and righteousness. Amen. Even so, Lord Jesus.

He laid the corner-stone of the old Bromfield-street church, in Boston, in 1806.[8] On the fifth of September, that same year, he was called home from his useful labors in the city of Boston, a young man of twenty-eight. "His early death was deplored by his brethren as the eclipse of a morning star."[9] The following item concerning his grave is from an article published in Zion's Herald several years ago:

Mr. Samuel Burrill was the richest man in the society, [First Methodist Episcopal church in Boston,] owned his house, his shop, and other real estate, and was evidently a man of standing in the community. He owned a tomb in Copp's Hill burial-ground, and in that (then) new tomb was laid Rev. Peter Jayne, of blessed memory—Jayne, who, on the 15th of April, 1806, laid the corner-stone of the Methodist chapel in Bromfield's lane, now Bromfield-street church. The next year, 1807, the owner of the tomb became an occupant.

---

[8] Stevens—Memorials of Methodism, p. 286.
[9] M'Clintock and Strong's Cyclopædia.

Willard S. Allen writes:

This old burial-ground is in the "North End" of Boston. The tomb may still be seen on the Snow Hill-street side of the burying ground, bearing the name of John H. Pitman; no inscription appertaining to Peter Jayne.

Mr. Jayne is said to have labored under the embarrassment of "a deafness not common to a man of his years,"[8] and yet, despite this infirmity, he rendered himself eminently acceptable. We have no portrait from which to judge of his personal appearance. He is described as "a handsome man, well-proportioned, with dark hair, refined and elegant in his manner."[9]

The following brief notice of him is found in the writings of Abel Stevens:

Peter Jayne was a well-beloved hope of the Church, a man of rare abilities and excellent qualities. His mind was capacious and critical, his information extensive, his style severe and forcible, his piety profound and uniform, and his manners were distinguished by a frankness and sincerity which marked him on all occasions. We regret that the resources of our information are so inadequate to the merits of such a man.[10]

SARAH, (CLARK,) the wife of Peter Jayne, survived him nearly forty years, and died the beloved and lamented widow of the Rev. Samuel Merwin. Her memorial is given in connection with the sketch of Samuel Merwin in this work.

We are indebted to the Rev. J. B. Merwin, D.D., for the following item concerning the three children of Peter and Sarah Jayne:

Peter, the oldest, named after his father, was a son of great promise. While on a trip to Albany, on a commercial enterprise of his own, at the age of fifteen, he was knocked overboard by the boom and drowned. The older of the two daughters was adopted by her grandmother in Marblehead, married, and is now deceased. *Eliza*, the younger, was in our family as one of us. Until we were quite large we did not know that she was not our full sister. She was married to Mr. Chappell, in Baltimore, while my father was stationed there.

---

[8] Conference Minutes, 1807, p. 146.
[9] This account of him was given to the author by the Rev. Dr. J. B. Merwin.
[10] Memorials of Methodism, first series, p. 392.

XXVI.
EZEKIEL CANFIELD.

HE REV. EZEKIEL CANFIELD was a noble specimen of the rank and file of early Methodist preachers. Stevens eulogizes him as "a veteran, mighty in labors if not in talents."[1] The records show that he was the successor of Peter Jayne in Brooklyn in 1803.

He was born in Salisbury, Conn., March 16, 1767. John Tooker, of Gloversville, N. Y., writes:

Ezekiel Canfield was my great-uncle. A friend, Mr. Wm. Cozens, who knew his parents, says that his father's name was Jonathan, and he thinks that both the parents were Methodists.[2]

The Minutes say that when twenty-four years of age "he was made a witness of justifying grace, and joined the Methodist Episcopal Church." The following is his

CONFERENCE RECORD: 1794, Herkimer and Otsego cir., N. Y., with S. Weeks and John Wooster; 1795, Cambridge cir., with S. Fowler; 1796, ordained deacon,—New Rochelle and Croton cir., with Joseph Totten and David Brown; 1797, Litchfield cir., Conn., with Wm. Thacher; 1798. Granville cir., Mass., with Daniel Webb; 1799, ordained elder,—Warren and Greenwich cir., R. I., with J. Hall and T. Bishop; 1800, Cambridge cir., N. Y., with E. Stevens; 1801, Brandon cir., Vt., with E. Washburn; 1802, not named on the list of appointments; 1803, **Brooklyn**; 1804, Albany city; 1805, sup'y; 1806, ditto, New Rochelle cir., N. Y., with Joseph Crawford and Henry Redstone; 1807, ditto, with Billy Hibbard, M. B. Bull and H. Redstone; 1808, ditto, with Billy Hibbard and Zalmon Lyon; 1809, Croton cir., N. Y., with J. Lyon; 1810, Cortland cir., with Billy Hibbard; 1811, Suffolk cir., with S. Bushnell, 1812, Montgomery cir., with Francis Brown; 1813, New Windsor cir., with N. Emery; 1814, Newburgh cir., with Z. Lyon; 1815, Croton cir., with Aaron Hunt; 1816, ditto; with Jesse Hunt; 1817, Stratford, Conn., with Reuben Harris; 1818, Goshen cir., with D. Ensign and T. Benedict; 1819, ditto, with D. Ensign; 1820–1825, superannuated.

Billy Hibbard in his autobiography mentions him as his colleague—a single man—in 1808. One year later, April 26, 1809, at the age of forty-two, he was married to Miss Alice Stow of Middletown, Conn.[3]

---

[1] Memorials of Methodism, p. 387.   [2] Letter to the author.
[3] Town Records.

Record of Ministers.

The late pastor in West Goshen, Conn., writes

The old records of this charge were burned in a dwelling-house, but it is definitely known that Ezekiel Canfield was twice on this charge, and he was the first Methodist who preached in the town. He delivered a sermon in a private house, standing on a half-bushel measure. This I learn from an old lady who was personally acquainted with him.[4]

His last days were spent in Mayfield, Montgomery county, N. Y., the home of his parents and other kindred. His life wore away with great suffering, which he endured with remarkable patience and resignation. "He declared that his faith was as unshaken as the pillars of heaven." With the prayer, "O Father, take me to thyself," trembling upon his lips, he passed on to his home in the skies, October 16, 1825, in the fifty-ninth year of his age. His funeral was attended by the Rev. Jacob Beeman, and his mortal form was laid in the Riceville cemetery, in the town of Mayfield. A tombstone marks his grave.

Ezekiel Canfield was a man of slender build, "a good off-hand speaker," modest in his deportment, cheerful and affable in his conversation, firm in his attachment to his friends, and plain and experimental in his preaching.[6]

ALICE, his wife, was the daughter of Solomon, Jr., and Alice (Abbott) Stow, of Middletown, Conn. She was converted in early life. Her husband found in her a faithful and useful sharer in his toils. After his death she returned to her childhood home, where she lived many years, esteemed and respected by all her acquaintances. Some are yet living in Middletown who distinctly remember "the little old lady," and often attended class-meetings in her house.

She died September 7, 1849, aged nearly seventy-six years. So sweetly did she fall asleep that one who watched her knew not the moment of her departure. Her last words were "Peace! peace! peace!"[7] She is buried in the Mortimer cemetery, in Middletown, Conn.

---

[4] Rev. George W. Hughes,—Letter to the author.
[6] Conference Minutes, 1826, p. 509.
[7] See The Christian Advocate and Journal, 1849.

XXVII.
WILLIAM THACHER.

SANDS STREET CHURCH numbered among her early pastors and presiding elders none more energetic and efficient than the REV. WILLIAM THACHER. Chief among the events of his ministry in Brooklyn was the erection of the "Old White Church."

He was born in Norwalk, Conn., April 3, 1769. His parents were decided adherents to the creed of the Congregational Church to which they belonged, and he and his two brothers were trained in the principles of piety. When a child of six years he declared his purpose to become a preacher. Two years later both his parents were removed by death. His father's dying request to a brother who expected to adopt him as a son, was to have him graduate at Yale College, and study for the ministry. His uncle died, and he never went to college; nevertheless, by diligent study he acquired an excellent education.

He began to learn the tailor's trade in New Haven at fourteen years of age. Five years later, (1788,) he removed to New York, where he attended a meeting among the Methodists for the first time, and heard one of their ministers preach. Though unconverted, he admired the simplicity and zeal of that people, and his prejudice against them was thoroughly removed.

At twenty years of age he was living with the family of a Methodist class leader and exhorter in the city of Baltimore. By these favorable associations he was influenced to become a Christian, and was admitted by Henry Willis to probation in the Methodist Episcopal Church, June 19, 1790. The following October he went to reside in the parish of Ripton, Fairfield Co., Conn., where the civil officers were petitioned to warn him to leave the town because he was a

William Thacher

REV. WILLIAM THACHER.

Methodist.[1] There he saw a member of the Methodist Episcopal Church, who lived seven miles away, and who invited him to a meeting held by that people near his home. He soon removed to New York, taking with him the following letter, written by the apostle of Methodism in the New England States:

> The bearer, William Thacher, calls himself a Methodist, and I hope he is a steady, well-meaning person. JESSE LEE.

He joined a class in the John-street church which met Sabbath morning at sunrise. He married Miss Anna Munson, of New Haven, and took up his residence there. His wife was converted one year after their marriage. He states that he heard the first Methodist sermon in New Haven,[2] and was one of five to form the first Methodist class in that place in 1795, of which he was appointed the leader.[3]

He was greatly exercised about preaching the Gospel. He writes:

> N. Snethen, who was then our preacher, advised me to exhort, but it soon appeared that I could not talk extemporaneously without a text. How discouraging! for how shall a man preach a sermon who cannot talk common sense five minutes by way of exhortation?

Another preacher advising him to take a text, he did so, and he gives the following account of his first effort:

> The text came, the day came, the people came, and I came trembling—the Lord came and helped me so that I was astonished at my liberty of speech.

His wife was at first unwilling that he should join the conference, but very soon gave her consent, and he entered upon his long and useful itinerant career.

MINISTERIAL RECORD: 1797, (New York Conf.,) Litchfield cir., Conn., with Ezekiel Canfield—the last few months, Pittsfield cir., Mass., with

---

[1] Manuscript autobiography. His memoir in the Conf. Min. (1857, p. 319) locates this incident in New Haven. This is probably a mistake. His own record makes no such reference to New Haven.

[2] Jesse Lee was the man who preached the first Methodist sermon in New Haven, June 21, 1789. See Stevens' Hist. M. E. Church, vol. ii, p. 421.

[3] New Haven was a conference appointment in 1790, and at the close of the year reported nine members. If the class formed in 1795 was the first, then the membership in 1790 belonged in New Haven circuit, but outside the limits of New Haven, which is probably true. It is possible that a class had been organized and afterward disbanded, and then it would remain true that Thacher and his wife were members of the first *permanent class* in that place.

158   Old Sands Street Church.

Cyrus Stebbins ;[4] 1798, Redding cir., Conn. ; 1799, ordained deacon by Bp. Asbury,—Pomfret, cir., Conn , R. I. and Mass. ; 1800, Dutchess cir., N. Y., with P. Jayne ; 1801, ordained elder by Bp. Whatcoat,—Dutchess and Columbia cir., with David Brown and Lorenzo Dow ; 1802, New Rochelle and Croton cir., with Geo. Dougharty ; 1803, New Rochelle cir., with A. Hunt ; **1804–1806, presiding elder, New York Dist.** ; 1807, Middletown, Conn. ;[5] 1808, New York city, with E. Cooper, John Wilson, F. Ward, L. Andrus, and P. Peck ; 1809, ditto, with Eben Smith and Wm. Keith ; **1810–1811, Brooklyn,** the first year he was to change with F. Ward, of Jamaica cir.; 1812, Jamaica cir., with Theodosius Clark ; 1813, New Rochelle cir., with Wm. Phœbus and O. Sykes ; 1814, ditto, with J. Lyon ; 1815, New York, with Wm. Phœbus, E. Washburn, M. Richardson, and A. Scholefield ; 1816, ditto, with L. Andrus, A. Scholefield, and D. Ostrander ; 1817, Poughkeepsie, did not go ; 1818–1819, Schenectady ; 1820–1821, New Haven, Conn. ; 1822, (Phila. Conf.) Philadelphia, St. George's, with T. Miller and H. G. King ; 1823, ditto, with T. Burch and D. Parish ; 1824–1825, Newark, N. J. ; 1826, Trenton and Bloomsburgh ; 1827, Trenton station ; 1828–1830, presiding elder, Phila. Dist. ; 1831–1832, (New York Conf.,) Poughkeepsie ; 1833, New Haven, Conn. ; 1834, Newburgh cir., N. Y., with P. R. Brown ; 1835–1836, Hudson and Print Works, with J. Carley ; 1837–1838, Flushing and Hallett's Cove, L. I. ; 1839, Williamsburgh and Newtown, with J. Rawson ; 1840, Norwalk and New Canaan cir., Conn., with J. A. Silleck ; 1841, Woodbury ; 1842–1843, Milan and Pleasant Valley cir., N. Y. ; 1844–1845, Dutchess cir., with Thos. Sparks ; 1846–1856, superannuated, residing at Poughkeepsie, N. Y.

When he started out to preach he paid $30 for a horse, and bought a second-hand saddle, bridle, and portmanteau. He was obliged to leave home with less than a dollar in his pocket, and to leave his wife nearly destitute. She and their child boarded in her father's family at $1 a week for both, and he was to be allowed only $128 salary, with little prospect of obtaining more than one half of that ; but he writes :

God had called me, and I must obey, nor did I stagger through unbelief.

He thus describes himself beginning the round of his circuit :

On a little gray mare, whose bones were prominent, sits a small man, pale and thin, dressed in a second-hand gray coat, and light-colored overcoat. The people say, " Brother Thacher, neither you nor your horse will stand this circuit. The rides are long, roads rough and mountainous—you must both fail." In a few months they say, " You have grown as fat as a farmer, and you've got a new horse, ha ? " The itinerant answers, " No, the same horse and the same rider."[6]

---

[4] Manuscript autobiography.

[5] In his MS. autobiography he states that Middletown was then a station and not a circuit, as would appear from the Conference Minutes.

[6] Manuscript autobiography.

A year or two later on the Pomfret circuit, he rejoiced in the conversion of many, among whom were four young men who afterward became itinerant preachers.[7]

As presiding elder he had charge of "the first camp-meeting ever published and held east of the Hudson River." It was held in Carmel, N. Y., Sept. 14-17, 1804. He writes concerning it:

> We had endeavored to prepare the ground beforehand, but who had ever seen a camp-meeting? Who could show us how to work it? It was like putting out to sea with captain and crew, all raw hands. But the Lord provided for this, also. Rev. Nicholas Snethen, a southern campaigner, and a large number of brethren came from New York, with sails of shipping for tents, and all provisioned for the four days. What a good instructor was Brother Snethen! Where could I have found such another? He gave directions in every thing pertaining to the meeting, and as for preaching, he was a host in himself.

In the following May he held another camp-meeting on Long Island. He says:

> We threw the Long Island quarterly meeting into a camp-meeting form, and held it in a place that we knew only by the name of Mosquito Cove.

Lorenzo Dow was at this meeting, and gives a thrilling account of it in his Journal. The New York preachers, Wm. Phœbus and Daniel Smith, judging from reports of such meetings, had been outspoken against them; but Thacher says:

> They came, they saw, they were conquered; and is it wonderful that these good and wise men should yield to a divine influence which has conquered thousands of foolish, bad men?

Another meeting in September, the same year, was held in Croton, N. Y. An old Methodist writes:

> I heard the Rev. Wm. Thacher give an account of the original act of locating the place of the meeting. A large forest had been designated by the proprietor for the purpose, and a committee, consisting of Mr. Thacher, the presiding elder, J. B. Matthias, then a local preacher of Tarrytown, and Nathan Anderson, of Callaborg, a layman, went out to fix the site for the meeting. When that had been done, and its chief points properly marked, they gathered at the foot of a great tree to offer up together a prayer of consecration, and to invoke God's blessing upon the work; and such was the baptism of the Spirit they received, that "Barney" Matthias sprang to his feet and ran about the grounds, gathering up stones with which to set up an "Ebenezer."[8]

---

[7] Stevens' Hist. M. E. Church, vol. iii, p. 441.
[8] The Methodist, New York, Sept. 17, 1881.

At a similar meeting conducted by Mr. Thacher in Tuckahoe, N. Y., in 1806, Marvin Richardson was converted. Many preachers were there, among whom was Bishop Asbury, who said that it excelled any camp-meeting he had ever attended, and from it most wonderful revivals spread in every direction.[*]

Wm. Thacher buried his wife in 1807, and in December, the following year, he married again. He states that Bishop Asbury publicly expressed his disapproval of this marriage, which was a sore trial to Thacher. He believed that the bishop was "ill-informed by some unfriendly tongue." Thenceforward for sixteen consecutive years his family resided in New York, his oldest daughter sometimes keeping house for him when his stations were distant from that city.

During his second year in New York, (1809,) Allen-street and Bedford-street churches were built. He carried the same enthusiasm for church-building to Brooklyn, and it was almost solely through his influence that the "old white church" was erected. Not a few were converted under his ministry in Sands-street. Among these were Judge Dikeman, who said to the author that he was led to seek the Lord under a sermon by Mr. Thacher from the text, "For Zion's sake will I not hold my peace." Of his appointment to Brooklyn with a monthly change for Jamaica circuit, he writes:

As to the monthly change, we made short work of it. I had the good fortune to be yoked with an unaccommodating and somewhat imperious brother, and I chopped the yoke in two, and told him to attend to his circuit, and I would mind my station, and risk the issue at the next annual conference. This ended the chapter of monthly changes, perhaps at the expense of peace, and the cost of some brotherly love.

He collected money for the rebuilding of John-street church in New York in 1816 and 1817, and was afterward active in church-building in Poughkeepsie, Newburgh, and Hudson. He was called "a bishop's favorite," and had a good deal of trouble at one time and another. He applied for a supernumerary relation in 1817, but the conference, in his absence, refused to grant it. His health, as he said, forbade his attending to his appointment at Poughkeepsie that year. In 1818 charges were brought against him for deserting his post, but they were not sustained. His next appointment was Schenectady, where two

---

[*] See Richardson's statement in Stevens' Hist. M. E. Church, vol, iv, p. 853.

revivals occurred in two years, and the membership increased from 54 to 190.

Concerning a public discussion which he held with a Universalist preacher in Newark, N. J., while stationed there, he says that the Universalists themselves acknowledged a defeat. Of his relation to the people on the Williamsburgh circuit, his last charge on Long Island, he says:

> The leaven of abolition was unhappily working among some of the members. I understood that my colleague [Jas. Rawson] was of that sentiment which might be the reason why they were so studious to show that they preferred him. This, however, gave me no displeasure. * * * A circumstance occurred that threw light on this mystery. On March 1, 1840, an order from the presiding elder made me a member of the committee to investigate charges brought against LeRoy Sunderland, of the New England Conference, who was editor of the abolition paper, entitled Zion's Watchman, then published in New York. The proceedings of said committee were canvassed by that conference, and L. Sunderland had to locate   From the time that I was appointed on that committee, a change of behavior on the part of many of the brethren was visible, resulting in the prevention of my re-appointment.

When he wrote his autobiography, (about 1850,) he said concerning " abolition " preachers;

> If they are contending for the truth once delivered to the saints, and their salvation depends on their boldness and perseverance, they will be worthy of the crown for which they contend ; but if at last it shall be said, " Who hath required this at your hands ? " alas for them !

He writes at some length of the New York Conference session of 1838, and the abolition discussion. He was strongly on the side of the conservatives. He records the suspension of three of the score of " abolition preachers " till they should give satisfaction to the conference, and says:

> The screws of our government were judiciously applied to some of our good brethren, which proved salutary to them and poor Zion's Watchman's editor, and all were subjected by able hands to a most severe and just castigation. * * * It was time to put in the subsoil plow, in hope of eradicating the snap-dragon from the soil. The effect of our measures was salutary. " As the partridge setteth on eggs and hatcheth them not," so these zealous men have had a long incubation ; there has been warmth enough, and feathers in abundance, yet where are the freed men ? What chickens have they hatched ?

The above reads strangely to us in the light of subsequent history. It is not often that our eye falls on a paragraph that so clearly unfolds the real animus of the opposition to the anti-slavery agitation of those days. Thacher and the larger majority of the conference, whose sentiments he thus boldly represents, all claimed, of course, to be antislavery men.

On the day of the seventieth anniversary of his birth, he wrote:

> Shall I superannuate? No; my powers, physical and intellectual, are not withered, and my heart is still delighted with the work of the ministry. My ability for pedestrianism and for mental labor was never better. Three services every Sabbath, and the usual meetings during the week, all give proof of this.

He continued to travel until he was seventy-five years of age, and retired to a comfortable home in Poughkeepsie, where he was cheerful and happy, and remarkably active, taking up the study of French, reading the Bible in the original tongues, and writing a history of his life. By invitation of the Rev. M. L. Scudder, he preached a semi-centennial sermon in Poughkeepsie, in 1847, which was repeated in other places. He wrote, July 6, 1848:

> I have now in my old age the satisfactory reflection that I entered the traveling connection in the spirit of sacrifice, in full faith in the promise of God for all necessary supplies of both the upper and the nether springs—spiritual and temporal grace, * * * and during my forty-eight years of effective service in the Church, God has liberally provided for me, and now my circumstances are as pleasant as heart could wish.

He recognized a kind Providence in all the events of his life, and recounted, with gratitude, twelve narrow escapes from death. His triumph culminated at the last, and often, in the midst of his severest agonies, he shouted, "Glory to God! I am happy in Jesus." Thus he finished his course with joy on August 2, 1856, in the eighty-eighth year of his age. His mortal remains yet slumber in a vault in the old Dutch burial-ground east of Poughkeepsie.

William Thacher was below medium size, possessing remarkable vigor and endurance, a close observer of men, sensitive, frank, fearless, and extremely positive in his opinions. "He was sometimes petulant—did not like to be contradicted."[10]

He took advanced ground in the temperance reform, lecturing on the subject in Poughkeepsie, Hyde Park, and Rhinebeck, as early as 1833, and although the pledge that was offered in those days was the old pledge against ardent spirits only, he writes·

---

[10] Statement of Judge Dikeman to the author.

I then advocated the teetotal principles before they were commonly known to be essential to the cause of temperance. The Holy Spirit set me right on the principles of temperance.

Few men ever had the ability to quote the Scriptures with greater pertinency and force. His brethren of the Conference adopted the following testimony :

His pulpit efforts were characterized by great earnestness, by clear exposition of the Scriptures, by terseness, brevity, and point. The general cast of his sermons was practical, while his closing appeals to the heart were often overwhelmingly effective. [11]

Chief among his published literary productions are " William Theophilus," (an autobiographical sketch,) and a sermon on secret prayer.[12] He was a member of the General Conference of 1808.

ANNA (MUNSON,) wife of William Thacher, was a holy woman. She "died happy," February 18, 1807, aged nearly thirty-four years.[13] She is buried in the old part of New Haven cemetery.[14]

MARTHA (OAKLEY,) his second wife, sought the Lord at the long-to-be-remembered camp-meeting in Croton, N. Y., in 1806, and first received the witness of her acceptance on board the returning sloop. She joined the Duane-street church in New York. She was married to Mr. Thacher Dec. 29, 1808. She shared the sorrows and rejoiced in the success of her husband. She was sick four days, and slept in Jesus, January 19, 1848, aged sixty-three years. She is "buried in the family vault of Josiah Williams," in Poughkeepsie, N. Y.

A son, named *William*, was adopted and educated by an uncle. He died at the age of thirty-four. Another son, *Israel*, died at the age of thirty-three. *Mary Ann*, one of the two daughters of William Thacher, married Luther Gilbert, of New Haven, Conn. One of her sons, William Thacher Gilbert, is a minister in the New York East Conference; another, Luther Munson Gilbert, is a physician in New Haven. Wm. Thacher's only surviving daughter, *Amanda*, married Wm. W. Reynolds, of Poughkeepsie, N. Y. A daughter, *Eliza*, married D. D. Richman, of Avondale, N. J. She died leaving a son, who is a physician in West Virginia.

---

[11] Minutes of Conference, 1857, p. 320.
[12] See Methodist Magazine, May, 1828.
[13] Thacher's manuscript. [14] Mrs. W. W. Reynolds, letter to the author,

XXVIII.

SAMUEL MERWIN.

HE name of the Rev. Samuel Merwin is honorably connected with the history of Brooklyn Methodism. Few men were better known in his time, or are better remembered to this day throughout the extensive region embraced in the old New York, New England, Philadelphia and Baltimore Conferences. His ancestors came from England, and settled in Milford, Conn. Daniel, his great-grandfather removed to Durham in the same state, where that branch of the family afterward resided. There Samuel Merwin was born, September 13, 1777, and when he was seven years of age, his father, Daniel Merwin removed his family into New York state, and with some of his former neighbors established the settlement of New Durham.

He was piously trained by his parents who were members of a Congregational Church: yet, like too many others, they were not "thoroughly furnished unto *every good work*," for his conference memorial states that he "fell back" from a religious life begun when a lad, "having no one to take him by the hand."[2] He was studious from boyhood, and taught school when eighteen years of age. About that time a Methodist itinerant dismounted in front of his father's house, and was invited to preach there. Samuel was brought back to the favor of God, and he and his parents united with the Methodists. With unquenchable zeal the young man engaged in the work of leading his neighbors to Christ, and the church soon discovered that he was called of God to a larger field of usefulness, "and thrust him out into her vineyard." The following is his

MINISTERIAL RECORD: 1799, a supply on Delaware cir., N. Y.;[3] 1800, (New York conf.,) Long Island cir., with James Campbell; 1801, Red-

---

[1]Sprague's Annals.   [2] Conf. Minutes, 1839, p. 670.
[3]Sprague's Annals. Stevens, following memoir in Minutes, says "Delaware District." There was a circuit, but no district by that name in 1799.

REV. SAMUEL MERWIN.

ding cir., Conn., with Isaac Candee; 1802, ordained deacon,—Adams, Mass.; 1803, ordained elder,—Montreal, Canada; 1804, New York city cir., with N. Snethen and M. Coate; **1805**, Redding cir., Conn., with Peter Moriarty,—last quarter, **Brooklyn**, with, or in place of, Ezekiel Cooper;[4] 1806, (New England Conf.,) Boston, Mass., with Peter Jayne; 1807-1808, Newport, R. I.; 1809, Bristol and Warren;[5] 1810, (New York Conf.,) Albany cir., with John Crawford; 1811, Schenectady cir., with H. Stead; 1812-1813, Albany city; **1814, Brooklyn; 1815-1817, presiding elder, New York Dist.**; 1819, New York city cir., with A. Hunt, Laban Clark, B. Hibbard, T. Spicer, and N. Morris; 1820, Albany; 1821-1823, presiding elder, New Haven Dist.; 1824, (Balt. Conf.,) Baltimore city, with Y. T. Peyton and N. Wilson; 1825, ditto, with B. Waugh, Y. T. Peyton, J. Summerfield, N. Wilson; 1826, (Phila. Conf.,) Philadelphia, St. George's, with L. Prettyman, R. Lutton, E. Cooper, sup'y; 1827, ditto, with S. Doughty and J. Lednum; 1828, (New York Conf., Troy, N. Y.; 1829, ditto, with J. C. Tackaberry; 1830, New York, with S. Luckey, L. Pease, S. Martindale, B. Goodsell, H. Bangs, and S. D. Ferguson; 1831, ditto, with L. Pease, S. Martindale, B. Goodsell, S. Landon, John Clark, B. Silleck, and C. Prindle; **1832-1835, presiding elder, New York Dist.**; 1836, New York, east cir., with J. Kennaday, S. Remington, H. Brown, and D. Smith; 1837-1838, Rhinebeck, N. Y.

The foregoing record brings to our view a man whose eloquence was in demand in all the great centers of Methodism in his day, from Montreal on the north to Baltimore on the south and Boston on the east. While in Boston, in 1806, he dedicated the old Bromfield-street church.[6] In 1807, when about thirty years of age, he married the widow of his friend and colleague, Peter Jayne. He was a member of every General Conference, except that of 1828, from 1812 to 1832.

He preached his last sermon about one month before his departure. On the 13th of January, 1839, in Rhinebeck, N. Y., at the age of sixty-one years, he bade a willing farewell to earth. Charles W. Carpenter preached his funeral sermon from Acts xx, 24. His remains were buried in Rhinebeck, and afterward removed to "Greenwood," where a suitable tombstone marks the place of his rest.

In the absence of a personal knowledge of Samuel Merwin, who had gone to his reward before the writer of this sketch was born, it will be the more appropriate to present an array of testimonies concerning his character and work by a few of his

---

[4] Church records.
[5] Stevens says, erroneously, "Bristol and Rhode Island." See Hist. M. E. Church, vol. iii, p. 455.
[6] Stevens' Memorials of Methodism, first series, p. 283.

intimate friends. Bishop Asbury, writing at New Haven, Conn., June, 1802, made the following record:

> I was pleased that the students of Yale College, as many as ninety or one hundred, had been under gracious impression. They would come to hear the Methodists, * * * God struck some of the vilest of them by the ministry of Samuel Merwin.

The Rev. Fitch Reed thus describes Mr. Merwin as he was in 1817:

> Our presiding elder was at our first quarterly meeting in Westfields, [Long Island,] June 28 and 29. This was my first introduction to him, and any one who ever saw him may readily imagine how a timid, inexperienced youth, constantly fearful of doing wrong, or of not doing right, would be impressed with his appearance and bearing. At that period he was just in his prime, about forty years of age, and in his personal appearance one of the finest and most noble-looking men I have ever seen. He was a little above the medium size, of perfect symmetry, with a high, broad forehead, fair complexion, and a brilliant eye, beaming with intelligence and benignity. His voice, especially when he addressed large audiences in the open air, was peculiar for its clear, rich intonations, and distinctness and force of utterance. Special occasions, which seemed to require special endowments, possessed with him a peculiar inspiration, more so, I think, than with any other man I ever knew; so that no extraordinary exigency could well take him by surprise. His preaching was often in the demonstration of the Spirit and with power. His memory is very precious to me.[7]

Just here it will be interesting to hear Dr. Bangs relate an incident in which many think his friend Merwin was quite misunderstood:

> Samuel Merwin sometimes became embarrassed in the pulpit. While he was preaching a missionary sermon in Allen-street, New York, feeling somewhat embarrassed in mind, and perceiving that his congregation were inclined to listlessness, he suddenly paused, and calling to a preacher who was in a slip in the body of the church, he said: "Brother B., you must come up here and help me, for I cannot get along with this great subject." The preacher replied with the same freedom with which he had been addressed: "It is in good hands, therefore go on, and you will conquer." This innocent artifice brought him out of the whirling eddies into which he had been carried, and, unfurling his sails, he gently glided off upon the sea of gospel truth.[8]

Many, to whom both of these men were well known, have been not a little amused on reading the foregoing paragraph. They affirm that the only rational view of the matter is that Mr.

---

[7] Reminiscences, Northern Christian Advocate, 1863.
[8] Hist. M. E. Church, vol. iv, p. 309.

Merwin, observing the listlessness of the audience, called on Dr. Bangs for help with the sole intent of startling his hearers, and gaining their attention. The doctor mistook this device for a token of embarrassment, and quite complacently tells of his "artifice" to help the preacher on.

A very excellent critic, Dr. Samuel Luckey, directs attention to his great power of imitation, and remarks that he would doubtless have excelled as an actor. He adds:

As a preacher, he was at once energetic and impressive, a model of correctness, power, and majesty, possessing a voice of great compass and uncommon melody. * * * As a ruler in the Church, he was firm, prudent, conciliatory, and successful.[9]

In words of similar import the Rev. Elbert Osborn describes Mr. Merwin's majestic appearance, and melodious yet powerful voice; he then quotes the following remarks, which he heard him make at a quarterly meeting many years ago:

When I was stationed in Albany I sometimes went into the capitol, and listened for a time to the learned, able gentlemen engaged in the debate, but I soon grew weary and uninterested, took my hat and retired; but I go from one quarterly meeting to another; every Sabbath I am in love-feasts, where I hear men, women, and youth, most of whom make no pretension to eloquence or learning, speak in artless language or broken accents of God's goodness to them, and it is still interesting, affecting, and, as it were, new to me every Sabbath.[10]

To these testimonies may be added a few lines from the portraiture written by Dr. Abel Stevens. After describing Mr. Merwin as a "perfect Christian gentlemen," he says:

He possessed superior powers of government, and discharged the functions of the presiding eldership with special ability. The invaluable talent of reconciling discordant brethren or societies was his in a rare degree. * * * His pulpit appeals were accompanied by a flowing and sweeping eloquence, sometimes rising to wonderful power and majesty.[11]

SARAH, wife of Samuel Merwin, was a daughter of Nehemiah Clark, of Milford, Conn. There she was born in 1776. In early life she was converted, and, although few if any of her relatives were Methodists, she chose to unite with that people.

---

[9] Sprague's Annals, vol. vii, p. 336.   [10] Life of Osborn, p. 52.
[11] Hist. M. E. Church, vol. iii, p. 457.

Right nobly she shared for eight years the toils and self-denials of her first husband, Peter Jayne, who fell at his post in the itinerant ranks in 1806, and whose memorial has a place in this book. She afterward married Samuel Merwin, spent thirty-five years more in this work, and, about eight years after his death, from the home of her son, the Rev. J. B. Merwin, in Poughkeepsie, N. Y., on the 8th of January, 1847, at the age of more than three-score and ten years, like a shock of corn fully ripe, she was carried to the garner above.

The children of Samuel and Sarah Merwin were five sons and two daughters. The eldest, *Samuel C.*, a physician, fell a martyr to his profession in Natchez, Miss., during the yellow-fever epidemic in 1839; next, *Andrew M.*, of the book firm of Bangs & Merwin; third, *John B.*, became his father's successor in the ministry and presiding eldership, and is numbered among the pastors of the Sands-street church; fourth, *Daniel O.*, a lawyer and judge in Massachusetts; fifth, *Elias*, a lawyer in Boston, Mass. One of the daughters, *Julia M.*, married Dr. Bangs' oldest son, Lemuel Bangs, of New York, and the other daughter, *Sarah M.*, married Merrels Ward, of Middletown, Conn.

XXIX.

Samuel Thomas

BROOKLYN station employed two pastors in 1806. One of these was the REV. SAMUEL THOMAS, at that time a supernumerary preacher. The following must be accepted as the only known record of his history antecedent to his becoming a traveling preacher.

It was early in life that this man of God became acquainted with the power of religion through the instrumentality of Methodist preachers, and became a member of the society in the early days of Methodism in the state of New Jersey where he then resided. His house for many years was a home for the preachers that came into that neighborhood.

For many years he was an acceptable local preacher, during which time—the latter part especially—his mind was much exercised about traveling feeling an ardent desire to be more extensively useful in the church of God.[1]

ITINERANT RECORD: 1796, (Philadelphia Conf.,) Flanders cir., N. J., with Thomas Woolsey; 1797, ditto, with T. Everard; 1798, Elizabethtown cir., with J. Tolleson and Thomas Morrell; 1799, ordained elder,—Freehold cir., with Robert Sparks; 1800, Newburgh cir., N. Y., with E. Woolsey; 1801, ditto, with M. Swaim and D. Best; 1802, Bethel cir., N. J., with B. Iliff; 1803, Elizabethtown cir., with G. Woolsey and G. Stevens; 1804, Freehold cir., with W. M'Lenahan; 1805, ditto, with D. Dunham; 1806, (N. Y. Conf.,) sup'y in **Brooklyn**,[2] with E. Cooper; 1807, sup'y, New York, with T. Bishop, E. Cooper, F. Ward and P. Peck; 1808–1811, superannuated.

Under his labors in connection with Ezekiel Cooper, Sands-street church was blessed with a remarkable revival in 1806. Among the converts were Marvin Richardson, Josiah Bowen and Charles Wesley Carpenter, who became eminent ministers of the gospel.[3]

His brethren of the conference declare that he was "a man of great prayer, and diligent in searching the Scriptures."

---

[1] Minutes of Conferences, 1812, p. 208.

[2] Sands-street records (1806) say he was appointed by Bishop Asbury to divide his time as supply between New York and Brooklyn.

[3] Richardson's MS. autobiography, quoted in Stevens' Hist. M. E. Church, vol. iv, p. 254. See also Conf. Minutes, 1853, p. 194.

Special mention is made of the fact that he was "a strict disciplinarian." "He was a man of slender constitution," suffering much pain and weariness, and, therefore, "subject to dejection, and frequently tempted and buffeted by the devil."

In the fall of 1811 he removed, with his daughter and son-in-law, to Cincinnati, Ohio. He passed the winter contentedly and happily, though suffering at times from severe attacks of sickness. His death, in the spring of 1812, after an illness of three days, was serene and peaceful.[4] At the time of his translation he was the only superannuated minister in the New York Conference.

The "In Memoriam" record in the recent editions of the New York Conference Minutes states that he was buried in Cincinnati, O. There is no record of his interment in the old Methodist burial-ground in that city.[5]

Concerning his family nothing definite has been ascertained.

---

[4] See Minutes of Conferences, 1812, p. 208. The exact date of his death is not known.

[5] John Dubois, Esq., of Cincinnati, attempted to find his grave, but without success.

XXX.
Oliver Sykes.

HE REV. OLIVER SYKES was born in the north-western part of the town of Suffield, Conn., January 12, 1778. During his boyhood and youth he had serious reflections bordering on despair. At the age of twenty-two he was residing in Westfield, Mass., and during a series of revival meetings among the Methodists, he sought the Lord in secret, and was saved from doubts "arising from Calvanistic instructions," and enabled to trust that the work of grace was already begun in his heart, "although" he writes, "the evidence was not so satisfactory as that of many." He continues as follows:

I was not far from twenty-three years of age when I was baptized by the presiding elder, Rev. Shadrach Bostwick, and not a great while after that time joined the Methodist society, of which I was appointed class leader, and used to go in general about four or five miles a week to attend class meeting; I also used to exhort at the close of sermons among the Methodists and Congregationalists."[1]

He was licensed to preach in February, 1805; visited the conference that year, and heard Bishop Whatcoat preach. He was much exercised and depressed, believing that he ought to give up his secular occupation, that of a clerk in a store, and enter the traveling ministry. After attending a few quarterly meetings with Daniel Ostrander, the presiding elder, he says, "I returned to Westfield pretty much the same dejected creature." He had put his hand to the plow, however, and was determined not to look back. His career as a conference preacher began in 1805, and may be traced by the following

MINISTERIAL RECORD: 1805, supply on Dutches cir., N. Y. three months with F. Ward and R. Dillon, and on Croton cir. nine months w.

---
[1] Manuscript Autobiography.

Billy Hibbard; **1806**, (N. York Conf.,) Redding cir., Conn., with N. Fitch; last half of the year, **Brooklyn**, with Samuel Thomas;[2] 1807, Middletown cir., Conn., with Reuben Harris;[3] 1808, ordained deacon,—Dunham cir., Canada and Vt.; 1809, Fletcher cir., Vt.; 1810, ordained elder,—Middletown cir., Conn., with J. Lyon; 1811, Redding cir., with Aaron Hunt and John Reynolds; 1812, sup'd; 1813, sup'y, without appointment; 1814, sup'y, Cortland cir., N. Y., with N. W. Thomas and Samuel Bushnell; 1815, Suffolk and Sag Harbor cir., with John Reynolds,—health failed; 1816, sup'd; 1817, sup'y, Dutchess cir., with Samuel Cochran and J. B. Matthias; 1818–1825, sup'd; 1826, sup'y, Redding and Bridgeport cir., Conn., with M. Richardson, H. Humphreys, and Aaron Hunt, sup'y; 1827, ditto, with Henry Stead and J. Lovejoy; 1828, sup'y, Stratford cir., with J. Lovejoy and H. Romer; 1830, sup'd; 1830, sup'y, Redding cir., with J. Youngs and J. Bowen; 1831, sup'y, Newtown, with L. Mead; 1833, sup'y, Saugatuck, with N. White; 1834, sup'y, Derby cir., with H. Humphreys and John Crawford; 1835, ditto, with J. Bowen; 1836, sup'y, Windsor cir., with E. Dennis and W. L. Starr; 1837, sup'y, Derby cir., with D. Miller; 1838, ditto, with O. Starr; 1839–1847, sup'd; 1848–1852, (New York East Conf.,) sup'd.

The early promise and popularity of Mr. Sykes are indicated in the following extract from a manuscript letter by Francis Ward, preacher in charge of Dutchess circuit, dated Rhinebeck, December 14, 1805, and addressed to Freeborn Garrettson, then stationed in New York:

I am afraid the cause will suffer if Brother Sykes is taken from us. He is a gracious and gifted man, and universally acceptable. To take him from us at this time is like breaking my bones. It would rejoice me exceedingly if you and Brother Thacher could so arrange matters as to leave him with us.

If his popularity did not greatly increase after that, it is probably due in a large measure to his physical infirmities. There is something pathetic in the continued repetition of "supernumerary" and "superannuated" in the foregoing record. He writes concerning it:

My relation to the Annual Conference varied according to circumstances, but for the most part I was on the list of worn-out preachers. I preferred this to supernumerary, as it left me more at liberty. However, I repeatedly took an effective relation, and was obliged to give it up on account of my health. At length Brother Bangs (now Dr. Bangs) told me he thought I had better make no more attempts to stand effective, but do the best I could in my condition. This course I have taken, and endeavored to labor as Providence opened the way.

---

[2] Autobiography.

[3] The Minutes add Wm. Thacher, but he was on the Middletown station. See sketch of Wm. Thacher in this work.

His active labors in Brooklyn and on the east end of Long Island did not much exceed a year in duration. He came to Brooklyn when Ezekiel Cooper went South, and boarded with John Garrison.

"He suffered patiently during his last sickness, which was severe and protracted," and departed this life "with an unclouded prospect before him."[4] He died at the house of Mrs. Joseph Curtis, of Stratford, Conn., who donates his manuscript autobiography to the New York East Conference Historical Society. The plain marble slab which marks his resting-place, in the Methodist cemetery at Stratford, bears the following inscription :

Rev. Oliver Sykes, of the New York East Conference of the Methodist Episcopal Church, died in the faith of the Gospel, triumphing over the fear of death, February 13, 1853, aged 75 years.

"What things were gain to me, those I counted loss for Christ."

It is doubtful if any portrait of Mr. Sykes was ever taken. He is remembered by the older preachers as a confirmed old bachelor, a tall man, a great pedestrian, almost invariably seen with an umbrella, rarely taking notice of children, opposed to instrumental music, remarkably gifted in prayer, fond of discoursing on the resurrection, seldom looking his congregation in the face, and often stealing away after service without speaking to any one. We have from his pen the following example of this last-named peculiarity :

My first Sabbath appointment at Rhinebeck was in the forenoon. I was so much harassed in mind in endeavoring to preach, that instead of going into the house, as was customary, to get some refreshment, after meeting, I immediately took my horse and started for my afternoon appointment, thinking, "You will never wish to see me at Rhinebeck again ;" * * * but when I came round to that place again I was told that Brother Sands, and I believe some others, were quite blessed under my sermon.

It was no unusual thing for him to walk nine miles from his lodging-place through the woods before breakfast, apparently with the sole motive of eating in a different place from where he slept. If he lodged at Redding, he would breakfast at Weston, and *vice versa*. He came at one time, by invitation, to see his friend, W. H. Dikeman, in New York, and was sincerely and cordially welcomed. In the morning, behold ! the guest

---

[4] Conf. Minutes, 1853, p. 212.

had abandoned his bed and his room secretly and without a word of explanation, before the family were awake, and his host never saw him afterward.

His property, about $25,000, he bequeathed to the Missionary Society of the Methodist Episcopal Church, for the benefit of the China Mission.

To some it may be interesting to read his own written testimony concerning the loss of physical strength, which he frequently experienced "while engaged in secret or family prayer, but sometimes in the class or prayer meetings, and even in the [public] congregation occasionally." He says:

> I do not recollect any instance of it, but when earnestly engaged in prayer. The effect, in a religious point of view, is salutary. It brightens my enjoyment, and nerves up my mind to pursue my religious course. Others may endeavor to account for these things by saying that the mind becomes greatly excited, and overpowers the body. But as to myself, I write from experience and what I know. The influence begins, progresses, till suddenly, as if it were by a stroke of lightning, my strength is gone and I fall to the floor. It may be a peculiarity with me, but I do not recollect any instance in which I could not soon rise up again. It seems to me, judging from its results, to be a baptism of the Holy Spirit.

XXXI.

Joseph Crawford

WHEN the Rev. Joseph Crawford was presiding elder of the New York District, and when later he was appointed pastor of the Sands-street Church, he ranked among the foremost men of the denomination.

He was a native of White Plains, N. Y. His active ministry began when he was twenty-four years of age, and the following is his

CONFERENCE RECORD: 1797, (New York Conf.,) Pomfret cir., Ct. with Stephen Hull; 1798, Vershire cir., Vt.; 1799, ordained deacon—Vershire and Windsor cir., with E. Chichester; 1800, Plattsburg; 1801, ordained elder, —1801–1802, Bernard, Vt.; 1803, presiding elder, Vermont District; 1804, (New England Conf., by change of boundaries,) same appointment; 1805, traveled with Bishop Asbury; 1806, (N. Y. Conf.,) New Rochelle cir., N. Y., with H. Redstone and Ezekiel Canfield, sup'y, 1807—1810, presiding elder, New York Dist.; 1811, Courtland cir., with Coles Carpenter; 1812, New York city, with Wm. Phœbus, Laban Clark, and Phineas Cook; 1813, ditto, with Phineas Cook, Samuel Cochran and Phineas Rice; 1814, Hudson; 1815, Jamaica cir., with Benj. Griffen; 1816–1817, Brooklyn ; 1818–1819, Albany.

His second circuit, Vershire, Vt., included all that part of the state east of the mountains, and under his labors large numbers were added to the church the first year, and he was still more successful in connection with his colleague, Elijah Chichester, during the second year, when "more than a hundren were added to the church, besides hundreds who were converted but entered other communions."[1] One of those converts was a young man residing in Bradford, Vt., twenty one years of age, Laban Clark by name, who afterward became one of the most distinguished members of the New York Conference. He thus describes Mr. Crawford's faithful labors in leading him to Christ:

---

[1] Stevens—Hist. M. E. Church, vol. iv, pp. 49, 63.

I left my work and went to hear him. He dwelt upon the ample provision of the atonement; the liberty of all to come ; the manner of coming by faith ; that the sinner was to come because he was a sinner, and not tarry to make himself better; and in conclusion he sang the hymn,

"Come, ye sinners, poor and needy," etc.

A few weeks later he visited that part of the circuit again, and Mr. Clark writes :

He came to my father's family. They collected together, the itinerant gave an exhortation and prayed, and in taking leave he took each person by the hand, and addressed a few words to them individually. When he came to me I was so affected that I could not refrain from weeping. He held on to my hand, exhorting me to receive Christ by faith, and lifting up his voice, he prayed earnestly for the Lord to bless me.[2]

The wife of the Rev. P. P. Sandford, when a child, " was melted into tears " under his powerful preaching, and after awhile gave her heart to Christ.[3]

Dr. Abel Stevens quotes Bishop Asbury's account of the affecting farewell of the bishop and Crawford at the close of their journey through the New England States. Asbury wrote :

Joseph Crawford came over the ferry with me. When about to part he turned away his face and wept. Ah, I am not made for such scenes! I felt exquisite pain.[4]

He was a member of the General Conference in 1804 and in 1808. It is related that on one occasion Mr. Crawford attended a meeting composed of Methodists and other people, and conducted by a Universalist preacher who had visited the place, and proposed to establish stated services. Mr. Crawford was invited to conduct the closing exercises, which consisted of singing and prayer. He announced the following hymn, " lining " it in the old-fashioned Methodist style :

"Jesus, great Shepherd of the sheep,
To thee for help we fly;
Thy little flock in safety keep,
For O, the wolf is nigh !"

That hymn and the prayer had a very discouraging effect on the Universalist preacher, and he never came again.

---
[2] Memoir of Laban Clark, Conference Minutes, 1869.
[3] See memorial sketch of Peter P. Sandford in this work.
[4] Hist. M. E. Church, vol. iv, p. 312.

The public career of this eminent standard-bearer was suddenly closed in 1820 by his exclusion from the ministry and the Church. Two trials and two appeals resulted in a final and adverse decision by the General Conference of 1828. A partial account of his subsequent history is given in the following communications from the State of Ohio, where he spent the last years of his life. The Rev. Cyrus Prindle writes:[5]

I was slightly acquainted with Mr. Crawford during the last of his connection with the New York Conference, and was in attendance as a member of that body when he had his last trial in 1825. Though I personally knew him after this, I knew but little of him. I incidentally learned that after doing business in New York or its vicinity for a season, he left, and went, *himself*, to Sandusky city, Ohio.

Visiting Sandusky, about 1848, he conversed with an aged and intelligent Methodist brother who had known Mr. Crawford during his stay in that city. His testimony Mr. Prindle records as follows:

He stated that from the time Mr. Crawford came to Sandusky until his death, which was by cholera, if I correctly remember, his deportment was good. He stated that at one period, when a considerable company were gathered together, the former life of Mr. Crawford was a theme of conversation, and it was voted to appoint a committee to call upon him and invite him to select a time and preach to them. This man informed me that Mr. Crawford was so overpowered that he wept as though his heart was broken, but finally consented, and preached the sermon as requested. The account to me at the time was a most impressive narrative.

The gentleman to whom I refer informed me where I could find his grave, with a plain tombstone, and his name on it. I went alone to the public burying-ground, and found all as it had been told me. I remained at the grave for meditation and reflection, thinking how Joseph Crawford, in his palmiest days, had swayed the multitudes while addressing them, as the winds of heaven the forests.

To the foregoing we may add the following note from a pastor in Sandusky, written August 29, 1881:

The Rev. Joseph Crawford is quite well remembered by several old citizens here. Of his previous history they know nothing, save the rumor that he left New York on account of certain irregularities. While here he was engaged as a clerk in two or more stores. He is not known to have been connected with any church, although he often came to the Methodist Episcopal church. Old Mr. Clemens states that he often led class, and frequently went out into the country to preach.

---

[5] Letter to the author.

This is not confirmed by others. He preached a funeral sermon at the burial of Mr. Boalt, which is remembered as a sermon of great power. He was considered a man of marked talent; was kind and gentlemanly, of dignified carriage, florid countenance, and gray, or slightly gray, hair.[6]

This correspondent makes note of conflicting statements by the aged people of Sandusky concerning the report that Mr. Crawford fell into a habit of drinking. He quotes the following, inscribed upon a tombstone in an old and neglected ground in the western part of Sandusky city:

In memory of Joseph Crawford, who was born in White Plains, N. Y., and died in this city Aug. 9, 1832, aged 59 years.

His wife long since found rest in heaven; and of their children, living and dead, many pages of merited eulogy might be written, but they are not required.

---

[6] Rev. Albert D. Knapp, letter to the author.

REV. ELIJAH WOOLSEY.

XXXII.

ELIJAH WOOLSEY.

SANDS-STREET Church was favored with the pastoral labors of the REV. ELIJAH WOOLSEY in the year 1807 He was born in Marlborough, Ulster Co., N. Y., July 26, 1771.[1] His memoir in the Conference Minutes states that "his parents were pious; his mother especially was deeply devoted to God, and no doubt imparted to him early religious instruction."

In his autobiography he relates that the Methodist itinerants were accustomed to visit his father's house. He was greatly affected when they took him by the hand, and affectionately urged him to seek the Lord. He was still more thoroughly awakened when his own sister was converted and became a Methodist In a short time he followed her example. He held meetings and exhorted his neighbors to repent. In 1792, he and his brother Thomas began their itinerant work; his brother on trial in the conference, and he as a supply on a very laborious circuit at the age of twenty-one. After that year he filled the following

APPOINTMENTS: 1793, (New York Conf.,) Cambridge cir., with Joel Ketcham; 1794, Upper Canada, upper cir.; 1795, ordained elder,—Bay of Quinte, with Sylvester Keeler; 1796, Redding cir., Conn., with Robert Leeds; 1797–1799, local; 1800, (N. Y. Conf.,) Newburgh cir.,N. Y., with S. Thomas; 1801, (Phila. Conf.) Flanders, N. J., with Benj. Iliff; 1802, ditto, with G. Bailey; 1803–1806, presiding elder, Albany Dist., N. Y., (from 1804, New York Conf.,) 1807, **Brooklyn**, with John Wilson; 1808, Croton cir., with Isaac Candee; 1809, Pittsfield cir., Mass., with Phineas Cook; 1810, Dutchess cir., N. Y., with Z. Lyon and Smith Arnold; 1811, ditto, with Peter Bussing; 1812, presiding elder, Rhinebeck Dist.; 1813, Middletown cir., Conn., with A. Scolefield; 1814, Stratford cir., with Henry Eames; 1815, Redding cir., with Reuben Harris; 1816, Dutchess cir., N. Y., with Noble W. Thomas; 1817, Cortland cir.,

---

[1] Minutes of Conferences, 1850. p. 453. This date nearly agrees with his age as inscribed on his tomb-stone. See Stevens' Hist. M. E. Church, vol. iii, 180, where 1772 is given as the date of his birth.

with B. Northrop ; 1818, Newburgh cir., with Heman Bangs ; 1819, Croton cir., with J. B. Matthias ; 1821, New Rochelle cir., with Wm. Jewett and Robert Seney; 1822, ditto, with Wm. Jewett and N. W. Thomas ; 1823, Cortland cir., with J. B. Matthias ; 1824, Redding cir., Conn., with John Reynolds; 1825, sup'y, Cortland cir., N. Y., with Elijah Hebard and Henry Hatfield ; 1826, Stamford cir., Conn., with Luman Andrus; 1827, ditto, with S. U. Fisher ; 1828, New Rochelle cir., N. Y., with S. Cochran and J. Bowen ; 1829, Cortland cir., with H. Bartlett and J. Reynolds ; 1830, sup'y, Cortland cir., with N. White and J. Reynolds ; 1831, ditto, with N. White, J. B. Matthias, and D. Stocking ; 1832, ditto, with H. Bartlett, J. B. Matthias, and W. M'Kendree Bangs ; 1833, ditto, with H. Bartlett and W. M'Kendree Bangs ; 1834, sup'y, no appointment ; 1835, sup'y, New Rochelle cir., with D. Ostrander and B. Daniels ; 1836, ditto, with P. R. Brown and Thomas Sparks ; 1837, ditto, with P. R. Brown, T. Sparks, and J. W. Le Fevre, sup'y ; 1838-1847, sup'd ; 1848-1849, (New York East Conf.,) sup'd.

It took nineteen days or more to reach his appointment in Canada. To accomplish that journey, which could now be made in a few hours with the utmost ease, he was subjected to almost incredible hardships, contending with the rapids in the Mohawk valley, facing storms of rain and snow on the Oswego River, wrecked on Lake Ontario, unsheltered by night, weary, famishing, and sometimes sick, but always happy in the Lord.[2] In that northern region he was remarkably popular, and successful in establishing Methodism in many places. One of the chroniclers of Canadian Methodism writes :

Elijah Woolsey reached a preaching place in Canada weary and hungry. The old lady showed him into the pantry and set a lunch before him. After quite a long time his hostess put in her head and found him still eating with a zest. " Brother Woolsey, the house is full of people," said she. " I will be out and at them in a minute," was his lively and energetic reply ; and our informant said that, sure enough, he went at them with a will, and with good and saving effect.[3]

Many wept when he left the circuit, and several small farms were offered to him if he would stay. He writes in his autobiography :

One man followed me down to the water side, and there we sat for some time and talked and wept together, and when I got into the boat, he threw his arms around me, and waded knee-deep into the water, and said, " If you will but come back again, as long as I have two mouthfuls of bread you shall have one." * * * It was to me a source of inexpressible satisfaction that I had been made useful to a few of my fellow-creatures, though of another nation, and the thought of meeting them on Canaan's happy shore, after the trials of life are over, and

---

[2] See full account of this journey in Stevens' Hist. M. E. Church, vol. iii, pp. 181-185.
[3] " Case and his Contemporaries," p. 44.

greeting them as my spiritual children, often gilds the shadows of my supernumerary hours, and gives brilliancy to the rays of my descending sun.[4]

Just before the conference in 1807 his wife's health declined, and is seems to have led to his appointment to Brooklyn. He writes us concerning this appointment and his experience there:

My wife was taken sick with what proved to be her last sickness. * * * I w wished to have my next appointment on Newburgh circuit, where she ed, and I sent my request to Bishop Asbury at the conference, accordingly ₂ did not see fit, however, to grant it, but chose that for me which was tter than if my own request had been granted. He appointed me to ooklyn, where I could fill my Sabbath appointments, and be with my fering companion most of the time. The friends of Brooklyn were exceedly kind; indeed, a kinder people I never saw. One day I saw my beved companion weeping, and said to her, "What makes you weep?" She d, "I want to live." I said to her, "What makes you want to live?" e said, "To compensate you for your kindness to me." This made me ep, and I felt unhappy for a time. A few days after I asked her if she was lling to give me up. She said she was. I felt thankful to God for it. She ₂n asked me if I could give her up. I told her I could. She appeared to glad. I continued to watch with her night and day as long as she lived.[5]

He was a member of the General Conference in 1804, 1816, id 1820. In his old age he wrote a history of his life, entitled The Supernumerary," a valuable contribution to the historic erature of our Church. He spent his last days in Rye, N. Y., here he preached occasionally and was held in great honor by l the people. His conference memorial states that "his dease was preceded by a long and gradual decline, during nich he exhibited Christian resignation and cheerfulness, and s spirit often rejoiced in God his Saviour."

Near the western boundary of a charming cemetery, owned ' the Methodist Episcopal Church, in the village of Rye, N. Y., a lot belonging to Dr. E. W. Finch, of New Rochelle, there a very tasteful monument of polished granite, surmounted ' an urn, and bearing this inscription:

REV. ELIJAH WOOLSEY,
IN THE MINISTRY OF THE METHODIST EPISCOPAL CHURCH 57 YEARS.
Died January 24, 1850, aged 79 Years.
In Labors Abundant.

PHŒBE, HIS WIFE,
DIED MARCH 27, 1874,
Aged 88 Years.
Gone Home.

---

[4] "The Supernumerary," p, 50.   [5] Ibid., pp. 93, 94.

Mr. Woolsey was twice married, but he left no posterity
was tall, well-built, and of noble bearing. The brief m
adopted by the conference says of him:

Father Woolsey was a man of great benevolence of character and a
of manners. He seemed to have a happy art of attaching himself
associates without effort on his part, and those attachments were las
life. He was a holy man, a good preacher, and he shall be held in evei
remembrance.[6]

He was a singer, and, like many of the early preachei
lighted in "China" and other old-fashioned minor tunes. H
gifted with a sharpness which convinced many a skeptic th
was a dangerous antagonist. W. H. Dikeman relates th
infidel once said to a friend of Woolsey's in Redding, C
"I tell you, the Methodist preachers don't know any
Woolsey is a fool. Invite me to your house sometime wh
is there, and I will expose his ignorance." The friend a
to the proposition, and warned Woolsey to þe on the lo
for some vexatious questions. The infidel propounde
following: "Mr. Woolsey, what is the soul?" The pre
replied: "Some people say it is the pith of the back-b
This answer was received with scorn and declared
ridiculous. "Well, then," said Woolsey, "if it isn't that,
is it?" He had the advantage at once. The infidel was
zled and ashamed, and acknowledged that it was easier
for a wise infidel to ask questions than to answer them.

The Rev. Elbert Osborn, who had often heard him pi
wrote of him as "animated in delivery," and Dr. Wakeley
said that he "possessed the spirit of the prophet whose
he bore."

ELECTA, his first wife, died among the Sands-street p
February 14, 1808, aged twenty-nine years. One week l
her death she declared to Father Garrettson "that the
had sanctified her soul more than two years before, and thi
had not seen one moment since that time in which she do
it any more than she doubted her own existence." In he
moments "she folded her hands together and said, ' Now,
Jesus, take me to thyself speedily.' These were her last woi

---

[6] Minutes of Conferences, 1850, p. 453.
[7] "The Supernumerary," pp. 94, 95.

he was buried on the east side of the Sands-street church-
l. On the head-stone are these lines:

> " Her sleeping dust, in silent slumber, lies
> Beneath this stone, till God shall bid it rise."

[N]one would now write such a couplet over the sleepers there.
[Wh]at changes have transpired! Little did those who laid their
[love]d ones to rest in the quiet slopes beside the village church
[anti]cipate that in less than a century their repose might be dis-
[turb]ed to make way for the busy throngs of a great and growing
[city].

[P]HŒBE (WILSON,) the second wife of Elijah Woolsey, has
[alre]ady been mentioned. Dr. E. W. Finch writes:

[M]rs. Phœbe Woolsey was aunt to my mother, who spent one year, when a
[gir]l, in Uncle Woolsey's home. The family ties are exceedingly strong in
[the] Wilson family. My dear Aunt Phœbe was like a mother to me. * * *
[Afte]r settling in New Rochelle I purchased a plot in the Rye cemetery, and
[findi]ng " the minister's plot " quite overrun with weeds and briars, I asked of
[the] Church authority to remove the remains of Uncle and Aunt Woolsey to
[my f]amily plot, which was readily granted. The plot seems more sacred since
[their] sacred dust was deposited there.[8]

Letter to the author.

XXXIII.

John Wilson

AMONG the most holy and useful of the early [Meth]odist preachers was the REV. JOHN WILSON [He] was born in Poulton, England, February 13[,] and, having been "taught by his parents the fear [of the] Lord," he became in very early life a Christian, and [while] yet a youth he cast in his lot with "the people called M[ethod]ists." At twenty years of age he came to New York, [bring]ing a recommendation from the Methodist preachers i[n Liv]erpool. Two years later he visited England on bu[siness,] and on the return voyage "experienced extraordinary [mani]festations of the love and presence of the Lord."[1] H[e ren]dered faithful service to the cause of Methodism i[n New] York city as class leader, exhorter and local preache[r. He] was thirty-four years of age, and had been in America [four]teen years when he entered the traveling connect[ion of] Methodist preachers.

CONFERENCE RECORD: 1797, (New York Conf.,) New [York] and Croton cir., N. Y., with David Brown and J. Baker; 1798, Lon[g Island] cir., with David Brown; 1799, ordained deacon,—ditto, with James C[ampbell;] 1800, New Rochelle and Croton cir., with David Brown and Elijah Ch[eney;] 1801, ordained elder,—ditto, with Jas. Campbell and Wm. Pickett; 18[02, New] York city cir., with T. Morrell and T. F. Sargent; 1803, ditto, with [Mor]rell, M. Coate, and R. Williston; 1804, assistant editor and gene[ral book] steward, associated with Ezekiel Cooper; 1805, New York, with F. G[arrettson,]

---

[1] Conference Minutes, 1810, p. 181.
[2] The appointment is "Brooklyn and Long Island" in the Conference [Minutes,] but the quarterly conference records show that the charges were not [united in] finances, and that Cyrus Stebbins was the Brooklyn pastor that year.

J. Snethen and Aaron Hunt; 1806, ditto, with A. Hunt, T. Bishop, and D. Crowell; **1807, Brooklyn,** with Elijah Woolsey; 1808, New York, with W. Thacher, E. Cooper, F. Ward, L. Andrus, and P. Peck; 1808-1809, chief book agent, with Daniel Hitt.

Lednum says he married Hester, a daughter of Frederick Deveau, a pioneer Methodist of New Rochelle, N. Y.,[3] but of her or her family nothing further is known.

In scholarship, John Wilson ranked among the foremost of the preachers. His memorial says:

> He was conversant with the Greek and Roman classics. Carrying with him his Greek Testament, he spent many of his leisure hours in the perusal thereof. He made great progress in polemical, experimental, and practical theology. He was an enlightened, able, and spiritual divine. In penmanship, for perpicuity and swiftness; in correctness of accounts and accuracy of calculations in business, he could be excelled by few.[4]

In all the graces which adorn the Christian character, his brethren declared him to be "a superior example worthy of imitation." His preaching was "in demonstration of the Spirit, and with power." Sinners and backsliders heard his monitory voice, and trembled; * * * mourners in Zion rejoiced at the consolation he brought;" and by his clear and powerful preaching on his favorite theme, *entire sanctification,* many were brought to the experience of that great blessing. The following passage by one of his contemporaries vividly illustrates his ability to overcome prejudice and doubt, when he spoke upon the doctrine of perfect love.

> On the sixth day of our session, [New York Conference, 1804,] the postponed subject of sanctification was called up, and Stebbins, its enemy, came in with his objections. Up rose John Wilson, whose soul flamed with the fire of it. His sanguine countenance, his sparkling eye, his animated frame and fervor of soul, all indicated that his heart was full of the subject; and, as in the case of Stephen, none could "resist the spirit and wisdom with which he spake." He sat down to wait a reply, but "none opened his mouth, or muttered, or peeped." The victory was complete; the debate was closed; all seemed love, and the angel of peace brooded over the consecrated assembly.[5]

He was several years secretary of the New York Conference, member and secretary of the General Conference in 1804, and member again in 1808.

---

[3] "Rise of Methodism," p. 103.
[4] Conference Minutes, 1810, p. 181.
[5] William Thacher's manuscript Autobiography.

During the last seven years of his life he suffered greatly from asthma, and while this affliction developed his patience, it did not quench his zeal. He died suddenly from suffocation, January 29, 1810, having conversed and prayed with his family a few hours before his death. His remains were deposited in a vault in the rear of the Forsyth-street church, New York.[6]

---

[6] See "Lost Chapters," p. 501.

REV. DANIEL OSTRANDER.

XXXIV.
DANIEL OSTRANDER.

John Wilson and Elijah Woolsey were succeeded in the Brooklyn charge by that "shrewd and far-seeing Methodist statesman," the Rev. Daniel Ostrander. He was born in Plattekill, Ulster Co., N. Y., on the 9th of August, 1772. He sprang from a rugged and vigorous stock—his ancestors were from Holland. His conversion at the age of sixteen years was followed by the earnest and sincere devotion of more than half a century to the noblest work that can engage the powers of a human being. Entering the itinerancy at the age of twenty one, he wrought grandly for God and the church in the following

APPOINTMENTS: 1793, Litchfield cir., Conn., with Lemuel Smith; 1794, Middletown cir., with M. Rainor; 1795, ordained deacon—Pomfret cir., with N. Chapin; 1796, Warren, R. I.; 1797, ordained elder—Boston and Needham cir., Mass., with Elias Hull; 1798, Pomfret, Ct., with Asa Heath; 1799, Tolland cir.; 1800, Pomfret cir.; 1801, New York with John M'Claskey, Thos. Morrell, and M. Coate; 1802-1803, New London Dist.; 1804-1805, (New Eng. Conf.,) same district; 1806, (N. Y. Conf.) Dutchess cir., N. Y., with F. Ward and Robert Dillon; 1807, ditto with Wm. Vredenburgh and Wm. Swayze; **1808, Brooklyn**; 1809-1810, Albany; 1811-1814, Hudson River Dist; 1815, Chatham cir., N. Y., with S. Minor; 1816, New York, with Wm. Thacher, E. Washburn, L. Andrus, and A. Scholefield; 1817, ditto, with N. Bangs, S. Crowell, and S. Howe; 1818, New Rochelle cir., with Coles Carpenter; 1819-1820, presiding elder, Ashgrove Dist.;1821-1822, Saratoga Dist.; 1823-1826, Hudson River Dist.; 1827, New Haven Dist.; **1828-,1831 New York Dist.**; 1832, New York city, east circuit, with B. Griffin, B. Silleck, P. Chamberlin, and P. R. Brown, 1833, ditto, with Laban Clark, B. Griffin, P. Chamberlin, and P. R. Brown; 1834, New Rochelle cir., with P. L. Hoyt and E. Woolsey, sup'y; 1835, ditto, with B. Daniels and E. Woolsey, sup'y; 1836-1839, **New York Dist.**; 1840-1842, Newburgh Dist.; 1843, superannuated.

He is classed among the founders of Methodism in New England, all his earlier appointments having been in that region. His first presiding elder's district "comprehended, during a part of the time, the entire field of Methodism in Connecticut, (except one circuit,) most of Rhode Island,

and a portion of Massachusetts."[1] Subsequently his labors were mostly in the State of New York. He was a member of General Conference *ten successive terms*, 1804 to 1840. His conference memorial, in reviewing his remarkable career, says:

> From the year 1793 to the year 1843, a full term of fifty years, so remarkably did the Lord preserve him, that only three Sabbaths in all that time was he disabled from pulpit service by sickness. Where, in the history of ministers, shall we find a parallel to this? For fourteen years he was on circuits, eight years in stations, (New York, Brooklyn, and Albany,) and twenty-eight years in the office of presiding elder.[2]

On September 3, 1798, he was married to Miss Mary Bowen. While pastor in Brooklyn he was the first to call out Marvin Richardson by "announcing him to preach without his knowledge."[3] One of his contemporaries, who, however, survived him many years, thus describes his appearance at the close of his effective ministry:

> Entering the New York Conference, your attention is attracted by the appearance of a venerable man occupying a seat near the platform directly in front of the presiding officer. His statue is small and slender, his form erect and sinewy, his complexion bronze, his nose sharp, his eyes small but clear and piercing, his mouth thin-lipped and compressed, his forehead high and broad, over which hang spare locks, well sprinkled with gray.
>
> He is attired in the costume of the early Methodist preachers; with black suit, the coat round-breasted, the vest buttoned to the chin, and the neck minus a collar, encompassed with a white neckerchief of excessive proportions. This is Daniel Ostrander, the Cromwell of the New York Conference. His face is indicative of vigor; his head, phrenologically viewed, of an iron will; in fact, the whole expression is that of a man of great energy, determination, and perseverance. Nor do his looks belie him. He is uncompromising in his antagonism to every form of wrong-doing, and this, when circumstances demand, finds expression in no ambiguous terms. His yea is emphatically yea! and his nay, nay!
>
> He is a Methodist from conviction and choice, and next to the Gospel he has faith in the ultimate ubiquity of the discipline, doctrines, and usages of the Methodist Episcopal Church. He has just concluded his fiftieth year as an effective preacher, and by a vote of the Conference he has been requested to preach a semi-centennial sermon. And how wonderful the record of those fifty years![4]

---

[1] Stevens' Hist. M. E. Church, vol. iii, p. 228.
[2] Minutes of Conferences, 1844, p. 472.
[3] Stevens' Hist. M. E. Church, vol. iv, p. 254.
[4] Rev. J. L. Gilder, in The Methodist, April, 1874.

Record of Ministers.

A large audience listened to this sermon in the Allen-street church, New York. At this time he insisted upon taking a superannuated relation, but it doubtless cost him a severe struggle of feeling to retire from his much-loved work. It is believed to have hastened his death. His memoir says:

> He preached occasionally, on Sabbaths, until his final sickness, and on August 29, 1843, at a camp-meeting near Newburgh, delivered his last sermon, from Psalm cxlvi, 8: "The Lord openeth the eyes of the blind," etc. It is said to have been an able discourse, and one of his happiest efforts.
>
> Through the whole of the summer he seemed to be ripening for heaven, and soon after this last message his health failed. * * * When asked if Christ was still precious, with his last and utmost effort he cried, "Yes!" and peacefully fell asleep in Jesus. So lived and labored, and so died Daniel Ostrander, literally worn out in the best cause—his life, from sixteen years of age to seventy-two, a living sacrifice to God.

The date of his departure is December 8, 1843. Bishop Hedding preached his funeral sermon from 2 Tim. iv, 7, 8.;[5] and his remains were interred in the old burial-ground in Plattekill, Orange county, N. Y., near the scene of his birth and childhood.

The best characterization of Daniel Ostrander that we have seen is from the pen of the Rev. J. L. Gilder. He describes him as "more aggressive than progressive—in fact, sternly conservative," and enlarges upon this point as follows:

> Jealous of the integrity and purity of Methodism, he regarded her peculiarities as constituting her chief excellence, and hence he viewed with suspicion whatever would tend to impair or destroy them. Therefore he resolutely resisted some measures which ultimately became an integral part of the economy of the Church.

He makes note of his punctuality, his frequent and pointed speeches in conference, his intuitive discernment of the right and wrong of every question, his consummate skill in unraveling difficulties which sometimes arose in the course of discussions, and his calm self-possession in the midst of intense excitement, on account of which he was sometimes called "the balance-wheel of the conference." As Mr. Gilder states,

> He was decided in his convictions, and his position once taken, he was immovable. In his administration he was rather severe and exacting. To the requirements of the Discipline he gave the most literal interpretation. It is not surprising, therefore, that instances arose in which he was regarded as

---

[5] Report in The Christian Advocate.

being dogmatical in his opinions and arbitrary in his measures. He was, however, thoroughly honest and conscientious in his convictions and acts, and no flattery on the one hand, nor threats on the other, would cause him to swerve one iota from what he conceived to be just and right.

The casual observer, forming his estimate of Mr. Ostrander by his general appearance and manner, might very naturally have considered him devoid of tenderness and sympathy, but to those who were brought into intercourse with him in social and private life, there was found underlying that rough exterior a stratum of almost womanly gentleness and kindness of spirit. Among his familiar friends he would throw off his usual reticence and be free and unrestrained. He would frequently enliven conversation with a spicy anecdote, and entertain by the narration of thrilling incidents connected with his itinerant career. While severe in his denunciations of what was simply meretricious, he was quick to discern and prompt to encourage real merit. Hence the young minister struggling with adverse circumstances, but consecrated to his work, found in him a judicious friend and a wise counselor.

As a preacher, he was distinguished for plainness of speech, depth of thought, scriptural language, and powerful appeals to the heart and conscience. If he had not elegance of diction or flights of oratory, he was free from verbiage. His style was compact, forcible, direct, incisive. He was mighty in exhortation, and there are those living who will recall the potency of his appeals.[6]

Though possessing a dignity bordering upon sternness, he is said to have had "a vein of the brightest humor, which was sometimes exhibited to the amusement of his friends." After a speech he had delivered in Baltimore, during which he was interrupted every few minutes by his opponents calling him to order, he met at a dinner party several of those who had attempted to silence him. One of them said, "Brother Ostrander, you beat all the men I ever saw; it seems to me that if twenty jackasses were to run over you when you were speaking, they could not break the thread of your discourse." Ostrander listened to the remark, then "bringing his fingers to his lips, and spitting rapidly three or four times, as if to get rid of some lingering bad taste, simply replied, in the most quiet manner possible, 'I think I have been pretty well tried in that way this morning.'"[7]

It is cause for gratulation that Mr. Ostrander, at the age of sixty-seven, withdrew his persistent refusal to sit for a portrait, and that the artist has given us an excellent likeness in oil, from which the engraving in this book is copied.

---

[6] Article in The Methodist.

[7] Dr. Samuel Luckey, in Sprague's Annals.

Record of Ministers.

MARY (BOWEN,) his wife, was born June 26, 1767, in Coventry, R. I. Her father, though regarded as an honorable citizen, was a man of deistic principles, who late in life, however, became a Christian. The gay pleasures of the world did not satisfy the daughter, and on hearing a Methodist preacher in her twenty-fourth year, she sought and found the Lord. In spite of great persecution, she united with the Methodists, under the ministry of Ezekiel Cooper, in 1793. Every two weeks she rode ten miles on horseback to attend class-meeting. Jesse Lee and George Roberts were her pastors, and she formed an early acquaintance with Asbury. She heartily accepted the lot of an itinerant's wife, and "forgot her own people and her father's house." She was an excellent wife and mother, noted for "industry," "frugality," "punctuality," and "neatness," and her many acts of charity. Through feebleness and watching over a dying son, in 1818, her reason gave way, and "for some weeks her mind became the sport of the enemy." Prayer availed for her recovery. She bore the death of her husband with amazing fortitude, and in five weeks and two days after his decease, on the 14th of February, 1843, she peacefully slept in Jesus, in the seventy-seventh year of her age. Her grave is beside that of her husband.[8]

Children of Daniel and Mary Ostrander: *Almira*, who was converted at the age of sixteen years, "drank at the fountain-head of Methodist doctrine and spirit by direct association with Bishops Asbury and George, and others of that noble band of pioneers," wrote for the press very creditable articles both in prose and poetry, and maintained a glowing religious zeal and devotion till her death, in 1879, in the seventieth year of her age;[9] *Richard*, who died young; *Daniel Bowen*, a highly cultivated physician, who, after preaching acceptably in the New York Conference a number of years, located, entered upon the practice of medicine, and died in 1877, leaving one child, a son; *Mary H.*, who married the Rev. Ira Ferris, of the New York Conference, and still survives him, (1884,) at the age of eighty-two, and among whose five living children is the Rev. Daniel Ostrander Ferris, of the New York East Conference.

---

[8] These facts were furnished for The Christian Advocate by her daughter, Miss Almira Ostrander.

[9] Rev. D. O. Ferris, in The Christian Advocate.

XXXV.
REUBEN HUBBARD.

BROOKLYN charge was the point of departure from which two of the early Methodist preachers entered the Episcopal Church. One of these was the Rev. REUBEN HUBBARD. He was a native of Brimfield, Mass. His father's ancestors were of English origin; his mother's name was Keep.[1] By his devoted parents "he was led on from his earliest infancy to regard himself as set apart for the ministry of the word," and he became a member of the Methodist Church "as early as his fifteenth year."[2] Joining conference about three years later, he continued in the Methodist ministry twelve years, and thereafter he was for half a century connected with the Protestant Episcopal Church. The following is an epitome of his entire

MINISTERIAL RECORD; 1798, Pittsfield cir., Mass., with Joseph Sawyer; 1799, Pleasant River cir., Me.; 1800, ordained deacon,—Bath and Union cir., with Timothy Merritt; 1801, Portland; 1802, ordained elder,—Greenwich and Warren cir., R. I., with Caleb Morris and C. H. Cobb; 1803, Needham cir., Mass., with Thos. Ravlin; 1804, Marblehead; 1805, Boston, with Peter Jayne; 1806, Newport, R. I.; 1807, Gloucester and Manchester cir.; 1808, (N. Y. Conf.,) Middletown and Hartford cir., Conn., with James M. Smith, P. Rice and Joseph Lockwood; **1809, Brooklyn**,—withdrew.

1809, Dec. 22, ordained deacon by Bp. Moore of the Protestant Episcopal Church; 1810, (Oct.,) missionary at Duanesborough and places adjacent; 1811 [or 1812]—1818, rector of the churches in Danbury, Redding and Ridgefield, Diocese of Conn.; 1819–1823, rector of St. Michael's, Talbot County, Md., 1824–1827, rector, St. James Church, Goshen, N. Y.; 1828, (June) to 1829, (Dec.) missionary at Sodus; 1830–1831, missionary at Waterloo and Seneca Falls; 1832–1835, missionary at Granville; 1836, several months at Sandy Hill and Fort Edward; 1837–1843, missionary at Stillwater and Mechanicsville; 1844–1845, residing in Waterford; 1846–1849, rector, St. Stephen's Church, Schuylerville; 1850–1858, residing at Yonkers.[3]

---

[1] The Rev. Wm. E. Ketcham obtained from Miss Mary Anna Hubbard, daughter of Reuben Hubbard, some of the facts here recorded. Dr. A. B. Carter states that "the father and other kindred" of Reuben Hubbard are buried in Cortlandville, N. Y   [2] Funeral address by A. B. Carter, D. D.

[3] His pastoral record in the Episcopal Church is obtained from Sword's Pocket Almanacs, Burgess' List of Deacons, and Diocesan Convention Journals of Conn. and N. Y.

REV. REUBEN HUBBARD.

He was a member of the General Conference in 1804. The following letter,[4] written while he was pastor in Massachusetts, was addressed to the Rev. Epaphras Kibby:

MARBLEHEAD, *April* 3, 1805.

Dear Brother: I was informed by Brother Robinson that you would be glad to make an exchange with me the second Sabbath in April. I should be very glad to exchange, but I don't know how it will be. Our collections are small. They have paid me nothing this quarter, and were able only to pay Mr. Bowler for my board, not any thing for interest. Mrs. Bowler talks of begging something to defray the expense of an exchange; (such is the people's attachment to you, not on my account.) If they conclude to do any thing, I will come to Boston on Thursday, if I have no further intelligence from you. If I cannot come on to Boston to change at the time appointed, would it not do a fortnight after, should any thing turn up to make it convenient on my part? If it will not, please inform me by letter. I am in good health, and tolerably good spirits, though nothing very encouraging appears among the people. Yours, R. HUBBARD.

It is likely that he raised money enough to meet the expense of a trip to Boston; at all events, he was stationed in that city at the ensuing conference. He was greatly beloved by the people to whom he ministered; yet, though popular and successful in the Methodist Church, he was for some years preparing to go over to the Episcopalians. Dr. Carter says:

In the last conversation I had with him he told me of his success as a preacher in those earlier years, and as a proof of the esteem in which he was held by the congregation to whom he ministered. In Newport, R. I., a large building was erected, and an urgent and repeated call given him to sever his connection with the Methodist Society, and become the independent pastor of this new church. But this his sense of duty would not allow him to do, as he had won their confidence and enlisted their sympathies as a Methodist preacher. The church had been built with the money of that denomination, and by their rule of discipline, to which he had subscribed and they had assented, he must leave, as his allotted time had then expired; which he accordingly did. He told me, however, that at this very time his mind was inclining to the ministry of the Episcopal Church, and not very long afterward he entered upon a course of study which was to prepare him for ordination. It had been suggested to him that he might, as a minister coming from another body, avail himself of the canon referring to such, and thus secure a dispensation from some of the studies, which would require more time and greater application, but he positively refused to be received upon any other than a full standard of requirements; and so he labored all the

---

[4] Copied from the original, on file in the library of the New England Methodist Historical Society.

more diligently, still, however, preaching to his Methodist brethren every Sunday until he felt himself equal to the preliminary examination. He was fully prepared, and consequently passed with credit.

He organized Episcopal churches in Whitehall, Seneca Falls, Glen's Falls, Mechanicsville, and several other places. His reports at the annual conventions of his diocese breathe the spirit of a true missionary, and bear witness to his great labors and privations, rarely surpassed by the most apostolic among the Methodist heroes. It cannot, it need not, be determined whether the same zealous devotion in the Methodist Church would have accomplished more good. It is true that he moved as often, traveled more, obtained less promotion, and probably received as little remuneration as when he was an itinerant of the itinerants among the Methodists. A few brief extracts from his reports may not be amiss.

In 1824. Goshen. Congregations are small, and they are obliged to make great exertions to meet their expenses.

1831. Seneca Falls. During the winter and spring I preached as often as six times a week, besides holding other services.

1835. Your missionary has been wholly unable to keep up the Sunday-school, for want of the support necessary from the people.

1838. Good seed falls on stony places.

1840. In these places the current of prejudice sets so strong against the Church that I have been able, with all the industry I could use, to produce but little inquiry concerning it. But few desire to read our books, or attend the services of the Church.

1843. Communicants in three Churches, thirty-nine.[5]

True to his Methodist instincts and education, he originated the plan which resulted in "The Fund for the Relief of the Aged and Infirm Clergy of the Diocese." Aged and worn he retired to a quiet home in Yonkers, N. Y., where he was honored as a patriarch among the people. On the last Christmas day preceding his departure he spoke to an assembly, while "the tears streamed down his furrowed cheeks, as he bade them listen to what might be his parting counsels." The rector says:

For nearly seven years he always stood beside me at the holy table, and helped me to distribute the precious symbols of a Saviour's dying love. He would go anywhere—do any thing—be always ready to assist, where his services were needed. Often has he joined me before the morning service,

---

[5] Journals of Conventions, Diocese of New York.

saying, as he would put on the priestly robes, "I like, even if I take no part in the service, to have my armor on." I never heard him speak an angry word, or give expression to an unkind thought, even when there was the greatest provocation for both. How many of us can leave behind so precious a memory as this?

Just before Mr. Hubbard's death, Dr. Nathan Bangs asked him if he would give him his reasons for leaving the Methodist Episcopal Church, and he answered that after his return from a visit he would; but he died while on that visit. Having introduced Episcópal services in Cortlandville, N. Y., where some of his kindred resided, he was invited when Grace Chapel was erected to visit his old friends, and join them in their rejoicings. This he did. It was the grandest outlook of his life—it was, indeed, his Mount Nebo, where he died in the Lord, February 10, 1859, aged seventy-nine years. The clergymen of the different denominations in Yonkers acted as pall-bearers at his funeral. He was buried in the St. John's cemetery, in Yonkers, where his tombstone may be seen.

ABAGAIL M., his wife, was a daughter of Dr. Lester, of New Haven, Conn., who was for some time president of the Medical Society in that city. Her grave is near that of her husband.

Of their children—six sons and three daughters—eight are still living. The eldest, *Miss Mary Anna Hubbard*, a member of St. John's Episcopal church, Yonkers, N. Y., resides in the Ashburton Cottage, where her father lived. One of the sons was educated at Union College, another at Hobart. Two sons are in the banking business. *John Lester, Samuel Seabury*, and *Murray* are the names of three of the surviving children.

XXXVI.

Tho. Drummond

HE REV. THOMAS DRUMMOND will occupy but a small space in these pages, "having," so far as any known record attests, "neither beginning of days nor end of years." He had a prosperous but brief career as a minister in the Methodist Episcopal Church. Two of those years—a part of each—he was pastor of Sands-street church. From the Conference Minutes and the church records we obtain the following list of his

APPOINTMENTS: 1808; (Phila. Conf.,) Cambridge cir., Md., with James Ridgaway; **1809**, Asbury cir., N. J., with P. P. Sandford,—the latter part of this year, **Brooklyn, N. Y.**, in place of R. Hubbard, withdrawn; 1810, Staten Island; 1811, ordained deacon,—located; **1813**, (N. Y.Conf.,) Stamford cir., Conn., with Benj. Griffin,—came to **Sands-street, Brooklyn**, the latter part of the year; 1814, New York, with Wm. Phœbus, S. Cochran, N. Emery, M. Richardson and Wm. Blagborne; 1815, ordained elder,—Albany city station; 1816, expelled.

That he was a popular minister is apparent from the high grade of his appointments. Reference has already been made to his faithful instruction of the children of Sands-street church before the days of Sunday-schools. At the close of each period of his service in Brooklyn he reported an increase of members.

It is painful to read the record of his expulsion. He might have been held in grateful and lasting remembrance, but if known at all in the history of the church, it will be as an admonitory beacon. The crime of adultery was the ground of the charges against him. On reliable authority it is stated that he ran away with the wife of a steward in his church, and did not return.

This man should not be confounded with the Rev. Thomas Drummond of blessed memory, who "died at his post" in St. Louis, in 1834, and concerning whom the Rev. Dr. Wm. Hunter wrote the touching and beautiful lines, commencing—

> Away from his home and the friends of his youth,
> He hasted, a herald of mercy and truth.

XXXVII.

Lewis Pease

WHILE as yet the Sands-street Church comprised the whole of Brooklyn Methodism, it was for more than three years under the able and successful leadership of the REV. LEWIS PEASE. He was born of Christian parents, in Canaan, Columbia County, N. Y., August 7, 1786. In early youth he was troubled with many anxious doubts concerning his immortal destiny. Upon this point his published memorial says:

> Having been educated in the peculiarities of Calvinism, he feared that the eternal decree had forever excluded him from divine mercy; and his distress and despair on that account became so great that he was strongly tempted to put an end to his own life, to know the worst of his case. But God delivered him from that temptation, and directed him to the Methodists, by whom he was taught a general atonement and free salvation.[1]

A divine voice whispered peace to his troubled spirit on the 30th of January, 1805. He was then in his nineteenth year. Soon afterward, while on a bed of sickness, the conviction dawned upon him that he was called to preach the gospel. He was licensed first to exhort, and then to preach, in the year 1806.

---

[1] Minutes of Conferences, 1844, p. 475.

ITINERANT RECORD: 1807, (New York Conf.,) Brandon cir., Vt., with Geo. Powers; 1808, Cambridge cir., N. Y., with Wm. Bull; 1809, ordained deacon,—Buckland, Mass.; 1810, Pownal cir., Vt., with Wm. Swayze; 1811, ordained elder,—Albany city; **1812 and part of 1813, Brooklyn;** 1814 -1815, sup'd; 1816, Pittsfield cir., Mass., with James Covel, Jr.; 1817-1818, sup'd; 1819-1820, Otis, Mass.; **1821-1822, Brooklyn;** 1823-1824, Hartford, Conn.; 1825-1826, (Phila. Conf.,) Philadelphia, Union church; 1827-1828, (New York Conf.,) presiding elder, Champlain Dist.; 1829, sup'y; 1830, New York, with S. Luckey, S. Merwin, S. Martindale, B. Goodsell, H. Bangs, and S. D. Ferguson; 1831, ditto, with S. Merwin, S. Martindale, B. Goodsell, S. Landon, John Clark, B. Silleck and C Prindle; 1832, sup'y, Lee cir., Mass., with Julius Field; 1833, sup'y, Lee and Lenox cir., with Thomas Sparks, Clark Fuller, and S. S. Strong; 1834, ditto, with J. B. Wakeley and E. S. Stout; 1835, sup'y, Richmond and Stockbridge cir., Mass., with G. Brown and A. Rogers; 1836, sup'y, New York, West cir., with C. W. Carpenter, Jas. Covel, Jr., Z. Nichols, and L. Mead; employed as chaplain to the New York City Hospital; 1837, sup'y, Richmond, Mass., with J. Hudson; 1838, ditto, with Wm. Bloomer; 1839, ditto, with A. G. Wickware and B. Hibbard; 1840, ditto, with T. Bainbridge, E. A. Youngs, and B. Hibbard, sup'y; 1841-43, sup'd; 1843, part of the year a supply in North Secondstreet, Troy, N. Y.

Mr. Pease was greatly embarrassed by feeble health, as might be inferred from the frequent occurrence of the words " supernumerary " and " superannuated " in connection with his name. He was attacked with bleeding at the lungs soon after his reappointment to Brooklyn in 1813, the hemorrhage recurring " almost daily for fifteen months." Resuming his labors in 1816, his health again gave way.

Concerning his appointment to Brooklyn for a second term, his memoir in the Conference Minutes says:

This was a great trial to him, as his health was poor, and he had once failed on that station;[2] but for his relief, the Church obtained the assistance of a local preacher the first year, and a revival of religion commenced in August of the first year, and continued to the close of the last, and two hundred souls were added to the Church.

It has already been recorded that the membership was nearly doubled under his ministry in two years—an unparalleled increase in the history of Sands-street church.

His retirement from the Champlain District was caused by a violent return of his disease. In 1835 he was called

---

[2] It was an unwelcome appointment, moreover, because "his predecessor, Alexander M'Caine, had left the station in a deranged condition."—Billy Hibbard, in Christian Advocate and Journal, October 25, 1843.

to part with his beloved wife. After a few months he married again.

His closing labors were performed while serving as a supply in Troy, N. Y., during the illness of the pastor. There, as in other places, he did the work of an evangelist, and made full proof of his ministry. Assisted by another preacher, he was permitted to gather 208 persons into the church in a few weeks.

From scrofulous affection of the lungs and of the other vital organs, he suffered months of pain almost beyond endurance; "but he was wonderfully supported by divine grace, and on the borders of the grave he was happy in prayer, and singing praises to God." To his ministerial brethren he sent this dying message :

Tell the conference that I died in the full faith of the Gospel, as taught by the Methodists; yes, tell the Bishops, the elders, and the preachers, that I love them, * * * and that I die in peace.

When he could speak no more, "he gave his weeping wife a silent token that all was well," and sweetly fell asleep in Jesus, on the 5th of September, 1853, aged fifty-seven years. The Rev. Thomas Bainbridge preached his funeral sermon, and the Methodist, Baptist, and Presbyterian clergymen acted as pall-bearers. He is buried in Canaan, N. Y.

Lewis Pease was greatly respected and beloved. His brethren elected him delegate to General Conference in 1828 and 1832. His early advantages were small, and perhaps his scholastic attainments were never remarkable; but he is declared to have been a diligent student, and, as a preacher, remarkably " efficient, impressive, at times pathetic, and always acceptable." Dr. Wakeley says:

Mr. Pease had great power as an exhorter. In May, 1834, I preached during the session of the New York Conference, in Sands-street church, Brooklyn, and he followed the sermon by an exhortation. He had been stationed in Brooklyn a few years before, when the population was comparatively small, and a powerful revival had occurred in connection with his labors, of which he gave many most touching reminiscences, particularly in respect to those who had with him fought the battles of the Lord and fallen at their posts. But he was an admirable preacher as well as exhorter. His sermons were chiefly of the expository kind, but they were well digested, and full of judicious, scriptural thought, and delivered in an earnest, impressive manner. He always preached well, but it required a great occasion to bring out his full strength. At quarterly meetings or camp-meetings he was very apt to appear as the master-spirit. I recall particularly an instance of his overwhelming power at a camp-meeting at Hillsdale, N. Y., in the fall of 1834. The text was highly charged with terror: "For in the hand of the Lord there is a cup, and the wine is red: it is full of mixture; and he poureth out of the same: but the dregs thereof, all the wicked of the earth shall wring them out, and drink them." For more than two hours there was a vast sea of upturned faces, gazing at him in breathless silence, as he delivered one of the most alarming sermons I ever heard. It seemed as if the preacher was actually standing between heaven and hell, with the songs of the redeemed and the wailings of the lost both vibrating in his ears, and throwing his whole soul into an effort to secure the salvation of his hearers. The description throughout was so unutterably terrific, that it seemed that every wicked man in the assembly must have been horror-stricken.

But his preaching was not always of the bold and alarming character. He knew how to present the most precious and consoling truths of the Gospel with great effect ; and sometimes, by an exhibition of the love of Christ, he would open fountains of tears all over the audience.[3]

The same writer—an intimate friend and colleague of Mr. Pease—thus describes his personal appearance:

He was tall and slender, with a long face, rendered thin and pale by disease, of light complexion, fine forehead, penetrating eyes, with a general expression of countenance at once grave and intellectual.

Of his first wife we have no definite knowledge, except that she died March 17, 1835, while he was attached to the Lee and Lenox circuit, that she was some years his senior, and that there were no children by this marriage.

MISS ANN ELIZA WHEELER became his second wife when he was in his fiftieth year, and she was twenty-two years of age. She was a native of Great Barrington, Mass. After his death, which was soon followed by the death of three of their five children, she remained a widow several years. Her second husband was Robert Disney, of Utica, N. Y., "a good but eccentric man, by whom she had one child that died in infancy. Then followed a second widowhood." Mr. Disney left her a comfortable home, and sufficient means of support.

In 1874 she was married to the Rev. James Erwin, a prominent minister of the Central New York Conference. This union lasted four years, and " the mortal scene closed " in Cazenovia, N. Y., November 19, 1878, in the sixty-sixth year of her age. Her last words were " Precious Jesus!" Dr. Wm. Reddy

---

[3] Manuscript prepared for Sprague's Annals.

preached her funeral sermon, and wrote an obituary for the Northern Christian Advocate, from which are taken most of the facts here recorded. She sleeps in Oakwood cemetery, in Syracuse, N. Y.

She was a woman of fine intellect, attractive social qualities, and uncommon energy; remarkably gifted in prayer and exhortation, a helper in the Gospel, and "a succorer of many." It was a great delight to her in her last days, as the wife of a presiding elder, to renew her personal connection with the itinerancy, and she spent much of her time in visiting, with her husband, the various churches in his extensive district.

A promising young man, son of Lewis and Ann Eliza Pease, whose initials were *W. P.*, died a few years ago in Brooklyn, N.Y.

Millie A., the only daughter who lived to maturity, was an estimable woman. She became the wife of the Rev. William C. Steele, of the New York East Conference, and died at Sea Cliff, L. I., September 20, 1873.

XXXVIII.

Nathan Emery

SANDS STREET CHURCH received for its pastor, in 1815, the REV. NATHAN EMERY. His ministry there is memorable on account of its connection with the origin of Sunday-schools in Brooklyn.

Mr. Emery was born in Minot, Maine, August 5, 1780. He was of the sixth generation descended from John Emery, who came from England with his brother, Anthony Emery, to Newbury, Mass., in 1635. Moses Emery, father of Nathan, was the first settler in Minot, and built the first mill in that town. His wife, Nathan's mother, was Ruth Bodwell before marriage, and (on the authority of her son Stephen) was one of the most pious of women, who "could not remember the time of her conversion, or the time when she did not love to pray." Such a woman could not fail to be blessed in her children. They were six in number. The eldest was Ruth, who married John Downing. "She never went to school, but learned to write so well that she taught her youngest brother, Stephen, and so anxious was she to help him to a college training, that she used to knit and sew, and actually peel bark with her own hands to obtain means to aid her brother in his struggle to acquire an education." Moses, the eldest son became a Methodist local preacher. The third child was Olive, who married Ezekiel Loring, and settled in Ohio. The fourth is the subject of this sketch. The fifth was Polly, who married Ebenezer Emerson, and lived and died in Bridgeton, Maine. The youngest was Stephen, a graduate of Bowdoin College, lawyer, judge, attorney-general, etc. He resided in Paris, Me., and died there in 1863. Two of his daughters married ex-Senator Hamlin, and a son, George F. Emery, to whom the author is indebted for the foregoing facts, was recently connected with The Boston Post.

When Nathan Emery was fourteen years of age, (1794,) he heard at his father's house the first Methodist preacher who ever visited that region. The next summer, he and several other members of the family became Christians, and joined the class. One year later, at the remarkably youthful age of sixteen, he was appointed class-leader.

Early in 1799, when nineteen years of age, he was licensed to preach, and served under the presiding elder as a supply until conference. Here follows his

CONFERENCE RECORD: 1799, Readfield cir., Me., with John Broadhead; 1800, Needham cir., Mass., with John Finnegan; 1801, ordained deacon, Union, Me.; 1802, (N. E. Conf.,) Norridgwock cir., Me., with N. Coye; 1803, (New York Conf.,) Middletown cir., Conn., with Abner Wood; 1804, (New Eng. Conf., by change of boundaries,) ditto, with E. Washburn; 1805, New London cir., with T. Branch; 1806, (New York Conf.,) Litchfield cir., with S. Cochran; 1807, Granville cir., Mass. and Conn., with P. Rice; 1808, Long Island cir., N. Y., with N. U. Tompkins and H. Redstone; 1809, Courtland cir., with H. Eames; 1810, Redding cir., Conn., with J. Russell; 1811, Newburgh cir., N. Y., with J. Edmonds; 1812, ditto, with J. Beeman and S. Fowler; 1813, New Windsor cir., with Ez. Canfield; 1814, New York city cir., with Wm. Phœbus, S. Cochran, M. Richardson, T. Drummond, and Wm. Blagborne; **1815, Brooklyn**; 1816, New Rochelle cir., with S. Arnold and Coles Carpenter; 1818, Burlington cir., Conn., with C. Silliman; 1819, ditto, with C. Culver; 1820, Goshen cir., with S. Dayton; 1821, sup'd; 1822–1828, located; 1828, traveled Columbus cir., Ohio, under the presiding elder; 1829–1830, (Ohio Conf.,) Zanesville, Ohio; 1831, Cincinnati station, with J. B. Finley, E. W. Sehon, S. A. Latta; 1832, ditto, with T. A. Morris, W. B. Christie, and E. W. Sehon; 1833, Marietta cir., with W. Young; 1834, Chillicothe; 1835, Worthington; 1836, chaplain of penitentiary, Columbus; 1836, Delaware cir., with J. B. Austin; 1838–1840, sup'd.

Ebenezer Washburn, his traveling colleague in 1804, describes him as "a loving companion in labor, pious, laborious, a good preacher, and a lover of Wesleyan Methodism." On the 20th of May, 1806, about the time of his appointment to the Litchfield circuit, he was united in marriage to Miss Clarissa Frothingham, of Middletown, Conn.

At the close of his pastoral term in Long Island, (1808,) he reported an increase of fifty members. The church in Brooklyn was in a flourishing condition when he was pastor there, and under his administration the first Sunday-school was organized in March, 1816. He was a member of General Conference in 1804 and 1816. Under his ministry, on the New Rochelle circuit, in 1817, a young man named David Holmes was led to the Saviour and licensed to exhort, who afterward became a prominent member of the New York Conference.

Soon after taking a superannuated relation in 1821, Mr. Emery removed to Blendon, (now Westerville,) Ohio, where he purchased a small farm. His health improved, and, being unwilling to burden his brethren, he asked for and obtained a location in 1822, but, as indicated above, soon resumed his itinerant labors. When permanently superannuated, though his health steadily declined, he labored both in the field and in the pulpit till near the close of his life. He preached on Sunday, May 20, 1849, and gave out an appointment for the succeeding Sabbath. On Thursday he was taken sick, and died on the morning of the following Sabbath, about the hour for the service to begin. His conference memorial says:

Father Emery, as he was familiarly and affectionately called, was no ordinary man. His preaching talents were not showy, but, far better than showy, they were useful. His ministrations were practical, and always characterized by good sense, great zeal for God, and a deep concern for the salvation of souls. Of a sweet and amiable spirit, he was greatly beloved of men—of deep and uniform piety, he was greatly honored of God.

He had always looked with some degree of dread to the conflict with his last enemy. And as he saw the hour of his dissolution at hand, he besought the Lord earnestly for dying grace. And dying grace was given. He took an affectionate leave of his friends, and especially his daughter, an only child, to whom he spoke many precious words of consolation. As he approached the Jordan of death his soul became more and more enraptured with the visions of glory that were revealed to him upon the other shore. And while passing through its chilling waters, he said, "O how gently my Saviour leads me through." Just as the spirit was about to take its flight, he looked upward, and fixing his eyes as if upon some object of unutterable loveliness, in a low whisper he exclaimed, "Up! up! up!" These were his last words on earth.[1]

The house in which he died is yet standing, (1881,) just outside the limits of Westerville. He is buried, with his wife, in the Methodist Episcopal cemetery of that place, about fifty

---

[1] Conference Minutes, 1849, p. 386.

yards from the parsonage. Some years ago "his nephew, Mr. Selah Sammis, erected upon his grave a marble stone that might be called a small monument."[2] Upon this stone is inscribed the following:

REV. N. EMERY,

Born in Minot, Maine, August 10, 1780.

Died May 27, 1849.

OUR BELOVED FATHER ENDURED THE HARDSHIPS AND SUFFERINGS OF AN ITINERANT LIFE WITH FIRMNESS AND PERSEVERANCE, AND FOR FIFTY-ONE YEARS HIS DAILY EXAMPLE WAS A CONSTANT COMMENT UPON THE GOSPEL HE PREACHED.

Mr. Emery rendered excellent service to the church, and wherever his name is remembered it is "as ointment poured forth." Much inquiry has been made in vain for a description of his personal appearance, and no portrait is extant. The bold and striking signature, written in 1816, in the Sands-street church record, might be taken to indicate grace of manner combined with decision of character.

His wife, CLARISSA (FROTHINGHAM,) was connected with a prominent family in Middletown, Conn. For nearly forty years they journeyed heavenward together. "Amiable, talented, gentle as an angel of light, she followed her husband from field to field of his labor;"[3] and on the 18th of December, 1845, less than four years previous to his decease, her sanctified spirit passed peacefully to the land of the blessed. She was sixty-three years of age. A plain marble slab designates the place of her repose, beside the grave of her husband.

They left an only daughter, *Mary.* "She was married to a Mr. Leanheart, who died; and she afterward married a Mr. Pierce, who lived four miles east of Lancaster, O. There she died and is buried near Emery chapel, on Sugar Loaf Grove circuit, of the Ohio Conference. Her children are all dead."[4]

---

[2] Letter of the Rev. L. F. Postle to the author.
[3] J. B. Finley, Western Methodism, p. 331.
[4] L. F. Postle's letter.

XXXIX.
WILLIAM ROSS.

HE veterans of Brooklyn Methodism unite with the "fathers" in other parts of the land in blessing the name of the REV. WILLIAM ROSS. Two different terms he was their pastor, and he died and was buried among them.

Mr. Ross was born in Tyringham, Mass., February 10, 1792. He was instructed in those branches of learning then commonly taught in the schools, but his desire and capacity for obtaining knowledge were far greater than his opportunities.

The story of his conversion at the age of sixteen years has been told as follows:

He was awakened under a sermon preached by the Rev. John Robertson. The conviction thus produced was lasting and pungent. When Mr. Robertson came to fill his next appointment in the neighborhood, a ball having been appointed at the same time, young Ross asked his mother to which he should go. Not receiving a direct answer, his inclination got the better of his judgment, now partially enlightened by the dawn of gospel truth, and he accordingly went to the ball. He had not been there long, however, before he was siezed with such agony of mind that he was constrained to leave this place of worldly mirth, and, retiring to a secluded spot, he poured out his soul "with strong crying and tears unto Him that was able to save;" and this he continued, with the use of other means of grace, from time to time, until he obtained deliverance from his sins.[1]

We united with the Methodists, instituted family prayer in his father's house, prayed and exhorted with great fervor and power, and, at the age of twenty years, was received into the ranks of the traveling ministry.

APPOINTMENTS: 1812, (New York Conf.,) Dunham cir., Vt. and Canada, with J. T. Addoms; 1813, Charlotte cir., Vt., with J. Byington; 1814, ordained deacon,—Plattsburgh cir., N. Y., with N. White; 1815, Grand Isle, Vt.; 1816, ordained elder,—Chatham and Hudson cir., N. Y., with Henry Eames; 1817, Pittsfield cir., Mass., with T. Benedict; 1818, **Brooklyn**; 1819,

---
[1] Methodist Magazine, 1825, p. 127.

REV. WILLIAM ROSS.

1820, Troy; 1821, New York city, with J. Soule, E. Hebard, M. Richardson, H. Bangs, and J. Summerfield ; 1822, ditto, with E. Washburn, M. Richardson, S. Martindale, H. Bangs, and J. Summerfield; **1823-1824, Brooklyn**.

His first appointment was in the region most affected by the excitement occasioned by the war with Great Britain, and he abandoned that part of the circuit belonging to Canada. How this came about is very pleasantly told by one of his friends, the Rev. Fitch Reed, as follows :

Preaching one evening in the town of Stanbridge, Canada, where was a large society of strict Calvinistic Baptists, he discoursed on the question of the possibility of falling from grace. In answer to the frequent assertion that although a Christian might fall away for a time, he could not die until he was restored, he replied : " In that case, sin is a sure preservative of life ; for if you would furnish me with an army of five thousand backslidden Christians, and they could be kept from praying, I could conquer the world, for no bullet could touch them as long as they could be kept from prayer."

This his Baptist hearers did not at all relish, and the next day some of them reported him to the commanding officer of the district, affirming that Mr. Ross had declared in a public congregation that with an army of five thousand men he could easily conquer all Canada. This, of course, was not to be allowed. Shortly afterward the officer waited on the preacher, and informed him that he must either take the oath of allegiance, or pass beyond the lines. He chose the latter.[2]

Mr. Ross wrote in his diary the following brief record of this experience :

The time has come which I have for some days expected ; that is, I am forbid to ride any more in the province, unless I take the oath. Accordingly, as soon as convenient, I shall take my departure for the States.

In addition to these embarrassments, he was in delicate health ; but his prudence, faithfulness, and zeal were crowned with success in winning souls to Christ.

While in his fourth appointment, at Grand Isle, Vt., in 1815, he preached a sermon which was the means of the conversion of Seymour Landon, and soon afterward received him into the church.[3] This young man became one of the most honored ministers in this region, and one of the successors of Wm. Ross in the Brooklyn charge.

While stationed in New York he was frequently invited to speak at the anniversaries of the Bible, missionary, and Sun-

---

[2] Quoted by Carroll, in " Case and His Contemporaries," vol. i, p. 278.
[3] Landon's " Fifty Years in the Itinerant Ministry."

day-school societies. An excellent address on education, which he delivered before the Wesleyan Seminary in New York, was published in full.[4]

Concerning his return to Brooklyn for a second pastoral term, his biographer says :

> He had to encounter a mass of prejudice, as formidable as it was unjustifiable, and which a less heroic mind would have shrunk from assailing ; but, being conscious of the purity of his motives and conduct, he entered upon the duties of his station with that Christian and ministerial firmness, meekness, and patience, "knowing no man after the flesh," which completely disarmed his enemies who had misjudged him, and finally won all hearts and established an empire in their affections which death only rendered the more firm and lasting.[5]

He was a member of the General Conference of 1824, and the author of "the luminous and able report of the Committee on Missions."[6] He returned from this conference to engage in protracted revival services in Brooklyn during the exhausting heat of summer, and his bodily health proved insufficient for the strain he put upon it. In the early part of the following winter he had engaged a substitute for a third service on the Sabbath : but the preacher failing to come, he stood in the pulpit with trembling and great weakness, and delivered his last public message. The sermon was attended with converting and awakening power, but the preacher went home to die. He had often spoken of premonitions of his departure. His last love-feast testimony in old Sands street church closed with these words :

> I *feel*, brethren, that my stay with you will be but short ; but, blessed be God ! when he calls, I am ready. • If I should die to-night you will take care of the body and God will take care of the soul, and all will be well.[7]

While wasting rapidly with consumption his faith triumphed over disease and the prospect of dissolution. Heaven seemed near, and he exclaimed, "Drop the curtain, and I am in glory ! "

To quote further from his biography :

> Mrs. Ross, sensible that he would not survive, said : "I hope you have given your friends and family up to God." "Ah, my dear," he replied, "you

---

[4] See Methodist Magazine, 1822, p. 139.
[5] Methodist Magazine.
[6] Sprague's Annals.
[7] Sketch in Methodist Magazine.

are the last that I shall give up." It was said to him: "I hope, whether you survive or not, that the Lord will be with you," He replied, with great firmness, " I have not a doubt of that."

As he lay dying he responded heartily to the prayers that were offered; and, while friends were raising him gently in his bed, he uttered those last words, " My work is done," and immediately fell asleep in Jesus, February 10, 1825, in the thirty-third year of his age. Dr. Bangs preached his funeral sermon. Soon after his death the widow and her children received a substantial token of affection from the people of Brooklyn.[8]

After slumbering about fifty years in the old Sands-street church-yard, his remains were removed to "Greenwood." The original head-stone was left to mark the spot where his weeping friends first laid him down to rest.

Many witnesses offer their eulogistic testimony concerning the talent and faithfulness of William Ross. They speak of him as " a gifted young preacher;"[9] " a natural orator, his sermons abounding in striking pictures and images;"[10] "a man of power in the pulpit, some of whose sermons would compare well with those of the most eloquent of his brethren."[11] One who knew him well from the time of his first appointment to Brooklyn says : " He was one of the most laborious and zealous ministers I ever knew ; he preached five sermons in one Sabbath not long before his death."[12] At the same time they tell us that he was "a man of great modesty and diffidence,"[13] and " very amiable, and greatly beloved."[14] As to his appearance, he is thus described :

> Mr. Ross was a man of engaging personal appearance. He was of moderate stature and well-formed, and of a benignant and agreeable countenance. His manners were at once genteel and dignified.

MISS HULDAH E. JONES was married to William Ross in 1816. It was the author's most delightful privilege to become acquainted with her as the widow of William Rushmore, of

---

[8] A gift of $1,200. See Bangs' Hist. M. E. Church.
[9] Rev. Myron Breckenridge in The Christian Advocate.
[10] Rev. Nathaniel Kellogg.
[11] Dr. Laban Clark, in Sprague's Annals.
[12] Judge Dikeman—conversation with the author.
[13] Conference Minutes, 1825, p. 476.
[14] Bangs' Hist. M. E. Church.

Brooklyn, N. Y. Bright, cheerful, intelligent—one of God's precious saints, she lived to a ripe old age, and was called home in the early part of 1884 to mingle with the pure spirits she had loved on earth.

To these parents four children were born, namely: *William Henry*, drowned in 1824, aged three years; *Lucy Almira*, married Stephen Crowell, Esq., of Brooklyn, died a few years since, a member of Summerfield Methodist Episcopal Church; *Mary E.*, married the Rev. Thomas H. Burch, died suddenly July 10, 1884, much lamented; *William G.*, died about 1860, in Brooklyn, N. Y.

REV. NATHAN BANGS, D. D.

XL.
NATHAN BANGS.

Two years as pastor and one year as presiding elder, the REV. NATHAN BANGS, D. D. was associated with Sands-street church. After Asbury died, no man in Methodism wielded a more potent and permanant influence than Dr. Bangs. He was born in Stratford, Conn., May 2, 1778. Removing to Stamford, Delaware Co., N. Y. when thirteen years of age, he grew up on a farm in that (then) frontier country, attended school when he could, and taught school at eighteen years of age. In 1799 he went to Canada, and, as teacher and surveyor, he resided in the Niagara region three years. There, through the faithful ministry of James Coleman, and later of Joseph Sawyer, he "was powerfully affected," and led to consecrate himself to Christ. This was in 1800, when he was twenty-one years of age. For opening his school with prayer he was persecuted and driven away; but this severe treatment only drove him to closer fellowship with Christian people, and a more decided renunciation of the world. Stevens says:

He conformed himself to the severest customs of the Methodists. He had prided himself on his fine personal appearance, and had dressed in the full fashion of the times, with ruffled shirt and long hair in a cue. He now ordered his laundress to take off his ruffles; his long hair shared the same fate, not, however, without the remonstrance of his pious sister, who deemed his rigor unnecessary, and admired his young but manly form with a sister's pride.[1]

He had been a Methodist about one year when he was licensed, first as an exhorter, then as a local preacher. He very soon disposed of his surveyor's instruments, bought a horse and saddle-bags, and "rode forth to sound the alarm in the wilderness." Thus we come to his

MINISTERIAL RECORD: 1801, supply on Niagara cir., Canada, with Joseph Sawyer and Seth Crowell; 1802, (New York Conf.,) Bay of Quinte and

---

[1] Hist. M. E. Church, vol. iii, p. 482.

Home Dist., with Jos. Sawyer and Peter Vannest ; 1803, ditto, with Jos. Sawyer and Thomas Madden ; 1804, ordained deacon and elder—River Le Trench ; 1805, Oswegatchie cir., with S. Keeler ; 1806, Quebec ; 1807, Niagara cir., with T. Whitehead and N. Holmes ; 1808, Delaware cir., N. Y., with Robert Dillon ; 1809, Albany cir., with I. B. Smith ; 1810, New York, with Eben Smith, J. Robertson, Jas. M. Smith, and P. P. Sandford ; 1811, ditto, with Wm. Phœbus, Laban Clark, Wm. Blagborne, Jas. M. Smith, and P. P. Sandford ; 1812, appointed to Montreal, Canada, but deterred from going on account of the war with Great Britain ; 1813–1816, presiding elder, Rhinebeck Dist. ; 1817, New York city, with D. Ostrander, S. Crowell, and S. Howe ; 1818, ditto, with Laban Clark, S. Crowell, S. Howe, and T. Thorp ; **1819, presiding elder New York Dist.** ; 1820–1823, senior book agent with Thos. Mason ; 1824–1827, ditto, with John Emory ; 1828–1831, editor of the Christian Advocate and Journal ; 1832–1835, editor of the Methodist Quarterly Review and books of the General Catalogue ; 1836–1840, resident corresponding secretary of the Missionary Society ; 1841–1842, president of the Wesleyan University ; 1843, New York city, Second-street ; 1844–1845, New York, Greene-street ; **1846, Brooklyn, Sands-street,** with J. C. Tackaberry, sup'y ; **1847, ditto,** with J. B. Merwin ; 1848–1851, (New York East Conf.,) presiding elder New York Dist. ; 1852–1862, superannuated.

He received fifty consecutive annual appointments, and yet, as pastor, presiding elder, book agent, editor, and superannuated preacher, he was a resident of New York for nearly half a century. His early efforts at preaching were attended with variable success, and he sometimes became quite discouraged ; but his zeal commended him to the conference, and, though absent, he was received on probation. Concerning the seven years of his heroic service in Canada his conference memorial says :

He braved the hardships of the itinerancy, traveling long circuits, sleeping on the floors of log-cabins or in the woods, fording streams, sometimes at the peril of his life, carrying with him food for himself and his horse, and eating his humble meals beneath the trees which sheltered him by night, preaching almost daily, facing wintry storms through unsettled tracts of land forty or fifty miles in extent, and suffering attacks of the epidemic diseases of the country, which sometimes brought him to the verge of the grave. He seldom received fifty dollars a year during these extreme labors and sufferings. He was sometimes assailed by mobs ; his life was imperiled by the conspiracy of persecutors to waylay him in the woods by night ; but he never faltered. He founded several new circuits and many societies. He preached from the westernmost settlement on the Thames River, opposite Detroit, to Quebec ; and, on leaving the country, records that he had proclaimed his message in every city, town, village, and nearly every settlement of Upper Canada.[2]

In one of his journeys he undertook to call on every family and pray with them ; and at only one house was he repulsed.

---
[2] Minutes of Conferences, 1863, p. 64.

Record of Ministers.

Dr. De Puy has thus described his return from the conference of 1804:

> He went from New York by way of Kingston, along the northern shore of Lake Ontario, and thence westward to the River Thames. He lodged for the night in a log-hut, the last in the settlement. The next day he traveled forty-five miles through an unbroken wilderness, without a dwelling of any kind, and being guided only by the marks on the trees. He arrived at sunset at a solitary log-hut, weary, hungry, and thirsty. The best possible fare was hospitably afforded him, namely, *some Indian pudding and milk for supper, and a bundle of straw for his bed. It was a real luxury.*[3]

How the young itinerant learned an important lesson by his experience is thus told by one of his friends and successors in Canada:

> While passing one day through a sparsely settled section of country, the weather being very cold and the newly-fallen snow quite deep, his mind became more than usually impressed with the value of souls, and his heart burned with desire to do all he could to save them. In the midst of his reflections he came opposite a dwelling that stood quite a distance from the road in the field. Instantly he was impressed to go to the house and talk and pray with the family. He could see no path through the deep snow, and he felt reluctant to wade that distance and expose himself to the cold, and perhaps, after all, accomplish no good. He resolved not to go. No sooner had he passed the house than the impression became doubly strong, and he was constrained to turn back. He fastened his horse to the fence, waded through the snow to the house, and *not a soul was there!* From that time he resolved never to confide in mere impressions.[4]

John Carroll says that Bangs had two sisters in Niagara circuit. One of them, who afterward married the Rev. Joseph Gatchel, could exhort, as a certain brother declared, "like a streak of red-hot lightning." Nathan Bangs was married while in Canada, in 1806, to Miss Mary Bolton, of Edwardsburgh, Ontario. On the Delaware circuit, in 1808, he received his brother, Heman Bangs, into the church.[5]

We have a striking illustration of his great zeal and endurance in his long ride on horseback from New York city to Detroit.[7] His standing and influence in the church may be inferred from his having been eleven times a member of General

---

[3] "One Hundred Facts," etc.
[4] Dr. Fitch Reed, in Northern Christian Advocate, Jan. 14, 1863.
[5] "Case and his Contemporaries," vol. i, p. 224.
[6] Stevens' Hist. M. E. Church, vol. iv, p. 256.   [7] Ibid., p. 352.

Conference, that is, of every one from 1808 to 1856, save that of 1848.

In eight years, by skillful management, he brought the Book Concern out of financial embarrassment, and became "the founder of that great institution in its present effective organization." His memorial says:

> At the time of his appointment to its agency it was sinking under debt; it was comprised in a small book-store on John-street; it had no premises of its own, no printing-press, no bindery, no newspaper; under his administration it was provided with them all.

During the same time he performed a very great amount of editorial work for The Christian Advocate and The Methodist Magazine. Of all his "vast and varied labors" the most honored and important were in connection with the missionary cause.

> He was one of the founders of our Missionary Society; he wrote its constitution, its first circular to the conferences, its first appeal to the churches, presided at its first public meeting, and during more than twenty years wrote all its annual reports. While its resident secretary, he devoted to it all his energies, conducting its correspondence, planning its mission fields, seeking missionaries for it, preaching for it in the churches, and representing it in the conferences. It will be monumental of his memory in all lands to which its beneficent agency may extend, and if no other public service could be attributed to him, this alone would render him a principal historic character of American Methodism, if not, indeed, of American Protestantism.[8]

No other man ever had a primary or initial agency in so many of the great interests of our denomination as Dr. Bangs. He founded Methodism in Quebec, and many other parts of Canada; assisted in the organization of the Delegated General Conference; is recognized as the founder of our periodical literature, the originator of our conference course of study, and "one of the founders of our present system of educational institutions." He was the first clerical editor of The Christian Advocate, and the first editor of the Quarterly Review. He is styled "the founder of the American literature of Methodism," and, as Dr. Stevens affirms, he "wrote more volumes in defense or illustration of his denomination than any other man, and became its recognized historian."[9] A writer for M'Clintock and Strong's Cyclopedia says: "Dr. Bangs was a man of vigor and

---

[8] Conference Minutes, 1863, p. 65.
[9] Hist. M. E. Church, vol. iii, p. 481. For complete list of his works, see Alumni Record, Wesleyan University, 1883.

force—a fighter, if need be, to the last." In his well-written conference memorial his character is thus described:

He was robust in intellect, in soul, and in body. In his prime he was a weighty preacher, a powerful debater, an energetic and decisive, if not an elegant, writer. He was a steadfast friend, a staunchly loyal Methodist, a charitable and truly catholic Christian.

He had his faults, and, like every thing else in his nature, they were strongly marked. But if he was abrupt sometimes in his replies, or emphatic in his rebukes, no man was ever more habitually ready to retract an undeserved severity, or acknowledge a mistake.

For about two years after his superannuation he went in and out among our metropolitan churches, venerated and beloved as a chief patriarch of Methodism. As he approached the grave his character seemed to mellow into the richest maturity of Christian experience. His favorite theme of conversation and preaching was "entire sanctification."[10]

He died in great peace, in New York city, May 3, 1862, aged eighty-four years and one day. His funeral took place in St. Paul's church, New York, and his remains were interred in "Greenwood." A valuable history of his life was written by one of our ablest men.[11]

MARY (BOLTON,) his widow, died in New York, May 23, 1864, in the seventy-eighth year of her age. She was a native of Canada, and was of French origin on her mother's side. She is buried by the side of her husband in Greenwood cemetery, and their graves are designated by a granite monument.

Seven of their eleven children are dead. The following list is copied from the Wesleyan University Alumni Record, 1883.

Nancy, b. 1807, d. 1807; Lemuel, b. 1809; Wm. M'Kendree, b. 1810, d. 1852; Nathan, b. 1813, d. 1856; Mary Eliza, b. 1815, d. 1857; Elijah Keeler, b. 1817; Grace Shotwell, b. 1819, d. 1847; Susan Cornelia, b. 1821, d. 1822; Joseph Henry, b. 1823, d. 1860; Rebecca, b. 1825; Francis N., b. 1828.

Lemuel Bangs is a well-known citizen of New York. *Wm. M'Kendree Bangs* was an honored minister of the Methodist Episcopal Church. *Elijah Keeler Bangs*, of Bangs & Co., New York, was graduated at the Wesleyan University. *Francis N. Bangs*, *LL.B.*, has been president of the New York Bar Association. *Mary Eliza* and *Rebecca Bangs* were members of Sands-street church.[12]

---

[10] Conference Minutes, 1863, p. 65.
[11] "Life and Times of Nathan Bangs," by Abel Stevens.
[12] See Book III of this volume.

XLI.

Alexander McCaine

ANDS-STREET church was the last pastoral charge to which the REV. ALEXANDER M'CAINE was appointed before entering the Protestant Methodist Church.

Mr. M'Caine was born in Tipperary County, Ireland, February 17, 1773. His father, Alexander M'Caine, a devout member of the Church of England, was "for many years employed as steward of the estates of the Earl of Farnham." The son was classically educated[2] in Dublin, with a view of his entering the ministry of the established church; but at the age of twenty-four he came to a decision which overthrew the hopes of his friends in that direction. Concerning this choice the Rev. Samuel E. Norton says:

In the year 1787 he united with the people called Methodists. It was then that he "formed the resolution that by the help of God he would strive to get to heaven and called upon God himself to witness the sincerity of his vow.[1] It was a most solemn act of an earnest, intelligent mind, * * * an act of very great moment, bred up as he had been, to come out in advocacy of a course so en

---

[1] Letter to the author by Mrs. Sarah A. Brett, daughter of the Rev. Alex M'Caine.

[2] Methodist Quarterly Review, 1830, p. 76.

tirely opposite not only to his own past experience, but to that of his entire family. He felt that it was to stand alone.[3]

Coming to this country in 1791, he joined the Methodist Episcopal Church,[4] and soon afterward began to preach.

MINISTERIAL RECORD: 1796, (traveling connection,) Broad River cir., N. C., with Rufus Wiley; 1798, Washington, D. C., with S. Cowles; 1799, ordained deacon—Norfolk, Va.; 1800, Huntingdon, Pa.; 1801, ordained elder—(Baltimore District,) Fell's Point, Md.; 1802, (Virginia Conf.,) Richmond, Va.; 1803, Greensville, Va., with Wm. Johnson; 1804, presiding elder, Salisbury Dist., Va.; 1805, (Baltimore Conf.,) Baltimore, Md., with G. Roberts and T. F. Sargent; 1806–1817, located; 1817, in Philadelphia, Union ch., with John Emory;[5] 1818, (Phila. Conf.,) Trenton, N. J.; **1819, 1820, Brooklyn, Sands-street**; 1821, located; 1829, president of the Va. Conf., Methodist Protestant Church; 18—, (S. C. Conf.;) 18—, (Alabama Conf.)

His daughter states that his location, in 1806, and again in 1821, was on account of physical infirmity, "which rendered him unfit for the *active duties* of a minister." She says:

In 1815 he was living in Cincinnati, where he had a book-store. There my mother died, which compelled him to bring his little children back to Baltimore. He taught school in that city in 1816.

In Philadelphia, in 1817, there was not a little friction between him and his colleague, John Emory, who afterward published an account of the troubles, in order to prove that Mr. M'Caine was captious and discontented.[6] During his pastoral term in Brooklyn, the colored members of the Sands-street church withdrew and formed an organization of their own. Concerning his ministry in Brooklyn his daughter writes to the author:

My recollection of Sands-street church is interwoven with my earliest impressions. The parsonage fronted on the street back of the church, the graveyard intervening. This was our play-ground while we stayed there. Even now I can see the form of my dear father as he entered the gate, while his voice echoed back, "I am the resurrection and the life," over the remains of a child that had died. The church was a white frame edifice, modest in its construction compared with houses of worship of the present day.

Writing of my father's inability to occupy the pulpit at times, calls to my

---

[3] Funeral Discourse, p. 6.
[4] Sprague's Annals.
[5] See Methodist Quarterly Review, 1830, p. 71. Compare Conference Minutes, which say James Ridgaway was appointed to that station.
[6] See Methodist Quarterly Review, 1830, pp. 71, 83.

mind a conversation I overheard when we lived in Brooklyn, to the effect that a stool be made high enough for him to *sit* while delivering his discourse. I am not certain, but I think he preached one or two sermons in this way. He went from Brooklyn back to Baltimore; could not preach, consequently had to teach school again.

Alexander M'Caine was ordained by Bishop Asbury; he was for years his confidential friend, and some time his traveling companion. Several letters addressed to him by Asbury have been preserved, and they show that the bishop loved him as "his own son." It is also said that the language addressed to him by Dr. Coke "could not have more clearly indicated the great respect in which he held the character and attainments of the person with whom he corresponded."[7] In the General Conference of 1804 he acted a prominent part; and he was secretary, but not a member, of the General Conference of 1820.[8] He appealed in 1820 from the decision of the Philadelphia Conference, condemning him for alleged maladministration, and the sentence was reversed by the General Conference.

After his location, in 1821, he became one of the foremost of the agitators who contended for lay representation in the chief councils of the church. From his own statement we gather that when the General Conference of 1824 decided adversely "to the complaints and demands of the laity and local ministers," he, "being fully convinced of the justice of those demands," was all the more inclined to investigate the subject and keep up the agitation. He writes:

New thoughts were waked up, and forebodings felt, which he [Mr. M'Caine] had never before experienced. He determined, therefore, to examine the grounds of such unheard-of claims. He was resolved, if possible, to ascertain the means by which traveling preachers had arrived at these pretensions, and find the authority which Mr. Wesley had given to justify them in saying he "recommended the episcopal mode of church government." [9]

In the course of these investigations he addressed letters of inquiry to several of the ministers then living, who had taken part in the organization of the church. The following is the letter addressed to Freeborn Garrettson, transcribed from the

---

[7] Mr. Norton's Sermon, p. 11.

[8] It was customary at that time to choose some person not a delegate as secretary. See Methodist Quarterly Rev., 1830, p. 99.

[9] Preface to "History and Mystery of the Episcopacy."

original, which is written in an exceedingly neat and beautiful hand. This letter was never before published:

BALTIMORE, *Sept. 25th,* 1826.

REVEREND SIR:

The General Conference of 1824 having in their circular denied the right of local ministers and lay members to be represented in that body; and having, moreover, intimated their determination to preserve to the traveling preachers forever the exclusive "authority to make rules and regulations for the church," it is, in my opinion, a matter of great importance, in view of the discussion growing out of this subject, to ascertain how the traveling preachers became possessed of this " authority." This inquiry carries me back to the origin of our church government, an account of which is published in the Minutes of Conferences for 1785, and in the book of Discipline, chapter 1, section 1. In this account I find it asserted that the conference, "following the counsel of Mr. John Wesley, who recommended the episcopal mode of church government, thought it best to become an episcopal church." This statement I have compared with the document on which it is professedly founded, (see Minutes of Conferences for 1785,) and cannot perceive in it any "counsel" or "recommendation" to adopt the episcopal mode of church government in "preference to any other." And as I have not been able to perceive, either in the documents alluded to, or in any part of Mr. Wesley's writings, any recommendation to adopt the aforesaid form of government, it has occurred to me, that as you are among the oldest preachers now living, and as you are supposed to have a knowledge of our church affairs at that early day, you may be able to give some information upon this subject. Permit me, then, to ask you,

1. If you have seen any document or letter in which Mr. Wesley *explicitly* "*recommended*" to the Methodist societies in these United States the episcopal form of government? If you have seen such a document, can a copy of it be procured?

2. Have you read Mr. Wesley's original manuscript letter, dated September 10th, 1784, an extract of which is given as the sole authority for the adoption of our present form of church government?

3. Have you ever seen any letter or paper in which Mr. Wesley gave any "counsel" or advice to Dr. Coke, Mr. Asbury, or any other person to ordain a third order of ministers in our church, meaning by that phrase, an order of bishops distinct from and superior to an order of presbyters? If so, can you tell if that paper can be produced?

4. Are you able to inform me in what year Mr. Wesley's name was left out of the Minutes? At what conference was the vote taken? By whom was it done? And for what reason?

That you may have a full understanding of the importance which I attach to this investigation, it may be proper to state to you that I have prepared an essay for the press, which, in my opinion, will have some bearing upon the *episcopal office* in our church. And, as my sole object is to obtain information, I would be extremely thankful to you if you could give me such information as would serve to correct the conclusions (if they be erroneous) to which I have been conducted by the perusal of those documents to which I have had access. And, before I close, it may not be amiss to remark, that if the liberty I have taken in making these inquiries be considered by you an improper one, I hope you will ascribe it to a good motive ; for truly it is my wish to obtain all possible information before I give my essay to the public.

With sentiments of respect I remain yours in the Gospel,

REVD. FREEBORN GARRETTSON.   ALEXANDER M'CAINE.

P. S.—Favor me with an answer as soon as convenient.

The "essay" to which he refers was published in 1827,[10] in pamphlet form, and was entitled "The History and Mystery of the Methodist Episcopacy." Mr. Garrettson's reply to the last question in the letter was quoted by Mr. M'Caine in the Appendix, as favoring the views of the author of the pamphlet, as set forth, also, in his letter to Mr. Garrettson, and blame was attached to him for withholding from the public the other portions of Garrettson's reply, which could not be so construed.[11] This "essay," which all admitted was ably written, stoutly denied the right of Coke and Asbury to the title of "bishop," and reflected somewhat severely upon the motives and action of those men. The work occasioned "no small stir" in the church, and called forth that same year a vigorous reply by the Rev. John Emory, entitled "A Defense of our Fathers." M'Caine issued a second pamphlet in 1829, entitled "A Defense of the Truth," etc. In the latter treatise he pronounced the name "Methodist Episcopal Church" a "boasted title," and the term "bishop" a "pompous appellation;" and, professing a "reverence unfeigned and profound" for Mr. Asbury, be nevertheless affirmed that the bishop's "ruling passion" was the "love of power," and that "he gave proof that he was willing to sacrifice every thing for the title of bishop."[12] In 1830 Emory and Bangs reviewed the whole matter in three numbers of the Methodist Quarterly Review.

The controversy became very bitter, and it was deemed proper to expel from the Methodist Episcopal Church a considerable number of the leaders in the disturbance. Emory mentions M'Caine's "expulsion," and his election to the presidency of the Associated Methodist Reformers, in Virginia, previous to 1830.[13] He was identified with the Methodist Protestant Church from its origin.

---

[10] Not 1829, as stated in Sprague's Annals, and M'Clintock and Strong.

[11] See Methodist Quarterly Review, 1830, pp. 340, 341.

[12] See "Defense of the Truth," pp. 91, 92, 96.

[13] Methodist Quarterly Review, 1830, pp. 80, 82.

Mr. M'Caine was married to Mrs. Kituel Hall, of Baltimore, Md., December 23, 1805. After her death he was again united in marriage to Miss Frances Griffith, of Baltimore, September 1, 1816.[14]

While in the South he wrote and published "Letters on Methodist Episcopacy," and "Slavery Defended from Scripture;" also, "Twelve Letters on the Catholic Issue." The papers concerning Catholicism were written a short time before his death, and published in the Montgomery (Ala.) Advertiser. They furnished additional proof of his remarkable ability as a writer.

He left a considerable amount of manuscript, but would not consent to the publication of any of it after his death. He retired for some time to Aiken, S. C., and his last days were spent at the residence of his daughter, Mrs. J. M. Brett, in Augusta, Ga., where he closed his mortal life on the first day of June, 1856, aged eighty-four years. His daughter writes:

His death was the calmest moment of existence, full of hope of a blessed immortality.[15]

Another eye-witness thus describes the closing scene:

Many a time had he prayed that God would grant him to retain his mental faculties to the close of life. He was heard in an eminent degree. The mind and heart of the man lived on when the great frame was dead; when hardly a vibration of life's chord could be felt, the light of his mind shone out like the dying glories of a splendid sun. * * * I talked with him day after day, and hourly during the day. He always accompanied me in my petitions,

---

[14] This lady is described as a woman of "brilliant" mind, but from certain statements, which the author has seen and heard, it is suspected that the union did not prove permanently happy, and was finally dissolved. Mr. M'Caine had trouble with one Rev. Will J. Walker, at Lynchburgh, Va., in 1829, who afterward indirectly accused him in the public prints of not only separating himself from his "ancient friends" in the church, but from "*very dear* relations."—*The Christian Advocate*, September 8, 1841. On the authority of Judge Dikeman this refers to a divorce granted to her by the courts. The Rev. Mr. Norton, after ascribing to Alexander M'Caine far greater depth and steadfastness of friendly affection than has generally been accorded to him, says: "It may have been observed that in these remarks I have been speaking of the *man* as to his general relationships to society. I have not alluded to his domestic life. My acquaintance does not extend farther than to a knowledge of Mr. M'Caine since his children have grown up and settled in life. Into that period of his life it does not now concern us to inquire. It may be remarked however, that at every period his habits of study and consequent seclusion must necessarily have modified the exercise of his moral qualities in a very considerable degree.—*Memorial Discourse*, p. 10.

[15] Letter of Mrs. Brett to the author.

and responded at the close with a hearty amen. At such times his heart seemed greatly to be encouraged. The light from above shined upon his mind, and he would speak very encouragingly to us all about his expected change, and then quietly clasp his hands upon his breast and close his eyes as if waiting for that change. * * * It came at last—calmly, peacefully. Not the desperate surging of the mad billows, but the gentle laving of the retiring tide. All is still, save the wailings of bereaved ones, burdening the night air. The race is run ; the fight ended. The soul is at rest.[16]

The funeral services were held in the "St. James Methodist Episcopal Church," in Augusta, on the 3d of June, and a sermon was preached by the Rev. Samuel E. Norton, who chose for his text the words of Paul, "I have finished my course, I have kept the faith." The preacher said :

The subject of this discourse was a man of large proportions intellectually and physically. His mind had been well trained by severe and critical study, and developed itself in a remarkable degree in the varied experiences of a long life. His powers of analysis were exceedingly acute, and served him eminently as a writer and controversialist. His judgment was most discriminating. It may be safely affirmed that he took nothing upon trust. He must go down to the root of the matter. He was not a retailer of other men's sayings. He wished to be certain that what he declared was so ; and he never remained satisfied until he could arrive at a conclusion based upon reason and common sense. * * * With him, language had no beauty, thought no charm, earnestness awakened no answering feeling, unless the author based his teachings, sustained his doctrines upon the immutable foundation of truth. * * * He was a most attentive listener to the sermons and speeches which he happened at any time to hear. Habitually closing his eyes and folding his hands, he sat patiently listening to the remarks that fell upon his ear, rarely looking up, unless something marked for strength, or peculiar for originality, or dangerous because erroneous, fell from the lips of the speaker.

He was a man of most methodical habit. * * * With him there was emphatically "a place for every thing, and every thing in its place." Nothing written—no correspondence was destroyed ; his letters and manuscripts, amounting to hundreds, dating back to the years of Asbury, Coke, and others, have been most carefully numbered and arranged for reference. * * *

His well-trained mind developed itself in the active duties of ministerial life. It was in that sphere he shone pre-eminent. He was emphatically a preacher. Christ was his subject. Calvary was ever before him. In his judgment a sermon without Christ was nothing worth. There was with him no time for trifling. * * *

In person he was one of the most remarkable men whom the speaker has ever beheld. Six feet four inches in height, and bulk in proportion, with no surplus ; hair white and flowing ; forehead high, brow prominent, from beneath which shot forth the glances of a sleepless mind ; a nose large, prom-

---

[16] Rev. S. E. Norton's Discourse, pp. 14, 15.

inent, and singularly expressive; all these characteristics combined to make him a man singularly venerable and influential, both as to mind and person. * * * A man of such large intellectuality and such varied experience in human affairs would be quite likely to act out the suggestions of his own mind oftener than to follow in a path marked out by others. Few men were less disposed to be led than was the subject of this discourse. Mr. M'Caine acted from conviction; hence he was independent in action. In this respect I think he has been greatly misunderstood. He has sometimes been regarded as adhering to his views with a tenacity amounting to stubbornness. He has perhaps, been regarded as somewhat arbitrary. Mr. M'Caine was as largely characterized by the exercise of indomitable will, as perhaps any man who has lived; but he was certainly not a stubborn nor an arbitrary man. Following out the convictions of his own independent mind, he may have often acted in opposition to the views of others; but it does not follow that it would have been wiser or more amiable to have acted differently. * * *

Mr. M'Caine's habits of study modified his intercourse with others. * * * His inflexibility in acting out the convictions of his own mind—his strong will, gave to his manners and language a sternness that sometimes seemed to amount to harshness. The speaker is entirely aware that his writings, particularly, have been thought open to this objection. * * * His intellectuality isolated him. Men of intense thought are not always good companions. Lions go not in herds. The eagle soars alone. Mr. M'Caine lived within as much as any man I ever knew. This was particularly the case for some years preceding his decease. Always inclined to study and reflection, he grew more disposed to the seclusion of his own heart and home, as his contemporaries passed from his companionship. It was at times difficult to draw him out of his silence and seclusion. * * * But when he could be removed from the influence of unfavorable circumstances—when he was among his brethren—when the elements of congeniality were around him—certainly no man could be more agreeable in manners, more entertaining in conversation.

We have given more space to the characterization of Mr. M'Caine than almost any other of the pastors of Sands-street church, partly because of the intrinsic interest and importance of the subject, and partly because very little can be learned concerning his personal history from the historical and biographical literature of our Church.

The grave of Mr. M'Caine, in the cemetery in Augusta, Ga., is inclosed with an iron railing, and marked by a plain, white marble head-stone, appropriately inscribed.

Concerning his two wives only a few facts are known to the author. The maiden name of the first wife was KITUEL MEZICK. As already observed, she was a widow when he married her.

Ten years afterward, May 17, 1815, she died, aged forty-one years, and was buried in Cincinnati, Ohio.

Of the second wife, FRANCES GRIFFITH, we only know this additional fact, that she died without children.

Five children were born to Alexander M'Caine by the first marriage.[17] Two of these died in infancy. The eldest son, *Alexander Mezick*, was a physician of fine ability, and died, in his thirty-third year, at Aiken, S. C., in the year 1844. The second son, *Baptist Joshua*, resides in Coleta, Clay county, Ala. The only daughter, *Sarah Anne*, was married to James M. Brett, of Barnwell District, S. C., in 1833. She is now a widow, and resides in Meridian, Miss.

---

[17] For most of his information concerning the family the author is indebted to James Brett, Esq., of Germantown, Tenn., and Miss Mary M. Brett, of Meridian, Miss., grandchildren of Mr. M'Caine.

REV. PETER P. SANDFORD, D. D.

XLII.
PETER P. SANDFORD.

ODI is the name of a town on the eastern shore of the Passaic River, in the state of New Jersey. There the Rev. PETER P. SANDFORD, D. D. was born, February 28, 1781. His ancestors were residents of the town, and were descended from an officer in the army of Great Britain, who came from the island of Barbadoes, and made himself a home with a few others in that hitherto uninhabited region. The Sandfords were a highly honorable and reputable people, possessing all the advantages resulting from easy financial circumstances and a good social position. To one branch of this family belonged Joseph Sandford, a local preacher, father-in-law of the Rev. Stephen Martindale. He resided in Belleville, and his generous hospitality to the early bishops and other ministers is widely known.

Peter P. Sandford's second initial does not stand for a name, but the letter "P." was adopted for his father's immediate family, to distinguish his children from other Sandfords bearing the same Christian names.

The memoir adopted by the New York Conference says:

At a very early age Brother Sandford gave evidence of being under strong moral and religious influence. * * * While as yet he was a child of but ten years, he was in the habit of gathering the children of his neighborhood into a chapel which he had prepared for the purpose, and read to them the liturgy of the Episcopal Church, and then preached to them as best he could.[1]

At seventeen years of age he gave his heart to the Savior, and obtained a clear and abiding witness of justification by faith. The conviction of a divine call to preach the gospel, which had been with him from his early childhood, now "revived with increased power;" some eight or nine years elapsed, however, after his conversion, before he began his itinerant career. He was spared to preach Jesus to men for about fifty years, as shown by the following

---
[1] Minutes of Conferences, 1857, pp. 320, 321.

MINISTERIAL RECORD: 1807, (Phila. Conf.) Trenton cir., N. J., with Wm. M'Lenahan; 1808, ditto, with Wm. Fox; 1806, ordained deacon, Asbury cir., with Thos. Drummond; 1810, (New York Conf.,) New York city, with N. Bangs, E. Smith, J. Robertson, and Jas. M. Smith; 1811, ordained elder—ditto, with N. Bangs, Wm. Phœbus, L. Clark, Wm. Blagborne, and James M. Smith; 1812, Troy; 1813, Newburgh cir., with Bela Smith; 1814, Albany; 1815-1818, presiding elder, Hudson River Dist.; 1819, Newburgh cir., with Josiah Bowen; **1820-1823, presiding elder, New York Dist.;** 1824, New York city, with P. Rice, T. Mason, J. B. Stratton, S. Bushnell, and E. Brown; 1825, ditto, with H. Stead, Wm. Jewett, J. Young, D. De Vinne, and H. Chase; 1826, New Rochelle cir., with P. Rice and Jno. M. Smith: 1827, ditto, with Josiah Bowen and Jno. M. Smith; 1828-1831, presiding elder, Rhinebeck Dist.; 1832, New York, west cir., with S. Landon, J. Bowen, G. Coles, and C. Prindle; 1823, ditto, with F. Reed, J. Bowen, J. C. Green, and C. W. Carpenter; 1834, White Plains cir., with Z. Davenport; 1835, White Plains and Greensburgh cir., with S. C. Davis; 1836-1837, Middletown; 1838-1839, presiding elder, Poughkeepsie Dist.; 1840, Poughkeepsie—elected book agent that year; 1841-1843, assistant book agent with George Lane; 1844-1847, presiding elder, New York Dist.; 1848-1849, Kingston; 1850-1851, Tarrytown; 1852, White Plains; 1853, Yonkers; 1854-1856, sup'd.

From the beginning to the end of his ministry he devoted himself unfalteringly to the great work to which God had called him.

In his memoir he is characterized as "a thorough divine, an able preacher, a judicious administrator of discipline, an eminent, honest Christian man." One who knew him well describes him in very similar terms, as "a man of great ability and the very soul of honor."[2] Another says of his sermons, "They were deep—he dug for hid treasure."[3] It was his apostolic preaching in Troy, N. Y., in 1816, which led Noah Levings, when but a lad, into the gospel light.[4]

His acknowledged pre-eminence is indicated by the fact that he was elected from among many worthy and strong men in the New York Conference as a delegate to every General Conference from 1816 to 1852. His son, Joseph Sandford, says that in the great discussion in 1844 he favored more extreme measures in the case of Bishop Andrew, and he afterward intimated that for that reason he should not be a candidate for re-election in 1848; but Dr. Bond, of the Christian Advocate and Journal, affirmed that that was a good reason why he should be a candidate.

---

[2] J. P. in The Methodist.
[3] Rev. Nathaniel Kellogg to the author.
[4] Sketch of Noah Levings in Sprague's Annals.

His ability as an author was considerable. He wrote an excellent book, entitled "Helps to Faith," 12mo, published by Harpers; also, "Wesley's Missionaries to America," published by the Methodist Book Concern. He received the degree of D.D. from the University of the City of New York in the year 1848. Coming from that source, it was deemed a signal honor.

He died of ossification of the heart, sitting in his chair, on the 14th of January, 1857, having almost completed the seventy-sixth year of his age. To the last moment he was "calm, triumphant, and assured of everlasting glory." In the face of death he exclaimed, "I have prayed for holy triumph, and I have it." His last words were, "Be ye therefore perfect, even as your Father which is in heaven is perfect." His grave is marked by a head-stone in the cemetery in Tarrytown, N. Y.

His first wife, ANN (WYLLEY) SANDFORD, "one of the excellent of the earth," died suddenly, after a brief illness, in Belleville, N. J., May 12, 1832, aged fifty years. She was a native of New York city, and was reared under the influence of the Episcopal Church. She is buried in Belleville, and a church is built over her grave.

BETSEY ANN, his second wife, survived him a little more than twelve years. She wrote concerning her early experience:

When about twelve years of age I was melted into tears under a sermon of Rev. Joseph Crawford, and the impressions which it made were not shaken off.

Five years later she found rest in Christ; and she obtained the blessing of entire sanctification about 1845, and her life ever after was a witness of its reality and power. She was a person of strange peculiarities, and "at times her mind seemed to be considerably affected." Her life was devoted to the church, and she bequeathed a part of her possessions to the missionary cause, and a part to the worn-out preachers of the New York Conference. On the 12th of May, 1869, at the age of sixty-nine years, she fell asleep in Jesus, in Poughkeepsie, N. Y., and she lies buried beside her husband.[8]

Peter P. Sandford was the father of thirteen children by the first marriage, seven by the second, making twenty in all. Four

---

[8] C. S. B., in The Christian Advocate.

of the thirteen—*Catharine, William, Joseph,* and *Wesley*—survived their mother. Only one of them—*Joseph*—is now living, (1884.) He has for many years been connected with the printing department of the Methodist Book Concern in New York, having assisted in the printing of the first copy of The Christian Advocate, in 1826. Most of the latter group of children reside in the vicinity of Tarrytown, N. Y. One daughter, *Mrs. D Miller*, of White Plains, died in 1874. Another, *Sarah M.*, wife of B. S. Horton, of Mount Pleasant, N. Y., died on the 1st day of June, 1881.[9]

---

[9] The Christian Advocate.

Henry Chase

REV. HENRY CHASE, M. A.

XLIII.
HENRY CHASE.

ALEXANDER M'CAINE'S unexpired term as pastor in Brooklyn in the year 1820, was acceptably filled by the REV. HENRY CHASE, A. M.

He was born in Hoosic, Rensselaer Co., N. Y., Sept. 10, 1790—the third child and eldest son of Daniel and Elizabeth Chase. His parents were reared as members of the society of Friends, and although they ultimately joined the Methodist Episcopal Church, they spoke the "plain language" through life.

Henry spent his boyhood on his father's farm, and attended the district school; but he longed for better opportunities, and with tears entreated his father to send him to an academy. A large family and limited means seemed to his father sufficient reason for denying his request. Yet the boy could not be turned aside from his purpose, and by dint of his own persevering effort, he obtained a superior classical, scientific and theological education.

At the age of eighteen he became a member of the Methodist Episcopal Church. We here transcribe his

MINISTERIAL RECORD;[1] 1809, supply, Pownal cir., Vt., with James M. Smith; 1810, Pittsfield cir., Mass., a supply with Seth Crowell,; 1811, in Ohio; 1812–1817, teaching, farming and preaching, mostly in his native town; 1818–1819, teaching in Troy, N. Y., and preaching statedly on the Sabbath; **1820**, teacher in Wesleyan Seminary, New York,—pastor in **Brooklyn** from Feb'y 21 till conference;[2] 1821–1822, teacher, Wesleyan Seminary, and preacher, Mariners' Church, assistant to John Truair; 1823–1824, wholly employed in the seamen's cause; 1824, (from November,) a supply in New York city, with P. P. Sandford, P. Rice, T. Mason, J. B. Stratton, S. Bushnell and E. Brown; 1825, (New York Conf.,) an elder—remaining in New York with P. P. Sandford, H. Stead, Wm. Jewett, J. Youngs and D. DeVinne; 1826–1847, New York, Mariners' Church, Roosevelt-st.; 1848–1851, (New York East Conf.,) ditto; 1852, a local preacher, retaining his place as pastor of Mariners' Church.

---

[1] His son, Prof. Chase, in Sprague's Annals gives the names of his appointments previous to his ministry in Brooklyn.

[2] Sands-street church records.

Such a record of nearly thirty years devoted to the work of a minister of Jesus Christ among the sailors, renders him worthy to take rank with Father Taylor, of Boston, among the noblest and best of philanthropists. In Sprague's Annals is the following, written by an intimate friend :

No sailor belonging to the port, or who had worshiped at the Mariners' Church, in Roosevelt-street, would ever pass him in the street without doffing his hat, no matter whether drunk or sober. And his success in founding and sustaining the Mariners' Temperance Society, for the reformation of intemperate sailors, may be regarded as among the greatest blessings with which God was pleased to crown his labors.

A number of sailors, having just landed after a long voyage, started Sunday morning for their own church ; but several of them were induced by some land-shark to drink on the way, and by the time they reached the church had become somewhat intoxicated. The spokesman inquired at the door whether the captain of the ship was on the quarter-deck—his way of asking if their own preacher, Mr. Chase, was in the pulpit ; and, on receiving an affirmative answer, they entered in a body. * * * A stranger being introduced as the preacher, one of these sailors said, in an audible tone, that as the preacher was not the captain of the ship he would pay him as far as he had gone, and, holding up a half dollar to the sexton, he made for the door, leaving the money for the usual collection at the close of the service. This was followed by an apology when the man became sober, and by his becoming a pledged member of the temperance society.[4]

This same friend describes him as a Christian, remarkable for his humility, rarely speaking of his personal experience; a minister, who won the affection and respect of Christian people of different denominations ; a preacher, whose sermons were well prepared but extemporaneously delivered, and whose prayers were offered with a pathos which often brought floods of tears to the eyes of the hardened sailors as they listened.

In society he was exceedingly courteous and affable, and much sought for in marrying people. It is stated by his son, Prof. Daniel H. Chase, that he united in holy matrimony *ten thousand couples*. A younger son, Sidera Chase, remarked to the author that when a youth he prepared an index to his father's large and well-kept marriage record book, and found that he had undertaken no inconsiderable task. The income from so many marriages, added to his moderate salary, enabled Mr. Chase to give to each of his large family of children an excellent education. His own scholarly attainments were well known,

---

[4] Rev. David Meredith Reese, M.D.

and the Wesleyan University conferred upon him the degree of A.M., in the year 1835. His appearance and bearing are thus described by the writer already quoted:

Mr. Chase was below the medium stature, strongly built, but not corpulent, and exhibiting an activity in his bodily movements corresponding to his quick perceptions and his ready utterance. His countenance was expressive of great benignity, and yet cheerfulness, which, instead of detracting from his solemnity, rather adorned it. He was regarded as a fine-looking man.

In answer to inquiries as to why he located and why the Mariners' Church dropped out of the list of Methodist appointments, it is stated that as the church was not sustained by Methodists alone, it seemed desirable to drop the denominational character it had assumed as a conference appointment.

Mr. Chase died of paralysis, July 8, 1853, in the sixty-third year of his age. During his fatal illness he was unable to speak, hence he left no dying testimony. His funeral sermon was preached by the Rev. J. B. Wakeley, and his body lay in the Mariners' Church after the funeral until the next day, and hosts of sailors, during the day and night, passed through the church and looked for the last time upon the face of their friend. Thence his remains were carried to the Indian Hill cemetery, in Middletown, Conn., where a monument has been erected to his memory.

RACHEL PINE, of Swansea, Mass., was married to Henry Chase, September 10, 1809, the day he was nineteen years of age. She died in New York, June 7, 1842, aged fifty-five years. From New York, where she was first buried, her remains were taken to Middletown, and buried by the side of her husband.

Children of Henry and Rachel Chase: *Arlina*, married, deceased; *Elizabeth*, died in mature life, leaving a family; *Daniel H., LL.D.*, first on the list of graduates of Wesleyan University, a successful educator; *George W.*, died in youth; *Sidera*, a graduate of Wesleyan University, formerly at the head of important educational institutions, now on the editorial staff of the *New York Tribune*; *Richard A.*, died, leaving a family; *Cornelia; Jane E.; Rachel*, wife of the Rev. N. J. Burton, D.D.; *Susan W.*, died in infancy. The daughters as well as the sons of Henry Chase enjoyed the best educational advantages of their time; two of them attended Rutgers' Female Seminary in New York.

XLIV.

LABAN CLARK.

HE REV. LABAN CLARK, D. D. was personally associated with the Sands-street Church as presiding elder of the New York District, from 1824 to 1827, and of the Long Island District from 1848, to 1851.

He was born in Haverhill, N. H., July 9, 1778, and during his infancy the family moved to Bradford, Vt. He was trained in the belief of his parents, who were Congregationalists, and strictly Calvanistic in their creed. But the lad was inclined to think independently, and often questioned certain points of the prevalent theology. The Wesleyan books brought into the neighborhood from England by a Mrs. Beckett, he carefully read, and his mind and heart were open to the teachings of the Methodist itinerants, when at length they made their way into that part of the state. John Langdon, of Vershire, who seems to have been the only Methodist except the Becketts, in all that region, petitioned the New York Conference for a preacher, and Nicholas Snethen in 1796,[1] after him Ralph Williston, and a year later, Joseph Crawford and Elijah Chichester were sent to that field, then comparatively a remote wilderness country. Clark heard Williston preach in a barn in Vershire. He writes:

> The day was pleasant, and seats were prepared in and out of the barn. I saw where they had prepared for the preacher to stand, and I took my position where I might see and hear to the best advantage. Under the first prayer an arrow seemed directed singly to my heart, and I felt that I was the very person he was praying for, and that I was the sinner who needed prayers. I there and then resolved that I would try to be a better man. I saw people, men and women. in the barn and out of it, on their knees in time of prayer, and I said to myself, This is the old Bible way, * * * and I went home with a fixed determination to live a new life. But how and where to begin I knew not. I was in perfect darkness.[2]

---

[1] Joshua Hall was appointed to the state of Vermont in 1794, but did not go. See Stevens' Hist. M. E. Church, vol. iii, p. 235.

[2] Quoted in an editorial article in the Christian Advocate.

REV. LABAN CLARK, D. D.

In our sketch of Joseph Crawford the overwhelming impressions produced upon Clark's mind by the public and private appeals of that earnest evangelist have been described. It was while Crawford held him by the hand, urging him to accept Christ by faith, and imploring God to bless him. that the burden of sin was lifted from his conscience and he enjoyed " a perfect calmness " which he could hardly understand. This was followed a few weeks later by an undoubted witness of his acceptance. On this occasion a class was formed, and he became one of the original members. He was then twenty-one years of age.

It has always been the glory of Methodism that it sets all its converts to work ; so young Laban Clark was soon called out to speak in public, and sometimes to expound and defend the doctrines taught by Wesley and Fletcher, with whose strong, logical discourses he was happily familiar. He was licensed to exhort in the year 1800. John Langdon, Rosebrook Crawford, and Martin Ruter were associates of Clark as exhorters or local preachers. By their pioneer labors the way was prepared for the itinerants, and the famous old Landaff circuit was formed. They were not dismayed by threats or violence, and even when Rosebrook Crawford was " ducked " in the river, at Lancaster, amid the jeers and shouts of the mob, they counted it all joy to be counted worthy to suffer in so good a cause.

Young Ruter, who afterward became a church historian and a missionary preacher, went with Clark to a quarterly meeting, and heard John Broadhead, the presiding elder, preach " with an effect that swept down the congregation so that scores of them lay as dead men." That was the starting-point in Ruter's itinerant career, and soon afterward Clark was also in the field. Sixty-eight years of ministerial life are embraced in the following

ITINERANT RECORD: 1800, supply under the presiding elder, place not known ; 1801, (New York Conf.,) Fletcher cir., Vt. and Canada, with Jas. Coleman ; 1802, Plattsburgh cir., N. Y., with D. Brumly ; 1803, ordained deacon—missionary at St. Johns and Sorreille, Canada, with E. Chichester ; 1804, Adams, Mass.; 1805, ordained elder—Lebanon cir., N. Y., with Geo. Powers ; 1806, Whitingham, Vt.: 1807, Buckland, Mass.; 1808, Granville cir., with J. Beeman ; 1809-1810, Litchfield cir., Conn., with Reuben Harris ; 1811, New York, with N. Bangs, Jas. M. Smith, and P. P. Sandford ; 1812, ditto, with Joseph Crawford, Wm. Phœbus, and Phinehas Cook ; 1813-1814, Troy ; 1815, Pittstown ; 1816-1817, Schenectady ; 1818,

New York, with N. Bangs, S. Crowell, S. Howe, and Thos. Thorp; 1819, ditto, with A. Hunt, S. Merwin, B. Hibbard, T. Spicer, and N. Morris ; 1820, Redding cir., Conn., with P. Cook; 1821, ditto, with A. Hunt ; 1822, Stratford cir., Conn., with E. Barnett ; 1823, ditto, with J. Nixon ; **1824-1827, presiding elder, New York Dist.**; 1828-1831, New Haven Dist.; 1832, agent, Wesleyan University ; 1833, New York, east cir., with D. Ostrander, B. Griffen, P. Chamberlin, and P. R. Brown ; 1834, ditto, with S. Cochran, J. Youngs, N. Bigelow, and J. Law ; 1835, sup'y, without appointment by his request ; 1836, sup'y, Haddam, Conn.—agent for Wesleyan University ; 1837-1840, presiding elder, Hartford Dist.; 1841, Wethersfield, Conn.; 1842, sup'y, Middletown, with A. M. Osbon ; 1843, Stepney and Weston ; 1844-1847, presiding elder, New Haven Dist.; **1848-1851, presiding elder, Long Island Dist.**; 1852-1868, sup'd, residing in Middletown, Conn.

He rode three hundred and forty miles to attend the conference in New York city and have his name enrolled among the itinerants in 1801. Of his experience on the Fletcher circuit, he says :

After traveling nine months I received three dollars only, and those to repair my boots. My spending money was exhausted, and I had borrowed five dollars of Mr. Coleman. At the quarterly conference the question came up how the money was to be divided. I told them that Mr. Draper, who had been sent to the east after the conference, had a family, and he must have his share. The elder then asked me for my traveling expenses. I told him that I had none, for I had just entered upon the regular work. He smiled, and told the steward to give me one dollar for shoeing my horse, and for quarterage money paid me seven dollars, so that I had enough to pay what I had borrowed, and a little to spare.[3]

He acted a prominent part in the eight different General Conferences of which he was a member—all from 1808 to 1836, except that of 1820. One of the many marked results of his ministry was the conversion of Noah Levings, in Troy, N. Y., while he was stationed there, in 1813. While pastor in New York, in 1819, he first suggested and helped to organize one of the noblest institutions known among men, the Missionary Society of the Methodist Episcopal Church. As presiding elder of the New Haven District, in 1829, his quick eye caught sight of the opportunity to obtain property for a Methodist institution of learning; and, with a faith that seemed inspired, he offered to purchase it, or find the men who, with himself, would purchase it for that purpose, and then brought the matter before the New York Conference. Laban Clark is recognized, therefore, as the father of the Wesleyan University, and he was

---

[3] Quoted by The Christian Advocate.

Record of Ministers.

president of the board of trustees from its inception, in 1831, to his death, in 1868. For this institution he very naturally cherished a paternal fondness; and, according to his desire, he lived and died and was buried almost beneath its shadow.

In the year 1851 he preached before the New York Conference a semi-centennial discourse, which was published. He was made a D.D. by the Wesleyan University in 1853. He finished his course, November 28, 1868, in the ninety-first year of his age. His life was longer than that of any other Sands-street pastor or presiding elder; he outranked, in this respect, Aaron Hunt, who also lived to be a little past ninety years of age. The cemetery, in the rear of the Wesleyan University, contains a brown stone monument, appropriately inscribed, which marks the place where the body of Laban Clark awaits the resurrection summons. His conference memorial says:

> He was a leader in the old New York Conference, and died the patriarch of the New York East Conference. As a preacher, he was sound, instructive, and, in his prime, frequently powerful.[4]

Dr. Stevens also describes him "as an able preacher, notwithstanding a marked vocal defect."[5] The author heard him address the conference when he was too far advanced in years to impress the preachers, except with a veneration for his age. He appeared at that time to be a man of medium stature and quite erect; his hoary head was a crown of glory, and his face, though deeply wrinkled, wore an expression of cheerfulness and peace. The memorial adds:

> He read much, and having a remarkably retentive memory was ready and instructive in conversation on almost any topic. There was a richly entertaining spirit in his conversation. He loved to talk, but never talked nonsense; he was fond of good stories, and had a very treasure of them. He wrote much, and left piles of manuscript. His piety was calm, steady, and deep.

He was very tenacious of his political opinions, and it has been affirmed that those who knew him well would hardly recognize a portraiture of Laban Clark that did not mention the fact, that he was a thorough-going Democrat of the old school, admiring Andrew Jackson in respect to politics as he did John Wesley in respect to theology.

---

[4] Minutes of Conferences, 1869, p. 97.
[5] Hist. M. E. Church, vol. iv, p. 70.

His first wife, HARRIET, was the daughter of Anson Fairchild, of Westfield, Mass.[6] She died February 8, 1836, aged fifty-three years.

SARAH (HANKS,) his second wife, was a resident of Hartford at the time of their marriage, April 17, 1837.[7] She died November 21, 1866, aged seventy-nine. In the announcement of her death it was said that she was "not a shouting, but a steadfast Methodist."[8]

Marianne, a daughter of Laban Clark, and wife of the Rev. Seneca Howland, died July 1, 1853. She was a true Christian and brilliant scholar.

---

[6] Rev. Oliver Sykes' manuscript autobiography.
[7] Notice in Christian Advocate and Journal.
[8] The Christian Advocate.

XLV.

Mitchell B. Bull

HE REV. MITCHELL B. BULL was born in Waterford, Ireland, January 30, 1778.[1] He experienced religion and joined the Methodists at the age of thirteen years.[2] A few months later, in 1793, he came to the city of New York. He was licensed to preach in 1802, and shortly afterward entered the itinerant ministry. The following is the record of his

APPOINTMENTS: 1803, (Phila. Conf.,)[3] Newburgh cir., N. Y., with Thos. Stratton; 1804, (New York Conf. by change of boundaries,) Saratoga cir, with John Finnegan; 1805; ordained deacon,—Montgomery cir., with Joseph Willis; 1806, Long Island cir., with James Coleman; 1807, ordained elder,—New Rochelle cir., with Billy Hibbard, Henry Redstone, and Ezekiel Canfield; 1808, Cambridge cir., with Lewis Pease; 1809, ditto, with W. Swayze and S. Sornborger; 1810, Saratoga cir., with John Finnegan; 1811-1852, local; 1824 **supply, Brooklyn, Sands-street**, W. Ross' unexpired term; **1853**, (N. Y. East Conf.,) **sup'y, Brooklyn, Sands-street**, with H. J. Fox, 1854-1855, **ditto**, with L. S. Weed; 1856-1857, **ditto**, with John Miley.

His private memoranda of the Newburgh, Saratoga, Montgomery, Long Island and New Rochelle circuits have been preserved. The author has not found among the papers of any others of the early itinerants such evidences of a personal knowledge of the members on the circuits. He kept complete records of the leaders and their classes, plans of appointments, preaching places, baptisms, marriages, texts from which he preached in the several appointments, etc. They are models of neatness, and besides the light they throw upon the character of the preacher and his work, they are exceedingly valuable contributions to the history of the church in the large number of localities over which his min-

---

[1] Dr. Nathan Bangs in the Christian Advocate, 1857.
[2] Conference Minutes, 1858, p. 99.
[3] That Conference then comprised much of New York state, as well as New Jersey, Delaware, and Pennsylvania.

istry extended. He was accustomed to preach thirty or forty sermons in four weeks. His retirement, after an active ministry of eight years, was on account of failing health. He was engaged in the dry goods business in New York city about seven years; thence he removed to a farm in the State of New Jersey, and finally took up his permanent residence in Brooklyn. He was prospered in his secular enterprises, and his generosity fully equaled his ability. He devoted one fifth of his income regularly to benevolent objects, and bequeathed $9,000 to religious institutions.

His conference memorial states that he was "active and useful in the church, a man of sterling integrity, and an able and earnest preacher."[4] His record of sermons from 1837 to 1849 indicates that he often preached in nearly every Methodist church in New York, Brooklyn, Jersey City, etc.

In social intercourse, as Dr. Bangs testified, he was "calm, courteous, kind." Judge Dikeman remarked to the author that Mr. Bull shared with many others in the expectation of the coming of the Lord in 1843. Hearing J. B. Matthias remark that he would like to live till Christ should come, Mr. Bull replied: "I don't expect to die; when Christ comes there will be no more dying."

The Rev. John Rossell, of Brooklyn, assures the author that no likeness of Mr. Bull was ever taken. Isaiah Scudder, of Huntington, L. I., who knew him well in 1806, describes him as tall of stature, with a pitted face and a marked Irish brogue. One eye had been put out. He was thrice married, but had no children.

He departed this life August 6, 1857, in the eightieth year of his age.[5] "During his last severe illness his mind was clear, calm, and cheerful," and "his last moments were gilded by the bright beams of the Sun of Righteousness. A head-stone in the Cypress Hills cemetery, lot No. 21, Moliere Path, designates the place of his burial.

A manuscript book, containing fifty-one admirable sketches of his sermons, and the valuable records mentioned above, fell into the hands of the Rev. Charles Stearns, and were presented by him to the New York East Conference Historical Society.

---

[4] Conference Minutes, 1858, p. 99.
[5] "In memoriam" record—Minutes of the New York East Conference.

ANN, his first wife, was a daughter of Henry Eames, a Methodist, (not the preacher,) who came hither from Ireland. She was converted in 1796, in the eighteenth year of her age, through the labors of Wilson Lee, and she at once gave her name to the church. Her marriage to Mr. Bull took place in May, 1799, and after fifty-three years the union was dissolved by her death, on the 18th of October, 1852, in the seventy-fifth year of her age. A head-stone marks her grave by the side of her husband's. Her health was never firm, but she was industrious and frugal, and aided her husband while in business to acquire a competence. Her modesty of deportment, her plainness and neatness of apparel, her kindness, affection, and piety, were remembered by her survivors. A little before her death she exclaimed, "Glory to God in the highest!"[6]

His second wife, ELIZA, resided in her youth at Dix Hills, L. I., and was converted in 1821, at a camp-meeting at Mosquito Cove, L. I. Her parents were named Goodwin, and the gospel was preached in her home. In 1830 she was married to Joseph Allen, and after being a widow two years, she accepted the hand of Mr. Bull, in 1854. It was her daily custom to read her Bible on her knees. She died October 12, 1856, aged fifty-seven years.

Mr. Bull was married to his third wife, ANN (SMITH,) of Brooklyn, February 16, 1857, when he was past seventy-nine years of age. His death occurred that same year, and she died in peace nine years later, August 1, 1866, aged sixty-four. Her father was a soldier of the Revolution. She is buried in the same grave with the first wife of Mr. Bull, but her name is not on the head-stone.

---

[6] Dr. Nathan Bangs, in The Christian Advocate.

XLVI.

Tho! Burch

AFTER the Brooklyn Methodists had buried their beloved Ross, the place was supplied by a local elder until the ensuing session of the New York Conference, when the REV. THOMAS BURCH, one of the most popular ministers of the denomination, was transferred from the Philadelphia Conference, and appointed to this charge.

He was born in Tyrone County, Ireland, August 30, 1778. His parents were people of culture, and highly respected members of the Church of England; but after his conversion, his mother, brother, and sister united with him in establishing a Methodist class in the place where they resided. His father never became a Methodist, having died previous to the formation of the society.

The chief agent in his awakening and conversion, while yet a young man, was Gideon Ouseley, the celebrated Irish evangelist.

In 1800,[1] Thomas arrived in the United States with his mother, his sister, and his younger brother, Robert,[2] and was soon appointed leader of a class in the vicinity of Boehm's chapel, in Lancaster County, Pa. He was encouraged by the Rev. Henry Boehm to enter the ministry, and accepted a license to preach. The following is his

CONFERENCE RECORD: 1805, (Phila. Conf.,) Milford cir., Del., with J. Aydelott; 1806, St. Martin's cir., Md., with J. Wiltbank; 1807, ordained deacon by Bp. Asbury,—Dauphin cir., Pa., with W. Hoyer and G. Harmon; 1808, ditto, with John Miller; 1809, Lancaster cir., Pa., with James Smith; 1810, Philadelphia, with T. F. Sargent, T. Bishop, T. Budd and T. Everard; 1811, Phila., St. George's, with S. G. Roszell; 1812–1814, (Genesee

---

[1] The memoir in the "Minutes" says 1803, but 1800 is the date named in the Rev. Henry Boehm's sketch in Stevens' Hist. M. E, Church, vol. iii, p. 434. He is a trustworthy authority, and became one of the earliest and most intimate friends of Mr. Burch after he reached these shores.

[2] This brother became a distinguished preacher in the Methodist Episcopal Church.

conf.,) Montreal, Canada—appointed the first year to Quebec, but stopped at Montreal ; 1815, (Balt. Conf.,) Baltimore city, with A. Griffith ; 1816, Georgetown, D. C., with Wm. Ryland ; 1817, Washington, Foundry church ; 1818, Georgetown ; 1819, Baltimore city, with M. Force and John Bear ; 1820, ditto, with R. Tydings ; 1821–1822, (Phila. Conf.,) Phildelphia, Union ch. ; 1823, Phila., St. George's, with Wm. Thacher and D. Parish ; 1824, ditto, with James Smith and H. G. King ; **1825,** (New York Conf.,) **Brooklyn ; 1826, ditto,** with S. L. Stillman ; 1827, New York, with N. White, R. Seney, J. J. Matthias, N. Levings, and J. Field ; 1828, ditto, with C. W. Carpenter, Jesse Hunt, J. J. Matthias, N. Levings, and Geo. Coles ; 1829–1830, Middletown, Conn. ; 1831, Albany, Garrettson station ; 1832, (Troy Conf.,) ditto ; **1833,** (New York Conf.,) **Brooklyn** and New Utrecht, with J. Kennaday and J. Luckey ; 1834, Brooklyn, same colleagues ; 1835, sup'y without app't ; 1836–1837, sup'y, Kingsbridge, (Yonkers,) with E. Oldrin and J. D. Bangs ; 1838, sup'y, ditto, with John Davies and S. C. Perry ; 1839, sup'y, ditto, with H. Hatfield and S. C. Perry ; 1840, Yonkers, with D. I. Wright ; 1841, New York, Vestry-street ; 1842–1843, Rhinebeck ; 1844–1845, sup'y, Yonkers, with J. C. Green ; 1846–1847, sup'y, ditto, with C. C. Keys ; 1848, sup'y, ditto, with S. C. Perry ; 1849, sup'y without app't.

His career is remarkable for the many conferences to which he belonged. He was transferred four times, and fell into the Troy Conference when it was formed by the division of the old New York Conference. One of the chroniclers of Canada Methodism says :

Thomas Burch holds the distinction of having entered Canada just as the war trouble was beginning, and remaining at his post till it had passed away.[3]

Stevens states that Burch made his way to Quebec in 1812, when Luckey and Bangs failed to reach their appointments on account of the war.[4] If he reached that city, it was not to remain ; for, as Carroll still further says,

Thomas Burch was designated to Quebec, but Bangs not going to Montreal, he made that city his head-quarters. It was no small boon to the Methodists in Montreal to obtain a man of such sterling piety and mature experience, and a preacher of such respectable talents, and to enjoy his labors for three full years.

One preacher only besides himself reached his appointment on British soil. That was Robert Hibbard, who was drowned shortly after, while attempting to cross the St. Lawrence River. Mr. Burch's prolonged stay in Canada seems to have had episcopal sanction, because he was the most suitable man for the work there. The Rev. T. H. Burch writes :

---

[3] Carroll—Case and his Contemporaries, vol. i, p. 281.
[4] See Hist. M. E. Church, vol. iv, p. 275.

Being then an unnaturalized citizen, and a subject of Great Britain, it was thought expedient, during the war, for him rather than an American citizen to labor there. He did not locate.[5]

He was one of the ninety chosen men of American Methodism who composed the first delegated General Conference in 1812. Twice subsequently a like honor was conferred upon him; namely, in 1820 and 1828.

He was married, May 25, 1816, to Miss Mary Smith, of Philadelphia. Ill-health compelled him to retire partially or wholly from active ministerial service for a number of years. After the death of his wife, in 1844, he resided in Yonkers, N. Y., till near the close of his life. His last sermon, ten days before his death, was delivered with great power from Paul's words concerning "the sufferings of this present time," and "the glory that shall be revealed in us." He died suddenly and alone, of heart disease, at the house of his son, Thomas H. Burch, in Nassau-street, Brooklyn, August 22, 1849, aged nearly seventy-one years, in the fifty-fifth year of his ministry. He was buried from the Sands-street church, the presiding elder, Laban Clark, officiating, assisted by other ministers. A monument in Greenwood marks the place of his rest.

Samuel Luckey writes admiringly of his friend, Thomas Burch, as "an amiable, sweet-tempered man," "of strong and heavenly aspirations," and of a "clear and well-disciplined mind." He says:

The most remarkable attribute of his preaching, and, indeed, of his character generally, was a charming simplicity. He was eminently fitted to discharge the duties of pastor, though I do not think he ever took a very active part in the general councils of the church.

He was a man of about medium size, was well-proportioned, and had agreeable and cultivated manners. The church showed in what estimate she held him, by keeping him always in her most important fields of labor.[6]

Dr. Bangs, in Sprague's Annals, says of Thomas Burch, that "he had a sharp, bright eye, that seemed to penetrate whatever it fastened upon;" that although "his mind was rather solid than brilliant," he was an animated preacher. "His voice," he says, "was musical, and his delivery fluent and graceful; his judgment was much confided in, and the influence of his whole character was extensively and powerfully felt in the denomination."

---

[5] Letter to the author.   [6] Sprague's Annals.

MARY, his wife, is said to have been "emphatically what a minister's wife should be." Having served the Lord faithfully thirty-eight years, she died at the residence of her daughter, Mrs. J. M. Van Cott, in Brooklyn, N. Y., April 24, 1844, in the fifty-third year of her age. Death came unexpectedly, but she was ready. Calling her children around her bed she commended them to God, and exhorted them to faithfulness; and, "with the word 'glory' faintly falling from her lips, slept in Jesus."[7] Her grave is beside that of her husband.

Children of Thomas and Mary Burch: *Mary Eleanor*, of Sands-street church, deceased;[8] *Sophia Gough*, died in infancy; *Thomas H.*, of the New York East Conference;[9] *Jane Sophia*;[10] *Anne Elisabeth*, deceased; *Robert Asbury.*

---

[7] Rev. L. M. Vincent in The Christian Advocate.
[8] See Van Cott, Book III, Record of Members.
[9] See Sketch, in Book III.
[10] Married J. M. Van Cott; see Book III.

XLVII.

Stillman

HE REV. STEPHEN LEWIS STILLMAN was born in Burlington, Conn., April 15, 1795. "His parents were Seventh Day Baptists; their seven children were piously trained, and all professed religion, and finally united with different denominations."[1] Stephen began his Christian life at the age of twelve, and six years later, in the year 1813, united with the Baptist Church. Some months later at a camp-meeting he obtained a deeper and richer experience in divine things, and from that time he was drawn toward the Methodist Episcopal Church, with which he united in Schenectady, N. Y., in 1817, under the ministry of Laban Clark. He was then twenty-two years of age, and had been married one year. He was licensed to preach in 1822.

CONFERENCE RECORD: 1823, (New York Conf.,) Burlington cir., Conn., with H. Hatfield; 1824, Winsted cir., with Eli Barnett; 1825, Wethersfield cir., with J. Z. Nichols; **1826, ordained deacon—Brooklyn**, with Thomas Burch; **1827, ditto**, with S. Luckey; 1828, ordained elder—Kingston cir., with Jos. D. Marshall; 1829, ditto, with E. Andrews and H. Wing, 1830-1831, Newburgh, N. Y.; 1832, Hudson and Print Works, with R. Little; 1833, ditto, with H. Humphreys; 1834, Hillsdale cir., with D. B. Ostrander, J. Carley, and William Lull; 1835, Hillsdale, no colleague named, 1836-1837, Poughkeepsie, 1838-1839, New York city, Eighty-eighth-street, 1840, New Haven, Conn.; 1841-1842, (Troy Conference,) Albany, Garrettson Station; 1843, Albany, West Station; 1844-1845, Troy, Second-street, (now Trinity;) 1846-1847,

---

[1] Mrs. Lucretia M. Stillman—letter to the author.

Ballston Spa. ; 1848–1849, Greenwich ; 1850–1851, Waterford ; 1852–1853, Shelburne, Vt. ;[2] 1854, without appointment on account of failing health ; 1855, chaplain of the Albany Bethel for Sailors and Boatmen ; 1856–1857, Bethlehem ; 1858–1859, Castleton, Vt. ; 1860–1861, Salem, N. Y. ; 1862, Clarksville and New Salem ; 1863, Albany, Free Central ; 1864, Hageman's Mills ; 1865, sup'y, without appointment ; 1866–1868, sup'y, Albany, Washington av., (now Trinity.)

It will be observed that he was first appointed to a charge including the neighborhood in which he was reared—an excellent comment upon the character and reputation of the young man. Burlington circuit then embraced twenty-eight different appointments, scattered over fifteen different townships. It is stated in his memoir that

> In each of these places he and his colleague were expected to preach once each in every four weeks, making an average of one sermon a day, and three on Sundays.[3]

His labors were not diminished on his subsequent appointments, the first of which embraced eighteen, and the second twenty-three, preaching places. Some account of his work in Brooklyn, in organizing the young men into a missionary society, has already been given on page 24 of this volume. The Christian Advocate, in 1837, reported a great revival under his labors in Poughkeepsie. His most remarkable success was in Garrettson station, Albany, where, during one series of meetings, about five hundred persons were added to the church. One of his parishioners writes :

> He entered upon his ministry with zeal and much religious fervor, and, as the result of his labors, old Garrettson station had one of the most sweeping revivals ever known in Albany in any one church. He became so worn down by midwinter that the official board secured the services of the Rev. Thomas Armitage to assist in continuing the meetings until spring. Many yet live who remember those stirring times, and the stately form and magnetic influence of the pastor, as he stood in that old tabernacle, with a great sea of faces before him, an audience of from 1,500 to 1,800 souls ; and many have gone up with their beloved pastor to swell the throng of those who sing the song of Moses and the Lamb.[4]

Mr. Stillman departed this life on the 2d of April, 1869, almost seventy-four years of age. Amid the closing scenes of his life he said to a committee of ministers in Albany : " Tell my

---

[2] Not Connecticut, as stated in his memoir in Conference Minutes.

[3] Minutes of Conferences, 1869, p. 116.

[4] William Dalton, of old Garrettson station, Albany.

brethren that I die in the full faith of the Gospel I have preached." Dr. Jesse T. Peck and other ministers addressed a large audience at his funeral in the Hudson-street church, Albany. His friends laid him to rest in the beautiful cemetery of Schaghticoke, Rensselaer county, N. Y., in a lot belonging to his father-in-law, Mr. Daniel Miller. A plain but neat Gothic stone marks his grave.

His brethren of the Troy Conference speak of him in his memoir as "a diligent and varied reader," perhaps all the more studious because of his consciousness "of the lack of early mental discipline, and of an educational foundation for scholarly attainment." They ascribe to him "a quickness of perception, a nicety of taste, an adaptation to the popular mind, a gentlemanly bearing, rare conversational powers, and a noble bodily presence." He was tall and erect at the age of seventy-three, "and his finely molded head, covered with a silvered crown of glory, made him conspicuous in any assembly."

MISS SARAH SPERRY was born in Connecticut, February 27, 1791, and was married to S. L. Stillman, August 12, 1816. One who was personally acquainted with her writes:

I remember her as a cultured Christian lady, dignified, courteous, kind, gentle, and universally beloved; a model wife and mother, domestic in her habits, and fond of her home. When Mr. Stillman was stationed in Troy she went on a visit to Westerly, R. I., and died while there, [July 10, 1846,] and was buried in the beautiful cemetery about half-way between Westerly and Watch Hill. A modest monument marks her grave.[5]

Mr. Stillman was married in 1848 to MRS. LUCRETIA MILLER EGGLESTON, who now resides in Valley Falls, N. Y.

Children of Stephen L. and Sarah Stillman: *Harlow Franklin*, of Chicago, Ill.; *William*, who died of consumption, in Albany, N. Y., the day he was twenty-two years of age, and was buried on the day he was to have graduated from a medical college in the city of New York; *George Henry*, of Portsmouth, Ohio; *Stephen Lewis, Jr.*, of Greenwich, N. Y., by profession a dentist. *William Olin*, the only offspring by the second marriage, was graduated from the Albany Medical College in 1871, was house physician five years at Dr. Strong's, in Saratoga Springs, and has since traveled and studied in Europe.

---

[5] Mrs. Lucretia M. Stillman's letter.

Saml Lucky

REV. SAMUEL LUCKEY, D. D.

XLVIII.

SAMUEL LUCKEY.

HE name of the REV. SAMUEL LUCKEY, D. D. is as ointment poured forth. His memory is fondly cherished by the old Brooklyn Methodists, and hosts of Wesley's followers throughout this country and Canada unite in the same admiring estimate of his character and his life.

He was born in Rensselaerville, N. Y., April 4, 1791. From certain statements of his we gather that he experienced a joyful hope in Christ before he was fifteen years of age.[1] With "a fair education, and a sound Christian experience," he began before he was twenty to travel a circuit under the direction of the presiding elder. Fifty-nine years of faithful service are included in the following

MINISTERIAL RECORD: 1810, supply, Montgomery cir., N. Y., in place of Datus Ensign or C. H. Gridley;[2] 1811, (New York Conf.,) Ottowa cir., Lower Canada; 1812, (Genesee Conf.,) assigned to St. Francis River, Canada, with J. F. Chamberlin, but unable to reach his appointment; 1813, (New York Conf.,) Dutchess cir., with W. Anson and Coles Carpenter; 1814, ordained deacon,—Saratoga cir., with Andrew M'Caine; 1815, Montgomery cir., with G. Pierce; 1816, ordained elder,—Pittstown, N. Y.; 1817, Troy; 1818, Troy and Lansingburgh, with E. Bancroft; 1819, Rhinebeck cir., with S. Howe; 1820–1821, Schenectady; 1822–1823, New Haven, Conn.; 1824–1826, presiding elder New Haven Dist.; **1827, Brooklyn**, with S. L. Stillman; **1828, ditto**, with S. Landon; 1829, New York, with Coles Carpenter, Jesse Hunt, G. Coles and S. D. Ferguson; 1830, ditto, with S. Merwin, L. Pease, S. Martindale, B. Goodsell and S. D. Ferguson; 1831, Albany, South Station; 1832–1835, (Genesee Conf.,) Principal of Genesee Wesleyan Seminary at Lima:—one year he had leave of absence from the seminary, and took the presiding eldership of the Rochester District on account of his health; 1836–1839, (New York Conf.,) Editor-in-chief of the Christian Advocate, Quarterly Review

---

[1] See his article entitled "Methodism Sixty-two Years Ago," in the Christian Advocate, January 17, 1867.

[2] Stevens,—Hist. M. E. Church, vol. iv, p. 259. Ensign was reported at the ensuing conference as having located.

and other publications of the Book Concern ; 1840, presiding elder, New York Dist. ; 1841, New York, Duane-street ; 1842, (Genesee Conf.,) Rochester, St. John's ; 1843, Rochester, First ch. ; 1844, presiding elder, Niagara Dist. ; 1845, Lockport, North ch. ; 1846-1847, presiding elder, East Rochester Dist. ; 1848-1849, (East Genesee Conf.,) presiding elder, Rochester Dist.; 1850, Penfield ; 1851, Rochester, Second ch. ; 1852, sup'y, Rochester, Third ch., with S. L. Congdon ; 1853, sup'y, Rochester, North-st., with A. Wright ; 1854, tract agent ; 1855, (Genesee Conf.,) Castile ; 1856, sup'd ; 1857, Gainesville, with J. M. Simpkins ; 1858, Scottsville ; 1859, (East Genesee Conf.,) Rochester, Cornhill ch. ; 1860, Rochester, North-st. ; 1861-1868, chaplain to the Monroe county penitentiary, the almshouse in Rochester, and the insane asylum ; 1869, sup'd.

Like Nathan Bangs, Elijah Woolsey, Thomas Burch, William Ross, Laban Clark, and many others who came to be princes in Israel, he received his early training as an itinerant in a foreign land. Not every young man would have accepted without flinching an appointment to Ottawa, Lower Canada ; but

Bishop Asbury had an interview with young Luckey after conference, and, finding him firm and dauntless, with only about twelve shillings in his pocket, opened his purse, which in those days was the missionary treasury of the Methodist Episcopal Church, and increased his frugal supply. A tedious journey on horseback of four hundred miles lay before him, and a poor and scattered flock awaited his arrival.[3]

He took with him his text-books in Latin and Greek and a few theological works, and diligently applied himself, both to immediate soul-saving effort and a thorough preparation for the work of future years. The following paragraphs afford us a very pleasing glimpse of him in his far-off post of labor :

Samuel Luckey, a young man, was sent to range the picturesque banks of the rapid Ottawa, among their simple, loving inhabitants. His youth, his comeliness, his pleasing manners, his piety and devotion, joined to his precocious ability as a preacher, took amazingly with the people. They spoke of him twenty-one years afterward, when the writer traveled the same interesting ground, with rapture. This young man was afterward known as the Rev. Dr. Samuel Luckey.[4]

On one of his long journeys Mr. Luckey suffered from hunger and cold. He stopped at a house in a French neighborhood and asked for food, and, as Mr. Carroll relates,

Not being sufficiently acquainted with the French language to indicate what he wanted, he pointed to his mouth. The Frenchman, observing the

---

[3] Minutes of Conferences, 1870, p. 280.
[4] "Case and his Contemporaries," by Rev. John Carroll, vol. i, p. 249.

gesture toward his face and the length of Mr. Luckey's beard, arising from want of facilities to perform his toilet for some days, inferred that he wished to shave himself, and, with true native alacrity and politeness, ran and brought him his razor. This was asking for bread, and receiving something worse than a stone. Whether he obtained the bread in the issue we did not distinctly learn.

The war prevented his going to his charge in 1812, and he seems to have spent most of that year in eastern New York and New England. While in Troy, in 1817, he witnessed, perhaps, the greatest revival which attended his ministry. Nearly one hundred and fifty members were added to the church. He recognized Noah Levings among the youthful helpers in the meetings, and gave him license to exhort.[5] About that time he published his book on "The Trinity," a work which increased his fame. Union College, by whose officers he was well known, honored him with the degree of A.M., and subsequently with the degree of D.D. These honors were unsolicited.

We have already alluded to his successful ministry in Brooklyn. An excellent sermon on "The Sure Word of Prophecy," printed and published while he was stationed there, may be regarded as a specimen of his discourses.[6] It is stated by W. H. Dikeman, of New York, that Samuel Luckey was the first clergyman outside of "the standing order" to preach the sermon at the opening of the assembly in the Connecticut legislature. In 1847 Dr. Luckey was elected by the legislature of New York to the important and honorable position of regent of the State University, and it is a noteworthy fact that he was the first clergyman holding office in the State under the amended constitution rendering clergymen eligible to civil offices. To the close of his life he remained one of the most active members of the board. He was a delegate to the General Conferences of 1828, 1836, and 1840.

As pastor, presiding elder, editor, principal of a seminary, regent of a university, chaplain to a prison, almshouse, insane asylum, all at once, " he performed," as Stevens has truly said, " an amount of public labor hardly surpassed by any of his contemporaries in the ministry." He wrote, in later life, an excellent treatise on "The Sacrament of the Lord's Supper," also "Ethic Hymns and Scripture Lessons for Children." When

---

[5] See sketch of Noah Levings in Sprague's Annals.
[6] See Methodist Magazine, 1828, p. 41.

almost at the close of his long and active life, he preached three sermons every Sabbath, besides devoting an hour in each of the institutions in which he preached in visiting and conversing with the inmates. When seventy-five years of age he said to the editor of The Christian Advocate that his work during the last twenty years had been performed with as much ease as at any preceding period.

But the end came at last, and " in peace, assurance, and victory, he passed away," October 11, 1869, aged seventy-eight years. The Rev. Geo. G. Lyon, pastor of the First Methodist Episcopal church in Rochester, visited him in his sickness, and wrote to The Christian Advocate :

His mind is clear and vigorous. He speaks calmly and intelligently of his approaching dissolution, and confidently and joyfully of his prospects beyond the grave. He has no will with respect to himself, but he inquires earnestly about the welfare of Zion. He is wrapped in his warrior's mantle, and is surveying the field of conquest and the embattled host before he retires to rest.

The resolutions adopted by the Rochester District Ministerial Association, while in session at Lima, Oct. 13, 1869, indicate that the preachers proceeded in a body to Rochester to attend his funeral. A grave marked by a head-stone in the Mount Hope cemetery, in Rochester, N. Y., contains the mortal remains of Dr. Luckey.

He is described as handsome in person, commanding, earnest, eloquent in delivery, respected in scholastic attainments, and firm in his religious convictions. Although he had been called no less than eight times to change his conference relations, thirty years of his ministry had been spent in the two Genesee conferences. When his brethren of the East Genesee Conference assembled after his death, they said in their report concerning him :

He was a thorough Methodist, and with the genius and historic development of his church he was as familiar as with the alphabet. He long stood among the magnates of his people, and his history is woven into the history of the church.[7]

His first wife, ELIZA, was a daughter of Richard Jacobs,[8] the heroic Methodist preacher who sacrificed his life in his perilous

---

[7] Minutes of Conferences, 1870, p. 280.
[8] Park's—Troy Conf. Miscellany, p. 35.

mission as the advance-guard of the Methodist army in the northern counties of New York State in 1796. It was no small honor to be the child of such a father. Stevens says:

He belonged to a wealthy Congregational family of Berkshire county, Mass., which had cast him out and disinherited him at his conversion to Methodism. "With his young wife he was thrown penniless upon the world." He joined Garrettson's famous young band of northern pioneers, and, in 1796, left his family at Clifton Park to make an expedition as far as Essex and Clifton counties, proclaiming the gospel among the scattered settlers in that remote region. Many were awakened and converted at Elizabethtown, and, promising them a pastor, he pushed along the western shore of Lake Champlain, preaching as he went, till, joined by a lay companion, he proposed to make his way back to his family through the Schroon woods to the head of Lake George. For about seven days the travelers were engulfed in the forests, suffering fearful privations and struggling against almost insurmountable obstructions. "Their provisions failed; they were exhausted with fatigue and hunger; and at last, in trying to ford the Schroon, Jacobs sunk beneath the water and was drowned. "All his family," adds the narrator of the sad event, "were converted," three of his sons became ministers, and two of his daughters married Methodist preachers.[9]

The widow of Richard Jacobs afterward married Judge Moe.[10] Eliza Luckey died in 1832, and was buried in Troy, N. Y.[11]

Samuel Luckey's second wife, LIDA M., was converted when very young. She shared her husband's lot for nearly thirty years, and died, of cancer, July 25, 1863, in the fifty-eighth year of her age. She was considered "faultless," a woman of pleasing person and address, attracting many friends. She met death in holy triumph.[12] She is buried beside her husband in Mount Hope cemetery.

His third wife, MARIA, after his death married a Mr. Utley. She died in Rochester in 1882.

Two children died in infancy. *Freeborn Garrettson*, a lawyer, resides in New York; *Caroline Amelia*, married Stephen B. Reynolds, of Danbury, Conn.; *Samuel Merwin*, died in 1883, in Rochester, N. Y. These are children by the first marriage. *John* died in Rochester; *Joseph L.*, the only living child by the second wife, is a lawyer and editor in Rochester.

---

[9] Hist. M. E. Church, vol. iii, p. 165.
[10] Statement of F. G. Luckey.
[11] J. L. Luckey—Letter to the author.
[12] J. R. in The Christian Advocate.

XLIX.

SEYMOUR LANDON.

THE REV. SEYMOUR LANDON is the first on our chronological list of the Methodist preachers of Brooklyn who was personally known to the writer. To have been favored with the counsel and blessing of so noble a patriarch as Father Landon, is a privilege to be highly esteemed.

Seymour Landon was born in Grand Isle, Lake Champlain, Vt., May 3, 1798. His father, Asahel Landon, first among the Methodist converts in that region, is mentioned in Stevens' "Memorials" as an honored local preacher. During Seymour's boyhood his father's house was a home for the pioneer Methodist itinerants, and "his barn and orchard their places of worship."[1]

On the 12th of September, 1814, the day after the naval victory of M'Donough over Downie on Lake Champlain, young Landon, who had witnessed the battle, stood on the gory deck of the flag-ship, Confiance, and said to himself as he looked upon the remains of Downie and his officers laid out for burial: "What is worldly honor to them *now?* What avails it to them if their souls are lost?" A few months thereafter, when he was seventeen years of age, his pastor, William Ross, preached a sermon which powerfully aroused his conscience, and led him to repentence and faith in Jesus Christ. Mr. Ross received him as a probationer in the church September 12, 1815, exactly one year after the scenes he witnessed on the deck of the Confiance had awakened those solemn thoughts in his mind. The same day and the next he accompanied the preacher to his appointments, and on the third day went with him in a sloop to a camp-meeting. On the way his pastor told him he believed God had

---

[1] "Fifty years in the Ministry," by the Rev. Seymour Landon, p. 10.

REV. SEYMOUR LANDON.

called him to preach. He soon began a course of preparation for the ministry, studying at an academy in St. Albans, Vt., and afterward with a Congregational minister, who strove to enlighten his pupil in Calvinistic doctrines, and succeeded in "confounding" the youthful Methodist. But it happened that young Landon had the company of J. B. Stratton, a sound and intellectual Methodist preacher, for two nights in a week during that time; and so, hearing both sides, he not only did not become a convert to Calvinism, but prepared himself to be a more successful defender of Methodist theology.

He was licensed to exhort, "without his knowledge or consent," and was soon afterward authorized to preach. Dissuaded from his cherished purpose of going to college, he accepted a recommendation to the New York Conference, which he joined in 1818, when twenty years of age.

CONFERENCE RECORD: 1818, (New York Conf.,) Charlotte cir., Vt., with N. White; 1819, Ticonderoga, N. Y.; 1820, ordained deacon,—St. Albans, Vt., with N. White; 1821, Ticonderoga, N. Y., again; 1822, ordained elder,—Chazy cir., with E. Crane; 1823, ditto, with Wm. Todd; 1824. Whitehall cir., including Poultney, Vt., where he resided; 1825, Poultney, a station;[2] 1826–1827, Sandy Hill and Glenn's Falls cir., N. Y.; **1828, Brooklyn,** with S. Luckey; 1829–1830, Lansingburgh and Waterford cir.; 1831, New York, with S. Merwin, L. Pease, S. Martindale, B. Goodsell, John Clark, B. Silleck, and C. Prindle; 1832, New York, West cir., with P. P. Sandford, J. Bowen, G. Coles, and C. Prindle; 1833–1834, Rhinebeck; 1835–1836, Newburgh; 1837, Sugar Loaf cir., with W. Miller; 1838, ditto, with T. Newman; 1839–1840, Hudson; 1841–1842, Brooklyn, 2nd church, (York-street,) and New Utrecht; 1843–1844, Hempstead; 1845–1846, Sag Harbor; 1847, Winsted, Conn.; 1848–1850, (New York East Conf.,) presiding elder, Hartford Dist.; **1851–1854, presiding elder, Long Island Dist.**; 1855–1856, Brooklyn, Gothic church; 1857–1858, Greenpoint; 1859–1860, Southport, Conn.; 1861–1862, Watertown, Conn.; 1863–1864, Mt. Vernon, N. Y.; 1865–1866, Astoria; 1867–1868, Amityville and Newbridge; 1869–1871, Springfield; 1872, Orient; 1873–1880, sup'd.

Here is a remarkable record of fifty-five years of effective service without a break, followed by eight years of quiet, peaceful waiting for his final remove to the "saints' everlasting rest."

He was married while on his second circuit, and the happy union lasted about fifty-eight years. In reference to his appointment to Brooklyn, in 1828, he writes:

I begged to be excused from being sent there, thinking it perfectly consistent with my vow to go wherever sent by the bishop, to decline an appointment which almost every other preacher coveted.

---

[2] Landon's account of the charge, which varies somewhat from the Minutes.

At the expiration of one year he was removed at his own request. Until the session of his conference, in 1879, the sixty-third from the time of his joining, he had never failed to be present. He spent about one year and three months of his life in attending the sessions of the conference to which he belonged.

He was a man of robust constitution, which did not entirely give way until a few months before his death, when he had been reduced almost to a skeleton by a series of heavy chills. He died at the residence of his adopted daughter, in Jamaica, L. I., July 29, 1880, in the eighty-third year of his age. Having outlived all the companions of his early ministry, he came down to his grave " as a shock of corn cometh in his season." As he saw death approaching, he exclaimed, " O what a salvation is provided for guilty men ! So rich, so full, so free ! I shall be saved ! It is all clear now ! " So did " the clouds that often troubled his faith in former years pass away " as he approached the entrance to glory, and heavenly light streamed through the " gates ajar."

The funeral took place in the Methodist Episcopal church in Jamaica, and the remains were laid away in the family plot in Winsted, Conn.

The character and career of Seymour Landon have been admirably portrayed in a memoir written by the Rev. George Lansing Taylor, D.D., and adopted by the New York East Conference. The following paragraphs are an extract from Mr. Taylor's sketch :

His early ministry was largely blessed with revivals, as was also his maturer work in some signal instances. As a preacher, while he was not remarkable as a profound or logical sermonizer, he was, nevertheless, a well-prepared, earnest, and often able, herald of the divine message. In his denunciation of popular sins and follies, he had something of the old Hebrew severity, and yet with it enough of the genial, and sometimes humorous, to retain the affection of his hearers.

His life-long regret at his privation of a college education, and the zeal and self-denial with which he and his companion sent all their children through college, are memorable points in his character ; yet, amid the collisions of the controversial times in which his ministry began, he never was put to the worse for want of enough of Greek, Latin, or English for the occasion. In the temperance reform he was prompt to sympathize with Dr. Fisk, when the latter threw his powerful influence into the rising total-abstinence movement, and he ever remained an earnest champion of the cause.

But the firm, though unostentatious, stand he took in the great antislavery contest, more than any other occasion of his public life, showed the moral fiber of the man. It is hard for us of this generation to comprehend the despotism of the pro-slavery sentiment that, to a great degree, ruled all the churches, and the whole fabric of society, North as well as South, in those days. The great struggle which divided the church in 1844 began eight years earlier. The General Conference of 1836, in its Pastoral Address, (see Bangs' History of the Methodist Episcopal Church, vol. iv, pp. 259, 260,) said to the church: "We * * * exhort you to abstain from all abolition movements and associations, and to refrain from patronizing any of their publications. * * * We have come to the solemn conviction that the only safe, scriptural, and prudent way for us, both as ministers and people, to take, is wholly to refrain from this agitating subject." An advice so contrary to all the primary rights of men, whether clergy or laity, probably no enlightened Christian body could be found on earth to give to-day. It is a phenomenon in religious history and psychology. But the bishops and annual conferences at once set about applying it as a law, giving it a weight which never properly belonged to any merely advisory deliverance, and enforcing it in an inquisitorial spirit. Following this cue, the New York Conference that year passed a resolution forbidding its members acting in any manner as agents for Zion's Watchman, the noted antislavery paper, then conducted by the Rev. Leroy Sunderland, of the New England Conference. Such action suggests to us of to-day that the modern term "bull-dozing" was invented forty years too late. It required uncommon manhood for Mr. Landon to stand up in his place and demand of the conference if "the resolution was intended to forbid my *taking* the paper *myself*, and paying for it?" The interrogation was resented as an insult to the conference, and at the following session, when the appointments were read off, Mr. Landon, whose previous charges had been wealthy Rhinebeck and prosperous Newburgh, found himself retired to the sylvan wilds of Sugar Loaf Mountain, where, like John the Baptist, he might riot on locusts and wild honey, and meditate on the folly of having opinions of his own.

At the session of 1838 James Floy, then in the bright promise of his youth, so nobly fulfilled in his manhood, was arraigned with several others at the bar of the conference for attending a Methodist abolition convention at Utica, N. Y., during the previous conference year. Although Floy and his friends took no part in the convention, save as spectators, yet for simply being present, and in the face of his own overwhelming defense for three hours before the conference, he was suspended from his functions as a deacon, by a vote of 124 to 17. Dr. Curry, in his memoir of Floy, (Quarterly Review, 1864. p. 117,) gives the now honored names of the courageous seventeen worthies; namely, "Daniel De Vinne, Charles K. True, Seymour Landon, Paul R. Brown, Harvey Husted, Cyrus Foss, David Plumb, C. W. Turner, Edwin E. Griswold, and probably John M. Pease, Humphrey Humphreys, Thos. Bainbridge, and Harvey Brown."[3] It must have brought a touch of honest pride to those brave men when, in after years, the New York East Conference sent four of them, Griswold, Floy, Landon, and Husted, to stand

---

[3] See sketch of Wm. Thacher in this book, p. 161, where he is quoted as expressing the sentiments of the majority on this subject.

up once more together as her delegates to the Buffalo General Conference, in 1860, to strengthen our testimony against slavery by passing the Kingsley amendments.

Mr. Landon, with every abolitionist of those and far later days, and as the pioneers of all reforms must always do in all organizations, frequently suffered in his appointments on account of his opinions. But he lived to reap in this life the honors and rewards of fidelity to righteousness ; to witness the triumphant overthrow and " extirpation of the great evil of slavery ; " to see his imperiled country free, united, and at peace ; and when he retired from the front of the battle, in 1873, his conference presented him, as an expression of affection, a purse of $1,681, one of the largest testimonials of the kind in the history of the church.

Doubtless the two most marked traits of Mr. Landon's character were his excessive, almost morbid diffidence, or self-depreciation, and his equally marked conscientiousness. His diffidence was so great on all personal points, as to subject him to occasional fits of despondency, and to unquestionably diminish his usefulness and power. It is, however, only in the light of this extreme native modesty that the sternness of his fidelity to great principles can be duly appreciated. These traits and his amiability and other charming personal qualities made him one of the truest and most lovable of personal friends.[4] Yet his sturdy honesty and independence were no less marked than his geniality. It is a significant token of his worth as a man, that *eleven* of the most valuable of the distinguished Olin's printed private letters, are addressed to Seymour Landon.

Mr. Landon's long career—the longest effective ministry in his conference—was crowned with serene brightness in his closing years. His always majestic and handsome face and figure (he was six feet tall and superbly proportioned) caught a new grace from that " hoary head," which " is a crown of glory if it be found in the way of righteousness." His presence was a welcome ornament in every circle of society, and he passed away amid the reverent affection of hosts of friends.[5]

PHŒBE, his wife, daughter of Levi and Charity (Miller) Thompson, was born in Granville, N. Y., Oct. 4, 1796, but, while an infant, removed with her parents to Ticonderoga. There she was received by the young itinerant, Seymour Landon, first into the church as a convert, and then into his home as a bride. It has been said that she made that home " a joy to its members, and a model to the parish." Her genial hospitality, her pure, sweet sympathies, her abounding good works, her timid and pathetic utterances in the social meetings, her

---

[4] In the New York Preachers' Meeting Dr. Curry said : " I *loved* Seymour Landon ;" adding, in his own peculiar way, " and the men I can say that of are *mighty few*."

[5] Minutes of the New York East Conference, 1881, pp. 57–59.

faithful training of her children, all conspire to make her memory precious. She died at the residence of her daughter, Mrs. James R. Alvord, in West Winsted, Conn., May 22, 1878, in the eighty-second year of her age.[6] W. H. Thomas, G. L., Taylor, and R. Codling were the ministers who took part in the funeral services. Her grave is near that of her husband.

Seymour and Phœbe Landon were the parents of four children : *Dillon S. Landon, M.D.*, whose memoir is found elsewhere in this book ; *Mrs. Louisa E. Burruss*, deceased ; *Mrs. Mary E. Alvord ;* and the *Rev. Thompson H. Landon, A.M.*, of the Newark Conference.

Amanda Covert was in her childhood adopted as a member of Mr. Landon's family. She married Jeremiah Hendrickson, and at her home in Jamaica, L. I., Father Landon was tenderly cared for during the last years of his life.

---

[6] For these facts we are indebted to the Rev. George Lansing Taylor, D.D. —sketch in The Christian Advocate.

L.

HE REV. NOAH LEVINGS, D. D., received his appointment to Brooklyn in the year 1829. He was a son of Noah Levings, and was born in Cheshire County, N. H., September 29, 1796. His parents moved to Troy, N. Y., when he was but a lad. They were in very humble circumstances, and their boy grew up with exceedingly limited opportunities, being sent from home to earn his own living at nine years of age, and apprenticed to a blacksmith at sixteen. He heard Peter P. Sandford preach in Troy, and, during a revival under the ministry of Laban Clark, in 1813, he united with the church on probation. He was small of stature, and bashful, and apparently about sixteen years of age. At the close of the second public meeting in which he in great simplicity attempted to pray,

> The official brethren gathered around the preacher; one inquired who the boy was; another said his forwardness must be checked; and a third that he must be stopped altogether. The preacher simply replied, "No, brethren, let that boy alone; there is something in him more than you are aware of;" and from that time no one questioned the right of the blacksmith boy to officiate in the public prayer-meetings.[1]

Thus actively from the first did he engage in Christian work but he did not receive the spirit of adoption until two years afterward. At this time, encouraged by his pastor, Tobias Spicer, he improved his gift in exhortation. Stevens quotes the following concerning him:

> After working at the anvil through the day, he would throw off his apron and paper cap, wash, and change his dress, and walk with Spicer to Albia, where he exhorted at the close of the sermons.[2]

---

[1] Clark in Meth. Quar. Review, 1849, p. 519.
[2] Hist. M. E. Church, vol. iv, p. 263.

ENGRAVED BY F.E. JONES, FROM THE ORIGINAL PAINTING BY JAMES PINE

In 1807 he received from his pastor, Samuel Luckey, an exhorter's license, and soon afterward he was licensed to preach. He was then twenty-one years of age. Samuel Luckey records that on coming to Troy he became deeply interested in the young blacksmith, finding him serious, modest, well-disposed, and of " an uncommonly brilliant mind ; " and he gives the following interesting account of a meeting conducted by Levings while visiting Troy, during the first year of his ministry, which sets forth in a strong light the zeal and faithfulness of the young itinerant :

At the close of the evening service I returned to my house and left him at the church with a large number of his companions, who remained behind for the purpose of practicing in sacred music. After I had been at home a short time there came a lad running in great haste to apprise me that I was wanted at the church. Without knowing for what purpose I was going, I made my way to the church as soon as possible, and there witnessed a scene which is more easily conceived than described. I found Mr. Levings at the altar engaged in prayer, and about forty, chiefly young persons, kneeling around it, and, upon inquiry, I ascertained that this was the explanation : Mr. Levings was sitting in the altar while the young people were singing, and he observed a young lady sitting near, weeping. He went and spoke to her, and found that she was deeply concerned on the subject of her salvation. He asked her if he should pray for her, and when she answered in the affirmative he requested that the singing might be suspended, and proposed that they should join in prayer ; they did so, and such was the effect of the announcement that forty came and knelt with her. I have rarely witnessed a more affecting scene than was passing when I entered the church.

We here transcribe a list of his

CONFERENCE APPOINTMENTS: 1818, (New York Conf.,) Leyden cir., Vt. and Mass., with I. Cannon ; 1819, Pownal cir., Vt., with D. Lewis; 1820, ordained deacon,—Montgomery cir., N. Y., with F. Draper ; 1821, Saratoga cir., with Jacob Hall ; 1822, ordained elder,—Middlebury, Vt. ; 1823–1824, Burlington ; 1825, Charlotte cir., with J. Poor ; 1826, ditto, with C. Meeker ; 1827, New York, with T. Burch, N. White, R. Seney, J. J. Matthias, and J. Field : 1828, ditto, with T. Burch, Coles Carpenter, J. Hunt, J. J. Matthias, and George Coles ; **1829–1830, Brooklyn,** with James Covel, Jr. ; 1831–1832, New Haven, Conn. ; 1833, (Troy Conf.,) Albany, Garrettson station ; 1834–1835, Troy, State-street ; 1836–1837, Schenectady ; 1838, presiding elder, Troy Dist. ; 1839, Troy, North Second-street ; 1840–1841, Albany, Division-street ; 1842, Troy, State-street ; 1843–1844, (New York Conf.,) New York, Vestry-street ; 1844–1848, financial secretary Am. Bible Society.

While on the Montgomery circuit he was married to Miss Sarah Clark. In Brooklyn, in 1829, he was called to mourn the death of one of his children, " little Charles Wesley." A few months subsequently he accompanied John Garrison to Salem, N. J., to erect a monument over the grave of Benjamin Abbott.[3] The Christian Advocate contains an account of a great revival under his ministry in Schenectady, in 1837. A warm personal friendship grew up between him and Dr. Nott, the president of Union College, on whose recommendation that institution conferred upon him the degree of D.D. While he was pastor in Schenectady he buried his mother. Four years later (1841) his father, who had been a Revolutionary soldier, died in Lockport, N. Y.

Dr. Levings was a member of General Conference in 1832, 1836, and 1840. A sermon of his on "The Foundation of the Church" was published,[4] also an important historic article concerning John Garrison and Brooklyn Methodism.[5] The original Methodist church edifice in Fair Haven, Conn., (now East Pearl-street, New Haven,) was built under his administration. He dedicated thirty-eight churches and preached nearly four thousand sermons. In the service of the American Bible Society he traveled more than thirty-six thousand miles, and delivered nearly three hundred addresses.

J. M. Van Cott, Esq., of Brooklyn, describes a sermon preached by Dr. Levings in the Sands-street church more than fifty years ago, exceeding, probably, all others he ever heard in its effect upon the congregation. It was on the eve of a revival effort. The text was, "Awake, thou that sleepest," etc. The preacher was all aflame with his subject. The excitement of the hearers reached a point beyond any precedent in the old Sands-street church. Though a Methodist people, they were an eminently cultured, decorous, dignified class of Methodists, and yet they all rose to their feet; some stood on the seats, weeping, laughing, shouting—a marvelous example of the power of the preacher over the minds and hearts of his hearers.

In an admirable memoir, written at his request by Dr. (afterward Bishop) Clark, is the following clear and discriminating account of his characteristics as a preacher:

The cast of his mind was not that which grapples with profound truths and evolves mighty thoughts, but rather that which would take the popular and

---

[3] Methodist Quarterly Review, 1849, p. 530.
[4] See Methodist Magazine, May, 1828, p. 201.
[5] Methodist Quarterly Review, 1831, pp. 258-273.

practical view of things. His reasonings generally were of this tone and character. * * * He combined, in an unusual degree, close argumentation with apt and striking illustration and an animated and attractive delivery. * * * His manner was self-possessed, the intonations of his voice well-managed, and his gesture easy and appropriate.[6]

His remarkable fluency of utterance, and his great success as a platform speaker, are a matter of frequent remark. The author just quoted says of his social qualities:

His manner was affable and winning ; his heart was warm and generous ; his mind naturally fertile and lively, and stored with an inexhaustible fund of anecdote, coupled with a retentive and ready memory, a brilliant imagination- a striking aptness at comparison, and fine colloquial powers, made him a most delightful companion in social life. * * * He was an almost universal favorite.

In person he was " of medium size," with " a form remarkably symmetrical," and " a countenance strongly expressive of benevolent feeling."[7]

In the early part of January, 1849, while on an extended tour in the service of the American Bible Society, he reached Cincinnati, Ohio, when sickness compelled him to halt. He was most lovingly cared for at the house of his very devoted friends, Mr. and Mrs. C. H. Burton, whose gratitude to him for the kind counsels and consolations he had imparted when he was their pastor in the East knew no bounds. From their hospitable home, far away from his family, he was summoned to his reward on the 9th of January, 1849, in the fifty-third year of his age. His biographer says:

His sufferings were great, but in the midst of them all he enjoyed perfect peace, and signal was his triumph, through grace, in the last conflict. When he found that the great object of his earthly desire—to see his family once more in the flesh and to die among his kindred—could not be realized, he only exclaimed, "The will of the Lord be done." On one occasion, when he was sitting up, Brother Burton placed a large Bible to support his head that he might breathe more easily. Observing the letters upon the back, he exclaimed, " Blessed book ! how cheerless would this world be without thy divine revelation." When Bishop Morris reached the city and hastened to the bedside of his dying friend, he said to him : " Thank God that I am permitted to see your face once more. I am not able to converse much, but I can still say, ' Glory to God !'" The Bishop inquired if he had any message to send to his brethren of the New York Conference. " Tell them," he said, " I die

---

[6] Methodist Quarterly Review, 1849, p. 540.
[7] Dr. Luckey, in Sprague's Annals.

in Christ; I die in the hope of the gospel. * * * All before me is light, and joyful, and glorious."

Bishop Morris preached his funeral sermon. His remains were buried in the city cemetery of Cincinnati; subsequently they were deposited in the Wesleyan cemetery, where it is said, "a suitable monument was erected to perpetuate his memory;"[8] and finally they were removed by the family to "Greenwood" in Brooklyn, N. Y. A head-stone marks his grave.

SARAH (CLARK,) his wife, was born in Amsterdam, N. Y., September 5, 1797. She died in New York, December 4, 1865, aged sixty-eight years, and was buried in Greenwood cemetery, by the side of her husband.

Their children are all dead. They were eight in number, as follows: *Noah Clark*, born in Middlebury, Vt., December 19, 1822; died February 12, 1823; *Noah Clark 2d*, born in Burlington, Vt., March 4, 1824, baptized by Buel Goodsell, died in New York, June 10, 1883, aged fifty-nine years—first a Methodist, finally an Episcopalian, a physician by profession; *Francis Asbury*, born in Monkton, Vt., June 17, 1826; died August 1, 1826; *George Suckley*, born in New York city, February 27, 1828; died January 14, 1865; *Charles Wesley*, born in Brooklyn, N. Y., July 18, 1829; died, July 30, 1829; *Wilbur Fisk*, born in New Haven, Conn., April 23, 1832; died October 9, 1833; *Martha Ann* and *Sarah*, twins, born in Troy, N. Y., April 7, 1835—Sarah died May 13, 1836, Martha Ann died July 24, 1840.

Allen Levings, M.D., of New York, son of the physician above named, is the only survivor among the descendants of the Rev. Dr. Noah Levings.

---

[8] Rev. Myron H. Breckenridge in The Christian Advocate, June 7, 1883.

REV. JAMES COVEL, Jr., M. A.

LI.

JAMES COVEL, Jr.

HE REV. JAMES COVEL, JR., A. M. ranks high among the honored pastors of the old Sands-street Church. His father, James Covel, Sen., as stated by Parks in the "Troy Conference Miscellany," was the son of a Baptist minister, whose wife was a Methodist. He joined the Methodist itinerancy in 1791, located in 1797, and was a practicing physician for many years. He was one of the three preachers who ordained the first elders in the African Methodist Episcopal Zion Church in 1822.[1] His wife, Sarah, mother of James Covel, Jr., became a Methodist in 1793, and stood firm and faithful in the midst of great persecution. She died at the residence of her son, Samuel Covel, in the city of New York, May 19, 1856, and her funeral was attended by the Rev. Dr. J. B. Wakeley.[2]

The elder Covel was stationed in Marblehead, Mass., in 1795, and there, on the fourth of September, 1796, the subject of this sketch was born. An interesting coincidence is noticed in the lives of James Covel, Jr. and Peter Jayne. Both were natives of Marblehead; both were converted at sixteen years of age; both began to preach within three years after their conversion, and both became pastors of the Sands-street Church.

The author of the memorial of James Covel, Jr., speaks of his early disrelish for study and the great improvement he afterward manifested in that respect.[3] At seventeen he joined the Methodist Episcopal Church, and when about nineteen years of age he received his first license to preach, signed by Nathan Bangs, as presiding elder. The church claiming his service, he relinquished his trade, and gave himself up to a

---

[1] Rush's Rise and Progress of the African M. E. Church, p. 78.

[2] Christian Advocate. In the Troy Conference Miscellany the maternal grandfather of the Rev. J. Covel, Jr. is said to have been a Methodist preacher. The same authority speaks of his brother as the Rev. Samuel Covel.

[3] Parks' Troy Conf. Miscellany.

life-long service as a minister of Christ. The following is his

PASTORAL RECORD: 1815, supply on Litchfield cir., Conn., with Samuel Cochran, Billy Hibbard, and Smith Dayton; 1816, (New York Conf.,) Pittsfield cir., Mass., with Lewis Pease and Timothy Benedict, supply;[4] 1817, Brandon cir., Vt., with D. Lewis and C. H. Gridley; 1818, ordained deacon,—Dunham cir., Canada; 1819, St. Albans cir., Vt., with B. Goodsell; 1820, ordained elder,—Ticonderoga cir., N. Y.; 1821, St. Albans cir., Vt., with A. Dunbar; 1822, Grand Isle; 1823, Charlotte cir., with C. Prindle; 1824, ditto, with L. C. Filley; 1825, Peru cir., N. Y., with O. Pier; 1826, ditto, with P. Doane; 1827–1828, Watervliet; **1829–1830, Brooklyn**, with Noah Levings; 1831, Williamsburgh, L. I.; 1832–1833, Newburgh; 1834, New Windsor cir., with N. Rice; 1835, ditto, with John R. Rice and T. Edwards; 1836, New York, west cir., with C. W. Carpenter, J. Z. Nichols, L. Mead, and E. E. Griswold; 1837, ditto, with C. W. Carpenter, J. Z. Nichols, A. S. Francis, and C. K. True; 1838–1840, (Troy Conf.,)[5] Principal Troy Conf. Academy West Poultney, Vt.; 1841, Fort Ann cir., N. Y., with W. Amer and W. Miller; 1842, ditto, with C. Devol and C. E. Giddings; 1843–1844, Troy, State-street, with John W. Lindsay, six months in 1844.

A venerable friend of Mr. Covel's wrote thus concerning the young preacher's labors as supply on Litchfield circuit:

His first and probably his only sermon preached in North Watertown, Conn., is in the recollection of the writer, then a lad of thirteen years. His youthful appearance is well remembered, as he applied himself to his work, with his coat off, on a winter's evening, in a crowded little school-house. It was near New-Year's-day, 1816.[6]

The people on his next circuit (Pittsfield, Mass.) were proud of their young preachers, Covel and Benedict, whom they called their "boy team." The boys while riding together one day were debating a biblical question, and agreed to leave it to Dr. Bangs, the presiding elder. "The doctor's decision favored Benedict's opinion. 'Well,' said Covel, with thoughtful earnestness, 'I will give it up, because I said I would, but I am no more convinced than I was before.'"[7]

While in Ticonderoga, July 16, 1821, he was married to Miss Anna G. Rice. His ministry in Brooklyn was attended with unusual success. While there he reported in "The Christian Advocate" a three-days' meeting, resulting in over one hun-

---

[4] Memoir of Covel in Troy Conference Miscellany.

[5] His memoir in Conference Minutes, 1845, p. 600, says erroneously that he was transferred in 1835.

[6] Manuscript sketch by Dr. A. J. Skilton, of Troy, N. Y.

[7] Parks's Miscellany.

dred conversions. The statistics on page 43 of this work show a large increase of members.

Mr. Covel was a good preacher. He indulged in no flights of fancy in the pulpit, but was "concise, clear, strong, and impressive," and intelligent people were exceedingly pleased with his sermons. The Rev. Tobias Spicer writes:

> He generally preached without manuscript, but sometimes had a brief outline of his discourse. His preaching was generally expository. He had a happy art of keeping the attention of his audience.[8]

However, he was not a "splendid" preacher. One of his old friends and parishioners says of him:

> Brother Covel, in the State-street charge, succeeded the Rev. Noah Levings, who was a Trojan, and at that time one of the most popular and able preachers of the day. Brother Covel was a man of the old stamp, able, sound, of good administrative ability, but he did not hold the congregation. In the fall of 1844 his health was poor, and the church asked for an assistant, and Bishop Hedding sent John W. Lindsay, then quite young, but he filled the place with perfect satisfaction. John Newland Maffit labored with us thirteen weeks, and there was a large number added to the State-street church, and all the churches in the city gained largely in numbers. * * * Of James Covel it may be said that his earnest and consistent life was a good example of the living gospel.[9]

Mr. Slicer gives a still further account of his friend:

> In the social circle Mr. Covel rendered himself at once instructive and agreeable. * * * When in company with his brethren in the ministry, he was fond of discussing some difficult passage of Scripture, or some knotty point of Christian theology.

In devout love of learning he had few superiors, and his attainments entitled him to a good position among educated men. The degree of Master of Arts was conferred upon him by the Wesleyan University in 1835. His son makes the following statement:

> My father was a great student. No time was lost with him, and his researches took a wide range; yet he kept close to the one purpose of his life, the Christian ministry. It seemed to be his first great ambition to read the Scriptures in the original Greek and Hebrew, and so thoroughly did he accomplish his purpose, that he was known frequently to recall from memory a quotation in the original, before he could remember the language of the translation.[10]

---

[8] See Sprague's Annals.
[9] Reuben Peckham, Esq.—letter to the author.
[10] Wm. B. Covel—letter to the author.

Like many others distinguished for their diligence in study, his abstractions sometimes led him into ludicrous mistakes. On one occasion, when a friend entered his study, he gravely bade him good-bye. In the midst of his studies he " forgot his appointment to preach."[11] It is said that some of the preachers, who could not appreciate his studious habits, were kind enough to admonish him that "knowledge puffeth up."

He was a member of General Conference in 1832 and 1844. His chief literary works were a series of Question Books for Sabbath-schools, and a Bible Dictionary, 18mo, which passed through several editions. At the time of his death he was engaged in the preparation of a work, entitled "The Preacher's Manual." The unfinished manuscript remains as he left it. The accompanying portrait was copied from a painting made when Mr. Covel was about forty years of age. The countenance, though that of a scholar, is not "sicklied o'er with the pale cast of thought," but indicates a robust physical condition. Tobias Spicer, in Sprague's Annals, says of him:

Mr. Covel was a man of noble appearance and bearing, rather above the ordinary height, and a little inclined to corpulency, but well proportioned. He had a full face, well-developed features, an intelligent expression, and a rather dark, sandy complexion. He was simple in his dress and manners, and as far removed as possible from even the semblance of ostentation.

He adhered with unswerving principle to " the conscientious performance of every conceived duty." In one of his last public acts he gave an instance of this fidelity. Our authority says :

At the great revival in the State-street church in Troy, when he was stationed there in 1844–45, a large number were added to the church, and of these there were eighteen or twenty who desired to be baptized by immersion, and it fell to his lot to perform that service. He baptized them against the advice of his family physician, in the month of March, in the ice-cold waters of the Mohawk, because he deemed it his duty to do so. The result was a fatal termination of his malady in about six weeks thereafter.[12]

After great suffering and a most beautiful and affecting farewell to his family, he passed into everlasting rest during the session of his conference, on the 15th of May, 1845, in the forty-ninth year of his age. The last words he uttered were, " Tell Brother Mattison that I died happy." His funeral was

---

[11] Park's Miscellany.
[12] Wm. B. Covel's letter.

attended by more than a score of his ministerial brethren, and Bishop Hedding preached from the words, " I am now ready to be offered," etc. He was buried in Mt. Ida cemetery, in Troy, and a plain head-stone marks the place of his rest. In the same lot are the remains of three other deceased members of the Troy Conference.

ANNA G., his wife, was born August 5, 1802, and was married to Mr. Covel before she was nineteen years of age, January 16, 1821. She died of paralysis, at the home of her daughter, in East Portland, Oregon, January 4, 1881, aged seventy-eight years. She spent the last ten years of her life with her children in the Far West. " She was dignified, cultured, thoroughly attached to the itinerant system—a noble woman in every respect." Her daughter writes :

At the time of her death no one would have supposed her to be in her seventy-ninth year. Her hair retained its glossy blackness, and her mind was bright and active. Until she lost consciousness she was in a very happy state of mind, beholding bright visions of angels and loved ones gone before.[13]

Her son pays the following tribute to her memory :

Of our dear mother we have only sweet and pleasant recollections. Though many years of her life were spent in suffering, she was always cheerful, patient, full of hope ; her light shone brighter and brighter to the close of her long and peaceful life. So delicate were her sensibilities, that she was frequently in some anxiety of mind, lest inadvertently, by word or deed, she had offended in some particular. She now sleeps in the Lone Fir cemetery, in East Portland, Oregon, but the body will soon be removed to Oak Hill cemetery, near San Jose, California.[14]

Of the five children of James and Anna G. Covel who arrived at maturity, the eldest died in Dubuque, Iowa ; *William B.*, resides in San Jose, Cal., (business, real estate ;) *James E.*, of Lawrence, Kansas, is proprietor of the Lawrence Tribune ; *Mary J.*, (Mrs. Briggs,) resides in East Portland, Oregon ; *Cornelia*, (Mrs. E. C. Lawrence,) resides in the State of New York.

---

[13] Letter of Mrs. Mary J. Briggs.
[14] Wm. B. Covel—letter to the author.

LII

HE REV. JOHN CHRISTIAN GREEN was born in the city of New York, May 2, 1798. His father, who was a physician, died when John was about twelve years of age. The marriage of John C. Green to Miss Esther Henry took place on the twenty-sixth of August, 1820. In less than two years thereafter he entered the itinerant ministry of the Methodist Episcopal Church.

PASTORAL RECORD: 1822, (New York Conf.) Newburgh cir., N. Y.; with Jesse Hunt; 1823, Coeyman's cir., with B. Sillick; 1824, ordained deacon —Pittstown cir., with Benj. Griffen; 1825, ditto, with N. Rice and W. H. Norris; 1826, ordained elder—Whitehall cir., with W. P. Lake and Lorin Clark; 1827, Poultney, Vt.; 1828, Middlebury; 1829-1830, Albany, N. Y., south; 1831, Brooklyn, with C. W. Carpenter; 1832, ditto, with C. W. Carpenter and J. C. Tackaberry; 1833. New York, west cir., with P. P. Sandford, F. Reed, J. Bowen, and C. W. Carpenter; 1834, ditto, with J. B. Stratton, F. Reed, D. DeVinne, and J. C. Tackaberry; 1835, Middletown, Conn.; 1836-1837, agent for Wesleyan University; 1838, New Paltz cir., N. Y., with E. Crawford; 1839, ditto, with Eben Smith; 1840, Montgomery cir., with S. Bonney: 1841, Montgomery and Middletown cir., with J. Davy; 1342-1843, New York, Green-st.; 1844-1845, Yonkers, with T. Burch, sup'y; 1846, Brooklyn, Centenary ch. and Flatbush; 1847, withdrew; 1848-1853, (August,) pastor First Congregational Methodist church, Brooklyn.

Mr. Green was charged before the New York Conference in 1826 with the intemperate use of ardent spirits, but on examination was acquitted.

In the year 1846, when Mr. Green was pastor of the Johnson-street church, Brooklyn, he allowed John Newland Maffit, whose character and authority as a minister were not at that time clear before the church, to preach in his pulpit, and refused to obey the bishop's instructions to erase his name from the church records.[1] For this offense Mr. Green was suspended from the use of his ministerial functions for one year. Potter J. Thomas, of Brooklyn, and others, who were cognizant of all the facts, affirm that the official board, rather than the pastor, insisted on employing Mr. Maffit; that Mr. Green presented the bishop's letter to the board, saying that he must act accordingly; but the trustees replied that they felt bound to keep their engagement with Maffit, and that they would assume the entire responsibility, should the pastor be arraigned before the conference. Viewing the matter from their stand-point, the friends of Mr. Green considered his suspension by the conference a great injustice, and some of the reasons for this belief have been published.[2]

After his trial and suspension he withdrew from the Methodist Episcopal Church; the Centenary church revolted, refusing to receive their new pastor, and undertook, as an independent organization, to retain Mr. Green. In the litigation which followed the courts decided that the Methodist Episcopal Church could hold the property; whereupon a large number of the members withdrew, and established, under Mr. Green's leadership, a Congregational Methodist church, in Lawrence-street, Brooklyn.

A few years later, (in 1849,) ex-Justice John Pierce, stepfather of Maffit's wife, having spoken of Green as a "drunken scoundrel," the latter brought a suit against Pierce for slander, and a verdict was given in favor of the plaintiff. John Dikeman and James M. Smith, Jr., were counsel for Mr. Green. Among the prominent witnesses in the case were the Revs. Nathan Bangs, George Peck, Valentine Buck, John C. Tackaberry, Bradley Silleck, and William H. Norris; also, Messrs. Jacob Brown, Joseph Moser, John Smith, Rufus S. Hibbard, J. Wesley Harper, Henry R. Piercey, and others. The entire

---

[1] See the Christian Advocate and Journal, January 9, 1847.
[2] See Rufus S. Hibbard's pamphlet, entitled "Startling Disclosures concerning the Death of John Newland Maffit," pp. 16-22; also "The Trial of Green vs. Pierce," p. 39.

ministerial life of Mr. Green was throughly canvassed. It was not proved by the evidence adduced, nor is it now claimed by the friends of Mr. Green, that he was a teetotaler; and it seems to us an error and a misfortune that, as a minister of Jesus Christ, he did not attain to that standard. That he was an inebriate, either before or after this trial, his most intimate friends declare to be false.[3] The tremulous, excitable state in which he was often seen, was declared by Dr. Reese to be due to a constitutional infirmity, or mobility of temperament.[4]

John C. Green is described as a fine-looking man, rather tall, an excellent speaker, with pleasant voice and winning manner, and a very happy and "impressive way of putting things." There was a nervous energy and a manifest unction attending his appeals under the excitement of revival services rarely surpassed by the best evangelists.

He survived his resignation as pastor of the Congregational Methodist church only about eight months, and died of paralysis, in the city of Brooklyn, on the 7th of April, 1854, aged fifty-six years. His grave in Greenwood cemetery is marked by a stone carved in the form of a pulpit.

ESTHER, wife of John C. Green, was born in the town of Newburgh, N. Y., May 2, 1798, and died September 14, 1875, in the 78th year of her age. She is buried by the side of her husband. One of their sons, *James Wilson*, attended the Wesleyan University in 1836, and afterward died in Texas. *John Henry*, another son, resides in New Jersey, and is engaged in business in the city of New York. One daughter, *Elizabeth*, died at the age of sixteen. *Mary C.* married a Mr. Porter, and for her second husband a Mr. Bellinger, of Davenport, Iowa. *Caroline* was married to Mr. Levi P. Rose. She is now deceased. *Emma E.* married Daniel Colgrove, of Brooklyn, and she, likewise, is dead.

---

[3] The author has conversed with William I. Steele, Potter J. Thomas, Rufus S. Hibbard, and others, and their testimony is decided and unanimous on that point.

[4] Trial, Green *vs.* Pierce.

LIII.

Chas W. Carpenter

A CONSIDERABLE number of young persons who began their Christian life in the Sands-street church became ministers of the gospel. Prominent among them in point of talent and usefulness, and preceding most of them in point of time, was the REV. CHARLES WESLEY CARPENTER, distinguished, moreover, as the only one of the Sands-street converts who became pastor of that church.

His father, Thomas Carpenter, was a native of Long Island, "and one of the noble men of early Methodism" in the city of New York. As an active business man, as a patriotic citizen in the Revolution, as an alderman of the city for several years, as one of the first managers of the American Bible Society, as a member of our missionary board, as trustee and class-leader in John-street church, he "served his generation by the will of God." He probably retained his membership in the John-street church until his death, but was buried in the Sands-street church-yard in 1825. Edith (Bunce), mother of Charles W. Carpenter, died before her son was sixteen years of age.[1]

---

[1] On her tomb-stone in the Sands-street church-yard it is stated that she died March 13, 1808, aged 46. For sketch of Thomas Carpenter and his second wife see Wakeley's "Lost Chapters," pp. 547-550.

The subject of this sketch was born in New York city, December 16, 1792. He was brought to a saving knowledge of Christ in Brooklyn, in 1806, during a gracious revival season, in which were converted two other young men—Marvin Richardson and Josiah Bowen—who became eminently honored and useful ministers of God. The following account of his conversion is in his own words:

Though at different times I was the subject of serious thoughts, yet no lasting impressions were made upon my mind until my fourteenth year?[2] At that time my parents lived in Brooklyn, where they retired in the summer season for the benefit of pure air. A revival of religion broke out under Mr. E. Cooper, then stationed at that place.[3] On a Sabbath evening, having loitered about the meeting-house until after the sermon had closed, I went in to see the exercises which took place among those that were under awakenings. My attention was caught by the earnest devotion of a young man just emerged from darkness into light. I looked at him for some time, when my heart became so affected that I could not refrain from shedding tears. I felt an earnest desire for the same enjoyment which he seemed already in possession of, but did not feel, in so great a degree as many, the horrors of a guilty conscience. This may have been in consequence of my tender years. I sat down with a sorrowful heart, when a godly man, James Herbert, noticing my agitation, came to me, and in an affectionate strain, urged the necessity of my being born again. His words, attended with the power of God, fastened conviction upon my mind. I remained in the meeting-house till quite late, my burden and sorrow of soul continually increasing. On Thursday evening, in conversation with a young disciple of Christ, P. Coopers, my mind seemed measurably relieved, but yet I was not satisfied. In the course of the Friday following I retired frequently, and poured out my soul to God in prayer. In the afternoon, while engaged in private, (the spot I well remember,) I felt a sudden and glorious change in my feelings. My burden was fully removed; my soul was filled with inexpressible peace.[4]

Thenceforward he was a happy and devout Christian. He entered Columbia College, but on account of ill-health was not able to complete the course.[5] When a little past nineteen years of age, he received from Freeborn Garrettson his first license to exhort, and on the 20th of October, in the same year, he was licensed as a local preacher by the quarterly conference in New York. He was married April 24, 1813,[6] being less than twenty-one years of age. One year later he was admitted to

---

[2] Not his eighteenth year, as stated in M'Clintock and Strong's Cyclopædia.
[3] Samuel Thomas was his associate.
[4] Quoted in his memoir—Conference Minutes, 1853, pp. 194, 195.
[5] Sprague's Annals and M'Clintock and Strong.
[6] Suffolk Circuit quarterly conference record.

the annual conference on trial, and the following, in brief, is his

MINISTERIAL RECORD: 1814, (New York Conf.,) Suffolk and Sag Harbor cir., N. Y., with A. Scholefield ; 1815–1827, local preacher, Savannah, Ga.; 1820, ordained deacon ; 1826, ordained elder ; 1828, (New York Conf.,) Suffolk and Sag Harbor cir., N. Y., with R. Seaman and O. V. Amerman ; 1829–1830, Sag Harbor ; **1831, Brooklyn cir.**, with John C. Green ; **1832, ditto**, with J. C. Green and J. C. Tackaberry; 1833, New York, west cir., with P. P. Sandford, Fitch Reed, Josiah Bowen, and J. C. Green; 1834, Sag Harbor and Bridge Hampton cir., with Harvey Husted ; 1835, Sag Harbor and East Hampton ; 1836, New York, west cir., with J. Covel, Jr., J. Z. Nichols, L. Mead, E. E. Griswold, and L. Pease, sup'y; 1837, ditto, with J. Covel, Jr., J. Z. Nichols, A. S. Francis, C. K. True, N. Bigelow, sup'y, and R. Seaman, sup'y ; 1838–1839, Poughkeepsie; 1840–1843, presiding elder New Haven District, Ct.; 1844–1845, Brooklyn, Washington-street ; 1846–1847, New Paltz and Plattekill cir., with John Reynolds ; 1847, ditto, with J. K. Still ; 1848–1849, North Newburgh, with J. W. Le Fevre, sup'y, and R. H. Bloomer, sup'y; 1850–1851, sup'y, Plattekill cir., with John C. Chatterton, sup'y; 1852, sup'y, Pleasant Valley, in the Newburgh District.

His retirement at the close of his first conference year was mainly on account of ill-health ; nevertheless, he was able to engage in business while in the South. Returning, he was warmly welcomed by a host of friends, recommended to the annual conference by the quarterly conference of Suffolk circuit, and re-appointed to his former charge. In Sag Harbor, where he was pastor three terms, the author has heard the older people speak of their exceedingly pleasant recollections of his ministry among them. He was secretary of his conference for many years, and in 1840 and 1844 was elected to a seat in the General Conference.

His last sickness was attended with extreme suffering, but greater than his bodily pain was his grief on account of not being able to meet his brethren in conference. He departed this life in peace, May 10, 1853, during the session of the New York Conference, in the sixty-third year of his age. His death occurred in the same house in Plattekill, N. Y., where Daniel Ostrander died ten years before. Dr. John Kennaday preached a sermon on his life and character.[8] His remains were first buried in Plattekill, but they now repose in Greenwood cemetery, on Long Island.

---

[7] Sprague's Annals.
[8] The Christian Advocate.

Charles Wesley Carpenter "held a high and strong position in the confidence of his brethren," who regarded him as pre-eminently " a Christian gentleman," and " an intelligent, able, and efficient minister of the New Testament."[9] Judge Dikeman said to the author:

> Brother Carpenter was familiar with almost every subject, but his conversation always savored of religion. His sermons were uniformly short and neat, and his appearance in the pulpit was the most clerical of all the men I ever heard.

One of the leading ministers of the conference writes:

> I knew him as a most amiable boy, and a most amiable and excellent man. * * * He was a tall, slender man, of a graceful form and delicate features, and an expression of countenance indicating rare gentleness and loveliness. * * * His labors found great favor with some of the most intelligent congregations in the denomination. * * * I doubt exceedingly whether his image still lives in any memory, where it is not associated with everything pure and lovely and of good report.[10]

His bland and peaceful spirit lulled many a rising storm in conference. He was too modest to be prominently active, and yet few men wielded a more persuasive influence in that body.

BETHIA (WALKER,) his wife, was a native of Smithtown, L. I., a quiet, unobtrusive, industrious Christian woman, greatly devoted to her husband, and interested in his work. It was the author's privilege to converse with her frequently, while he was her pastor, in 1869 and 1870. She survived her husband about twenty-two years, and fell asleep in Jesus, in Newburgh, N. Y., in May, 1875, aged about eighty years.

Their only children were *Anna Maria*, and *Albert.* The former died, an infant, in 1815; the latter was connected with the Sands-street church and Sunday-school for several years, and afterward removed to Newburgh, N. Y., where he died only a few years ago.[11]

---

[9] Memoir in the Conference Minutes.
[10] Dr. Samuel Luckey, in Sprague's Annals.
[11] See notice of Albert Carpenter, in Book III.

J. Tackaberry

REV. JOHN C. TACKABERRY.

LIV.

JOHN C. TACKABERRY.

HE REV. JOHN CRANWILL[1] TACKABERRY was born in the town of Wexford, Ireland, September 8, 1799. His parents, John and Jane (Cranwill) Tackaberry, were connected with the people called Methodists. Fossey Tackaberry, a brother of the subject of this sketch, was a very distinguished Methodist preacher in the Irish Conference, whose life was written by the Rev. Robert Huston and published in Belfast.

When J. C. Tackaberry was eighteen years of age he emigrated to America, and resided some time in Quebec. There, in July, 1817, soon after his arival, he obtained the joy of pardon, and before many days united with the people of God. His conference memorial says:

In 1819 he received license as an exhorter, and faithfully and zealously served the church in that capacity until 1821, when he was licensed as a local preacher. For a year or two subsequently he was employed under the presiding elder to labor within the limits of the Canada Conference. In 1826 he was ordained as a local deacon by Bishop Soule.[2]

Thenceforward he received the following

APPOINTMENTS: 1827, (Pittsburgh Conf.,) Greenfield cir., Pa., with P. Buckingham; 1828, Washington cir.; 1829, ordained elder,—(New York Conf.) Troy, N. Y., with S. Merwin; 1830, Kingston, with F. W. Smith and E. Andrews, 1831, Catskill and Saugerties cir., with D. Poor; **1832, Brooklyn**, with J. C. Green; 1833, Stratford and Bridgeport cir., Conn.; 1834, New York, west cir., with J. B. Stratton, F. Reed, J. C. Green and D. DeVinne; 1835, ditto, with J. B. Stratton, D. DeVinne, L. Mead and E. E. Griswold; 1836, visited Europe on business and to see his friends; on his return, Harlem mission, with John Luckey and D. DeVinne; 1837, Montgomery cir., with David Webster; 1838, Harlem mission, with J. Floy; 1839, ditto, with S. H. Clark; **1840**, Stamford, Ct., and Poundridge, N. Y., with S. J. Stebbins and I. San-

---

[1] This is said to be one form of the celebrated name Cromwell. The widow of J. C. Tackaberry says Cranwill was her husband's name, not Cranville, as it is spelled in the Conference Minutes and elsewhere. He usually omitted the second name in writing his own signature. See Life of the Rev. Fossey Tackaberry, p. 298, where his grandmother Cranwill is mentioned.

[2] Conference Minutes, 1852, p. 42, and Hist. St. James' M. E. Church, New York, p. 57.

1841–1843, sup'd; 1844, New York, Seventh-street, with A. M. Osbon; **1845, sup'y, Brooklyn, Sands-street,** with H. F. Pease; **1846, ditto,** with N. Bangs; 1847, sup'y, New York, Forsyth-street, with J. B. Stratton; 1848–1849, sup'y, New York, Greene-street, with Daniel Smith; 1850, sup'y, ditto, with Davis Stocking; 1851, sup'y, New York, Bedford-street, with Addi Lee.

His ministerial life, as above outlined, comprises many important details, of which no record has been preserved. We must be content with a few interesting incidents. In a letter addressed to the Rev. W. H. Dikeman, of New York, and published in one of our church papers, he describes a terrific storm at sea, which he encountered on his return from Europe, April 19, 1837. The following extract conveys a vivid impression of the thrilling event:

At half past two A. M. a black cloud arose above the horizon to the northwest. The first mate called the captain on deck. Suddenly the wind hauled round to the north-west, blowing violently and took the ship all aback, driving her stern foremost at about five knots. The hands were immediately called to bring the ship about and shorten sail. While the sailors were performing this duty, a ball of fire or a flash of lightning struck the ship and passed down the rigging, exploding with a noise equal to the report of a cannon, and with such force that it knocked down almost all the men on the deck. The sparks of fire fell in every direction, and for some moments seemed to cover the deck. The sailors exclaimed that the ship was going down, while some of them ran to the forecastle. * * * In a few minutes another flash struck the ship and passed down the rigging, exploding the same as the first, and again knocking down several of the men. * * * The sail was shortened immediately, and a little after three o'clock the wind died away, and there was a dead calm. A few minutes before this phenomenon took place, I had been observing the progress of the vessel; but, perceiving no danger, I had turned into my berth again, when the ship received the first shock. As I had heard all hands called on deck, and knew that they had been taking in sail, my first thoughts were that some of the passengers on board had a quantity of powder which had exploded; or that some of the hands had fallen from aloft and were killed. And as the shock jarred the skylight over the cabin, I thought whoever had fallen must have struck upon it, and that the large lamp which usually hung under it, being shaken, had caused the waving light which I had observed when the first flash took place. When I went to the lobby there was a smell of sulphur, as strong as if several guns had been discharged in it. I dressed as soon as possible, intending to go and render any assistance in my power to those who might be hurt, as I knew the hands were all employed. When the second explosion took place I was satisfied that it was lightning, and supposed that the vessel and all on board would be at the bottom in fifteen minutes.

While I feel grateful to God for his goodness in preserving me amid the perils of the sea, I feel the highest satisfation in being permitted to meet my numerous friends on this side of the Atlantic. My travels through Europe have only increased my attachment to our country and institutions, and I am fully satisfied there is really nothing (even in these embarrassed times) to prevent our being the happiest people under the sun.[3]

In his fortieth year, on New-Year's-day, 1839, he was married to MISS SARAH L. TIEMAN, an estimable lady, who still survives, (1884,) in the thirty-fifth year of her widowhood.

As appears from the list of his appointments, he was colleague of John C. Green, in Brooklyn, in 1832. Seventeen years later the testimony of Mr. Tackaberry, in the case of Green *versus* Pierce, revealed the fact that there was a lack of harmony between the two preachers while they were associate pastors in this charge. He says:

> I was removed at the end of one year. I did believe that Mr. Green and Judge Dikeman obtained my removal. * * * There was a difficulty between Mr. Green and myself. I told Mr. Merwin he was trying to keep people away from my congregations. * * * I stated the circumstances to prove it.[4]

Farther on in the testimony it is faintly intimated that Green found fault with his playing on the violin. These slight infelicities were unquestionably more frequent formerly than now.

In his best estate, before his health declined, his preaching was fervent, pungent, and often pathetic. He particularly excelled in "doctrinal discourses." W. H. Dikeman, who knew him intimately from 1833, said to the author:

> Mr. Tackaberry wrote his sermons with great care, but preached without notes. It was his habit always to cite authorities, sacred or secular, and he was often called "Book, Chapter, and Verse," from his method of quoting Scripture in his sermons.
>
> In social intercourse he was bright. Few excelled him in wit and repartee, but his language was always chaste. I tested his friendship for nearly twenty years, and I never knew a man to show more unswerving fidelity to his friends in storm and in sunshine.

Many others have spoken of him as "a walking concordance," and it has been affirmed that he knew the New Testament by heart.

He was a man of slender build, taller than the average, of light complexion, and pleasant countenance. The likeness accompanying this sketch, is copied from an oil portrait in the possession of the family.

---

[3] The Christian Advocate and Journal, August 18, 1837.

[4] "The trial of the Rev. John C. Green against John Pierce for slander," p. 13.

In his later years he preached only occasionally. He longed for a return to the active ministry, but the derangement of his nervous system, and a tendency to congestion of the brain, made the labors of the pulpit impracticable. He died in the fifty-third year of his age, in New York city, May 9, 1852, of Southern fever, contracted while he was chaplain and physician upon a New York and Nicaragua steamer. In one of his intervals of consciousness he said: "In the word of God is my trust; its promises are my support."

His remains were first deposited in the vault of the 125th-street church, afterward they were removed to Greenwood.

Of his six children all except *Albert*, who died in youth, are now living, (1884,) and continue to revere God and the church of their father. They are *John A.*, *William G. H.*, *Jane C.*, *Emily G.*, and *A. Antoinette*.

REV. JOHN KENNADAY, D. D.

LV.

JOHN KENNADAY.

WHEN the "fathers" repeat the names of the most admired and beloved of the earlier Methodist preachers of Brooklyn, the REV. JOHN KENNADAY, D.D., is never omitted from the list. He was born in the city of New York, November 3, 1800. When he was quite young his father, who was a native of Ireland and a Roman Catholic, was drowned. His mother was a native of this country.[1] He learned the printer's trade when a youth, but devoted his leisure hours to reading and study. A more minute account of the boyhood of such a man as Dr. Kennaday could not fail to be interesting and instructive. What there was in his training and his early habits to inspire hope for his success in life would then be more apparent. Probably, however, there was little previous to his conversion, except his love of learning, to suggest the character of his subsequent career.

On New-Year's Day, 1822, when twenty-one years of age, he was awakened in John-street church, New York, under a sermon preached by Heman Bangs, who thus graphically describes the beginning of young Kennaday's noble Christian career:

In those days we took advantage of all the holidays to hold public worship, and in John-street we had a public service on New-Year's Day. My brother Nathan was to preach the sermon; I went to the church; he did not come, and I had to rise on the moment and preach myself; and Providence directed this young man (Kennaday) into the church, and God was pleased to awaken him. I held always, once a week, a meeting for seekers in my house. He attended and made known his desires, and I took him into the church. I exhorted him to preach and recommended him to travel, and was present when he received his first license. I remember the first speech he ever made in public. It was in John-street, the occasion being a love-feast. Our city (New York) was then one circuit, and we all came together for love-feast into one church, and consequently the church was crowded. Among

---

[1] The author learned these facts from the widow of the Rev. Dr. Kennaday.

others, a young man arose in the back part of the church, near the gallery, and began to speak. The moment he opened his mouth it seemed like pouring the oil on Aaron's head ; the odor was such that it seemed to diffuse itself all over the congregation, and the fragrance was such that every one seemed to catch it. The inquiry was made : " Whose silvery voice is that ? " I believe that eloquence which he then manifested, and which seemed to be natural, easy, and unaffected, continued with him to the last, more or less.[2]

After a few months he was licensed to exhort and to preach, and labored without a break for more than forty years in the following

APPOINTMENTS : 1822, supply on ―――― cir., N. J.; 1823, (New York Conf.,) Kingston cir., N. Y., with J. D. Moriarty ; 1824, ditto, with D. Lewis ; 1825, ordained deacon,—Bloomingburgh, N.Y.; 1826-1827, (Phila. Conf.,) Paterson, N. J.; 1827, ordained elder; 1828-1829, Newark ; 1830-1831, Wilmington, Del.; 1832, Morristown, N. J.; **1833-1834, Brooklyn,** with Thomas Burch and John Luckey—New Utrecht was included in this charge in 1833 ; 1835, New York, east circuit, with S. Cochran, J. Youngs, N. Bigelow, and J. Law; 1836, ditto, with S. Merwin, S. Remington, H. Brown, and D. Smith—this east circuit embraced all the churches east of Broadway; 1837-1838, Newburgh, N. Y.; 1839-1840, (Phila. Conf.,) Philadelphia, Union ch.; 1841-1842, Phila., Trinity ch.; 1843-1844, Wilmington, Del.; 1845-1846, Wilmington, St. Paul's ; 1847-1848, Phila., Union ch.; 1849, Phila., Nazareth ch.; 1850-1851, Brooklyn, Pacific-street ; 1852-1853, Brooklyn, Washington-street ; 1854-1855, New Haven, Conn., First ch.; 1856-1857, Brooklyn, Pacific-street ; 1858-1859, Brooklyn, Washington-street, with S. H. Platt, sup'y; 1860-1861, New Haven, Conn. First ch.; 1862, Hartford ; **1863, presiding elder, L. I. Dist.**

The following account of his labors in his first circuit in New Jersey is taken from his diary. It is a very remarkable record, even for those times. He says :

In every 28 days I preached 42 sermons, walked 113 miles, and rode 152—making in 252 days, 369 sermons ; traveled on foot 1,017 miles, and rode 1,368 ; total, 2,385—besides leading classes, attending Sunday-schools, visiting almshouses, etc.

On the twenty-third anniversary of his birth, and soon after joining the New York Conference, he was married to MISS JANE WALKER. While preaching in Wilmington, about 1845, he was invited to Schenectady to deliver an address, and at that time Union College conferred upon him the degree of D.D.

Referring to the list of his appointments, the writer of his conference memorial says :

---

[9] Conference Minutes, 1864, p. 89.

The noticeable fact of this record is the number of times Dr. Kennaday was returned as pastor to churches that he had previously served. Of the forty years of his ministry twenty-two years, or more than half, was spent in five churches. No fact better attests his long-continued popularity, and his power of winning the affections of the people.

His death was sudden and unexpected. On Tuesday evening, Nov. 10, 1863, he was in the act of delivering an exhortation in the chapel of the Washington-street Methodist Episcopal church, of Brooklyn, when he was struck with apoplexy; he was borne unconscious to his bed, and died the following Saturday, November 14, aged sixty-three years. Thus did the Lord Jesus permit his faithful servant to

"Preach him to all, and cry in death,
'Behold, behold the Lamb!'"

Bishop Janes preached his funeral sermon, a sketch of which was published in the Brooklyn Eagle. Heman Bangs and others took part in the services. The remains were deposited in "Greenwood."

Dr. Kennaday's career is a marked "illustration of the beauty and glory of a life devoted to the pastorate." He was a model pastor. "To preach Christ and to watch over Christ's flock seemed his highest joy." Bishop Janes penned the following beautiful tribute soon after the death of his friend:

As a Christian pastor, Dr. Kennaday was eminent in his gifts, in his attainments, and in his devotion to his sacred calling, and in the seals God gave to his ministry. In the pulpit he was clear in the statement of his subject, abundant and most felicitous in his illustrations, and pathetic and impressive in his applications. His oratory was of a high order. His presence, his voice, his fluency of speech, his graceful action, his fine imagination, and his fervent feelings, rendered his elocution effective and powerful, and gave to his preaching great attractiveness and popularity.

Out of the pulpit the ease and elegance of his manners, the vivacity and sprightliness of his conversational powers, the tenderness of his sympathy, and the kindness of his conduct toward the afflicted and needy, and his affectionate notice of and efforts for the childhood and youth of his congregation, made him the greatly endeared and beloved pastor.

The Rev. A. Manship describes the flocking together of his numerous friends to hear him preach the dedicatory sermon in the Hedding church, in Philadelphia, and then adds:

He has labored much within the bounds of the Philadelphia Conference, and is deservedly a popular minister, and his popularity among us has never waned. Several of our best church edifices have been reared through his instrumentality. He has assisted in relieving many from pecuniary embarrassment within our bounds. He is abundant in labors, perfectly at home in the work of revival. Who ever witnessed his management of a protracted meeting or a camp-meeting, and could not well say, he is a good tactician? He has the happy art of interesting the children.[3]

A book of exercises, adapted for use in Sunday-school concerts and exhibitions—one of the earliest and best of its kind—was compiled by Dr. Kennaday.

It was the author's privilege on one occasion, at a camp-meeting in Milford, Conn., in 1861, to listen to Dr. Kennaday's moving appeals to the unconverted. Many penitents knelt in front of the stand after the sermon, and it was a delight to see how eagerly and thankfully they listened to his affectionate and helpful words, as, with wonderful adaptation to each, he directed their faith to the Lord Jesus Christ.

JANE (WALKER,) widow of the Rev. Dr. Kennaday, lingered among us in patient, happy hope of heaven, until September 13, 1884, when she died, in her eighty-second year, at the residence of Mrs. Joshua Brooks, in Highland, N. Y., where she had spent the summer. Her memorial says:

She was born in New York city, March 27, 1803. and early became a member of John-street Methodist Episcopal church. * * * She was a person of great gentleness, which, combined with a most exemplary Christian character, made her beloved by all. * * * Her health gradually failed until she sank peacefully to rest, with her family, except one daughter, around her bedside.[4]

The Rev. E. L. Allen, pastor of the Highland Methodist Episcopal church, preached her funeral sermon. The remains were interred in Greenwood cemetery. The author visited Mrs. Kennaday, in New York city, about a year before her death. She talked beautifully and affectionately of her husband, of his life and death, and the near prospect of a happy re-union.

Children: *John R.*, a lawyer, was four years a member of the N. Y. Legislature—two years as senator; died in 1884, soon after the death of his mother; *James H.* resides in Rochester, N. Y.; *Catherine* died January 17, 1884; *Jane W.* married Wm. G. Stille; *Maria B.* (Mrs. John Sawyer) died about 1864; *Lavinia R.* died in infancy; *Helen Cornelia*; *Caroline Virginia*.

---

[3] "Thirteen Years in the Ministry," page 334.
[4] J. R., in The Christian Advocate.

LVI.

John Luckey

THE subject of this sketch, the REV. JOHN LUCKEY, was brother to Samuel Luckey, who preceded him by a few years as pastor of Sands-street church. The Luckey family originated in Scotland; thence, it is said, in a time of religious persecution, they fled to the north of Ireland, where they held a very respectable social position. Three brothers emigrated to this conntry, and after a time they separated, one going west, another south, and one settled near New Hamburgh, N. Y., where the old homestead of "Squire Luckey" may still be seen. Joseph Luckey, Sen., the father of the two Methodist preachers, was a farmer. He died at his home in Auburn, N.Y., in 1833. His wife was from Holland. The old family record says of her: "Lanah Wagner, born July 6, 1763, married 1787, died suddenly August 6, 1816." She was a devout Christian, and her children always spoke of her with loving reverence.

John Luckey was born March 13, 1800.[1] He gave his heart to God before he was nine years of age.[2] His widow writes:

He left home when a mere boy, lived with his brother Samuel, went to school, and became a teacher. The love of the brothers for each other was like the love of David and Jonathan to the end of their lives.

---

[1] Presumably in Rensselaerville, N. Y., the birthplace of his brother Samuel.
[2] I. J. T. Lumbeck—memoir in "The Christian Advocate."

PASTORAL RECORD : 1820, supply, Delaware cir., N. Y., with John Finnegan and James Quinlan; 1821, (New York Conf.,) Durham cir., Conn., with Josiah Bowen ; 1822, Burlington cir., with C. Silliman ; 1823, ordained deacon,--Wethersfield cir., with E. Barnett ; 1824, missionary to the west end of Long Island ; 1825, ordained elder,—New Haven and Hamden, with H. Bangs; 1826, sup'y, Stratford cir., with S. D. Ferguson and Valentine Buck ; 1827, Hampshire mission in the Rhinebeck Dist., N. Y.; 1828, Hampshire cir., with Hiram White ; 1829-1830, Southold cir.; 1831, Saratoga cir., with W. Anson, sup'y, J. D. Moriarty, sup'y, D. Ensign, sup'y, and T. Newman ; 1832, New Utrecht ; **1833, Brooklyn** and New Utrecht, with T. Burch and J. Kennaday ; **1834, Brooklyn,** with T. Burch and J. Kennaday ; 1835, Harlem mission ; 1836, ditto, with D. De Vinne ; 1837-1838, Goshen, Conn. ; 1839-1846, chaplain, Sing Sing prison, N. Y. ; 1847-1848, New Castle and Pinesbridge ; 1849-1850, Pleasantville ; 1851-1852, New York, Five Points mission ; 1853, White Plains ; 1854, Fishkill, west; 1856-1865, chaplain, Sing Sing prison ; 1866, sup'y ; 1867-1875, sup'd, Rolla, Phelps County, Mo.

He organized the Flushing circuit in 1824. On the 18th of May, 1829, he was married, by Bishop Hedding, to Miss DINAH RUTHERFORD, of the Sands-street church. He repaired with his young wife to his appointment, the Southold circuit, on the east end of Long Island. More than fifty years afterward Mrs. Luckey furnished the author with interesting reminiscences of their experience on that circuit.

As the foregoing record shows, Mr. Luckey spent more than twenty years in ministering to the poor people of the city and the criminals of the prison. C. C. North, Esq., who was Sunday-school superintendent and class-leader at the Five Points mission when Luckey entered upon his work there, writes as follows :

The first Sabbath of Mr. Luckey's pastorate was memorable. The society still occupied the old saloon, corner of Cross and Little Water streets. Services and Sunday-school had been held in this room for one year, with temperance meetings on Wednesday nights. Class-meetings on Thursday nights were held in an adjoining dingy old room, where the writer dealt out for one year to hungry souls the bread of life.

Sifting from the doubtful company twelve who, amid surrounding temptations of debauchery, had stood with heroic fidelity and proved that they were, indeed, disciples of the Lord Jesus, they were presented to Mr. Luckey as the foundation of the church which he came to establish. On the morning of May 18, 1851, these twelve knelt at the altar, Mr. Luckey and the writer within, while the noble ladies of the society, with deep solicitude, saw the twelve received on probation, and then joined them in the Lord's Supper. Under Mr. Luckey's administration the work prospered in all departments, until the capacious mission buildings were erected. It could not do otherwise. His fine sense, his industry, his integrity, his humor, his patience, and his transparent piety were guarantees of success. I loved to see him in his work. He was charity personified as he stood with bread and garments for the poor and words of counsel for the erring. The Five Points mission was and is a colossal work, and he was the colossal figure in it. The dignity of his person and the integrity of his character drew to the mission the support of many of the best men and women of all the churches.[3]

From personal knowledge the same writer gives the following glowing account of Mr. Luckey in the peculiar work of the prisoners' chaplain, which occupied a very large share of his ministerial life:

In 1855 he was called to the chaplaincy of the Sing Sing prison. This was his second appointment. His first, including the years from 1839 to 1846, was so eminently successful that many distinguished men of both parties were deeply interested in his renewed service. In 1861 the writer moved to the neighborhood of Sing Sing, and was at once sought out by Mr. Luckey to assist him in his Sunday services among the prisoners. During five years the custom was for me to address the prisoners once a month. The frequency of these visits gave me a thorough acquaintance with his personal traits and his successful administration. During that whole period I never heard an unkind word said against him from inspectors, wardens, keepers, or even prisoners, except from those who feared his incorruptibility. I called at each of the 1,000 or 1,200 cells, and conversed with every prisoner. In these conversations Mr. Luckey's name was generally if not always introduced, and the sentiment was unanimous that his character for piety, probity, and unselfish devotion to his work was without a flaw. The convicts might berate the inspectors, wardens, and keepers, but the name of Luckey closed at once the lips of derision and scorn. With the tenderness of woman he would listen on the one hand to the sad stories of the convicts, and on the other penetrate with rare sagacity the schemes of corrupt men. He was loved by the worthy and sincere, while the false dreaded no man more than him whom they were wont to call "old Luckey." When he discovered in a young man the promise of a better life, with what tenacity did he follow the case, not only through prison-life, but also into the great outside world, until the young man was restored to the family and society from which he had fallen ! No one on earth can know how numerous were his visits to the wives and children and parents of the convicts, nor how countless were the little benefactions he conferred on the families and friends of those unhappy men.

The last ten years of his life were spent on a farm near Rolla, Mo. His pastor says:

He donated to the church six acres of land and a small house, which, repaired, became " Luckey's Chapel." He preached once a month and worked in the Sunday-school till his health utterly failed. His last public discourse was to the children of this little school, and it was very affecting.[4]

---

[3] The Christian Advocate, May 9, 1876.
[4] I. J. K. Lunbeck in The Christian Advocate.

His old-time friend, C. C. North, visited him in his Western home. He tells the story thus:

> Business called me a few years since to St. Louis. On Saturday the inquiry arose in my mind where I should spend the Sabbath. Rolla and the Luckeys flashed on my mind. Taking an afternoon train a ride of eighty miles brought me at midnight to Rolla. I learned at the hotel that my friend lived four miles away. Curbing my impatience, I remained till early morning, and then, mounting a horse, rode out to their home in the woods. It seemed a long and devious way, my road winding around "settlements," until, perched upon a side hill and flanked by a forest, was the picturesque, yet plain and unadorned home of the Luckeys. They had spied a stranger emerging from the woods, had seen him fasten his horse and enter the gate, and then came the recognition, followed by a scene which the reader will not expect me to describe. I found that religion in the new relations was just as marked and prominent as at former periods of Mr. Luckey's history. His home that Sabbath was the gathering-place for Christian worship. The neighbors looked upon him as a patriarch to whom they might come for counsel, sympathy, and help.
>
> I was the only one of his eastern friends who had visited him. My presence, therefore, that day was a comfort to him, while the visit was to me a feast. Amid an apparent serenity the presence of one from the East renewed the yearnings he felt for his old friends. The shades of evening drew on, and I and my beloved friends waved the last farewell as the family group, cottage, and hill-side faded from sight.

He was exceedingly affable, child-like, perfectly unostentatious, counseling with the youngest preachers as with equals, notwithstanding he was "the associate and peer of the ablest men of the church." The weak, suffering, and penitent always found in him a friend. His piety burned the brighter as the lamp of life grew dim. He delighted in hearing the gospel proclaimed, and had preaching in his room when he could not go to the chapel. He never missed his family worship until the morning of his death. When it became necessary for him to move into town, where he might be near a physician, he would not leave his farm until he had arranged for a tenant who would care for his little church. This done, he expressed himself as fully satisfied and ready to meet his God.

On the morning of the 10th of January, after he had moved into town, he arose as usual, with no premonitions that death was at the door. Mrs. Luckey describes the closing scene:

> He sat in a rocking-chair at the table, eating his breakfast. He indulged in a little pleasantry, just like himself, but I observed that he leaned over on

his left side. Eliza and I succeeded in getting him into the bed; his eyes closed, he lay like one in a deep sleep, and in a few hours "he was not, for God took him."[5]

Funeral services were held in the Methodist Episcopal church in Rolla, Mo., and in Sing Sing, N. Y. In Dale cemetery, in Sing Sing, is a head-stone suitably inscribed, which marks the resting-place of John Luckey.

His widow resides in Haverstraw, N. Y., with their only surviving child, *Helen Eliza*. Two children, *Mary* and *John*, died while Mr. Luckey was stationed in Brooklyn, and their graves are in the Sands-street church-yard. Two others, *Samuel* and *Emma*, are at rest by the grave of their father; and another, *Isabella*, is buried in Newcastle, Westchester County, N. Y.

Mrs. Luckey is a daughter of Christopher Rutherford, an honored local preacher of the Sands-street church.[6] Her letters to the author contain evidence of rare talent and culture, and a character worthy of fellowship with her noble husband both in labor and reward.

---

[5] Letter to the Rev. Elbert Osborn.
[6] For an extended account of the Rutherfords, see Book III.

LVII.

BARTHOLOMEW CREAGH.[1]

THE REV. BARTHOLOMEW CREAGH was born in Dublin, August 23, 1804. His ancestors on his father's side were Scotch-Irish, while his mother's family were of English extraction and of high social position. His maternal grandfather, John Hawkins, of Dublin, was an eminent barrister. His father was a gentleman of culture and ability, but it was to his mother, a refined, accomplished lady, that he owed his religious training. Mrs. Creagh felt that upon her devolved the responsibility of moulding the religious character of her children. Although a member of the Episcopal Church, she became deeply interested in meetings held under the auspices of the Methodists. About this time her oldest son, Bartholomew, who had already been baptized and confirmed, became deeply exercised upon the subject of religion. To his mother's great joy, at one of these meetings he dedicated himself to God's service, and there never was a more entire consecration. The habitual tendency of his soul was toward the object of its supreme love; he seemed to watch for opportunities for communion with God, and testifies in his diary to the blessedness of his intercourse with his "soul's Beloved", and this habit followed him through life. He was eminently a man of prayer, a firm believer in the immediateness of Divine help in daily duty. He entered upon this life of faith when sixteen years of age.

Born in a home of luxury, with expectation of handsome inheritance, he had intended to follow a legal profession; but God's thought for him was of higher things. These plans were relinquished that he might preach the gospel, and ev-

---

[1] This elegantly written memorial is from the pen of his daughter, Miss Fidelia M. Creagh, of Brooklyn, N. Y.

ENGRAVED BY S.E. JONES FROM A DAGUERREOTYPE BY HEALY

B.I.Creagh

ry energy was devoted to preparation for the work of his hoice. He was richly endowed by nature and by grace, and hese gifts were supplemented by a classical education. He ras a fine linguist, reading Greek, Hebrew, and Latin with ease, nd was also conversant with some of the modern languages.[2] Ie was, perhaps, most remarkable for the beauty and purity of is English. One of the most eminent instructors of the age aid of him : " His language was perfect, so simple that a child night understand, and always critically correct."

Unexpected loss of fortune induced his family to seek prosperity in the New World. He accompanied his father to New York at the age of eighteen years. He began to preach in 1826 t Flushing, L. I. This event is noted in his diary:

A few days since I left my pleasant home, and a large circle of friends, hose society had been a joy to me, but it was under firm conviction that ecessity was laid upon me to preach the gospel.[3]

This entrance upon the work of the ministry was not a cause f small import. This, the struggles of his heart as expressed n his diary, amply testify. He says:

I am led to think if I could always preach with satisfaction to myself, I hould in some measure forget that my help cometh from the Lord. I continually cry, " Who is sufficient for these things?"

Again he writes :

Lo! I see another year. With what propriety can I adopt the words of he venerable Jacob, " Few and evil have the days of the years of my fe been." I am greatly humiliated with a sense of my imperfections, nd would ever cry, Lord pardon what I have been, and order what I hall be. If I know myself, I more ardently long for inward purity than allness of joy.

---

[2] [His children say that he was educated in Dublin. The statement in M'Clintock and Strong's Cyclopedia that he studied Greek and Latin in Belast is an error.—E. W.]

[3] [Thus began a ministerial career of more than twenty-five years, of which comprehensive view is furnished in the following record of successive **APPOINTMENTS:** 1826, Flushing cir., N. Y., a supply, with Richard eaman and O. V. Amerman ; 1827–1828, (New York Conf.,) Hempstead ir., with D. De Vinne and D. Holmes ; 1828, ditto, with N. W. Thomas nd D. I. Wright ; 1829, ordained deacon ; 1829–1830, Plattsburgh ; 1831, rdained elder; 1831–1832, Rhinebeck; 1833–1834, Middletown, Conn. ; **1835– 836, Brooklyn, Sands-street ;** 1837–1838, New York, Vestry-street ; 839–1840, Rhinebeck ; 1841–1842, Red Hook mission ; 1843–1846, presiding lder, Hartford Dist., Conn. ; 1847–1848, (the latter year, New York East onf.,) New York, Allen-street ; 1849–1850, New York, Seventh-street ; 851–1852, Williamsburgh, South Fifth-street.—E. W.]

Modest and tender, gentle and strong, compassionate to the weak, he was most severe with himself, for self was continually arraigned before the stern bar of his own tender conscience. He seemed clothed with humility as with a garment, and it was of no scanty pattern. While those who knew him best were rejoicing in the light which his consistent life threw upon the pathway to the skies, he was often in secret places, deploring as in dust and ashes his own short-comings, and pleading the merits of Jesus, as his only hope.

In the pulpit he was a fervid, impassioned speaker.[4] Preaching was not an opportunity for the display of natural gifts, but rather the outpouring of a full heart, that sought to free itself from solemn responsibility. He seemed literally to persuade men, and under his soul-stirring appeals many dead hearts were touched, and blind eyes opened to the beauty of holiness. It was not strange that one who so continually communed with his "soul's Beloved," the one "altogether lovely," should have many seals to his ministry. An extract from a memorial sermon by that eminent man of God, the Rev. Nathaniel S. Prime, D.D., of the Presbyterian Church, will be appropriate. He says:

> It is not my intention to pronounce a eulogy upon the great man whom God has taken from our midst ; but I cannot withhold the spontaneous tribute of my heart, and I predicate my right upon the fact that when such a man as Bartholomew Creagh is removed from a community, it is a greater loss to the public than to his own particular church. During the past year it has been my privilege to hear him oftener than any other clergyman, and always with intense interest and profit. His sermons gave evidence of careful preparation and deep thought, and were delivered with a pathos that could only be obtained in the closet. From the first time I heard him proclaim the gospel of our common Master, I understood more fully than ever before the force of that simple record, "It came to pass when he had made an end of speaking, that the soul of Jonathan was knit unto the soul of David, and Jonathan loved him as his own soul." Being his near neighbor, my privilege of social intercourse was considerable, sufficient to show me that he was every-where the same warm-hearted, consistent, catholic Christian. To express in a few words my estimate of his character, I would say that to a vig-

---

[4] [Daniel De Vinne, a fellow-countryman of Mr. Creagh, said in his Semi-centennial Sermon: "Brother Creagh had been fitted for Trinity College, Dublin. He was naturally eloquent, while his piety, earnestness, and wholeheartedness gave a peculiar force and beauty to his enunciation. I have heard John Summerfield in his best days, but would as soon have heard Bartholomew Creagh." Bishop Davis W. Clark says, in Sprague's Annals: "As a preacher he was always interesting and impressive. * * * He was extremely tender and earnest in his appeals; indeed he was sometimes overwhelmingly eloquent."—E. W.]

rous, discriminating intellect, and a heart transfused with love to God and man, there was added a clearness of perception and an originality of thought, expressed in chaste and beautiful language, that is rarely equaled.

In private life he was courteous and genial; he had always the right word at the right time, and it was given to young or old, high or low, as the case might be, with a simple courtesy that won all hearts.[5] To intimate friends he revealed much of that humor which is the heritage of his countrymen; still, this was guarded with a watchful eye, and he was careful that the last impression should be a serious one.

He was an ardent lover of Nature; all fair forms and beautiful colors were a joy to him, and he always ascended into spiritual meanings. The cultivation of flowers was a favorite recreation, and he found keen enjoyment in music, sometimes resting himself with his flute. A letter from Boston to his little daughter illustrates these tastes. He says:

I have seen many interesting things, about which my little dame and I will have nice talks on my return. Are you careful to feed the birds? These little creatures are not more dependent upon our thought, than we are upon our heavenly Father's care. Do not forget to water the flowers; they will amply repay you in sweetness and beauty. I know you will not neglect your books; but, more than all, seek the wisdom that is more precious than rubies. A long letter from my little girl will rejoice the heart of her loving father.

His valued friend, Miss Garrettson, thus speaks of him:

His visits were always occasions of deep interest, and hailed with delight by all the household. I recall, with peculiar pleasure, a time when he was about to leave Wildercliffe, but was delayed by a severe storm. After tea, he read to Mrs. Olin and myself, Mrs. Browning's drama of "Exile." Absorbed in the theme, he swept us along, by the alternation of strong feeling and tender pathos. As he ceased the old clock in the hall rang out the midnight hour. He exclaimed, "Is it possible!" and retired. Mrs. Olin turned to me with radiant face, and said, "Well, cousin Mary, I never really heard it before!"

One great element of power was his strong personal influence. This was largely the result of devotedness to God. A few

---

[5] [Bishop Clark says: "Nowhere, perhaps, did his fine qualities display themselves more beautifully than in the house of mourning, and at the bedside of the sick and dying. He seemed to know intuitively how to adapt the consolations of the gospel to each particular case." See Sprague's Annals. E. W.]

words from his diary will indicate the cast of his thought. He says:

My people love me too much, receive me with too much pleasure ; it is sweet to the human heart. Lord, save me from undue regard to men. I have been under a cloud, but, thanks be to God, such an outpouring of glory! Bless the Lord ! my help alone cometh from him.

A gay man of the world, not reverent toward holy things, once said to a relative, in whose house he was a frequent guest : " No one could be with Mr. Creagh without wishing to be good, and I do not believe any one could think of wrong in his presence."

His exceeding modesty forbade his being prominent in debate, but when he departed from his usual custom, his opinions were received with marked attention. Liberal toward all Christians, he was loyal to his own church. Thrice in the course of his ministry he was solicited to enter another denomination, but it was no temptation to his steadfast soul. In 1848 he led the New York delegation to the General Conference, in Pittsburgh, and again in Boston in 1852. About this time he preached a sermon on Christian perfection, which so impressed the lamented Dr. Horace Bushnell, who was one of his hearers, that he sought an introduction, which resulted in a correspondence that promised mutual pleasure, but was soon ended by the death of Mr. Creagh.

Upon leaving New York, in 1851, he became pastor of the South Fifth-street (now St. John's) church, Brooklyn. He entered upon his work with accustomed zeal, and proved himself to be "a workman that needed not to be ashamed." In the spring of 1852 the death of Bishop Hedding, whom he loved as a father, deeply affected him. He preached, by request, a memorial sermon in New York. So great was the effect upon his sensitive nature, that for days he suffered extreme nervous prostration. In May he attended the General Conference, after which he returned to pastoral duties with not quite his usual strength. Specially endearing were the relations of pastor and people, which resulted in frequent claims upon his time and sympathy outside his own church. These were rarely disregarded, for he counted not his life dear unto himself. On the first of August, with peculiar significance, he preached from the words, " Though I walk through the valley," etc. Little thought he that its chill shadows were even then fast closing around him. The next day he lay pale and feeble upon a bed of languishing, and after ten days of extreme prostration his pure spirit escaped its frail prison house to be "forever with the Lord."[6] Once he was heard to murmur, "My wife and children; my dear people!" but for the most part they were days of exceeding quiet, his spirit was still before God. Fully conscious that the time of his departure was at hand, with great tenderness he bade farewell to his loved ones, not forgetting a valued servant, saying, as she turned sobbing away, " Poor Bessie, a stranger in a strange land." He sent messages of love to the different churches of his care, South Fifth-street, Seventh-street, Allen-street. Vestry-street, and Sands-street. He said: ' That blessed Jesus, whose gospel I have endeavored to preach, does not forsake me now; he is my all-sufficient Saviour; he is intimately nigh." His countenance shone with heavenly radiance, as again and again he cried, " Victory! Victory! through the blood of the Lamb. Glory! all is glory!" Faith seemed to o'erleap the confines of dim sense, and view the angel of release, as with beckoning motion he said, " Come quickly, haste, haste!" To those who knew his devoted life there was fitness in the rapturous triumph of his farewell to the earth. As naturally as a liberated bird seeks its native air, his pure spirit swept up exultingly into the glorious unfoldings of infinite love.

According to man's measure, brief was his career, but rarely have forty-eight years been more richly endowed with earnest labor and sublime faith. Lovely in private life, untiring in duty, devoted in holiness, triumphant in death.[7]

Some of the most useful lives are those of which the world hears little, whose fragrance is no less pervasive because withdrawn from noisy comment. This thought was suggested by

---

[6] [The date of his death is August 10, 1852. Clark, in Sprague's Annals, says: " When death was approaching, after he had been apparently engaged in silent prayer for some minutes, he cried out, "O for an honest view! O for an honest view! I trust I have taken it!" Then looking round upon his friends, he said, ' Dig deep, dig deep! lay a good foundation !' He asked those present to sing ' Rock of Ages,' and after the singing he exclaimed, ' Yes, cleft for me.'"—E. W.]

[7] [J. B. Wakeley mentions Bartholomew Creagh as a "son of consolation, one of the sweetest spirits that ever tabernacled in clay tenement." He describes his person as neither corpulent nor slender, of light complexion, blue eyes, and head of great classic beauty. He says, furthermore, " I was a bearer at his funeral, and I could but feel that seldom had the church on earth lost a brighter ornament." See Sprague's Annals.—E. W.]

the life of ELIZA A. WELLING, who was born in New York, January 30, 1800. Her ancestors on one side were English, and Anglo-French on the other. Her father, William Welling, was an attendant of St. Paul's Episcopal church, but was attracted by the fervor of the services in John-street Methodist church, where, among the sweet singers in Israel, was Miss Hester Le Page, who afterward became his wife. Eliza Welling was the third child by this marriage.

She entered upon a Christian life when sixteen years of age, and gave to her Master no half-hearted allegiance. Possessed of a voice of singular sweetness, from that time it was employed only in singing the praises of her King. Her education was more thorough than was usual at that period, gained partly at Mr. Parker's school, in New York, (where, among her friends was Theodosia Burr, whose sad fate she always deplored,) and then completed in Baltimore, when she became an inmate of the household of her uncle, that eminent servant of God, Dr. George Roberts.

Skilled in domestic arts, she also took delight in the more active ministries of life, was engaged in home mission work, and a teacher and superintendent in the Allen-street Sunday-school, to which, years later, she returned as a pastor's wife.

In 1829 she was married to Rev. B. Creagh, and cheerfully accepted the sacrifices incident to the position. Years of sweet companionship and tender association followed, shadowed by the death of her first-born son. Never in rugged health, the full measure of her strength was given to the ways of her household, which was a home for the Lord's people, where many a one rested from the stress of life, as in the "palace beautiful." In four brief years a devoted husband, a son in the dawn of manhood, a father and mother, were taken from her home. Mrs. Creagh bore these keen afflictions with patient acquiescence, and abiding confidence in Him "whose compassions fail not."

Naturally shy and fond of quiet places, she now more than ever shunned publicity, and found content in the care of her two younger children, whom she sought to impress by word and life with the inestimable value of spiritual things.[8]

She was thoughtful, but never melancholy; extremely reserved,

---

[8] [The names of the children here referred to are *Anthony H.* and *Fidelia M. Creagh*, highly esteemed members of St. John's Methodist Episcopal church, Brooklyn, N. Y.—E. W.]

and therefore often misunderstood, revealing the depth of her nature only to the few who came into intimate nearness. Love of truth and simplicity were among her distinguishing characteristics; nothing was ever done for effect, and perhaps conventionality sometimes paled before this necessity of her nature.

More than three-score years and ten had passed in quiet usefulness; peace and serenity were the seal of what had been. Eyes sharpened by intense solicitude saw that natural powers were declining, but knew that, like the King's daughter, she was "all glorious within."

It sometimes seemed as if she lived between two worlds and held acquaintance with the skies. Frequently, when a soft, low utterance escaped her, in reply to her daughter's question, if she wished any thing, would come the answer, "No, dear, I was only speaking to my best Friend." Nothing in her life so well became her as the leaving it. The last day of health was spent as usual in useful occupation, and then suddenly, peacefully she took "the grand step beyond the stars" into limitless life and love.

"Their works do follow them," and in the home consecrated by her presence, her gentleness and serenity are a power and inspiration, and the loved voice still speaks from that other shore.

LVIII.
WILLIAM H. NORRIS.

SANDS-STREET CHURCH enjoyed the services of the Rev. WILLIAM HENRY NORRIS during two full ministerial terms; also, as presiding elder five years. He was identified with some of the most important events connected with the history of that church.

Mr. Norris was born in Orono. Maine, Oct. 28, 1801. His parents were orthodox, thrifty, intelligent people, and they "trained him in habits of filial piety." With them he came to the city of New York when fifteen years of age. At sixteen he was converted, and joined the Duane-street Methodist Episcopal Church. He heard a divine call, and abandoned fine lucrative mercantile prospects to enter the itinerancy, at the age of twenty-four. The following is his

MINISTERIAL RECORD: 1825, (New York Conf.,) Pittstown cir., N. Y., six months with J. C. Green and N. Rice;—last part of the year, Saratoga cir., with B. Crfffin, W. P. Lake and W. Anson, sup'y;[1] 1826, (Maine Conf.,) Belfast, Me.; 1827–1828, Bath,—ordained deacon in 1827; 1829, ordained elder,—Portland cir., with S. Lovelle; 1830, ditto, with J. Horton; 1831–1832, Hallowell; 1833, presiding elder, Portland Dist., 1834, Portland circuit, with E. Wiley; 1835–1836, Bangor; **1837–1838**, (New York Conf.,) **Brooklyn, Sands-street**, 1839–1841, missionary to Montevidio, S. A.; 1842, New York, Vestry-st.; 1842–1846, miss'y to Buenos Ayres; 1847. agent of the American Bible Society in Mexico; 1848–1849, **Brooklyn, Sands-street**; 1850–1851, New Haven, Conn., First church; 1852–1853, presiding elder, New Haven Dist.; 1854–1855, New York, Forsyth-street; 1856–1858, P. E., New York Dist.; 1859–1862, presiding elder, Long Island Dist.; 1863, appointed agent American Bible Society, Panama and Central America, but prevented by sickness from filling the appointment;[2] 1864, appointed missionary to South America, but change of plan by missionary board interfered with his going;[3] 1865, missionary presiding elder, Nashville, Tenn.; 1866, sup'y; 1867–1868, Durham, Conn.; 1869–1878, sup'y,[4] residing in Hempstead, N. Y.

---

[1] Conference Minutes do not mention his appointment to Saratoga, but see "Trial of J. C. Green vs. J. Pierce," p. 10.

[2] Mrs. Norris,—Letter to the author. [3] Ibid.

[4] His relation was not superannuated, as stated in his conference memorial, and he received no appropriation as a conference claimant.

REV. WILLIAM H. NORRIS.

He was married in 1831 to MISS SARAH MAHAN. The Maine Conference elected him to a seat in the General Conference in 1832 and in 1836. His return for a second term to three important appointments, namely, Portland, Bangor, and Sands-street, Brooklyn, indicates the high esteem in which he was held by the churches he was called to serve.

It is said that his early labors in Maine were marked by a continuous revival. He found 432 members and probationers in the Sands-street church, and two years later reported 667. A most wonderful revival crowned his unceasing, earnest labors there, and there are living witnesses of his glowing zeal and his manifest agony for souls, as he preached and prayed, and sometimes stood leaning against the pillars of the church weeping aloud for the perishing around him. He labored indefatigably during his second term in this charge, and under his leadership the church recovered from the loss of its buildings by fire, and rebuilt 'the church and parsonage. His labors in the First ehurch, New Haven, were characterized by the same fervent spirit, and attended with singular success.

He always appeared to have a painful sense of the high demands of the ministerial calling, and of his own insufficiency to meet the claims of God and the church upon him, yet, when assigned to any work, he always went cheerfully, and the church never had a more obedient servant. Personal considerations weighed nothing in his mind, when he heard the voice of the church, which was to him always the voice of God. One of his brethren writes:

The measure of the man may be best taken by reflecting on the estimate which the church itself made of him, and which may be seen in the varied and often delicate missions with which he was charged. He was a safe man, and one in whom the largest trusts could be reposed, and also one whose clear sense of right and ready ability of placing any matter of controversy in the simplest relations, made him at all times sought after for these valuable qualities.

As a preacher, the same conscientious painstaking was always apparent. Methodical, logical, and scrupulously conscientious, his sermons were models of exactness and forcible conclusions. His chief excellence, perhaps, lay in the pastorate. Indeed, it often seemed to us that if a man was ever called to a special work, Mr. Norris was called to this. Systematically dividing his time and his parish, he would go from house to house, mingling with his people, carrying their sorrows, advising in their perplexities, and especially sympathizing with the poor and fatherless; going as a man of God, and going with both hands and heart open to minister to whatever necessities might crave his sympathy.

Equally conscientious in his benevolence, his habit of giving was as exact as his habit of prayer. Whatever income he had was measured into its appropriate parts, and out of it must come the proper proportion which belonged to God. The best epitome of his character is that which the Scriptures give of the centurion, Cornelius. He was "a devout man, one that feared God with all his house, and gave much alms to the people, and prayed to God always." [5]

To some observers there was in him an appearance of sternness, on account of his extreme conscientiousness and strict sense of justice. Dr. Curry, in a memorial address, ascribed to him a severe purity, which caused a man of ordinary integrity, when thrown in contact with him, to question whether his own heart was right.

The author of his conference memorial says:

His extended travels and long association with the best societies of different countries, and his extensive reading upon subjects connected with his work, made him eminently capable of advice in times of grave inquiry. In the prosecution of his mission in South America, although chiefly directed to the English-speaking population of the cities where he labored, he gave himself to a diligent study of the Spanish language, that he might reach the natives through their vernacular; and also closely observed their manners and customs, and afterward became a valuable contributor to a published history of that interesting portion of our southern continent. And when the American Bible Society contemplated establishing an agency in Spain, Mr. Norris was selected for that work.

He was the author of two biographical works—abridgements—namely, a "Life of George Whitefield," and a "Life of Thomas Coke." [6]

The appearance of Mr. Norris was rather striking. His hair was long and dark, his eyes and complexion dark also, and there was upon his face what seemed to be a scar. Though he was of a strong constitution, he suffered much during a large part of his life, the result of an attack of acute bronchitis, brought on by exposure during his early ministry in Maine. In Tennessee a miasmatic fever was developed, from which he never entirely recovered.

A dark shadow enveloped him some two years previous to his death—the eclipse of his intellectual powers, accompanied

---

[5] Rev. Dr. Francis Bottome, in The Christian Advocate.

[6] Copies of these books are in the library of the Philadelphia Conference Historical Society.

Record of Ministers. 299

by physical decay. His memorial says that, as the closing hours drew near, " this curtain of night was lifted for a moment, that he might recognize and smile upon the dear ones who watched for his departure, and then he was at rest."

So died this faithful servant of the church, on the 19th of October, 1878, having nearly completed the seventy-seventh year of his pilgrimage. His burial-place, in Greenfield cemetery, Hempstead, is marked by a granite monument.

His widow resides in Hempstead, Long Island, with a married daughter. The two surviving sons are active members of the Presbyterian Church in a Western State. The other children, five in number, " are in the better land."

LIX.

THE REV. FITCH REED, D. D. was born in Amenia, N. Y., March 28, 1795. He was reared under Calvinistic instruction, but when he heard the Methodist preachers, he readily embraced the reasonable and scriptural doctrine of free grace and unlimited redemption. In the nineteenth year of his age he was awakened and converted under the ministry of Marvin Richardson, the junior preacher on the Dutchess circuit.

He soon abandoned his studies for the medical profession under a strong conviction that it was his duty to devote his life to the work of the Christian ministry. He writes:

In the ear of conscience the call was as distinct and emphatic as if a voice from heaven had audibly declared, "Preach or be lost forever!"[1]

He received his first license to preach at the age of twenty, and thereupon was immediately employed by Nathan Bangs, presiding elder, to labor on a circuit.

APPOINTMENTS: 1815, last part of the year, supply, Rhinebeck cir., N. Y., with Wm. Anson and Thos. Thorp; 1816, supply, Goshen cir., Conn., with S. Cochran and Daniel Coe, supply; 1817, (New York Conf.,) Suffolk cir., N. Y., with William Jewett; 1818, Sag Harbor, 1819, ordained deacon by Bishop Roberts,—Dunham circuit, Vermont and Lower Canada; 1820, missionary to York, Canada; 1821, ordained elder—missionary to York and New

---

[1] Semi-centennial sermon, p. 7.

settlements, with K. M. K. Smith; 1822, Ithaca and Caroline cir., N. Y., with Dana Fox; 1823, presiding elder, Susquehanna Dist.; 1824, Ithaca; 1825-1826, Cazenovia; 1827, Utica; 1828, (New York Conf.,) Rhinebeck; 1829, Amenia cir., with A. S. Hill; 1830, ditto, with Lorin Clark; 1831-1832, Middletown, Conn.; 1833, New York city, west cir., with P. P. Sandford, J. Bowen, J. C. Green, and C. W. Carpenter; 1834, ditto, with J. B. Stratton, . C. Green, D. De Vinne, and J. C. Tackaberry; 1835, agent for Wesleyan University; 1836, Amenia cir., with D. Holmes, and J. P, Ellsworth; 1837, Amenia and Sharon cir., with D. Holmes and G. L. Fuller; 1838, presiding elder, New Haven Dist.; **1839, Brooklyn, Sands-street;** 1840, Poughkeepsie, with P. P. Sandford; 1841, Poughkeepsie, 2nd ch.; 1842-1843, Sharon, Conn.; 1844-1845, Danbury; 1846-1847, Peekskill, N. Y.; 1848-1849, Oneida Conf.,) Ithaca; 1850, presiding elder, Susquehanna Dist.; 1851, Newark Dist; 1852, Ithaca Dist.; 1853-1856, Auburn Dist.; 1857, Ithaca, Seneca-street; 1858-1859, Port Byron; 1860-1861, Asbury; 1862-1868, sup'd; 1869-1871, (Central New York Conf.,) sup'd.

His delay in joining conference was on account of sickness and the fears which he and others entertained that he was too frail to endure the toils and privations of an itinerant preacher's life. His published writings contain many interesting reminiscences of his early ministry. On Goshen circuit, while but a youth, he was permitted to lead a man one hundred and four years old to a saving trust in Jesus. He thus describes his journey to the Suffolk circuit, in 1817:

As soon as I received my appointment I went to my father's and spent a few days at the dear home of my childhood. * * * Tuesday, June 24, the farewell was spoken, and I started to find my new field of labor. On horseback and alone, and by roads I had never traveled before, I journeyed to my destined place of toil, about one hundred and forty miles distant. That journey I shall never forget. I instinctively smile when I think of it, and call to mind several little incidents associated with my natural bashfulness and easily excited embarassment among strangers. I had been instructed to inquire at certain places for Methodist families, where the preachers were accustomed to call, and where I would find welcome entertainment. It was exceedingly embarrassing to me to call on entire strangers, introduce myself as a preacher, and virtually ask entertainment for myself and beast as a gratuity.

To find my way through the city of New York and to Long Island, that was the great question of my journey. I dreaded it beyond measure. What places and whom should I inquire for? I thought that as " a fool when he holdeth his peace is counted wise," I would keep my own counsels, and, if possible, not expose my verdancy. But I was driven from my circumspection. I found myself on Broadway, and, as it seemed to be a well traveled road, I pushed on, knowing it would lead me *somewhere*. And it did. I came in sight of the Battery and the waters of the bay beyond. Now what shall I do? Here is a gentlemanly looking man; I will ask him to direct me. "Can you tell me, sir, if there are any Methodists living about here?" O dear! now I have betrayed myself. I have told him that I am a green country boy. A very significant smile and a shake of the head was his only reply. Turning to retrace my steps, I saw upon the corner of a house, "John-street." It instantly occurred to me that I had seen this name in the imprint of our hymn book. Turning down the street, I soon came to our "Methodist Book Room," where I received a cordial greeting by Joshua Soule, the senior book agent, and I once more felt like myself.

Crossing the East River into Brooklyn, I traveled that day as far as Jamaica, where, by direction of friends in New York, I called at the hospitable mansion of Brother Disosway, whose friendly greetings and kind attentions made ample amends for my previous embarrassments and perplexities. Friday I reached Hauppauge, a principal appointment on the circuit, and a short morning ride from Westfield, where the next day our quarterly meeting was to commence. I reached there on Saturday in time for the meeting, where I found my colleague, Rev. Wm. Jewett, and our presiding elder, Rev. Samuel Merwin.[2]

Concerning his appointment to Dunham circuit, whose northern limit was in sight of Montreal, he writes:

Frail as I was, I did at first wonder that the lot should fall to me just here, and thought that possibly the bishop had made a mistake in my appointment; yet, before the year had expired, I most clearly perceived that it was the Lord, more than the bishop, who had supervision of the case. The harsh climate, the hard work and plenty of it, and the harder fare, were just what infinite Wisdom saw I needed. I praise the Lord to this day for Dunham circuit. It saved me from an early grave.[3]

In the following year, 1820, he was the gospel pioneer in the wilderness lying north of Lake Ontario. He says:

The distance to be traveled in reaching it, including my journey to and from conference, was nearly *one thousand miles*. No circuit had been formed; no one had preceded me as a messenger of mercy; not a sermon, I believe, had been preached in all that region; little more, indeed, than twelve months had elapsed since the ax was first heard to break the stillness of the forest. There were no roads, no bridges, no food for a horse; so that all my travel, by no means very limited, was of necessity on foot. I was directed by a compass, without regard to the marks or monuments of the surveyor. I carried with me a common Indian hatchet, both as a defense against ferocious wild beasts, and as a means of constructing bridges over streams of water too deep to ford.[4]

It is not a little surprising that one so well entitled to the

---

[2] "Reminiscences," in the Northern Christian Advocate, 1863.
[3] Semi-centennial Sermon, p. 9.
[4] Ibid., p. 11.

rank of a pioneer should have so little prominence in the standard histories of the church.

He was married in 1823 to Miss Almeda Dana, sister of the late eminent Judge Amasa Dana, of Ithaca, N. Y.[5] He was a member of the General Conferences of 1824, 1832, 1840, and 1844.[6] In 1860 the Genesee College requested the Oneida Conference to designate some member of that body upon whom the degree of D.D. should be conferred. His daughter writes:

> The conference selected my father. He valued the honor, coming in that way, as a mark of their respect, though he had no fondness for degrees in themselves.[7]

During the ten years of his retirement he resided in Ithaca, N. Y., where he had been pastor several terms, and where his wife's relatives resided. Notwithstanding a troublesome bronchial and asthmatic affection, he was able to preach occasionally, and was not confined to his room until one week previous to his death. His uniformly clear and blessed experience became manifestly more glowing and exultant during the last year of his life; and "when finally too weak to do more than whisper now and then a word, he still strove to tell how unspeakably precious Jesus was to him."[8] Thus he passed away on the 10th of October, 1871, in the seventy-seventh year of his age. A plain head-stone designates his grave in the cemetery in Ithaca, N. Y. His widow and two or three daughters reside in or near Ithaca.

Fitch Reed was one of the golden links uniting this generation of Methodists to the early fathers of the church. He is thus characterized in his conference memorial:

> Dr. Reed was a man of scholarly attainments, possessed of an active, logical mind, refined taste, quick, sound judgment, pure, strong, and noble impulses. His preaching was at once instructive, entertaining, convincing, and persuasive. By his labors and sympathies he was always identified with the progressive spirit of the church. His piety was ardent and transparent. All knew its source; it bore the seal of Christ, and could meet the approval of heaven.

---

[5] Smith's "Pillars in the Temple," p. 187.
[6] The conference memorial says, incorrectly, 1820, and omits 1832 and 1834.
[7] Miss Kate Reed—letter to the author.
[8] The Rev. O. H. Warren, in The Christian Advocate.

LX.
STEPHEN MARTINDALE.

LONG ISLAND having been detached from the old New York District in 1840, the REV. STEPHEN MARTINDALE, one of the leading ministers in the conference, then fifty-two years of age, was placed in charge of the district as its first presiding elder. He was a native of the Eastern Shore of Maryland. He hailed from a state in which Methodism was early established and has always flourished; a state which gave to the denomination the first native American preacher, Richard Owen, and the first native American itinerant, William Watters;[1] and after them such renowned and heroic men as Freeborn Garrettson, Wm. Phœbus, Laurence M'Combs, George Pickering, Bishops Emory and Scott, and many others of equal power and fame. Tuckahoe Neck, the neighborhood from which he came, "furnished its quota of preachers for the itinerancy in the Reverends Ezekiel Cooper, Solomon Sharp, Stephen Martindale and Thomas Neal."[2]

Stephen Martindale was born near the Choptank River in the year 1788. His grandfather was a clergyman of the Church of England. His father, Daniel Martindale, was a Methodist class leader and local preacher. Ezekiel Cooper was a member of his class. A large part of his property was in slaves, but he set them free. He was a holy man. The mother of Stephen Martindale was named Mary Mead. He was the youngest of a family of ten children, and was two years old when his mother died. While he was yet a child his father was taken from him, and he was placed under the care of his sister, a woman of rare accomplishments, from whom he received an excellent training, and toward whom he ever cherished the deepest and truest affection.[3]

---

[1] Lednum—Rise of Methodism, p. 21.   [2] Ibid., p. 165.

[3] The author is indebted for these facts to the daughters of Stephen Martindale, Mrs. Dr. A. S. Purdy of New York, and Miss Mary Martindale of Tarytown.

REV. STEPHEN MARTINDALE.

He engaged in the work of the ministry under the direction of his presiding elder in the year 1808. The name of his charge is not known.

PASTORAL RECORD : 1808, supply ; 1809, Somerset cir., Md., with David Best; 1810, Dover cir., Del., with J. Sharpley ; 1811, ordained deacon, —Snow Hill cir., Md., with W. Wickes ; 1812, Morris cir., N. J., with J. Van Shaick ; 1813, ordained elder,—Essex cir., with John Finley ; 1814, Bergen cir., with Phineas Price ; 1815, Philadelphia, St. George's, with Robert Burch and L. Laurenson ; 1816, ditto, with Robert Burch and Martin Ruter ; 1817, Talbot cir., Md., with W. Quinn ; 1818, Queen Ann's cir., with Thos. Ware ; 1819, ditto, with Wm. Ryder ; 1820, Kent cir., with T. Smith ; 1821, Newark, N. J. ; 1822, (New York Conf.,) New York city cir., with E. Washburn, M. Richardson, Wm. Ross, H. Bangs, and J. Summerfield ; 1823, ditto, with E. Washburn, P. Rice, J. B. Stratton, S. Bushnell, and E. Brown ; 1824, New Rochelle cir., with H. Bangs, L. Andrus, sup'y ; 1825, ditto, with P. Rice, L. Andrus, sup'y : 1826–1827, Troy ; 1828–1829, (New England Conf.,) Boston, Mass., with E. Wiley ; 1830, (New York Conf.,) New York city cir., with S. Luckey, S. Merwin. L. Pease, B. Goodsell, N. Bangs, and S. D. Ferguson; 1831, ditto, with S. Merwin, L. Pease, B. Goodsell, S. Landon, J. Clark, B. Sillick, and C. Prindle ; 1832, Stratford cir., Conn., with L. C. Cheney ; 1833–1836, presiding elder, New Haven Dist., Conn. ; 1837, White Plains and Greensburgh cir., N. Y., with D. I. Wright, R. Harris, sup'y ; 1838, ditto, with J. A. Sillick, S. U. Fisher, sup'y, and R. Harris, sup'y ; 1839, presiding elder, Rhinebeck Dist. : **1840–1843, presiding elder, Long Island Dist.** ; 1844–1845, New York, Eighteenth-street ; 1846–1847, New York, Norfolk-street ; 1848–1850, presiding elder, Delaware Dist. ; 1851, Newburgh Dist. ; 1852–1854, New York Dist. ; 1855–1858, Poughkeepsie Dist. ; 1859, Irvington, N. Y, ; 1860, superannuated.

His daughter writes :

I heard my father say that when he went out to preach he was but nineteen years of age and had only one shilling in his pocket, but that he had never wanted for money.[4]

Having traveled four years, he was married in 1812. His wife taught school to supplement their insufficient salary. He was ordained by Bishop Asbury, and was on familiar terms with all the earlier bishops. "He came North," says his daughter, "on account of slavery. His wife was greatly opposed to the system, and told the Southerners that some day all their slaves would be free."

Remarkable revivals attended Mr. Martindale's labors in Troy, Bowery Village, and Boston. He was greatly interested in the work of his friend, Father Taylor, of Boston, and he aided in the formation of the Port Society of that city.

---

[4] Mrs. Dr. A. E. Purdy—letter to the author.

With R. R. Roberts, L. M'Combs, Joseph Totten, Ezekiel Cooper, and other famous men, he represented the Philadelphia Conference as General Conference delegate in 1816 and 1820, and with Garrettson, Merwin, Bangs, Ostrander, Washburn, Sandford, Waugh, Richardson, Clark, Rice, Olin, Peck, and others of like standing, he formed a part of the New York Conference delegations in 1824, 1828, 1836, and 1844.

After more than half a century of devoted, heroic, and useful service in the active ministry, he departed this life in great peace, May 23, 1860, in the seventy-third year of his age. His illness was of about two months' duration. To an aged friend who visited him he said, "I have always believed in the doctrines I have preached, and they sustain me now." [b] To the Rev. John J. Matthias, who called upon him, he quoted with animation some of the most triumphant strains of the psalmist. That was an hour of supreme interest to these two men of God. They were to meet no more on the shores of time, but were destined to hail each other very soon on the plains of heavenly glory. The memorial in the Conference Minutes contains the following:

> Mr. Martindale's eldest daughter states that about a week before his death he awoke from sleep with an expression of joy on his countenance. She inquired why he looked so joyous. "O," said he, "I rejoice with all my heart. * * * My work is done. * * * I am a sinner saved by grace!"

His friend, John J. Matthias, wrote for The Christian Advocate as follows:

> His funeral sermon was preached by the writer on 2 Tim. iv, 7, 8: "I have fought a good fight," etc., in the presence of a numerous congregation, in the Methodist church in Tarrytown. Rev. Mr. Wakeley offered prayer at the house, and Rev. Drs. M'Clintock and Foster, and Rev. Mr. Todd, of the Dutch Church, led the devotions of the congregation. Among the pall-bearers were the pastors of the village (Baptist, Episcopalian, Dutch Reformed) and others. The neighboring gentlemen sent their carriages to convey the people to the grave.

He and his wife are buried in a neatly inclosed plot in Sleepy Hollow cemetery, in Tarrytown, N. Y., and modest head-stones mark their resting-place.

Mr. Martindale is uniformly described by those who knew him as a man of uncommon amiability, cool self-possession, and good judgment. Many remember him as a sound theolo-

---

[b] Minutes of Conferences, 1861, p. 113.

gian, a good pastor, a loved presiding elder, (twenty years in that office,) a popular preacher, a sweet singer, and "remarkably gifted in prayer." His "diction was always correct and often elegant." He was "tall and well-proportioned, with a countenance fair and ruddy, expressive of intelligence and benignity," and he spoke with "a voice whose rich intonations flowed and rippled like a brook."[6] In all his varied relations he maintained a consistent piety. His daughter says—and her words are quoted in his obituary—

It was my father's example that made me a Christian. It was his daily walk in the privacy of family and home that preached and made us love the religion which he illustrated.

Twenty-one years after his death his younger daughter wrote:

I often heard my father say that if he thought he had one drop of bigotry in his veins, and knew where to find it, he would take an instrument and let it out. Nevertheless, both of our parents were the most intense Methodists; and we children gloried in Methodism because it was the religion of such parents, and was progressive. Yes, my father made us intelligent Methodists. He said he wished us to choose Methodism for ourselves; and so, as soon as we came to years of discretion, he procured the standard books of each church, as well as "Hurd on all Religions," and frequently conversed with us on any mooted point; not forcing us, but leaving us alone to read and inquire at our own option. In looking into my father's face I always thought of the glory of a June day—the deep-blue eyes were like the sky, and his smile was like the sunshine. Seldom are children nurtured amid such elevating influences. * * * Both parents were singularly fond of young people, especially such as were struggling to rise. Our house was a home for many such, and many have been sent forth therefrom rejoicing. When my brothers were in college (we lived in the town part of the time) they were urged to bring their college mates home; for both father and mother were aware that there was no safeguard for these young men like such a home as they knew ours to be. Dr. Fisk, his compeers and successors, were household friends, and loved to come to our house for relaxation and social cheer. Excuse me for writing so freely—it is seldom I do this. * * *

My father was morbidly sensitive in regard to any parade of services rendered. We used to talk often about this, but I could not change his mind. I sometimes playfully told him, "I might some day support myself by such things," but his invariable, gentle, reverent reply to me was, "God knows." To-day, when papers and books do so laud human service, I love the memory of my sainted father all the more intensely because of this reticence. I have two manuscript volumes of sermons and outlines to tell me what he did in public. His home life is in my heart.[7]

---

[6] Conference Minutes, 1861, p. 114.
[7] Miss Mary Martindale—letter to the author.

MARY (SANDFORD,) his wife, daughter of Joseph Sandford,[8] was born in Belleville, N. J., September 26, 1788, and died in Tarrytown, N. Y., November 6, 1868, in the eightieth year of her age. Dr. Joseph Holdich wrote a beautiful sketch of her life for The Christian Advocate, in which he says :

> Mrs. Martindale used to tell the story of her own conversion. When she was twenty years of age her father, [an Episcopalian at the time,] one evening soon after his own awakening, went to a prayer-meeting held at a neat neighbor's. "Tell Mary," he said to her mother, "to come to the prayer-meeting." Mary was accustomed to say, "If my mother had told me my father was dead, I could not have felt worse than when she told me that he had gone to a Methodist prayer-meeting, and directed me to come likewise." But she never dreamed for an instant of disobeying him. That prayer-meeting resulted in the conversion of both father and daughter. She gave her heart to Christ, and both united in membership in the same "household of faith." At the age of twenty-four she was united in marriage to the Rev. Stephen Martindale, then in the zenith of his popularity ; * * * but the Methodist Church, then in its infancy, was feeble, poor, little understood, and not in good repute among the more cultured classes, or in the world at large. But none of these things moved her. She became the devout and devoted wife of a Methodist preacher, and cheerfully shared all his toils. She was his helpful companion, encouraging, counseling, sustaining him, manifesting a happy temper, and looking naturally at the bright and hopeful side. She could put up with inconveniences without complaining ; while, by a prudent but not pinching economy, she made the small stipend of a minister of that day not only meet their wants, but sustain a reputable appearance. She brought up their children with great propriety and respectability, securing them educations adapted to any station in society. * * * Her children and grandchildren have in her sweet life and example a blessed treasure that shall not be forgotten.

Her pastor, the Rev. Charles S. Brown, in an address at her funeral, said :

> I shall never forget—those who sat near her, and especially the daughter who was with her, will never forget—the rapture of her spirit the last time she filled her seat in the house of God. It was her custom to retire, leaning on the arm of her beloved daughter, before the closing services, to escape the excitement of passing out with the congregation. But on that day she could not go. She joined with unusual fervor in singing the last hymn, and at the close, turning to a lady who sat near her, expressed her desire, if it might be the will of God, to go from the earthly directly to the heavenly sanctuary.[9]

The day before her death this pastor found her too feeble for distinct utterance, but giving other signs of peace that is

---

[8] See sketch of the Rev. P. P. Sandford in this work.
[9] Quoted by the Rev. Dr. Holdich in his memorial sketch.

"like a river." The Rev. J. W. B. Wood, a former pastor, was with her when she departed. Mr. Brown said further:

She was a member of the New York Female Bible Society, and active as a Bible visitor. She was also a member of the Female Assistance Society, and for some time one of its managers. * * * Not only her husband and her children shared the fruits of her self-denial, but strangers and the poor always found in her a friend. Take the following specimen: Twelve little children coming in yesterday to look at her remains, one of them said to the rest, "Who will give us cake, now Grandma Martindale is dead?"

Dr. C. K. True, who knew her long and well, wrote a loving testimonial to her children after her departure. Our limited space forbids us to quote from it. The following tribute by her daughter is too good to be omitted:

My mother learned by heart many of the poems of standard English authors, and in the last year (eightieth) of her life would repeat page after page of Pope, Pollock, Cowper, " dear old Goldy," (Goldsmith,) and lots of others. My father, even, with his fine mental qualities, always deferred to my mother on that score. She was wonderfully appreciative and brilliant, even in her eightieth year, quick at repartee, and well posted in all important political, social, and intellectual questions in home and foreign lands. She was, moreover, one of the best and most sympathizing of friends to the poor and lowly. I was but a child when we lived in Boston, I remember, and my sister was a lovely young lady. One of my brothers had a little hand wagon. Often, after night-fall, my mother would fill this wagon with fuel, and, giving my sister a basket filled with good things, would send the two out on missions of love to some distressed home. We were always taught by both parents that any loving, unselfish act never degraded us, however poor and miserable might be the recipient.

When my parents were young, father's salary was so small that my mother opened a little school, and in after years she used laughingly to say she "made much more money than did my father." * * * We lived one year in Brooklyn while father was presiding elder of Long Island District, and he advised us each to unite with a different church. My mother went to York-street, brother Stephen to Centenary, I to Washingson-street, and all rallied at Sands-street.[10]

As we might expect, we are able to make a gratifying record of the children of Stephen and Mary Martindale: *James Alexander*, after studying medicine at Yale, lost his health, took a sea-voyage for restoration, (his passion was the sea,) rose to rank, and died in Santo Domingo, of yellow fever, November 15, 1844. *Anne Sandford*, wife of Dr. Alfred S. Purdy, of New

---

[10] Miss Mary Martindale—letter to the author.

York, who died December 2, 1883, was for nearly twenty years first directress of the New York Female Assistance Society for the Relief of the Sick Poor, and for a long time a manager of the New York Female Auxiliary Bible Society, (with both of these societies, as we have seen, her mother was connected many years ago;) she was also a manager of the New York Branch of the Woman's Foreign Missionary Society, and of the M'Clintock Association, and of the Five Points' Mission. She is also remembered as connected with the Soldiers' Relief Association in the work at the hospitals during the war for the Union. *Stephen, Jr.*, a true Christian gentleman, was graduated with honor at the Wesleyan University, practiced law in the city of NewYork, and died May 28, 1852. *Joseph*, a druggist by occupation, died May 24, 1853. *Mary*, twin sister of Joseph, was never married. She wrote, July 9, 1883, to the author:

I am trying to follow my father as he followed Christ, which was lovingly and faithfully. I am a lone woman, fighting the world with my own two little hands, but the memories of the departed are my strongholds, and, please God, when the fight is over the reunion and rest will be glorious.

She entered that "glorious rest," from her home in Tarrytown, N. Y., on the 15th of February, 1884, and near the graves of her parents a new mound was made over her mortal remains. *Daniel*, a younger brother, was graduated from Wesleyan University at the head of his class, entered the legal profession, was State's attorney in Jackson, La., and died a victim of yellow fever, November 1, 1853—" a martyr to his own kindness of disposition, as he caught the fever from nursing a friend."[11] Mary wrote in a letter:

My three younger brothers all died within eighteen months—all noble sons, our great hope and dependence. My parents never fully recovered from the pain of this bereavement, yet never let the shadow of our great loss fall upon others. It seemed to ripen them for heaven.

---

[11] Dr. Holdich in The Christian Advocate.

LXI.

P. C. Oakley

WE are informed that the Oakleys sprung from the substantial yeomanry of old England. The name can be found as far back as the eighth century. At a[n] early period in the history of this country, three members of the Oakley family came hither and landed in Boston. [For] a while one of them settled in the county of Westchester, N. Y. George Oakley, one of his descendants, was father [of the] subject of this sketch. He became a Methodist in Westchester county, moved to New York city, joined the old [John-]street church, and finally moved "up town," casting in [his lot] with the Forsyth-street brethren, and his remains [were] laid to rest in the burial ground of that church.

[The] REV. PETER CANNON OAKLEY was born in the city of [New] York, August 20, 1800. From early childhood he attended the Methodist meetings, but his mind was not permanently impressed with divine truth until he read in a book [called] "Russell's Seven Sermons" a discourse on "Time and [Eternity]." About this time his father died instantly from a [stroke] of apoplexy. This terrible bereavement strengthened [his] purpose to choose God for his Father and guide. A [kind] Providence had prepared for him an excellent Christian home with the parents of "Harper and Brothers," where, [thoug]h he was but an apprentice, he was treated as one of [the fa]mily. Gradually, by the leadings of the Spirit and the [encou]ragement afforded by "Father and Mother Harper," he [was b]rought to the enjoyment of divine favor, and joined [the Jo]hn-street church when about seventeen years of age. [Rec]alling this event he writes: "I am probably the only [ma]n now living who was then in the old hive."[1]

---

[1] [Let]ter to the author.

His first license as an exhorter was signed by Ebenezer Washburn, preacher in charge, New York city, November 11, 1822. About twelve months later, after he had been traveling some time under P. P. Sandford, presiding elder, as a supply, he received a local preacher's license, and a recommendation to the New York Annual Conference.

Previous to his conversion he had gained but a limited knowledge of reading, writing, and arithmetic. His conversion aroused in him an ardent thirst for knowledge, and though working at the printing press fourteen hours a day, he found "much time to read," and, in company with J. Wesley Harper and Nicholas Murray, (afterward the Rev. Dr. Murray,) he studied English grammar. Having served his apprenticeship, he entered the Wesleyan Seminary, in Crosby-street, New York, where he acquired some knowledge of the Latin and Greek languages.

MINISTERIAL RECORD: 1823, supply, Croton cir., N. Y. with Marvin Richardson; (New York Conf.,) Croton cir., with M. Richardson; 1825, Granville cir , Mass. and Conn., with Smith Dayton ; 1826, ordained deacon,—ditto, with D. Miller and Job Allen ; 1827, Pittsfield cir., Mass., with B. Sillick and S. C. Hurd ; 1828, ordained elder,—ditto, with B. Sillick and C. F. Pelton ; 1829-1830, Poultney, Vt. ; 1831, Middlebury; 1832, (Troy Conf.,) Middlebury ; 1833, Charlotte and Shelburn cir.; 1834, ditto, with J. Gobbett ; 1835-1837, presiding elder, Plattsburgh Dist. ; 1838, Troy N. Y., North Second-street, with J. Cannon, sup'y ; 1839, Oneida Conf., Ithaca ; **1840-1841,** (New York Conf.,) **Brooklyn, Sands-street;** 1842-1843, New York, Willett-street; 1844-1845, Stamford, Conn.; 1846, Hartford, Conn., with C. Fletcher ; 1847, Hartford ; 1848-1849, Saugerties, N. Y.; 1850, agent, New York State Colonization Society ; 1851-1852, Yorkville, N. Y.; 1853-1854, Goshen; 1855-1858, presiding elder, Rhinebeck Dist.; 1859-1860, Cold Spring ; 1861, Ashford and Greensburgh ; 1862-1863, North Newburgh ; 1864-1866, Shrub Oak ; 1867-1869 Sugar Loaf ; 1870-1871, Milton ; 1873-1874, sup'y ; 1875-1884, sup'd.

He traveled and preached fifty years without losing six months during the entire period. In a letter to the author he says :

In my earlier circuits I preached about thirty sermons in a month, leading class after each public service. The custom was on Sunday to preach three times and lead three classes. But I performed the work as a matter of course, and never thought it hard. The pay was small—one hundred dollars a year for a single man, and I was counted such for four years—but I never grieved at that, for I did not preach for money.

Mr. Oakley was married, September 12, 1827, in Windsor, Conn., to Miss MARIA LOOMIS. His brethren elected him delegate to the General Conference of 1836. He was married a ond time, in 1844, to Miss HARRIET SILLICK, daughter of friend and former colleague, the Rev. Bradley Sillick. This e still survives, and the two are enjoying a serene and happy age in the town of Milton, N. Y.

Concerning his connection with Sands-street church, Mr. kley writes:

ly pastorate in Brooklyn was interesting and very pleasant, but the incits were not remarkable. The longest confinement I ever had in my min-/ was there. In consequence of visiting a sick sister, I caught the oloid, and was kept in-doors some weeks. I have pleasant memories of V. Harper and family, Jacob Brown, John Smith, David Coope, Father rbert, etc., etc. But most of them are gone—I hope to meet them on the er shore.[3]

That he has learned the art of growing old gracefully, is dent from the following statement:

s it regards myself *now*, my eyesight is good, my hearing a little defective, hand, as you see, trembles; otherwise my mental and physical powers are fair order for one who has passed through eighty-three summers. My dren are all gone, except a daughter, who is unmarried and remains at 1e. Myself, wife, and daughter form a trio to be broken by and by; but re is a "sweet by and by," where we hope to meet, not as a little trio, but t part of the general assembly and church of the first-born in heaven.

MARIA, his wife, died in the Willett-street parsonage, April 1844, in the forty-seventh year of her age. She was born in 98, in Windsor, Conn., and experienced religion a short time or to her marriage. Her piety was uniform and genuine. e spent her last Sabbath, though feeble, in the house of God. he was her husband's best earthly friend and confidential viser. As a mother, she loved her children, and by every ans in her power, sought their present and future welfare."[4]

Letter to the author.
Dr. Noah Levings in The Christian Advocate.

LXII

Leond M. Vincent

HE ministry of the REV. LEONARD M. VINCENT in the old Sands-street church was a very marked success. At the close of his term in the year 1844, the full members and probationers had increased to six hundred and sixty-four, the largest membership to which the church ever attained.

Like Peter P. Sandford's second initial, the "M." in Leonard M. Vincent's name is only a distinguishing letter. Mr. Vincent is the only surviving ex-pastor of this church whom the writer has never seen—a lack only partly compensated by a pleasant but very brief correspondence. This fact makes the task of writing the present sketch more than ordinarily difficult and delicate.

The date of Leonard M. Vincent's birth is October 16, 1814; the place one of the villages on the eastern shore of the Hudson—town of Washington, Dutchess, County, N. Y. His childood home was a little cottage by the river's brink.

From its windows in front, vessels could be seen passing up and down. Hard by, at the end of the cottage, was a creek, emptying itself into the river. Near the mouth of the creek was a beautiful waterfall. This was backed by a large pond of water, the motive power of mills and factories that stood below. The location of the cottage was picturesque in the extreme. Here he spent his early days, and spent them happily, in the society of an affectionate mother and a devoted sister near three years his senior.[1]

Leonard was very young when his father died, and his mother, though not a Christian, trained him in "the strictest morality." In accordance with his father's expressed desire, the boy was placed at the age of ten years in the care of his uncle, to be brought up on a farm. At fourteen he returned to the home of his mother, to spend a year in

---

[1] "The Farmer Boy" pp. 13, 15. This volume is from the pen of Mr. Vincent—an autobiography; disguised, however, by the use of an assumed name. Most of the facts here narrated are gleaned from this little book.

school. Although his religious instruction had been very limited, he was placed in charge of a class of boys in the Sunday-school. By this means he became acquainted with the minister and other pious persons, who "taught him the way of the Lord more perfectly." In a short time he was powerfully convicted of sin and happily saved. His struggles with his own heart, the firmness of his resolution, the bitterness of his repentance, the fierceness of his temptations, and the rapture of his deliverance, were quite remarkable in the experience of one so young. He exhibited great conscientiousness and sincerity from the beginning of his Christian life. Following his convictions of duty he asked the privilege of erecting a family altar in his mother's home; and, in the presence of the family and several visitors, none of whom were professors of religion, he offered prayer. The joy of the lad was complete when, a short time afterward, he learned that by manfully bearing the heavy cross in the presence of his mother, sister, uncle, and aunt, he had been the means of leading them all to Christ, and erecting two family altars instead of one.

His call to the ministry was simultaneous with his conversion, but not very promptly obeyed. He abandoned the idea of farming, and entered the employ of his sister's husband as clerk of a store in New York. During his stay there he was connected with the Duane-street church, where he became associated with the lamented Dr. Emory and other eminent Christians. Leaving the city at the end of one year, he returned to his native village, served as a clerk in a store two years, then engaged in mercantile business on his own account. After his marriage, which occurred about this time, he applied himself the more closely to business for two or three years, "toiling on under constant convictions and struggles of mind" concerning his call to the ministry.

Receiving license as a local preacher in the summer of 1832, he preached his first sermon in a school-house on a Sunday afternoon. A horn was blown to call the people together. It was the last message to which some of the hearers ever listened, for the cholera seized five persons of that congregation soon after the service closed, and they were *dead and buried* before eleven o'clock the next day.

Providence opening the way for a satisfactory disposal of his business interests, he entered the itinerant ministry in the year 1837.

316   *Old Sands Street Church.*

CONFERENCE RECORD: 1837, (New York Conf.,) Dutchess cir., N. Y., with John Reynolds; 1838, ditto, with S. Cochran; 1839, ordained deacon by Bishop Hedding,—Mount Pleasant cir., with S. Van Dusen; 1840, ditto, with D. Holmes; 1841, ordained elder,—Johnsville, with J. A. Chalker; **1842-1843, Brooklyn, Sands-street**; 1844, Rhinebeck; 1845-1846, New York, Allen-street; 1847-1848, New York, Duane-street; 1849-1850, Poughkeepsie, Washington-street; 1851-1852, Matteawan; 1853-1854, New York, Sullivan-street; 1855-1858, presiding elder, Newburgh Dist.; 1859-1862, presiding elder, Poughkeepsie Dist.; 1863, Poughkeepsie, Washington-street; 1864-1884, superannuated.

In Sands-street church, as already intimated, Mr. Vincent was exceedingly industrious and successful. He endeared himself to the young, the sick, and the poor—to all, indeed, as a man of warm sympathy, sound judgment, and remarkable adaptation to the pastor's vocation. He was there during "a year of revivals," and Sands-street church shared in the general visitation. Mention has already been made of the demolition of the old white church, and the erection of a new, brick edifice during his ministry there.

Several incidents of Mr. Vincent's pastorate in Sands-street are recorded in the story of "The Farmer Boy." In the humble home of a pious widow, a native of Scotland, her little son, John, sickened and died. He had been found by a kind teacher and led to the Sands-street Sunday-school; the mother had followed her boy to the church, and both had learned the blessedness of trusting in the Lord. Their home was an attic in an obscure "alley;" but the pastor found it to be the abode of heavenly peace. He writes:

Frequent interviews with John confirmed my very favorable opinion of his piety and preparedness for heaven. The same calm resignation to the Divine will, the same sweetness of spirit was manifested up to the hour of his departure. * * * He whispered, "I am ready," and sweetly slept in Jesus. * * * John was buried on a Sabbath afternoon. It was one of those bright and glowing days of summer, when nature seemed loudest to proclaim the goodness and mercy of the Lord. Early in the afternoon the corpse was taken from the home in the alley, and borne to the church-yard. Here it was placed upon a bier, beneath the shade of a majestic willow, whose branches, gracefully bending, swept the green earth, as moved by the winds of heaven. All then retired into the church and listened to the funeral sermon. This service being concluded, a procession was formed for the place of burial, headed by a band of Sabbath-school scholars, bearing the remains of the deceased. Then followed his mother, some three hundred children, and a great number of the congregation, each anxious to show respect to the piety and worth of the mother and her son. After the body was deposited in the ground, and the burial service was read, the vast group of children joined in a sweet and touching hymn, the melody of which was occasionally interrupted by the sobs and sighs of the multitude. It was a tribute shown not to wealth, or fame, or worldly distinction, but to piety, such as commanded the approval of God and the admiration of men.[2]

Another incident is worthy of being transferred to these pages, since it furnishes an example of Mr. Vincent's diligent pastoral service, and illustrates the grand work done by the Sands-street Sunday-school. It is recorded as follows:

Soon after my entrance upon my ministerial duties in this charge I was called to visit a poor widow. She was the mother of an interesting and much-loved daughter, aged, perhaps, eleven years. She was a stranger in the place. Her birthplace was beyond the wide Atlantic. Her home was there, and her kindred. Her heart yearned to visit her native shores, and she desired that her dust might mingle with the soil of the country where she was born. In my visits I was frequently led to mark her holy triumph. There was joy in her countenance in the midst of her sufferings. Resignation was upon her brow, and the language of sweet submission fell from her lips. There was only one tie, she said, that bound her to earth. Its strength is best known to a mother's heart. That tie was her orphan child, a member of our Sabbath-school. Never shall I forget the scene I witnesssed—that mother gazing with tearful eyes upon her offspring, and commending to God, as her last sacrifice, her girl. She had just asked me to pray for her, that God would give her a complete victory. We prayed. The struggle was severe and somewhat protracted, but the mother triumphed By faith the daughter was committed willingly, and in holy confidence, to God; and there was a holy calm in the mother's breast. To gratify her earnest wishes, it was resolved that she should cross the wide waste of waters to the shores of France, if her wasted energies would permit it. She hoped thus to die amid the scenes of her childhood. Kind friends came to assist her. The mother and daughter left us, followed by the prayers of pastor, friends, and especially Mary's Sabbath-school teacher and classmates. The mother lived to see the land of her birth, but not to tread on its shores. The pilot boat that towed the ship to her anchorage bore to the wharf the lifeless remains of the mother.

But the little girl, the orphan; you ask, what became of her? She found the home sought by her parent, but O! how desolate! The joy of her life was wanting. No parental ear was there to hear the tale of her sorrow. No breast heaved with emotion, on which to pillow her little head and find comfort. She was alone. Though among her kindred, they were strangers. Months passed, and then a letter came to the Sabbath-school teacher, bearing tidings of this lone child of sorrow. In that letter, she, in substance, said: "I am hastening to meet my mother in a better world. I am dying; consumption takes me as it did mamma; but I wish to tell you that my heart cherishes its attachment to my Sabbath-school in America. I have not forgotten nor ceased to love my teacher, schoolmates, and friends. Though far

---

[2] "The Farmer Boy," pp. 128-130.

away, my heart still clings to you who received us, strangers ; yet cared for us, and taught us the things of God. I am dying ; but my Sabbath-school lessons I learned with you (for I have no minister now) have shown me where to go in the hour of trouble, and in whom to trust. I believe that I have the prayers of those who cared so much for me in a land so distant. I have gone to my Saviour ; I have offered my prayers to him ; I have been brought into his favor, and feel that I am his child. I am ready to go and meet mamma in heaven. Farewell ! I am dying ! happy, happy, happy !"

This letter came with a postscript : "She is dead." O! ye Sabbath-school teachers and friends, see the fruits of your toil ! God waters the seed you sow, and gives you a hundred-fold. Toil on, then. Here is one saved, at least,—yea, two, the mother and the daughter. When the mother landed on our shores she was a French Catholic. It was a Sabbath-school teacher that won the mother by winning the child ; both by this means were led to Christ.[3]

Mr. Vincent was married to a daughter of the Rev. Marvin Richardson. One of their sons is the Rev. Marvin R. Vincent, D.D., of the Church of the Covenant, New York city, and their daughter is the wife of a minister.

---

[3] "The Farmer Boy," pp. 138-142.

REV. JOHN J. MATTHIAS.

LXIII.

JOHN J. MATTHIAS.

JOHN B. MATTHIAS was a sturdy pioneer Methodist preacher, whose name will not cease to be honored in the annals of the church. His visits to the little society in Brooklyn soon after it was organized, and his prominent agency in the introduction of camp-meetings into this region, we have already noted. His son, the REV. JOHN JARVIS MATTHIAS, was born in the city of New York, January 7, 1796. The name Jarvis was given him in honor of his mother's family. Her parents, Nathaniel and Phœbe Jarvis, were devoted Methodists in the town of Huntington, L. I. Of the same family were Bishop A. Jarvis and the Rev. S. F. Jarvis, of Connecticut.[1]

Bishop Janes, an ardent friend and admirer of John J. Matthias, wrote thus concerning his early life:

At a suitable age he went to Brooklyn to learn the art of printing, but the decease of his employer prematurely closed the engagement. While in this persuit he became the subject of converting grace, and soon felt that he was called of God to the Christian ministry, which he entered at the age of twenty-one.[2]

He was charged with various responsible offices during his active ministry as appears from the following list of his

APPOINTMENTS: 1817, (New York Conf.,) Goshen cir., Conn., with E. P. Jacob; 1818, Pittsfield cir., Mass., with E. P. Jacob; 1819, ordained deacon,—Stow cir., Vt., with H. Dewolf; 1820, Luyden cir., Mass., with John Clark; 1821, ordained elder,—Cortland cir., N. Y., with G. Lyon; 1822, ditto, with.R. Harris; 1823, Middlebury, Vt.; 1824, St. Albans cir., with S. Covel; 1825, Pittsfield, Mass., with G. Pierce; 1826, Cortland cir., N. Y., with H. Hatfield; 1827, New York city, with T. Burch, N. White, R. Seney, N. Levings and Julius Field; 1828, ditto, with T. Burch, C. Carpenter, J. Hunt, N. Levings and George Coles; 1829–1830, Albany, North ch.; 1831–1832, (Phila. Conf.,) Newark cir., N. J., with A. Atwood; 1833–1835, presiding elder, East Jersey Dist.; 1836, Philadelphia, Nazareth ch.; 1837–1841, sup'd; 1837, governor of Bassa Cove, Africa; 1842, (New York Conf.,) Flushing, N. Y.; 1843,

---

[1] Sprague's Annals.   [2] The Christian Advocate, Jan. 9, 1862.

Rockaway; **1844-1847 presiding elder, Long Island Dist.;** 1848-1849, (New York East Conf.,) Williamsburgh, Grand-street, (Gothic ;) 1850-1851, New York, 27th-street ; 1852, sup'y, Hempstead, with S. W. Smith ; 1853, Jamaica ; 1854, sup'd ; 1855-1858, chaplain Seamen's Friend Retreat, Staten Island ; 1859, sup'y; 1860-1861, sup'd.

His appointment, in 1837, as governor of Bassa Cove, on the West Coast of Africa, was given him by the Colonization Societies of Pennsylvania and New York. He remained in Africa about one year, " filling the station of governor with ability and usefulness, and to the satisfaction of the societies." There his wife died of African fever, and he barely escaped death from the same disease. After his return he was employed for a while in the Methodist Book Concern, and some time on his farm in Bloomfield, N. J. He was married, in 1839, to MISS MARY C. BEACH, of Newark, N. J.

While serving as chaplain in the " Retreat," he discharged his duties well, and " was held in the highest esteem by the officers and managers of that institution." He resigned the chaplaincy on account of feeble health, and retired to a quiet and comfortable home in Tarrytown, N. Y., where he spent the remnant of his days. Bishop Janes says:

Perhaps none of the positions he had filled in his active ministry was more difficult than this retired one ; * * * but he pleasantly moved in this circumscribed sphere, ornamenting the church, and honoring his profession to the last.

He preached the Sabbath but one before his departure, from the text, "And there shall be no more death." Though afflicted a long time with dyspepsia and clergyman's sore throat, he was prostrated only a few days. In the midst of his greatest suffering he requested his wife to repeat the hymn commencing,

"Jesus, thy blood and righteousness
My beauty are, my glorious dress ;"

and exclaimed, " How beautiful ! " A little later he said to Mrs. Matthias, " If disembodied spirits are permitted to return to this world, I will love to be with you." Though he talked thus of his departure, he did not seem to apprehend that it was so very near. He wound up his watch as usual, and within half an hour he slept in Jesus, on the 25th of September, 1861, aged sixty-five years. The funeral services were conducted by the Revs. C. K. True and G. W. Woodruff, and the remains were interred in the Sleepy Hollow cemetery, in Tarrytown, by the side of his friend, Stephen Martindale. A head-stone designates his grave.

His brethren, at the ensuing session of the conference, put on record an appreciative testimony, in which they say:

In all his work he was punctual and patient, firm and affectionate, sparing no labor or sacrifice to promote the cause of God and the comfort of his brethren. As a presiding elder he was much beloved. "He was a high-minded, intelligent, and honorable man," of refined taste, delicate feelings, with dignified and affable manners. He was faithful as a pastor, and particularly devoted to the interests of the Sabbath-school. He was often truly eloquent in preaching, and exceedingly happy in his illustrations.[3]

Fitch Reed, who was ordained deacon by Bishop Roberts at the same time with Matthias, his conference classmate, says of him:

John J. Matthias was a buoyant and cheerful companion, and for his earnestness and fidelity, as a preacher and pastor, stood high in the favor and praise of all the churches.[4]

He was a model of devotion and consistency in his domestic and private life. Besides attending strictly to family worship, it was his life-long custom to retire morning, noon, and at evening twilight for secret communion with God.

A brief extract from one of his sermons may serve as an example of his style. His text was the language of Paul, "I have fought a good fight," etc.:

We behold him, as it were, standing on an eminence, with both worlds in view. On the one hand he looks down the line of his past history, and finds dotted thickly on the record, shipwrecks, encounters with beasts at Ephesus, stoning, scourging, hunger, and nakedness; the contempt and ignominy of the world, the multiplied care of churches, and, in fine, all sorts of privations, hardships, and frequent deaths. On the other, he beholds the blissful plains of Paradise, the river of God, the New Jerusalem with its streets of gold and gates of pearl; thrones, dominions, principalities; a crown jeweled with works of faith, purified and fitted by the hand of Christ. This in reserve for him! O, the rapture of that view![5]

---

[3] Minutes of Conferences, 1862, p. 80.

[4] Reminiscences, in the Northern Christian Advocate, 1864.

[5] Memorial sermon, at the funeral of Stephen Martindale; published in The Methodist, May 11, 1861.

His wife, CHARLOTTE, shared the toils and pleasures of his itinerant life until suddenly cut down by death, soon after their arrival in Africa. She is buried by the side of Cox and the other missionaries.

The widow, MARY C. MATTHIAS, and her only son, (who bears his father's name,) are journeying homeward, where a happy reunion awaits them at the close of their pilgrimage. Mrs. Matthias resides in Newark, N. J. *John J. Matthias* resides at New Haven, Conn.; is a member of the First Methodist Episcopal Church there, one of its trustees, and superintendent of its Sunday-school. He is the author of a service of song, entitled "Saint Paul;" also, of a volume, entitled "An Experiment in Church Music."

LXIV.

H. F. Pease

OHN and Patty Pease, the parents of the REV. HART FOSTER PEASE, were members of a Congregational church, and showed their pious care for their son by dedicating him to God while an infant in holy baptism. He was born in Ashfield, Franklin County, Mass., on the 27th of December, 1811. In the same month that he was eighteen years of age, he gave his heart to God. In 1830, while pursuing his occupation as merchant in the city of Rochester, N. Y., he was there received into the Methodist Episcopal Church by the Rev. Gleason Filmore.

He prepared for college at Wilbraham, and entered Wesleyan University in 1833, but left during his Freshman year. His first license to exhort he received while he was a student at Wilbraham Academy in 1832. It was signed by Orange Scott, presiding elder. The following year, while teaching school in Cheshire, Conn., he received a local preacher's license, bearing the signature of the presiding elder, Stephen Martindale. These names and dates remind us that Mr. Pease was connected in his earlier Christian life with a generation whose foremost men have nearly all passed away; yet we have never thought of our brother as having attained to old age. He seems like a veteran in labors rather than in years.

PASTORAL APPOINTMENTS: 1834, (New York Conf.,) Fair Haven, Conn.; 1835, Cheshire; 1836, ordained deacon by Bp. Hedding; 1836-1837, Fair Haven; 1838, ordained elder by Bishop Andrew; 1838-1839, Guilford; 1840-1841, Sharon; 1842-1843, Poughkeepsie, N. Y., 2nd ch.; **1844-1845, Brooklyn, Sands-street**, with J. C. Tackaberry, sup'y; 1846-1847, New Rochelle cir., with R. C. Putney; 1848-1849, (N. Y. E. Conf.,) Stamford, Ct.; 1850-1851, New York, Second-street; 1852-1853, New York, Willett-st.; 1854, Essex, Ct.; 1855, Essex and Deep River; 1856-1857, Redding; 1858-1859, Norwalk, 1st

Ch.; 1860-1861, Bethel; 1862, sup'y, at Bethel; 1863, Williamsburgh, N.Y., North Fifth-street; 1864-1866, presiding elder, L. I. North Dist.; 1867-1870, presiding elder, New York Dist.; 1871, presiding elder, L. I. North Dist.; 1872, Brooklyn, Broadway Mission; 1873-1878, sup'y; 1878-1880, Berlin, Conn.; 1881-1884, superannuated.

The author has often heard old people in Meriden speak of their pleasant recollections of Mr. Pease, the youthful teacher and exhorter who was with them fifty years ago. He succeeded Leonard M. Vincent in Sands-street, soon after the first brick church was built. The older people of the church remember vividly his ministry among them. They speak of his sermons in that day as always interesting, remarkable for pith and point.

He was granted a supernumerary relation in 1862, in order that he might remain a third year at Bethel, Conn., to complete the building of a church there.

When Mr. Pease was presiding elder, the author took great pleasure in greeting him on his quarterly visits to his charge, always enjoyed his sermons exceedingly, and found him a warm and true friend, in whom he could safely confide.

The New York East Conference elected him a delegate to the General Conference in 1868, and a reserve delegate in 1872.

Mr. Pease was married by the Rev. Stephen Martindale to Miss LOUISA L. IVES, of Meriden, Conn., April 3, 1836. Of their seven children, *Mary L.* and *Rowena C.* are deceased. The latter was converted at the age of ten, lived a "singularly pure and consistent Christian life of thirty-two years, and died a most happy and triumphant death" in Hartford, Conn., July 19, 1882. She was the wife of Gen. Wm. R. Pease, U. S. A.[1] The other children are *Maronette A.*, *Frances J.*, *Emma L.*, and *Hart E.*

---

[1] Obituary notice in The Christian Advocate.

REV. JOHN B. MERWIN, D. D.

LXV.
JOHN B. MERWIN.

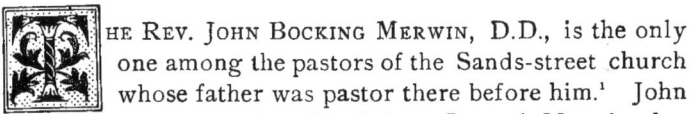

HE REV. JOHN BOCKING MERWIN, D.D., is the only one among the pastors of the Sands-street church whose father was pastor there before him.[1] John was two years old when his father, Samuel Merwin, began to hold forth the word of life in the "old white church." When Dr. Nathan Bangs was re-appointed to Sands-street in 1847, he was not in good health, and the associate preacher had practically full charge of the station; indeed, some pleasantly said that he had a double charge—that of Dr. Bangs and the church. Mr. Merwin was then in his youthful prime, about thirty-five years of age. His continuance in Poughkeepsie for a fourth year was desired, and it was arranged that he should remain supernumerary and be returned, but for the sake of Dr. Bangs this plan was changed at conference, and Mr. Merwin was appointed to Brooklyn with him.

John B. Merwin was born in Albany, N. Y., May 14, 1811. He gave his heart to God at a very early age, and was received into the old Light-street Methodist Episcopal church in Baltimore in September, 1824, by his father who was pastor there at that time.

He graduated at Augusta College, Kentucky, in 1832, completing the course in three years. Martin Ruter was president, Henry B. Bascom was professor of moral science, and J. P. Durbin, professor of languages when young Merwin entered that institution. He accompanied Dr. Durbin on his return from a visit to New York, and

---

[1] See Sketch of the Rev. Samuel Merwin in this book.

was a member of his family. He preached his first sermon at a watch-meeting on the last night in 1832, and was soon after licensed as a local preacher and recommended to the New York Annual Conference by the quarterly conference of Brooklyn. The following is his

MINISTERIAL RECORD: 1833, (New York Conf.;) White Plains cir., N. Y., with R. Seney; 1834–1835, Smithtown cir., L. I., with W. K. Stopford; 1835, ordained deacon; 1836, agent for Plattekill Seminary; 1837, ordained elder,—Newington, Conn.; 1838, Newington and Wethersfield; 1839–1840. Patchogue, L. I.; 1841–1842, Lenox, Mass.; 1843, Glenham, N. Y., and Troy, Second-street; 1844-1845, Poughkeepsie, Cannon-street; 1846, ditto, sup'y; **1847, Brooklyn, Sands-street,** with N. Bangs; 1848–1849, (New York East Conf.,) Flushing, L. I.; 1850–1851, Danbury, Conn.; 1851–1852, Westville; 1854–1855, Middletown; 1856, Bloomfield; 1857, sup'y, agent Wesleyan University; 1858–1859, Nichol's Farms, Conn.; 1860-1861, Watertown; 1862, New York, Ninth-street; 1863-1865, Hempstead, L. I.; 1866-1868, Brooklyn, Grand-street; 1869-1870, presiding elder, L. I. North Dist.; 1871-1874, New York Dist.; 1875, New York, Forsyth-street; 1876, Ridgefield, Conn.; 1877, Brooklyn, Simpson Ch.; 1878-1880, Hamden, Conn.; 1881-1883, Brooklyn, Gothic ch.; 1884, East Norwich, L. I.

Mr. Merwin received the degree of A.M. from his *alma mater* in 1836, and the Iowa University conferred upon him the degree of D.D. in 1875. He was a delegate to General Conference in 1856, and in 1872 he was first reserve delegate, taking his seat on the election of Bishop Andrews.

A few of the many incidents connected with his long and busy career may serve to illustrate the work and character of the man. During his pastorate in Flushing, L. I., he organized the Methodist Episcopal church in Whitestone. Some years ago he performed an "itinerant feat, which has seldom, if ever, been paralleled." The Christian Advocate published the following account of it:

After attending the Sing Sing camp-meeting, on a Saturday afternoon, he started from his father's, at White Plains, at four and a half o'clock P. M., for his Sabbath work (morning and afternoon) in eastern Long Island, the whole involving a journey of over one hundred and twenty-four miles and two sermons. Driving hastily to New Rochelle, he hoped to go by the evening steamer across the sound. On reaching the wharf in time he was met by the unwelcome announcement that the steamer would not land, and the alternative was presented of continuing the journey by carriage, or disappointing the congregations on the Sabbath. The conclusion was quickly made—to meet, if possible, the appointments. The horse was hastily rubbed down and the ride renewed. The ninetieth mile was reached by sunrise; then followed a change of horses and a renewal of the ride. The thing was done! At three and a half P. M., Mr. Merwin had, in twenty-three hours, journeyed one hundred and twenty-four miles, (by private carriage, 107; on foot, 5; on horseback, 12; total, 124,) and preached twice. What pastor, presiding elder, or bishop has ever outdone that? Does not that beat the fathers?

While at Poughkeepsie, in 1846, he was appointed a representative of the Ministerial Union of that city to the Evangelical Alliance in London, and he availed himself of the opportunity to visit various parts of Europe. The California Christian Advocate of May 31, 1877, published the following:

Rev. J. B. Merwin, of the New York East Conference, gave us a call last week. He has gone to *do up* Yosemite. On returning he may possibly visit Oregon. Brother Merwin is a member of the Mission Committee, and is taking a deep interest in our missions on this coast—German, Chinese, and Indian.

Dr. Merwin is a bachelor. The dates make it certain that he is seventy-two years of age, but he seems more like a man of fifty. Time has dealt kindly with him, and, judging from his erect form and elastic step, we should say he could even now perform an amount of work that some of the youngest of his brethren would not care to undertake. Sands-street church was re-enforced by about one hundred converts during his ministry there, and it was found, one year later, that of that number ninety-seven were members in Sands-street church or some other, or were in heaven. In every other charge, save one, God has favored his labors with a revival. Few men among us have made a more honorable record, or gained a higher place in the esteem of their brethren, than the Rev. Dr. Merwin.

LXVI.
JOHN W. B. WOOD.

WILLIAM HAWKINS WOOD, father of the subject of this sketch, was a native of Wilmington, Delaware. He became an importer and manufacturer in Baltimore, and an honored local preacher in the Methodist Episcopal Church. His wife, Anna Bond, was the only daughter of Thomas Bond, Esq., of Harford County, Md., one of the earliest converts to Methodism in America, under the labors of Robert Strawbridge. She was sister to the Rev. John Wesley Bond,[1] and to the eminent Dr. Thomas E. Bond, who was for twelve years editor of "The Christian Advocate and Journal."

The REV. JOHN WESLEY BOND WOOD is one of a family of five children, He was born in Baltimore, Md., January 15, 1804. In early childhood he was the subject of deep religious impressions, and from the age of seven years confidently expected to be a preacher of the gospel. From his godly mother he received faithful instruction in the Holy Scriptures. After the death of his parents, he and one of his sisters (now the widow of the Rev. John Poisal, D. D.,) found a home with their uncle, Dr. Thomas E. Bond, who then resided in Harford County, Md.

It being intended by his friends that he should study for the medical profession, he entered Asbury College, in Baltimore; but that institution failed, and the result was a decided change in the course of his whole life. He went to sea at the instance of the merchants of Baltimore, who were determined to change the character of the whole mercantile marine, and so introduced educated young men into the service. After a voyage of twenty months, having doubled Cape Horn in safety, he returned to Baltimore, but was induced to go again and again, crossing the ocean eighteen times. Returning at last from a voyage of several years, he left his ship in New York city, determined to revisit his native town. He took passage on a coasting clipper which was overtaken in

---

[1] For memorials of this excellent minister see Minutes of Conferences, 1819, p. 324, also Methodist Magazine, 1819, p. 284.

REV. JOHN W. BOND WOOD.

the night by a terrific gale and seemed destined to be driven on the shoals and wrecked. The thought came to him, "I shall not be lost; for am I not appointed to preach the Gospel?" Kneeling down he solemnly vowed that his heart and service from that moment should be given to God. Instantly his fear was gone, and he exclaimed, "Lord, give me the assurance of the acceptance of my vow by breaking the gale at midnight." Upon this he fell into a sound sleep. At twelve o'clock he was startled by the midnight call for the watch below. The gale was broken. A voice within said, " Remember your vow," and he cried, " My Lord, I will." When he reached Baltimore and stood upon the shore the same voice was repeated and the same answer given. It was Sunday evening. His friends had gone to church, a mile distant, and he followed them, still hearing the divine voice, " Remember your vow," and answering anon, " My Lord, I will." The next morning he followed the advice of Mrs. Bond, his aunt—his best Christian counselor, then living—took one of the farm horses, and went to camp-meeting and there found joy and peace in Christ. This was in the year 1831, when he was twenty seven years of age.

MINISTERIAL RECORD: 1831, supply on Jay cir., N. Y., with Orris Pier; *1832*, (Troy Conf.,) Chazy and Champlain cir,, N. Y., with E. Goss and M. H. Stewart ; 1833, Peru cir., with D. Stevens ; 1834, ordained deacon,—Grand Isle cir., Vt.; 1835, Granville and Hebron cir., with O. E. Spicer; 1836, ordained elder,—Fort Ann cir., N. Y., with J. B. Houghtaling, H. W. Steward, and D. Brayton, sup'y ; 1837, ditto, with J. B. Houghtaling, and ——, supply ; 1838, East Whitehall and Whitehall Mission, with J. Squire ; 1839-1840, sup'd ; 1841, located ; 1842, (Troy Conf.,) Stowe cir., Vt., with S. Hewes ; 1843-1844, (New York Conf.,) Tarrytown, N. Y.; 1845-1846, Matteawan ; 1847, Flushing, L. I.; 1848-1849, New York, Forsyth-street ; **1850-1851, Brooklyn, Sands-street ;** 1852-1853, Rockaway cir., L. I.; 1854, Williamsburgh ; 1855-1856, Brooklyn, Carlton ave.; 1857-1858, Sag Harbor ; 1859, Westchester and West Farms, with D. De Vinne, sup'y.; 1860, (New York Conf.,) Rondout ; 1861, Coxsackie and Baltimore Corners, with G. C. Esray ; 1862-1863, Tarrytown ; 1864-1866, Hancock ; 1867-1868, Goshen ; 1869-1870, Monroe ; 1870-1872, Highland Mills ; 1873-1875, West Point ; 1876, chaplain Sing Sing prison ; 1877-1883, sup'y ; 1884, superannuated.

On his first charge in the Adirondack Mountains his labors were greatly owned of God ; nearly two hundred souls were gathered into the fold. A revival of remarkable extent and power occurred under his labors on the Hancock circuit. Tarrytown and other places were divinely blessed through his ministry. In Sag Harbor the writer found excellent results of his faithful labors there, after he had been gone from that charge ten years.

He was married in 1834 to Miss Juliet C. Ketchum, daughter of Benjamin Ketchum, of Plattsburgh, N. Y., whose death—the greatest affliction he was ever called to endure—occurred while he was among the Sands-street people. He was greatly comforted by their friendly sympathy.

Mr. Wood is a man of marked individuality. He seems to have been fitted by nature and by his long experience as a sailor to gain ready access to rough, godless men, and few ministers are able to exert so strong an influence over that class of persons. He was doing excellent work among the convicts of the Sing Sing prison, when, through political influence, he was suddenly removed. He is genial, exceedingly frank, and sometimes droll in his utterances. One of the oldest preachers in the New York Conference, he appears to be enjoying pleasantly the evening time of life.

JULIET CAPULET KETCHUM was married to J. W. B. Wood at the age of nineteen years. She died of consumption, in the parsonage of the Sands-street church, in 1852, after suffering six years. Living and dying she was the Lord's.

Of their seven children only four survive. *Jennie*, the eldest, has been her father's housekeeper many years. At her mother's death she took charge of three younger children, though but a child herself. *John Wesley Bond, Jr.*, has resided for some years in Montana. *Juliet C.* (named for her mother) is the widow of the late James Bishop, of New Brunswick, N. J. *Emma* married Henry Malcomson, an English gentleman, a merchant, and resides in New York city.

REV. HENRY J. FOX, D. D.

LXVII.
HENRY J. FOX.

A NUMBER of the learned and eloquent pastors of Sands-street church are distinctively recognized as "self-made men." Among these the REV. HENRY JOHN FOX, D. D. should be prominently named.

He was born—the second of a family of nine children—in the parish of Sculcoates, Kingston-upon-Hull, England, May 13, 1821. His parents, Thomas and Sarah (Clarke) Fox, were devoted members of the Wesleyan Connection. The former lived to be ninety-one years of age. He is buried in Columbia, S. C., where he died in 1877. The latter died and was buried in Ashland, Greene Co., N. Y., in December, 1858.

Henry J. Fox, when a lad, attended a private academy in his native town, conducted by Thomas Ager, Esq. He was powerfully awakened under the preaching of Rev. Robert Atkin, a distinguished minister of the Established Church, but on entering upon a Christian life, he chose to connect himself with a small sect of Methodists, of which Dr. Warren was the most prominent founder. His class leader was Geo. Cookman, Esq, mayor of the town, a local preacher, and father of the distinguished Methodist orator, the Rev. George G. Cookman, who was lost in the ill-fated steamer President, in 1841.

In a short time he left this small seceding body, and united with the Wesleyans. Being placed on the "plan" as a local preacher at nineteen years of age, he preached his first sermon Nov. 15, 1840, at Analby, an appointment on the Hull circuit.

Four years later he left England intending to go to Canada, but was detained in New York by the Rev. George Taylor, afterward one of his successors in the Sands-street

I invited him to spend the Sabbath with me at Harlem, and preach for me. He consented, and his preaching was so simple, so earnest, and so profitable to my people, that we felt he ought to give himself wholly to the ministry.[1]

Mr. Taylor introduced him to the Rev. Samuel D. Ferguson, who persuaded him to go to Durham, Greene County, N. Y., where he was employed for some time as a pastor, the preacher in charge being sick. Thus, providentially and unexpectedly, he entered upon his public ministry, and his services thenceforward are briefly epitomized in the following list of

APPOINTMENTS: 1844, Durham cir., N. Y., a supply, with J. D. Bouton and William C. Smith ; 1845, Prattsville cir., supply, with William Bloomer and Wm. C. Smith ; 1846–1847, (New York Conf.,) Newfield and Plymouth, Conn ; 1848,(New York East Conf.,) ordained deacon ; 1848–1849, Farmington ; 1850, ordained elder,—Hartford ; 1851, Hartford, Second ch.; **1852–1853, Brooklyn, Sands-street;** 1854–1855. Williamsburgh, South Fifth-street; 1856, Hempstead, L. I.; 1857–1860, President Ashland Collegiate Institute ; 1860, (New York Conf.;) 1861–1862, New York, Forty-third-street ; 1863–1865, New York, Central ch.; 1866–1868, Carmel and Drewville ; 1869–1871, (South Carolina Conf.,) Oro, S. C., with W. H. Scott ; 1872–1873, Charleston, with S. Weston ; 1873–1876, Prof. of English Literature and Rhetoric in the University of South Carolina; 1877–1878, (New England Conf.,) Hyde Park, Mass.; 1878–1881, East Saugus ; 1882–1883, Wilbraham ; 1884, North Andover.

Beginning his ministry with comparatively limited literary attainments, Mr. Fox commenced and kept up a rigid course of study. He found time on his six-weeks' circuits, with twenty-two appointments, to make rapid and thorough advancement in literature and science. He was honored with the degree of M.A. by the Wesleyan University in 1857, and nine years later he was made a Doctor in Divinity by Union College. About the same time he was elected secretary of the New York Educational Society.

In 1863, in company with Dr. (now Bishop) Foster and the Rev. W. F. Watkins, he spent two weeks in the service of the Christian Commission on the battle-field of Gettysburgh. As a delegate from the American Branch of the Evangelical Alliance he attended a meeting of the World's Alliance, in Amsterdam, in 1867.

He was exposed to great danger during the first years of his residence in the South, and experienced no small amount of suffering and pecuniary loss by the persecutions of the Ku-klux Klan. His name appears in the Minutes as secretary of the South Carolina Conference.. The charge to which he was appointed in Charleston was a large church in Wentworth-street. The Legislature gave him his position in the university, and he held it until the institution was closed.

Dr. Fox has achieved a good reputation as a lecturer. As a writer he is well known by his numerous contributions to The Christian Advocate and Zion's Herald. Articles from his pen on the Negro, Plagiarism, and Shakespeare, in the Methodist Quarterly Review, do credit to his ability. His chief works are a " Quadrennial Register of the M. E. Church," of which 10,000 copies were sold, " The Land of Hope," " The History of our Mission in Cape Palmas," "The Student's Commonplace Book," and " The Student's Shakespeare."

His success as a man of letters is believed to be more than equaled by his usefulness as a preacher and pastor. Very large accessions to the church were the result of his ministry in Hartford, Sands-street church, Brooklyn, and Forty-third-st., New York. Among those received by him into the Sands-street church' were Richard Vanderveer, Mrs. Richards, (afterward the famous Mrs. Tilton,) also an old man, Joseph Riley, who had sat under the preaching of John Wesley.

Dr. Fox was married to MISS CLARINDA S. WHITE, in Ashland, Greene County, N. Y. Of their nine children five are living at this date, (1883.) *Belle Amelia* was born in the parsonage of the Sands-street church. *Gilbert D.*, the eldest son, has been for seven years secretary to one of the committees of the United States Senate. He is a steward of the Metropolitan M. E. church, in Washington, D. C., and a worker in the Sunday-school of that church. *Henry A.*, a graduate of the South Carolina State University, an attorney-at-law, was instantly killed by a collision on the Charleston and Savannah railroad. *Clarence W.* is engaged in business in the city of Boston. *Irving P.* was graduated at the Boston University in 1883, and is now connected with the Boston Courier.

LXVIII.
LEVI S. WEED.

HE name of the Rev. LEVI STEVENS WEED, D. D., is a household word among all the members and friends of old Sands-street church. This excellent minister was born in Darien, Conn., May 29, 1824. His parents moving to Williamsburgh (now Brooklyn, E. D.,) and thence to New York, much of his early life was spent in those two cities. At that time neither his father nor mother professed religion, but his mother was "a truly exemplary woman," and later in life became a faithful member of the church.

In 1843 the family were living in Durham, Greene county, N. Y. Meetings were held under the direction of the Rev. Reuben Bloomer; and our friend, then nineteen years old, with several others gave his heart to the Lord. It is said that before the extra meetings closed, he and another of the converts, A. H. Mead, were out on the circuit, filling the pastor's appointments.[1] An exhorter's license was given him about this time, and he began a course of theological studies under the direction of the Rev. S. S. Strong. In 1844 he entered upon the work of preparing for college in the Delaware Literary Institute, in Franklin, N. Y. While there he was licensed as a local preacher. By close application to study his health was somewhat impaired, and his earnest desire for a college training was overborne by the urgent protest of the older ministers. He says: "They told me it was a wicked waste of time while souls were perishing. I yielded; but it has been the regret of my life." "Yet we doubt," says his conference memorial, "if his cherished desire realized, would have added to the luster of his long and prosperous ministry."

PASTORAL RECORD: 1845, supply, Catskill cir., N. Y., with E. S.

---
[1] This statement was made to the author by the Rev. E. S. Hebberd.

REV. LEVI S. WEED, D.D.

Hebberd ; 1846, supply, Prattsville cir., with Wm. Bloomer and W. C. Smith ; 1847, supply, Franklin cir., with Addi Lee ; 1848–1849, (New York East Conf.,) Southampton, L. I.; 1850, ordained deacon,—Orient ; 1851, Southport, Conn.; 1852, ordained elder ; 1852–1853, Colebrook River; **1854–1855, Brooklyn, Sands-street,** with M. B. Bull, sup'y ; 1856–1857, Hartford, Conn.; 1858–1859, New Haven, First ch.; 1860–1861, Stamford, Conn.; **1862–1863, Brooklyn, Sands-street;** 1764–1865, Brooklyn, Summerfield ch.; 1866–1868, New York, Allen-street ; 1869, Mamaroneck ; 1870–1872, New York, John-street ; 1873–1874, Brooklyn, Carroll Park ; 1875–1877, New Haven, First ch.; 1878–1879, Harlem, 118th-street ; 1880, New York, John-street ; 1881–1882, Brooklyn, New York Avenue.

Before coming to Sands-street, as the record shows, he had been assigned to small country appointments. While assisting the pastor, Henry J. Fox, in a series of extra meetings, he manifested so much ability and piety that the brethren of this church expressed a strong desire that he might become their next pastor, and he was appointed in accordance with their wishes. Thenceforward he was always stationed in the most prominent appointments in the conference. Three of these— Sands-street, First Church, New Haven, and old John-street, New York—he served a second term.

In 1849 he was married to Miss Julia M. Stephenson, daughter of P. Stephenson, of Coxsackie, N. Y., who after twenty months was called to her reward. Two years later he married a younger sister of the deceased wife, Miss Cornelia A. Stephenson. His little girl, an only daughter, aged about four years, died in 1855 ; and in 1880 his wife, who had been the light of his home for nearly thirty years, was taken from him. While the shadow of this last great affliction was upon him he remarked to some of his relatives, "I take up my work as if nothing had happened; yet," said he, with a sigh and a tear, "every moment of my life I know that something has happened." Thus thoroughly was he prepared to sympathize with the sorrowful.

Mr. Weed was remarkably genial and kind toward his ministerial brethren, and they took pleasure in his promotion. He united with the New York East Conference at the beginning of its history, and wrought nobly within its bounds to the last, without a break or a transfer. By appointment he preached the missionary sermon before the conference in 1865, which was delivered with rare eloquence and power. The following

As I look upon the not-distant future I see devout disciples from our humble mission in Foochow threading every province of the "Flowery Kingdom," and preaching Christ to the millions of the capital of China itself. I hear the words of truth sounding out from Bulgaria, and waking to a new life all of Russia from the wilds of Siberia to the palace of the czars. From altars and temples which Christian efforts have planted in the very heart of the domain of the "man of sin" himself I hear the sweet music of the untrammeled gospel as it swells from the classic banks of the "Yellow Tiber" through all the Alps made sacred by martyr blood. From the chapels of an unpretending worship which the gifts and prayers of the good are even now planting on the very soil, and in the metropolitan city where the Huguenots were slain, the notes of gospel grace go out over all France, and, touch, with strange and solemn power, the land of sorrow and of song. From Bremen and Copenhagen, and other centers of Christian life which mission efforts are now creating, I hear strains sublime borne on every breeze over Germanic States, while Scandinavia's old heroic heights send back their responses to the now-united song that sweeps from gulf to sea over all our new and grander realm. * * *

I would have every one feel that this is a privileged time in which we live, and while continents are trembling to the tread of coming and great events, and clouds of distress and the storm of battle are sweeping the nations as the thunder-gusts do, only to usher in the sweet serene of a blessed millennial day, I long to have every Christian and every Christian minister rise in thought and noble living to the real grandeur of his blessed privilege of being a co-worker with God in bringing the whole race into loving allegiance to our Lord Jesus Christ.

He was one of the chief speakers at the great centenary celebration—a union meeting of the two New York Conferences in 1866—and his address on that occasion has been rarely equaled in breadth and beauty and power.

In 1872 the Indiana Asbury University conferred upon him the degree of Doctor in Divinity. He represented his annual conference in the General Conference of 1880. At the time of his death he was chairman of the New York Preachers' Meeting and a member of the Board of Managers of the Missionary Society.

On Monday, June 12, 1883, he inquired at the office of The Christian Advocate concerning Bishop Foss, who was then in a critical condition. He proceeded to the preachers' meeting, where he presided as usual. In the afternoon he assisted in laying the corner-stone of the Methodist Episcopal church in Harlem, where he had been pastor a few years before. On the morning of Wednesday, the 14th, he left his home, in Brooklyn, apparently in good health, and, hurrying to overtake his friend on Fleet-street. Leaning against an ice-box, he said, I am faint." He settled down upon the floor, and instantly " as noble a heart ceased to beat as ever dwelt in house of clay."

At his funeral, in the New York Avenue church, Brooklyn, the house was densely packed, and many persons could not obtain standing room. The ministers who took part in the services were Drs. Kettell, Curry, Goodsell, Sanford, Merwin, and Pullman, and the Revs. G. Hollis, T. H. Burch, and W. T. Hill.

Dr. Weed was a man of striking appearance, a little above the average height, with broad, square shoulders and erect carriage. His head was of good size, but his features were unusually small and delicate, and it was sometimes a matter of remark that a man with so small a mouth could be so fine an orator. His eyes were gray and of a clear expression, his hair black and glossy, and his smoothly shaven face gave him the appearance of a Roman Catholic priest, for which, it is said, he was sometimes taken. Dr. Buckley, in The Christian Advocate, wrote thus concerning him :

He was always a gentleman and absorbed in the work of the ministry, attaining more uniform success than is common to ministers who make frequent changes. As a pastor he had no superior. The writer twice followed him, first at the Summerfield church, in the city of Brooklyn, and then in Stamford, Conn. No neglect of duty, in a single instance, was alleged against him, and the personal hold that he had upon many individuals and families, and the use which he made of it, evinced the qualities which make the efficient pastor. * * *

Conscientious fidelity marked his whole career, conscious painstaking devotion to all things, small and great. This, when applied to the improvement of his powers as a public speaker, showed itself sometimes in a painful attention to details of pronunciation. His public efforts, however, were always interesting to the great mass of his hearers. It was possible for him to surprise even his best friends by an occasional effort of rare excellence. * * *

He was a special friend of John B. Gough, the temperance orator, who had a high opinion of his powers as a speaker, and of the late Dr. Woodruff, who requested him on his death-bed to prepare the memorial of his life for this paper.

His sermons were thoughtfully prepared and usually written, but he used only brief notes in the pulpit, and preached with the ease and animation which belong more particularly to extemporaneous address. His voice was strong and penetrating, not especially musical, but resounded like a trumpet, and

truths of the gospel to the hearts of men. One of his brethren writes from an intimate acquaintance with his habits as a preacher:

> His subjects, usually practical, were selected and treated with an obvious aim to be useful. Tenaciously holding the grand verities of the evangelical system, he assumed them as settled points in all his pulpit work, seldom or never opening them for an analysis or debate. A worker, even more than a thinker, regarding truth rather with a view to immediate practical uses, he was never trammeled with doubts, but aimed, by a natural logic, to work such truths into the convictions of his hearers, and by fervid natural eloquence to impress them upon their hearts.[2]

His great heart was always young, and earnestly enlisted in the Sunday-school work. He never lost his interest in the Sands-street Sabbath-school, and he was often seen and heard at its anniversary gatherings. His attachment to the Sands-street church was only equaled by his devotion to the old John-street church. No man in later years did more than he to promote the honor and usefulness of that venerable home of Methodism in New York. His virtues are appropriately commemorated by a marble tablet on the walls of the old church.

JULIA M., his first wife, experienced the pardoning love of God in her sixteenth year. She died during the second year of her married life, June 21, 1851, leaving a helpless babe; but "every object and interest this side of the grave was committed to the çare of God. She requested that her husband might admit to her room all the neighbors and friends, that they might see how a Christian could die."[3]

His second wife, CORNELIA AUGUSTA, after six years of intense suffering from cancer, closed, in Christian triumph, a pure and exemplary life, December 17, 1880. Both wives, with the husband, sleep in the Greenwood cemetery. Two sons by the second marriage are the only surviving members of the family.

---

[2] Rev. T. H. Burch, in The Methodist.
[3] A. H. Mead, in The Christian Advocate.

REV. BUEL GOODSELL.

LXIX.
BUEL GOODSELL.

ONG ISLAND was detached from the old New York District in 1840, and thenceforward till 1864, the Long Island District, including the entire island, was a presiding elder's charge. To this field the REV. BUEL GOODSELL was appointed in 1855, and during his term of four years the number of pastoral appointments increased from 48 to 58, and the number of members and probationers from 8,384 to 11,380. The pastors of Sands-street church during this time were Levi S. Weed, John Miley and John B. Hagany. Mitchell B. Bull was supernumerary pastor with Weed and Miley, and Wilbur F. Watkins was preacher in charge for a short time as a supply.

It is a matter of regret that so few of the facts of Mr. Goodsell's history are now within our reach. He was born July 25, 1793, in the town of Dover, Dutchess County, N. Y. When about sixteen years of age he professed conversion and joined the Methodist Episcopal Church in Dover. Zenas Covel, the elder John Crawford, and Smith Arnold were the preachers on the Dutchess circuit that year. Five years later, when not quite twenty-one years of age, he joined the New York Conference with Charles W. Carpenter, Wm. M. Stillwell, and seven other young men.

CONFERENCE RECORD: 1814, (New York Conf.,) Granville cir., Conn. and Mass., with C. Culver; 1815, Stowe cir., Vt., with G. Lyon; 1816, ordained deacon,—Plattsburgh cir., N. Y. with E. Barnett and J. M'Daniel: 1817, Middlebury, Vt.; 1818, ordained elder,—St. Albans, with J. B. Stratton; 1819, ditto, with J. Covel, Jr.; 1820-1821, Chazy, N. Y.; 1822, Charlotte cir. Vt., with L. Baldwin; 1823-1826, presiding elder, Champlain Dist.; 1827, Pittstown[1] cir., N. Y., with C. Prindle and M. Bates; 1828-1829, Schenectady; 1830, New York city cir., with S. Luckey, S. Merwin, L. Pease, S. Martindale, H. Bangs, and S. D. Ferguson; 1831. ditto, with S. Merwin, L. Pease, S. Martindale, S. Landon, J. Clark, B. Sillick, and C. Prindle; 1852-1833, (Troy Conf.,) Troy; 1834-1837, presiding elder, Troy Dist.; 1838-1839, (New York Conf.,) New York, John-street; 1840-1841, North Newburgh

---

[1] Erroneously printed "Fitchtown," in the conference memorial.

1842–1843, White Plains; 1844–1845, Brooklyn, York-street; 1846–1847, New York, Willett-street; 1848–1849, (New York East Conf.,) Norwalk, Conn.; 1850–1851, Hempstead, L. I., N. Y.; 1852–1853, New Rochelle; 1854, Brooklyn, Franklin ave.; **1855-1858, presiding elder, Long Island Dist.;** 1859–1860, Greenpoint; 1861–1862, Far Rockaway and Foster's Meadow; 1863, East Chester and City Island.

His prominence among the preachers is indicated by the high grade of his appointments, and by his election as General Conference delegate in 1828, 1832, and 1836.

After he had traveled as a conference preacher about seven years, he was married to MISS EUNICE WILLIAMS. At thirty years of age he was appointed to preside over a district embracing both sides of Lake Champlain, extending eastward to the Green Mountains, and manned by some of the strong men of the conference, such as John J. Matthias, James Covel, Jr., Noah Levings, and Seymour Landon. While on this Champlain District he was sorely bereaved by the death of his wife and infant child. He was married on 18th of April, 1827, to MISS ADELINE FERRIS, of Peru, N. Y.

The Carlton avenue (now Simpson) church, of Brooklyn, was organized by him in the summer of 1844; and, on Sunday, July 13, 1845, he dedicated the first chapel erected by that society. His conference memorial gives the following account of his death:

> He went to his appointment, [East Chester,] the next Sabbath after receiving it, and preached with great power, greatly exciting the hopes and strengthening the faith of the brethren. He returned [to Long Island] the next day (Monday) for his family and effects. The latter part of the same week he set out with his wife and daughter in his own carriage for their new home, was arrested by disease on the way, called on his friend, Dr. Van Ness, [once a member of Sands-street church,] in Brooklyn, where he received all the attention that affection and medical skill could suggest, and after lingering about a fortnight, amid alternate hopes and fears for the results, he died in great peace and holy triumph on the 4th of May, [1863, almost seventy years of age.][2]

He is buried in Cypress Hills cemetery. His record in the church is that of "a laborious, faithful, and successful servant of the Lord Jesus Christ," a scholar of respectable attainments, and a preacher of marked ability, more thoughtful and profound than his memoir in the Conference Minutes would imply, and at the same time often producing a marvelous emotional

---

[2] Minutes of Conferences, 1864, p. 89.

effect upon his hearers. He did the work of an evangelist, and made full proof of his ministry, and many are the stars in his crown.

EUNICE WILLIAMS, the first wife of Buel Goodsell, was born December 4, 1797. She was left fatherless at ten years of age. At nineteen she sought the Lord at a camp-meeting near her home, and five years later she was married to Mr. Goodsell. She departed this life on 16th of March, 1826, aged twenty-nine years. A circumstantial account of her farewell to earth was written by her husband and published as a magazine article.[3] It is a most affecting story of resignation and faith and triumph in the last hours of life. After comforting her weeping husband, she called her eldest daughter to her bedside, and imparted to the child a dying mother's blessing. Then followed most impressive appeals to others:

She said: "I shall soon be gone, I must improve the moments that remain." She began by addressing herself to her mother, saying, "Mother, I expect to meet you in heaven; pa, too. Tell my sisters and brothers I expect to meet them in glory. Tell the rest of the family they have a heaven to gain and a hell to shun." After this she addressed an exhortation to every one present; and O! with what words of fire and feeling did she exhort some of her unconverted acquaintances to seek religion and prepare for death, * * * adding, "I shall soon be with holy angels, with the great and good God, with the holy and blessed Redeemer! Come, Lord Jesus! come quickly! Glory! glory! glory!"

Besides the infant, deceased, there are two daughters by the first marriage, *Lucy Elliott*, who married Jordan Searing, of Brooklyn, and *Elizabeth Williams*, who married James H. Chipman, of Albany.

Mr. Goodsell's second wife, the faithful partner of his ministry for thirty-five years, is now in the twenty-second year of her widowhood. She bore him seven children, the eldest of whom, *Charles Buel*, was graduated from the University of the City of New York, studied medicine, enlisted in the volunteer army, was wounded, and at the time of his death, in 1867, in his thirty-eighth year, was principal of a school in Yonkers, N. Y. The second son, *Henry*, died in infancy. *Julia Adeline* married Dr. Geo. A. Dewey, of Brooklyn, N. Y. The *Rev. George Henry Goodsell* and the *Rev. Daniel Ayers Goodsell, D.D.*, are useful and honored members of the New York East Conference. *Mary C.* married Thomas R. Ball, of Brooklyn, N. Y.

---

[3] Methodist Magazine, 1826, p 293.

LXX.

Jno. Miley

OHN and Anna (Miller) Miley, the parents of the Rev. JOHN MILEY, D. D., LL. D., were natives of Pennsylvania. Their ancestry was German. They were highly respectable people and Methodistic in their creed. In the year 1810 they emigrated from their home near Brownsville, Pa., and settled in Butler County, a little way east of Hamilton, in the state of Ohio. There John Miley was born and reared on his father's farm. His father died when he was twelve years of age, and his mother when he was eighteen. He is now the only surviver of the family of five sons and two daughters.

When a boy he manifested an unusual taste for reading and study, and was sent to such schools as the neighborhood furnished, and later to a good school in Hamilton. At length he entered Augusta College, Kentucky, where Drs. Tomlinson, Bascom, M'Cown, and Trimble were professors, and where he was graduated in 1838. One other Sands-street pastor, J. B. Merwin, was graduated at the same college six years earlier, and one of the same professors, H. B. Bascom, was a member of the faculty in Merwin's time.

Dr. Miley was converted in Hamilton, Ohio, in his fifteenth year, under the ministry of the late Rev. John. A. Baughman. The church was in an active state at the time, but there was no special revival. Young Miley improved his gifts in the meetings, and was licensed to exhort in 1833, and to preach in 1834.

MINISTERIAL RECORD: 1838, (Ohio Conf.,) Batavia cir., O., with D. Whitcomb; 1839, Cincinnati, Western charge, with W. H. Raper; 1840, ordained deacon—Hamilton and Rossville circuit; 1841, Chillicothe circuit; 1842, ordained elder—ditto, with John Barton; 1843-1844, Columbus; 1845-1846, Zanesville, 7th-street; 1847, Cincinnati, Wesley Chapel; 1848-1849, professor of languages and mathematics in Wesleyan Female College; 1850-1851,

Cincinnati, Morris chapel; 1852-1853, (New York East Conf.,) Brooklyn, Pacific-street; 1854-1855, Williamsburgh, South Second-street; **1856-1857, Brooklyn, Sands-street,** with M. B. Bull, sup'y; 1858-1859, Danbury, Conn.; 1860, New York, Forsyth-street; 1861, ditto, with E. L. Janes; 1862-1863, Bridgeport and Fairfield, Conn.; 1864-1865, New Rochelle, N. Y.; 1866-1868, (New York Conf.,) Newburgh; 1869-1871, Sing Sing; 1872, Peekskill, St. Paul's; 1873-1884, professor in Drew Theological Seminary, Madison, N. J.

He was married, June 9, 1840, to OLIVE C. PATTERSON, in Batavia, Ohio. His ministerial brethren elected him to the General Conferences of 1864, 1872, and 1876. The Ohio Wesleyan University conferred upon him the degree of D.D. in 1859, and the degree of LL.D. in 1872.

As preacher, pastor, and teacher, Dr. Miley has proved himself to be a workman that needeth not to be ashamed. Revivals have attended his labors on several charges. He is now faithfully serving the church in one of those eminent and responsible positions which only the best and ablest men can acceptably fill.

Dr. Miley has written extensively for various periodicals, and is the author of two important works, which have been widely read and highly commended. The first is entitled "Class-Meetings," and the second, "The Atonement in Christ."

OLIVE CHICHESTER, his wife, died in Madison, N. J., August 29, 1874. " She was rich in the best womanly endowments, true and good, intelligent, bright, full of kindly sympathy, but for many years feeble in health. During her extreme suffering she exhibited, in a remarkable measure, the sweet graces of the Christian life."[1] She is buried in a beautiful cemetery in Morristown, N. J. Three months previous to her death a beloved Christian daughter, a teacher in Dr. Van Norman's school in New York city, passed on to the heavenly rest. The entire list of the children is as follows: *Annie Brooks, Olive Comfort, Sallie Foster, John William.*

---

[1] Editorial note in The Christian Advocate.

LXXI.

W. F. WATKINS.

As a supply for a brief season, the REV. WILBUR FISK WATKINS, D.D., when a very young man, was pastor of the Sands-street church. A recently-published sketch contains the following account of his birth and childhood:

He first saw the light on the 9th of July, 1836, in the city of Baltimore, Md. His early youth was spent in that city, where his father hoped to establish him at a proper time in a mercantile life. But in his young boyhood Wilbur was noted for his religious impressionability and exemplary conduct, and his dreams and hopes for life were quickly centered on the ministry.[1]

After studying at the Govanstown Academy, he entered Dickinson College when sixteen years of age; but severe application to study undermined his health, and for this reason he left college at the close of his sophomore year, and being less than eighteen years of age, began his ministerial career as a junior supply on one of the circuits in the mountains of Pennsylvania. He rode horseback with saddle-bags, after the fashion of the fathers. The biography already referred to says:

This exercise in the bracing air of the mountains brought back the wasted vigor, and imparted additional strength, developing the slight youth into a sturdy and robust man. His first sermon was preached on Manor Hill, Pa., from the text, "I have fought a good fight," etc., thus beginning his proclamation of the good news of God by anticipating the close.

This brings us to his

MINISTERIAL RECORD: 1854, supply in the Allegheny Mts.; 1855, (Balt. Conf.,) Manor Hill cir., Pa., with J. W. Haughawout; 1856, West Harford cir., Md., with F. Macartney; 1857–1858, "located," student in Biblical Institute, Concord, N. H.; **1858, (April and May,) Brooklyn, Sands-street,** supply; 1858, (several months,) Lawrence, Mass., supply; 1859, (New York East Conf.,) Mamaroneck, N. Y.; 1860, ditto, with N. Tibbals, sup'y; 1861, ordained deacon; 1861–1862, New

---

[1] Hanson Place Quarterly, October, 1883. Sketch by the Rev. Charles A. Tibbals.

REV. WILBUR F. WATKINS, D. D.

York, Twenty-seventh-street ; 1863–1865, Brooklyn, Washington street ; 1866-1868, Brooklyn, Hanson Place ; 1869-1870, New Haven. Conn., First ch.; 1871, withdrew ; 1871, ordained deacon in the Protestant Episcopal Church by Bp. Littlejohn, of Long Island,—assistant minister, St. James Church, Brooklyn, in charge of St. Barnabas Mission—later in the same year, ordained priest—rector, St. Barnabas ; 1872-1875, rector of the Church of the Epiphany, Washington, D. C.; 1876-1880, rector of Christ Church, Baltimore, Md.; 1881-1884, rector of the Church of the Holy Trinity, New York.

As the " boy preacher " in Pennsylvania and Maryland, it is thought that " he enjoyed the sweetest notoriety of his life ; " but, being conscious of the need of a systematic theological training, he stepped aside from the conference and entered the theological school in Concord, N. H. There the author formed his acquaintance, heard him preach, and spent many pleasant hours in his company.

In the midst of his theological course Mr. Watkins visited Brooklyn, and was invited to address the Juvenile Missionary. Society of the Sands-street church on the first Sabbath in April, 1858. That was the spring of the " great revival." It happened that year that the New York Conference met in May, several weeks after the session of the New York East Conference. Dr. Miley, of the latter, was the retiring pastor ; Dr. Hagany, of the former, was the coming pastor. Services were held in Sands-street every night. Mr. Watkins preached several times during the week succeeding the missionary anniversary, and considerable interest was manifested. The pulpit being vacant, and this young and talented minister being on the ground, the official board of Sands-street church passed very complimentary resolutions concerning Mr. Watkins, and petitioned the faculty at Concord to grant him leave of absence until Dr. Hagany's transfer. That petition was granted, and, by appointment of the presiding elder, Buel Goodsell, he was in charge of Sands-street church for a few weeks. He preached every night during the week and twice on Sundays, and there were many conversions.

His work at Sands-street led to his invitation to the church in Mamaroneck. Under his administration a new church was built at the latter place, and Methodism received a new impulse. While there, in 1860, he was married at the age of twenty-four to MISS ESTHER GRIFFIN, daughter of the late Schureman Halstead, one of the most eminent Methodist laymen of New York. During his pastoral term in the Washington-street church, as the successor of Dr. De Hass, that church nearly reached its zenith in respect to members and strength. In Hanson Place church he followed the Rev. George W. Woodruff, and his ministry was there, as elsewhere, a very marked success. He was prostrated by a severe illness while serving this church, but a three-months' stay in the West Indies restored his health.

An Episcopalian rector, who likewise was formerly a Methodist pastor, gives the following history of the change which took place in Mr. Watkins' church relations:

> From Hanson Place Mr. Watkins went, in response to a call, to the First Methodist Episcopal Church of New Haven, Conn., where he was admired and beloved as pastor and preacher, as he had been in all places where he had exercised those holy offices. But here a change was made in his views and convictions which was destined to alter his whole after-life. It was not suddenly or quickly done, but rather it was the expression of thoughts and purposes which had been growing within him for years. Although so remarkably successful in his work, and to all appearances so admirably adapted to it, Mr. Watkins had for years been feeling less and less at home in the Methodist connection. It was in New Haven that the conclusion forced itself upon him that if he were to make the change, of which he had thought so long and earnestly and prayerfully, it must be done at once, without further delay.
>
> This is not the place to enter into any discussion upon the reasons of the departure of Mr. Watkins from the Methodist communion, and his entrance into the Protestant Episcopal Church. Suffice it to say that it was upon no grounds of selfish expediency, nor because of the friction of the itinerancy, but upon conscientious grounds.[2]

In Brooklyn he took charge of a small mission; lots were purchased, a chapel erected, and a prosperous Sunday-school and congregation gathered. As rector of the Church of the Epiphany he ministered to the largest congregation, with one exception, (Metropolitan Methodist,) in the city of Washington, and numbered among his hearers some of the first men of the nation. Here he was again prostrated, but restored by rest and a European tour. While serving Christ Church, in Baltimore, he received from William and Mary College in Virginia the degree of Doctor in Divinity. He wrote from Baltimore to the Bibliothean Fraternity—composed of his earlier friends and associates in the Biblical Institute—assembled in their triennial re-union, that he warmly cherished the old fraternal feeling,

---

[2] The Rev. C. A. Tibbals, in "Hanson Place Quarterly," October, 1883.

fully believed in evangelical Christian work, stood by Moody in the revival in Baltimore, and had established a weekly prayer-meeting in his church, largely attended by persons converted in the Moody meetings.

In his present parish he is successor to the younger Dr. Tyng, and here his former popularity and usefulness are, if possible, surpassed.

Dr. Watkins is a fascinating speaker, engaging in his appearance, easy and graceful in manner, with a voice of uncommon melody, and a fluency rarely excelled. To quote Mr. Tibbals again :

As a speaker, Dr. Watkins possesses natural gifts of rare excellence, which have been finely developed by cultivation. His style of composition, though in the beginning of his career florid and highly rhetorical, has become, by intellectual growth, terse and nervous to a marked degree. Full of energy, his thoughts come forth in clear-cut sentences, and by an impressive and fascinating delivery, are impressed upon the mind, never to be forgotten. At times, carried away by the grandeur or solemnity of his theme, our preacher rises to flights of eloquence, startling in their power and beauty. And so he is said to be in the best sense the most popular preacher in the communion of which New York can boast. His social qualities are equally delightful and engaging. His genial cordiality, united to unusual conversational powers, his kindly humor, and noble generosity, all combine to make friends for him every-where, and attach them with a genuine and lasting enthusiasm. Dr. Watkins' fondness for and interest in young men are proverbial. He is always befriending, helping, and attracting to himself young men, over whom he exerts the best possible influence.

His estimable wife, ESTHER G. (HALSTEAD), "entered into rest" December 16, 1884. From her father's home, which echoed with Methodist shout and song, she passed well-trained into the position of an itinerant's wife, where she was happy and useful; yet she heartily concurred with her husband in his latter choice as to their church relations. One year ago Mr. Tibbals wrote concerning the children :

The eldest, *Wilbur Fisk, Jr.*, is a deacon in the church, and at present (1883) assisting his father. He is a young man of bright promise and of studious habits, devoted to his calling. The second son, *S. Halstead*, is studying in preparation for holy orders in the Berkeley Divinity School, at Middletown, Conn. The third, *Thomas Coke*, is a young lad who looks forward to a mercantile life. The youngest are two charming girls ; the elder is just budding into sweet girlhood, and the other a child of seven years. One child, *Ruth*, has passed on to make heaven more attractive to this family, who enjoy in their happy life a taste of that love which is the gate to the Paradise of God.

LXXII.

JOHN B. HAGANY.

THE REV. JOHN BISHOP HAGANY, D.D., the much esteemed pastor of the Sands-street church in 1848 and 1849, was successor to Dr. Miley. He was born in Wilmington, Del., August 26, 1808. His father was a Methodist local preacher, a devout man, and somewhat over-strict and severe in the government of his family. Becoming restless under discipline, John, at two different times, ran away from home to try the fortunes of a sailor's life. The father's prayers were answered at length, and his heart made glad by the conversion of the young man at the age of nineteen, and his entrance upon the work of a traveling preacher at the age of twenty-two.

ITINERANT RECORD: 1831, (Phila. Conf.,) Talbot cir., Md., with M. Hazel and B. Andrew; 1832, Port Deposit cir., with Thos. M'Carroll; 1833, ordained deacon,—Elkton; 1834–1835, Easton, Pa., ordained elder in 1835; 1836, (New Jersey Conf.,) Burlington, N. J.; 1837, (Phila. Conf.,) Philadelphia, Kensington ch.; 1838–1839, Elkton, Md.; 1840, Pottsville and Minersville, Pa.; 1841–1842, Philadelphia, St. George's, with E. Cooper, sup'y; 1843–1844, Philadelphia, Ebenezer; 1845–1846, Middletown, Del.; 1847–1848, Pottsville, 1st ch., Pa.; 1849–1850, Philadelphia, Trinity; 1851–1852, (New York Conf.,) New York, Vestry-street; 1853–1854, New York, Mulberry-street; 1855–1856, Yonkers; 1857, New York, Sullivan-street; **1858–1859**, (New York East Conf.,) **Brooklyn, Sands-street**; 1860–1861, (New York Conf.,) New York, St. Paul's; 1862–1863, New York, Bedford-street; 1864–1865, New York, Thirtieth-street.

His pastoral term was duplicated in Elkton, in Pottsville, and in the Mulberry-street charge, New York, after it had become St. Paul's. His stations were six years in Philadelphia and a little over nine years in New York city. He was a member of four different annual conferences. While in the Philadelphia Conference he was the friend and associate of George R. Crooks, William H. Gilder, John A. Roche, John S. Inskip, John Kennaday, and the venerable Ezekiel Cooper; all of whom, either before or afterward, were prominently connected with the Methodism of Brooklyn and New York. His conference memorial says:

No man among us was more uniformably acceptable to the people, or retained to the last a more controlling power in the pulpit. * * * As a Christian, he was devout without the ostentation of superior piety. * * * As a preacher, Dr. Hagany possessed the advantage of a fine physique, a voice of extraordinary compass and sweetness, and a quiet self-poise which always rendered him a most agreeable and captivating speaker. * * * His sermons were rarely thrilling, but always pleasing, and sometimes overwhelmingly emotional. * * * In the social circle he shone the brightest; as a companion one of the pleasantest, and as a conversationalist racy and sparkling; yet he never forgot or forsook the dignity of the minister.[1]

His familiar friend, the Rev. Dr. George R. Crooks, contributes the following testimony:

Dr. Hagany was an eloquent preacher. He had a sweet-toned voice, a calm rather than a fervent temperament, a quick, tender sympathy, by which he was readily affected himself, and could readily affect others to tears. His memory was retentive, and enabled him to command instantly all his resources. In the early Methodist literature and the English classics of the seventeenth century he was unusually well-read, and his citations from his favorite authors pleasantly spiced his conversation. Withal there was a vein of humor running through his speaking and writing which gave a flavor to both. His literary remains consist chiefly of essays contributed to religious and other periodicals. One of these, on John Wesley, furnished to Harper's Magazine, is one of the most striking characterizations of the great reformer extant.[2]

Dr. Hagany is elsewhere described as "a writer of force, exquisite polish, humor, and pathos."[3]

While pastor in New York and Brooklyn it was his uniform habit to dine once or twice a week at the house of Fletcher Harper, and usually in company with his choice friends, Drs. Milburn, Prime, Stevens, and M'Clintock. Dr. Stevens, on meeting a daughter of Dr. Hagany in Switzerland years afterward, recalled those pleasant hours of conversation, assuring the lady that her father's genial and sparkling humor was the very life of those meetings.

Dr. Hagany's death was sudden and unexpected. He preached to his congregation on the last Sunday in June, 1865, from the text, "Let me die the death of the righteous, and let

---

[1] Minutes of Conferences, 1866, p. 73.
[2] M'Clintock and Strong's Cyclopedia.
[3] Simpson's Cyclopedia.

my last end be like his," and proposed to resume the interesting subject the next time he preached. In the evening he was too unwell to go into the pulpit. Three days afterward, Wednesday, June 28, he sat reading aloud to his wife some passages from the sermons of the Rev. Jonathan Seed, an old favorite of John Wesley, when suddenly he was seized with a spasm of pain in the heart, the book dropped from his hand, he leaned forward upon the table, and almost instantly expired. He had nearly completed his fifty-seventh year, and the thirty-fourth of his ministry.

Dr. Crooks preached his funeral sermon in the Thirtieth-street Methodist Episcopal church, and his remains were carried to their resting-place in the Wilmington and Brandywine cemetery, Wilmington, Del. His grave is marked by a white marble tomb-stone on which is inscribed the text of his last discourse.

His wife, CAROLINE S. (FORD,) was, previous to their marriage, a resident of Elkton, Md. She died in the month of August, 1877, aged sixty years, and is buried by the side of her husband.

One of their two daughters, *Mary*, wife of John E. Fay,[4] died in the year 1876; the other, *Emma*, is the wife of Mr. Henry Bartlett, of Brooklyn, N. Y.

---

[4] See account of the Fays in Book III.

REV. BERNARD H. NADAL, D. D.

LXXIII.

BERNARD H. NADAL.

A BRIGHT star in the galaxy of the Sands-street pastors was the REV. BERNARD HARRISON NADAL, D.D., succ essor of Dr. Hagany. Bernard Nadal, his father, was a native of Bayonne, France. He was very early placed in training for the Roman priesthood, but when a lad of twelve years he threw down his books in the street, ran away from his parents, and came to the United States. As we observe concerning our beloved and honored Kennaday, and De Vinne, and others prominently connected with the Sands-street church, we see here also another marked illustration of the fact that the Roman Catholic Church not only is now, but has been for generations, losing her children and her children's children, and furnishing Protestantism with some of her best and grandest champions. From Dr. Buttz we quote the following additional statement concerning the elder Nadal:

He was married twice; his second wife, whose maiden name was Rachel Harrison, became the mother of three children, Bernard being the youngest.

The father died five months previous to Bernard's birth. The boy's maternal grandfather was a man of decided moral convictions. He freed all his seventy-five slaves, although they constituted the greater part of his wealth. Bernard's mother was a member of the Methodist Episcopal Church from her childhood—a woman "of much intelligence and force of character," teaching school and making many sacrifices to support her children respectably. From 1821 to her death she resided with her brother in Hookstown, Md., five miles from Baltimore.

Bernard Harrison Nadal was born in Talbot County, Md., March 27, 1812. While very young he entered the employ

352   *Old Sands Street Church.*

of a chemist and liquor merchant in Baltimore. At seventeen he was apprenticed to a saddle-maker, John Bear by name, in Hanover, Pa. While there, at the age of twenty, he found the pearl of great price. He began the study of Latin, learning the paradigms and rules from his book on a little frame before him, while his hands and eyes were occupied in stitching saddles. He took little interest in his work, and thought he had missed his calling. Leaving this place, he was hired as a clerk in a store in Woodstock, Va. A young lawyer gave him assistance in his mathematical studies. The next we know of him he has entered the traveling ministry.

CONFERENCE RECORD: 1835, (Baltimore Conf.,) Luray cir., Va., with M. Goheen ; 1836-1837, St. Mary's cir., Md., with W. S. Evans,—or dained deacon in 1837 ; 1838, Bladensburgh cir., with F. M'Cartney ; 1839, ordained elder,—Baltimore city station, with John Bear, G. Morgan, W. B. Edwards, and T. Myers ; 1840, ditto, with I. Bear, C. B. Tippett, John A. Henning, and T. Myers ; 1841-1842, Lewisburgh, Va.; 1843, Lexington cir., with W. Krebs ; 1844, ditto, with F. H. Richey ; 1845-1846, Baltimore, Columbia-street ; 1847-1848, Carlisle, Pa.; 1849, agent Baltimore Conf. Female College ; 1850-1851, Baltimore, High-street ; 1852, Baltimore city station, with John Poisal, S. Register, and E. A. Gibson ; 1853, ditto, with S. M'Mullin, S. Register, and T. A. Morgan ; health poor, visited Europe ; returning, supplied the pulpit of Dr. Duncan's Presbyterian church ; 1854, appointed (sup'y) to Baltimore city station, but continued to supply the Presbyterian church ; same year appointed Prof. of History and English Literature in Indiana Asbury University ; 1855, (North Indiana Conf.,) retaining his position as professor ; 1857, (Baltimore Conf.,) remaining at the university during the first part of the year ; last part, presiding elder, Roanoke Dist., Va. ; 1858-1849, Washington, D. C., Foundry church ; **1860-1861,** (New York East Conf.,) **Brooklyn, Sands-street;** 1862-1863, New Haven, First church ; 1864-1865, (Baltimore Conf.,) Washington, D. C., Wesley Chapel ; 1866-1867, (Philadelphia Conf.,) Philadelphia, Trinity ; 1868-1871, Professor of Historical Theology in Drew Theological Seminary.

When he came to travel his first circuit he realized some advantage from having been an apprentice, for he was able to make his own saddle. During his second year in Lewisburgh, Va., he was married to MISS SARAH JANE MAYS, daughter of John Mays, Esq., of that place. During the years he was stationed in Carlisle, having previously made preparation to enter an advanced class in Dickinson College, he read up the entire course, was examined, and took the degree of A.B. in 1848. This he is said to have done " without neglecting any of the proper duties of his office."

While at the Indiana Asbury University he was the associate

of Dr. Curry, who speaks very highly of his ability, thoroughness, and efficiency as an instructor of young men. He received the degree of D.D. from Dickinson College in 1859, nine years after his graduation at that institution.

His presence in Washington amid the closing scenes of the war, and his influence both in public and in private, are believed to have been of great value to the cause of the Union. He enjoyed the confidence of President Lincoln and other foremost men of the nation, and was recognized as a stanch supporter of the Union. His biographer says:

> He preached the funeral sermon of Governor Hicks, of Maryland, in which he portrayed his excellent services to the nation in her hour of peril; and while at all times he maintained his views of right with great conscientiousness, yet he secured the respect of those from whose principles and aims he was compelled to dissent.[1]

His position as professor in Drew Theological Seminary he had held only about two years when he speedily followed his friend and associate, Dr. M'Clintock, to the world of blessed rewards.

He first complained of indisposition on Thursday of the week preceding his decease, but no alarm was felt either by himself or his family until the succeeding Sunday. Then it was found that his old chronic complaint, a disease of the kidneys, without causing much pain or prostration, had really weakened his constitution to such an extent that congestion of the lungs and brain seemed to be inevitable. When informed of his extremely critical condition he replied promptly that he had left the issue entirely with the Lord. As the evening advanced he gradually sunk into a stupor, from which he did not awake. Thus on Monday morning, June 20, 1870, in the village of Madison, N. J., at the age of fifty-eight, Dr. Nadal came suddenly to the end of his race, " dying ' in warm blood,' running at the top of his speed, but he failed not, for he gained the prize of his high calling."[2] He was buried in the Laurel Hill cemetery, in Philadelphia.

Dr. Wm. M. Punshon, in his memorable address before the General Conference, in Brooklyn, a few months after the death of Dr. Nadal, assigned him a prominent place among the recently crowned victors of whom he spoke. He said:

---

[1] Dr. Buttz in " New Life Dawning," p. 36.
[2] Minutes of Conferences, 1871, p. 47.

And then I think of John M'Clintock, that *anax andron*,[3] almost an Admirable Crichton in versatility of attainment, Melanchthon in tenderness, and Luther in courage, but all whose wise, rare gifts he cast at the feet of him who was the Man of Sorrows, but upon whose head are many crowns ; of Nadal, who dropped so soon after his friend that it seemed as if, in preparing his memoir, he had got to long so much for nearer communion that he must needs ascend to join him in the presence of the Master whom they both loved.

Bishop Foster mourned for him as his " dear Nadal," and penned a beautiful tribute, in which he said :

To rare beauty of mind he added the superior charm of perfect candor and unflinching bravery. He was no trimmer. The church had in him a true and faithful son, always ready to do valiant service. But he was no bigot ; his catholicity was broad and genial ; many of his most attached friends were found in other churches than his own.[4]

In the pulpit Dr. Nadal was instructive, convincing, persuasive, and often eloquent. In doctrinal statements and opinions he was decidedly evangelical and Methodistic in the best sense of those terms. In his early ministry he often wrote and delivered his sermons *verbatim*. Later in life he quite frequently used his manuscript, but always with good effect.

He was oppressed by a conviction, which he frequently and strongly expressed to his nearest friends, that he was not adapted to the itinerancy—that he might have accomplished vastly more good in the settled ministry; yet his love for Methodist theology led him to decline very flattering invitations to become a permanent pastor of a Calvinistic church.

He attained a high rank among educated men, and may be cited as a marked example of successful achievement by diligent application in spite of great disadvantages. " He loved knowledge for its own sake." The trustees of the Drew Theological Seminary published the following :

We desire to record our sense of his eminent abilities as a scholar, a preacher, a writer, and a professor ; in all of which respects he has made a marked impression on the students, and left a brilliant example.[5]

Dr. Nadal attained his chief pre-eminence as a writer. As his brethren testify—

The range of his writings included theology, ethics, politics, social life, nature, and art ; and each was treated in a masterly way. Lectures, addresses, sermons, newspaper editorials, were continually pouring from his tireless pen.[6]

---

[3] Prince or king of men—ἄναξ ἀνδρῶν.
[4] Introduction to " New Life Dawning," p. 7.
[5] Extract from a resolution published in The Christian Advocate.
[6] Memoir in Conference Minutes.

A posthumous volume, entitled "New Life Dawning and Other Discourses," accompanied by an excellent memoir from the pen of the Rev. Dr. H. A. Buttz, has attracted considerable attention.

The Rev. L. M. Vernon, in The Christian Advocate, ascribes to Dr. Nadal a "marvelous analytic power," "glowing imagination," and "instinctive profundity of thought," while his "heart was a glowing furnace that warmed to blood-heat every thought of the brain." Dr. Crooks classes him with those "who ripen slowly, and have a long period of fruitage." Another, who knew him intimately, writes:

His religion tinged all the habits of life as well as his duties. * * * The following resolutions found in his diary, supposed to have been written about 1865, show the practical character of his mind, as well as his earnestness in improvement: "I promise, God helping, the following, namely: 1. To do my best not to lose my temper; 2. Not to smoke; 3. To eat nothing for supper beyond bread and butter; 4. To try to be in bed before eleven o'clock; 5. To visit more diligently.—B. H. N." "I further promise, by the help of God through Christ, never to speak favorably of myself, except to my most intimate friends, and sparingly even to them.—B. H. N." How this simple record, intended for no eye but his own, reveals his character.[7]

The same writer describes his person and manner thus:

Dr. Nadal was about five feet seven inches in height; though short, he was rather thick-set and very erect and active in his bearing. His step was firm and decided; he carried himself well, and there was nothing uncertain in his demeanor. He could be stern at times, but was, as a rule, winning and pleasant. His eyes were bright, and, when his mood was a happy one, they had warmth in them, a fireside glow, delightful to all that came near him.[8]

Dr. Buttz describes the "cheerfulness" and "hospitality" of his home, and quotes from his beautiful tribute to his "little Lizzie," who died.

The home of MRS. SARAH JANE (MAYS) NADAL, his widow, is now (1884) in the city of New York, where all but one of his surviving children also reside. The following are the children: 1. *Ehrman S.*, formerly an *attaché* of the American Legation in London, now secretary of the Municipal Civil Service Examining Board, New York city—author of a work on his observations in England, and a volume of essays, etc. 2. *Thomas W.*, a

---

[7] Dr. Buttz in "New Life Dawning," pp. 77, 78.
[8] Ibid., pp, 88, 89.

physician in Jamaica, L. I. 3. *Rebecca M.*, joined Sands-street church by letter, with her mother and brother, in 1872, and removed by letter in 1876. 4. *Bernard Harrison*, a student in Wesleyan University in 1868, member of Sands-street church 1872–1876, for years past employed in the Custom-house, New York. 5. *Charles C.*, a lawyer in New York. 6. *Frank*, a youth of great promise, was a member of the senior class of Columbia College at the time of his death by drowning in Bernardsville, N. J., in 1879. A beautiful memorial, by Mrs. Mary Stevens Robinson, was published in The Methodist. 7. *Jennie.* 8. *Grace M.*

REV. D. CURRY, D.D., LL.D.

LXXIV.
DANIEL CURRY.

E have knowledge of the ancestry of the REV. DANIEL CURRY, D. D., L L. D. as far back as Richard Curry, who was born in East Chester, just above the city of New York, in 1709.

About 1730, having married, he took his young wife and all their effects, and, mounting themselves on a single horse, they rode northward into the almost unbroken forests in the northern part of Westchester County, then still, occupied by the wild Algonquins. He located in the valley of Peekskill Creek, a few miles back from the Hudson, where he became an extensive land owner reared a large family, and died in 1806.[1]

Stephen, second son of Richard Curry, was the father of four sons and a number of daughters. Thomas, second son of Stephen Curry, reared a family of nine children, six of them sons, the fourth of whom is the subject of this sketch. The longevity of several persons in the different branches of the family has been remarkable. Richard, the great-grandfather of Dr. Curry, died in his ninety-seventh year, and an uncle, Stephen Curry, celebrated the one hundredth anniversary of his birth about the year 1870, at which date all the five brothers of Dr. Curry were living, the eldest seventy years of age. The family name has been honored by several persons who have attained considerable distinction. A brother of Daniel Curry was candidate for Governor, and afterward Chief Justice of the Supreme Court of California, about the time of the war of the Rebellion.

Daniel Curry was born near Peekskill, N. Y., November 26, 1809. At that date the Methodist Episcopal Church had been organized just twenty-five years; there were less than six hundred traveling preachers and only about one hundred and sixty three thousand (163,000) members in the

---

[1] Article in the Christian Advocate about 1870.

United States and the Canadas. A comparison of these figures with the statistics of the present centennial year will convey some idea of the growth and development of the church during Dr. Curry's life-time.

His youth was divided between the occupations of farmer and student. At home, when twenty years of age, he gave his heart to the Saviour. He was baptized by Peter P. Sandford, at Shrub Oak, N. Y. At White Plains, N. Y., where he prepared for college, he received his first license as a local preacher in 1834. He was graduated from the Wesleyan University in 1837, and was employed that same year as the first president of the Troy Conference Academy, in Poultney, Vt. Two years later he was appointed to a professorship in the Georgia Female College, in Macon. He was ordained local deacon by Bishop Andrew, in the State of Georgia, in 1841. He entered the itinerant ministry that year, and the following is his

CONFERENCE RECORD: 1841, (Georgia Conf.,) Athens, Ga.; 1842, Athens and Lexington; 1843, ordained elder,—Savannah; 1844, Columbus; 1845, (New York Conf.,) New York, Twenty-third street, with Z. Davenport, sup'y; 1846–1847, New Haven, First ch.; 1848–1849, (New York East Conf.,) Brooklyn, Washington-st.; 1850–1851, Brooklyn, Fleet-st.; 1852–1853, Hartford; 1854, New York, Twenty-seventh-st.; 1855–1857, (Indiana Conf.,) Pres't Indiana Asbury University; 1857, (New York East Conf.,) Brooklyn, N. Y., South Third-st.; 1858–1859, Middletown, Conn.; 1860–1861, New Rochelle, N. Y.; 1862-1863, New York, Thirty-seventh-st.; **1864, presiding elder, Long Island South Dist.**; 1864–1876, editor of The Christian Advocate; 1876–1880, editor of The National Repository; 1880–1881, associate editor of The Methodist, with D. H. Wheeler; 1881–1882, New York, Eighty-second street and South Harlem; 1883, New York, Bethany chapel; 1884, New York, Trinity ch., with T. H. Burch until May, then elected editor of the Methodist Quarterly Review.

Dr. Curry was married, February 16, 1838, to Miss Mary Halstead, daughter of A. L. Halstead, of White Plains, N. Y. The degree of D.D. was conferred upon him by the Wesleyan University in 1852, and that of LL.D. by the Syracuse University in 1878. He has been a member of every General Conference from 1860 to 1884, inclusive, leading his delegation five times out of seven. He was a delegate to the Methodist Ecumenical Conference, in London, 1881.

Daniel Curry has been prominently before the public for nearly half a century; with voice and pen, as teacher, preacher, platform speaker, author, and editor—one of the busiest men of his age; and to this day his "bow abides in strength." More than forty years ago he took rank among the ablest writers in the Methodist Episcopal Church, a pre-eminence which he still maintains. Besides the incalculable product of eighteen years of editorial work, scores of elaborate contributions from his pen have appeared in cyclopedias and magazines, and about twenty-five of his best articles are in the Methodist Quarterly Review. He is the author of a "Life of Wicklif," "The Metropolitan City of America," and "Platform Papers." The works of Dr. James Floy and Southey's "Life of Wesley" were edited by him. His last book is a revision of Clarke's "Commentary on the New Testament," an "elaborate, scholarly work," upon which he "has spent the energies of his ripe, rich genius."

Great satisfaction has been expressed concerning the almost unanimous election of Daniel Curry to the difficult and honorable position of editor of the Methodist Review. Few, even among the ablest men of Methodism, would have been trusted to take charge of this highest periodical of our Church, especially as the successor of that mighty theologian, scholar, and writer, Dr. Daniel D. Whedon.

Since one of the boldest of men has written, "Dr. Curry is too much alive for us to risk a characterization," the author of this book ought surely to be prudent enough to resist any temptation in that direction. But Dr. Buckley proceeds to say: "No man living ever taught the writer more than Dr. Curry;" which statement is, perhaps, as great a climax as this chapter can reach.

Three sons of Daniel and Mary Curry, namely, *Edward Coxe*, *Francis Shay*, and *David Stanford*, died in childhood. Their only daughter, *Georgia*, is the wife of Mr. James Armstrong.

LXXV.

CHARLES FLETCHER.

THE REV. CHARLES FLETCHER was born near Leeds, Yorkshire, England, January 10, 1811. His wife was often heard to speak of her acquaintance with him as a boy in the Sunday-school, where he showed uncommon talent and won the admiration of many. At sixteen he was converted, and began to preach when eighteen years of age. His educational advantages were exceedingly limited. After a short time spent at school, the only opportunities of his youth were such as a factory life affords; a fact which afterward elicited the question, "Whence hath this man such wisdom?" He developed a fine talent for business, and came to this country as a wool-buyer in 1842.

It would seem that he had ceased to be a preacher, if, indeed, he was a church-member at the time of his coming to America. Some important facts in Mr. Fletcher's history, occurring about this time, are vividly presented in a communication by the Rev. Aaron Foster. He writes:

In the year 1842, I resided in Glenham, Dutchess County, N. Y., had charge of the village school, and was one of the class-leaders in the church of that place. My first interview with the lamented subject of this tribute was soon after he arrived in this country, when, while walking apparently for pastime, he halted in front of my residence where I was standing, and seemed inclined to make my acquaintance. I recognized in him a stranger. Moved by what proved a mutual impulse, I reciprocated his advances. We had not conversed long, till his pleasant manner, together with the ease, grace, elegance and fluency of his conversation, convinced me that he was more than ordinary. In this conversation I learned he had belonged to the Wesleyan Church in the old country, and also that he had been a local preacher, and he showed himself conversant with the Church, its institutions, and leading standard-bearers in that country. Indeed, he seemed, comparatively as a luminous star bursting from behind a dark cloud—such a man as one seldom meets. I at once sought a closer acquaintance, and invited him to my class-room. He

Rev. CHARLES FLETCHER.

came. I introduced him to our pastor, he joined on probation, and his utterances were fragrant with a deep and rich experience. His words thrilled our souls. While he spoke our hearts burned. In due time he was licensed to preach.[1]

Thenceforward to the close of his life, Mr. Fletcher continued, either as a local or an itinerant preacher, to proclaim the glad tidings of salvation to men. Indeed, while he was outside the conference, his field, as a commercial traveler, was even more extended, and his transient visits and mighty sermons, in widely distant parts of the country, will not soon be forgotten. His record as a pastor in this country is briefly contained in the following list of

APPOINTMENTS : 1845, (New York Conf.,) Hartford Conn., with W. K. Stopford;[2] 1846, ditto, with P. C. Oakley ; 1847-1851, a local preacher; 1850, last part, Brooklyn, Washington avenue. (Summerfield)—a supply ;[3] 1852 (New York East Conf.,) ordained deacon,—Brooklyn, Summerfield chapel; 1853-1854, Birmingham, Conn.; 1855, ordained elder ; 1855-1856, Bridgeport, Conn.; 1857-1858, New York, Seventh-street ; 1859-1860, New York, Twenty-second-street, the first year with J. J. Matthias, sup'y ; 1861-1862, Mamaroneck ; 1863, Meriden, Conn. ; **1864-1866, Brooklyn, Sands-street** ; 1867-1868, New Haven, Conn., First ch.; 1869-1871, Brooklyn, Pacific-street; **1872-1875, presiding elder, Long Island South Dist.**, 1876-1879, presiding elder, New York East Dist.; 1880, supernumerary.

His field of labor in his first appointment was not in the city of Hartford, but, as the junior preacher, he was assigned to an outlying village, which afforded him an inadequate support, and he left the charge and engaged in mercantile business before the second year had expired. He was not happy, however, until he had re-entered upon the work to which he was conscious the Head of the Church had called him. He was providentially led into a hitherto unoccupied but hopeful field, and, by the blessing of God, he became the founder of the strong and prosperous Summerfield church, in Brooklyn.

When Mr. Fletcher was stationed in New Haven he had reached the height of his fame. It was then that the author, as a neighbor, had opportunity to witness the power of his influence, and to observe the cause and the extent of his popularity. In his sermons he almost invariably presented the greatest

---

[1] " Reminiscences," etc., in The Christian Advocate, 1880.

[2] His memoir in the Conference Minutes, 1881, p. 79, is inaccurate and misleading, as it speaks of " his conference work, begun in 1852."

[3] Quarterly conference record.

and grandest topics of revelation. "The finished sacrifice," "the transfiguration," "the Christian's spiritual foes," "the sovereignty, majesty, power, dominion, and government of the Almighty," were some of the subjects in which his great heart and intellect found ample scope. He seemed to lose himself in his subject, and there was a clearness, depth, and grandeur, and "a steady march to the climax," which captured the attention, and made a most powerful impression upon the minds and hearts of his hearers. His conference memorial says:

> People of mature judgment and scholarship, and of cultured taste, sat under his ministry with delight. The professors and students of Yale College were fond of dropping into his church.

The official board of the First Methodist Episcopal church in New Haven, in resolutions adopted after his death, declared:

> Though we have been favored with the devoted pastoral care of many of the eminent ministers of the church, none have left a more fragrant memory, or a more salutary Christian influence.

The author remembers to have heard him preach a sermon at the Plainville camp-meeting from the text, "It is finished," which swept like a mighty torrent over the assembly. A minister in the stand, most remarkable for his equanimity, seemed as much overwhelmed by his thoughts and emotions and as violently demonstrative as the others. The following is an extract from the Rev. Dr. Buckley's excellent memorial article in The Christian Advocate:

> As a man, he had the advantage of a large stature, a dignified bearing, and a deep yet musical voice. When in repose, or as he stood before an audience about to begin a discourse, his presence was imposing. In reading the Holy Scriptures he was very impressive. The late Canon M'Nejl, of Liverpool, had a high reputation as a reader, but having heard both, we are of opinion that in solemnity, dignity, and pathos Charles Fletcher nearly equaled him; perhaps, aided by similar externals, he would have attained the same excellence. * * *
>
> Ordinarily reticent in social intercourse, when with a few kindred spirits, he was the charm of the occasion. He was capable not only of wit, but of that which is higher than wit, genuine humor, which was illustrated at the union of the New York East and New England Conferences a few years ago. There those who did not know the rich vein of humor in his composition were surprised and delighted by his happy speech. Every conference has a few men who, if they do not stand above, stand out from the body, not in

seclusion, but in marked individuality. When such men die, they should be fitly described; and so we have tried to represent this man, unique, reserved, not unkind, always a gentleman, and a truly great preacher.

If he had possessed the adaptive facility of some others in prayer-meetings and the Sabbath-school, or had preached from the elevated pedestal of a college presidency, or an episcopal position, his fame would have been as wide as the nation.

While it is not true, as some have believed, that Mr. Fletcher never wrote his sermons, it is a fact that of some of his greatest sermons not a written line or word have his friends been able to find. His memory was well trained. Mr. Foster, already quoted, says:

His reading was select and close, yet various and extensive. He made the best thoughts of the best writers his own, but every thing he borrowed was perfected by the ordeal of a powerful original analysis.

This statement is strikingly exemplified in a manuscript sermon, which Mrs. Fletcher placed in the author's hands. If there were space in this work to publish it, many of his friends would recognize therein the style and spirit of Mr. Fletcher's discourses. After he began to decline in health he spent some time at his son's residence near the writer's home in Great Neck, L. I. He was affable, genial, entertaining, though evidently suffering, and apprehensive of his approaching end. He remarked with a weary smile, when invited to preach, "I feel just now as if I could endure about as much rest as any other man." He was confined to his room in Brooklyn during the session of the conference in 1880; but, prisoner as he was, he took great interest, and even participated in the work of the conference. As death approached he talked some, though not much, about his departure. His theme was Christ. He recited again and again the lines,

"Jesus, our great High Priest,
Hath full atonement made."

After repeating impressively "The burial of Sir John Moore," he added: "And more gloriously the Christian warrior dies." Thus he entered into rest on the 20th of April, 1880, having reached the age of sixty-nine years. His funeral was attended in the Sands-street church, Dr. Curry and other ministers participating in the services, and his remains were borne thence to their last resting-place in Greenwood cemetery.

SARAH (MARSDEN,) his wife, was born near her husband's birthplace, in Yorkshire, (date unknown.[4]) Her father was brother to the noted Australian chaplain and pioneer missionary to New Zealand, the Rev. Samuel Marsden, who was, during his earlier Christian life, a Wesleyan. She had known and loved Charles Fletcher from childhood, and none could fail to observe that she regarded his character, his talent, his work, with a fondness and pride rarely equaled. She stood guard at his study door to prevent unnecessary interruption of his preparation for the pulpit, assumed the cares of the household, and performed an untold amount of pastoral work. It is safe to say that the usefulness of her husband's ministry was largely due to Mrs. Fletcher. Having, on account of studious habits and peculiar tastes, less adaptation than some to certain kinds of pastoral duty, he fortunately found in his energetic and devoted wife a valuable assistant. It is a fact known to some that Mr. Fletcher was subject to despondency, and at times strongly tempted to withdraw from the ministry, but the cheering words and tender persuasions of his wife held him to his work. She never attempted to conceal her admiration for her husband's pulpit ministrations. Forty years of familiarity with his thought and voice and manner only intensified her interest in his sermons.

Mrs. Fletcher was an ardent Methodist, well informed and thoroughly decided on all questions agitating the church. She cherished a profound interest in the welfare of Methodist ministers. She knew and placed her own estimate upon nearly every member of the New York East Conference.

After her husband's death she looked and talked like one homesick for heaven. With all her tender affection for the living, she could not refrain from conversing about the dead, and the hope of meeting them above. Thus she lingered about one year, and died in peace at the residence of her son, Charles M. Fletcher, in Great Neck, L. I., August 14, 1881, aged (probably) about seventy-two. John Pegg, E. Warriner, Geo. Hollis, and others, took part in the funeral services. She sleeps in Greenwood by the side of her husband. Their two sons, *Sydney* and *Charles M.*, survive them, and will never cease to remember their virtues, their counsels, and their prayers.

---

[4] She was peculiar in this particular. Though it was understood that she was older than her husband, she would never tell her age, even to her children.

REV. B. PILSBURY, D. D.

LXXVI.

BENJAMIN PILSBURY.

SOUTH LONG ISLAND DISTRICT was in charge of the REV. BENJAMIN PILSBURY, D. D. from June, 1864, to April, 1868. These were years of great prosperity to the church. Large sums were contributed in the "centenary offerings," and many debts of long standing were liquidated. Sands-street church paid a debt of ten thousand dollars. Several new societies were organized, and some dead ones revived; several new houses of worship were built, and thousands of souls were converted to Christ. The number of pastors employed increased fifty per cent., and the amount paid for ministerial support nearly one hundred per cent.

Benjamin Pilsbury was born in Boscawen, N. H., October 25, 1824. His ancestors came to this country from England, in 1651, and settled in that part of Newbury, Mass., called Belleville. The site where the first log-cabin was built has descended from father to son through all the subsequent generations. Here Daniel Pilsbury. the grandfather of Benjamin, was born; but in early life he emigrated to Boscawen, N. H., where he raised a numerous family, of whom Daniel Jr., the father of Benjamin, was the eldest.

The mother of Benjamin Pilsbury was Betsey Burleigh, daughter of Joseph Burleigh, Esq., of Salisbury, (now Franklin,) N. H., whose farm adjoined that of the father of Daniel and Ezekiel Webster. She became the second wife of Daniel Pilsbury, Jr., and Benjamin was her youngest child, and the only one who lived to maturity.

While he was yet an infant, his parents moved from Boscawen to a farm on Baker's River, in Plymouth, N. H., and there and in that vicinity remained until he was fifteen years old. In 1839 they moved to West Newbury, Mass., where they died at a good old age.

Benjamin's early advantages for schooling were not great. The district school was distant, of short continuance, and not always well taught. In Massachusetts his opportunit[ies] were much better, and he commenced to prepare for colle[ge]. Two winters he studied at the celebrated Dummer Academ[y] in Newbury, and one year at the Wesleyan Academy, Wilb[ra]ham, Mass., but a large part of the required studies were m[as]tered by him alone, by the "midnight oil," while helping [his] father on the farm. He entered the Wesleyan University [in] 1843, and at once took a high position in his class; but his e[x]cessive labors had so exhausted his physical system, that [he] soon fell sick with typhus fever. When this subsided, his ph[y]sician commanded rest, and he went home. This sickness, [al]though a serious interruption, was not altogether disadvant[a]geous. Hitherto his father had opposed his seeking a collegia[te] education, but now he desired his return and promised sor[ne] assistance. His mother had always sympathized with him [in] his efforts, and aided him as much as she was able. He return[ed] to college at the beginning of the second term, and althou[gh] obliged to teach and preach to pay part of his expenses, and [at] times suffering from ill-health, he was able to graduate hon[or]ably with his class in 1847.[1]

Mr. Pilsbury experienced religion while studying at Wilbr[a]ham, in April, 1842, and this event soon changed all his pla[ns] for the future. He had in view the legal profession; but t[he] voice of the Spirit and the leadings of Providence pointed hi[m] to the ministry as the work of his life. In order to earn fun[ds] for the further prosecuting of his studies he taught a distri[ct] school in Agawam, Mass., in the winter of 1842–1843. [He] found there a Methodist class, without a pastor, but holdi[ng] meetings in the school-house on the Sabbath. Of course t[he] teacher, though young and but just received into the churc[h], was pressed into the service; and in that place, without licens[e] and with no intention of seeking one, he commenced to lead t[he] meetings, and call sinners to repentance. A precious reviv[al] followed, and in consequence a little church was soon erecte[d].

While in college Mr. Pilsbury was an active worker [in] holding meetings in the school-houses and little churches [in] Middletown and vicinity; and at length yielded to the convi[c]tion that he must make the "preaching of the cross" his lif[e] work. He was first licensed to preach by the quarter[ly]

---

[1] Bishop Andrews, Dr. Winchell, and other eminent men were members [of] this class.

conference held in Middletown, Conn., August 4, 1845. Bartholomew Creagh was presiding elder, and by his appointment Mr. Pilsbury had the pastoral charge of a little church in Rocky Hill during his last collegiate year.

Feeling the need of additional preparation for the ministry, he resolved to pursue a course of study at some theological seminary, and a providential opening led him to New Haven. The Methodist church in Westville desired him for their pastor, and consented to allow him all the advantages of the theological department in Yale College. Here he spent one year as a supply, and two years as a conference preacher, graduating from the seminary in 1850. Combining pastoral duties with attendance at school was an arduous task, but boarding at Westville, the long and regular walks gave him vigorous health, which he has generally enjoyed ever since.

MINISTERIAL APPOINTMENTS: 1846-1847, Rocky Hill, Conn. a supply; 1847,Westville, a supply; 1848-1849, (New York East Conf.,) returned to Westville ; 1850-1851. Guilford , 1852, New Britain ; 1853-1854, Waterbury; 1855-1856, New York, Seventh-street ; 1857-1858, Hempstead, L. I.; 1859, Rye, N. Y.; 1860-1861, New Haven, Conn., St. John-street; 1862-1863, Brooklyn, N. Y., South Third-street; **1864-1867, presiding elder, Long Island South Dist.**; 1868, West Winsted, Conn.; 1869, Middletown, with J. H. Knowles, (nominal appointment;) 1870-1871, Watertown; 1872-1875, presiding elder, New Haven Dist.; 1876, Danbury; 1877-1879, Stratford; 1880-1881, Woodbury ; 1882-1883, Durham ; 1884, Forestville.

In Waterbury (1853) the large brick church on East Main-street was built. In 1856, under his ministry, an old debt of $5,000 was paid by the church in Seventh-street, New York. A parsonage was built by the people of South Third-street church, Brooklyn, under his administration. His nominal appointment to Middletown was at his own request, that his wife might care for her sick mother residing there. Mr. Pilsbury has witnessed many conversions under his ministry, in some appointments receiving additions to the church every month ; but we have not space for details. The great revival in Hempstead, L. I., in the winter of 1857-1858, however, requires special notice. One hundred and sixty professed faith in Christ, of whom one hundred and thirty-five united with the Methodist church on probation. The society about doubled its membership during his administration and became one of the strong churches of the conference. One of the converts is now a useful minister in

the New York East Conference. Mr. Pilsbury rendered
ceptable service as delegate to General Conference in 1864
1868. He received the degree of D.D. from the East Ten[n]
see University in 1875.

During his first year as a conference preacher, on the 2[?]
of April, 1848, Benjamin Pilsbury was married to MISS
MARIA CHANDLER, only daughter of Theophilus Chandler[,]
Middletown, Conn., and sister of the late Rev. T. B. Chand[ler]
of the New York East Conference. Two children have b[een]
born to them—a son and a daughter. The son, *Benja[min]
Chandler*, was graduated at the Wesleyan University in 18[??]
taught Latin and Greek in two conference seminaries, stud[ied]
in Yale Theological Seminary, and is now a member of [the]
New York East Conference. The daughter, *Sarah Ma[ria,]*
"after sixteen beautiful years," departed "to be with Chri[st.]"
Both were converted young.

BISHOP EDWARD G. ANDREWS, D. D., LL. D.

LXXVII.

EDWARD G. ANDREWS.

SANDS-STREET Methodist people do not disguise their pleasure in numbering among their pastors the REV. BISHOP EDWARD GAYER ANDREWS, D.D., LL.D. The church desiring for its pastor "the office of a bishop, desireth a good work." The helpful influence of pastors and churches is mutual; noble, godly laymen may therefore expect not only to be gratified, but even honored and "admired," through the well-deserved promotion of the ministers with whom they have faithfully labored, and in whose success they have been personally and actively interested. While many others among the eighty-nine pastors and presiding elders of the Sands-street church may have been worthy of this office, Dr. Andrews stands alone among them as bishop.

His ancestry was of New England, and related to the many families of the name of Andrews, residing near Hartford, Conn., particularly in New Britain, whence his grandfather migrated to Oneida County, N. Y., in the early part of this century, settling in Whitestown, near Utica. George Andrews, father of the bishop, was married to Polly Walker, a lady of Quaker descent, connected not remotely with the Coffins and Gardiners of Nantucket. In early life she was a member of the Presbyterian church in Whitesboro, but when her husband, about the time of the birth of their son Edward, was converted, both together joined the Methodist Episcopal church in New York Mills, not far from their residence. The following, written by Dr. Buckley, appeared in The Christian Advocate, November 11, 1880:

> The mother of Bishop Andrews celebrated her eighty-third birthday last Friday. She was born on Gunpowder Plot day. When she was a little girl more was said about it than now. One hundred and ninety-two, minus eighty-three, runs back to within one hundred and nine years of the landing of King William, and the recent rush of events had not obscured the memory of that great crisis in modern English history. We had the pleasure to be the pastor of this venerable woman eighteen

years ago, and in view of her character and that of her family, congratulat her that God has satisfied her with long life and shown her his salvation ; tha she has seen "her sons come to honor;" yes, she has seen her children children, and their children.

Edward G. Andrews was born August 7, 1825, in New Hart ford, Oneida County, N. Y. He was one of eleven childrer all but one of whom lived to adult years, and became membei of one or other of the evangelical churches—" so graciously di God, our Father, give his blessing to parental piety."

Having had elementary instruction in the common schoo young Andrews subsequently studied for a while in the Oneid Institute, then under the care of the well-remembered and abl Dr. Besiah Green. He began to study Greek with the Rev. Ir Pettibone, pastor of the Presbyterian church, New York Mill: and, very early, when not ten years of age, was sent, in the car of an elder brother, to the Cazenovia Seminary, (George Pecl D.D., principal,) forty miles from his home. With considerable ir termission he attended this school until he was nineteen years c age, when he entered the Wesleyan University, graduating there from in 1847, with Orange Judd, Benjamin Pilsbury, Alexande Winchell, and others who have become an honor to the college

While a student at the seminary he early made a profession c religion and united with the church. His precise age at th time we have not ascertained. He was licensed to exhort an to preach when eighteen years of age, in Hartwick circuit, Ot sego County, N. Y., where he was teaching a private schoo Nelson Rounds, D.D., was presiding elder, and Calvin Hawley a man of wonderful power in prayer and exhortation, was th preacher in charge.

MINISTERIAL RECORD: 1847, supply, Morrisville and Pratt's Ho low cir., with D. A. Whedon; 1848, ordained deacon,—(Oneida Conf.,) Hamilto and Leeville cir.; 1849, Hamilton; 1850-1851, Cooperstown; 1852, ordaine elder; 1852-1853, Stockbridge; 1854-1855, teacher in Oneida (now Central Ne York) Conference Seminary, Cazenovia ; 1855, elected President of Man: field, Ohio, Female College, and filled that position about one year, but th Minutes make no mention of it ; 1856-1863, Principal of Oneida Conferenc Seminary; 1864-1866, (New York East Conf.,) Stamford, Conn., with W. C Hoyt; **1867, Brooklyn, Sands-street;** 1868-1870, Brooklyn, St. John' 1871-1872, Brooklyn, Seventh ave.; 1872 (May)-1884, bishop, residing mo: of the time in Washington, D. C.

His turning aside from the pastorate, in 1854, was occasione by the failure of his voice, which he attributes to his " fault manner of speech " in the early years of his ministry. Having engaged in educational work, which he intended to be only a temporary relief from pulpit labor, he continued therein for ten years, until, at length, unwilling longer to be kept from the occupation that was congenial to his tastes and desires, he returned to the pastorate.

The degree of D.D. was conferred upon him by Genesee College in 1863, and that of LL.D. by Allegheny College in 1881. He preached a missionary sermon before the New York East Conference which was very highly appreciated. He was chosen orator at the twenty-fifth anniversary of his college class in 1872. At the semi-centennial of the Cazenovia Seminary, in 1875, he delivered the historical address, which was published. He was elected a trustee of the Wesleyan University in 1881, and the same year delivered a response to the address of welcome at the semi-centennial exercises of the college.

The records of Sands-street church were carefully revised by Dr. Andrews, and they bear testimony to the conscientious and painstaking attention which he gave to every part of the pastor's work. While in the New York East Conference (of which he has all along been claimed by his brethren to be a member, his name appearing on the roll in the Minutes for ten years after he was made a bishop) no minister was held in greater esteem among us. He was always recognized as a master spirit in the deliberations of the conference. His marked ability in debate was often strikingly displayed by his bringing forward at the opportune moment the suggestion or proposition that was sure to receive the unanimous approval of the preachers. He represented the Oneida Conference in the General Conference of 1864. His election to the General Conference, held in Brooklyn, in 1872, and his promotion by that conference to the highest position in the church, gave great satisfaction to his many friends, and his eminent efficiency and usefulness as a bishop prove the wisdom of the choice.

The accompanying portrait represents Dr. Andrews as he appeared when pastor of the Sands-street church. He now wears side whiskers, which have turned very grey, yet he seems to have retained much of the vigor of former years. The Christian Advocate describes him as " well built, with ruddy and pleasant

---

[1] Semi-Centennial, Wesleyan University, pp. 8-15.

countenance, and eyes shaded with glasses; neat in habit, of courteous yet dignified mien, retiring and unassuming, but exceedingly social among friends."

The day he was twenty-six years of age, (August 7, 1851,) E. G. Andrews was married to MISS SUSAN M. HOTCHKISS, of Cheshire, Conn. *Eva*, their first-born, died in infancy. The other children are: *Winnifred Elizabeth ; Helen*, (Mrs. W. G. Nixon;) *Edward Hotchkiss*, (class of 1885, Wesleyan University,) and *Grace*.

REV. E. E. GRISWOLD, D. D.

LXXVIII.
EDWIN E. GRISWOLD.

THE REV. EDWIN ELIJAH GRISWOLD, D. D., son of Elijah and Lydia Griswold, was born in Windsor, Ct., August 20, 1802. The family were descendants of the original settlers of that town. Among his relatives was Bishop A. V. Griswold of the Protestant Episcopal Church.

Dr. Griswold's mother was of Puritan descent, and of the Adams family. She with her husband joined the Episcopalians, but was an ardent admirer of Jesse Lee and his successors, who were often entertained at her home. She survived her husband, and in her later years became a Methodist and lived with her son.

Mr. Griswold records that during his infancy he was once so very sick that he lay a long time as if he were dead, and then recovered. When about commencing his public labors for Christ, he overheard his mother relating this incident to a friend, and saying,—"I then felt that my child was raised up to do or suffer a great deal in this world." This remark made a lasting impression upon his mind. He experienced religion at the age of fifteen, through the pastoral care of the Revs. Micah and Aurora Seager. He never ventured to determine the exact moment of his conversion, but he always remembered the strange, sweet peace which he experienced one day while following the plow, and humming the lines he had heard in the Methodist prayer-meeting—

"O! Christian, are you ready now
To cross the narrow flood?"

there came to his heart a comfortable assurance that he was ready. This was in June, 1817. The following March he joined the little society in the neighborhood, and as he was the only male member, he was appointed leader, and held the position until, some years later, he left home to join the itinerant ranks. His few early advantages he faithfully improved, attending the public school when he could, and studying by candle-light, and sometimes by fire-light, and even by moonlight, while others were asleep. Concerning his diligence as a student, and his call to the ministry, the Rev. George A. Hubbell writes:

> In early youth he showed a fondness for study, reading all the family library, which contained a Bible. Prayer Book, Fox's Martyrology, Hervey's Meditations, Seneca's Morals, and Mason on Self-knowledge. At twelve years of age he began to draw books from the district library, selecting Josephus, Rollins' History, Robinson's Charles V., and books of biography, voyages, and travels, to which he added two or three works of fiction. The practical character of his early reading stamped his mind with certain common-sense peculiarities which were prominent in all his public life,[1]

How he was led step by step to enter upon the life of an itinerant preacher is thus told by the same writer:

> Thoughts of the ministry were familiar to him from his childhood, when his grandfather laid a hand of blessing on his head and said, "This boy must be a minister." Soon after his conversion he heard the divine call to this work. The preachers urged it upon his attention; and when he was seventeen years old, Rev. Cyrus Culver, unsolicited, gave him license to exhort. From this time he became more studious, and read all the Methodist literature within his reach. Six years later he was in doubt respecting his duty, and decided to settle down to business. He married Miss Nancy Webster, an amiable and estimable Christian lady, and engaged in farming and school-teaching. But he was not at rest. After two years of vacillation the conviction became strong that he must give himself up wholly to the work of the ministry, in which, as an exhorter, he had been partially engaged for nearly ten years. Rev. E. Osborn, preacher in charge, gave him appointments on the circuit, and he was licensed to preach at the district conference held at Richmond, Mass., in October, 1827. In the spring of 1829 he was admitted on trial in the New York Conference.

He continued in the active work forty-three successive years, serving the church with acceptability and success, filling the entire pastoral term in every circuit or station. The following list of his appointments and his colleagues will enable the reader to follow the faithful itinerant from place to place, and may suggest many reminiscences of his work and his fellow-workers.

---

[1] Memorial sketch, in The Christian Advocate.

CONFERENCE RECORD: 1829, (New York Conf.,) Monkton cir., Vt., with Elias Crawford ; 1830, Monkton and Charlotte cir., with T. Seymour and A. Hazleton ; 1831, ordained deacon,—Windsor cir., Conn., with W. M'Kendree Bangs ; 1832, Windsor ; 1833, ordained elder ; 1833–1834, Wethersfield ; 1835, New York, west cir., with J. B. Stratton, D. De Vinne, J. C. Tackaberry, and L. Mead ; 1836, ditto, with C. W. Carpenter, J. Covel, Jr., J. Z. Nichols, L. Mead, and L. Pease, sup'y ; 1837, New Haven, Conn.; 1839–1840, Brooklyn, York-street ; 1841–1842, Newburgh ; 1843–1844, Middletown, Conn.; 1845–1846, Hempstead, L. I.; 1847, presiding elder, Hartford Dist., Conn.; 1848–1849, New York, Mulberry-street ; 1850–1851, New York, Ninth-street ; 1852–1853, Essex, Conn.; 1854–1855, Danbury ; 1856–1859, presiding elder, Bridgeport Dist.; 1860, presiding elder, New Haven Dist.; 1861-1864, presiding elder, New York Dist.; 1865-1867, presiding elder, New Haven Dist.; **1868-1871, presiding elder, Long Island South Dist.**; 1872–1877, superannuated.

He was a member of four successive General Conferences, 1852, 1856, 1860, and 1864, once (1856) at the head of his delegation. In 1864 he received the degree of D.D. from Mt. Union College, Ohio. Dr. Griswold was twice married. At the close of this article the reader will find a sketch of his first wife. By a second marriage he became the husband of a very estimable lady, the widow of an honored Methodist preacher. His last six years were spent in comparative retirement at his home in Danbury, Conn., and from thence he "crossed over" on the 3d of April, 1878, in the seventy-sixth year of his age. About the time when the preachers had assembled in New York, and the secretary was calling the conference roll, he answered to the roll-call of heaven. Like Carpenter and Covel and Stillman, already sketched in this book, he closed his earthly life while his conference was in session, from whose annual meetings he had failed to be present only once in forty-nine years. Revs. G. A. Hubbell, B. Pilsbury, S. H. Bray, and John Crawford took part in the funeral services. He was buried in Wooster cemetery, Danbury, Conn.

Father Griswold was an able and interesting preacher, though his delivery was not the most attractive. In his later years his voice was husky at times, and his naturally stout frame and rounded shoulders, his broad face and bristling gray hair, gave him a unique appearance in a stranger's eyes; and yet, wherever he was known as a minister of Christ, he was universally revered for his eminent piety and talent. In all his public ministrations his thoughts were practical and clear, his rhetoric chaste and beautiful, and his prayers—what marvels of appropriateness, simplicity, and tenderness they were!

His friend, Mr. Hubbell, writes:

As a preacher, he was always interesting. His sermons were thoroughly studied and were models of good, practical sense. He indulged in nothing speculative, fanciful, or sensational, but preached the gospel only. * * * He fed the people with knowledge. Rarely did he preach controversially; but when occasion demanded, he proved a master in this field, as discomfited immersionists in Newburgh and Millerites in Middletown freely conceded. Having no collegiate education to fall back upon, he continued to study and grow in useful knowledge until the end of his ministry. He was a careful student of nature and of man. He kept abreast of the growing science and progressing thought of the age, and his sermons and conversation were enriched with the ripest thought. Few have been better versed in the English classics, or Christian theology, or current literature.

During the terms of his pastoral service in New Haven and Middletown he availed himself of most of the public lectures in science in connection with the colleges. The writer already quoted, adds:

As a pastor, he was singularly devoted to his work, being rarely absent for a single day, and with impartiality and fidelity looking after every member of his flock. Very gracious revivals attended his earlier ministry, especially in New York, New Haven, Brooklyn, and Newburgh, nearly two hundred souls being gathered into the church in the latter place.

During the seventeen years of his presiding eldership he manifested a deep interest in the prosperity of the churches, and a sympathetic interest in the welfare of the preachers. His administrative abilities were good. His quarterly visitations were genial, conciliatory, and edifying.

The name of "Elder Griswold" will never cease to be dear to the present generation of preachers in the New York East Conference. The young men on his districts studied his character closely, and all learned to admire the soundness of his judgment and the kindness of his heart. Now that he is gone the younger race of preachers find it no small honor and no easy task to wear his mantle and to wield his sword.

NANCY (WEBSTER,) his first wife, was nearly seven years his senior. She was born in Bloomfield, Conn., December 16, 1795. Having been converted under Methodist influences, she joined that "almost unknown and every-where derided people," against the wishes of her father's family, who, like their ancestors, were connected with the Congregational Church.

Her memorial says:

When, four years after her marriage to Mr. Griswold, he entered upon the work of the ministry, although she would sometimes in pleasantry say that she was not responsible for the duties of a minister's wife—not having married a minister—yet she entered heartily with him into the great enterprise; and, so far as the care of her young family and enfeebled health would permit, bore her full share of its responsibilities.[2]

She suffered extremely for twenty-five years from nervous prostration and neuralgic disease, and "finally consumption of the lungs supervened, and in a few days opened to her the gates of eternal life." After some days of terrible spiritual conflict, she gained a complete triumph. "As the breath grew short and the pulses still, a luminous smile, completely indescribable, overspread her countenance, and she died with it beaming there." Thus she passed away, April 3, 1870, exactly eight years prior to the death of her husband. Their bodies repose side by side.

His widow, ARTEMESIA (WHITE,) is a daughter of the Rev. Nicholas White, of blessed memory, and was formerly the wife of the lamented Rev. John M. Pease, of the New York East Conference. Her present residence is Plainfield, N. J.

Children of Edwin E. and Nancy Griswold: *Fannie E.*, residence, Danbury, Conn.; *Edwin C.*, graduate of Wesleyan University, 1847, teacher in Wyoming Seminary, clerk on North River steam-boats, employee in Methodist Book Concern, New York, moved to Elyria, Ohio, book-seller there, now farmer—a lay delegate to General Conference in 1876; *Harriet W.*, (now Mrs. E. B. Stevens;) *Anne Augusta*, (now Mrs. Horace Purdy;) *Mary Victoria*, who died in childhood.

---

[2] "X," in The Christian Advocate.

LXXIX.

A. H. Wyatt

SANDS STREET CHURCH was left to be supplied in the spring of 1868, and the REV. ALBERT HARMON WYATT. A. M., having taken a supernumerary relation in the New York Conference, was placed in charge for a short time, until the arrival of Mr. De La Matyr who was transferred from Western New York.

Wyatt is a name which Methodists have reason to honor. The church has preserved a memorial of Peter Wyatt, of the Virginia Conference, who in comparative youth closed a life of great usefulness in 1817.[1] Lednum mentions a Joseph Wyatt, one of the early Methodist itinerants from the state of Delaware, a man of marked talent, who served as chaplain to the legislature of Maryland.[2] William Wyatt, the father of the subject of this sketch, was a Methodist itinerant preacher of remarkable pulpit power. His parents before him were godly Methodists, pioneers of the denomination in Danby, N. Y. William's father was of English extraction; his mother of French. "From her" it is said "he took his physique and fire. The author formed the acquaintance of Chaplain William Wyatt in the army, attended a camp-meeting with him in Maryland in 1863, and heartily concurs in the following statement concerning him.

As a preacher he was *sui generis*. His sermons were written, elaborated, and thoroughly memorized. His style was eccentric and very impressive. His voice

---

[1] Minutes of Conferences, 1817, pp. 291, 292.
[2] "Rise of Methodism," pp. 226, 227.

was clear and strong, and his enunciation distinct. Hs sermons were "arousements." Who that ever heard him preach on " The Closet," "Jacob's Ladder," "Sampson," "Stone Kingdom," or " The Valley of Dry Bones," can forget the impression made? His life and labors were a grand success. He was a good man, and, like Enoch, walked with God.[3]

The widow of William Wyatt, mother of Albert, is a daughter of the late Rev. Reuben Reynolds, of the Northern New York Conference.

Albert H. Wyatt was born in Speedsville, Tompkins County, N. Y., October 16, 1839. Before he was seventeen years of age, on the 6th of September, 1856, at a camp-meeting in the Wyoming Valley, Pa., he experienced the pardoning love of God. That same year he was licensed to exhort in Wilkesbarre, Pa., and he received local preacher's license October 16, 1857. He was ordained local deacon by Bishop Scott in 1862, and in the fall of that year he was appointed chaplain of the 109th Regiment N. Y. Volunteer Infantry. He prepared for college in the Wyoming Seminary, and was graduated at the Wesleyan University in 1864, having joined the New York Conference in April of that year. The following is his

CONFERENCE RECORD: 1864-1865, (New York Conf,) West Harlem, N. Y.; 1865, ordained elder; 1866-1867, White Plains; 1868, sup'y, supply, Brooklyn, Sands-street, a few months, then traveled in Europe; 1869-1871, New York, Washington Square; 1872-1873, (Wyoming Conf.,) Wilkesbarre, Pa.; 1874, (Erie Conf.,) Jamestown, N. Y.; 1875, (New York East Conf.,) Brooklyn, Summerfield ch.; 1876-1877, sup'y; 1878-1879, Durham, Conn.; 1880-1881, Brooklyn, South Second-street; 1882-1883, Middletown, Conn.; 1884, New Haven, St. John-street.

Mr. Wyatt was married, April 27, 1865, to MISS ANNIE E. BROWN. She died April 1, 1867. Her brief memorial says:

Her married life, of but two years' duration, was exceedingly happy; yet with holy joy she bade farewell to husband and friends, and passed away to rest with Jesus.[4]

June 30, 1868, he was married to MISS MARTHA WASHINGTON PRESTON, of Buffalo, N. Y. This excellent Christian lady, after a brief illness, died in Durham, Conn., February 18, 1879. The writer was intimately associated with Brother Wyatt and his family during the time of their residence in Glen Cove, L. I.,

---

[3] Rev. H. Brownscombe, in The Christian Advocate.
[4] Rev. B. M. Adams, in The Christian Advocate, May 23, 1867.

in 1876 and 1877; and a more amiable and beautiful character than Mrs. Wyatt's he has rarely known. She was sister to William I. Preston, Esq., whose name appears in this book as a prominent member of the Sands-street church.

MISS GERTRUDE E. FIELD, daughter of the Rev. Julius Field, of the New York East Conference, was married to Mr. Wyatt, September 14, 1880. Two of his children died in infancy; a daughter and a son are now living.

Albert H. Wyatt shone conspicuously among his associates in college, and has ever since been regarded as one of the most eloquent and useful men in our ministry. He speaks with remarkable ease and fluency, and his sermons sparkle with beauty and glow with heavenly fire. It would be impossible for any Christian, and difficult, indeed, for any sinner, not to love such a man as A. H. Wyatt; yet he strikes telling blows against sin in the church and out of it, and has never been suspected of seeking popularity for its own sake. His modesty is often noticed and admired. In appearance he is rather tall and erect, with a broad forehead, dark complexion, raven locks, large nose, pleasant mouth, dark, full, and somewhat drooping eye, with an unusually calm and benignant expression.

Providence has been pleased to send upon Brother Wyatt repeated and severe afflictions. By the failure of his health while pastor of the Summerfield church, in Brooklyn, in 1876, which rendered absolutely necessary a suspension for two years of his active ministerial work, and by the death of two wives, a father, a sister, Lizzie, (Mrs. Rev. Dr. W. P. Abbott,) and two infant children, all occurring within a few years, the gold in his character has been abundantly tested, but by no means diminished or destroyed.

LXXX.

G. De La Matyr

THE REV. AND HON. GILBERT DE LA MATYR, D.D., was pastor of the Sands-street church from June, 1867, to April, 1869. He was born in Pharsalia, N. Y., July 8, 1825. His father yet lives, (1884,) aged eighty-one years, and has been at least sixty years a local elder in the Methodist Episcopal Church. His mother, a devout Methodist from her youth, died in 1858, and is buried in Middletown, Wis. Four of the six sons of this family entered the ministry. John H. is a presiding elder in the Nevada Conference; David died at the age of twenty-five, having been seven years a preacher; the third is the subject of this sketch; the fourth, George W., is a member of the Nevada Conference. Another brother is a teacher by profession, and the youngest is a physician.[1]

Gilbert De La Matyr was educated at Rushford, N. Y.,[2] He was converted when about sixteen years of age. In this particular he is classed with other eminent ministers of Sands-street: Jayne, Ross, Covel, Creagh, Norris, Goodsell, Fletcher, Wyatt, and Kettell, all of whom reached the happy crisis in their lives at the same age, sixteen years. About four years afterward he began to preach, and in his twenty-fifth year we mark the beginning of his more public

MINISTERIAL RECORD: 1850, (Genesee Conf.,) Boliver, N. Y.; 1851, Olean cir., with S. Parker; 1852, (ordained deacon,) Portville; 1853, Friendship; 1854, ordained elder; 1854–1855, Wyoming; 1856–1857, Pike; 1858, Leroy; 1859–1860, Albion; 1861, Medina; 1862–1864, Chaplain 8th N. Y. Artillery; 1865–1866, presiding elder, Wyoming District; 1867, Alexander; **1868–1869**, (N. Y. E. Conf.,) **B'klyn, Sands-st.**; 1870–1871, (Neb. Conf.,) Omaha,

---

[1] Letter of the Rev. G. W. De La Matyr to the author.
[2] Simpson's Cyclopedia.

Neb., 1st ch.; 1872-1873, (St. Louis Conf.,) Kansas City, Mo., Grand ave.; 1874-1876, (Southeast Indiana Conf.,) Indianapolis, Roberts Park chapel; 1877, Indianapolis, Grace ch., 1878-1883, local; 1883, supply, Denver, Colorado.

The author formed a very delightful acquaintance with Chaplain De La Matyr in Baltimore, Md., in the year 1863, and was frequently permitted to hear him preach in the Methodist pulpits of that city. A ride together by carriage to and from Gettysburgh, on the occasion of the dedication of the national cemetery, occupying a number of days, was an incident too rare and too pleasant to be easily forgotten.

While presiding elder of the Wyoming District, in 1867, Mr. De La Matyr was elected a delegate to the Republican State Convention, and was by that body put in nomination on the S ate ticket for the office of inspector of State prisons. This drew him somewhat into politics, but he continued to receive appointments as a regular conference preacher for several years thereafter. While in Omaha he published a sermon on "The Relation of Church and State," opposing the taxing of church property in Nebraska. He received the degree of D.D. from the Willamette University, of Oregon. In 1878 he was elected to Congress on a Greenback ticket in Indiana. While in Washington he identified himself with the Metropolitan church. About this time he became somewhat famous throughout the country as a political speaker and lecturer. His lecture on " Daniel, the incorruptible statesman," was often referred to in the papers as "abounding in glowing descriptions and lofty flights of eloquence." He preached nearly every Sabbath, however busily occupied he may have been with other matters during the week.

While many questioned the wisdom of Dr. De La Matyr's acceptance of the civil promotion which his political friends saw fit to confer upon him, it cannot be doubted that he followed conscientiously the guidance of his judgment in the matter. As the foregoing record shows, he now has pastoral charge of a church in one of the great and growing centers of the West.

Dr. De La Matyr is a man of pleasing manners, a genial friend and companion, quiet in his movements, but always terribly in earnest. When he speaks "his lower jaw closes like a vise, and seems to open sparingly for his words, which he utters in a deep bass voice that gets lower instead of higher when he reaches a climax."

His first wife, LUELLA C., was with him at Fort M'Henry, in Baltimore, and the writer was very favorably impressed with her piety and intelligence. Her health was then feeble, and continued to be until her departure to that land where " the inhabitants never say, I am sick," on the 29th of January, 1866, aged forty-three years.

MARYETTE, his second wife, a native of Lima, N. Y., was an occupant of the parsonage of the Sands-street church. They were married April 28, 1868. She was converted at fifteen. Previous to her marriage she was enthusiastically devoted to her profession as an artist, and her paintings were much admired. Her memorial says:

She possessed beauty of person, unusual force of character, excellent judgment, and cultivated taste. She had little hesitation in approaching persons privately on the subject of personal religion, but found it difficult to take much part in public religious services. Those who knew her best esteemed her most highly.

She was ill for about four years, and for more than a year before her death an acute sufferer, having endured several painful operations for the cure of cancer. Her faith grew as the end approached, and toward the last she was flooded with the most glowing emotions. She spoke of what she saw and heard as indescribable in human language; and thus she passed away in Indianapolis, Ind., August 18, 1877, aged forty-two years. Her remains were taken to Albion, N. Y., for burial. She left a little boy, whose real loss was only increased by the fact that he was too young to comprehend it.[8]

---

[8] Rev. J. H. Bayliss in The Christian Advocate.

LXXXI.

Geo F. Kettell

SINCE the preparation of this work was begun three honored ministers of the Sands-street church—Fletcher, Weed, and Kettell—have been summoned from active service to their heavenly reward, making the whole number of the deceased sixty-six, and leaving about one third as many survivors, namely, twenty-three. Of each of those so lately called hence the author has exceedingly pleasant personal recollections. Their relations to the Sands-street people were exceptionally interesting, one (Dr. Weed) having been their pastor two full terms, and the other two (Mr. Fletcher and Dr. Kettell) having had charge, first of the station, and afterward of the district of which it forms a part, on which district they both performed their last work as ministers of Christ.

An admirably written memoir of the REV. GEORGE FREDERICK KETTELL, D.D., adopted by the New York East Conference, contains the following:

George F. Kettell was born, May 18, 1817, in Boston, Mass. His earliest New England ancestors settled in Charlestown, Mass., in 1630. Thomas Prentice, the patriotic pastor of the Congregational church of that place during the war of the Revolution, was his great-grandfather. At the battle of Bunker Hill the parsonage which he occupied and the church in which he had preached many a powerful sermon were destroyed by fire. From the burning home an infant was rescued. The child, when grown to manhood, became the father of the subject of this memorial sketch. In early infancy our friend was baptized in the "Old South Church" of his native city.

His father at that time, and for years afterward, maintained successful mercantile connections with Germany; and the home of his boyhood, which he gratefully remembered, was one which afforded every facility for the proper training of his richly gifted nature. Then followed reverses, and the Boston merchant removed with his household to Hamburg. For five years his son enjoyed the rare advantages of instruction and discipline in the schools of that famous free-city of Germany.

At the age of fifteen he returned to his native land, and we find him in Danbury, Conn., for the first time in his life, fully thrown upon his own resources. He entered the employ of a thrifty hatter, who being an old-time family friend, treated him with unusual consideration.

From a few facts which have floated down to us it is made evident that he was an uncommonly brilliant and attractive lad. He was a Puritan in his upright, downright love for honesty and truth; his German culture had trained and quickened his naturally acute powers, and the inimitable humor which fascinated his friends to the last, threw a charm over all his words and ways.

He was a leader among scores of fellow-workers, but the leader was led one day to the old Methodist meeting-house. A turning-point in his history was thus reached. The pungent appeals to the conscience, and the winning words of invitation which he heard from the pulpit and in the prayer-meeting brought him very soon as a penitent to the Saviour. When he was sixteen years of age, though sternly opposed by all his kindred, he identified himself with the Methodist Episcopal Church. He kept himself at this period under self-appointed rules of study, and the fruits of his efforts were manifest to all. There is a tradition that at the age of eighteen he delivered an address in Danbury, upon a topic of public interest, which a high officer of the State pronounced a most extraordinary production. At this time, too, he seemed, without loud professions, to have made steady progress in the Christian life. Upon a fly-leaf of one of his private note books, he wrote, in a bold hand, this brief but characteristic prayer: "O, for wisdom, for heavenly wisdom!" In the social meeting he would now and then speak briefly, but always to the point, and sometimes with great power![1]

January 5, 1836, before he was nineteen years of age, he was married to LUCRETIA HAWLEY, in Danbury, Conn. All this time he was advancing toward the point of applying himself to the great life-work to which God had called him. Dr. Hunt writes further:

Not hastily, but after long consideration, he accepted from his pastor, the late Rev. John Crawford, a license to exhort. This paper bears the date of April 26, 1840. On the 19th of September, 1841, he received a license to preach. This document bears the honored name of Charles W. Carpenter, who was always regarded by our brother as a model presiding elder. Six months later he removed to New York city, and became a member of the Forsyth-street church.

PASTORAL RECORD: 1842, supply, Haddam, Conn.; 1843, (New York Conf.,) returned to Haddam cir., with C. Brainard; 1844–1845, Madison; 1845, ordained deacon; in 1846, Windsor cir., with C. Brainard; 1847, ordained elder; 1847–1848, New York, Vestry-street; 1849–1850, Poughkeepsie, Cannon-Street; 1851–1852, (Phila. Conf.) Philadelphia, Union church, with James Mitchell, sup'y; 1853, (New York Conf.,) sup'y at Poughkeepsie, Cannon-street, with R. A. Chalker; 1854, sup'y, ditto, with John W. Beach; 1855–

---

[1] Rev. A. S. Hunt, D.D., in Minutes New York East Conference, 1883, p. 57.

1856, agent Tract Society, practically sup'y; 1857, sup'y, Poughkeepsie, Cannon street; 1858, Poughkeepsie, Cannon-street; 1859–1862, presiding elder, Rhinebeck Dist., N. Y.; 1863–1865, Rhinebeck; 1866, stationed at Peekskill— went to Europe; 1867–1868, sup'y, in Europe; **1869 (latter part)–1871, Brooklyn, Sands-street**; 1872–1874, Hartford, Conn., First ch.; 1875, presiding elder, New York Dist.; 1876–1878, Brooklyn, Summerfield ch.; 1879, Brooklyn, Greene ave.; **1880–1882, presiding elder, Brooklyn Dist.**

He was assigned, as we have seen, to an important pastorate in the city of New York (Vestry-street) after a brief experience in small country charges, but "he promptly impressed the entire Methodism of the city as a remarkably gifted and efficient preacher of the gospel." A serious accident in his childhood, by which one eye was lost and the other injured, accounts for the appearance of his name on the supernumerary list for a number of years.

His wife died in Poughkeepsie, November 2, 1858, and he was again united in marriage to MISS MARY A. ANDREWS, on the 11th of December, 1860, in the town of Richmond, Mass. In 1866, he was appointed United States consul at Carlsruhe, Germany, where he received skillful and successful treatment for the improvement of his sight. The Wesleyan University conferred upon him the degree of Doctor in Divinity in 1873.

When speaking of death he had often expressed a preference for a sudden departure, and this desire was not denied him. He died of neuralgia of the heart at his home in Brooklyn, March 19, 1883. It was the day after a Sabbath of very wearisome labor; he went home to take a little rest before holding a quarterly conference in the evening, but before the sun set "he passed out of our sight." His funeral service was held in the Summerfield church. The pall-bearers were the Rev. Dr. J. O. Peck, Mark Hoyt, the Rev. George E. Reed, Judge Reynolds, the Rev. I. Simmons, W. W. Wallace, the Rev. J. S. Breckinridge, and ex-Mayor Booth. The exercises were under the direction of the Rev. Thomas H. Burch, presiding elder of the New York District, and the other preachers who participated were G. P. Mains, W. T. Hill, G. A. Hubbell, W. D. Thompson, Henry Baker, W. L. Phillips, A. S. Hunt, Thomas Stephenson, H. A. Buttz and O. H. Tiffany. Mr. Burch said:

Twelve months ago there were four of us, members of the same conference, dwelling not far apart, and closely related to each other; at least I felt the three to be closely related to me. Two of them were my friends of thirty years' standing; the other I had known scarcely a third of that period, but so sweet and tender had been the fellowship between us as to seem equally long-established. One of the four, Dr. George W. Woodruff, died last March. At the funeral services which followed, the other three officiated, one of them, Dr. Weed, directing the exercises. Less than four months afterward Dr. Weed died suddenly, passing, apparently, without a pang to his rest. A great throng gathered in the church of which he was pastor to give him reverent and tender burial. Dr. Kettell presided at those services, and I was permitted to take part. The sad year, well-nigh spent, had yet a day to run, when, unanticipated by himself or his family, and to the sore amazement of us all, Dr. Kettell ceased to breathe. And now, the survivor of the four, I am charged with the direction of these funeral rites.[2]

The following day the remains were taken to Poughkeepsie for burial. Dr. Buckley, who was one of Dr. Kettell's Sunday-school boys in Philadelphia, in 1852, wrote as follows, in The Christian Advocate:

The editor of this paper has seen Dr. Kettell as the pastor of his youth, twice as his presiding elder, once as his successor in the pastorate, in the business of the annual conference, the less formal debates of the New York Preachers' Meeting, and the stately proceedings of the Board of Managers of the Missionary Society. He has wandered with him among the hills and valleys and along the waters of Mount Desert, and at all times admired his remarkable clearness of intellect, his unusual felicity of statement, his wide range of thought, his abundance of instructive anecdote, his genuine humor, his candor, his marked ability in the pulpit, his unfailing good temper, his easy refinement of manners.

The results of his life-work are not to be measured by statistics. He was not a pioneer; he was not one who burst upon a community like an army in battle array; he did not excel in the "management of meetings." But the sum of his influence was to command respect for the church, reverence for the truth, esteem for himself as a minister and a man. A philosophic and semi-humanitarian vein, doubtless to some extent traceable to his New England origin and his long residence in Germany, ran through his preaching, which made it very interesting to the intellectual, but diminished its immediate effects. Fear in the utterance of what he believed true he seemed never to know.

His conference memorial says:

His mind was one of great breadth and fullness, and was well poised. He had keen analytic power, a wonderful memory, especially for matters of history, in which he found perpetual delight. He was loyal to truth as he saw it, and if he sometimes saw as we could not see, we knew, nevertheless, that his integrity and genuineness were unimpeachable. The law of conscience was to him clothed with the might of God. To his healthful sense of humor, allusion has already been made, and it may be added that his conversation and his extemporaneous utterances sparkled at times with

---

[2] The Christian Advocate, March 29, 1883.

dignified but pungent wit. He was master of terse and idiomatic English, exhibiting in his chain of words the most extraordinary felicity. Large words and high-sounding words he did not use, but fitting words, so fitting that ordinary men might search for hours and yet fail to find the delicately-shaded epithets which fell from his lips with perfect naturalness and inimitable grace.

In the pulpit he was, perhaps, less skillful in his appeals to the unconverted than in his addresses to believers. It must not be understood from this statement that he did not sometimes stir the consciences of sinners, for he certainly proved his ability to do this, but as a preacher upon themes aiming at the edification of the church he was one of a thousand.

LUCRETIA, his first wife, was a native of Danbury, Conn. She was nine years his senior—a woman " of a very quiet, retiring disposition, and faithful to her duties." She died in Poughkeepsie, N. Y., as already stated, in the forty-second year of her age. Three daughters were the fruit of this union. They are all married, and are still living. Dr. Kettell left a widow, who, with their only son, resides in Brooklyn, N. Y.

REV. T. G. OSBORN, M. A.

LXXXII.

THOMAS G. OSBORN.

THE ancestors of the REV. THOMAS GILBERT OSBORN, A.M., were among the early settlers of East Hampton, Long Island. They came from Lynn, Mass., but were originally from Maidstone, in Kent, England. Thomas Osborn and John Osborn were named in the charter of East Hampton when it was incorporated under the colonial government of New York by a patent from Governor Nicoll, March 13, 1666.[1] From one of these was descended Daniel Osborn, of East Hampton, who was born before 1700, and to whom the ancestry of T. G. Osborn is definitely traced. Daniel Osborn, grandfather of Thomas G., was a graduate of Yale College. He practiced law in Cutchogue, L. I., and was a member of the New York Legislature in 1787 and 1788. His son, Dr. Thomas Osborn, of Riverhead, had an extensive practice in Suffolk County for many years. Elizabeth, wife of Dr. Osborn, and mother of the subject of this sketch, was granddaughter of Colonel Phineas Fanning, of the Revolution. Her father was Deacon Enoch Jagger, of the Presbyterian church in West Hampton, L. I. Being always of Arminian views, Deacon Jagger at once hailed the coming of the Methodist preachers into his neighborhood, joined their communion, and assisted in building the first Methodist Episcopal church in the town. Dr. and Mrs. Thomas Osborn, although educated in the strictest creed of the Presbyterian Church, were always Arminian in belief, and for years before they united with the Methodists, their house was a home for the itinerant preachers. Their son writes:

---

[1] See Bayles' History of Suffolk County.

Richard Wymond used to tell, with a good deal of pleasure, the story of his first meeting with my father. He had been sent to a large circuit on the east end of Long Island, including no small part of Suffolk County. He was an entire stranger in those parts. As he drew near to the pleasant village of Riverhead he drove into the pond to water his weary horse. He was feeling lonely and sad. Just then a portly man in a gig drove in from the opposite side. Looking keenly at his broad-brimmed hat and strait coat, he said, "You are a Methodist preacher. Just drive up to the house you see there; give your horse to the men, and make yourself at home until my return. I am Dr. Osborn, and my house is a home for all the preachers."

My mother united with the church under the ministry of the Rev. John Trippett, and my father became a member while Dr. James Floy was pastor in Riverhead. My father contributed most of the funds to build the original Methodist church in that place. He died in peace in 1849, aged seventy years, and my mother died triumphantly in 1867, while visiting her daughter, the wife of Professor T. Stone, in the Cooper Institute, New York. [2]

Thomas G. Osborn was born in Riverhead, L. I., October 15, 1820. He prepared for college at the Franklin Academy, near Riverhead, where he remained three years under the instruction of the Rev. Phineas Robinson, of the Presbyterian church, and a graduate of Hamilton College. Having spent four years in the Wesleyan University, he was graduated in 1840, with J. W. Lindsay, Joseph Cummings, Chauncey Shaffer, and other men of note. While a thoughtless youth in college, he and young Lindsay, his intimate friend, by mutual agreement gave their hearts to Christ. He was then about nineteen years of age. Dr. Francis Hodgson, pastor in Middletown at the time, was the chief agent in his conversion.

Mr. Osborn was made a member of the Phi Beta Kappa Society after he left the university, and received the degree of A.M. in 1843. His time, for the first three years after graduation, was divided between the law office of Judge Miller, of Riverhead, the Harvard Law School at Cambridge, Mass., and the Union Theological Seminary in New York. He received an exhorter's license June 27, 1843, and two months later he was licensed to preach, the paper being signed by the presiding elder, Stephen Martindale.

CONFERENCE RECORD: 1844–1845, (New York Conf.,) Southampton, L. I.; 1846, ordained deacon by Bp. Hedding; 1846–1847, Bridgehampton; 1848, ordained elder by Bp. Waugh; 1848–1849, (New York East Conf.,) Patchogue; 1850, sup'd; 1851–1852, Birmingham, Conn.; 1853, Bridgeport and East Bridgeport; 1855–1856, Waterbury; 1857–1858, New

---

[2] Letter to the author.

York, Twenty-seventh-street; 1859, New York, Allen-street; 1860, ditto, with J. Ellis; 1861, Brooklyn, Summerfield ch.; 1862-1863, New Haven, St. John-street; 1864, sup'd one month, then presiding elder, Bridgeport Dist.; 1865-1866, sup'd, residence New Haven; 1867-1868, Riverhead; 1869-1871, presiding elder Bridgeport Dist.; 1872, **presiding elder, Long Island South Dist.**; 1873-1874, Portchester; 1875-1876, sup'y; 1877-1879, Riverhead, L. I.; 1880-1884, sup'y.

In Southampton, where he began his ministry, he organized the first Methodist society, which has grown to be a large and flourishing church. The friends of Methodism had purchased the Presbyterian church, and were rejuvenating that solid structure. Their young minister preached in the village school-house until the lecture-room of the church was finished. As the fruit of a revival during the first year seventy were added to the church by conversion, and about a dozen by letter from the Presbyterian church. About one hundred and fifty members were received during a revival in Birmingham, Conn., while he was laboring there. In Allen-street, New York, during his ministry, about two hundred were converted. The most signal outpouring of the Spirit under his ministry was in 1857, in East Twenty-seventh-street, New York. Here, during the revival, more than five hundred professed conversion at the altar, and joined the Methodist church. It was considered the most wonderful work of grace in the city of New York during that year of general revival. The astonishing magnitude of the work was largely due to " unintermitted *pastoral visitation.*" At that time John Stephenson, who was superintendent of the Sunday-school, trustee, steward, class-leader, and chorister, co-operated most heartily with the pastor. Every Monday morning a list of all new scholars who had attended the Sabbath-school was left at the parsonage. The paper was in Mr. Stephenson's handwriting, and contained the names of all new scholars, and the names, nationality, occupation, and religious preference (if any) of their parents. All these families were systematically visited the same week by the pastor, with this valuable directory in his hand, their temporal and spiritual wants inquired into, and, if they were not attendants upon any place of worship, they were invited to the Twenty-seventh-street church. In this way scores were gathered in who never previously attended any church, and were made happy followers of the Lord. Among the converts were Edwin F. Hadley and J. Stanley D'Orsay, who afterward became preachers in the New York East Conference.

Joseph Pullman (now the Rev. Dr. Pullman, of Brooklyn) was at that time a Bible-class scholar in Twenty-seventh-street Sunday-school, and a student in the New York Free Academy.

Mr. Osborn's health was seriously impaired by exposure and incessant labor on the Bridgeport District, on account of which he has been compelled at two different times to resign his place as presiding elder, and to hold a superannuated or supernumerary relation for several years. He was a delegate to General Conference in 1872. By invitation of the Methodist people of his native village he has been with them two terms—five years in all—as their pastor. He recommended the Rev. E. F. Hadley as a suitable person to take his place in 1869 and supervise the erection of a new church. Desirous of assisting in the good work, he sent the trustees a check for five hundred dollars, and, while serving as pastor there the second time, in order to sweep off all the debt from the church and parsonage, he contributed an additional hundred dollars.

The accompanying portrait is a very correct likeness of Mr. Osborn as he appeared when, as presiding elder, he was associated with the Sands-street church. He is a man of more than medium height, light complexion, blue eyes, auburn hair sprinkled with gray, quick movement, and ready and rapid utterance. His sermons are intellectual and practical, and usually delivered with an unction that renders them eminently effective.

Mr. Osborn's domestic life has been one of uncommon bereavement, as appears from the notices of his three wives and two children, deceased, which are published at the close of this sketch. His present wife, GRACE E., to whom he was married in 1869, was formerly the consort of Captain Elbridge Colburn, of the First Connecticut Cavalry, who died in the service of his country. Surviving children of Thomas G. Osborn: *Mary E.*, born 1849; *Thomas S.*, born 1857.

JERUSHA L. (COOK,) first wife of the Rev. T. G. Osborn, was married March 23, 1846, and died in the parsonage in East Twenty-seventh-street, New York, August 25, 1857, aged thirty-one years. On her tombstone are inscribed the precious words, "Forever with the Lord."

MARIA JANE, his second wife, sister of the above, was born

in Bridgehampton, L. I. She was converted at ten years of age, and joined the church at fifteen. She was married to Mr. Osborn September 1, 1858, and was "a good mother to the children of her sainted sister." She died in the St. John-street parsonage, in New Haven, March 5, 1863, aged thirty-two years.[3]

CALISTA E. (BARTON,) Mr. Osborn's third wife, experienced religion at the age of ten years, at South Hadley Falls. She was married May 18, 1864, and died in Riverhead December 22, 1867, aged thirty-three years. Her obituary notice says:

In class her seat was seldom vacant, and one of many similar passages from her Journal will suffice to show her estimate of this means of grace : "Attended class this evening, and had a blessed meeting ; have felt like rejoicing all the day long." She was an exemplary Christian, amiable in all the walks of life, and universally beloved. The closing words of her Journal, written but a little while before her death, are as sweetly expressive of her whole life as words can well be : " I will try to submit without murmuring to my heavenly Father's will, and feel sure that it is right." Her last audible words in reply to her husband, who asked, "Is it all well ?" were, "All is well."[4]

The three wives repose side by side in the cemetery in Riverhead.

Children deceased: *Thomas G.*, infant, died December 21, 1853 ; *Isabel C.*, died March 7, 1865, in the eleventh year of her age.

---

[3] Notice by Heman Bangs, in The Christian Advocate.

[4] Dr. L. S. Weed, in The Christian Advocate.

LXXXIII.

FREEMAN P. TOWER.

THE REV. FREEMAN PRATT TOWER is of the seventh generation descended from one John Tower, who was born in England in 1609, and who came to this country in early life and settled near Boston. Those familiar with the genealogy say that all the " Towers " in this country are the posterity of this man.

F. P. Tower was born in Eastford, Conn., February 13, 1838. When he was two years old the family moved to Dudley, Mass., and three years later to Southbridge, in the same State.

He studied awhile in Rawson's family school, in Thompson, Conn., but his preparation for college was chiefly made at the Nichols Academy, in Dudley, Mass. He was assistant principal of this academy several terms, and one term principal of a public school in Pomfret, Conn.

Most of the good and useful men whom God has chosen to be his ministers were converted in very early life, and Mr. Tower is not an exception to this rule. It may prove to be one part of the mission of this series of biographies to furnish examples of the great honor Christ confers upon those who seek him in early life. From eight years of age, and even farther back in unremembered infancy, to the ages of sixteen and eighteen, by far the larger number and the best and most useful of the Christians herein mentioned, gave their hearts to the Lord. At Southbridge, Mass., under the ministry of the Rev. W. R. Bagnall, in the year 1850, at the age of twelve, Freeman P. Tower exercised saving faith in Christ. He was licensed as a local preacher when nineteen years of age, and very soon thereafter his presiding elder, the Rev. Jefferson Hascall, employed him as pastor of one of the churches on his district.

Mr. Tower entered the Wesleyan University a sophomore in 1860, and was graduated in 1863. He was pastor of a church during two years of his college course.

REV. F. P. TOWER, M. A.

Record of Ministers. 395

MINISTERIAL RECORD: 1859-1860, Hardwick, Mass., a supply; 1861-1862, Plantsville, Conn., a supply; 1863-1865, (New York East Conf.,) Cheshire; 1865, ordained deacon; 1866-1868, Meriden; 1867, ordained elder; 1869-1871, Brooklyn, Greenpoint Tabernacle; **1872-1873, Brooklyn, Sands-street;** 1874, South Norwalk, Conn.; 1875, (California Conf.,) Alameda, Cal.; 1876-1878, (Oregon Conf.,) Salem, Oregon; 1879-1884, agent, Willamette University; 1880, also presiding elder, Portland Dist.

Mr. Tower's pastoral labors in the East, beginning with his youthful ministry in Hardwick, were signally blessed in the conversion of sinners. The young, especially, were won to Christ in great numbers. While in Meriden, besides witnessing spiritual prosperity, he gained great credit for his successful management of an important church-building enterprise, and in his later charges he has proved himself "the right man in the right place," by his persevering energy in promoting the financial interests of needy churches, and of the oldest Protestant institution of learning on the Pacific coast. The church in Alameda nearly doubled its membership and began to build a new church edifice during his administration. The carpenters were putting the roof on the building when he was invited to Salem, Oregon, and appointed by the bishop to that place. The church had been struggling for six years, with partial success, to erect a house of worship, and he found the congregation holding services in the lecture room. The church edifice, the best in the state of Oregon, was completed during his second year, and a new parsonage built, the total cost being about $40,000.

While he has been the agent of Willamette University, the financial condition has been improved to the amount of about $40,000, more than $10,000 of which was raised in the Eastern States. He is at present (1884) engaged in raising $20,000 to endow a Bishop E. O. Haven memorial professorship in this institution.

It fell to his lot to deliver the principal address at the funeral of Bishop Haven—"a very able paper, which gave a full statement of the bishop's career, and a just analysis of his character." [1]

We might content ourselves with this brief outline of facts, and leave the rest to the memory of Mr. Tower's friends. They will not fail to call to mind occasions when the gospel

---

[1] Rev. George W. Woodruff, in The Christian Advocate.

27

message from his lips was attended with marvelous power; for example, the sermon on "the judgment," at the Forestville camp-meeting, in 1864. His sermons are intellectual and logical, and extemporaneously delivered ; his manner is earnest and persuasive; his voice full and clear. In conversation and in preaching he speaks with deliberation, and in company has an air of abstraction, which is sometimes very noticeable. A more conscientious Christian, and a more unselfish, honorable friend, one rarely finds.

Mr. Tower was married, August 20, 1863, to MISS JULIA A. CLEVELAND, of Barre, Mass. She was educated at Mt. Holyoke Seminary, and has been a devoted Christian from her childhood. They removed to the Pacific coast in search of a friendlier climate, and mainly for the benefit of Mrs. Tower's health. Only one of their three children survives, namely, *Olin Freeman*, now twelve years of age.

REV. GEORGE TAYLOR

LXXXIV.

GEORGE TAYLOR.

HE REV. GEORGE TAYLOR is a native of the village of Honley, near Huddersfield, Yorkshire, England. He was born on the 12th of May, 1820. His godly Methodist parents taught him the fear of the Lord, and with them he went very early to class and prayer meetings and the public worship of God. Through their efforts and the pious influence of Sunday-school teachers, and especially of an earnest local preacher named Edward Brooks, little George Taylor, at the age of eight years, became a happy Christian and joined the class. He received his first love-feast ticket from the hand of the Rev. John Bowers. We have here another example of the reality and blessedness of childhood conversion. Not only do most of the subjects of these biographical sketches stand forth as witnesses of the adaptation of converting grace to the heart of a child, but they show that of all who believe in Christ, the very young, when properly cared for, are most likely to steadfastly maintain their faith. We have no backslidings of this little eight-year-old convert to record, nor of scarcely any other who made a like early and noble choice.

He attended the common school, and received classical instruction from the Rev. J. Lowe, of the Episcopal Church. In his eighteenth year he began to labor as a local preacher on the Glossop circuit, in the Manchester district. After attending the Rev. Thomas Allin's theological school in Altringham, (now merged into the college of the Methodist New Connection, in Sheffield,) he came, in 1843, to this country, recommended to the Methodist Episcopal Church, there being no opening for young men in the ministry of his church in England at that time. He became a member of the Second-street church in New York city, of which Dr. Bangs was pastor. After a few months he entered upon the pastoral work.

APPOINTMENTS: 1843, Wolcottville, Conn., a supply; 1844, (New York Conf.,) Harlem, N. Y., with R. Seaman, sup'y; 1845, Westerlow; 1846, ordained deacon; 1846-1847, Delhi; 1848-1849,

(New York East Conf.,) Astoria, L. I. ; 1849, ordained deacon ; 1850, Bristol, Conn.; 1851–1852, Brooklyn, Eighteenth-street ; 1853–1854, Bridg.-hampton, L. I.; 1855–1856, New York, Twenty-seventh-street ; 1857–1858, Rye, N. Y.; 1859-1860, Brooklyn, First Place; 1861-1862, Greenpoint ; 1863-1865, Williamsburgh, Grand-street (Gothic); 1866-1868, Jamaica, L. I.; 1869-1871, Flushing; 1872-1873, New York, Willett-street ; **1874-1876, Brooklyn, Sands-street ;** 1877-1879, Greenwich, Conn. ; 1880, Parkville, L. I.; 1881-1883, Patchogue ; 1884, Southold.

After traveling five years he was married to MISS SUSAN HATFIELD, of Delhi, N. Y. Their living children, *Josephine, Jennie L.*, and *Susie H.*, are members of the Methodist Episcopal Church. The records of the Sands-street church and Sunday-school show that Mr. Taylor received in that place (as elsewhere) no little assistance from the several members of his family.

Mr. Taylor is singularly modest, and his voice is rarely heard upon the conference floor, yet his talent and usefulness are well known. His countenance, voice, and manner are exceedingly attractive. He stands very high in the confidence and esteem of the preachers and people within the bounds of the New York East Conference. His brethren elected him a delegate to the General Conference in 1868.

LXXXV

A. S. Graves

HE REV. ALBERT SCHUYLER GRAVES, D. D., was born of Methodist parents, Augustus and Lydia (Kelsey) Graves, in Salisbury, Vt., January 17, 1824. In 1839, at the age of fifteen, he was baptized and received into the Methodist Episcopal Church, in Salisbury, by the late Rev. David P. Hurlburd, of the Troy Conference. He prepared for college at West Poultney, Vt., and was graduated at Wesleyan University in 1846.

MINISTERIAL RECORD: 1846, West Troy, N. Y., a supply; 1847, Groton cir. N. Y., with W. N. Cobb; 1848, ditto, with Alonzo Wood; 1849, ordained deacon by Bishop Janes; 1849-1850, Moravia; 1851, ordained elder by Bishop Hamlin—Ithaca, Seneca-street; 1852-1853, Oxford; 1854, Utica, Bleeker street; 1853-1856, Cortland; 1857-1858, Auburn; North street; 1859, ditto, sup'y; 1860-1863, presiding elder, Cortland Dist.; 1864-1869, Principal of Oneida (now Central New York) Conf. Sem., Cazanovia, N. Y.; 1870-1871, (New York East Conf.,) Fair Haven, Conn.; 1871, traveled in Europe; 1872-1873, West Winsted; 1874-1875, New Rochelle, N. Y.; **1876, presiding elder, L. I. South Dist.; 1877-1879, presiding elder, Brooklyn Dist,**; 1880-1881, Brooklyn, South Third-st.; 1882-1883, Southold; 1884, Port Jefferson.

He was secretary of the Oneida Conference several years, and was honored by that body with a seat in the General Conference in 1864 and in 1868. He was also a member of the New York East Conference delegation in 1880. That same year the preachers of the Brooklyn District presented him with an elegant watch as a token of their esteem. Mr. Graves is an able minister, and as teacher, pastor, and presiding elder, has been uniformly successful. He has a genial countenance and a pleasant voice, and his manner is attractive both in and out of the pulpit.

On the 19th of October, 1851, he was married by the Rev. Elias Bowen, to MISS HARRIET A. GRANT, of Ithaca, N. Y., who died July 20, 1858. He was married to MISS ISABELLA G. MCINTOSH, of Vernon, N. Y., April 19, 1862. Of the children, seven in number, a son and a daughter alone survive. Their names are *Arthur Eugene* and *Belle Evangeline*.

LXXXVI.

AMES PARKER, father of the REV. LINDSAY PARKER, was a Methodist and a "prayer leader" in Ireland. He married Miss Jane Lindsay, an Episcopalian, who joined the Wesleyans with her husband. Lindsay, their son, was born in Dublin. He attended the Wesleyan school in that city, of which the Rev. Robert Crook, LL. D. was head master. Young Parker was converted when about fifteen years of age. After spending some time in a lawyer's office, he yielded to the earnest solicitation of the Rev. Charles Lynn Grant, superintendent of Abbey-street circuit, Dublin, and joined the Irish Conference of the Wesleyan Methodist Church. Having preached in his native country nearly four years, he came to America in August, 1873, and joined the Twenty-seventh-street Methodist Episcopal church in New York city, whose quarterly conference immediately licensed him as a local preacher, and recommended him to the traveling connection. He rendered efficient service in the Methodist ministry about ten years longer, and then joined the Protestant Episcopal Church, in which he has been advanced to full orders.

MINISTERIAL RECORD: A few years prior to 1873, (Irish Conf.,) Dungannon; Portadown; Knock, a suburb of Belfast; 1873, supply, Hoboken, N. J.; 1874, (New York East Conference,) ordained deacon by Bishop Wiley—Darien, Conn.; 1875-1876, Ansonia; 1877, ordained elder by Bishop Peck; **1877-1879, Brooklyn, Sands-street**; 1880-1882, New York, Sixty-first-street; 1883, withdrew; 1884, first assistant of the Rev. W. S. Rainsford, rector of St. George's Protestant Episcopal Church, New York.

Mr. Parker was married in Darien, Conn., to Miss Frances A. Reed. His pulpit talent and his fine social qualities render him exceedingly popular, especially with the young. He writes to the author concerning the transfer of his church relations as follows: "The main cause of my change of base was dissatisfaction with the itinerancy.

REV. JOHN S. BRECKINRIDGE, M.A.

LXXXVII.
JOHN S. BRECKINRIDGE.

A PROMINENT place on the roll of the pastors of old Sands-street church belongs to the REV. JOHN STORRY BRECKINRIDGE, A. M. He was born July 12, 1837, in Augusta, N. Y., and named after the Rev. John Storry, an eminent English clergyman.

His father, the Rev. E. W. Breckinridge, is a native of Dover, England, and came to this country while yet a young man. He was already married, and a local preacher in the Wesleyan Church. Having united with the Duane-street Church in New York city, he was soon urged to give himself wholly to the ministry, and in 1836 joined the Oneida Conference. In the year 1876, after forty years of faithful service, he was entered upon the list of the retired and superannuated ministers of the Wyoming Conference.

The mother of J. S. Breckinridge was born in Ramsgate, England, and died in 1867. She was a woman of superior mind and profound piety. She took her son with her when a child to class meeting, and counseled him in his youth, and prayed with him always. She was a strict disciplinarian, and taught her children to fear God and honor their parents, and before she died, saw them all happily converted and received into the Methodist Church.

Mr. Breckinridge experienced religion at the age of sixteen years. The immediate agent, next to his praying mother, was the Rev. Mr. Francis, a Baptist evangelist, who held a series of meetings in Gibson, Pa., where young Breckinridge resided. His conviction was pungent, his deliverance was complete. For three weeks he had been fighting the suggestion that if he experienced religion, he would have to preach. He prefered any other occupation. At last he yielded and exclaimed, "Lord, save me, whatever the consequences may be!" The power of Satan was broken, and his heart was thrilled with unspeakable joy. In some of the circumstances his conversion bore an exact resemblance to that of Freeborn Garrettson. He was on horseback at the time, riding through a bit of woods, and he could hardly keep his seat, so overcome was he with heavenly emotion. The forest seemed illumined by a thousand suns, so brilliant was the light which broke upon his mind. He longed for an auditor to whom he might tell the glad tidings, and found his first one in the blacksmith who shod his horse. He seemed amazed, but said nothing. In the evening, before a school-house full of people, the young convert stood and tremblingly told "the old, old story," while some wept, and others shouted. His father received him on probation in the church, and six months later extended to him the right hand of fellowship.

He soon became anxious to obtain an education, and entered a select school for boys, taught by a Mr. Judd, near Berkshire, where his father was then stationed. On the removal of his father to Binghamton, he entered the Susquehanna Seminary, superintended by the Rev. Dr. J. W. Armstrong. Prof. J. C. Van Benschoten, now of Wesleyan University, was one of the teachers, and when he went to the Oxford Academy, as principal, Mr. Breckinridge followed him thither. He entered Wesleyan University in 1857, taught school each winter during his college course, and, being licensed as a local preacher in Middletown, in 1858, he frequently occupied the pulpits of neighboring churches. In his freshman year he was elected orator of his class, and in his sophomore year he won the prize for elocution. In his senior year he was elected a member of the Phi Beta Kappa Society as a recognition of superior scholarship.

CONFERENCE RECORD: 1861, (New York East Conf.) Middlebury, Conn.; 1862, Plymouth; 1863, ordained deacon; 1863-1865, Bethel; 1865, ordained elder; 1866-1868, Norwalk, Second, ch.; 1869-1871, Birmingham; 1872-1874, Middletown; 1875-1876, Brooklyn, Greenpoint Tabernacle; 1877-1879, Brooklyn, Seventh av., known as Grace Church in 1879; **1880-1882, Brooklyn, Sands-street church;** 1883-1884, Meriden, Conn.

During his pastoral term in Bethel a revival began in his church which swept over the town, and resulted in one hundred and fifty conversions, abundant fruit of which is still to be seen. About $1,200 was paid on the church debt. At Norwalk he found a revival in progress; the religious interest continued throughout his three-years' term, and about one hundred were added to the church. A beautiful parsonage was built, and the debt considerably lessened. While at Norwalk he was elected a delegate to the International Convention of the Young Men's Christian Associations of the United States and Canada, held at Montreal, and was also made a life-member of the American and Foreign Christian Union.

During his pastorate in Birmingham about one hundred were converted, and the entire indebtedness of the church, amounting to nearly $6,000, was canceled, and a surplus of $500 left in the treasury. His appointment to the city of Middletown, within less than eleven years after his graduation at its college, was accepted in a full sense of the peculiarly trying character of the position, and there, as in other fields, he enjoyed a prosperous ministry. Fifty were added to the church and over one hundred received on probation. While pastor there he visited Europe, and in company with Professors Harrington and Hibbard, and the Rev. Arza Hill, he traveled through the British Isles and over the continent as far as Vienna. An interesting account of the trip was written by him, in a series of magazine articles, and published in Philadelphia. He also prepared two lectures on the tour, one entitled " European Odds and Ends," and the other " European Cities," which were delivered in Middletown and elsewhere. He preached in Middletown a series of sermons which were largely attended, and extensively reported in the Hartford Post and other papers. The one on " Eternal Punishment " aroused much interest, and was replied to by the Universalist minister of Middletown.

His administration as pastor of the Greenpoint Tabernacle was in every respect successful. He was placed in charge of the Seventh Avenue Methodist Episcopal Church, in Brooklyn, by the unanimous desire of the official board of that church, after the resignation of the Rev. Emory J. Haynes, who united with the Baptist denomination. The church was in financial trouble and in danger of going to pieces. He remained three years, and during that time it was re-organized, placed upon a sound footing, and $8,000 was secured in cash and reliable subscriptions toward the payment of its debts. Old Sandsstreet church prospered under his administration.

While in college Mr. Breckinridge enlisted at the beginning of the war as a three-months' volunteer, but shortly afterward all the three months' troops were disbanded, and he was not called into service. Later he spent several weeks in Chesapeake Hospital, near Fortress Monroe, as an agent of the Christian Commission. Some years since he was constituted a life director of the American Bible Society, and he has been, since 1876, one of the managers of the Tract Society of the Methodist Episcopal Church.

Mr. Breckinridge is a valuable contributor to the department of Christian experience in the literature of our church. The following brief extract concerning religious growth is taken from The Christian Advocate:

One state of grace differs from another only in degree. A river is like a rivulet, only larger. As water is water, whether it be an ocean or a drop, so religion is religion, whether it be that possessed by an ignorant beginner or a matured saint.

The distinctions made by theologians between little piety and much are often merely nominal. They are like the different terms given by geographers to varied formations of land, such as isthmus, cape, mountain, etc. These are all in reality one, and the drowning man who reaches either is saved, and may, by traveling on, reach the rest. He who has become in the lowest degree religious, has touched the shore—the continent of all spirituality. * * * Religion is, from beginning to end, not only the same in kind, but the way in which we obtain one degree of it is the only way in which we can obtain any degree of it, even the most exalted. As the earth grows lustrous by steadily turning toward the east, so Christians grow pure by steadily approximating God. The price paid by one who rises in the scale of experience becomes constantly larger, but it is ever one currency—the gold of self-surrender; that, and that only, is legal-tender, and must be paid whether the blessing sought be initial or completive. One progresses in spirituality as in any thing else, by a process of repetition. * * * We receive Christ by faith, and can grow up into him only by a repetition of that exercise. It is the alphabet of all religion, and spells every possible experience.

His sermons abound in metaphor, and are always interesting, practical, useful, and often truly eloquent. He is rather below the medium height, and stouter than the portrait would indicate; of blue eyes and light complexion.

Mr. Breckinridge was married, in June, 1863, to MISS MARY ADELINE ASHLEY, daughter of the Hon. R. T. Ashley, of Susquehanna County, Pa. Their children are *Rollin Ashley B.*, aged seventeen, and *Florence B.*, ten years of age.

REV. ICHABOD SIMMONS, M. A.

LXXXVIII.

ICHABOD SIMMONS.

SANDS-STREET CHURCH has enjoyed the services of thirty-one different presiding elders. After the saintly Foster and Willis came Garrettson and Morrell, and other high-minded and noble men, who "hazarded their lives for the name of the Lord Jesus Christ." A little later the district was placed in charge of such royal presiding elders as Samuel Merwin, Peter P. Sandford, Laban Clark, Daniel Ostrander, Buel Goodsell, John Kennaday, and others of equal fame and power. The last in the succession thus far is the REV. ICHABOD SIMMONS, M.A.

He is the son of Ichabod and Marcia B. Simmons, and was born in Duxbury, Plymouth County, Mass., December 24, 1831. His strong attachment to Methodism is not an inheritance, his father having been a Universalist, and his mother not a member of any church. He was converted in Newport, N. H., in October, 1852, before he was twenty-one years of age. The pastor was the Rev. S. Holman, by whom he was shortly afterward baptized, received into the Methodist Episcopal Church, and licensed to exhort. His first license to preach bears date February 4, 1854.

He had learned the cabinet-making trade in Newport, but a divine voice bade him seek an education and enter the work of the ministry. He spent two terms at Newbury Seminary, Vt., and two years at the Biblical Institute, Concord, N. H., after which he completed his preparation for college at the seminary in Northfield, N. H. He then took a four years' course in the Wesleyan University, where he was graduated in 1860. The degree of M.A. he received in 1863. For some months he taught a Bible class in the State-prison in Concord, N. H., but he had the responsibility of a pastorate nearly all the time while pursuing his studies. The following is his entire

MINISTERIAL RECORD: 1854, supply, Pembroke, N. H.; 1855, (N. H. Conf.,) Amherst; 1856, (conf. relation discontinued at his request,) supply at Amherst a few months; 1856-1857, supply, Saybrook, Conn.; 1858, ordained deacon by Bishop Baker,—supply, Vernon Depot; 1859, supply, West Meriden (Hanover) and West Rocky Hill, alternating with W. H. Wardell; 1860-1861, (New York East Conf.) Simsbury; 1862-1863, New Haven, George-street; 1863, ordained elder by Bishop Baker; 1864-1865, Bridgeport; 1866-1868, Birmingham; 1869-1871, Norwalk, Second Ch.; 1872-1874, Brooklyn, Eighteenth-street; 1875-1876, Brooklyn, South Third-street; 1877-1879, Brooklyn, Fleet-street; 1880-1882, Brooklyn, Janes church, Reid Ave.; **1883-1884, presiding elder, Brooklyn Dist.**

Mr. Simmons exhibited remarkable energy and perseverance in working his way through college, and has ever since manifested the same earnestness of purpose. He wrote to a friend: "I entered the ministry with joy, and have stayed in it from the love of it and for the Master's glory." He is a modest but faithful and happy witness to the blessed experience of perfect love, into which he entered at a camp-meeting in Milford, Conn., on the 15th of August, 1870, when, as he declares, his "soul and body were thrilled with glory and filled with light." Some ten years ago he was elected a member of the Ocean Grove Camp-meeting Association, and in 1878 he became a member of the National Camp-meeting Association for the Promotion of Holiness.

On recovering from a severe illness, while pastor of Janes church, Brooklyn, he was granted a leave of absence to visit Europe. When Bishop Warren, in 1883, desired a man for presiding elder who would "carry a pentecost to every charge on his district four times a year," he looked through the conference, and wrote at the head of the appointments to the Brooklyn District the name of Ichabod Simmons. Our dear brother has been greatly successful in his ministry, and is pre-eminently a man of one work. His talents command respect, and his genial manners win for him a host of friends.

He was married, July 4, 1860, to Miss HARRIET NEWELL BULL, of Old Saybrook, Conn. They have three daughters, *Marie Annette*, *Harriet Ellen*, and *Marcia Ann*, all of whom "were converted when they were little children, and joined the church, and are walking in the light."

LXXXIX.

L. R. Streeter

AST in the honored succession (to date) of the Sands-street pastors we are permitted to record the name of the REV. LEWIS RICHARD STREETER. He was born in the village of Westfield, county of Sussex, England, June 13, 1850. George Streeter, his father, was a local preacher twenty-seven years. He was a gifted man, an exceedingly fluent preacher, and greatly in demand, preaching once or twice nearly every Sabbath. He married a woman of the sensible, sturdy, English type. Both were converted young.

Lewis is the seventh child in a family of twelve—nine sons and three daughters. He was converted in his tenth year, became a Sunday-school teacher at the age of twelve, and having been impressed from early childhood that God had called him to preach the gospel, he was licensed as a local preacher on trial in his eighteenth year. His early tuition was received in the national schools of England.

On coming to the United States he at once entered the itinerant ministry, pausing in the midst of his conference work to pursue a course of study at the Drew Theological Seminary.

CONFERENCE RECORD: 1872-1873, (North Indiana Conf.,) Sharpsville; 1874, ordained deacon; 1874-1876, Centerville; 1876, ordained elder; 1877, until Sept.—five months, Greenfield; 1878-1879, sup'y, Drew Seminary; 1880-1882, (New York East Conf.,) New York, Beekman Hill; **1883-1884, Brooklyn, Sands-street.**

He was married in the summer of 1883 to a very estimable lady, of Philadelphia, grand daughter of Daniel Fidler, one of the early itinerant ministers of the Methodist Episcopal Church. Mr. Streeter is highly esteemed by his people, and has proved himself worthy to be enrolled among the eighty-nine distinguished itinerant preachers who have ministered by appointment in the old Sands-street church during the last hundred years.

BOOK III.

ALPHABETICAL AND BIOGRAPHICAL RECORD OF MEMBERS.

PRELIMINARY.

To the *Annals* of "Old Sands-street church" and the personal history of her honored *Ministers* we now propose to add some account of the *Laity*, by whose diligent, constant, and wise co-operation the pastors achieved success. A complete history of any church must include a history of its members.

The noble rank and achievements of Methodism in Brooklyn, and the past and present prosperity of the city, may be largely attributed to the agency of the early members of old Sands-street church. They were people of sterling character and unusually influential position, taking the lead in every important moral, social, educational, and financial enterprise at its beginning, and for many years thereafter.

Faults and foibles they had. They were possessed of like passions with us; (there were lapses, trials, and expulsions, which for obvious reasons are not recorded here;) yet, taken one with another, they compose a company of men and women probably unsurpassed for practical, sensible, useful, godly living by any church of modern times. For confirmation of this statement the reader is referred to the memorials of the Garrisons, Mosers, Van Pelts, Strykers, Kirks, Harpers, Merceins, Snows, Herberts, Dikemans, Odells, and many others. The records show that nearly seventy of the members have been licensed to preach the Gospel, and a score of these joined the ranks of the traveling ministry.

A star (*) indicates that the person whose name is thus designated is known to be deceased.

Those whose names are prefixed by two stars (**) were members of Sands-street church at the time of their death.

The names printed in CAPITALS are found on the membership roll in 1884.

When authorities are cited they are included in brackets.

ABBREVIATIONS.

b. for born,
bro. for brother.
bur. for buried.
cem. for cemetery.
cl. ldr. for class leader.
ch. for church.
Ch. Ad. for Christian Advocate.
conv. for converted.
d. for died.
dau. for daughter.
exh. for exhorter.
j. for joined.
lib'n. for librarian.
loc. pr. for local preacher.
mar. for married.

off. for officer.
rem. for removed.
rem. by c. for removed by certificate.
sec. for secretary.
supt. for superintendent.
S.S. miss'y soc. for Sunday-school missionary society.
S.S.t. for Sunday-school teacher.
std. for steward.
treas. for treasurer.
trus. for trustee.
w. for wife.
wid. for widow.
yr. for year.

RECORD OF MEMBERS.

ABBOTT, ANNIE.—ABRAMS, AMELISSA.—ABRAMS, SARAH A.—**Abrams, Wm.**, rem.—****Acker, Egbert,** std., S.S.t., S.S. sec. and treas. many yrs.; first treas. S.S. miss'y soc.; clerk in custom house, N.York, 29 yrs.; mar. Miss Elizabeth E. Haff; d. calmly and triumphantly, Sept. 4, 1882, age 56; bur. Cypress Hills.—****Elizabeth E.,** w. of the above; b. in Brooklyn; j. Sands-st. S.S. in infancy; j. the ch. at 14; a devoted S.S.t.; very active and prominent in temperance work; d. in Brooklyn in Oct., 1884; bur. beside her husband.—ACKER, JOS. H., son of Egbert and Elizabeth E.—***Acker, Mrs. Laney,** only child of John and Sarah Cornelison; appears as Leanah Smith, on church roll, 1798; afterward mar. Acker; went to N. York and d. [Mrs. J. W. De Grauw.]—****Ackerman, John H.,** b. 1811; some time cl. ldr. in York-st. ch.; subsequently exh. and cl. ldr. in Sands-st.; a sweet singer; mar. Gertrude Speer, 1836; d. 1865, age 64.—**Gertrude,** wid. of the above, rem. by c. to Sum'f'd ch., 1878.—ACKERMAN, JOHN H., JR.—**Adams, Mary,** rem. by c., 1849.—ADAMS, MRS. MARY.—**Addy, Mary,** rem. by c., 1873.—**Albro, Mary,** rem. by c.—**Alexander, Alex.,** S.S.t.; rem. to N.York, 1850.—**Allen, Ann,** rem. by c., 1850; **Allen, David,** exh. 1856.—**Allen, Edward,** S.S.t.; rem. by c. to Sum'f'd ch., 1879.—ALLEN, EMMA.—**Allen, Geo. H.,** rem. by c. to Sum'f'd ch., 1879.—**Allen, G. W.,** rem.—ALLEN, HEWLETT D.—ALLEN, HEWLETT G., sexton.—ALLEN, PHŒBE; **Allen, James,** j. Prim. Meth. in B'klyn, about 1841.—**Allen, Jas. S.,** rem. by c., 1880.—ALLEN, JENNIE.—**Allen, John,** rem. by c.— —***Allen, John W.,** sec. of Sands-st. S.S.; eldest son of Edward and Mary Allen, was brought to repentance by the death of a loved sister, and was converted in his room at home; j. Sands-st. ch.; rem. by c., 1879, to Sum'f'd ch.; faithfully attended the class-meeting where he led the singing 5 yrs.; always carried his Bible with him and studied it; conducted family prayers in his father's absence; d. victorious, Oct. 15, 1880; mourned by many friends. [C. N. Sims, in Ch. Ad.]—**Allen, Mary**, rem. by c.—**Allen, Mary Ann**, mar.; see Burrows; **Allen, Mary F.**, rem. by c. to Sum'f'd ch.—ALLEN, PHŒBE ANN.— **Allen, Robert L.**, and **Susan A.**, rem. by c., 1879.—ALLEN, WALLACE A.—ALLEN, WM.—**Allen, Wm. C.**, rem. by c. to Sum'f'd ch., 1879.—****Allison, Sarah**, d. in peace, 1880.— **Alvord, Edwin P.** and **Mary**, rem. by c., 1872.—**Alvord, Mary**, rem. by c., 1848.—**Ambler, Jas.**, loc. pr., 1817. One Jas. B. Ambler j. the N. E. Conf. in 1818, and was app't'd to Lyon, Mass., with E. Hedding. After that date name disappears from the Minutes.—**Amerman, Nicholas**, and **Ann Eliza**, rem. by c., 1874.—***Amerman, Oliver Valentine**, b. in Brooklyn., June 10, 1804; at 4 yrs. of age left fatherless; his mother d. 12 yrs. later, but not until she had made deep and saving impressions upon the minds of her children, and heard the promise of her son Oliver that he would seek the Lord. At 17, while attending a camp-meeting in Haverstraw, N. Y., on the 22d of Aug., 1821, he experienced the joy of salvation. B. R. Prince says he was remarkably exercised, and lay in a trance for a long time. He j. Sands-st. ch. at once, won the confidence and esteem of all, and was licensed to preach, Dec. 17, 1824. "His services were in immediate demand. He was accustomed to preach two or three times each Sabbath, and often on secular evenings to the people who had known him from infancy." [M. D'C. Crawford, in Ch. Ad] His ministerial appointments and colleagues were as follows : 1826, Flushing cir., L. I., a supply with R. Seaman and B. Creagh ; 1827, (N. Y. Conf.,) Suffolk cir., with N. W. Thomas and C. Foss; 1828, Hempstead cir., with N. W. Thomas and D. I. Wright; 1829, ord. deacon—Stamford cir., Conn., with D. DeVinne; 1830, Redding cir., with E. Washburn; 1831, ord. elder—Sag Harbor; 1832, Sag Harbor and Bridge Hampton, with J. Trippett; 1833, "without app't, on account of ill-health;" 1834, Stamford cir., Conn., with C. Stearns; 1835, Fair Haven; 1836–37, Salisbury ; 1838, Hillsdale, N. Y. ; 1839, New Haven, Conn.; 1840, Woodbury; 1841–42, Saugerties cir., N. Y., with H. Lamont and D. Buck; 1843–44, Salisbury, Conn.; 1845–46, Red Hook miss'n, N. Y.; 1847–48, New York, Bedford-st.; 1849–50, New York, Duane-st. ; 1851–52, Goshen ; 1853–54, Rhinebeck; 1855–56, Red Hook miss'n; 1857–58, Sheffield, Mass.; 1859–1860, Shrub Oaks, N. Y. ; 1861–62, Dobb's Ferry ; 1863, Kensico and North Castle; 1864–65, Hillsdale; 1866–68, Fishkill Landing; 1869–79, sup'd. On June 23, 1828, he was mar. to Miss Eliza B. Greenwood. Fifty years afterward they celebrated their golden wedding. With great heroism and faithfulness the wife fulfilled her share of the itinerant's mission. She is living still, (1884,) "as for several years past, a suffering invalid, but so cheerful, so intelligent, so beautifully illustrating the excellence of our holy religion, as to excite wonder in all who enter her still charming home." While Mr. A. was jr. preacher on L. I. one of his colleagues chided him for preaching too short. "It isn't my criticism," he added; "but they all say so." Amerman replied, "But they all say you preach too long." He was a general favorite, often powerful in preaching and exhortation, enthusiastic in whatever he undertook, "a man of remarkably cheerful temper, and of most tender sympathies." In early manhood his personal presence was attractive and impressive, and his bearing and manner were those of a cultured Christian gentleman. In later years, when his physical force abated, he retained the same loving, evangelical spirit. [Conf. Min., 1880, p. 42.] He d. Apr. 23, 1879, in Peekskill, N. Y., age 75. A monument marks his grave in Greenwood cemetery, L. I. Children of Mr. A.: Richard Seaman, formerly a member of the N. Y. Conf.—obliged to retire on account of feeble health; Greenwood—residence, Matteawan, N. Y.; Frances Amelia, (Mrs. Alsdorf;) Anna Louise, (Mrs. H. N. Hinman.)—*Anderson, Fred R., exh. 1834, cl. ldr. 1837; afterward one of the original members and a cl. ldr. in Johnson-st. ch.; active; member of a praying-band; d. in New York.—**Anderson, John S.**, and **Mary A.**, rem. by c. 1873.—ANDERSON, KATIE.—**Anderson, Margaret**, rem.—**Anderson, Sam'l T.**, trus. about 1820.—**Applegate, Mehetable**, d. about 1831.—**Appleyard, Wm.**, j., the Primitive Methodists about 1841.—**Archer, Fanny (Moore)**, w. of Joseph, reared from infancy in the family of J. J. Studwell; member of Bible-class; d. in May, 1881, age 26.—**Archer, Joseph**, rem. by c., 1883.—**Archibald, Wm. F.**, rem. by c., 1866.—ARMSTRONG, MRS. ELIZABETH. —**Armstrong, Margaret**, rem. by c., 1880, to E. B'klyn. —**Armstrong, M. J.**, rem.—ARMSTRONG, PHŒBE.— **Arthur, Isabella**, w. of Wm., d. 1880, age 33; brought up in Boston; conv. young.—ARTHUR, WM.—ARTHUR, MRS. WM. T.—**Ash, John** and **Jane**, rem. to N. York, 1849.—**Ashton, Jas. H.**, rem. by c., 1883.—**Attlesby, Rebecca**, rem.— **Austin, Catharine**, rem. by c.—AUSTIN, ELIZABETH F. —AUSTIN, WM. C.—AVILA, HARRIET.—*Ayers, Ann, wid. of David; dau. of Geo. Smith; d. about 1878 in Galveston, Texas, and is bur. there. AYERS, MRS. ARMINDA.— **Backman, Peter**, S.S.t., (bro. of Rev. Chas. Backman,) and **Mary**, his w., rem. by c., 1868; said to have gone to Cal.— **Backman, ———**, rem. by c. to Johnson-st. ch., 1849.— **Bacon, Ann**, d. in triumph, May 22, 1808, age 73 [grave-stone, old ch. yard].—**Baggott, Ann M.**, rem. to W'msburgh, 1850. **Baggot, John** and **Leonora**, of Red Hook Lane class, 1826–

1828.—**Baggott, Jos.,** of Red Hook Lane class, 1826; loc. pr., 1827; on Flushing cir. plan, 1828; rem. about 1830.— ****Bagnell, Hannah,** d.—**Bagshaw, Oratus,** rem. by c.— BAILEY, FRANCIS.—**Bailey, Jas.,** rem. by c., 1841.— **Bailey, Polly,** charter member of Yellow Hook (Bay Ridge) class, 1822.—****Bailey, Wm.,** d. about 1830.—BAKER, DANIEL.—BAKER, EMILY.—**Baker, Jas. R.,** rem. by c. to Newark, N. J., 1849.—****Baker, Sophronia,** d. about 1822. —BALDWIN, HATTIE.—BALDWIN, LIZZIE.—**Bangs, Mary Eliza,** dau. of Dr. Nathan Bangs, d. peacefully in N. York, Oct. 21, 1857, age 41; conv. in 13th yr. at a camp-meeting on L. I., to which she went with her father. " Even the trees seemed to break forth into rejoicing." [Ch. Ad.]—**Bangs, Rebecca,** sister of the above, rem. to N. York. See sketch of Dr. Nathan Bangs in this work.—**Banta, John W.,** loc. pr., 1866; rem. by c., 1868.—****Barber, Joseph,** a native of Flatbush, L. I., d. 1866; bur. near Hempstead M. E. ch. See headstone.—**Mary Ann,** wid. of the above, rem. by c., 1874.—BARGOLD, MARGARET.—BARNETT, SUSAN.—BARNIER, JOHN J.—std., trus., S.S.t., S.S. supt., off. S.S. miss'y soc.; a native of Eng.; one of the stanch supporters of Sands-st. ch. and S S. for upward of 16 yrs.—ELIZABETH, w. of the above, is a dau. of the excellent John Brice.—ELIZABETH, dau. of the above.—**Barstow, Caroline S.,** rem. by c., 1849.—**Basker, Elijah C.,** rem. to N. York.—**Battu, Jane,** rem. by c., 1877. —****Bayles, Gilbert,** grocer, d. in great peace, 1866.—BEACH, IDA.—****Bedell, Daniel,** d. in peace. He was a barber, afterward a real estate agent.—****Bedell, Jane,** member of A. Mercein's class in 1824; d. soon after.—BEDELL, MISS LOUISA R.—*****Bedell, Moses,** name spelled " Beagle," then " Beadle," and finally " Bedell;" b. in East Meadow, L. I., May 10, 1781; conv. in 1805; cl. ldr. in Brushy Plains, (East Meadow,) L. I., as early as 1806; kept a grocery store in the country, subsequently rem. to B'klyn, and engaged in the milk business, member of C. Hempstead's York-st. class, which met in the " new c." in 1825; loc. pr. in East Meadow in 1826, later in Turtle Hook, (Uniondale,) L. I.; returned to B'klyn about 1831; cl. ldr. on B'klyn charge about 1835; std. in De Kalb ave ch., 1841; loc. pr., Johnson-st., 1849; d. in B'klyn, Dec. 27, 1849, age 68.— *****Elizabeth,** w. of the above, a native of Merrick, L. I.; d. June 2, 1860, aged 77.—**Bedell, Sam'l,** loc. pr. about 1839.—*BEEKMAN, MRS. CATHARINE.—BEERE, MRS. ANNA.— BEERE, ELLEN.—**Beers, Edwin,** S.S.t. and lib'n; became an Episcopalian.—BEERS, JOSEPH.—**Beers, S. Lucinda,** S.S.t., rem. by c. to Huntington, L. I., about 1850.—BEHLER, LILLIE.—****Biester, Eleanor,** d. in peace, Aug. 25, 1849, age 91.—**Bell, Mrs. T. A.,** rem. by c. 1877.—**Bell, Peter C.,** cl. ldr. in Sands-st., 1830; in Hempstead, 1837; in York-st.,

B'klyn, about 1845; a true Methodist of the olden type.—
**Rebecca, w. of the above; conv. at 15; became a Methodist and worthily served the ch. 56 yrs. " Death came suddenly, but found her prepared." [F. C. Hill, in Ch. Ad.] Their son, J. J. Bell, was once a pastor in B'klyn.—BELLOWS, CHAS.—
**Bellows, Edward P., S.S.t.; drowned at sea, Jan. 8, 1865; sutler in the army; excellent young man. His wid. is a dau. of Barzillai Russell, of Sands-st. ch.—BELLOWS, ELIZABETH.
—Bellows, Joseph R., rem.—Benjamin John, cl. ldr., 1843; rem., ("J. H. Benjamin" was a S.S.t. in 1839.)—*Bennett, Abraham, j. Sands-st. ch. in 1807; some time cl. ldr. in Sands-st. and many yrs. in Hempstead, whither he removed; d. Jan. 5, 1867, age 79; bur. east of the M. E. ch., Hempstead; no stone.
—Ann, w. of the above, eldest dau. of Jeremiah and Ann Booth; conv. in B'klyn at 17; rem. to Hempstead in 1834; highly esteemed; d. March 30, 1838, age 45; funeral sermon by Joseph Law: tombstone in M. E. ch. yard, Hempstead. Children of Abraham and Ann Bennett: William, Andrew Mercein, and others.—BENNETT, AMY.—**Bennett, Ann E., d.—Bennett,'Benj. and Louisa, rem. by c.,1849.—Bennett,Catherine H., rem. by c.—Bennett Clarinda, rem. by c.—**Bennett, John, d. 1829; probably this is the man mentioned in the list of cl. lds., 1808.—**Bennett, P. Wynant, a shoe dealer; d. 1849.
—**Joanna, his wid., d., 1839.—Bennett Walter L., cl. ldr. about 1864.—Benoit, Mrs. Sarah, rem. by c.—BETTZ, HENRY.—BILLINGS, ANN E.—Bingham, Chas., rem. by c. to Mich.—Bishop, David H., rem. by c., 1867.—BISHOP, NICHOLAS.—BISHOP, SARAH.—BLACKWOOD, CHRISTIANA.—*Blagborne, Wm., loc. pr., 1811; b. in Eng.; was preacher on Leeds cir., probably in 1798; [Everett's "Life of Wm. Dawson," p. 117.] Conf. App'ts in America: 1811, (N. York Conf.,) a deacon; N. York city, with N. Bangs, Wm. Phœbus, Laban Clark, Jas. M. Smith, and P. P. Sandford; 1812, no app't named; 1813, ord. elder—Jamaica cir., L. I., with J. Lyon and S. Bushnell; 1814, sup'y N. York cir., with Wm. Phœbus, S. Cochran, N. Emery, M. Richardson, and T. Drummond; 1815, name disappears—returned to Eng. Some of the old people recall pleasant memories concerning him. While in Brooklyn he was accustomed to attend the debates held by the young men. The elder men—honorary members—were often called upon to sum up the arguments. Judge Dikeman relates that on one occasion the question being whether married or single life is most conducive to happiness, Mr. B. was called upon to weigh the arguments and render a decision. He said the weight of the argument was in favor of single blessedness; but, though he had had two wives and was a widower, if he were not so old and had a good chance, he would surely get married again. The Rev. Henry Hatfield described him as a large,

noble-looking man, and a good preacher. The venerable Moses Rogers, of Northport, L. I., remembers him as a preacher on Jamaica cir. in 1813, a widower with two daughters; his niece kept house for him. Rogers says that the natural color of his hair was white. Elbert Osborn [Life, p. 38] speaks of having heard Mr. B. preach from 1 Pet. ii, 2, and mentions his "florid countenance" and his "somewhat peculiar voice and enunciation;" also his death in Eng. some years after his return. In the "Life of Wm. Bramwell" (chap. xv) is the following sentence: "O the blessed state of that holy man of God, Mr. Blagborne, when he was about to depart. I saw him in London a short time prior to his death, when he exclaimed with joy, 'Glory! glory be to God, who hath made me fully ready for my change!'"—BLAIR, MRS.—**Blair, Eliza,** rem.—**Blair, Walter,** cl. ldr., rem. by c., 1830.—**Blanchard, Nathan H., and Rebecca H.,** rem. by c., 1842.—**Blatchley, Sarah,** rem. —**Blew, Wm. H.,** rem. by c.—**Blewit, Sarah,** rem. by c.— ****Bliss, Sam'l W.,** d. 1884.—BLISS, MRS. ANNA J.— ***Bogart Adrian,** written sometimes "Orion," first j. the M. E. ch. in Newtown, L. I., [Meth. Mag., 1825, p. 165.] Thence he rem. to Yellow Hook, (now Bay Ridge,) and united with Sands-st. ch. Through his influence preaching was established and a class formed in Yellow Hook in 1822, which soon grew to be a separate society. He was a licensed exh., and was a cl. ldr. also from 1824 till his death, Oct. 6, 1849, at the age of 78. He d. in the very room in which the first Methodist sermon was preached in Bay Ridge. [Rev. J. D. Bouton, in Ch. Ad.] A head-stone in the old Meth. grave-yard in Bay Ridge marks his resting-place.—***Phœbe,** first w. of the above, a native of Newtown, L. I., mar. at 23. 11 yrs. later, under a sudden and powerful conviction, she went away alone to pray, and soon returned to her work shouting aloud for joy. She, with her husband, remained faithful amidst great persecution. She d. in her husband's arms in Dec., 1824, age 53. She had just finished saying, "How long before Jesus will come?" [Meth. Mag., 1825, p. 165.] —***Bogart, Getty,** one of the original members of Yellow Hook class, Sands-st. ch., in 1822; sister to Adrian; mar. Wm. Kelly, rem. to N. J., and died about 1850, a Methodist; bur. in the Reformed ch. burial-ground, New Utrecht.—***Bogart, Peter,** charter member of Yellow Hook (Bay Ridge) class in 1822; probably son of Adrian; bur. in old Methodist burial-ground in Bay Ridge.—***Bogart, Wynant,** early member Yellow Hook (Bay Ridge) class; d. in Bay Ridge, May 3, 1855, age 76; left a good record. [Rev. E. K. Fanning, in Ch. Ad.] Bur. in old Methodist grave-yard. He left a family.—**Bond, Benj. W.,** S.S.t. and loc. pr.; native of B'klyn; conv. and j. Sands-st. ch. under the ministry of H. J. Fox; rem. by c. to Sum'f'd ch., thence to N. York ave. ch., (six yrs. std. there,) thence to Grace ch., and was S.S. supt. 2 yrs. He is a graduate (1862) of the N. York Univ. He interested himself in the religious education of the colored people while residing 2½ yrs. in Norfolk, Va.— *Bond, Hannah, mother of the above, d. 1867, age 56.— BOND, MARY.—Bond, Newall, S.S. supt.—*Bonnell, Nathaniel, cl. ldr., trus., and std. in Sands-st ch.; afterward a member of the original board of trustees in Hanson Pl. ch., an honored member of which he was at the time of his decease. He carried on an extensive business as mason and builder. His son, C. L. Bonnell, M.D., is a worthy successor of the father in various departments of Christian work.—Bonnington, Catharine, rem., 1850.—BOOGAREDST, ELIZABETH.— **Booth, Eliza, d. about 1822.—Booth, Geo. B., cl. ldr., 1833; an Englishman; went to York-st. ch., where he was S. S. supt.; mar., and d. soon after.—Booth, Walker, loc. pr., 1839. —BORDEN, JAMES D.—Bottome, Francis, first named on the records of Sands-st. ch., in 1849, as a loc. pr. from Canada. Two other recorded items are: " Recommended to the traveling connection," and " Removed by Bp. Janes to Rahway." *Conference Appointments:* 1850, (N. York East Conf.,) Southampton, L. I.; 1851-52, Meriden, Conn.; 1852, ord. deacon; 1853-54, Saybrook; 1854, ord. elder; 1855-56, Norwalk; 1857-58, Birmingham; 1859-60, Hempstead, L. I.; 1861-62, W'msburg, Grand-st., (Gothic;) 1863-65, N. York, 7th-st.; 1866, Bridgeport, Conn.; 1867-69, N. York, Beekman Hill; 1870-71, (N. York Conf.,) Yonkers, 1st ch.; 1872-74, N. York, Central ch.; 1875, Marlborough; 1876-78, Tarrytown; 1879-81, N. York, Tremont; 1882, sup'y; 1883-84, Tuckahoe. Mr. B. mar. Miss Margaret M'Donald, of the Sands-st. ch., in Sept., 1850; visited Europe in 1881; a few years since received the degree of D.D.; is a gifted preacher, and widely known as a poet of extraordinary talent. He has a son, who, as we understand, has become an Episcopal clergyman.—**Bowman, Wm., S. S. t., d. 1836.— **Bowne, Ann M., d. in peace, 1848—" a loss to the ch."— **Box, Ann, "d. in the Lord," 1841.—BOYD, FANNY J.— **Boylhart, Christian, d. 1867.—BOYNTON, FRANK.— BOYNTON, SARAH.—BRADFORD, ANNIE L.—Bradley, Deborah, rem.—*Bradstreet, John M., a native of Ohio, a friend of the Rev. J. B. Finley, and one of the founders of the Finley Chapel, in Cincinnati. He came to B'klyn, and established the " J. M. Bradstreet Commercial Agency." His services in Sands-st. ch., as S. S. t., sec. of the S. S. miss'y soc., and cl. ldr. were very much appreciated. He d. in June, 1863, a member of St. Paul's M. E. ch., N. York. He mar. twice, the 2d time to Catharine, a dau. of Ira Perego, Sen. She was a S. S. t. in Sands-st. After his death she was mar. to Dr. Ranney, of N. York. Mr. B. left 2 sons and 2 dau. Henry resides in N. York. Milton in Texas.—**Brakey, Elizabeth, d.

1870.—**Brand, Susan,** rem.—**Branner, Mary F.,** rem.—**Breckinridge, David A.,** withdrew, 1850.—**Brewer, Sidney,** cl. ldr., 1835; exh., 1842; soon after he was loc. pr. in Washington-st. ch. It is said that he embraced the views of the Second Adventists.—**Brewster, Lucius G.,** and **Julia,** rem. (Julia Ringwood Brewster wrote for the Brooklyn Eagle a fine poem on the death of M. F. Odell.)—****Brice, Ann E.,** mar. See Seffern.—****Brice, John,** loc. pr. and cl. ldr.; j. the Wesleyans in Eng., his native country, in his 16th yr.; became an itinerant preacher, colleague of Joseph Benson, at 19. After about 8 yrs. his health failed, and he came to B'klyn in 1831. He was a druggist. Thousands of times did he dispense medicines to the poor and sick, saying, "May this do thee good, by the blessing of God." He was studious, and his excellent memory served him when he had become almost totally blind. Four hours after he had, as usual, prayed with his family, on June 9, 1849, he d. of apoplexy, age 77. [Rev. W. H. Norris, in Ch. Ad.]—****Elizabeth,** w. of the above, was b. in Eng., and conv. in childhood. Her father, "honest Isaac Brown," was one of Wesley's most honored preachers, and was remembered by him in his will. [See Wesley's Works, vol. vii, pp. 145, 181.] She preceded her husband to the heavenly glory by about 3 mos., age about 76. Mr. B. said, as he bowed over her coffin, "I shall soon follow." Her funeral was attended by W. H. Norris and J. J. Matthias. [Matthias, in Ch. Ad.] Both are bur. in "Greenwood."—**Brice, Sarah L.,** rem. by c., 1849.—****Brice, Susan,** d. in triumph, about 1839.—**Briggs, Ira,** cl. ldr. about 1850.—**Briggs, John,** rem., 1837.—****Bright, Wm.,** a native of Ireland, d. 1829, age 45. [Stone in old ch. yard.]—**Brisbee, Ann,** rem.—****Bristol, Thos.,** d.—****Bristol, Sarah,** d.—**Bristow, Eleanor,** (colored;) "truly pious;" d. in great peace, 1849, aged 91.—BROOKS, CAROLINE.—BROOKS, PHILIP, S.S.t.—Brower, Calvin, rem. by c., 1873.—Brower, John, cl. ldr., 1806; exh., 1811. Mrs. Wm. Rushmore states that he mar. a sister of Mrs. Israel Disosway, and that a dau. of his mar. Daniel Ayers, of Brooklyn.—**Brown, Mrs. Anna,** rem. by c., 1884.—****Brown, Ellen,** d. in peace, 1864.—BROWN, MRS. ELLEN, from the Reformed ch.—***Brown, Jacob,** one of the best examples of the old-fashioned, noisy Methodists; was early made cl. ldr., std., and trus., (pres't of the board.) He was b. in

ERECTED IN MEMORY OF JACOB BROWN.
By the Class which he led in this Church FOR FORTY YEARS.
Born April 26th 1790.
Died Sept. 13th 1865.

"Thanks be to God who giveth us the Victory through our Lord Jesus Christ."
"Therefore my beloved Brethren, Be ye stedfast, unmoveable, always abounding in the work of the Lord."

Babylon, L. I., Apr. 26, 1790; "lived 75 yrs. in B'klyn, was widely known as an upright, honest citizen, and for a long time the foremost man in the Meth. ch. in the city; 60 yrs. connected with the Sands-st. ch." [Brooklyn paper.] He d. in B'klyn, Sept. 13, 1865, in his 76th yr. His pastor, C. Fletcher, preached his funeral sermon. A head-stone designates his grave in "Greenwood." The memorial tablet in the church (a fac-simile of which is given on p. 416) very worthily commemorates the esteem and reverence of the church for their good father and friend.— **Ann (Furman),** his w., was b. in B'klyn, May 16, 1793; at 18 mar. Mr. B.; d. Dec. 28, 1870, age 77; bur. beside her husband. She, also, was a member of Sands-st. ch. over 60 yrs., and what is said in praise of Jacob Brown may be as truly said of his wife. Of their 11 children, 5 are living, viz: John F., Emeline, Noah Levings, Almira, and Wesley, "belonging to different churches, and cherishing bright hopes of a happy union in heaven." [Letter of John F. Brown to the author.] —**Brown, L. L.,** rem. by c., 1878.—BROWN, MARIA.— **Brown, Margaret,** rem. by c., 1875.—**Brown, Martha,** rem. by c., 1884.—****Brown, Mary,** d. about 1834.—BROWN, MRS. NELLIE.—BROWN, RICHARD A.—**Brown, Sam'l,** rem. by c.—****Brown, Wm.,** son of Jacob, d. in peace, 1841; not married.—**Brown, Hester,** rem. without c., 1845.—BROWNE, LA GRANGE, S.S.t.—****Brush, Deborah,** d. about 1819.—****Bryant, John,** S.S.t. and S. S. supt., d. 1841, a young man.—****Buckley, Mrs. Elizabeth,** d. 1870.—**Budd, Richard** and **Gertrude,** j. by c., 1876, rem. by c., 1879.—BUELL, ADA.—**Bull, John,** loc. pr., 1866, from Eng.—BULWER, MARY C., rem. by c.—****Bumford, Catharine,** w. of Edward, d. 1870.—BUMFORD, SARAH, S.S.t.— BUNCE, RICHARD, cl. ldr. since 1866; clerk in hardware store in B'klyn.—**Burch, Thos. Hardin,** son of Thomas Burch, a Sands-st. pastor, was b. in Phila., June 8, 1823. We cannot give the date of his conversion. Studied in Wes. Univ.; left college in junior yr., (1842;) studied law 3 yrs. in the office of Anthon and Van Cott, N. York, and practiced law about 6 yrs. in that city. He was S.S.t. in Sands-st. ch. in 1842, afterward S. S. sec. He took part in the election of the first board of trustees of Fleet-st. ch., Brooklyn, [Records;] was licensed to preach by the quar. conf. of Sands-st. ch., and recommended to the Annual Conf. at the same meeting. *Conf. Record:* 1850-51, (N. York East Conf.,) Flatbush, L. I.; 1852, ord. deacon; 1852-53, Flatlands; 1854, ord. elder; 1854-55, Brooklyn, Hicks-st., (First Pl.;) 1856-57. Flushing; 1858-59, N. York, Forsyth-st.; 1860-61, Hartford, Conn.; 1862-63, Stamford; 1864-66, New Haven, 1st ch.; 1867-69, Danbury; 1870-72, N. York, 37th-st.; 1873-74, B'klyn, Greenpoint Tabernacle; 1875-77. N. York, 2d ave.; 1878-80, B'klyn, Central ch.; last part of 1880, P. E., N. York Dist.; 1881-82, P. E., N. York Dist.; 1883-84, N. York, Trinity ch. He was mar. in 1844 to Miss Mary E. Ross. Their children are: Thos. R., Wm. R., Charles R., Mark H., and Mary E. [Alumni Record, Wes. Univ.] Mr. Burch has descended from a noble stock. He is a bright man and a popular preacher.—*Mary E., w. of the above. Her father, the Rev. Wm. Ross, was twice pastor of the Sands-st. ch. She rem. by c. to Flatbush, to enter upon the duties of a pastor's w., in 1851; d. suddenly at her parsonage home, in N. York, July 10, 1884. Funeral services in Trinity ch., Harlem, were conducted by Bp. Harris, Dr. Curry, Dr. A. S. Hunt, and the Rev. Wm. C. Steele, all intimate friends of the family. "Mrs. B. was a woman of decidedly domestic habits, and her household gathered around her with the most sincere and loving devotion." [Ch. Ad.]—*Burnett, Wm., rem. by c. The Rev. Geo. Coles mentions meeting him at Red Hook, on the Hudson, in 1820. [" My First Seven Years in America," p. 173.] He was an exh. in Sands-st. ch. in 1822, afterward loc. deacon in Wash'gt'n-st. ch. He labored long and faithfully among the soldiers on Bedloe's Isl. and Governor's Isl., and through his efforts hundreds were rescued from the lowest depths of sin. Subsequently he turned his attention to seamen —head-quarters on a receiving ship in B'klyn Navy Yard; finally hired a little Bethel in Catharine-st.; where he preached and held temperance meetings. He was pastor of the Bethel about 25 yrs., with success very rarely equaled. On hearing of his death in B'klyn, Jan. 1, 1861, his friends, the sailors, begged, as a favor, that they might be pall-bearers at his funeral; sermon by the Rev. F. S. De Hass, of Wash'gton-st. ch.; procession escorted by the Sons of Temperance. [T. B., in Ch. Ad.]— *Mary Ogden, wid. of the above, b. in N. London, Conn.; d. at the residence of her son-in-law, Edward Storer, Esq., in B'klyn, Dec. 12, 1881, aged 81, a member of Wash'gt'n-st. ch.; nearly 70 yrs. a devoted and faithful Methodist. [F. S. De Hass, in Ch. Ad.]—Burns, Mary, mar. See Fay.—**Burr, Frances, d. 1848, age 45; bur. in "Greenwood."—Burrows, Joshua L., loc. pr.; came from Gt. Britain to Sands-st. ch. in 1853. *Pastoral Record:* 1854, (N. York East Conf.,) North Hempstead cir., L. I.; 1855, Northport and Centerport; 1856, name disappears; became rector of an Episcopal ch. in Huntington, L. I.; 1884, and many yrs. previously, rector of the Ch. of the Evangelists, Oswego, N. Y. The titles D.D. and Ph.D. appended to his name, are indicative of his scholarly attainments.—Burrows, Lemuel and Mary A., rem. by c., 1875. Mr. B. came from Mystic, Conn., in 1848; j. the M. E. ch. when a lad; was S.S.t. in 1854; went from Sands-st. to Hanson Pl.; afterward a member and pres't board of trustees in Greene ave. ch.; later j. the Nostrand ave. ch. He is now

an assessor in Brooklyn.—**Burrows, Mary T.**, rem. by c.—
Burrows, Thos. Coke, j. the Sands-st. ch. when a S. S. boy,
(J. B. Hagany, pastor;) rem. to Carlton ave. ch. in 1861; now
cl. ldr. and Bible-class teacher in Simpson ch.—**Burtis, Margaret,** rem. by c., 1882.—BURTIS, MRS. MARY E.—BURTIS, WM.—**Burtnett, Kate R.,** rem. by c., 1873.—**Burton,
Mrs. Catharine,** rem. by c., 1881.—BYRNE, SARAH A.—
Cadmus, Richard, S.S.t. and std., went to Gowanus.—CADMUS, RICHARD and MRS. RICHARD.—**Cady, Henry M.**
and **Sarah H.,** rem. by c., 1882.—CAMPBELL, MRS. CLARA
—CAMPBELL, MRS. CORNELIA.—CAMPBELL, GEO.—
**Campbell, John, a native of Scotland; d. Jan. 3, 1809, age
67; bur. in old ch. yard. [See headstone.]—CAMPBELL,
MRS. LETITIA.—CAMPBELL, WM.—**Canfield, J. B.** and
Mary A., rem. by c. to Schenectady, 1849.—****Cannon,
Rachel;** [see Moser.]—****Carl, Eliza,** d. 1871.—CARL,
ELIZA.—**Carman, Albro R.,** rem. by c., 1866.—****Carman,
Sarah,** d. 1852.—***Carpenter, Albert.** His father, the Rev.
Chas. W. Carpenter, was a Sands-st. pastor. Mr. C. was S.S.t.
and sec. of S. S.; rem. by c., 1839; d. in Newburgh, N. Y., not
many yrs. ago. He was mar. to Mary, a sister of David Coope.
It is said that she and her son reside in Newburgh.—**Carpenter,
Carman R.,** rem., 1850.—CARPENTER, ELIZABETH.—
CARPENTER, JANE.—**Carpenter, Rob't,** rem.—**Carpenter, Ruth,** rem.—CARROUGHER, GEO. W.—CARROUGHER, JOSEPH, and ISABELLA, his w.—CARSON, JOSEPH.—CARSON, MRS. ANNA F.—CARTER, BARNABAS.
—**Carter, Chauncey,** cl. ldr. 1826; also a S. S. supt., much
esteemed.—**Cartwright, Wm.,** cl. ldr., 1846; one of the
founders and original off. of the S. S. miss'y soc.; more recently
sexton of Wash'gton-st. ch.—**Chadwick, Hannah,** rem. by c.,
1848.—**Chadwick, Ruth A.,** rem. by c., 1849.—****Chadwick,
Thos.,** a mason, rem. to B'klyn from Monmouth Co., N. J. He
was killed by the falling of a chimney, in the summer of 1817;
bur. in the old ch. yard. His w., ***Keziah,** " was of a gentle,
loving spirit, and trained her children in the fear of the Lord."
Her son writes: "Well do I remember my mother taking my
two sisters and myself to father's grave, and weeping for our
loss."—**Chadwick, Thos. Worthley,** son of the above, S. S.
sec., treas., and supt., and cl. ldr. in the Sands-st. ch., was b. in
B'klyn, Sept. 27, 1817. His boyhood was spent partly in school
and partly in a crockery store. David Coope, of Sands-st. ch.,
was his employer. He was conv. and j. this ch. at 15, (Thos.
Burch, pastor.) At 18 he obtained a situation in the Kings Co.
clerk's office, and remained in the office 10 yrs.; at 21 was
made deputy cl'k. In 1842 he was mar. by his pastor, P. C.
Oakley, in the old white church in Sands-st., to a member of
this ch., Miss Mary Frances Akins, stepdaughter of Thos.

Frazier. For 12 yrs. he strove against a divine call to preach the gospel. He rem. to N. York and j. Bedford-st. ch. in 1849, and 4 yrs. later, at a camp-meeting love-feast on L. I., conducted by Dr. Bangs, he submitted fully to God's will in respect to his life-work, and was wonderfully blessed. Soon after the camp-meeting he preached his first sermon in a tent, where the 7th ave. M. E. ch., N. York city, now stands. Obtaining license 1st as exh., then as loc. pr., he was immediately put into the field. *Pastoral appt's:* 1853, last part, supply at Dobb's Ferry, N.Y.; 1854-55, (N. York Conf.,) Dobb's Ferry Miss'n; 1856, ord. deacon; 1856-57, Red Hook and East Chatham; 1858, ord. elder; 1858-59, Hudson; 1860-61, Red Hook; 1862-63, Middletown; 1864-66, Kingston; 1867, N. York, 24th st.; 1868-71, P. E., Prattsville Dist.; 1872-73, Peekskill, 1st ch.; 1874-76; Pleasantville; 1877, White Plains, 1st ch.; 1878-80, Coeyman's and S. Bethlehem; 1881, Woodstock; 1882-84, Coxsackie. Church edifices have been erected under his ministry at Dobb's Ferry, Ashland, and East Chatham; one was rebuilt at Red Hook; another finished and dedicated at 24th st., N. York. He has witnessed gracious revivals at Dobb's Ferry, Hudson, Middletown, Kingston, and Peekskill. He was sec. of the N. York Conf. 5 yrs. His surviving children are: Walter Augustus, an alumnus of Wesleyan Univ. and of Drew Theolog. Sem.; member of the N. York Conf. since 1872; Ann Louisa, a grad. of Drew Ladies' Sem.; Chas. Wesley, a grad. of Wes. Univ., now studying art and engraving in N. York city.—**Mary F.**, w. of the above, rem. by c., 1848.—****Chamberlain, Sarah**, d. 1868. (Mrs. S. E. Chamberlain was S.S.t. in 1864.)—**Chapman, Maggie**, rem. by c. to Embury ch., 1880.—**Chappelle, Caroline**, S.S.t., 1855; rem. to Elm Pl. Cong. ch., 1877.—CHEESEBORO, FRANK S.—CHEESEBORO, MATTIE.—CHEETERTON, ALFRED.—CHEEVER, A. C.—CHESHIRE, CHAS. B.—CLARK, ARCHIBALD G.—**Clark, Geo.**, rem.—**Clark, Leverett** and **Ruah**, rem. by c.—**Clark, Rebecca**, rem. by c., 1872.—**Clark, Rhoda**, rem. by c., 1883.—CLARK, S.—**Claxton, (Susan) Emma**, mar. See Hudson.—CLAYTON, JAMES; from Eng.; loc. pr. in Sands-st. ch. since 1849; S.S.t., 1858.—CLAYTON, MRS. PHŒBE.—CLOFFY, SOPHIA.—**Cobb, E. R.**, rem.—**Cobb, Rachel M.**, rem. by c., 1883.—COFFREY, **Amelia**.—****Cole, Moses**, d.—**Collett, John**; from Eng.; loc. pr. in 1836; rem. by c. about 1839.—**Collins, Richard**, rem.—****Colvert, Hannah**, d. in peace, 1865.—COLVIN, JENNIE.—COLVIN, SARAH.—**Combs, Daniel A.**, rem. by c.—****Compton, Mrs. Elizabeth J.**, d.—****Compton, Henry**, d. 1882.—***Conger, Peter**, (colored,) exh., 1814.—**Conklin, Catharine,**, rem. to N. York.—CONKLIN, MARTHA J.—**Connoly, Hugh G.** and **Elizabeth**, rem. by c., 1867.—***Connor, Leah**, member in 1798.—****Cook,**

Benj. S., cl. ldr , d. about 1860.—**Cook, Hannah,** rem. by c., 1877.—*****Cooke, David A.,** S.S t., 1856; cl. ldr., 1862; nephew of C. C. Smith; b. in B'klyn, when a young man studied with Fowler & Wells; lectured on phrenology established the first daguerreotype gallery in B'klyn ; engaged in literary work; a writer of force and elegance; editor of the Willow Magazine, and the Lyceum Reporter contributed to various papers ; finally, compositor in office of New York Tribune highly honored by his friends for his active mind, generous impulses, and great kindness of heart, a successful infant-class teacher, a model husband and father In size, gait, manner, countenance, and voice, he is said to have resembled Dr. J. M. Buckley. He rem. by c. to Hanson Pl. ch. in 1870; d. in B'klyn, Feb. 1, 1877, aged 57, and is bur in " Greenwood."—**Mary E.,** his w., rem. by c., 1870. Of their 7 children, 2 sons and 1 dau. are living.—******Cooke, Elizabeth,** mother of David A., dau. of Geo. Smith rem. to Ithaca, N Y , returned; d. in B'klyn, April 7, 1884, bur. in Evergreen cem.—**Cooke, Emily V.,** dau. of David A.; rem. by c., 1870.—******Coope, David,** S.S.t., S.S. supt., std., cl. ldr., trus., (sec. and treas. of the board;) brother in-law to Albert Carpenter; began business in B'klyn as a china merchant with a few pieces of crockery in a store on Fulton st. opposite Henry ; business prospered C. C. Leigh was his partner some yrs. Mr. C. was a prominent and useful officer in the ch., and when taken away was greatly lamented. He d. in 1877, aged about 70.—**Coope, Edison,** rem. by c., 1879.—*****Coope, Edward,** brother of David; rem. 1837 ; has since d. [Mrs. J J Studwell.]—**Cooper, Caroline,** rem. to N York —**Cooper, John,** ldr. of a colored class, 1808.— **Cooper, Wm.,** rem. by c., 1866.—**Copeland, Chas. J.,** rem. without c —**Copeland, Geo.** and **Harriet F.,** rem. by c. (Geo. M. Copeland was S.S.t. in 1839.)—******Cornelison, John,** trus. before 1800; rope-maker; d. in faith, 1819, aged 75. [Tombstone in old ch. yard.] Mrs. J. W. De Grauw described him as a good man, very devout; she often heard him pray when the tears rolled down his cheeks.—******Sarah,** his w., called sometimes " Auntie Cornelison," was an energetic woman of the olden type. She used to row a small boat across the ferry from Brooklyn to N. York. [C. C. Smith.] See sketch of her dau., Mrs. Lanie Acker.—CORNWELL, MARY A.—*****Cornwell, Richard,** chorister, also S.S.t., one of the first. He entered into politics, and fell away from the ch., but is believed to have been restored to God's favor during his last illness. He d. about 1845, and his pastor, C. W. Carpenter, at his funeral, spoke of his happy death and beautiful visions of heaven.—*****Mary,** w. of the above, dau. of James Herbert, S.S.t., one of the first; d. about 1800, and was bur. from the Washington st. ch. Children of Richard and Mary Cornwell:

Rich'd Herbert; James, d. 1882 in B'klyn; Timothy, member Classon ave. Presb. ch.; John, d. in B'klyn; Sam'l; Mary, (Mrs. Campbell;) Amanda, d.; Anna, d.; Katie, wid. of ―――― Brewer, lives at Flatbush.—CORNWELL, MRS. SARAH.—**Corson, Dr. John W.**, cl. ldr., 1842; rem. by c.; b. at Grimsby, near Niagara, C. W., Aug. 2, 1816; son of a Meth. pioneer missionary, the Rev. R. Corson. He was an industrious and ambitious lad, and was greatly aided "by the heroism and counsels of his gifted mother." He studied the classics at Cazenovia Sem.; was graduated in medicine at Albany in 1842; began his practice in B'klyn; traveled and studied in Europe; published a vol. entitled, " Loiterings in Europe;" was chosen visiting physician to B'klyn City Hospital; rem. to N. York; mar. a dau. of the late Calvin Condit, Esq.; adopted as his specialty diseases of the chest and throat; wrote papers; lectured in the colleges; served as recording sec. of the Am. and For. Xn. Union; health failed; rem. to Brampton, near Toronto, C. W.; rallied; lectured in Victoria College, Toronto; rem. to Orange, N. J.; for years physician to the Orange Memorial Hospital. He was a faithful worker in the S.S. and the ch., and d., greatly lamented, about Jan. 1, 1882, age nearly 66.—CORWIN, MRS. MARY E.—COSTELLO, HENRY.—COSTELLO, MRS. LETITIA.—COSTELLO, MRS. MATILDA,—**Cottier, John**; loc. pr., 1849, and later S.S.t., S.S. sup't, trus., std., and cl. ldr. He was b., of Wesleyan Meth. parents, in Peel, Isle of Man, in 1809; conv. at 21; j. the Wesleyans; 5 yrs. later began his work as loc. pr.; came to N. York in 1844; to B'klyn soon after; devotedly served the Sands-st. ch. for 30 yrs. in many different relations. He was one of the originators, and for a time the highly-honored pres't, of the Nat'l Loc. Preachers' Assoc'n, also an active member of the Loc. Prs. Assoc'n of N. York and B'klyn, by whose agency many souls were converted and many churches established in those two cities. He d. in 1879, age 69, and is bur. in "Greenwood." His memoir says: "He was diligent in business, which secured him a competency to support a large family, and to educate and fit his children to move in the most refined circles. At his funeral, and at the 'memorial services,' held in the Sands-st. ch., pastors of the churches and his brethren of the local ministry spoke of him as a distinguished, courteous, consistent Christian gentleman, who gave time and money freely to advance the kingdom of God. In the pulpit his manner was solemn, earnest, fervent; the melody of his voice, his clear, sincere utterance of gospel truth, his graceful manner and dignified person, and, above all, his acknowledged purity of character, insured him a welcome to most of the pulpits of N. York and B'klyn." He left a w., a son, and 3 daus.—COTTIER, MRS. MARY A.—COTTRELL, MRS. SARAH.—COULTER, JOHN J.—

COWELLS, W. W.—**Cox, Sam'l**, rem. by c.; identified with the most active laymen of B'klyn and W'msburgh Methodism for many yrs.; now a member and off. in the Glen Cove (L. I.) M. E. Ch. The author was his pastor 3 yrs.—**Cozine, Addie**, rem. by c., 1883.—**Cozine, Gertrude J.**, rem. by c., 1883.—COZINE, MRS. ROSANNAH.—**Craig, James B.**, rem.—**Crane, Josephine A.**, rem. by c., 1882.—**Crangle, Susan**, rem. by c., 1876.—**Crans, Josephine**, rem.—CREED, SARAH.—CRESHULL, MRS. SARAH J., S.S.t.—CRESHULL, WM.—*****Cromwell, Benj.**, conv. at Matteawan, on the Hudson, in early manhood; removing thence, j. the 27th-st. ch., N. York; afterward one yr. a member of Sands-st. ch.; thenceforward he belonged to York-st.; and at the time of his death was pres't of the board of trustees and sec. of the joint board. For years he led or assisted in leading the service of song in the ch. and S.S. In 1880 he d., age 60. His memoir says: " He was a member of the Good Samaritans, and Worthy Patriarch of the Sons of Temp. For 14 yrs. he was at the head of the Cadets of Temp. in B'klyn, and for many months previous to his death he was Worthy Chief of the Star Lodge of Good Templars." He was bur. in the Evergreen cem.; left a w. and 2 children, with a large circle of friends. [A. C. Stevens in Ch. Ad.]—CROOK, MRS. KATIE.—**Crosby, Jane**, d. 1866; member one yr.—**Crosby, Louise**, rem. by c., 1872.—**Crosby, Sarah**, rem.—CRUM, SARAH.—****Cumberson, Thomas**, d. 1882.—****Cunningham, Mrs. Sophronia**, d. 1883.—**Curry, Emma**, rem., by c. 1849; went West.—**Cursiner, Mrs. Elsie**, rem. by c. to Sum'f'd. ch., 1880.—CURTIS, CORNELIA.—CURTIS, MRS. ELIZABETH.—**Cutter, Julia**, dau. of S. Virginia, rem. by c. to Nostrand ave. ch., 1878.—*****Cutter, S. Virginia**, w. of Britton P., sister of A. B. Thorn; b. in Richmond, Va.; S.S.t. some time; S.S. supt. 13 yrs.; d. in peace, Jan. 5, 1870, age 48; bur. in "Greenwood." See headstone. Her counsels were wise, and her influence always good. She was a wid. 20 yrs.; left a dau. as above.—*****Dale, Betsey**, member in 1798.—**Dalton, John**; loc. pr.; recommended to traveling connection, 1817; name does not appear in Conf. Minutes.—**Damon, Mary**, rem. by c., 1867.—**Dann, Isaac N.**, rem. to N. Haven, Conn., about 1855.—**Dannath, E.**, rem.—**Danney, Ellen**, rem. by c., 1848.—**Darcey, Harriet**, rem. by c., 1867.—**Darling, James**, S.S.t., rem. by c., 1867.—**Darling, Mary A.**, rem. by c., 1867.—DARLING, MARY JANE.—**Darrow, Mrs. Emily**, withdrew.—DAVIDSON, ELIZABETH.—DAVIDSON, EMMA.—**Davidson, Mrs. Zilla**, rem. by c.—DAVIS, ELISHA.—DAVIS, HEZEKIAH.—**Davis, John**, S.S.t., rem. to N. York, 1851.—*****Davis, Rebecca**, conv. on Staten Island; d. 1848, age 22. [Ch. Ad.]—*****Davis, Sarah**, w. of Wright, dau. of Geo. Smith, rem. by c , 1848, to Oyster Bay, L. I., where she is believed to have been a Meth. as long as she lived. She d. in B'klyn about 1868; bur. in "Greenwood."—DAVISON, JOSEPHINE.—**Davison, Kate,** rem. by c., 1876.—**Dawson, Wm.,** loc. pr., 1815, from Eng.; nothing further known; same name as the brilliant and famous loc. pr. of Eng., commonly known as "Billy Dawson."—*__Day, Anna,__ member in 1798.—DAY, EMMA.—**Dayton, Amelia,** mar.; see Miller.—DAYTON, ANNIE.—DAYTON, CARRIE.—**Dayton, Frances,** d. 1866.—**Dayton, John,** withdrew about 1831.—****Dayton, John,** d. 1881.—DAYTON, MARY E.—**Deacon, John,** rem. by c.—DE BEVIS, FRANCIS.—*__De Graw, Ida,__ dau. of James De Graw, j. Sands-st. ch. at the age of 12, (Lewis Pease, pastor;) elected S.S.t. about the same time; received the first Bible ever given by the B'klyn S. S. Union. [Letter of Isaac Carhart.] She rem. by c., 1850; was a member several yrs. at Parkville, L. I.; d. 1877, age 66. She was quiet, but very earnest and faithful; distributed tracts, visited the sick and poor, studied God's word, communed with her Saviour, and was a witness for him wherever she went. [Rev. H. Aston, in Ch. Ad.] "The Bible she received from the S. S. Union," says Miss Vanderveer, "was her daily companion during all her subsequent life. As death approached she asked Mrs. Carhart to read, 'Blessed are they that do his commandments,' etc.; then saying, 'Now I feel as if I could go to sleep,' she sweetly fell into the repose of death."—****De Graw, James,** a pioneer cl. ldr. and trus. of this ch. In 1801 he mar. Elizabeth Debevoise. His birth, baptism, and marriage occurred on the holy Sabbath. Of his six children it is said that two still survive. He d. in his own house in Sands-st., May 8, 1835, age 68; bur. in the old grave-yard. When the ch. was enlarged it was built over his grave. [Isaac Carhart's letter.] He was sometimes irregular in his habits, but it is believed that he retained his membership in the ch.—****Elizabeth,** his w., d. Oct. 29, 1839, age 68.—**De Graw, Maria,** rem. 1850.—**De Gray, Deborah,** rem.—**De Gray, James,** cl. ldr., S.S.t., and S. S. supt.; one of the founders and 1st trustees of Fleet-st. ch. in 1850. His name stands on the list of the 1st board of stewards in Sum'f'd ch. in 1851.—**De Groff, John,** member of Yellow Hook (Bay Ridge) class in 1822.—**Delaney, Ann,** rem. by c.—DELANEY, MRS. MARGARET.—**Demmon, Isaac** and **Fanny M.,** rem. by c., 1866.—**Denike, Thos. S.,** went from Sands-st. to York-st. ch.; cl. ldr. in York-st., 1845-1849.—**Dennison, Sarah,** rem. by c., 1848.—*__Denton, Mary,__ member in 1798. —*__De Vinne, Daniel,__ b., of Catholic parents, in Londonderry, Ireland, Feb. 1, 1793. "Soon after his birth his father became involved in the Irish troubles and came to America with his family. They first settled near Troy. Young De V.'s earliest

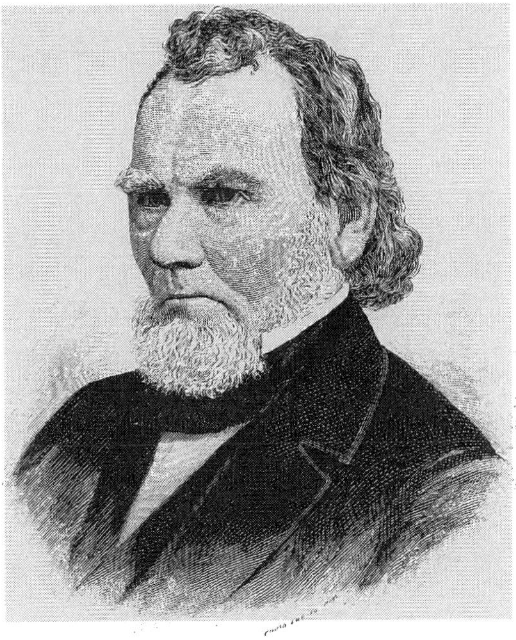

Danl. De Vinné

recollection was of the removal of the family soon after to the little village of Charleston, which, though less than 40 m. from Albany, was then a frontier town, with plenty of bears, wolves, and other wild animals, to annoy the settlers. He remembered well the excitement caused in the little township when the news came of Geo. Washington's death in 1799. The settlers were obliged to wait for particulars until spring opened and they could get a newspaper from Albany." [N. York Tribune.] At the age of 10 the boy was sent to school, and "learned something in spite of his teacher." He was called the "little Roman" by the school-boys because he stoutly upheld the Rom. Cath. faith. His mother was his only religious teacher, and her only source of instruction was a Bible which she sometimes borrowed. He was the subject of deep religious impressions, and in later years he wrote: "At the age of 9 I promised the Lord that I would be his forever, and when I became a man, I would be a priest." His mother d. when he was 11, having charged him "to obey his father, love his brothers and sisters, and, above all, to love and serve God." John Miller DeVinne, his father, was afterward drowned in the Hudson. Mary, a sister, became a Meth., mar. Peter Miller, and d. in Pine Grove, Mich., in 1881. The boy continued to receive Catholic training from his grandparents in Albany after his mother's death, but his heart was not satisfied. At 15 he made a tour of all the churches in Albany, except the Meth., which was deemed too heretical to be worthy of notice, in order to ascertain which was the true, but the result was he only became the more unhappy and "stood upon the verge of infidelity." At length, when nearly 16 yrs. of age, on the last night in 1809, he dropped into a watch-meeting in N. Pearl-st. M. E. ch. to warm himself, and he immediately felt "These are the people." He returned the next evening and knelt at the altar, and continued seeking till he found favor with God, just after midnight, Jan. 3, 1810. He wrote to the author, Jan. 8, 1875 : " Last week was my 65th anniversary in the M. E. ch. The Lord brought me into this ch. When I j., 7th Jan., 1810, I had never heard a whole Meth. sermon, had attended none of the meetings, never saw a Meth. book, no Meth. had ever spoken to me; the Lord led me." He had no one to guide him in his studies, but bought some old books at auction, and wasted much time and labor in studying "Locke on the Understanding," and "Lavorsier's Chemistry," and in trying to learn Eng. grammar from "Eutick's Pocket Dictionary." In much the same way he sought and actually gained a considerable knowledge of Latin and Greek, adding subsequently the French and Hebrew. He made practical use of this knowledge, and some yrs. previous to his death he had read the Greek Test. through 41 times. He heard Bp. Asbury, in Albany, in 1815. That same yr. he was in New York a short time, and identified with the first S. S. organization in that city; that same yr. opened a private school in Kirk's printing-house, B'klyn. He writes in his Journal: "B'klyn, at that time, was a mere village—one, too, of very modest dimensions. It was confined to the ferries at the foot of Fulton and Catharine sts., with a few scattering houses in the gore of land between said ferries, on land toward the navy-yard, and a few other ones on the turnpike toward Jamaica. Had any one at that period asserted that within 40 yrs. it would have contained hundreds of inhabitants, he would have been deemed insane. I attached myself to the Meth. ch. in Sands-st., the only one in the village." He assisted in the organization of the 1st S. S. in B'klyn. (See pp. 17, 19 of this vol.) He was the only one among the founders of this S. S. who lived to see the Rob't Raikes Centennial. After teaching 3 yrs. in B'klyn he sold out his school in 1818. That yr. "he j. an association formed in N. York for the support of a miss'y in N. Orleans—a society which was the germ of the Miss'y Society, organized a few months later. The same yr. he went to N. Orleans, and began a S. S. for slaves." [Stevens' Hist. M. E. Ch., vol. iv, p. 442.] This was a great offense, and the school was broken up. He was licensed as a loc. pr. about this time, and preached his first sermon, in Feliciana, Sept. 10, 1819, from Prov. viii, 36. *Ministerial Record:* 1819, short time, supply on Natchez cir., Miss., with John Manifee; 1819, Nov., (Miss. Conf.,) Opelousas (then called Attakapas) cir., La., with Ashley Hewit; 1820, ditto, without colleague; 1821, ord. deacon,—Amiti cir., with J. A. Blackburn: 1822, Claiborne cir., Miss., with M. Henderson; 1823, Lawrence cir., Ala., with T. Burpo; 1824, ord. elder,—(N. York Conf.,) Sullivan cir., N. Y., with Ira Ferris; 1825, N. York city cir., with P. P. Sandford, H. Stead, Wm. Jewett, J. Youngs, and H. Chase; 1826, Hempstead (previously called Jamaica) cir., L. I., with D. Holmes and B. Creagh; 1828, Stamford cir., Conn., with S. U. Fisher; 1829, ditto, with O. V. Amerman; 1830, N. Rochelle cir., with E. Hebard; 1831, ditto, with E. Washburn and Ira Ferris; 1832, Mt. Pleasant cir., with J. Reynolds; 1833, ditto, with Theodosius Clark; 1834, N. York, west cir., with J. B. Stratton, F. Reed, J. C. Green, and J. Tackaberry; 1835, ditto, with J. B. Stratton, J. C. Tackaberry, L. Mead, and E. E. Griswold; 1836, Harlem miss'n, with J. Luckey and J. C. Tackaberry; 1837, ditto, with Jas. Floy; 1838, Catskill and Durham cir., with A. C. Fields; 1839, ditto, with W. F. Gould; 1840, White Plains and Greenburg cir., with V. Buck; 1841, Peekskill cir., with Lorin Clark; 1842, Peekskill and Shrub Oak; 1843, Amenia; 1844–45, Cold Spring; 1846, New Castle and Pine's Bridge; 1847, Huntington cir., L. I., with W. M'K. Bangs; 1848, (N. York East Conf.,) ditto, with G. Hollis; 1849, New Rochelle cir., with C. B. Sing—his special charge, Rye; 1850, Rye;

1851-52, East Chester; 1853-54, Newtown, L. I.; 1855-56, Union Place, (Cypress Hills;) 1857-82, sup'd. On the Opelousas cir. "he preached every day except Monday to the whites, and every night to the slaves, besides leading classes and traveling from 30 to 40 m. a day, over prairies without roads or bridges; fording the bayous, or, when they were high, swimming them, or passing over by boats—decayed logs tied with grape-vines." His cir. was a range of 564 m., from Alexandria, on the Red River, to the gulf. He writes: "I have smiled many times since, and I suppose others did then, at my grotesque appearance—saddle-bags sticking out on both sides, crammed with books and tracts." [Ch. Ad.] His salary the 1st yr., after paying ferriage and horseshoeing, was less than $13; the next yr. it advanced prodigiously to $67; " and be it borne in mind that he was sent thither "*by his own request.*" At St. Mary's Court House the colored people made him a formal donation, amounting to nearly 50 cts.! He "lodged one night with pirates without knowing it," but "found that they could talk about religion." He was a member of Gen. Conf. in Balt., in 1824. On his way thither he visited ex-Pres. Jefferson, at his residence in Monticello, and was not agreeably impressed with his infidelity or his pro-slavery. To reach the Sullivan cir. that yr. he traveled on horseback 2,074 m. He writes of that cir., as the Shawangunk Mts., "where he saw frost in dog-days;" but the Lord blessed his labors, and he had "good times." There he and his colleague together rec'd $85. While in N. York (1825) he mar. Miss J. Augusta Low, a lady of uncommon personal attractiveness and culture, who is now passing the calm, evening of a beautiful Christian life in the company of her children. Of their introduction to the Hempstead cir., the following yr., he writes: "When I called upon the stewards of the cir. they said they had no parsonage, nor any hired house, and did not know where one could be hired. When leaving, they reminded me that the circuit allowed only $25 for house-rent. There was nothing personal in all this; it was the custom of the times. The people were not particular in regard to the preacher sent to them, and they were not solicitous in regard to his support. Many seemed to think that it was enough remuneration to the preacher simply to come and hear him. Many a well-to-do farmer gave only a shilling, or 25 cts., per quarter, for himself and family. If any one gave half or a whole dollar, it was a matter of surprise. Nor were the sisterhood any more provident or active in ch. matters. It was some weeks after our arrival before any of them looked in upon us. . . . I received that yr. $180, out of which I had to pay part of my rent and find hay for my horse, when at home. The cir., however, gave $30 additional by a 'spinning.' This was the technical name for a donation or surprise, from the fact that the present usually

consisted chiefly of flax, which the young women had spun for
the preacher's family." On this cir., in 2 yrs., he preached 560
serm., traveled 4,800 m., and received 471 probationers. At
Stamford, in 1830, there were 100 conversions. [Ch. Ad.]
" He was banished in 1836, (in the estimation of his friends,) for
his abolition sentiments, to a place on L. I., [the appointment
does not appear in the printed Minutes,] where they did not
desire, because they could not support, a preacher; but by the
intercession of others he was transferred to the Harlem miss'n,
then embracing 27th-st. and all north to the Harlem River, with
$275 to sustain a family of 9, and flour at $13 a bbl. The next
was the memorable Greene-st. Conf. of 1838, in which he, with
others, who felt that 'every thing could be borne, but nothing
conceded' to the 'monster evil,' slavery, was proscribed and
punished by being sent to Catskill." [N. York East Conf.
Minutes, 1883, p. 55. See also Stevens' History M. E. Ch.,
vol. iv, p. 423, in reference to his hatred of slavery.] During
his 40 yrs. of effective service on 24 cir. and sta., he traveled on
horseback, or in very poor carriages, 61,678 m., and preached
8,440 serm., a little over 4 per week, and aided in the erection
of 13 new churches. He personally received 3,756 probationers,
averaging 94 per annum for 40 yrs. His receipts averaged $327
a yr. [See Min. of Conf's, 1883, p. 91.] He preached in 1869
a semi-centennial sermon, from which we have quoted above.
The following paragraph, by the Rev. S. H. Platt, will be read
with great satisfaction : " His later years were blessed far beyond those which usually fall to the lot of the retired minister,
in the rare devotion of sons who vied with each other to promote his welfare and do him honor; in the tender ministry of
daughters who delighted to display the noblest qualities of
womanhood in his service ; and in the matchless charm and
peerless comfort of the wedded tie that had been cemented by
the mutual toils of 58 such years." [N. Y. East Conf. Min.]
Not long before life's close he was seen at the annual conf. and
the N. York preacher's meeting. He d. at his home in Morris-
ania, N. Y., Feb. 10, 1883, age 90 yrs.; funeral, Feb. 14, from
the M. E. ch. in M. Dr. D. Curry and the Revs. S. H. Platt
and G. Hollis made addresses. Among the other ministers
present were A. N. Molyneaux, J. H. Stansbury, R. Crook, J.
A. Roche, T. N. Laine, C. T. Mallory, and W. C. Smith. The
interment took place in " Woodlawn." " Daniel De V. was a
man for his times. Conscientious to the very verge of monastic
rigidity, catholic in his instincts, and kind in his feelings. . . .
In his habits of study he was a model." His published writings
are : " The M. E. Ch. and Slavery ; " " The Irish Primitive
Ch.," pronounced by Dr. G. L. Taylor a " treasure " and a
" gem ; " " A History of the M. E. Ch. in New Rochelle," (in
Meth. Quar., 1832 ;) and various other articles written for our

church periodicals. He wrote to the author: " Now, my dear brother, let us be holy. Most Christians are living far below St. Paul's standard. I fear the present working of affairs will not convert the world." He was short and stout, with a countenance of unique expression, well represented by the portrait, a musical but rather monotonous voice, and articulation somewhat indistinct, particularly in his old age.—*De Voe, Isaac, b. in B'klyn; cabinet-maker by trade, and a vet. of 1812, [Stiles, Hist. B'klyn, vol. i, p. 453;] trus. and cl. ldr. in Sands-st. ch. In 1819 his plain-spoken pastor wrote opposite his name, at the head of his class record, " rather crooked." The exact meaning of the comment and the occasion of making it are not quite apparent at this time. He was certainly much esteemed in later years. After removing from the mother ch. in Sands st., he was cl. ldr. in Wash'gt'n-st. ch., in the fellowship of which he d. in 1859, age 72. [Ch. Records.] His confidence and faith were unshaken. He said, " I don't hope, but *I know* I am going to heaven." Bur. in Evergreen cem. His first w. was Mary (Cook.)—**Rachel, (Bourdette,)** wid. of the above, was received into Sands-st. ch. by Wm. Ross; rem. to Wash'g'ton-st. ch., and finally to 18-st. ch.; was living, (1882,) age 91. Their surviving children are 1 son and 3 daus.—*De Vosnell, John, member in 1798.—De Vosney, John, rem. by c.—Dey, John, rem. by c.—DEYO, GEO. A.—Dickerson, Jas., rem. —*Dikeman, John, was b., in the town of Hempstead, L. I., Mar. 31, 1795; clerk in a store in the small village of B'klyn at 15; not pleased with the business, went to Phila.; returned shortly after to B'klyn, and studied law with Judge Radcliffe, teaching school to pay expenses. In 1815 he j. the society to prevent and suppress crime in B'klyn; mar. Miss Susan Remsen, and in 1816, became principal of the first public school ever opened in B'klyn. That yr. he and his w. taught in the 1st B'klyn S. S., and he never afterward lost his interest in secular and religious education. He opened a law-office cor. Fulton and Henry; at 29 was village trustee and clerk of the board; in 1820 appointed Judge of the Court of Common Pleas, an office at that time filled by the governor and State senate—term, 5 yrs. He received license as a loc. pr. in 1827, which office he resigned in 1830. His name appears among the loc. prs. in the plan of Flushing cir., 1828. He was cl. ldr. in 1839; among the founders of the Wash'gt'n-st. ch. in 1831, and remained a member thereof till his death. Until 1825 he was known as a Jacksonian Democrat, but was that yr. elected a member of the Assembly on the Native American ticket. He became one of the lessees of the South and B'klyn ferries in 1839; afterward one of the managers of the B'klyn Union Ferry Co.; elected Co. Judge by Republicans a 2d time in 1864; w. d. that yr.; vice-pres. King's Co. Inebriate Home in 1867; next yr. retired to private life; d. at his residence, Aug. 23, 1879, in his 85th yr. Flags on the court-house and city-hall in B'klyn were placed at half-mast. In appearance Judge D. was tall and spare, with an

JOHN DIKEMAN.

interesting but not handsome countenance, indicative of great strength of intellect and of will. He was a close observer of men and things, and well informed on secular and religious topics.— *Susan, w. of the above, dau. of Isaac Remsen, and step-dau. of Burdet Stryker; j. Sands-st. ch. in early life; d. Mar. 20, 1864, in her 70th yr. Judge D. and w. are bur. in "Greenwood." [See tombstones.] Of their 9 children, 4 were living in 1882.—**Dillont, Frederick** and **Sadie**, rem. by c., 1882.— **Dillont, John Frank**, S.S.t.; came from London; received by C. Fletcher into Sands-st. ch. by c. from Tarrytown, Asbury M. E. ch.; rem. by c., 1881, to Hanson Pl. ch., thence to Grace ch.; publisher of The Prospect Quarterly, and vice-pres. of the Young People's Association of Grace ch.— ****Mahala**, w. of the above, d. in 1877, age about 36.—DIONIAN, CHRISTINA.—**Dirgin, Mrs. Maria**, rem. by c., 1883.—**Dixon, Jos.**, rem. by c., 1873.—**Doane, Mary**, rem. by c., 1866.—**Dodge, Emma H.**, rem.—**Dolgbrest, Elizabeth**, rem. by c., 1865.—DONALDSON, WM.—**Donnelly, Jane**, mar.; see Goodwin—**Dorlon, Alice**, rem.—DORLON, EDWIN W.—DOUGHTY, MRS. MATILDA.—

DOUGLAS, D. H.—DOUGLAS, GEORGIANA.—**Douglas, Mrs. Georgiana W.**, d. 1852.—DOUGLAS, MAMIE.—**Dow, Andrew** and **Catharine**, rem. by c., 1869.—**Drake, C. W.**, loc. pr., Drew Sem., 1869; rem. by c., 1869; member 1 yr.—DREDGE, ALFRED, cl. ldr.; b. in Somersetshire, Eng., in 1827; parents were Baptists; at 25 conv. among the Methodists in Quebec; moved to Toronto; ldr. of the largest class in Richmond-st. ch. of that city; trus. many yrs.; std. 20 yrs.; came to B'klyn in 1880.—DREDGE, MRS. ALFRED.—DREW, CORNELIA.—**Drew, Eliza**, wid. of Geo.; d. 1874.—**Drew, Geo.**, d. in Texas, 1849; dealer in house-furnishing goods; a true Xn.—**Drew, Mary**, rem.—DRUMGOLD, MRS. ARMINDA.—DRUMMOND, AMANDA.—DUCKER, MRS. ELIZA A.—DUCKER, MARIA E.—*Ducker, Wm.**, exh. and loc. pr., 1827; cl. ldr., 1834; trus. in Wallabout (De Kalb ave.) ch., 1838; an Israelite indeed. He was a lighterman, plying his vocation on the East River; dressed somewhat after the Quaker fashion. The Rev. Geo. Hollis writes: " I heard him preach his trial sermon in the Sands-st. ch. He was my friend when I needed one." He is said to have embraced Millerism in 1843. He d. some yrs. ago, and is bur. in "Greenwood."—**Duffour, Nicholas**, d. 1850.—**Duncey, Timothy**, rem. by c., 1848.—**Dunkinson, Bethia**, mar. A. Van Horne.—**Dunn, Deborah**, d. 1870.—**Dunn, Francis** and **Amelia**, rem. by c., 1866.—**Dunn, James**, rem. by c., 1866.—**Dunn. Rebecca**, rem. by c.; 1866.—**Dunn, Mrs.**, d. 1874.—**Dunn, Mrs. Sarah**, rem. by c., 1874.—DUNN, MRS. VIRGINIA.—**Dunn, Wm., Jane, and Margaret**, rem. by c., 1870; members 1 yr.—**Dunn, Mrs.** and **Miss Ada**, rem. by c., 1872.—**Duren, Henry**, S.S.t., at the same time supt. of a German M. E. S. S. in Wyckoff-st.; rem. to Fleet-st. ch.; then to First Pl. ch.; then to Carlton ave. (Simpson) ch.; cl. ldr. there 12 yrs.—**Duston, Walter**, rem. by c.—**Dykes, Jos.** or **Sam'l**, cl. ldr., 1835.—EAGAN, JENNIE.—**Eaton, Marietta W.**, d. Sept. 1, 1870, age 25.—**Edmonds, John Albert**, b. in London, Eng., Jan. 25, 1813; parents belonged to the Established ch.; conv. Apr. 1, 1831, and j. the Wesleyan Connection; mar. Charlotte Fields, March 3, 1833, and 4 yrs. later came with wife and 1 child to N. York; j. Bedford-st. ch.; soon afterward rem. by c. to Franklin-st. ch, Newark, N. J., and was licensed, first as an exh. and then as a loc. pr., and preached frequently in Orange, Belleville, and other places. His grocery business not succeeding in Newark, he rem. to B'klyn in 1839; j. the Sands-st. ch., also became a member of the Loc. Prs'. Association, preached nearly every Sabbath, generally twice, sometimes thrice, always walking to and from his app'ts. E. B'klyn, Gravesend, New Utrecht, and E. New York were among the country places visited. He preached also in Sands-st., York-st., and Wash'gt'n-st. churches. He labored in Patchogue, L. I., in the early part of 1840, (J. B. Merwin, the pastor, being called South to settle the affairs of his deceased brother,) and his efforts were abundantly blessed. The ensuing spring the quar. conf. of Sands-st. recommended him to the Annual Conf. *Pastoral Record:* 1840, (N. York Conf.,) Huntington cir., L. I., with J. Nixon; 1841, ditto, with O. Starr; 1842, ord. deacon,—Westhampton; 1843, Cutchogue and Southold; 1844, ord. elder; 1844–45, Guilford, Conn.; 1846, New Britain; 1847, Bloomfield; 1848, (N. York East Conf.,) ditto; 1849–50, King-st, N. Y.; 1851–52, Sag Harbor; 1853–54, (N. York Conf.,) Red Hook; 1855–56, Rondout; 1857–59, sup'y; 1860, Milton; 1861, Hyde Park; 1862, Pleasant Valley; 1863–65, Spencertown and Chatham Four Corners; 1866–67, Pawlings; 1868–73, sup'd; 1874, Pawlings and Reynoldsville; 1875, N. York, Greene-st. and Duane; 1876–77, N. York, Asbury; 1878–79, Hartsdale; 1880–84, sup'd, residence, Sag Harbor, N. Y. His 1st w., Charlotte, a devoted Xn., d. Jan. 25, 1859. On the 6th of May, 1861, he was mar. to Miss Sarah A. Bassett, his present w. She is nearly blind, several yrs. having elapsed since she was able to read a word, and, in addition, she has been confined to her bed as a paralytic for sevaral months past; yet, with a mind clear and bright, she rejoices in the God of her salvation. Mr. E., though suffering intensely from rheumatism, is cheerful, bearing uncomplainingly the trial of his superannuation and the loss of his property (now so greatly needed) through the dishonesty of another. He has done excellent service for the church, and is gratefully and affectionately remembered by many.—**Edsall, Wm.**, off. S. S. miss'y soc.; became a Presbyterian.—**Edwards, Abbie C.**, rem.—**Edwards, Phœbe**, rem.—**Edwards, Rebecca A.**, rem.—****Eichell, Eliza**, d. 1872.—**Elmendorf, D. K.**, cl. ldr., about 1866; rem.—**Embree, Isaac**, rem. by c., 1865.—**Embree, Isabella**, rem. by c., 1868.—**Emmons, A. W.**, rem. by c.—EMORY, FLORENCE.—EMORY, GRACE A.—EMORY, MARIA L.—**Emsley, Harriet**, rem. by c., 1864.—***Engle, Sam'l**, member in 1798, father of James C. Engle.—***Engle, Sarah**, member in 1798. —**Ensign, Elizabeth**, rem.—**Erwin, Mary Jane**, rem., 1846. —ESPENSCHEID, JOHN M., S.S.t., std., cl. ldr., S. S. supt., and several yrs. financial sec. of the ch.; was b. in Sodus, N. Y., of pious parents, who were natives of Germany, and members of the German Evangelical Association, and whose children all became Xns. He was conv. at 15, at a union prayer-meeting in a country school-house; came a probationer to Sands-st. ch., B'klyn, in July, 1858, (J. B. Hagany, pastor.)—ESPENSCHEID, HELEN.—ESPENSCHEID, MARGARET, w. of John M.—ESTES, EDWIN C., S.S.t. b.; in N. C.; went to Ala.; came thence to B'klyn in 1836; most of time a member of Sands-st.

ch.—**Everitt, Richard,** trus., one of the 1st, in 1794, and some time treas. of the board; d. of yellow fever in 1798—the 1st *recorded* death among the members. Hannah Stryker had preceded him to the home above, but there is no book containing a record of that event. Mr. E. had a stall in the old Fly Market in N. York. [Stiles' Hist. B'klyn, vol. ii, p. 127.]—**Sarah,** w. of the above; was a member in 1798. Their son, Thomas Howard, b. 1796, was baptized by Bp. Asbury. She mar. after his death, and d. in the faith; see M'Kenney.—**Fanning, Martin,** cl. ldr., and his w., **Margaret,** rem by c.—**Fanning, Mary A.,** mar. Mr. Campbell.—**Farley, Clara,** mar. a Mr. Campbell, and after his death a Mr. Fisher.—FARLEY, JOHN C.—**Farnell, Alfred F.,** the last man licensed as a loc. pr. in this ch.; came from Eng. to N. Haven, Conn.; thence to B'klyn, and j. Sands-st. ch., about 1866; rem. by c., 1873; formerly dealt in gents' furnishing goods, now proprietor of "Ye Olde Booke Shoppe," B'klyn; not connected with the M. E. ch. at present.—**Farnell, Jane,** rem. by c., 1873.—**Faucett, Ellen,** rem. by c. to Eng., 1881.—**Fay, John G.,** (often called by his friends Governor Fay,) was S.S.t., off. S. S. miss'y soc., cl. ldr., S. S. supt., and loc. pr. When a young man he rem. from Eng., his native country, to S. A.; was conv. in Buenos Ayres; aided the Rev. John Dempster in his S. American mission work; came to B'klyn about 1852. He was a pure-minded, conscientious Xn., distinguished for gentleness in his deportment toward all. He exerted a remarkable power over young men, drew a large number into his Bible class, developed their self-dependence and self-respect, organized a debating society, and by various means cultivated in them a literary taste. He d. in May, 1865, in his 65th yr., meeting the grim messenger with the calmness of one fully prepared. Only a few hours before his death, when his eldest son said, "Father, rest upon my arm," he replied, "Underneath me are the everlasting arms." He is bur. in "Greenwood."—**Elizabeth P.,** his w., was b. in Eng., and mar. to Mr. F. in S. A. She d. in Sept., 1873, in her 75th yr.—FAY, JOHN E., son of the above; S.S.t. and sec. of S. S.; was b. in Buenos Ayres; j. Sands-st. ch. in 1853, (H. J. Fox, pastor.)—*Mary H., his w., dau. of the Rev. John B. Hagany, D.D.; rem. by c., 1872; d. in Jan., 1877.—**Fay, Henry G.,** youngest son of John G., was b. in Buenos Ayres; j. Sands-st. ch in 1853; was S.S.t., S. S. supt., std., and pres't of the S. S. miss'y soc.; rem. by c. to Sum'f'd ch., in 1878, where he was made std. in 1880.—*Mary (Thorn), w. of Henry G. Fay, sister of A. B. Thorn; was S.S.t., treas. of the W. F. M. S., a co-worker in the "Home for Friendless Women and Children," and the "Home for Aged Men" in B'klyn, and in the "Five Points' Mission" in N. York. She was b. in N. York city; j. Greene-st. M. E. ch. in early life, (S. D. Ferguson, pastor.) In 1851, with her family, she moved to B'klyn, and j. Sands-st. ch.; after many yrs. of efficient service she rem. by c., with her husband, to Sum'f'd ch., where she manifested the same diligence, zeal, and fidelity, until she d. from congestion of the brain, May 30, 1880. She was bur. in "Greenwood," amid the most eloquent tokens of affection and respect. "Mrs. Fay possessed many eminent and engaging qualities. Her intellect was bright and comprehensive, distinguished alike for feminine delicacy and masculine strength. Her temper was kind and genial, her manner polished, graceful, and winning. Her force of character made her eminently competent for practical affairs. She discharged her trusts with a conscientious fidelity which won the esteem of all who knew her." [Rev. G. F. Kettell, in Ch. Ad.]—*Fellows, Chas. H., S.S.t., one of the original officers of the S. S. miss'y soc.; was b. in Stonington, Conn., Jan. 26, 1819; conv. in New London at 20; came to B'klyn, and j. Sands-st. ch., in 1848, (Dr. N. Bangs, pastor;) rem. by c., and helped to organize Fleet-st. ch., in 1850; thence went to Central ch.; thence to Gothic; ultimately to S. 3d-st., where he remained nearly 35 yrs., and was S. S. supt. from 1857 to his death, Dec. 18, 1880—23 yrs. "He built for himself a noble memorial in the character of the young men and women who grew up under his influence." [Rev. A. S. Graves, in Ch. Ad.]— Feltham, Wm., rem. by c., 1849.—*Fenn, Hannah, rem. by c., 1850.—*Ferguson, Eleanor, member in 1798.—Ferguson, Sarah E., rem. by c., 1880.—Ferman, Eliza, of Yellow Hook (Bay Ridge) class, 1822.—Ferris, M. A., rem. —Fichter, Wm. H. and Mary C., rem. by c., 1882.—Field, Dan'l, exh., and 1st ldr. of the Yellow Hook (Bay Ridge) class in 1822.—Field, Eliza, rem. to Flushing.—Finch, Wm. Stanbury, nephew of the late alderman, John Stanbury, of B'klyn; b. in South Zeal, Devon, Eng., Nov. 28, 1821; baptized in the South Tawton English parish ch., of which his parents, Wm. and Mary Finch, were members; educated in the village school and at Jendle and Vissicks' establishment in Plymouth. At the latter place he worshiped in the Ebenezer Meth. ch.; attended S. S. at Sticklepath; was conv. under the earnest ministry of Dan'l Blamey, who afterward came to America; taught in the S. S. and worked as a loc. pr. until about 1840; then went to London to finish his business training; was enlisted in the large S. S. of the Queen-st. Meth. ch., of that city; aided in the circuit work; listened frequently to eloquent sermons by Dr. Beaumont, Dr. Jabez Bunting, the inimitable "Billy Dawson," and many others; was present at the ordination of the 1st 6 missionaries to the Fiji Islands—Dr. Newton's text that day, "What hath God wrought!" In 1844 he returned to his early home, and mar. Miss Amelia Moore; came as a loc. pr., with letter of removal, to Sands-st. ch., B'klyn, in 1846, (Dr. N.

Bangs, pastor;) after the great fire, in 1848, rem. by c. to Toledo, O.; afterward to Delafield, Wis.; back to Toledo; finally settled in Toronto, Canada, in 1854; j. the Richmond-st. ch., and there " organized the first infant-class in the Meth. Ch. of Canada—a wonder in those days, born of recollections of the Sands-st. infant-school, where Bro. Cartwright taught the little ones." For 30 yrs. Mr. F. has taught classes of little children, numbering on an average, 100. Some of these lambs of the flock have grown to maturity, and are now moving in spheres of large usefulness in the ch., while others have passed into the "upper fold." On the erection of the Metropolitan ch. (cathedral of Methodism) in Toronto, he rem. by c. to that ch., and taught the infant-class, working with great profit and joy; is still a member of the quarterly board, and "rejoicing in a present and full salvation." He j. about the first total abstinence society some 50 yrs. ago, and has helped many others to do the same. He is not an ordained minister, but has been a co-laborer in the gospel with the foremost preachers of Canadian Methodism, such as the Rev. Drs. Egerton Ryerson, Lachlan Taylor, Anson Green, and Wm. M. Punshon, and with many princely laymen, of whom John M'Donald is one. He rejoices greatly in a united Methodism, extending from Newfoundland, on the east, to Vancouver's Island, on the Pacific, toiling faithfully alongside of our mighty M. E. ch. to spread scriptural holiness over these lands.—**Amelia,** his w., is a dau. of Dr. Denis Moore, of Exeter, Devon., Eng., and sister of the late high-sheriff and mayor of Exeter, Wm. D. Moore; rem. by ç. from Sands-st. ch. with her husband, and is still active in the ch. and other benevolent associations.—**Fink, Wm.,** rem. by c., 1849.—***Fish, Elizabeth,** sister to Mrs. Jane Vanderveer; j. Sands-st. ch. in 1819, (A. M'Caine, pastor;) after more than 60 yrs., rem. by c. to Sum'f'd ch.; her home was with Mrs. M. F. Odell, where she d. in May, 1881, age 95 : bur. in " Greenwood." She never married.—**Fisher, Elizabeth,** rem.— **Fisher, Geo. M.,** rem. by c.—**Fisher, Georgiana,** w. of Geo. M.; rem. by c., 1868; see Vining.—**Fitch, Sarah A.,** rem. —FLAMMIE, ELIZA.—FOLGER, ELLA, S. S. supt. 14 yrs. —**Fonnham, Mary E.,** rem. — FOSTER, HORACE.— **Forbes, Louisa H. S.,** rem. by c., 1866.—**Forbes, Maria M.,** rem. by c., 1871.—**Foster, Marsh,** rem. by c.—**Foster, Mary,** rem. to Johnson-st. ch., 1850.—**Foster, Solon C.,** conv. under the labors of J. N. Maffit; cl. ldr. in Sands-st. ch.; j. Johnson-st. ch.; went with J. C. Green to 1st Cong. Meth. ch., and remained a short time. Mr. Green boarded with his family. Mr. F. and his w. have for years resided in Hempstead, L. I., and are members of the M. E. ch. in that place.— ****Foster, Wm.,** member in 1798; made cl. ldr. 1808; afterward trus.; by occupation a butcher, and later engaged in the lumber business with his son-in-law, B. R. Prince ; lost the most of his property. He was regarded as one of the stanch citizens of B'klyn, a thorough Meth., and a member of the Society to Suppress Vice and Crime. [See Stiles' Hist. B'klyn, vol ii, pp. 14, 38.] At his house Meth. preachers always found a good home. He d. in 1846, age 67, and was bur. in the old ch. yard, in the same grave with his 1st w., **Anna, who " d. in the Lord," in 1826. Children : Elijah Woolsey, deceased ; Wm. A.; Sarah Ann, who mar. B. K. Prince ; Electa ; and Hannah.— **Catharine, 2d w. of the above, one of the early members of Willett-st. ch., N. York ; j. Sands-st. ch. years ago ; d. 1870; bur. in Tuckahoe, N. Y.—Foster, Wm., 2d., cl. ldr.; came from Johnson-st. ch., where he was cl. ldr. in 1850 and std. in 1857 ; a zealous, earnest Meth. He and his w., Sarah, rem. by c. to Cal., whither one or more of their children had preceded them.—FOWLER, ABBY J.—Fowler, Corrina, rem. by c., 1868.—**Fowler, Mary, "d. happy," 1832.—FOWLER, MRS. SARAH E.—Frazier, Elizabeth, rem.—Frazier, James, rem. to N. York, 1850.—Frazier, Hannah. rem.— Frazier, Sarah E., dau. of Thos. ; mar. Benj. Payne ; rem. to Painted Post, N. Y.—Frazier, Stephen Richardson, std. and cl. ldr. With his w. j. by c., 1866 ; rem. by c., 1867 ; and again rem. by c., 1873.—*Sarah W., his w., d. in Ill., where they had resided for some time.—*Frazier, Thos., cl. ldr. and trus.; conv. at a camp-meeting, in 1813 ; soon j. the Meth., with whom he remained in fellowship for more than 50 yrs. He was rem. by c. to N. J., in 1849 ; subsequently j. at Nostrand ave., and was a std. in that ch. at the time of his death, June 9, 1868. He had arrived at his 80th yr., but he d. without any premonition. He had led in family prayer, as had been his custom from the day after his conversion, and that morning had prayed particularly for every one of his children. Breakfast over, he was engaged in conversation, when his heart suddenly ceased to beat. He was ready. [Ch. Ad.] He was mar. thrice ; 10 of his 12 children are living, (1883.) Mrs. Nathan T. Beers, of B'klyn, is his dau. [See also Frazier, Chadwick, and Powell.]—**Ann, his 1st w., sister of Simon and Rev. Marvin Richardson; d. about 1829, age 29 ; bur. in old Sands-st. ch. yard ; afterward in " Cypress Hills," by the side of her husband.—**Frederick, Eleanor, " d. in the Lord."—**Freeman, Fanny, d. 1837.— Freeman, Matthias, rem. by c., 1866.—FREY, MRS. AMELIA.—FREY, ANNIE.—Frey, Elizabeth, rem. by c., 1873.—FROST, SARAH.—Fulcher, Eliza, rem. by c., 1878.— Fuller, Edwin, rem. by c., 1881.—Fuller, Wm. J., rem.— Fulton, Margaret, rem. to Gravesend.—FURLONG, MARIA.—**Furman, Elizabeth, d. 1818.—FURNAVEL, SAM'L.—**Gable, Conklin L., sexton ; was b. in Riverhead, L. I.; conv. about 1836 ; d. 1859 ; bur. in " Cypress Hills."—

Ellen A. (Cregg,) w. of the above, d. about 1836.—GABLE, ELLA.—Gable, Julia E., dau. of Conklin L.; rem. by c., 1879; now of Hanson pl. ch.—**Gage, Susan, d. suddenly, 1840.— **Gale, Addie, w. of Frank A.; d. 1861, age 27; bur. in "Greenwood."—Gale, Frank A., S.S.t. and off. S. S. miss'y soc., rem.—Gale, Andrew D., cl. ldr.; b. in Harrison, Westchester Co., N. Y.; j. Allen-st. ch., N. York; then John-st., where he was S. S. supt.; rem. to Sands-st. ch., B'klyn; and finally to Jersey City; a member of Emory M. E. ch. His w., Susan, rem. by c.—Galloway, John, withdrew.—Gandishand, Mrs. Harriet, mar. Wm. M'Donald.—Gandishand, Mrs. H., d. 1873, age 49; bur. in "Greenwood."—GARDNER, FRANK.—Gardner, Stephen H. and Mary A., rem. by c., 1882.—GARRICK, MRS. MARY.—*Garrison, Jacob, son of John; cl. ldr.; a butcher by occupation. It is said that he became quite deranged, and d. at the home of his brother in Flatlands. He left a w. and a number of sons and daughters.— *Huldah, his w., sister of the Rev. Marvin. Richardson, d.— **Garrison, John, known as Judge Garrison, was an early cl. ldr. and trus. in this ch. He was of Dutch extraction, and a native of Gravesend, but during nearly his entire life-time a resident of B'klyn: for some yrs. in a farm-house on Fulton-st.,, opp. Hicks-st., afterward in a large yellow dwelling, cor. Wash'gt'n and High sts. He had some time a stand in the Fly Market, N. York. Having entered the legal profession, he held the office of Judge of the Municipal Court. He was one of the presidential electors who cast the vote for Andrew Jackson in 1828. When 29 yrs. of age he heard a discussion by two clergymen (one a Calvinist and the other a Meth.) which established his belief in unlimited redemption and human freedom, and confirmed his purpose to repent of his sins and cast in his lot with the little band of Methodists. The following yr. (1794) he was appointed cl. ldr., probably as the immediate successor of N. Snethen, and retained the office until his death. From the 1st election, in 1794, he was a trus., and some time treas. of the board. He sternly resisted innovations and so-called reforms, and used his powerful influence to prevent divisions in the ch. His extreme conservatism led him to withhold sympathy and support from the S. S. long after more progressive men had given their aid and indorsement to

JOHN GARRISON.

the cause. Against the name of John Garrison the words
" Earnest, strong-willed " may be seen upon the margin of the
ch. register, written with pencil, in 1819, by the pastor for the
benefit of his successor. Stiles gives the following description
of Judge Garrison : " He was 6 ft. 2 in. high, remarkably large,
weighing 300 lbs. . . . He was invariably dressed in a suit of
' pepper and salt ' mixed clothing, cut very loose. Many pleasant
stories are told of his queer ways and sayings. . . . In
politics Mr. G. was a violent Democrat of the old school, and
was naturally regarded by some as a man of vindictive feelings,
while, in fact, a kinder-hearted man never lived." [Hist. B'klyn,
vol. ii, p. 79.] The portrait on preceding page was copied by S.
E. Warren from Guy's celebrated " snow-scene," painted in 1820.
Mr. G. was overcome by heat and fatigue while visiting the
grave of Benj. Abbott, for the purpose of erecting a monument
to the memory of the old hero, and d. shortly afterward (1831)
in Christian triumph, pronouncing blessings upon each of his
dear ones, and saying, " Farewell; meet me in heaven." His
age was 67. [N. Levings, in Meth. Quar. Rev., 1831, p. 258.]
He is bur. under the ch.—**Garrison, Mary C. H.**, wid. of
the above, sister to Isaac and Jos. Moser, d. 1839, age 69. She
was a woman of great loveliness, one of the early Sands-st. members,
very active, and sometimes led the class. [See notice of
her mother, Margaret Moser.] The names of John and Mary
Garrison are inscribed on a memorial tablet on the interior wall
of the ch. Of the sons, Jacob, John Fletcher, and Thomas
were with the father in the butcher business. [Stiles' Hist.
B'klyn, vol. ii, p. 38.] Nelson was a physician, and Sam'l was
a lawyer. They are all dead. One dau., Mary, resides in
Mechanicsville, N. Y.; another dau., Rachel, mar. a Mr. Stanley.
She is dead.—**Garrison, Mrs. Mary J.**, rem. by c., 1874.
—GASCOIGNE, FRANK.—**Gascoigne, James B.**, b. in
Yorkshire, Eng.; conv., and j. the Meth.; came to Amer. while
a young man; j. John-st. ch., N. Y.; engaged in the hardware
trade; rem. to B'klyn; served the Sands-st. ch. faithfully as
S. S. supt. and std.; highly honored for his integrity and good
judgment. His name appears on the list of the 1st board of
managers of the parent Miss'y Soc'y, elected in 1819. He d.
about 1859, age 76. His 1st w., Ann (Taylor), d. His 2d
w., *Sarah (Mortimer), survived him about 4 yrs.—**Gascoigne,
Joshua I.**, son of Jas. B., was one of the original off.
of the S. S. miss'y soc'y, sec. and treas. of S. S., and std. When
a child he was a scholar in the Sands-st. S. S.; conv. at a campmeeting
in N. J., whither he went with M. F. Odell. In 1872
rem. by c. Now a std. in Nostrand ave. ch.—**Lavinia**, w. of
the above, sister of Mrs. H. G. Fay and Abia B. Thorn; rem.
by c., 1872.—**Gascoigne, Mrs. Phœbe**, rem. by c., 1881.—
Gascoigne, Phœbe B., dau. of Jas. B., a S.S.t., rem. by c.,

1881.—GASNER, MARY.—GILBERT, HELEN.—**Gill, Jos. Hamilton,** was b. in Londonderry, N. of Ireland, where in early life he united with the Meth. He came to this country when about 21. Having been engaged in the dry-goods business in Belfast, he followed the same occupation in N. York and B'klyn. Following the advice of Bp. Foster, he went to Evanston, Ill., and was graduated at the N. Western Univ. and Garrett Bib. Inst. *Ministerial Record:* 1871, (E. Maine Conf.; transferred to Rock River Conf.,) no app't named; 1872, (India Conf.,) Moradabad and Sambhal, with F. M. Wheeler; 1873, Moradabad; 1874, ord. deacon; 1874–75, Paori; 1876, ditto, with T. S. Johnson, sup'y; 1877, ord. elder—(North India Conf.,) Paori; 1878, Gurhwal; 1879–80, ditto, with F. W. Greenwold; 1881–82, sup'y; 1883, Moradabad cir., with I. Fieldbrave.— **Gillen, Cordelia F.** and **Mrs. Harriet E.,** rem. by c. to Fleet-st. ch., 1879.—**Glendenning, Wm.,** rem.—*Gold, Ellen, w. of James; one of the original members of Yellow Hook (Bay Ridge) class, 1822; d. a Meth. in Bay Ridge.— **Goodell, Oliver,** rem. by c., 1882.—GOODWIN, EMILY A. —GOODWIN, MRS. E. A., (one **Mrs. Emily A. Goodwin** rem. by c., 1867.)—**Goodwin, Maria,** mar.; see Furlong.—**Goodwin, Michael** and **Jane E.,** rem. by c. to Simpson ch.— **Goodwin, Susan,** mar. Mr. Bassett.—**Goodwin, Wm. J.,** rem.—**Gould, Brewster,** rem. to Cal., 1849.—GOULD, DEBORAH.—**Gould, Eliza,** rem. to Huntington, L. I., 1849.— GRACE, VICTORIA.—GRAHAM, ISABELLA.—**Graves, Milo A.,** rem. by c.—**Green. Jas. H.,** withdrew.—**Gray, Anna,** mar.; see Sheriden.—**Gray, Jacob M.,** cl. ldr., 1843. —****Gray, Mary L.,** d. May 27, 1872, age 23.—GREEN, CHAS. E —GREEN, JOANNA.—**Green, Mrs. Catharine C.,** mar.; see Henderson.—**Greener, Ann,** rem.—**Gregory, Geo. E.** and **Elizabeth,** rem. by c., 1866.—GRIFFIN, HENRY E.—****Griffin, Jemima,** "d. in the Lord," 1842.— GRIFFIN, ORLANDO; (a person of the same name rem. by c.)—GRIGGS, A.—GRIGGS, ARTHUR L.—GRISWOLD, BESSIE. — GRITMAN, MRS. JANETTE. — GRUMAN, MRS. PHŒBE J.—**Gurley, Mrs. Ella,** rem. by c., 1871.— **Guhraner, Addie,** rem. by c., 1883.—GUHRAUER, HENRY H., S. S. sec. and lib'n.—GUMBLE, LINAS.—GURLITZ, AUGUSTUS T., cl. ldr., std., and S.S.t.; a Russian by birth; lawyer in N. York.—GURLITZ, AMY, w. of the above; dau. of Dr. D. S. Landon.

Habberton, E. S., rem.—**Habberton, S. F.,** rem. by c. to Flushing, L. I., 1850.—HACKETT, AMELIA.—**Haddon, Mary,** rem.—**Haff, Benj. A.,** bro. of Mrs. Egbert Acker; S.S.t.; conv. in 1846; now an official member of the Hempstead M. E. ch.—***Haff, Amelia,** sister to Mrs. E. Acker; mar. W. S. Wright; rem. by c. to Johnson-st. ch.; d. a member of Carlton ave. ch. in 1857; bur. in "Cypress Hills."—**Haff, Amelia M.**, S.S.t.; mar. John J. Welsh; now of 18th-st. ch.—*****Haff, Elizabeth E.**, mar.; see Acker.—**Haff, Esther A.**, sister of Mrs. Egbert Acker; rem. to Centenary; thence to Warren-st. ch.; now of 1st Pl. ch.; wid. of Jas. S. Shutes.—**Haff, Olive D.**, rem. to Hempstead, L. I.; wid. of Ebenezer Haff.—*****Haff, Sarah**, sister of Mrs. E. Acker; mar. Geo. W. Johnson; d. 1862; bur. in "Cypress Hills."—**Hagenback, Frank**, rem. by c., 1875.—HALBERT, MRS. MARY E.—**Halderan, Abram**, withdrew.—******Hall, Edward**, d. 1873.—**Hall, Jeannette**, rem. by c., 1867.—**Hall, Mrs. Mary E.**, rem. by c., 1870.—**Hall, Rebecca**, rem. by c., 1864.—**Halldom, Jane**, mar.; see Mattesen.—HALSTED, FRANCES.—HAMILTON, MRS. CHARLOTTE.—HAMILTON, ELLEN.—******Hamilton, Watson**, d.—**Hammond, Amelia**, rem. by c., 1866.—**Hammond, Anna**, rem. by c., 1867.—**Hammond, Eliza**, rem. by c., 1866.—HAMMOND, MRS. FRANCES.—**Hammond, Geo. P.** and **Frances M.**, rem. by c., 1872; (persons of the same names were previously rem. by c.)—******Hammond, Miss Maria**, d., after a long illness, 1850.—**Hammond, Mary E.**, rem. by c., 1866.—******Hammond, Sam'l**, d., after a long and painful illness, July, 1850.—**Hammond, Sam'l J.**, rem. by c., 1868.—**Hammond, Wesley A.** and **Eliza**, rem. by c., 1870.—*****Handley, Benj.**, S.S.t. and cl. ldr.; said to have d. not a member of the ch.—*****Hanford, John E.**, son of Andrew Hanford; b. in Peekskill, N. Y.; conv. in early life; j. Allen-st. ch., N. York; rem. to old John-st. ch.; afterward to Sands-st., where he was cl. ldr. in 1846. He became one of the founders of the Fleet-st. ch. in 1850; supt. of its S. S. from its beginning till his death, a period of 13 yrs. He served the Fleet-st. ch., also, as std. and trus. There was scarcely a man at the head of any S. S. in B'klyn more beloved or more successful. He d., greatly lamented, Apr. 5, 1863, age 39. An elegy was written and published, as an expression of the ardent love of the Fleet-st. S. S. for their departed friend and supt. [See My S. S. Scrap-Book, p. 23.] Mr. H. is bur. in "Greenwood."—**Maria A.**, his w., was also one of the founders of Fleet-st. ch.; now a member of Sum'f'd ch. Their sons are: Solomon, Farrington, and Wm. Stone.—**Hanford, Solomon H.**, older bro. of John E., was cl. ldr. in Sands-st. ch. before 1839. He has been a member successively

J. E. HANFORD.

JOSEPH WESLEY HARPER.

Engraved by F Halpin from a Photo by Rockwood

of Allen-st. and John-st. chs., in N. York, and of Sands-st, Wash'gt'n-st., Fleet-st., and Sum'f'd chs., in Brooklyn. He was one of the most energetic and liberal of the founders of Fleet-st. ch.; pres't of the 1st board of trus. His w., **Hannah (Wright)**, rem. by c.—**Hannah, Lillie**, rem. by c., 1871.— ****Hannah, John**, d. 1883.—****Hannah, Elizabeth**, w. of the above d. 1883.—HANSEN, ABIGAIL.—HARDMAN, MRS. GRACE.—**Hare, Mrs. E. Ann**, rem. by c., 1865.—**Hare, Mrs. Elizabeth W.**, rem. by c., 1868.—**Hare, Jos. Knowles**, rem. by c., 1868.—**Harman, John**, withdrew.—****Harker, Benj.**, d. 1865; member 1 yr.—****Harker, Demaris**, d. 1863, age 68; unmarried. "Her memory is like ointment poured forth." [L. S. Weed, in Ch. Ad.]—**Harker, Elizabeth**, rem. by c., 1866.—**Harley, Mary**, rem.—**Harman, John**, withdrew.—**Harper, Augusta**, rem.—**Harper, Emma**, mar.; see Dodge.—****Harper, James**, native of England; father of Joseph; grandfather of the 4 original Harper bros.; trus. of Sands-st. ch. in 1800, and some time treas, and sec. of the board. His connection with this ch. began in 1799. He had previously been a Meth. for a number of yrs., and was pre-eminent among the founders of the denomination on L. I. When a resident of Newtown, (Middle Village,) in 1768, at the age of 26, he welcomed Capt. Thomas Webb into his house, where the Meth. soldier preached and formed a society, which still exists, the oldest on L. I.; and it may be presumed that the name of James Harper was the first on the list of members. [See Bangs' Hist. M. E. Ch., vol. i, p. 298, and Life of Abbott, p. 179.] His home was the home of the preachers. Mrs. J. W. De Grauw informed the author that Jas. Harper kept the B'klyn town poor-house on Sands-st. His tombstone in the old ch. yard contains the record of his death, in 1819, at the age of 77.—****Rebecca**, his w., was one of the excellent of the earth. She d. in 1821, age 82, and sleeps beside her husband.—****Harper, Joseph Wesley**, grandson of the above, was made cl. ldr. in this ch in 1837. He was std. also, and for many yrs. sec. and treas. of the board of trus. Smith's "Pillars of the Temple" contains an extended biography, from which some of the facts recorded in this brief sketch are taken. Wesley Harper, as his friends always called him, was b. in Newtown, L. I., Xmas day, 1801—third child of Jos. and Elizabeth Harper, whose names will be ever fragrant in the annals of L. I. Methodism. They were hard-working farmers, in comfortable circumstances, and Wesley always cherished fond recollections of the quiet, rural home of his boyhood. J. C. Derby, in "Reminiscences of Authors and Publishers," says: "Joseph Wesley Harper, the 3d of the 4 brothers, was of slighter physique than the rest. He was fond of telling, with quiet humor, that when he was a child an old presiding elder said to his mother: 'Sister Harper, why don't you give one of your boys to the Lord to be a preacher?' 'Why,' said she, 'that is just what I expected to do, and I have already selected one of them.' 'Which one have you selected?' inquired the gratified elder. 'I have selected Wesley,' was the reply. 'And why Wesley, rather than James, or John, or Fletcher?' 'O, well,' replied Mrs. Harper, 'Wesley seems to be the most feeble and delicate in health, and he is rather lazy—' Then, perceiving from the elder's perplexed and rather mortified look that he had put a wrong interpretation on her motives, she hastened to add, 'I thought that if I gave Wesley to the Lord, he would take him and make him over again, so that he would be all right.' . . . As a young man, Wesley Harper visited a theater but once, and his experience, as described by himself in later life, was any thing but agreeable. 'One evening,' he said, 'some of the boys persuaded me to go to the theater with them. We went together and took our seats in the pit. The performance had not begun. The people were assembling, and my companions sat joking and laughing; but I could not enter into their fun. A dreadful feeling came over me. It seemed as though all the prayers of my mother, all the instructions of my father, rushed across my mind at once. I felt as though I was at the very mouth of perdition, and that I could hardly hope to escape alive. At length I could endure it no longer, and, remembering that the hour of family prayer was approaching, I seized my hat, and fled from the house.'" This incident strikingly illustrates the reverent simplicity and filial devotion of the son and the powerful influence of the pious parents. Before he was 20 he was apprenticed, with his younger bro., Fletcher, to their older bros. of the firm of "J. & J. Harper, Publishers." He learned the printer's trade, and as proof-reader of the excellent reprints of the house, he became familiar with much of the best English literature. In a few years Wesley and Fletcher had both become partners in the house, and the style was changed to " Harper & Brothers." He was a most thorough Meth. from his youth; his money and influence were at the service of the ch. He was a wise counselor of his official brethren, and a useful cl. ldr., but so shy and unobtrusive that he was never heard in the public assembly. Once, indeed, at the 1st Xmas celebration by the S. S., it being the anniversary of his birth, he felt moved to whisper in the ear of the supt. that he had a word to say, and the announcement that Wesley Harper was about to speak was received as a signal for the most profound and respectful silence. "Soon after joining the firm he mar. and settled in B'klyn, and gradually a large family clustered around him. The business prospered. As the correspondent of the house he was brought into contact with men of every kind, and his acquaintance was very wide. His shrewd observation, his retentive memory, and his genial humor made his rem-

-iniscences of noted persons very charming. The impression made by him upon all who came to the office was that of an intelligent, courteous, unassuming man. But it was well said, that if the question were asked, 'Which is the head of the house, and which is the Harper, and who are the Brothers?' the only accurate answer was: 'Either one is the Harper, and all are the Brothers.'" [Pillars in the Temple, p. 256.] "As his part of the business he, for many yrs., managed the literary department, receiving authors' MSS., and frequently reading them himself. . . . If a MS. was to be declined, the declination was always made in the kindest manner, and the disappointment softened, not infrequently, with suggestions and advice that gave the unsuccessful applicant fresh heart and hope." [Derby's Reminiscences.] One of his old friends recently testified: "He was a devout man, with a temper like that of John in the Gospel—so sweet and gentle." [Dr. S. I. Prime, in Ch. Ad.] He built a house on Clark-st., which some of the members of his family still occupy— a spacious, cheerful dwelling, a "kind of image of himself." For some months his health gradually failed. "One afternoon his three brothers paid him a visit at his house. What took place during that interview has never been told. It was the last meeting of the four on earth. The next day James met a fatal accident. Wesley, deeply afflicted by the break in the harmonious circle of brothers, predicted that he would be the next to go." [Derby.] About the beginning of the yr. 1870 a sudden and startling illness warned him that his end was nigh. "Then came the confinement to the house, to the room, to the bed ; but in no happy home was there a more cheerful room than the chamber of the dying man." [Pillars in the Temple, p. 258.] He received visits from his friends, and talked cheerfully about dying. On

Monday morning, Feb. 14, 1870, he received a drink from the hand of his sister, smiled upon her, and said, "Thank you," with all his accustomed gentleness, and immediately there was a change; and before his friends could be called into the room, his pure spirit had taken its flight. His funeral was held at the ch. When his memorial in Greenwood Cemetery and the tablet on the wall of the ch. shall have crumbled to dust, the memory of Jos. Wesley Harper will live in the hearts of those whom his noble life has blessed.—**Hannah**, wid. of the above, dau. of Chas. Peck, d. June 17, 1882, age 72. "Her church life was exceptionally exemplary, her home life strikingly beautiful, . . . her last months were filled with longings for heaven." [J. S. Breckinridge, in Ch. Ad.] Children of the above: Jos. Wesley, Chas. Wesley, John Fletcher, Adaline P., and 4 other daughters.—**Harper, Sam'l**, trus. about 1826. One Sam'l B. Harper was a member of the 1st board of managers of the present Miss'y Soc'y. [Stevens' Hist. M. E. Ch., vol. iv, p. 478.]—*Harris, John, member in the 18th century; d. 1836; tombstone near the ch.—HARRISON, MRS. FRANCES.—HARRISON, GEORGE.—**Harrison, Geo. R.**, rem. by c., 1877.—HARRISON, H. A.—HARRISON, MRS. HENRIETTA.—**Harrison, Horace N.**, S.S.t. and off. S. S. miss'y soc.; rem. by c. to Centenary ch., 1849.—**Harrison, Pamelia**, rem. by c. to Albany, 1848.—HART, EDGAR F.—**Hart, Francis** and **Catharine**, rem. by c., 1866.—**Hart, Mrs. Hannah**, d. 1877: 40 yrs. a member.—HART, MRS. JANE.—HART, WM. H.—HART, WM. H., JR.—**Harvey, Ann M.**, rem. by c., 1864.—**Harvey, Chas.**, rem. 1846.—**Harvey, Henry E.**, rem. by c.—**Harvey, Sarah**, d.—**Haskins, John** and **Emily**, both S.S.ts.; rem. by c., 1869.—**Haskins, Lewis N.**, S.S.t., and **Jane**, rem. by c., 1864.—**Hassell, Jas.**, rem.—HASTINGS, MRS. ANNA M.—**Hastings, John**, a gardener, lived opposite the ch., one of the members before 1800; mentioned by Stiles. [Hist. B'klyn, vol. i, p. 450.]—*Deborah, his w., was a most excellent woman.—HAWKINS, JOHN B.—**Hawley, Mary B.**, mar. Mr. M'Vay.—**Hayman, Amelia**, rem. by c., 1880.—**Hayman, Geo.**, d. 1878.—**Heary, Julia**, mar. Wm. Lardler.—HECHLER, ADDIE L.—HEGEMAN, ABBIE, S.S.t.—HEGEMAN, LOTTIE.—HEGEMAN, WM. R., std.—**Hedges, Harriet**, mar. John Berry.—*Hempstead, Christopher M., cl. ldr. and trus. His class became a part of York-st. ch. He was elected a member of the separate board of trustees for York-st. at the 1st meeting, in June, 1835. He appears in the Sands-st. record about that date as having rem. by c. He was a rope-maker, and is remembered as an excellent man, one of the great multitude of worthies concerning whom the church has a very inadequate record. He is said to have d. a member of the E.

B'klyn (De Kalb ave.) ch. [C. C. Smith.]—HENDERSON, MRS. CATHARINE C.—HENDERSON, GEO. E.—**Hendrickson, Henry**, rem.—****Hendrickson, Jemima**, " d. in faith."—****Hendrickson, Stephen**, member of 1st board of trustees; excluded from the ch., 1798; cause not stated. [Trustees' record.] He mar. a dau. of the senior Geo. Powers. [Stiles' Hist. B'klyn, vol. ii, p. 187.]—**Henry, Ida**, rem. by c., 1883.—**Henry, James**, rem.—**Henry, Nancy C.**, rem. by c. to Jersey City, 1849.—**Henry, Wm.**, trus. about 1808.—**Henshaw, Hattie**, rem. by c.—***Henshaw, Linus K.**, b. in N. York city, Jan., 1800; mar. a Miss Van Pelt; moved to B'klyn when a young man; name appears in Sands-st. ch. record as cl. ldr., about 1831. He was cl. ldr. and trustee in York-st. ch. in 1837 or earlier; also a loc. pr., and some time pres't of the Loc. Prs'. Association of B'klyn. He preached the opening sermon, in a hired room in Carlton ave., at the inception of what is now the Simpson ch. He was a grocer; afterward engaged in the banking business; d. in B'klyn, a member of Sum'f'd ch., 1875, age 75. See tombstone in "Greenwood." The Rev. J. L. Gilder says: " He was cautious and considerate in judgment; he had a clear conception, a ready utterance, a voice of remarkable flexibility, sweetness, and penetration. His emotional nature was highly susceptible and readily stirred. As a speaker, he was distinguished for tenderness and pathos." [Hist. York-st. ch., p. 12.] His only surviving children are: W. W. Henshaw, of Sum'f'd ch., B'klyn, and a Mrs. Charlotte, of N. York.—****Herbert, Chas. A.**, d.—***Herbert, Isaac**, son of Joseph; b. Apr. 9, 1812, d. March 4, 1846, age 34; bur. in "Greenwood." Of 6 children, 3 are living: Geo. R., Isaac H., and Wilbur Fisk.—****Herbert, James**, a member as early as 1798; styled by his pastor, Jos. Crawford, in a comment in the ch. record, " the excellent ;" very early a cl. ldr. and trus. of Sands-st. ch.; d. 1825, age 55. See gravestone in old ch.-yard. His remains may have been removed. He brought up his bros., Jos., Dan'l, and Sam'l, to the shoe-maker's trade, after the death of his father. [Stiles' Hist. B'klyn, vol. ii, p. 112.] He was a pious, useful man. For an example of his noble Christian efforts, see memorial sketch of the Rev. C. W. Carpenter, in this volume, p. 272. One of his daughters mar. Richard Cornwell, who was for yrs. chorister in the Sands-st. ch.—****Caty**, wid. of the above, dau. of Sam'l Engle, sister to James C. Engle, (or Inglis;) d. in B'klyn, about 1844. She is bur. in "Greenwood." Of 6 children, 2 dau. survive: Eliza, wid. of Henry Case, of B'klyn, and Sarah Ann, wid. of Alfred Todd.—HERBERT, JAMES.—****Herbert, Joseph**, cl. ldr., trus., and S. S. supt., was bro. of James Herbert. He came with his father to B'klyn shortly after the Revo. War; commenced the shoe business for himself about 1806; mar. and moved into his new house on

Sands-st. "No name," says the historian of B'klyn, "is more uniformly identified with every important social, religious, and educational movement in the early history of the village than that of Joseph Herbert." [Stiles, ii, 112.] He commanded the Fusileers, a military co., in 1812. The Apprentices' Library Assoc'n, established in 1823, the 1st of its kind in B'klyn, was much aided by his efforts, he being one of its 1st officers. [Stiles, iii, 888.] But the brightest luster is imparted to his name by the fact that he was the associate of Snow, Mercein, Sands, Murphy, and De Vinne in the founding of Sunday-schools in B'klyn. These were all Sands-st. Methodists, but Herbert alone had been a member as far back as the previous century; and he maintained a connection with the school for a much longer period than either of the others, and was for many yrs. its honored supt.—successor to Rob't Snow. The portrait is copied from a painting, which has hung for many yrs. upon the wall of the S. S. room. "Pleasant, yielding, agreeable, good," was the character given him by his pastor in 1819. [Ch. Records.] He is described as of medium size, stout, verging on corpulency, with a fresh, clear complexion and white hair. [Stiles' Hist. B'klyn, vol. ii, p. 113.] He d., Oct. 16, 1861, in his 83d yr.; funeral in the ch.; bur. in "Greenwood."—**Frances, (Hand,)** his w., "d. in peace," 1850, age 74; her grave is beside her husband's. She was reared a Calvinist; j. the Sands-st. ch. about 1800, (D. Buck, pastor.) The author has heard old Sands-st. people mention the following names of their children: Isaac, (see above;) Julia A.; (see Swift;) Wm.; Sidney, who went to Cal.; Amelia.—**Herbert, Julia A.**; mar.; see Swift.—**Herbert, Rebecca**, w. of Dan'l, (a bro. of James and Joseph Herbert;) d. about 1830. —**Herrick, G. B.**, rem. by c., 1876; member 3 yrs.—**Herrick, Mrs. Mary E.**, rem. by c., 1876.—**Hewett, Eliza**, rem. by c., 1851—**Hewett, Maria**, dau. of Wm.; S.S.t.; conv. about 1845; d. June, 1850, age 21; bur. in "Greenwood;" remains rem. to Rural cem., Huntington, L. I.—**Hewett, M. Lankton**, rem. by c.—**Hewett, Sarah A.**, dau. of Wm.; S.S.t.; j. about 1847, (Bangs and Merwin, pastors;) rem. by c.; now Mrs. Henry Funnell, of Huntington, L. I.—**Hewett, Wm.**, b. in Eng., 1802, where he was for some time a Wesleyan Meth. loc. pr. There he mar. Eliza Chambers. Coming to N. York, about 1833, they attended Bedford-st. ch. Shortly afterward they came to B'klyn, and j. Sands-st. ch. He did not continue to be a loc. pr. in Amer.; rem. to Huntington, L. I., 1851; d. Aug. 29, 1868, age 66; bur. in Rural cem., Huntington. See headstone. He was a Xn. indeed, strong, true, useful. While sick he called in the pastor and several of the members to unite with him in celebrating the sacrament of the Lord's Supper. Occupation: sailor in Eng., hat-presser in B'klyn, druggist in Huntington.—**Eliza,** his w.; rem. by c., 1851; resides in Huntington; an aged and estimable Xn. The writer was her pastor 2 yrs.—**Higbie, Elizabeth,** rem. to Fleet-st. ch., 1850. —**Hill, John B.,** b. in Newark, N. J., in 1828; conv. at 11 yrs. of age: student for a time in the Wesleyan Insititute, in Newark; an apprentice for a yr. or two in B'klyn; rem. by c., 1850, to Newark. He writes: "My stay at Sands-st. was one of the most delightful periods of my life. It was full of the joy of a greatly quickened spiritual life, and of the blessedness of spiritual associations and activities." He became a licensed loc. pr. soon after leaving Sands-st. ch. *Conf. Record:* 1852, (W. Va. Conf.,) California Mission; 1853, (Cal. Conf.,) Benica and Martinez; 1854, ord. deacon,—Grass Valley; 1855, Grass Valley and Rough and Ready; 1856, ord. elder,—Downieville; 1857, San Francisco, Bethel ch., with Wm. Taylor; 1858-59, Stockton; 1860-61, Santa Clara; 1862-63, Nevada; 1864, Maysville; 1865-66, San Francisco, Central ch.; 1867-70, P. E., Sacramento dist.; 1871, P. E., Marysville dist.; 1872-84, ag't Meth. Book Depository, San Francisco. (See his portrait in Simpson's Cyclopedia.) His mother, Mrs. Mary G. Hill, was a useful temperance worker in Newark more than 50 yrs.—***Hillear, Sarah,** member in 1798.—**Hilliard, James,** withdrew.—****Hilliard, Letitia,** d. Aug., 1849, age 48; bur. in "Greenwood."—**Hillmuth, Christopher,** rem. to a Lutheran ch., N. York.—**Hinman, Heman,** rem. to Little Falls, 1850.—**Hinton, Ann,** rem. by c., 1873.—**Hobart, C. B.,** cl. ldr. He and **Mary A.** rem. by c., 1866.—**Hobart, David** and **Almira E.,** rem. by c., 1866. Mrs. H. was a S.S.t.—**Hobday, Charlotte,** rem.—HOGINS, MRS. JOSEPHINE.—**Holland, Mary,** rem.—****Holland, Sarah Ann,** S.S.t.; d. in B'klyn, 1847, much beloved; her associates in the S. S. erected a stone over her grave in Conn. [Mrs. Acker.]—**Holliday, Catharine,** rem. by c.—**Hollis, George,** S.S.t. in Sands-st. ch. in 1836, and loc. pr. in 1841. We are in ignorance respecting his early life. *Conf. Record:* 1842-43, (N. York Conf.,) Greenport and Orient, L. I.; 1844, ord. deacon,—Westhampton; 1845, Smithtown cir., with M. R. Lent; 1846, ord. elder,—ditto, with J. Robinson and Z. Davenport; 1847, Greenport; 1848, (N. York East Conf.,) Huntington cir., with D. DeVinne; 1849, Huntington; 1850, North Hempstead cir., with H. C. Glover; 1851, ditto, with J. J. Bell (supply) and R. R. Thompson, (supply;) 1852, Bridge Hampton;

1853-54, Greenpoint mission; 1855-56, Southport and Fairfield, Conn.; 1857-58, Mamaroneck, N. Y., with N. Tibbals, sup'y; 1859-60, Greenwich, Conn.; 1861, Nichol's Farms; 1862-63, Redding; 1864, Westport and Poplar Plains; 1865, Mamaroneck, N. Y., with Abel Stevens; 1866, N. York city miss'n; 1867-69, ditto, with Wm. Ross; 1870, Roslyn and Searingtown, L. I.; 1871, N. York city miss'n, with W. Ross and F. Brown; 1872-74, B'klyn, N. Fifth-st.; 1875-76, Springfield, L. I.; 1877, sup'y, filled vacancy, B'klyn, Leonard-st.; 1878-79, B'klyn, Leonard-st.; 1880, B'klyn, Cook-st.; 1881-84, sup'y; 1882, supply, B'klyn, Francis ch. He mar. Lucinda Wiggins, of Orient, L. I., one of the 6 Meth. ministers' wives taken from that village within a few yrs. Mr. H. re-organized the churches in Bayville and Cow Bay, (Port Washington,) L. I., after Methodism had become extinct in those places. Churches were built during his ministry at Mt. Sinai and Smithtown Branch, and these are but specimens of many monuments which tell of his laborious and faithful service. He suffered a severe loss, a few years ago, in the death of his only son.—**Hollis, Mrs. Jane,** d. Nov., 1883.—**Holly,** ———, cl. ldr., 1842.—HOLMAN, JESSE.—HOLMES, MRS. JANE.—**Holmes, John C.,** d. before Apr., 1867. [Records.] —Hoole, Catharine E., rem. by c., 1870.—Hoole, Mary E., mar.; see Hall.—**Horton, Jeremiah H.,** rem. by c., 1865; member a short time.—HORTON, MRS. MARGARET.—HORTON, PHILANDER.—HORTON, T. F.—**Houghton, Albert G., Mrs. Harriet C., Albert F., Miss Hattie,** and **Miss Marilla,** j. by c., 1867; rem. by c.—**Howard, Ethalinda,** d. 1852.—HOWARD, JOSEPH.—**Howe, Edward J.,** d. 1873.—**Howzy, Sally,** member in 1798; d.—**Hoyt, Frederick,** rem. by c., 1868; member 1 yr.—**Hoyt, John O.,** S.S.t., rem. by c., 1865; member successively in Newark, N. J., Rochester, N. Y., Sands-st., B'klyn, and Elizabeth, N. J.—**Eliza H.,** his w., was S.S.t.; rem. by c., 1865.—**Hoyt, John O., Jr.,** rem. by c. to Elizabeth, N. J.—**Hoyt, Joseph A.,** son of John O., S. S. lib'n; j. Sands-st. ch. about the time of Dr. Hagany's pastorate; rem. by c., 1864.—*Hubbell, Harvey, b. in Stepney, Conn., 1797; conv. at 14. "His 1st effort at public speaking Nathan Bangs heard and encouraged." For yrs. he was S. S. supt. in old John-st. ch.; later, trus. and cl. ldr. in Sands-st.; a subscriber for the Ch. Ad. from the 1st No., in 1826, till his death—55 yrs. He and his w. rem. by c.; resided at Long Hill, Conn., 20 yrs.; d. July 2, 1882, age 85. As he entered the harbor he exclaimed, "It is smooth sailing! All is well!" He was an active, useful, happy Xn.; "left a faithful w., loving children, and hosts of friends." [A. H. Goodenough, in Ch. Ad.]—**Hudson, Mary,** d. about 1818.—HUDSON, (SUSAN,) EMMA.—HUGHES, WM. and MARGARET.—**Hume, Mrs. Ruth,** w. of Henry, rem. by c., 1884.

—**Humphrey, Belinda M.**, mar. Mr. M'Cogg.—**Humphrey, Thos. J.**, exh., 1846.—**Hurd, Alvin**, rem. by c.—*****Hurlburt, Sam'l**, cl. ldr., 1843; std., 1844; came hither from Allen-st. ch., N. York; rem. to Orange, N. J.; resided in Middletown, Conn., while his 2 sons were in college; d., 1874, in Newark, age about 81; bur. in Orange, N. J.—*****Evelina P.**, wid. of the above, d. at the residence of her son, Rev, J. L. Hurlburt, in Hoboken, March 6, 1879, age 73. The son above referred to, the Rev. Dr. J. L. H., is author of the notes on the International Lessons, published in the S. S. Journal.—**Hussey, Eliza**, mar. Mr. Flam.—**Husted, Sam'l**, cl. ldr., about 1832.—**Hyde, Eliza M.**, w. of Wm.; j. John-st. ch., N. York; then Mulberry-st. ch.; rem. thence to Wash'gt'n-st. ch.; later Sands-st. ch., 8 yrs.; rem. by c., 1876; now of Hanson Pl. ch. Her husband, nephew of Jas. N. Hyde, and official member of Fleet-st. ch., d. about 1861.— HYDE, MRS. ELIZABETH E.—**Hyde, Emma L.**, sister of Erastus; S.S.t.; rem. by c., 1876; j. Fleet-st. ch.; now of Hanson Pl. ch.—**Hyde, Erastus**, grandson of Wm. A. Mercein, was b. in N. York; j. Fleet-st. ch., B'klyn; sec. of the S. S. 9 yrs.; went thence to Pacific-st. ch., an officer there; then Sands-st. ch.; std., 1875; rem. by c., 1876; now of Hanson Pl.—**Hyde, George** and **Abagail**, rem.—*****Hyde, James N.**, cl. ldr., 1831; rem. to Wash'gt'n-st. ch.; cl. ldr. there before 1839; went to N. Orleans; d., of yellow fever, at an advanced age.—**Hyde, Maria M.**, S.S.t.; sister of Erastus; j. Fleet-st.; rem. to Pacific-st.; thence to Sands-st.; now of Hanson Pl. ch.

Ibbotson, Rob't, b. in Derbyshire, Eng., Apr. 3, 1806; j. the Wesleyans at 12 yrs. of age; when about 15 moved to Sheffield; was a loc. pr. at 19, occupying from time to time the several pulpits on the circuit; came to U. S. in 1830. His name appears on the books of the Wash'gt'n-st. ch. as a cl. ldr. as early as 1842; loc. pr. in Sands-st. ch. in 1849, and std. about 1850. A meeting was held, Jan. 27, 1851, at his residence, in Clinton Ave., B'klyn, which led to the organizing of the Sum'f'd ch. He was a prominent associate of the Rev. Charles Fletcher in that important enterprise. His present residence (1884) is Montclair, N. J. In his 79th yr. he is waiting patiently for his heavenly Father's call.—******Ingraham, Anne**, w. of George Ingraham, sister to John G. Murphy, step-mother to the Rev. Rob't Seney, mother-in-law to C. C. Smith, and grandmother to Sam'l, Rich'd, Wm., and Henry Ingraham; j. Sands-st. ch. previous to her marriage; rem., with her husband, to Amenia, N. Y.; after his death came to live with her dau. in B'klyn, and re-united with Sands-st. ch. The following incident illustrates her large-hearted hospitality: A quar. meeting was held near her house in Dutchess Co. A large attendance was anticipated, and there were few homes of Methodists thereabouts, where the people could stay. She expected to entertain 30 or

40 people, and was prepared for them; but on Sat. noon, lo! 100 hearty, hungry guests came crowding into her house. 70 chickens had been kept for winter use, and other things had been laid up for cold weather, but there seemed to be little left after that meeting. The horses devoured a good-sized stack of hay. It must have been a heavy strain on the good woman's generosity, but she deemed it a privilege to serve and entertain her brothers and sisters in Christ, and doubtless felt that she was lending to the Lord and laying up treasure in heaven; and her Father never permitted her to come to want in this world. She d. in Christ, in 1863, age 85; bur. in "Greenwood."—**Ingraham, Sam'l**, from Amenia, N. Y.; came to B'klyn in 1836; clerk in a grocery store; after a few yrs., rem. by c.; went back to his father's farm. Later, rem. to Ontario Co., N. Y.. where he still resides.—IVES, BETSEY.—***Inslee, Elizabeth**, w. of Abraham Inslee, eldest dau. of Orrin Swift; b. in B'klyn; was a Sands-st. S.S.t.; rem. to 2d Pres. ch., to which her husband belonged; d. in Sept., 1872, age 42; bur. in "Greenwood," family plot.—**Inslee, Caroline E.**, sister to the above; 2d w of Abraham Inslee; rem. by c., 1872.

Jackson, Ann, rem.—**Jackson, Ann S.**, rem. by c. to Wash'gt'n-st. ch., 1848.—**Jackson, Tanner**, rem.—**James, Lucinda**, rem. to Albany, 1850.—****Jane, Catharine**, d. 1833, age 21. See head-stone in old ch. yard. She fell when 8 yrs. of age, and never walked afterward; conv. and j. Sands-st. ch. in 1830, (N. Levings, pastor.) [J. Luckey, in Ch. Ad.]— ****Jarvis, Catharine**, w. of Henry; b. in Eng.; last 50 yrs. in America; 22 yrs. in B'klyn; "d. sweetly in Christ," July, 1879, at the residence of her dau., Mrs. Gassner, age 70; bur. in "Greenwood." Lindsay Parker, her pastor.—**Jarvis, David S.**, rem.—**Jayne, Sam'l F.**, rem. by c., 1867; member a short time.—**Jeffrey, John**, S.S.t., cl. ldr., and loc. pr.; rem. by c., 1868. He was b. in Southampton, Eng., and came to the U. S. about 1850; conv. at Sands-st. in 1853, (H. J. Fox, pastor;) licensed to preach while Dr. Nadal was preacher in charge. He was for a long time sec. of the Loc. Prs'. Union, of B'klyn, and preached frequently in Cypress Hills and many other places, and was pastor in Flatlands, as supply under the P. E. It is said that when he was a young man, M. F. Odell secured him a position in the custom-house in N. York, where he still remains.—**Margaret**, w. of the above, rem. by c., 1868.—JENKINS, MRS. DEBORAH.—JOHNSON, ALICE.—***Johnson, Catharine**, member in 1798.—JOHNSON, MRS. CATHARINE.—**Johnson, Emma**, rem. by c.—JOHNSON, FANNIE.—JOHNSON, FRANCES P.—JOHNSON, HATTIE.—JOHNSON, HELEN. —**Johnson, Jane E.**, rem. by c.—JOHNSON, JENNIE.— **Johnson, Matthew**, rem. by c. to Wash'gt'n-st. ch., 1849.— **Johnson, Rudolphus H.**, rem. by c., 1865; member a short time.—**Johnson, Thos.,** " d. in peace," 1850.—**Johnston, Mrs. Elizabeth,** rem. by c.—JOHNSTON. MRS. JANE.— JONES, MRS. EMMA M.—**Jones, Mrs. Isadore,** rem. by c. —**Jones, Rob't Owen,** loc. pr., 1861.—**Julius, Cha's J. Fox,** loc. pr. about 1853; from the West Indies, Wesleyan Connection.

Kelsey, Melville, cl. ldr. about 1852; rem. to Cal.— ****Kemp, Elizabeth,** d. since 1850.—**Kempshall, W. H.,** rem. by c., 1865.—KESSLER, SOPHIA.—**Ketcham, Wm.,** rem.—*Kimball, Aaron, sexton and cl. ldr.; said to have d. a member of York-st. ch.—**Kimball, Myron H.** and **Eliza,** j. by c., 1873; rem. by c.—****King, Ellen,** 2 yrs a member; d. Aug. 3, 1877; one " Ella King" was bur. in " Greenwood," Aug., 1877, age 21.—KING, F. C.—KING, MRS. F. C.— ***King, Gamaliel,** b. in Riverhead, L. I., Dec. 1, 1795; in 1816 rem. to B'klyn; in 1819 mar., and about the same time j. Sands-st. ch.; spent the winter of 1826 in Charleston, S. C. With Jos. Moser he built the York-st. ch. in 1823, and he was architect of the Washg't'n-st. ch., 1831. He attended the latter ch. from its organization, but for some time it seems he was not a member anywhere. He renewed his connection with the Wash'gt'n-st. ch. about 1846, (Chas. Shelling, pastor;) d. in the faith, Dec. 6, 1875, age 80. His w., ***Catharine (Oliver),** adopted dau. of Rob't Snow, was b. in N. York, Nov. 25, 1789. She has been called a " Dorcas " on account of her kindness to the poor. She d. a member of Wash'gt'n-st. ch., Nov. 20, 1874, age almost 75; bur. with her husband in " Greenwood." Children of G. and C. King: Mary, wid. of James Herbert Cornwell, Jamesport, L. I.; Rob't Snow, d. 1825, an infant; Martha M., wid of Alfred Bridgeman, Newburgh, N. Y.; Geo. L., drowned 1869, age 41; Sarah S., w. of Geo. B. Jellison, Tenafly, N. J.; Orpha V., member of Wash'gt'n-st. ch., B'klyn.— ****King, John,** j. 1823; d.— ****Kingsland, Aaron,** trus. and cl. ldr.; b. in N. York; j. Sands-st. ch. about 1843, (L. M. Vincent, pastor.) He was not learned, but was remarkable for practical common-sense, integrity, and benevolence. He was a wholesale fish dealer, but his diligence in business did not interfere with his devotions. He hired a room convenient to his office, (Fulton Market,) as a place to which he could retire for meditation and prayer. His habit was to pray every time he came into his house from his business. He kept a charity fund, and

AARON KINGSLAND.

gave away one tenth of his income. He d. in 1868, age 63. His grave in "Greenwood" is marked by a head-stone.—
KINGSLAND, ELIZA, wid. of Aaron, still lingers "in age and feebleness extreme." Of the 13 children 4 survive; Daniel, Aaron, Joseph, and Charlotte—the last a member of Sands-st. ch.; see Weeks.—KIRK, CATHARINE.—**Kirk, Geo.** and **Catharine,** rem. to Paterson, N. J., 1851.—*****Kirk, Thomas,** cl. ldr. and trus. in 1807; pioneer editor, publisher, bookseller, and printer; one of the foremost among the enterprising contributors to the early growth and prosperity of B'klyn; b. in Cork, Ireland, in 1772; became a printer in his youth; was conv., and j. the Wesleyans at 17; came to Amer. prior to 1790; established a printing, book-selling, and publishing business in N. York; came to B'klyn, where, in 1799, he commenced the publication of the L. I. Advertiser, the 2d paper established on L. I. [Stiles' Hist. B'klyn, vol. iii, p. 927.] The L. I. Star was started by him in 1809. Some time after this he sold out his paper and all his publishing interests, confining himself to his job-printing office, but subsequently we find him a publisher in N. York, conducting the largest establishment of that kind in the city. By this house was issued the first ed. of Clarke's Commentary published in this country. Commercial reverses interfered with his amassing a fortune, as his success in business promised. Having again returned to B'klyn, he became closely identified with the interests of the growing town, and for some time occupying the position of one of the associate judges of the county. His name, as we have seen, is pleasantly connected with the origin of Sunday-schools in B'klyn, the first gatherings having been in a house provided by him. (See engraving opposite p. 18.) He was the 1st vice-pres. of the "Apprentices' Lib'y Assoc'n" in B'klyn, in 1823, and one of the 1st officers of the "B'klyn City Bible Soc'y," in 1840. Leaving Sands-st. ch., he became an official member of Wash'gt'n-st. ch., subsequently one of the chief founders of Pacific-st. ch., and its 1st cl. ldr. He was present with the class, in their usual place of meeting, just one week prior to his death. On the evening of his departure the class-members, hearing, after they had met, of his dangerous illness, repaired to his house. "There, surrounded by the family, and all the members of his class but one, while his pastor and class were bowed in prayer, and at the very hour in which he was accustomed to close his class, he 'ceased at once to work and live.'" Thus, on Thurs. ev'g, Oct. 9, 1851, this noble, honored Xn. d., at the age of 79. He was the 1st to be bur. from the Pacific-st. ch., in whose erection he had taken so deep an interest. Dr. Kennaday conducted the services. A vast concourse of people assembled, embracing, it is said, all the public functionaries of the city. Mr. K. was a man of uncommon culture, generosity, and piety, and profoundly respected by all.

[J. Kennaday, in Ch. Ad., 1851, and Stiles, in the Hist. B'klyn, vol. iii, pp. 860, 888, 927.]—*Sarah (Campbell), his w., was a relative of Peter Cooper's. She was a paralytic for some time, and her speech was affected. She d. Dec. 28, 1855. Granite stones in Mr. Cooper's beautiful and spacious round plot, at the junction of Central and Grove aves., in "Greenwood," commemorate the virtues of Mr. K. and his worthy Xn. wife. On the one is inscribed: "The sweet remembrance of the just shall flourish when he sleeps in death;" on the other: "Blessed are the dead," etc. Children: Amelia, mar. Capt. (afterward Com.) Newton—she d. some time since; James, d. at sea about 1820; John, a captain in the navy-yard; Asbury; Julia Salena, w. of Augustus T. Post, d. in New Haven, Conn., June 16, 1868—her grave is beside those of her parents; Thomas, the youngest, d. Mrs. Wm. Rushmore, who furnished the author with the above list, stated that Julia was an Episcopalian, and that none of the children became Methodists.— *Kissam, Jemima, member in 1798.—Kissam, Mrs. Mary J., withdrew.—Kittle, Sam'l P., cl. ldr. and S.S.t.; b. in Groveland, Livingston Co., N. Y., where he was conv. at 17, and j. the M. E. ch. Removing to Buffalo, he j. the Niagara-st. ch., (only M. E. ch. in the city;) became one of the founders of the Swan-st. (now Grace) ch.; rem. by c. to Sands-st. ch., B'klyn, about 1861; thence, 1869, to St. Paul's, Newark, N. J.; ass't supt. of S. S. there, and pres't Y. M. C. A. Rem. thence to Beekman Hill ch., N. York; S. S. supt. there 4 yrs.; now of W. Harlem ch. His w., Catharine E., rem. by c.—Knighton, P. H. and Cornelia, rem. 1847.—KNOWLES, WM. A., S.S.t. —Knowlton, Calvin, S.S.t. many yrs. ago; rem.—KNOWLTON, PERRIN.—**Kollinger, Margaret, d. 1867.—Kollinger, Charlotte, mar.; see Scudder.

Laine, Thos. N., loc. pr.; a native of the island of Guernsey; called to preach before his conversion; 1st a member of the French Wesleyan ch., afterward of the English; a loc. pr. in his native home; came to B'klyn, and j. Sands-st. ch. in 1860; cordially received and helped. *Pastoral Record:* 1861, supply, Union Pl. Mission, (Cypress Hills,) L.I.; 1862-64, supply, Southampton; 1865, ord. deacon; 1865-66, Riverhead; 1867, ord. elder; 1867-68, Trumbull and Nichol's Farms, Conn.; 1869, Stepney; 1870-71, Bethel; 1872-74, Watertown and N. Wat'n; 1875-76, Milford; 1877, Georgetown; 1878-80, City Island, N. Y.; 1881-83, North N. York; 1883, removed to fill a vacancy in Stamford, Conn.; 1884, Essex. He was mar. in 1864; has 2 daughters.—Lambard, Mrs. Frances, rem. by c., 1873.—Lambard, Jessie, mar.; see Longacre.—LAMPE, MARY A.—Lamson, Lewis, rem. by c., 1882.—LANDLER, JULIA, w. of Wm.—**Landon, Dr. Dillon Stevens, son of the Rev. S. Landon, was b. near L. Champlain; named for one of the N. York Conf. preachers, a friend of his father's; was graduated at the N. York Univ., and then studied medicine there; cl. ldr. in York-st. ch., 1842; later a S.S.t. and cl. ldr. in Sands-st. He was trus. of the Polytechnic School, and physician of the B'klyn City Hospital. Prominent, respected, beloved. He d. in 1874, age 52; bur. in J. Wesley Harper's plot in "Greenwood."—LANDON, ELIZABETH H., wid. of the above, dau. of J. Wesley Harper.—LANE, EBER and SUSAN J.—**Lane, Wm., a shoe-dealer; d. 1850, at an advanced age.—LARKIN, MRS. MARGARET. —La Roza, Mrs. Abagail, rem. by c., 1879.—La Roza, Mrs. Alma, rem. by c.—La Roza, Eliza, rem.—**La Roza, John, d. 1874.—La Roza, John L., rem. by c., 1872.—**La Roza, Zebulon, d.—Latimer, Ebenezer, cl. ldr., 1831.— Lawrence, Amanda, rem. by c.—Lawrence, Bennella, rem.—Lawrence, Mary, rem. by c., 1840.—**Lawrence, Rich'd, app'ted cl. ldr. about 1846; b., of Quaker parents, in Middletown, Monmouth Co., N. J., in 1805; coming to B'klyn, he was apprenticed to Gamaliel King, and became a builder. One Sabbath Mrs. King invited the Quaker lad to the Sands-st. S. S., where he heard announced a camp-meeting prayer-meeting, which his curiosity led him to attend. At that meeting he gave his heart to God. He was then 16 yrs. of age. He soon j. this ch.; rem. by c., 1839, to assist in founding Johnson-st. ch.; returned about 1847; rem. by c. to Harlem, 1850; returned again in 1855. The last 16 yrs. he was practically identified with the Nostrand ave. ch., but until his death his name was found on the Sands-st. record. His last words were, "Blessed Jesus!" "Destitute of early advantages of education, God made him great—great in his love, his zeal, and the heroism and power of his faith." [Rev. G. E. Reed, in Ch. Ad.] He d. Mar. 9, 1882, age 76. It is said that his funeral was attended by 1,000 persons, including the Society of Old Brooklynites, to which he belonged. Bur. in Cypress Hills cem.—MARY (DRAKE), his w., is a native of N. J. Though she is probably recognized as a member of the Nostrand ave. ch., her name remains on the Sands-st. ch. record. The children are 6 in number: Benj., Mrs. Stone, and 4 other daughters.—*Lawrence, Wm., nephew of Rich'd; rem. by c., and d. a member of Hanson Pl. ch.—Lay, Lucy Ann, rem. by c., 1869.—**Lay, Sylvia M., d.—LAYTON, ELSIE.—LAYTON, MRS. MEREENA. —Leach, Adam, rem. by c.—Leach, B. F. B., loc. pr., 1864; rem. by c., 1865.—Leach, Eliza, rem. by c.—*Leaneigh, John, member in 1798.—**Leary, Mrs. Sarah E., d 1867, age 25.—*Leavens, Geo., cl. ldr., 1866; exh., 1867; rem.; became deranged and d.—LEIGH, CHAS. C., S.S.t., S. S. supt., exh., cl. ldr., and loc. pr.; b. Dec. 25, 1812, in the city of Phila.; parents moved to Po'keepsie, N. Y.; both d. before he was 12 yrs. of age. At 16 he j. the M. E. ch. in Albany; rem. by c. to

Sands-st., B'klyn, in 1833 ; was ordained a loc. deacon in 1835 ; aided in forming the Loc. Prs'. Assoc'n in B'klyn ; subsequently became one of the founders of the National Loc. Prs'. Assoc'n ; supplied, as pastor, Astoria (part of Newtown cir.) in 1844. He resided in N. York for some yrs. after 1846, and held his membership in Bedford-st. and in 7th ave. ; was pres't of the N. York City Temp. Alliance ; a member of the N. Y. Legislature 2 terms ; renominated and elected by the temperance party, and was chairman of the Com. on Temperance. That com. reported favorably on the Maine Law, which was adopted by the Legislature. He was nominated by the same party for governor, and afterward for sec. of state. He has delivered without fee or reward hundreds of temperance addresses in various parts of the U. S. All his preaching, likewise, has been without pay. Mr. L. was one of the prime movers in the formation of the Nat'l Freedmen's Assoc'n, of which the Rev. Dr. Tyng was the 1st pres't. He was chairman of the executive com., and devoted all his time to the asso'n until after the close of the war. Collections were taken in all parts of the North, and in Europe also. Many thousands of pkgs of goods were sent from Eng. and Holland, all directed to him, and the U. S. gov't gave instructions to the Collector of the Port of New York to deliver all pkgs directed to Mr. Leigh without opening them—an expression of confidence perhaps never made to any other citizen. He visited several European countries in the interest of this cause, made addresses and formed assoc'ns. The speech he made in the Meth. Centennial Hall, in London, was printed in all the European and some Asiatic languages, and not a little aid was received from the heathen of the Old World. Observing that, in case of war with Gt. Britain, telegraphic communication between the U. S. and Europe would be cut off, Mr. L. interested himself in the formation of a cable line between our country and France, conducted the necessary negotiations, and witnessed the success of the scheme. Mr. L. was in early life, and is now, a dealer in crockery in B'klyn.—LEONARD, BENJ.—**Lessner, Priscilla,** rem. by c., 1868.—LESTER, CATHARINE.—**Lewis, Epenetus,** rem. by c., 1839 ; became an off. in York-st., Johnson-st., and Carlton ave. chs. successively. His 1st w. was a dau. of Joshua Rogers, of York-st. Ch. Rem., more than 30 yrs. ago, to Westbury, L. I., where he has been cl. ldr., trus., and S. S. supt.—LEWIS, MRS. FREE-LOVE W.—LEWIS, HANNAH.—**Lewis, Jane Ann,** rem. to N. J.—LEWIS, MRS. JULIA A.—**Lilly, Arthur,** rem. by c., 1868 ; a member 1 yr.—**Linden.** ———, loc. pr., 1809.— **Lindsay, Alfred** and **Emma D.,** from Simpson ch., rem. by c., 1879.—LINESBURG, C.—LINESBURG, CAROLINE L. —**Litchult, Mrs. Ann M.,** rem.—**Lock, Walter,** cl. ldr.; rem. by c., 1869 ; member 2 yrs.—LOCKE, ELIZABETH.—

Lockwood, Robert M., S.S.t., off. S. S. miss'y soc., cl. ldr., and S. S. supt.; rem. by c., 1866. He was b. in Alexandria, Va., Apr. 14, 1818, the 2d of a family of 7 children. His parents, Aquila and Cassandra M. (Dallam) Lockwood, were Methodists from Harford Co., Md. Mrs. Cassandra Lockwood's early home, "The Cranberry," was one of the visiting places of Bp. Asbury on his horseback journeys from Balt. to Phila. It is related of the bishop that having arrived very weary at "The Cranberry," one Saturday night, and having requested the family not to call him in the morning, he staid in his room that he might not be seen by a circuit-rider, who had an appointment at that house on Sunday morning. Just as the sermon commenced the old bishop came quietly down stairs, and seated himself behind the door opening into the hall. He made 32 scratches on the door with his penknife, and when Cassandra's mother asked him what they meant, he replied, with a quizzical smile: "They are the mistakes the young brother made in preaching." Mr. Lockwood's uncle succeeded to the possesion of the old mansion, and would never, in all the repairs that were made in the score of yrs. succeeding, allow the back of the door to be painted; and Mr. L. states that he has often seen the marks when visiting the old homestead. When the father of R. M. Lockwood visited B'klyn, being about 80 yrs. of age, the Sands-st. S. S. visited him in a body, to express their respect for him, and as an evidence of affection for his son; the mother lived to see her 2 older children conv., and went home to her Saviour in 1833. Robert was conv. under the ministry of the Rev. Norval Wilson, father of one of the bishops of the M. E. ch., South, July 31, 1832, age 14; rem. to Balt., 1835; cl. ldr. in Balt. city station, 1840 to 1850; supt. of Light-st. S. S. (called Asbury S. S., No. 1) from 1839 to 1850. This was the oldest S. S. in the city, and from the date of its organization to 1850, the time when Mr. L. left it, there had gone forth to preach the gospel 39 of its members. On its honored roll are the names of Bp. Cummins, of the Ref. Epis. Ch.; Dr. Dashiel, our late miss'y sec.; Drs. W. F. Watkins and John D. Easter, of the Prot. Epis. Ch., and many others. Mr. L. was transferred to the Charles-st. ch. in 1850, and was S. S. supt. there till 1856. That yr. he rem. to Sands-st. ch., B'klyn, and served the ch. and S. S. as above. He rem. thence to South Orange, N. J., and j. the Jeffersonville charge, Newark Conf. His 1st license as a loc. pr., in 1867, was signed by Jas. Ayars, P. E. He had pastoral charge in Jeffersonville for more than a yr.; then went south and united with the Savannah Wesley Monumental ch. of the M. E. Ch., South, where he was std. and S. S. supt. *Pastoral Record:* 1868–69, Jeffersonville, N. J., a supply; 1872, ord. deacon by Bp. Wightman, (South Ga. Conf.)—Hawkinsville, Ga.; 1873, ord. elder by Bp. Keener,—E. Macon; 1874–75,

REV. ROBERT M. LOCKWOOD.

Darien; 1876-77, Bainbridge; 1878, Sandersville; 1879-82, Conf. S. S. sec.; 1880, Eastman; 1883, Hamilton; 1884, Columbus. His w. was the dau. of Francis J. Dallam, Esq., of Balt. They were mar. in 1849. She d. in 1865, soon after the death of a son and a dau. in B'klyn. Another dau. d. in 1867. A dau., the only surviving child, resides in Savannah, Ga. Bro. L. writes: "The darkest hour of my home-life was when sickness and death made their inroads into my happy family in B'klyn. The prayers and sympathies of the Sands-st. ch. and S. S. were a sweet solace to me, and have left a precious memory." After the death of his 3d child he determined, as soon as he could settle up his business, to leave the scene of so much sorrow; and, in a new and unknown country, to devote the remainder of his life to the work of the ministry. Mr. L. is one of the best-remembered men of the old Sands-st. ch. and S. S. The result of his useful labors will endure forever.—**Long, Anna,** mar. a Mr. Hart.—**Longacre, Mrs. Jessie,** rem. by c., 1873.—**Longstreet, Maria,** mar. T. Wales.—LONGWORTH, CATHARINE.—****Loper, Isaac,** d. Mar., 1872; remembered as a man of strange peculiarities and petty prejudices. See Beecher's allusion to him, p. 36 of this work.— LOPER, MRS. MARIAN.—LORCKE, HERMAN.—LORD, GEO. H.—LORD, MARY A.—LOSANO, FRANK W.— LOSEE, FRANK.—**Lott, Mrs. Maria,** rem. by c., 1868.— **Lounsbury, Phineas C.,** rem. by c., 1864 and 1869.—**Lovejoy, James,** S.S.t.; rem.—LOWE, WM. E.—LOWE, MRS. ABBIE E.—**Luckey, Ann,** rem.—LUCKEY, GEO.— LUCKEY, MRS. MARY.—LUNT, THADEUS.—**Lush, Geo. W.,** rem.—***Lynch, Rebecca,** member1, 798.—**Lyon, Jonathan,** was a loc. elder in Sands-st. ch. in 1823. He was a son of Peter and Jerusha Lyon, of North Castle, N. Y. His father, Peter Lyon, Esq., was an off. in the Revolution. Jonathan was conv. at 12, and j. the M. E. ch. He was mar., Dec. 5, 1794, to Freelove Forman, of Bedford, N. Y., and 11 children were born to them, of whom 2 are living, (1884:) namely, the wid. of Fletcher Harper, (youngest of the original Harper Brothers,) and the wid. of Dr. Thos. Henry. *Ministerial Record:* 1807, (N. York Conf.,) Litchfield cir., Conn., with A. Hunt; 1808, Redding cir., with N. W. Thomas; 1809, ord. deacon,—Croton cir., N. Y., with E. Canfield; 1810, Middletown cir., Conn., with O. Sykes; 1811, ord. elder,—Croton cir., N. Y., with P. Cook; 1812, New Rochelle cir., with Eben Smith; 1813, Jamaica cir., L. I., with S. Bushnell and W. Blagborne; 1814, New Rochelle cir., with W. Thacher; 1815, Middletown cir., Conn., with Wm. Jewett; 1816-49, located. This record shows that he served a second time on 3 different circuits. He located on account of physical infirmity, but preached considerably until old age prevented. Moses Rogers, of Northport,

L. I., remembers that when Lyon came to the Jamaica cir., in 1813, a stranger, he saw a board nailed to a tree, where a lane leading from a farm-house intersected the highway, and on it was printed, in rude letters. " Bro. Lyon, turn down here." He followed the direction, and found a welcome in a good Methodist home. Judge Dikeman relates that immediately after a sermon in the " old white church," which he had delivered in his usual stormy and vociferous manner, the sexton, with a notice in his hand, went up to the high octagon inclosed pulpit, in which the preacher stood. A little child watched the movement, and whispered to his mother : " Now, mamma, he is going to be good, and the man will let him out!" From the Rev. Henry Hatfield and Dr. Griswold we learn that Mr. L. engaged in business—wharf-building and other public works—and was not altogether successful. In his last brief, painful sickness he was not able to converse much, but was sustained by faith; d. in peace, in the neighborhood of Middle Village, L. I., Aug. 21, 1849, in the 76th yr. of his age. Plain marble slabs, close beside the head-stones of Joseph and Elizabeth Harper, in the Meth. ch.-yard in Middle Village, designate the graves of J. L. and Freelove, his wife. She d. Feb. 12, 1850, age 80 yrs., one of the excellent of the earth. [B., in Ch. Ad.] On his tombstone is inscribed : " A devoted Christian, an affectionate husband, and kind father;" on hers : " A devoted w. and mother, whose life was a practical illustration of piety and virtue."—**Lyon, Lorenzo G., went to the war, and d.

*Macfarlan, Frederick D., loc. pr., 1830. His father, a graduate of the College of Edinburgh, gave him classical instruction. About 1825, in B'klyn, he was brought to Christ by " a pious w. and mother ;" rem. to N. York ; from thence entered the itinerancy. *Pastoral Record:* 1832, (N. York Conf.,) Sullivan cir., N. Y., with N. Rice; 1833, Ellenville ; 1834, ord. deacon,—New Platz cir., with E. Washburn and D. Webster; 1835–36, Rossville ; 1836, ord. elder. He visited his parents in N. York, in Oct., 1836, and was taken sick after preaching in the Greene-st. ch. ; partially recovered ; overworked in a 4 days meeting in Nov. ; dropsy ensued, and he d. Jan. 1, 1837, age 40. The attending physician did not inform him of his danger until a few hours before his death. He replied: " You ought to have let me know, but I am not afraid to die." The conf. gave him a good record as a " studious, modest, acceptable, useful minister of the Lord Jesus Christ." [Minutes, 1837, p. 493.] He is bur. in Rossville, N. Y. He left a wid.—*Macreading, Chas. S., (name written " M'Reading " in earlier yrs.;) b. in Portsmouth, N. H., Feb. 5, 1811 ; left motherless when very young ; " thrown out into the wide world," but kindly cared for by Providence ; conv. in Dorchester, Mass., (L. Johnson, pastor,) age about 17 ; licensed to preach in 1830. We observe

REV. WILLIAM M'ALLISTER.

an unusual number of locations and changes in the following *Ministerial Record:* 1831, (N. E. Conf.,) Scituate and Marshfield, Mass., with J. J. Bliss; 1832, Andover and Bradford, with Leroy Sunderland; 1833, ord. deacon,—Randolph and Abington; 1834, Salem; 1835, ord. elder,—Dighton and Taunton cir., with E. C. Scott; 1836-37, Newtown; 1838-44, located; part of 1839, loc. elder in Sands-st., and part of the yr. supply, B'klyn, Wash'gt'n st., in place of B. Griffin, rejected; 1845-46, (N. E. Conf.,) Lynn, South-st.; 1847-48, Webster, with J. Ireson, sup'y; 1849, Southbridge; 1850, Fitchburgh; 1851, Mendon; 1852-53, Boston, Meridian-st.; 1854, Newtown Upper Falls; 1855, Cambridge, Howard-st.; 1856, located; 1856-57, (Wis. Conf.,) Milwaukee, Spring-st.; 1858, located, supplied Belvidere, Ill.; 1859, (Peoria Conf.,) La Salle, Ill.; 1860-66, (N. E. Conf.,) sup'd; 1860, supplied Channahon, Ill.; 1861, chap. 39th Ill. infantry; 1865, supplied, Lisbon, Ill. As chaplain he was in several battles in the Peninsula, and was loved and honored by his reg't. "He was by nature warm and impulsive, and frank to a fault;" a "sincerely good man," and an "accepted and talented minister." He "early engaged in the antislavery cause, and rejoiced in its final triumph." In his home-life he was affectionate and cheerful. He d. suddenly, but peacefully, in Plainfield, Ill., Apr. 12, 1866, age 55. His last words for Christ were in a protracted meeting, in which many were converted. [Conf. Min., 1867, p. 61.] He left a wid. and several children. His eldest son, C. S. Macreading, Jr., d. in 1875, a member of Prov. Conf. [Conf. Min., 1876, p. 74.]—**M'Adam, Rob't,** rem. by c., 1868 and 1871.—*__**M'Allister, Wm.,**__ S.S.t., 1841; loc. pr., 1843. He was b. in 1820, in the N. of Ireland. His ancestors were Scotch, his father a vestryman of the Ch. of Eng. Wm. attended a parochial school, learned the linen-draper's trade, and when a very young man came to B'klyn, and j. the Sands-st. S. S.; was conv., and j. this ch. while W. H. Norris was pastor. He developed a remarkable talent for business, which promised large wealth; but he heard and obeyed a call to abandon secular schemes, and engage in the ministry of the word. *Appointments:* 1845, (N. York Conf.,) New Britain and Berlin, Conn., with S. W. Law—Berlin his special charge; 1846-47, Farmington; 1847, ord. deacon; 1848-49, Cornwall cir., with Isaac Sanford; 1849, ord. elder; 1850-51, New Milford; 1852-53, Southport; 1854-55, N. York, 9th-st.; 1856-57, N. York, Willett-st.; 1858-59, Meriden, Conn.; 1860-61, N. York, 37th-st.; 1862-63, N. York, Willett-st.; 1864-66, B'klyn, Johnson-st.; 1867-69, N. York, 37th-st.; 1870-72, N. York, Allen-st.; 1873-75, N. York, 2d st.; 1876-78, Birmingham, Conn.; 1879, N. York, 76th-st., (Cornell Memorial.) When he went to his first charge some were very anxious to know where he was graduated. He told them, "Sands-st. M. E.

ch., class-room No. 3—Jacob Brown, pres't." [Rev. T. W. Chadwick, letter to the author.] He was mar., in 1846, to Miss Esther Hollis, sister of the Rev. George Hollis, a lady " eminently fitted to share his trials and make his victory sure." Their silver wedding, in 1871, was attended by many friends, among whom was the Rev. H. F. Pease, who married them. Mr. M. visited Europe, and his lecture on " Glimpses of Great Britain " was heard and enjoyed by many. He was a member of Gen. Conf. in 1872, and was chairman of the Com. on Sunday-schools and Tracts. He was for some yrs. a member of the general miss'y board. During his last yrs. he was greatly interested in the doctrine and experience of entire sanctification. His last sermon to his people, on the Sabbath before his death, was concerning " The Pentecost." On Monday he was attacked with inflammation of the bowels, and from the first was assured that he must die; but he was ready; his work had been fully and faithfully done. During his sickness, in his delirium, he was talking about the young people who had requested prayers on the previous Sabbath ev'g. " There they are," said he, " a great company of them, right by the pool. They will take another plunge." " On the next Saturday ev'g, in the same hour in which Bp. Gilbert Haven took his flight homeward, Bro. M'Allister was called to his reward. Two worthy and blood-washed souls from the walls of Zion side by side went through the gates of the city into the excellent glory. What a pleasant surprise it was for these brothers to meet on their journey homeward. Perhaps the Bishop said, ' Well, Bro. M., I appointed you, at the last session of your conf., pastor of Cornell Memorial. What are you doing here?' The Irishman would be sure to answer, ' Yes, and it was a good appointment; but the Bishop of our souls has given me a better.'" [Dr. Fowler, in Ch. Ad.] His funeral was held in the ch. in which he was appointed to minister. A large concourse of sorrowing people thronged the ch., and many ministers appeared as chief mourners. Mr. M. is remembered as a " first-class pastor," " a strong, forcible preacher," " a good debater," and a most active friend of his unfortunate and poorly-paid brethren. Providence is said to have favored him, so that he was always above financial want, and left his family in possession of means for a comfortable support. His wid. resides in N. York. Of their 2 sons, the elder, the Rev. Wm. H. M'Allister, formerly of the N. York East Conf., is now pastor of the Bethany Indep't Meth. ch., Balt., Md., and the younger was a student in N. York when his father d. The dau. is the w. of Dr. Taneyhill, of Balt. All are members of the household of faith.—M'ARDELL, J. W.—M'ALPERIE, SIMON.—M'ALPERIE, TEMPERANCE.—**M'Alpine, Josephine**, mar.; see Van Dyke.—**M'Chesney, Catharine H.**, dau. of Rob't; rem. to a Dutch Ref. ch.; mar. Edward Burnett.

—**M'Chesney, Geo. W.**, son of Rob't; b. in B'klyn, 1837; member of infant-class in Sands-st. S. S., under Cartwright; j. the ch. when H. J. Fox was pastor; entered the choir young, and was chorister there 7 yrs. By his suggestion the 1st musical instrument was introduced. Rem. by c., 1865, to Wash'gt'n-st. ch.; thence to Pacific-st.; thence to Embury, and finally to Hanson Pl. Has been very efficient as chorister or precentor in most of the churches to which he has belonged. —**Abbie**, his w., rem. by c., 1865.—**M'Chesney, John D.**, son of Rob't; rem. Deacon in Pres. ch., (Dr. Bartlett's,) Wash'gt'n, D. C., 1883.—****M'Chesney, Rob't**, cl. ldr.; b. in Monmouth Co., N. J., in Sept., 1807; conv. and j. Sands-st. ch. in his youth; faithful worker, always at his post; d. in Dec., 1845, age 38; funeral attended by H. F. Pease, his pastor; bur. in Wallabout; rem. to "Cypress Hills," grave marked by headstone.—****Sarah (Dey)**, wid. of the above; d. Jan. 28, 1875, age 67. She was b. in N. J.; mar. in 1829; j. Sands-st. in 1833, and was a S.S.t. Left alone with 4 small children, she spent her life in self-denying labors for her family and her ch. In 1867 her youngest son was killed in the discharge of his duty as a public officer. The shock was too great, and she gradually sunk to the grave. Funeral attended by L. S. Weed and Geo. Taylor. Children of Rob't and Sarah D. M'Chesney: Catharine H., (Mrs. Burnett;) Geo. W.; John D.; Rob't S., who d. Oct. 19, 1867.—M'CLOUD, MRS. JEAN.—**M'Coy, Thos.**, cl. ldr., 1835. One Thos. M'Coy d. 1850, a member of S. 2d-st. ch.— **M'Coy, Jane**, rem. to Johnson-st. ch, 1850.—**M'Cormick, C. F.**, rem., 1850.—M'CREADY, MARGARET.—M'CULLY, MARY.—**M'Donald, Edgar**, of Nassau Bank, B'klyn; son of Wm., (1st,) S.S.t., lib'n, off. S. S. miss'y soc., and cl. ldr.; b. in B'klyn; conv. and j. Sands-st. ch. under Dr. Miley's ministry; rem. by c. to Sum'f'd ch., 1878.—**Emma**, w. of the above, dau. of J. H. Ackerman; rem. by c. to Sum'f'd ch., 1878.—**M'Donald, J. F.**, rem. by c., 1861.—**M'Donald, Fletcher**, youngest son of Wm. (1st;) rem. by c., 1876.—**Mary**, his w.; rem. by c., 1876. At a recent date both were members of Wash'gt'n ave. Bap. ch.—**M'Donald, Jennie**, (or **Virginia**,) mar.; see Moore.—**M'Donald, Margaret**, mar.; see Bottome.—**M'Donald, Mary**, mar.; see Tate.—M'DONALD, MRS. MARY.—**M'Donald, Rebecca**, rem. by c., 1878.—***M'Donald, Wm.**, (1st.;) b. in N. York city; conv. at 18; j. Forsyth-st. ch. In 1832, age 25, came to B'klyn and j. Sands-st. ch., where he became cl. ldr., trus., and S. S. supt. Rem. later to Fleet-st. ch., where he was a std. and a very superior Bible-class teacher. By occupation, a cooper and gauger; elected a member of the city council; a man of energetic and progressive spirit; an ardent Meth., but no bigot. He d. in great peace, March 24, 1852, age 45. [C., in Ch. Ad.] Resolutions of respect and affection were adopted by the

Sands-st. quar. conf.—*Mary (Willis), wid. of the above, d. May 4, 1880, age 74. She j. Forsyth-st. ch , N. York, at the age of 12. Came with her husband to Sands-st. ch. After her decease more than one writer for the Ch. Ad. paid a loving tribute to her memory. One appropriately applied to her Paul's beautiful description of a wid. indeed : " Well reported of for her good works, if she have brought up children, if she have lodged strangers, if she have washed the saints' feet, if she have relieved the afflicted, if she have diligently followed every good work." During her sickness "her room was rather a place of social greetings and constant religious joy and service, than of any sadness and tears. . . . Her conversations were remarkable for their cheerful wisdom and persuasive unction, so much so, indeed, that several of her visitors, until then strangers to God, were induced to seek the same grace that so wonderfully transformed that chamber of death into the vestibule of life." She is bur. with her husband in " Greenwood." These godly parents left 7 children : namely, Margaret, (Mrs. Rev. Dr. F. Bottome ;) Carrie, (Mrs. Rev. Dr. T. H. Pearne;) Jennie, (Mrs. R. M. Moore ;) Mary, (Mrs. W. J. Tate ;) Willis ; Edgar ; Fletcher. —**M'Donald, Wm., (2d,) a plumber; d. Oct., 1878.— M'DONALD, WILLIAM, (3d.)—M'Donald, Willis, son of Wm., (1st ;) S.S.t., cl. ldr., and std. ; rem. by c., 1872, to Hanson Pl. ch.; publisher of Hanson Pl. Quarterly.—Mary, his w.; rem. by c., 1872.—M'FARLAND, MRS. MARTHA J.—M'Gee, Eliza L., mar. ; see Phillips.—**M'Gee, Mary Ann, S.S.t., and for 21 yrs. an excellent S. S. supt.; d. suddenly, of heart affection, at the house of her bro., Jas. R. M'Gee, on Sunday P. M., Sept. 6, 1868, age 68. She was at her post that day in two sessions of the S. S. She is bur. in " Cypress Hills."— M'GEE, REBECCA.—M'Gee, Sarah Ann ; mar. A. M. Bradshaw in 1861 ; rem. to Lakewood, N. J.—M'Gill, Edward F., rem. by c.—**M'Gill, Elizabeth, d. 1842.—M'Gill, Henry F. and Elizabeth, rem. by c.—M'Gill, John and Pauline, rem. by c., 1865.—M'Grady, Elizabeth, mar. John Carter.—M'HARG, BELINDA.—**M'Intyre, Martha, d. at the Old Ladies' Home.—**M'Kay, Elizabeth, d.—M'KAY, ELLEN.—M'KAY, EMELINE (STRINGHAM), S.S.t.; w. of Alex. M'Kay.—M'Kee, Wm., rem. by c., 1865.—M'Keon, Sarah J., mar. ; see Smith.—*M'Kenney, John, was at one time a member; d.—**Sarah, w. of John M'Kenney, was previously the w. of Rich'd Everitt, one of the original trustees of this ch. She d. about 1850.—M'LEAN, ROB'T.—M'LEAN, ELIZABETH.—M'LEOD, MRS. JENNIE.—M'NEELY, ANDREW.—M'WILLIAM, JAMES, S.S.t. and std.; shipping and commission merchant in B'klyn. He was a member of Miss Griswold's infant-class; j. the ch. in his youth; many yrs. pres't of the Young People's Assoc'n.—M'WILLIAM, LIZZIE

R.—MAIN, S. D. and MRS. S. D.—MALCOLM, AMELIA.—
MALCOLM, MATTIE.—MALCOLM, ROB'T.—**Mallery,
Henry,** S.S.t., 1837; rem. by c.—**Mallory, Charlotte,** S.S.t.,
1849; rem. by c.—**Mandeville, Edwin,** of L. I. Bank, B'klyn;
b. in N. J.; rem. to N. York; j. Greene-st. ch., (W. P. Corbit,
pastor;) rem. to Sands-st. ch. about 1863, (L. S. Weed, pastor;)
rem., 1865, to Fleet-st. ch.; afterward trus. in Nostrand ave. ch.
—**Emma,** his w., was rem. ditto.—**Markle, Jos.,** rem. by c.,
1867.—****Marsden, Rachel,** d. 1848.—MARSH, HIRAM.—
Marsh, T. Pliny, rem. by c., 1865; member 1 yr.—MAR-
SHALL, HANNAH.—MARSHALL, JOHN.—**Marshall,
John** and **Elizabeth,** rem. to Pa.—MARSHALL, JOS.—
MARSHALL, MARY.—**Martin, Humphrey,** rem.—MAR-
VIN, RACHEL.—**Marvin, Wm.,** rem. W. C. Marvin was
S.S.t. in 1844.—MASON, SUSAN H.—MATLOCK, MRS.
ELIZABETH A.—**Mattesen, Mrs. Jane,** rem.—**Matthews,
Jane,** rem. by c., 1875.—**Matthews, Louisa,** rem. by c. to
Mass., 1849.—MATTHEWS, MRS. MARIA.—**Matthews,
Rich'd,** rem. by c., 1874.—**Maybee, Thos. B.** and **Jean-
ette,** rem. by c.—**Maynard, Mary Ann, Sarah E.,** and
Rosina, rem. by c.—**Mazarine, Catharine,** rem. by c. to
Bushwick, 1848.—**Megill, John** and **Pauline,** rem. by c.,
1865.—**Megill, Henry F., Mrs. Elizabeth,** and **Edward
L.,** rem. by c.—**Melins, Esley,** rem. by c.—****Melvin,
John C.,** cl. ldr. and exh.; rem. by c., 1835, and returned;
d. 1850.—****Mercein, Andrew**; his parents were Swiss Huguenots, who came to this country in 1753, and j. the settlement
in New Rochelle, N. Y. There
he was b. in 1763. The father, a
watch-maker, with mother and
child, moved to the city of N.
York, where shortly afterward he
d. A young lad, living with his
mother, and she a foreigner, Andrew remained in the city during
its occupancy by the British, but
he steadfastly refused to enlist in
their cause. When about 16 yrs.
of age, he was seized by a press-
gang, and carried to a vessel which
was kept in the Hudson R. to receive recruits, and he escaped
during the night by swimming to
the shore, unhurt by the shots that were fired after him. He
was otherwise connected with the thrilling events of the war.
In 1780, previous to the "evacuation," he was mar., at the age
of 17, to Elizabeth Royce—a most happy union of 50 yrs'. continuance. He j. old John-st. ch. in 1786, and while serving

ANDREW MERCEIN.

as a trus. and cl. ldr. there, he aided in the erection of the Forsyth-st., Duane-st., and Bowery Village chs. He was successfully engaged in the cracker-baking business for many yrs. Before 1798 he purchased a country residence in Newtown, L. I. In this hospitable retreat many a weary itinerant found repose. Jesse Lee records of his brother John, that on Saturday, June 23, 1798, " he started with Dr. Phœbus for L. I., but after crossing the ferry they had traveled but a short distance on the island before he began to raise blood by the mouthful. The doctor bled him, and, after resting a little, they went on in the chaise to Bro. Mercein's, in Newtown." [Life of Lee, p. 144.] There Lee was attacked with a violent hemorrhage, and in the presence of his bro. Jesse, who came to visit him, he made his will. By careful nursing he soon became strong enough to return to his home in Va. After a few yrs. Mr. M. rem. to B'klyn, where he passed the remainder of his days. He was cl. ldr. and trus. in Sands-st. ch. from 1808. As a public-spirited man no one in B'klyn excelled him. Every interest pertaining to the welfare of the community shared his thought and labor. He was named as one of the trustees of the village of B'klyn in the act of incorporation in 1816. He and Rob't Snow labored hard for the establishment of free education. They were members of the 1st board of trus. of pub. schools in B'klyn, and "performed their services gratuitously, visiting every house in order to examine for themselves the condition of the children." [Stiles' Hist. B'klyn, vol. ii, p. 866.] His own educational advantages had been small, but by persevering study he had become a man of unusual intelligence. He hailed the opportunity to join with others in the formation of a S. S. in B'klyn. His granddaughter, Mrs. Barry, of Stamford, (to whom the author is indebted for many facts and incidents concerning this good man,) well remembers his taking her, a child of 10 yrs., to see the S. S. in B'klyn, when a little boy named Henry C. Murphy (afterward an eminent citizen of B'klyn) was placed under her charge to be taught—his alphabet or spelling-lesson, probably. With the largest liberality toward other denominations, he was an intensely zealous Meth. He was one of the founders of York-st. ch., and when the building was erected he devoted a liberal contribution "and the whole of his time" to that object. He also aided in the erection of the Wash'gt'n-st. ch. Indeed, his obituary states that not a ch. of his denomination was built in N. York and vicinity, up to the day of his death, toward which he did not contribute. During all his advanced yrs. he was an off. of the Bible, tract, S. S., and miss'y societies, savings-banks, and other secular institutions, attending faithfully the services of God's house, and visiting almost daily, with prayers and with gifts, the homes of the sick and the poor. He d. in B'klyn, June 19, 1835, age 73. His pastor, Bartholomew

Creagh, preached his funeral sermon in the Sands-st. ch., from " Precious in the sight of the Lord," etc. [See Lost Chapters, p. 561.] He had been a member of York-st. ch. for a time during his residence in that neighborhood, but had returned to his old communion. He was bur., by the side of Ross and Summerfield, near the old ch. The grave was afterward covered by the new and larger edifice, and the headstone placed against the outside of the building. His portrait, taken in middle life, bespeaks the character of the man.—**Elizabeth, his 1st w., " was worthy of her husband. She approved of his every good work, and welcomed, in her quiet way, all whom his largehearted hospitality invited to their home. She was the mother of 12 children, only 2 of whom survived the age of infancy." [Mrs. Barry: letter to the author.] She d. in 1830, age 68, and was bur. beside her husband.—**Charlotte (Galt), his 2d w., was a S.S.t. previous to her marriage, and an esteemed friend of the family. She had been an Episcopalian, but had j. Sands-st. ch., with the approbation of her friends. Those who knew her speak of her as modest, intellectual, benevolent, devout, a faithful S.S.t., tract-distributor, and visitor of the poor. She was a suitable companion for Mr. M., watching over him in his declining years. She d. in B'klyn, about 1850, in her 70th yr. Falling from her chair at the table, she suddenly expired. Two sons of Andrew and Elizabeth Mercein attained to manhood. One, Thos. R., was a well-known citizen of N. York 60 yrs., a man of culture, philanthrophy, and social position, a graduate of Columbia College, founder of the Mechanics' Society School and of the Apprentices' Library, comptroller of the city, and col. of one of its best regiments during the war of 1812; one of the projectors of the N. York Univ., and for the last 20 yrs. of his life pres't of the Equitable Ins. Co. The brilliant and distinguished young minister, the Rev. T. F. R. Mercein, author of " Natural Goodness," was a son of Thos R. Imogen, a dau. of Thos. R. Mercein, was an eminent Christian and an author of some note. By appeals and personal labors, as sec. of the Ladies' Home Miss'y Soc., in N. York, " she was the chief agent in the successful establishment of the Mission at Five Points." [N. Mead., in Ch. Ad., Apr. 27, 1882.] Her sister, Mrs. Eliza Mercein Barry, (another most worthy descendant of Andrew Mercein,) is a member of the M. E. ch. in Stamford, Conn. Wm. A., another son of Andrew Mercein, was in the war of 1812, and prominently connected with the Mechanics' Soc'y School of N. York. He was one of the 1st board of managers of the parent Miss'y Soc'y, in 1819. [Stevens' Hist. M. E. Ch., vol. iv, p. 478.] He came from John-st. ch., N. York, to Wash'gt'n-st. ch., B'klyn. John Summerfield and other eminent preachers were often entertained at his hospitable home. He d. in B'klyn. A son, Thos. R. Mercein, and 2 daughters, Mrs. Wm. Hyde and Mrs.

Chas. W. Thomas, with their families, reside in B'klyn, and cherish the church and the faith of their ancestors.—**Mercein, Miss Susan,** dau. of Wm. A., granddau. of Andrew; now a member of Hanson Pl. ch.—****Merriam, Mrs.,** d. 1869.— ****Merriman, Georgiana,** mar.; see Douglas.—**Merritt, M. J.,** rem.—MICKLEBOROUGH, AMANDA.—**Milford, Wm.,** rem., 1849.—MILLARD, ELIZA.—****Miller, Catharine,** d. June, 1875.—MILLER, CHAS.—MILLER, MRS. DEBORAH H.—**Miller, John,** rem.—**Miller, Jos.,** rem. by c. —MILLER, SAM'L.—MILLER, MRS. SARAH.—MILLER, MRS. S. EMMA.—MILLER, WM. H.—MILLS, MRS. CAROLINE.—MILLS, LUCILLA.—**Mills, Mary,** mar. Mr. Pitt. —MOLYNEAUX, MRS.—MOON, MRS. CATHARINE.— ****Moore, Fannie A.,** mar.; see Archer.—MOORE, JASON and MRS. MARY IRENE.—****Moore, John,** S.S.t., d. "suddenly in peace and hope," 1849, probably a member. See stone in ch.-yard.—****Moore, Jos. J.,** d.—MOORE, RICH'D.— **Moore, Rob't M.,** S.S.t., loc. pr., and cl. ldr.; came from Allen-st. ch., N. York, 1866; succeeded M. F. Odell as cl. ldr.; member of Sands-st. ch. 2 yrs.; rem. by c., 1868; j. Simpson ch.; thence rem. to Elizabeth, N. J.—**Jennie,** his w., dau. of Wm. M'Donald; rem. by c.—**Moore, Sam'l G.,** rem. by c., 1866.—**Moore, Wm.,** bro. of Jason and Rob't M.; a Wesleyan in Ireland; member of Sands-st. ch., 1 yr.; rem. by c., 1870.— **Lizzie,** his w., a Pres. in Albany before coming to B'klyn; rem. by c., 1870.—**Morehouse, Eliza,** "gone to Green's establishment," Cong. Meth. Ch. [Ch. records.]—MORGAN, BENJ. F.—MORGAN, CHARLOTTE A.—**Morley, Mrs. Sarah,** rem. by c., 1868.—**Morrell, Elisha B.,** withdrew, 1839.— ****Morrell, Jane,** d. about 1829.—MORRELL, MRS. MARIA. —****Morris, Mrs. Elizabeth,** d. 1871.—**Morris, Hannah,** rem. to Johnson-st. ch., 1850.—MORRIS, LUCY.—****Morris, Mary,** d. about 1830.—**Morris, Nelson,** cl. ldr.; rem. by c. to Johnson-st. ch., 1849.—MORRISON, CARRIE.—****Mortimer, John,** d. 1846.—**Mortimer, John,** rem., 1847.—***Moser, Ida,** a member in 1798.—****Moser, Isaac,** trus. in 1794, one of the 1st. and some time treas. of the board; cl. ldr. as early as 1798, and again ldr. of Red Hook Lane class in 1830. He was b. Apr. 12, 1768. Stiles mentions him as a grocer in B'klyn, in 1816. [Hist. B'klyn, vol ii, p. 114.] His store was located cor. Fulton and High. [Mrs. R. E. Wakefield.] Thos. L. Rushmore remembers calling to see him a short time before his death. Jacob Brown, John Smith, and Jos. Moser were present at the same time. When they prayed by his bedside the good man did not respond to their petitions for his recovery, but shouted when they spoke of heaven. At length one of them said, "He longs to depart; let him go!" On a Sabbath (perhaps the same occasion) he was thought to be dying, but revived, and, in a tone of disappointment, said: "I was born on the holy Sabbath, baptized and married on a Sabbath, and I thought I was going to die this Lord's day." He lived one week longer, and d. Sunday, Oct. 18, 1846, age 78. J. C. Green, his pastor, preached his funeral sermon.—**Susanna, commonly known as "Aunt Susan," w. of Isaac Moser, was a woman of sweet and even temper, wore a Methodist bonnet, and always sat in the "saints' corner," that is, in one of the side seats near the pulpit. She was universally beloved; j. Sands-st. ch. in 1800; d. 1850, age 74; bur. with her husband in "Greenwood." Mrs. R. E. Wakefield writes: "Grandmother, Susanna Moser, was sister to Joseph Harper. Grandma was a very handsome widow when grandpa mar. her; he, also, was a widower." Here is a list of the children of Isaac Moser: Isaac S.; Joseph; Sam'l H.; Lydia, (see Reynolds;) Susan A, mar. a Mr. Biglow, whose son is of the firm "Biglow & Main;" Eliza, mar. a Mr. Green.—**Moser, Isaac Snow,** son of the above, was named for Rob't Snow; j. Sands-st. ch. at 17; rem. to Hanson Pl. ch.; thence to Camden, N. Y., where he still resides. While living in B'klyn he fell from a building, and remained insensible two weeks. On a Sabbath, during that time, mighty prayer was offered for his recovery in Hanson Pl. ch., and he was almost miraculously restored. [Letter to the author.]—**Maria H. (Farrington),** his w., S.S.t. before marriage; left the Society of Friends to j. Sands-st. ch. Their son, Cap't Sam'l H. Moser, a devoted member of Hanson Pl. ch., was wounded 5 times in the War for the Union, and at length killed in battle, in 1864.—***Moser, Joseph,** bro. of Isaac, familiarly known as "Uncle Josey," was b. in Stamford, Conn., in 1776, and came to B'klyn in 1783. When a youth he sought the Lord, and was gloriously converted in a cornfield between Fulton-st. and Columbia Heights. [E. C. Estes.] He was cl. ldr. in 1806, afterward trus. and some time pres't of the board. During the last 20 yrs. of his life he was one of the chief pillars in Wash'gt'n-st. ch. He and Gamaliel King were the builders of the 1st York-st. ch. By industry and enterprise he amassed a competence, but through others, whom he unwisely and generously trusted, he lost the whole of his hard-earned property. He was P. M. under Pres. Jackson in 1831 and in 1834, and he was one of B'klyn's 1st board of aldermen. [Stiles' Hist. B'klyn, vol. ii, pp. 236, 243.] Before his death he was

SUSANNA MOSER.

appointed inspector of customs in N. York, and of pavements in B'klyn. He d., it is said, at the house of Geo. I. Seney, Esq., Feb'y 8, 1854, age 77. A sketch by Stiles [Hist. B'klyn, vol. ii, p. 81] describes him as "peculiar in gait, clean-shaven, round-

JOSEPH MOSER.

shouldered, and dressed in dark-colored clothes," and says further: "His ministrations to the sick and the heavy-laden, his labors in the S. S., his untiring interest in the youth of the place—counseling them and originating entertainments for them, in which instruction and amusement were most judiciously blended—endeared him to the hearts of both old and young."— *Rachel, his w., appears to have j. the Sands-st. ch. in its very infancy. She was at that time the w. of Peter Cannon, the cooper, in whose shop the 1st stated services by the Meth. were held in B'klyn in 1787, and in whose house the 1st trustees were elected in 1794. The name of Rachel Cannon is on the oldest known register of Sands-st. ch., (1798,) and it is not unlikely that her name was recorded on the 1st class paper in 1787, and that by her influence her husband, who was not a member, (at least in 1798,) was ever active and generous in his friendship toward the ch. After his death she was mar. to Jos. Moser. She d., a member of Wash'gt'n-st. ch., July 9, 1848. Jos. and Rachel Moser had no children, but 2 nieces lived with them. One mar. a Mr. Simonson, another a Mr. Morehouse.—

Moser, Joseph, son of the elder Isaac, d. His grave is under the S. S. building. He was an excellent young man.—
Moser, Lucretia, of Red Hook Lane class, 1826. [Records.] Possibly Lucinda Moser is meant.—**Moser, Margaret,** w. of John, mother of Isaac and Joseph, mother-in-law of John Garrison; d. June 3, 1811, age 67. [Headstone in ch.-yard.] Believed to have been a member.—**Moser, Rachel,** dau. of the elder Isaac, is bur. under the S. S. building. [Mrs. R. E. Wakefield.]—*****Moser, Sam'l Harper,** son of Isaac, was a native of B'klyn, and a cl. ldr., trus., and std. in Sands-st. ch. "He kept a grocery-store near his father's." [Mrs. R. E. Wakefield.] It is believed that he did not retain his membership in the ch. He d. in N. York.—*****Lucinda Vail,** his w.; d., and was bur. in "Greenwood." They left 2 daughters: Phœbe, w. of Geo. l. Seney; and Eliza, w. of Thos. L. Rushmore.—**Mott, Eliza,** rem. by c.—MULDOON, WM. S.—MULDOON, MRS. S.—MULDOON, EMMA C.—**Mumford, Adeline,** rem. by c., 1867.—**Mumford, Anna L.,** S.S.t.; rem. by c., 1867.—
*****Mundell, Wm.,** boot and shoe dealer; b. Apr. 28, 1789; became a loc. pr. in this ch. in 1827; his name is in the printed "plan" for Flushing cir., 1828. "At his suggestion the Loc. Prs'. Assoc'n was formed in B'klyn about 1835." [C. C. Leigh.] He was transferred at an early date to Wash'gt'n-st. ch., and in that communion he d., Aug. 27, 1840, age 51. Children: Jeremiah, David, and John, deceased; Chas., Geo., Elizabeth, and another dau., living, (1883.)—*****Martha,** w. of Wm. Mundell, was b. on the Isle of Wight, Eng.; conv. and j. the Meth. when very young. Her spirit and example were admirable. She trained her children well; was one of the managers of the Female Miss'y Soc'y, and active to the last. She d. in triumph, March 3, 1852, age 56.—**Munson, Amanda,** S.S.t.; b. in Broome Co., N. Y.; conv. at 14; d. 1847, age 21; fine scholar and faithful follower of Christ. [N. Bangs, in Ch. Ad.] Useful in S. S.; bur. in Utica, N. Y. [Minutes in S. S. Teachers' Record.]—*****Murphy, John Garrison,** S.S.t.; b., 1783, in Middletown, N. J. Timothy Murphy, his father, was a native of Ireland, and belonged to the American army in the Revolution. Stiles' Hist. B'klyn (vol. ii, p. 24) contains a sketch to which we are indebted for many facts concerning Mr. M. He mar. Clarissa Runyon, of Princeton, N. J., and rem. to B'klyn in 1808. By his industry and mechanical genius he established a profitable business as millwright. He was the inventor and patentee of the machinery for the team-boats used on the East River ferry and other ferries in the U. S. and Canada. He was school commissioner, justice of the peace, and judge of the Municipal Court. The Jeffersonian Democrats of Kings Co. regarded him as a leader in their party. The Sands-st. ch. people esteemed him highly as a S.S.t., trus., and

cl. ldr. His name, as we have seen, was signed to the 1st printed statement to the people of B'klyn concerning the establishing of a S. S., in 1816. After many yrs. he became a member of Wash'gt'n-st. ch. "He was a tall, fine-looking man, and possessed much prudence, reticence, and self-reliance." He d., Feb. 11, 1853, age 69, leaving 4 daughters and 2 sons, one of whom was the Hon. Henry C. Murphy, late pres't of the trustees of the B'klyn bridge.—***Clarissa**, his w., d. 1824, age 38, and was bur. in the old ch.-yard. See tombstone.—**Murray, Mary**, mar.; see Luckey.—MURRAY, THEODORE W.—MURRAY, MRS. FREELOVE.—**Myers, Mrs. Frances**, came from John st. ch., N. York; d., "suddenly in peace and hope," 1849, age 85. [N., in Ch. Ad.]

Nadal, Chas., Mrs. Sarah J., Rebecca M., and **Bernard H.**, rem. by c., 1876. See sketch of the Rev. Dr. Nadal.—****Napier, Thos. A.**, d. many yrs. ago.—**Nash, Israel**, rem. by c.—**Nast, Albert J.**, rem. by c., 1866.—NAST, FREDERICK A., S.S.lib'n.—NAST, GENNETT.—**Nast, Martha**, rem. by c., 1876; member 1 yr.—NATRASS, EDWIN C.—**Natrass, Emma**, rem. by c., 1879, to Sum'f'd ch.—**Neal, Charity**, rem. without c., 1850.—**Nelson, Paul** and **Magdalene**, rem.—**Newell, Mrs. Phœbe N.**, rem. by c.—****Newman, Elizabeth**, d.—**Newman, Sarah**, rem., 1851.—**Newton, Julia E.**, S.S.t.; rem., 1846.—**Nichols, Anthony**, loc. pr., 1818. The Records say: "1820, expelled."—****Nichols, Hannah Ann**, d.—**Nichols, John**, rem.—**Nickerson, John**, loc. pr.; rem. by c., 1819, to Danbury, Conn., where he d. about 1850, age 56; a loc. pr. till his death; truly a man of God. He was the father of the Rev. L. D. Nickerson, of the N. York East Conf.—*****Nickerson, Mrs. J.**, was also a member of Sands-st. ch.—NICKERSON, ROB'T.—**Niles, Isabella C.**, rem. by c., 1865.—**Niles, Virginia K.**, rem.—**Noden, Ann**, rem.—**Noden, Thos.**, loc. pr., 1852, from Wis.—**Nordhoff, Chas.**, S.S.t.; rem. by c., 1867, to Mich.; also **Chas.** and **Mrs. Chas.**, rem. by c., 1870.—NORDHOFF, LAWRENCE.—**Norfolk, Geo. H.** and **Mrs. G. H.** They were of Flatbush; rem. by c., 1865.—**Norris, Chas. T.**, rem. by c., 1867.—**Northridge, N. T.** and **Ann**, rem. by c., 1870.—NORTHROP, WM. B.—**Norton, Electa C.**, rem. by c., 1848.—**Norton, Mary C.**, rem. by c.—NOSTRAND, FRANCIS.—**Nostrand, Isaac**, trus. about 1824.

**Odell, Moses Field, son of Wm. D.; S. S. sec., off. S. S. miss'y soc., cl. ldr., and S. S. supt.; of Huguenot descent; b. in Tarrytown, N. Y., reared in N. York and B'klyn; held a position in the N. York custom-house during most of the active yrs. of his life. As member of Congress, during 4 yrs. of Lincoln's administration, he was personally intimate and friendly with the president. He voted conscientiously, and almost alone of his party, (Dem.,) for the abolition of slavery in the Dist. of

Hon. MOSES F. ODELL.

Columbia, and for the constitutional amendment prohibiting slavery throughout the land. He was a member of the Com. on the Conduct of the War. His total abstinence principles were known at Wash'gt'n as well as at home. Pres. Johnson appointed him naval officer for the port of N. York, which position he held till his death. He was religiously trained, a member of the S. S. from his childhood, a constant attendant upon the ch. services, and strictly upright in his life. Placed at the head of the S. S., he plainly saw the need of a spiritual preparation for his work, and gave his heart to God at a camp-meeting, when 28 yrs. of age. Thenceforward, to the close of his life, he was recognized as the prince of S. S. supts. He was a good singer, and pre-eminently successful as a leader of social meetings. For a number of yrs. he was actively connected with the Gen'l Miss'y Board. He d. of cancerous affection of the throat, in 1866, age 48. The Sands-st. quar. conf. adopted a memorial pronouncing him "eminently useful in every sphere of private, social, religious, and public life, in which, in the providence of God, he was called to act, and from which he was so early called." His death was lamented by thousands of friends, and especially by the S. S. Many successful business men have said to the writer: "He gave me counsel and assistance when I was one of his S. S. boys." "He was the best friend I ever had." He was worthily eulogized in the Ladies' Repository, June, 1867, and in the Ch. Ad. The B'klyn Eagle published a fine poem on the same subject by a member of the S. S. A tablet in the ch. commemorates his services.—**Sarah F.**, his w., dau. of Abraham Vanderveer, was a S.S.t.; rem. by c., 1880, to Sum'f'd ch.—****Odell, Sam'l U. F.**, bro. of Moses F., was S.S.t., off. S. S. miss'y soc'y, S. S. supt., std., and cl. ldr. He was the chosen delegate from this ch. to the 1st electoral conf. of laymen, in 1872. He was one of the managers of the General Miss'y Board. At the time of his death, and for several years previous, he was American Consul-general for the Kingdom of Hawaii, and he superintended the arrangements for the reception of King Kalakaua, when he visited the U. S. In business he was senior partner of the firm of Barclay & Livingstone, in N. York. He d. of erysipelas, which developed into Bright's disease of the kidneys, in the yr. 1875, age 44, and was bur. in "Greenwood." [Ch. Ad.]—***Belinda (Vanderveer)**, his w., sister of Mrs. M. F. Odell, was likewise a S.S.t. She rem. by c.,

1880, to Sum f'd ch.; d. in Oct., 1884. She was possessed of a quiet dignity, and was a person of true refinement and culture. —**Odell, Wm. D.,** cl. ldr.; father of Moses and Sam'l; a merchant in N. York; afterward, for 25 yrs., cl'k in the auditor's division of the custom house, where, even at his great age, his services were highly valuable. [Ch. Ad.] He d. in 1875, age 81.—****Susanna,** his w., d., in the "faith and peace of the gospel," in 1878. —**Oliver, Wm.,** rem., 1850.—OLLIFFE, MRS. ANNA.—OLLIFFE, ANNA.—OLLIFFE, ELIZA W.—**Olliffe, Emma,** mar; see Strong.—**Olliffe, Henrietta,** mar.; see Smith.—OLLIFFE, MRS. SPEARS.—**O'Neill, David,** S.S.t., cl. ldr., sec. and treas. of S. S., off. S. S. miss'y soc.; rem. to Fleet-st. ch.; actively and successfully engaged in S. S. work there, with J. E. Hanford and others from Sands-st. ch.; rem. at length to Orange, N. J. —**O'Neill, Mary,** rem.—**O'Neill, Oliver C.** and **Harriet E.,** rem. by c., 1869.—**O'Neil, Wm. Percival,** withdrew.—**Osborn, Augusta,** rem. by c., 1874.—**Osborn, Joshua,** withdrew.—**Osborn, Virginia,** rem. by c., 1874.—**Osborn, Wm.,** rem. Wm. S. Osborn was a S.S.t.—**Owen, Thos.** and **Eliza,** rem. by c., 1865. He was a loc. pr. in 1863.—****Owens, Margaret,** d.

PALMER, ARMENIA.—PALMER, ROB'T.—**Palmer, Wm. P.** and his w., **Sarah J. (Winters),** rem. by c. to N. J, 1883.—**Parcell, Ellis,** cl. ldr., 1838, in Sands-st. ch.; ditto, about 1860, in Johnson-st. ch.—**Parkinson, W. J.,** rem. by c., 1865.—PARKER, DAVID.—**Parker, Mrs. Frances Augusta,** rem. by c.; see sketch of Rev. L. Parker.—**Parker, Henry,** son of Wm.; rem. by c., 1870.—**Parker, Jane,** rem. by c., 1866.—**Parker, John,** S.S.t., and **Sarah,** rem. by c., 1869. —**Parker, Longworth,** bro. of Rev. L. Parker, rem.—**Parker, Wm.,** S.S t. and cl. ldr.; came with his family from Somerset, near Bristol, Eng., and brought 6 children at once into the S. S.; rem. by c., 1870, to Simpson ch.; then, changing his residence, j. Dr. H. M. Scudder's (now Dr. Berhend's) ch. Still retains his attachment to the doctrines and usages of Methodism. He was a barber yrs. ago, on Fulton-st.—**Susan,** his w., rem. by c., 1870.—**Parkinson, W. J.,** rem. by c., 1865.—****Parmelee, Walter,** d. 1849.—**Parmlee, Walter,** rem. 1849.—**Parsons,** ———, rem. to Pacific-st. ch., 1850.—**Parsons, Rachel,** rem.—**Patience, Wm. H.,** rem.—PAYNE, BETHUNE D. —**Payne, Shepherd H.,** son of Silas W., of York-st. ch.; b. in B'klyn; conv. and j. Sands-st. ch. when 11 yrs. of age, (H. J Fox, pastor;) rem. by c. to Amityville, L. I.; after 9 yrs., rem. to Carlton ave. ch., B'klyn; thence to 18th-st. ch., N. York, and finally returned to Carlton ave. (Simpson) ch., B'klyn; trus. and S.S.t. in several places.—**Peacock, I.,** rem. by c., 1867.— PEARSALL, M. E.—**Pearsall, Mehitable,** rem.—PEARSON, ELIZABETH.—**Pease, R. L.,** rem.—PECK, BELLA.

—*Peck, Capt. Chas., rem., 1849, to N. Haven, Conn., where he d. some time afterward. He was father of Mrs. J. Wesley Harper.—**Elizabeth, his 1st w., j. the M. E. ch. in her youth. She d. Aug. 7, 1847, age 56. During her long illness her mind was stayed on God. [J. B. Merwin, in Ch. Ad.] She is bur. in "Greenwood." Capt. P. was mar. again, in N. Haven, to the wid. of the Rev. John Mott Smith. Her maiden name was Amanda Day, and her early residence was Norwalk, Conn.—**Peck, Chas. Benson, captain of steamboat "American Eagle," was conv. at 18, and j. Sands-st. ch. He d. in 1841, age 22; bade w. and friends good-bye, and shouted, "All is well! He comes!" [P. C. Oakley, in Ch. Ad.]—Peck, Chas. Benson (2d) and Frances B., rem. by c. to Hanson Pl. ch., 1881.—**Peck, Laura C., " d. in peace," about 1848.—Peck, Mary W., rem.—Peck, Rachel S., rem. by c.—*Peck, Rob't W., b. in Orange Co., N. Y.; conv. in 1839, when 33 yrs. of age. He was made cl. ldr. in Sands-st. ch. in 1843; afterward he rem. to Fleet-st. ch.; thence to Nostrand ave. Energetic and wholly consecrated, he served the ch. as cl. ldr. 30 yrs., and passed through the gates of death with shouts of glory on his lips, May 2, 1870, age 74. [C. E. Glover, in Ch. Ad.] He was father-in-law of the Rev. E. H. Dutcher, of the N. Y. Conf.—**Peckham, Thos. G., S.S.t.; b. in R. I.; conv. and j. the M. E. ch. at 16. He was S. S. supt. 16 yrs. and cl. ldr. 25 yrs. in New Market, N. H., before coming to B'klyn. He d. in 1873, age 72. His last words were "Jesus! Jesus! Jesus!" He was a pious, thoughtful, genial Christian. [F. P. Tower, in Ch. Ad.]—Peckham, Frances E., mar.; see Scofield.—Peckham, Mereena; see Layton.—PECKHAM, MRS. THANKFUL.—**Pell, Albert, d. Oct. 28, 1881.—Pell, Annie, wid. of the above, rem. by c., 1884.—Pellett, Dan'l, rem.—Pelton, E. R., rem.—Pelton, R. S. and Catharine, rem. by c., 1866.—Percey, A. J., Eliza L., and Allie F., rem. by c., 1870.—*Perego, Carrie A., grand-dau. of Ira, Sr.; rem. by c., 1867; d. in New Orleans.—*Perego, Ira, Sr., cl. ldr., trus., std., and S. S. supt.; came from John-st. ch.: rem. by c., 1867, to 7th ave (now Grace) ch.; d. April 25, 1876, age 75.—*Frances Eliza, his w.; a member of John-st. ch., N. York, before joining Sands-st.; rem. to 7th ave. ch.; d. Nov. 27, 1867, age 62. See headstones in "Greenwood."—Perego. Ira, Jr., S. S. supt., off. S. S. miss'y soc'y, and cl. ldr. in Fleet-st. ch.; now a member of Grace ch.—Perego, Margaret, S.S.t.; a dau. of the senior Ira Perego; rem. to N. York.—PETTINGER, RHETTIE.—**Pettit, Mary E., d. —Pettit, Rob't, b. in Near Rockaway (Rockville Center) about 1810; j. M. E. ch. there, (Gershom Pearce, pastor;) rem. to B'klyn, and j. Sands-st. ch., about 1835; returned to Rockaway; a merchant there; later, engaged in business in N. York.

—*Elizabeth, his w., was b. in Hempstead ; d. July 22, 1881, age 74 ; a member of Nostrand ave. ch.—PHILLIPS, DAN'L B., S.S.t., std., S. S. sec., off. S. S. miss'y soc'y, and financial sec. of the ch.; b. in Phila; attended S. S. of Bap. ch., to which his parents belonged; came to B'klyn in 1845 ; was conv. and j. Sands-st. ch. when Dr. Nadal was pastor; clerk in Department of City Works 13 yrs.—ELIZA L. (M'GEE), w. of the above; S.S.t.—**Phillips, Edward,** rem. by c., 1831.—**Phillips, Geo. W.,** b. on L. I.; came to B'klyn in 1838 ; j. Sands-st. ch., 1858, (J. Miley, pastor;) rem. by c., 1865, also rem. by c., 1869, to Warren-st. ch., then to Janes ch., (Reid ave.,) 1882.—**Margaret,** his w., a native of N. York city ; j. Sands-st. about 1858 ; rem. by c.—**Phillips, Phœbe A.,** rem. by c., 1865.—*Piercey, Henry R., cl. ldr., 1827 ; became one of the chief founders and supporters of the Cong. Meth. ch. in B'klyn, (J. C. Green, pastor.) " He owned the 1st power-press in N. York city, and printed the Herald before the elder Bennett owned a press. He was a Republican and an advocate of the abolition of slavery in the early days when it was dangerous to proclaim that doctrine. He also published The Emancipator, and printed the 1st copies of the N. York Sun. He j. the N. York Typographical Soc. in 1820, and the surviving members were present at his funeral." [B'klyn Eagle, Oct. 17, 1881.] The Cong. Meth. ch. became the Union Cong. ch., of which Mr. P. was a prominent member when he d., Oct. 14, 1881, age 84.—**Pierson, Geo.** and **Eliza,** rem. by c.—**Pickering, Phœbe,** rem. by c., 1850.—PILKINGTON, SARAH.—**Pinkney, Andrew,** S.S.t.; rem. by c., 1835.—**Pitt, Sarah,** mar.—**Pitts, Chas. L.,** cl. ldr., about 1868.—**Plummer, Lucy,** rem. by c., 1849.—*Pomeroy, Chas., loc. elder in 1833. *Conf. Record:* 1822, (N. York Conf.,) Sharon cir., N. Y., with Jas. Quinlan ; 1823, Jefferson cir., with Jesse Pomeroy and Q. Stewart; 1824, app't not recorded ; 1825, ord. deacon; 1825-26, Montgomery cir., with H. Eames, Jacob Beeman, Theodosius Clark, and J. Elton; 1827-28, Peru cir., with J. Leonard and Elijah Crane; 1828, ord. elder; 1829-30, Bridport, Vt., with C. R. Morris, Wm. P. Lake, sup'y, and R. Westcott; 1831, Leicester cir., with Lewis Potter; 1832, located. The Rev. P. C. Oakley writes: " I knew Chas. Pomeroy in 1832, but have no recollection of him since. He was a devout man, but a little eccentric; for example, he would commence with a mild and pleasant voice, but suddenly elevate it so that his hearers said it made their heads ache. He had a strong intellect. I heard him once at a camp-meeting preach one of the ablest sermons on the divine government that I ever listened to. It was clear and profound. I think that in his latter days he was subject to mental aberration."—**Potter, Mrs. Abagail,** rem. by c., 1869.—**Potter, Abbie J.,** rem. by c., 1871.—**Potter, Joseph,** withdrew.—**Powell, Alma,** rem. by c., 1867.—**Powell, Amanda,** rem.—**Powell, Anna,** mar.; see Carson.—**Powell, Annie,** rem. by c., 1880.—**Powell, Mrs. Hannah,** rem. by c., 1874.—**Powell, Hannah E.,** rem. by c. to De Kalb ave. ch., 1880.—POWELL, HULDAH.—**Powell, Jos.,** rem.—****Powell, Mrs. Kate,** d. March 6, 1868, age 20.—****Powell, Matilda,** mar., and d.—**Powell, Rob't J.,** cl. ldr., about 1864. He and **Augusta** rem. by c., 1867.—**Powell, Ruth,** rem. by c., 1876. —POWELL, WEALTHY.—POWER, MRS. ELLEN.— ***Powers, Mary,** w. of Geo. (2d;) j. Sands-st. ch. (probably in 1797;) one of the honorable women whose name is fragrant with blessed memories. It is said that the Dean-st. (afterward Hanson Pl.) ch. was organized at her home. The house stood on what is now the N. E. cor. Flatbush ave. and Hanson Pl. It was in the center of extended grounds with little to obstruct the view of out-lying fields and hills. She gave 4 lots on Dean-st., that is, a plot 100 feet square, for the building, and made other large donations. One of her last acts, as she lay on her death-bed, was to place $500 in the hands of her pastor, Sam'l Law, for her loved Hanson Pl. ch. Her grandson, Geo. A. Powers, counted the money for her in $1 bills. A memorial tablet, near the pulpit in Hanson Pl. ch., contains the following inscription: *In memory of Mrs. Mary Powers; b. Apr.* 20, 1771, *and d. in peace, Aug.* 2, 1857, *aged* 86 *yrs.,* 3 *mos., and* 13 *days. For* 60 *yrs. a faithful member of the M. E. ch. Charitable, humble, devoted; a liberal contributor to this ch.* "*Blessed are the dead who die in the Lord.*" Her husband was the 2d in a succession of 6, in a direct line, by the name of Geo. Powers. Stiles' Hist. of B'klyn contains a sketch of his father, who was an Episcopalian. The husband of Mary Powers d. 1829, age 51, and a headstone in the old Sands-st. Meth. ch.-yard shows that

MRS. MARY POWERS.

he was bur. there. C. C. Smith and Geo. A. Powers are of the opinion that he was a member of Sands-st. ch., but his name is not found on any existing record of the ch. Mr. Smith was present at his funeral, and recollects that Geo. Smith and Judge Garrison were pall-bearers. His son, George, d. in 1832, and is bur. in Sands-st. ch.-yard; probably not a member. A dau. of Geo. and Mary Powers, w. of Wm. Jenkins, d. 1828, age 25. See headstone in the old ch.-yard.—*Pray, John G., cl. ldr. and trus. in Sands-st. ch.; a native of Kittery, Me.; commenced a sea-faring life when very young; after his marriage came to B'klyn, and j. the St. Ann's Episcopal ch. Having experienced converting grace at a camp-meeting, he united with the Methodists; after some time left Sands-st. ch., and became a cl. ldr. and S. S. supt. in Wash'gt'n-st. ch. Stiles, in Hist. of B'klyn, states that he was a member of the "Society to Prevent Vice" in 1813, and later became one of the 1st members of the B'klyn S. S. Union. He was a successful ship-master; made a number of profitable voyages to the East Indies; then his friends— ministers and prominent members of the ch.—urged him to give up the sea, which he somewhat reluctantly did, and engaged in the printing and publishing business—firm, "Pray & Bowen." One of the older Harpers and J. J. Matthias were employed by them, and lived in Mr. Pray's family for a time. His dau., Mrs. Spinney, thinks he made a mistake in leaving his former occupation for one with which he was not acquainted. He d. Jan. 24, 1839, age 57.—**Hannah (Lord), his 1st w., was mar. to Mr. P. in Portsmouth, N. H., in 1805, became a member of Sands-st. ch. [So writes Mrs. Capt. Spinney.] She d. in 1825, age 44.—*Lucy (Emerson), his 2d w., was from a Meth. family in Malden, Mass. She d. in 1832, age 32, and is bur. in Sands-st. ch.-yard. [Hannah Stryker.] The following are the names of the children by the 1st marriage who lived to maturity: Mary A., wid. of Capt. Jos. Spinney, of B'klyn; Hannah, wid. of Thos. Staples, of Cal.; Elizabeth, w. of Rich'd H. Cornwell, of N. J.; John W., mar. Matilda, dau. of Judge Dikeman, of B'klyn—both dead. Children by 2d marriage: Lucy M. C., d. in Balston Spa, N. Y., member of Wash'gt'n-st. ch., B'klyn; Geo., d. in childhood; Jos. M., of B'klyn, mar. Mary B., dau. of Judge Dikeman.—PRESCOTT, MARGARET G.—**Preston, Andrews,** rem. by c., 1882.—**Preston, Wm. Irvine,** son of Andrews and Eliza Ann (Ferris) Preston, grandson of Sam'l and Louisa (Abbott) Preston, and great-grandson of Jacob Preston, is a native of Cato, Cayuga Co., N. Y. He was b. Sept. 3, 1828, the 3d of a family of 11 children. His father was greatly respected as a man of integrity and ability, and was thrice elected a member of the N. Y. Legislature. As a boy, Wm. was "adventurous, daring, generous," and was called "General Put," from his likeness to the intrepid Putnam of

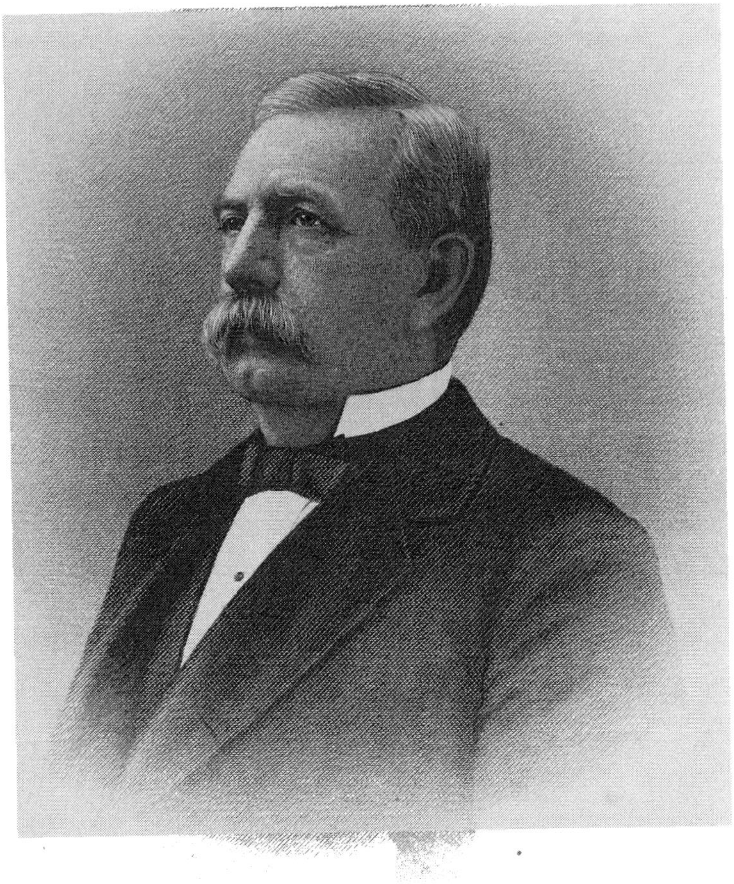

Wm J Preston

Eng^d by H.B. Hall's Sons New York

Revolutionary fame. "Many anecdotes are related of his narrow escapes from the use of small cannon ; of many instances when his face and hands were severely burned with powder; of his falling into a caldron of lye, which took the skin from his entire body. On one occasion young Preston, as the champion of the village boys, in a contest with the country boys, was soundly thrashed by the leader of the latter." At 15 he attended a high school in Victory, N. Y., (the Rev. J. C. Vandercook, principal;) one yr. later, his father having established himself as a merchant in Red Creek, N. Y., he entered the academy in that town as a student. He was soon taken into his father's employ, and subsequently became a partner in the firm of "A Preston & Son." When 19 yrs. of age he j. the M. E. ch. in Red Creek, was devoted and exemplary, and in a short time was chosen S. S. supt. It is said that "the manner in which he discharged the duties of this position highly distinguished him and led to the most pleasing results. He seemed peculiarly qualified to blend instruction with delight." At 21 he was town-clerk of Wolcott; at 22, postmaster; subsequently supervisor of the town. He was mar. Oct. 21, 1851, and the same year he engaged in the hardware business in Auburn, N. Y., and became cl. ldr., trus., and S. S. supt. in the North-st. ch. of that city. "Being very fond of music, he used his influence to advance the musical interests of the ch. At this time instruments were almost unknown in Meth. churches. Through Mr. Preston's influence a melodeon was purchased and placed in the ch. The morning it was first used old father Cherry came early to ch., taking his seat near the pulpit. As the singing began he caught the sound of the melodeon, and, indignant at the innovation, he marched down the aisle, exclaiming in a loud voice, striking the floor with his heavy cane, 'I cannot and will not stand the growling of that bull-dog!'" Mr. P. returned to Red Creek in 1853, and removed thence to Oswego in 1854, where he began his successful career in the grain commission trade. He j. the 1st M. E. ch. of Oswego, "and was soon made trus., std., cl. ldr., and S. S. sup't. The society was in debt, and for a long time was subjected to a severe struggle for existence. Among other difficulties was the intrusion of the slavery question." The calm reasoning of Mr. Preston availed, a disastrous rupture was averted, and the ch. grew to be one of the strongest in the conf. "A chapel was erected in the southern portion of the city, which the friends of Mr. P. desired to name 'Preston Chapel,' but as he would not consent to this, it was finally called Fifth-st. Chapel." During the war our friend advocated the Union cause, and induced many to enlist. When the N. Y. 110th was ready for service, by appointment of the citizens of Oswego, and of the Board of Trade, of which he was pres't, and in behalf of the donors, Mr. Preston presented, with a fitting speech, to Col. De Witt C.

Littlejohn, a sword and a caparisoned horse. As Dem. candidate for mayor of Oswego and for member of assembly he was defeated by small majorities. In 1865 he rem. to N. York, and 6 mos. later to B'klyn; j. Sands-st. ch. in 1867; became S.S.t., cl. ldr., trus., and S. S. supt.; rem. by c. from this ch. in 1882; j. the M. E. ch. in Sea Cliff, " having accepted the office of pres't of the Sea Cliff Assoc'n, for the express purpose of aiding in extricating that corporation from its financial troubles." We learn that Mr. P. is intensely interested in St. Paul's M. E. ch., in B'klyn, and is devising liberally and (no doubt) wisely a new departure in the practical methods of ch. work. He is actively identified with the Amer. Bible Soc'y, the Miss'y Soc'y of our ch., the B'klyn City Bible Soc'y, the Syracuse Univ., (as trustee,) and the very efficient and useful B'klyn Ch. Soc'y, (as chief founder, pres't, and honorary life patron.) He holds a prominent position in the Masonic fraternity, is connected with the Fulton Bank and with the Historical Societies of L. I. and N. York. [Condensed from a work on B'klyn, published 1884.]— **Laura L.**, his w., dau. of the late Rev. Reuben Reynolds, of the Northern N. Y. Conf., was teacher in the Sands-st. S. S.; rem. by c., 1882.—**Price, Jennie,** mar.; see Tayleure.— PRICE, MARY H.—PRICE, MRS. SARAH H.—*****Prince, Benj. R.,** b. on Shelter Island, Sept. 8, 1800; worked in the summer and attended school in the winter, like other farmer boys. In 1818 he commenced learning the carpenter's trade with Jos. Glover, of Southold. An incident is related by Mr. P. which illustrates the drinking customs of those days. " My boss," he says, " built a house for Mr. C. at Rocky Point. The contract was $900 and board, with a pint of rum a day for himself and two boys. The boss used all the rum." [L. I. Traveler.] His happy conversion on the 18th of July, in that yr., in the private house where the Methodists held their meetings, marked the beginning of a revival which continued until 80 converts were numbered with the Xn. disciples in the neighborhood of Southold, and a ch. was built. The young convert was appointed cl. ldr., and several of the veteran ch. members were in his class. His comrades called him " deacon." Having completed his apprenticeship, he came to B'klyn and hired out to Jos. Moser. He presented his ch. certificate to the Sands-st. ch. In 1823 he was mar. to the eldest dau. of Wm. and Anna Foster, members of this ch. After working at his trade 6 yrs., he started a lumber-yard at the foot of Jackson-st., accumulated $100,000 in 10 yrs., but lost it all in the crash of 1837. He subsequently turned his attention to inspection of lumber for a number of yrs. He was trus. of B'klyn village, and alderman of the city 3 yrs. During the cholera epidemic in 1832 he faithfully visited the sick and cared for the dead in his ward. All the work devolved upon him, as his colleague became frightened and

REV. ELNATHAN RAYMOND.

ran away. He was connected with the fire dep't of B'klyn
14 yrs. Leaving Sands-st. ch., he was cl. ldr. in York-st. ch.
for some time. At length he returned to Southold, and spent
his last yrs. amid the scenes of his youth. He received exhorter's and preacher's license about 1854, [Southold quar. conf.
record,] and was cl. ldr. and S. S. supt. The writer was for 3
yrs. favored with the fellowship and co-operation of B. R. Prince
in Christian labor on the Southold charge. He suffered greatly
from asthma, but glowed with seraphic fervor of soul, and
labored to the last limit of his strength for the church of his
Redeemer. He d. in Southold, Jan. 28, 1878, age 77, having
been about 60 yrs. a Meth. He went through life singing, for
his religion made him uniformly happy. He often said that
most of his early Christian companions had gone on before him,
and he was not unwilling to enter their ranks and join their
victorious song.—*Sarah Ann, his 1st w., was conv. under the
ministry of Lewis Pease, and j. Sands-st. ch. at the age of 14.
She d. in 1847, age 40; an excellent woman and faithful worker
in the S. S. Mr. P. was mar. in 1849 to Temperance Brown,
and she survives him.—*Prince, Martin, rem. by c., 1832;
probably the Martin Prince, bro. of Benj. R. He was subsequently for many yrs. a member of the Presbyterian ch. on
Shelter Island; d. in Babylon, L. I., Oct. 27, 1883, age 71.—
Pritchard, Mary Irene, mar.; see Moore.—PROUSE, MRS.
HARRIET.—Pullman, George, rem. by c., 1876.—Purdy,
Mary E., mar.; see Walling.

Quale, Jane, rem. 1846.—Quereane, Elizabeth, rem.—
QUIMBY, DAVID S., trus.; b. in Marlboro, Ulster Co., N. Y.;
came to N. York city in 1829; j. Bedford-st. ch.; rem. to B'klyn
in 1832. He cherishes a strong affection for the Sands-st. ch.
He has been from early manhood in the stove business—dealer
and manufacturer.—Quimby, David S., Jr., S.S.t, S.S. sec., off.
S. S. miss'y soc'y, trus., and std.; rem. by c. to Sum'f'd ch. in
1878; was in real estate business; later, in the establishment
formerly occupied by his father.—Maria L., his w.; rem. by
c., 1878.—Quimby, Mrs. Elizabeth, rem. by c., 1883.—
**Quimby, Rob't A., d.

RATHBURN, MRS. MARIA.—RAYERCRAFT, ELIZA
E.—RAYERCRAFT, MARTHA.—RAYERCRAFT, MRS.
MARY J.—*Raymond, Elnathan, loc. pr. and cl. ldr. in this
ch.; b. Apr. 23, 1789, in Norwalk, Conn., the 6th son of Nathaniel
and Dolly Raymond, who were Methodists. His brothers j. other
denominations, but he adhered to the ch. in which he was reared.
While an apprentice in N. York, age 17, he j. the old John-st.
ch. He mar., in 1811, Miss Lydia Bess, of Norwalk, Conn., by
whom he had 3 sons, only 1 now living. In 1817 he moved to
Muskingum Co., O.; in 1818 his w. d.; in 1819 he mar. Rachel
Banning, dau. of a loc. pr. of Mt. Vernon, O.; that yr. a supply

on Knox cir.; returned in 1821 to the East, and engaged in the furrier business with his 2 bros., in B'klyn; member of Sands-st. ch. until 1831; then of Wash'gt'n st. ch. He is mentioned in the Meth. Mag., 1823, p. 118, as the chief founder of Methodism in Bay Ridge, L. I. In 1834 he returned to Mt. Vernon, O., and 3 yrs. later j. conf., having been ordained deacon and elder. *Itinerant Record:* 1837, (Mich. Conf.,) ag't Norwalk Sem., O.; 1838, Mansfield cir., with O. Monett; 1839, Martinsburgh cir.; 1840, (N. Ohio Conf.,) Galena cir., with S. B. Guiberson; 1841, Frederick cir., with H. Camp; 1842, ditto, with O. Burgess; 1843, Bellville cir., with J. Burgess; 1844-45, P. E., Wooster Dist.; 1846-47, P. E., Tiffin Dist.; 1848, Frederick cir., with T. H. Wilson; 1849, Amity cir., with O. Mitchell; 1850, ditto, W. M. Conant; 1851, sup'y; 1852, East Union cir., with Wm. Boggs; 1853, Utica cir., with J. M'Nabb; 1854, Newcomerstown cir., with Wm. Boggs; 1855, Chesterville cir., with S. Faut; 1856, sup'y, Mt. Vernon, O., Banning chapel, with D. Rutledge; 1857-58, ditto, with Wm. M. Conant; 1859, ditto, with Jas. Wheeler; 1860-73, sup'd. He d. July 31, 1874, age 85. Mr. R. was an excellent man, zealous, faithful, and "always happy in the Lord." His 1st. w. d., as already stated.—*****Rachel (Banning),** his 2d w., d. in blessed hope, July 23, 1880, age 84. She is bur. with her husband in Mt. Vernon cem. Children of Mr. R. by 2d marriage, living in 1883: Mrs. G. A. Jones, Mrs. D. Blanchard, and Mary Raymond, of Mt. Vernon, O.; a widowed dau. in Ala.; and a son in Kan.—*****Read, Mrs. Margaret,** w. of Wm., sister to Mrs. Wm. M'Donald, b. in B'klyn; rem. to Fleet-st. in 1850—a "charter member;" d. at her country home in Allendale, N. J., Apr. 3, 1882, age 79; bur. in "Greenwood." An active, faithful, consistent Xn.—**Reast, Alpha,** rem. by c.—**Reast, Fred J.,** off. S. S. miss'y soc'y, cl. ldr., and financial sec. of the ch., was b. in Eng., of Episcopalian parents; conv. under the labors of Jas. Caughey, June 21, 1846, age 15, and j. the Wesleyans; came to N. York at 21; j. 9th-st. M. E. ch. in 1852; rem. by c. to Sands-st. ch., B'klyn, when H. J. Fox was pastor; as ldr. took Jacob Brown's Sunday-morning class; rem. by c., 1884.—******Margaret (Stryker),** his w., dau. of John and Hetty Stryker, was a S.S.t.; connected with the school from her infancy until her death, Nov. 30, 1878, at the age of 43. She is bur. in Evergreen cem. Left a family of children.—REAST, FRANCIS S.—**Reast, Herbert Odell,** rem. by c., 1884.—**Reast, Mary H.,** rem. by c., 1884.— REAST, WM. J.—**Redfield, John,** loc. pr.; rem. to N. York, 1848.—REED, DAYTON.—**Reed, D. I.,** loc. pr., 1846.— REED, MRS. FANNIE.—REED, FANNIE M.—**Reed, Jane R.,** rem.—**Reed, John** and **Mrs. J.,** rem by c. 'to Nostrand ave., 1878.—*****Reed, Thos.,** S.S.t.; j. Sands-st. ch. when J. W. B. Wood was pastor; one of the founders of

Fleet-st. ch. in 1850; cl. ldr. and std. there; d. July 28, 1872, age 43; bur. in "Greenwood."—**Sarah A. (De Gray)**, w. of the above; j. Sands-st. ch. about 1847, (W. H. Norris, pastor;) was S.S.t.; rem. to Fleet-st.—among the 1st members; thence to Sum'f'd ch.—**Reed, Thos. P.**, rem. by c., 1868; member a short time.—**Reed, Wm.**, rem. by c. to Nostrand ave. ch., 1878.—**Reeve, Emily**, rem. by c., 1882.—**Reeve, Tappan**, was trus. in 1855.—**Reid, Gilbert H.**, rem. to Johnson-st. ch., 1850.—**Reynolds, Israel**, rem. to N. York.—REYNOLDS, KATE P.—**Reynolds, Mrs. Lydia**, dau. of Isaac Moser; rem.—RHINEHART, LAVINIA.—RICHARDS, GEORGE S., b. in Troy, Me., March 4, 1845. His ancestors came from Dorsetshire, Eng., and landed at Plymouth, Mass., in 1632. His father, Rob't R. Richards, was a Meth. preacher in the Me. and E. Me. Confs. 25 yrs. Geo. S. Richards commenced teaching school in Me. when 17 yrs. of age. Three yrs. later (1865) he settled in Richmond, Va., where he connected himself with the M. E. ch., in 1870; was std. and trus. 12 yrs., having official relation to the ch. prior to membership in it. He was collector of internal revenue for 2d Dist. of Va. from Dec., 1870, to Dec., 1877; rem. to B'klyn in 1878, engaged in the wholesale oil business, and is now treas. of the N. York Refining Co. He j. Sands-st. ch. on coming to B'klyn, and has been for some time a cl. ldr. He is a member of the Board of Managers of the B'klyn S. S. Union. In 1870 he was mar. to Mary M., dau. of Dr. Jesse Nichols, of New Bedford, Mass. Mr. R. is brother-in-law to the Rev. Dr. J. R. Day, of the N. York Conf.—RICHARDSON, MRS. HARRIET.—RICHARDSON, LIZZIE.—RICHARDSON, MRS. ISABELLA.—****Richardson, Marvel**, (1st,) d. 1831, age 67. [Headstone in old ch.-yard.] Probably a member. Left 3 sons, Benj., Hiram, and Marvel, and 2 daughters, Elizabeth and Mary.—****Richardson, Marvel**, (2d,) a shoe-maker; d. 1849.—***Richardson, Marvin**, son of Stephen and Huldah, was cl. ldr. in this ch. in 1807, loc. pr. in 1808, and was recommended by this ch. to the traveling connection in 1809. He was b. in Stephentown, N. Y., June 10, 1789. While a youth came with his parents to B'klyn, and attended Sands-st. ch.; was awakened in the fall of 1805, and j. the ch. on probation. At a camp-meeting in Tuckahoe, N. Y., May 10, 1806, he found peace in believing. The Rev. L. M. Vincent states that Ezekiel Cooper appointed him cl. ldr. in 1807, but his name is omitted (doubtless by mistake) from our list of cl. ldrs. taken from the ch. records. Having spoken to his pastor, Dan'l Ostrander, in the summer of 1808, concerning his convictions in regard to the gospel ministry, "he was overwhelmed by an announcement from the pulpit on the succeeding Sabbath, that Marvin Richardson would preach in that ch. on the following Thursday ev'g. He came and preached his 1st sermon from Matt. xvi, 24. He was licensed to preach at the ensuing quar. conf., Oct. 1, 1808." [Conf. Min., 1877, p. 41,] He was then only 19 yrs. of age. *Ministerial Record:* 1808, supply on Croton cir., with E. Woolsey; 1809, (N. York Conf.,) Charlotte cir., Vt., with Andrew M'Kain; 1810, Granville cir., Mass. and Conn., with G. Pearce; 1811, ord. deacon,—Buckland, Mass.; 1812, Dutchess cir., N. Y., with W. Anson and W. Swayzey; 1813, ord. elder,—New Haven, Conn.; 1814, N. York, with W. Phœbus, S. Cochran, N. Emery, T. Drummond, and W. Blagborne; 1815, ditto, with W. Thacher, E. Washburn, and A. Scholefield; 1816, Jamaica cir., L. I., with Thos. Ware; 1817–18, Middletown, Conn.; 1819–20, New Rochelle cir., N. Y., with S. Bushnell; 1821, N. York, with J. Soule, E. Hebard, W. Ross, H. Bangs, and J. Summerfield; 1823, Croton cir., with F. Reed, a supply; 1824, ditto, with P. C. Oakley; 1825, Redding and Bridgeport cir., Conn., with H. Humphreys and F. W. Sizer; 1826, ditto, with H. Humphreys; 1827–28, Po'keepsie; 1829, Dutchess cir., with A. M. Osbon; 1830, ditto, with M. Mallinson; 1831, P. E., Hudson River Dist.; 1832–34, P. E., Newburgh Dist.; 1835–37, P. E., Po'keepsie Dist.; 1838–39, N. York, Duane-st.; 1840–41, N. York, Willett-st.; 1842, Bushwick and Wallabout, L. I.; 1843–46, P. E., Newburgh Dist.; 1847–50, P. E., Po'keepsie Dist.; 1850, sup'y, Po'keepsie, Wash'gt'n-st., with W. H. Ferris, and Wm. Jewett, sup'y; 1852, sup'y, N. York, Duane-st., with R. A. Chalker; 1853, ditto, with Z. N. Lewis; 1854–76, sup'd. This record covers a period of nearly 70 yrs. Thos. Thorp was led to Christ by his 1st sermon on the Croton cir., in 1808, and became a useful preacher; but the young evangelist was so diffident, and sometimes so discouraged, that his colleagues with difficulty restrained him from abandoning his work. To the next cir., 300 m. distant, he went on horseback, " carrying his clothing and books, all that he possessed, in his portmanteau; . . . 200 souls were added to the membership of the circuit." [Stevens' Hist. M. E. Ch., vol. iv, p. 254.] One of the converts under his ministry on the Dutchess cir. became the honored and useful Dr. Fitch Reed, one of the pastors of Sands-st. ch. In those early days his experience consisted of " long, weary days of travel on horseback, through forests, fording rivers, sleeping in log huts, with beds often covered with snow, preaching from 6 to 10 times a week, and winding up the years. toil with empty pockets and threadbare garments—but with a harvest of souls." [Conf. Min.] He " became one of the representative men of his conf., and was called the finest-looking member of that body—in person well-proportioned and dignified, with an expressive face, simple but most courteous manners, of few words, extreme modesty, great prudence in counsels, and tranquil uniformity of temper and life—the perfect Christian gentleman and unblemished Christian minister." [Dr. Abel Stevens.] The writer is assured from personal acquaintance that all this is true of Marvin Richardson. He was a member of 8 successive Gen. Conferences, including 1820 and 1848. The Wes. Univ. gave him the degree of D.D. in 1868. In his last speech in conf., in feeble and trembling tones, he said: "I am one who never asked a presiding elder or a bishop for an appointment. I have been asked where I wanted to go, but have replied,

REV. MARVIN RICHARDSON, D.D.

'That is not my work.' I have never received a dollar of the public funds of the ch. Money has been put into my hands, but I have transferred it to those more needy. . . . I j. the Methodists in 1805. Since we last met I have been close to the cold waters of Jordan, but I have been preparing for it for years." The day before his death he said, "All is bright; I have no fear!" and, with reason unclouded and faith triumphant, he sweetly fell asleep, in Po'keepsie, N. Y., June 14, 1876, age 87. A headstone marks his grave in the Po'keepsie cem. (See sketch of M. R. in Simpson's Cyclopedia.) His w., Sarah, was b. in Dutchess Co., N. Y., in 1791; conv. under the ministry of Nathan Bangs; mar. to Mr. R. in 1813; d. in New York, Aug. 12, 1856, age 65; funeral text: Job xiv, 14. [J. S. Mitchell, in Ch. Ad.] She is bur. beside her husband. Of their 4 children, 3 are living, (1884.) One, the w. of the Rev. L. M. Vincent, resides in her father's old home in Po'keepsie.—RICHARDSON, MARVIN, (2d.)—**Richardson, Mary,** mar.; see Sales.— *Richardson, Simon, bro. of Marvin; conv. in 1805; j. Sands-st. ch.; made cl. ldr. in 1807; an early member of Wash'gt'n-st. ch.; cl. ldr. there; subsequently j. Cook-st. ch., where he was cl. ldr. and trus. He was circumspect, industrious, generous. His emotions often gushed forth in tears. On the 28th of Oct., 1854, he d., age 66. Last whisper: "O how bright, how lovely!" [Dr. J. Kennaday, in Ch. Ad.] He was a grocer in B'klyn; afterward a rope manufacturer in "Cross Roads."—**Sarah,** his w.; d. about 1819.—**Richardson, Stephen,** was father of the Rev. M. Richardson, who writes concerning the revival in N. York, which followed the camp-meeting in Tuckahoe, in 1806: "Many were led to Christ, and among the number, to my great joy, our whole family, consisting of father, mother, and 3 bros. and 3 sisters, found peace with God and connected themselves with the M. E. ch. [Quoted in Stevens' Hist. M. E. Ch., vol. iv, p. 254.] He d. in 1826, age 65. See headstone in Sands-st. ch.-yard.—**Huldah,** his w., d. in 1837, age 77, and was bur. by his side. Their sons were Marvin, Simon, Lemuel, Gideon, and Benj. Among his grandchildren are Mrs. N. T. Beers, and the wid. of the late Mayor Powell, of B'klyn.—**Richmond, Mary C.,** w. of Henry C., dau.-in-law of Warren Richmond; d. 1865, age 35. —RICHMOND, WARREN, cl. ldr., was b. of Meth. parents in Killingworth, Conn., April 3, 1797. The family moved to Southold, L. I., when he was 4 yrs. old. After learning the carpenter's trade, he came to N. York, at the age of 21. In 1823 he rem. to B'klyn, and after a few yrs. established himself in the grocery business, on the N. E. cor. Pearl and Sands, moved thence some time afterward to Fulton-st., opposite Clark; remained there until 1853, when he sold out his interest in the business. He was conv. and j. Sands-st. ch. in 1828, (S. Luckey, pastor.) The writer was intimately associated with him in Southold, where he owns a farm and spends a large share of his time. He is a veteran in the church, thoughtful, independent in his views, conservative, and thoroughly reliable. He was on the ch. building committee in 1848. The records show that he served with J. Wesley Harper a long time as the committee to visit the S. S., and from the reports we infer that he discharged his duty in an admirable manner.—**Jemima (Wheeler)**, his 1st w., was b. in Smithtown, L. I., and d. suddenly in 1859, age 62. She was ready. Her grave is in "Greenwood." Their sons: Warren P., deceased; Albert S., deceased; Henry C.—RICHMOND, BETSEY (GRISWOLD), w. of the above. She was an efficient S.S.t., in charge of the infant class many yrs.—RICHMOND, HENRY C., son of Warren.—**Riddle, Elizabeth**, rem., 1845.—RIDER, MRS. EMILY.—RIEGE, WM.—**Riencke, Chas.**, d., 1865.—**Riencke, Mrs.**, a wid.; d. 1872.—**Righter, C. A.**, rem.—**Riley, Joseph**, b. in Ireland; heard John Wesley preach; came to the U. S. when 18 yrs. of age; mar. Miss Lydia Baker in 1799; was reclaimed from sinful wandering under the ministry of H. J. Fox, and j. Sands-st. ch.; d. 1857, age 80. [H. B., in Ch. Ad.]—**Lydia**, his w., was b. in N. York; j. old John-st. ch. previous to her marriage; was a genuine, old-fashioned Meth.; d. about 1862. Both are bur. in "Cypress Hills." One of the daughters mar. Sam'l Herbert, of Sands-st. ch.—**Ringwood, Catharine C.**, rem. by c. to Elm Pl. Cong. ch., 1877.—**Ritchie, Wm. M.**, rem. by c.—**Roach, Bridget,** "d. in the Lord."—**Roberts, Emma** and **Mrs. Hannah**, rem. by c., 1871.—**Roberts, Matilda**, mar. C. A. Barnard.—ROBERTS, WM. H.—ROBERTSON, ALEX.—**Robertson, Annie**; see Pell.—ROBERTSON, AUGUSTA.—**Robertson, Elizabeth**, rem. by c., 1847.—ROBERTSON, JAS. D.—ROBERTSON, JAS. W., cl. ldr. and std.—ROBERTSON, MRS. MARIA H.—**Robertson, Rob't**, rem.—**Robinson, Henry H.** and **Maria H.**, rem., 1846.—ROBINSON, LUCY.—**Robinson, Mrs. Maria**, rem., 1874.—**Robson, Maria J.**, rem., 1870.—**Robson, Rob't**, loc. pr. from Canada, 1861; loc. pr. in 18th-st. ch., 1867-71.—**Rogers, Abbie A.**, rem.—**Rogers, Elizabeth**, S.S.t., 1822; left and j. York-st. ch.; mar. Ira C. Buckalew. Her son, J. R. Buckalew, was for some yrs. a member of the N. Y. E. Conf.—**Rogers, Jas. L.** and **Catharine**, rem. to N. J., 1850.—*Rogers, Joshua**, b. in Centerport, L. I., Oct. 11, 1784; mar. Desire Higbie, dau. of Dan'l Higbie, of Old Fields; rem. by c. from Sands-st. ch., probably to become one of the founders of York-st. ch.; cl. ldr. and trus. there many yrs.; a Meth. more than half a century. "His name was the synonym of all that is humble in spirit, unostentatious in manner, pure in purpose, and consistent in piety." [J. L. Gilder, in Hist. of York-st. ch.]—ROGERS, RICH'D L.—**Rolph, Augustus**, cl. ldr., 1831.—**Romer, Jas. L.**, cl. ldr., std., and off. S. S. miss'y soc'y; went to Sum'f'd ch. Reported deceased. Left w. and children.—**Roscoe, Jackson** and **Mary**, rem. by c., 1865; members 1 yr.—**Ross, Julia** and **Jane**, rem. by c. to Embury ch., 1879.—**Rossell, John**, loc. pr. and cl. ldr.; b. in Englishtown, Monmouth Co., N. J., in 1815; conv. at 16 in old Halsey-st. ch., Newark, under

J. N. Maffit's labors; mar. 1834; came to B'klyn 1839; preached his 1st sermon in Leonard's hotel, Sheepshead Bay, L. I. The old lady tended bar while the proprietor attended the meeting. Mr. R. left Sands-st. ch. in 1850 to become one of the "charter members" of Fleet-st. ch.; now a cl. ldr. and loc. deacon there. He was associated for a time with Chas. Battersby, as pastoral supply at Sheepshead Bay; had charge, as a supply, of Warren-st. ch. when the society was worshiping in a private house; afterward preached at Cypress Hills, and still later filled unexpired term of pastor in Fort Lee, N. J.—**Rebecca H. (Smith)**, his w., when a young lady, went out and gathered 18 new scholars for the Wash'gt'n-st. S. S., some of whom have become valuable members of the church. She rem. by c. from Sands-st. to Fleet-st. ch. in 1850.—**Rossell, Virginia or Jennie**; see Johnson.—*****Rote, Elizabeth**, member in 1798.— ****Ruggles, Nath'l**, loc. pr., was b. in Danbury, Conn.; conv. at 25; j. N. York Conf., with Rob't Seney and others, in 1820, and was appointed to Burlington cir., Vt., with Datus Ensign; located after 1 yr. on account of impaired health; established his residence in Bridgeport, Conn., where a ch. was built under his pastoral care; labored as loc. pr. in various places; came to B'klyn and j. Sands-st. ch. in 1845. His voice was often heard in the pulpit and in the social meetings. In 1847 he was seized with paralysis, affecting seriously his intellect, " but to the last glimmer of its expiring light it beamed for Christ and purity." He d. in 1850, age 55. [J. W. B. Wood, in Ch. Ad.]—**Ruland, Henrietta**, rem. by c., 1880.—**Ruland, Mary L.**, rem. by c., 1882.—****Ruland, Sophronia**; see Cunningham.—RUNDLE, CATHARINE E.—**Runyan, Jas.**, rem., 1842.—RUSHER, WM.—****Rushmore, Rebecca G.**, w. of W.; d. 1828. Her grave is in the Hempstead Presbyterian ch.-yard. Her husband mar. the wid. of Wm. Ross. [Thos. L. Rushmore.]—**Russell, Alex.**, rem.—RUSSELL, BARZILLA I.—RUSSELL, ELIZABETH, w. of the above; S.S.t., 1822.—**Russell, J. T.**, rem. by c., 1866; member 2 yrs.—**Rutherford, Chas. H.**, son of Christopher, Jr., was b. in White Plains; j. M. E. ch. in Nyack; rem. to Sands-st. ch., 1867; thence to Nostrand ave. ch., 1872. —**Elizabeth S.**, his w., was also a member in Sands-st. 5 yrs.; rem. by c., 1872.—*****Rutherford, Christopher, Sr.**, was a loc. pr. and cl. ldr. His father was Christopher Rutherford, of the Scottish ch. at Newcastle-upon-Tyne, Eng. Young Christopher attempted to attend a Meth. love-feast, but "the door was shut." This caused serious thoughts and finally led to his conversion. He became a warm friend of Wm. Bramwell; was placed on the "plan" of Newcastle cir. as a loc. pr.; walked frequently from 5 to 10 m. on a Sabbath, preaching and organizing S.-schools, carrying his luncheon in his pocket, dining beside a brook or hedge. At the time of his leaving Eng. (1821) he was a commission merchant, dealing in hides, wool, etc. He was welcomed by the Sands-st. ch., placed on the "plan" of Flushing cir. in 1824, made ldr. of Yellow Hook (Bay Ridge) class, and ord. deacon by Bp. Hedding in 1826. He owned a morocco factory, lost heavily in that year of disaster, 1837, and moved to a farm in Wells, Hamilton Co., N. Y. After a few yrs. he made his home with his eldest son, James, in Hempstead, L. I., where resided also 2 other sons, Christopher Rutherford, Jr., A. M., afterward a preacher, and the Rev. Collingwood Rutherford, associate principals of the Hempstead Sem. He and his w. afterward resided with their children in Nyack, Sing Sing, and Haverstraw, N. Y., and in Hyde Park and Chicago, Ill. Warned by heart-disease that his end was drawing nigh, he wrote in his last letter to his son-in-law, the Rev. John Luckey: "I have committed to God every member of my family, young and old.... God has been, and still is, abundant in mercy toward me. By faith in an atonement once offered for all, I prove its power in my case; it gives me rest and peace in Jesus." His dau., Mary Nelson, wrote: "His mind is clear and composed; indeed, he is joyful, and it is delightful to wait upon him." He d., repeating the hymn, "O, Lamb of God, I come," on the 12th of Nov., 1870, age 86.—***Mary,** his w., was a dau. of Wm. Collingwood, who left the Ch. of Eng. to j. the Meth., and entertained the early prs. She was b. in 1785, and mar. to Mr. R. in 1805. Their dau., Mrs. Luckey, writes: "I never knew a couple so lovingly devoted to each other." In the same letter she adds: "My mother would not brook the least irreverence toward God, or his word, or his ministers, or the ordinances of his house; and so decided was her influence in these things that we had no trouble in the family of 5 sons and 2 daughters." Mrs. Rutherford d. July 3, 1870, age 85. Her aged husband wrote to his dau. on the day after the funeral: "Your dear mother, now doubly dear to me, is no longer an inhabitant of earth.... On the first shock, last Wednesday ev'g, my mind was thrown back along the 65 yrs. we had toiled together. I lost sight of all her childishness and all the infirmities of a feeble and wasting nature, and felt the touches of our first love in all its strength. I also felt the force of the bereavement, but I accept it all at the hands of the Lord." She sleeps beside her husband in the cem. at Hyde Park, Ill., and their names are (or are to be) inscribed on the family monument. They are honored in their posterity. Two sons, James Rutherford and the Rev. Christopher Rutherford, Jr., came to the close of faithful, useful lives in peace. Another son, the Rev. Collingwood Rutherford, was an itinerant minister 9 yrs., and has long held an honorable position as loc. pr. and pres't of a commercial college in N. York. The daughters' names are Dinah and Mary.—**Rutherford, Dinah,** dau. of the above. (See sketch,

of her husband, the Rev. John Luckey, pp. 288-295 of this book.)
—**Rutherford, John,** son of Christopher, Jr.; rem. and j. Mulberry-st. ch., N. York; now a farmer in Iowa.—***Rutherford, Rosannah Augusta,** w. of James, dau. of Col. Porter, U.S.A., was conv. at 15 and j. Sands-st. ch.; d. a member of York-st. ch. in 1851. She was lovely as a child, sister, wife, mother, and friend. Her voice was often heard in the social meetings. [W. C. Hoyt, in Ch. Ad.]—**Rutter, H. C.** and **Mrs. Maria,** rem. by c., 1868. He j. by proba.; she from Bap. ch. in 1867.

****Saffern, Ann E.,** "d. in peace after much suffering," March 28, 1849.—****Sales, Mary R.,** w. of Sam'l, dau. of Marvel Richardson; d. 1866.—**Salmon, Thos.,** rem.—**Saltanoff, Andrew,** rem. by c., 1867.—**Saltar, Caroline,** rem. by c., 1871.—**Sanders, Dan'l** and **Mathilda.**—***Sands, Thomas,** loc. pr., (?) is mentioned on pp. 18 and 19 as the man who first proposed the establishing of a S. S. in B'klyn, and as the 1st treas. of the B'klyn S. S. Union. He was b. in Leeds, Eng., Jan. 8, 1791, and by his father's death was left to the sole care of his mother, who was an intellectual and energetic woman, and a Wesleyan. He mar. Sarah, oldest dau. of Anthony Branson, Esq., of Sheffield, Apr. 21, 1814. From a cloth-worker in Leeds he came to be a commercial traveler, moved to Liverpool, was connected with a business firm in that city, and came as its representative to N. York. His dau., Miss Susannah Sands, writes to the author from Stirling, Scot.: "I have often heard my father speak of his early efforts to establish a S. S. in B'klyn." She was not aware that he ever had a loc. preacher's license, but J. Wesley Harper mentions him as a loc. pr. in Sands-st. ch. in 1816. [See trustees' records.] Returning to Europe he was Mayor of Liverpool in 1843. After enjoying unusual success in business he met with reverses, by which all his property was swept away. While in prosperity his gifts to the ch. were large. His portrait is in the Meth. Centenary picture, the more prominent and shorter of the two standing figures. He d. at the residence of his dau., Mrs. Black, on the Clyde, near Glasgow, Apr. 4, 1867, age 76, and was bur. in the Necropolis, Glasgow, where his w. was laid 4 yrs. previously. The stone he erected over her grave bears his name. List of the children: Thos. Branson, who resides in France; Hugh Spooner, who d. in Jamaica, W. I.; Sarah Ellis; Susannah; Mary, (Mrs. Black;) James Stopford, who was in

THOMAS SANDS.

business with his father in N. York, and afterward d. there, (1879,) leaving a wid. and 4 children. Three daughters of Thos. Sands reside in Scotland. It is said that most of his descendants, including those in N. York, are Episcopalians.—
Sanford, Watson, S.S.t., cl. ldr., off. S.S. Miss'y Soc.; was a stove dealer in N. York; resides in B'klyn.—**Savage, Wm. L.**, rem. by c., 1849, to E. B'klyn.—SAYRE, MRS. ELIZABETH.—**Saywell, Wm.**, rem. by c., 1871; member 3 yrs.—SCHENCK, MRS. REBECCA.—**Schenck, Sarah J.**, rem. by c., 1864.—****Schnell, Anna**, w. of John, dau. of Henry Shawver, d. Oct. 14, 1805, age 52. [See stone in ch.-yard.]—***Schnell, John**, member in 1798. One "John Snell" d. Oct. 5, 1812, age 72. [See stone in old ch-yard.]—SCHRIVENER, HENRY.—SCHRIVENER, MRS. HENRY.—**Schureman, Catharine**, rem. by c., 1876.—**Scofield, Frances E.**, rem. by c., 1872.—SCOFIELD, GEO. F.—**Scudder, Mrs. Charlotte**, rem.—*** Seabury, Adam**, a baker, ldr of a colored class in Sands-st. about 1828; had charge of the 1st class formed in Washington-st. ch., 1831, and was, in 1868, still ldr. of the same class, and the only survivor among those who originally composed his little band. [Stiles' Hist. B'klyn, vol. iii, p. 706.] He was a trus. of Washington-st. ch. as early as 1839, and d. a member of that ch. He was a "noisy Methodist," and a very peculiar but truly godly man. The name of his 1st w. was Hulsehart. He outlived his 2d w., who was a member of Washington-st. ch.—**Seabury, E.**, rem. by c., 1868.—****Seabury, Miss Emeline**, d.—****Seaman, Mrs. Abby**, d.—**Seaman, Jacob**, rem. by c., 1880.—****Seaman, Sarah**, w. of Jacob, d. in Sept., 1872.—***Searles, Isaac**, trus., 1825, father of Mrs. Rev. Dr. D. D. Whedon; did not continue in the ch.—**Searles, Wm. N.**, exh., 1831.—**Seawright, Agnes**, mar. Mr. Stryker.—**Seckerson, Rich'd**, rem. by c.—**Seeley, Ellen B.**, rem.—****Seffern, Ann E. (Brice)**, w. of G. W. Seffern, d. in peace after much suffering, 1849.—**Sellick, E.**, and **Mary E. (Waterbury)**, rem. by c., 1879.—**Sellick, Noah**, std., 1841. He and **Mary j.** by c., 1868, and rem. by c., 1870. Said to have moved to Staten Island; see Silleck.—**Sellick, Thos. A.**, rem. about 1831.—****Selover, Mrs. Charity**, d. 1871.—**Selover, Mary A.**, rem.—**Selvey, John O.** and **Mary A.**, rem. by c., 1876; members 1 yr.—SERVANT, FLORENCE S.—**Shackerly, Henry E.** and **Mrs. Catharine S.**, rem. by c., 1868.—**Shapton, R.**, cl. ldr. about 1866.—***Sharp, Richard**, chorister, went to Fleet-st. ch.; d. about 1879; age about 72; an excellent man.—***Eliza**, his first w., sister to Mrs. Wm. M'Donald, foremost in every good work, d. about 1877, age 61; no children. [Mrs. J. Rossell.]—**Shattuck, Harriet A.**, rem by c., 1877.—**Shaw, Ann M**; see Litchult.—SHAW, ELIZABETH.—**Shaw, Ellena**, rem.—

SHAW, JOHN.—SHAW, JENNIE M.—SHAW, ROB'T.—
SHEDD, ELIZABETH.—**Shepherd, Janette,** w. of Sam'l;
b. in Edinburgh; came to U. S. at 10 yrs. of age; in 1822, 3
yrs. after her marriage, conv. at a camp-meeting in Ill; in 1824
j. Sands-st. ch. by c. She was a patient sufferer; d. shouting
"Glory! glory! Come, Lord Jesus!" [Ch. Ad.]—**Sheriden,
Mrs. Anna,** rem. by c.—**Showard, Margaret,** rem. to Phil.,
1849; mar. J. M. Morrell.—*Shreeve, Caleb, member in
1798—*Shreeve, Meliscent, member in 1798.—**Shultz, Esther, A.,** rem. to Johnson-st. ch., 1850.—**Schultz, Leek** and
Maria, rem.—*Sickerson, Mrs. Rosannah, conv. at 17 in
Sands-st. ch., B. Creagh, pastor; d. 1853. [S. A. Seaman, in
Ch. Ad.] Supposed to have j. the ch.—SIKES, HELEN.—
Silence, Mrs., rem. by c., 1868.—SILLECK, AUGUST.—
Silleck, Noah, rem. by c., 1873; see Sellick, Noah and Mary.
—*Silleck, Mary Ann, w. of Noah, rem. by c. 1873; d. some
time afterward. [Mrs. J. J. Studwell.]—SILVERY, JOHN O.—
SILVERY, MARY A.—**Simmons, Amelia,** rem.—**Simmons,
John N.,** rem. by c.—*Simmons, Thos. S., cl. ldr; in 1850 became one of the founders, one of the 1st cl. ldrs., and one of the 1st
trustees of Fleet-st. ch.; and shortly afterward a std.; d. in N.
J.—*Simonson, Carman A., cl. ldr., 1835; rem. by c, 1849, to
Johnson-st. ch.; d. in the Lord, Apr. 10, 1858. By occupation
a butcher. A consistent, patient, happy Xn.—**Ann,** his w., rem.
by c. to Johnson-st. ch., 1849; d. 1884.—*Simpson, Ellen, d.
1837.—**Skidmore, Delia,** rem. by c., 1872.—SKIPPON, MRS.
LUCY L.—SLADE, HATTIE, w. of W.—**Slater, Mrs. Mary
H.,** rem. by c., 1884.—SLATER, THOS. W. and MRS. MARY
H.—**Slawson, Rufus,** rem.—*Smead, Ithiel, cl. ldr., 1804;
loc. pr., 1809, and recommended for deacon's orders. Wm.
Thacher, in his MS. autobiography, relates that during one of
his visits as P. E. at the house of Jas. Harper, in B'klyn, Ithiel
Smead entered, ghastly and weak from what threatened to be a
fatal illness. It was the time for morning prayer. Mr. and
Mrs. Harper, Wm. Thacher, Ezekiel Cooper, and Ithiel Smead
knelt together, and as prayer was offered for Bro. Smead's recovery, an effusion of divine power was immediately felt by all
the little group. Mr. Smead, declining to remain to breakfast,
quickly withdrew, though when he entered he was scarcely able
to walk. In the ev'g he appeared at the quar. conf. entirely restored, declaring that he was suddenly healed in answer to the
prayers offered for him that morning. Mrs. Jane Vanderveer
knew him as a school teacher about 1818 in Greenburgh, N. Y.,
and frequently heard him argue with her father, who was a Presbyterian, on the subject of free grace. When Smead became
excited, his Presbyterian friend would say, "Speak low," and he
would reply, "I am not ashamed to proclaim these sentiments
aloud, and I tell you I would as soon be an atheist as believe

Record of Members. 491

in an infinite tyrant." Such discussions were very frequent in those days. Mr. Smead had a w. and 1 child.—**Smith, Adaline, d.—Smith, Anna,** rem.—**Smith, Benj. and Jane E.,** rem. by c.—**Smith, B. F.,** rem.—**Smith, Clark,** a very exemplary member, d. 1874.—SMITH, MRS. CORNELIA.— SMITH, CRAWFORD C., trus. and std.; son of Geo. and Mary G. Smith; b. in B'klyn, 1809, and now the only surviving member of the family. He was for some time treasurer of Kings Co.; afterward, treasurer of the city of B'klyn; a few yrs. cashier of the Nassau Bank, and the past 20 yrs. its pres't. He has been familiar with the pastors and members of the Sands-st. ch. from his infancy, and there is no person living, probably, who cherishes a warmer interest in the old ch. than he.—SMITH, REBECCA, w. of Crawford C., dau. of Mrs. Anne Ingraham.— SMITH, EDWARD A.—SMITH, ELIZA.—**Smith, George,** cl. ldr. and trus.; b. in Middletown, N. J.; a carriage maker by trade; came to B'klyn in 1800; d. 1826, age 57; bur. in the old ch.-yard, where the headstone was left when his remains were rem. to "Greenwood." He was an intimate friend and associate of Judge Garrison, and they were nearly always seen together at funerals, and in other public assemblies. The contrast in their size was noticed. "Uncouth, honest," are the words by which his pastor described him in the ch. records about 1819.—**Mary Garrison,** his w., was b. in Phila.; came to N. J. when a child; was conv. after her marriage; d. about 1849; age about 72; bur. in "Greenwood" beside her husband. She was a Dorcas, "full of alms-deeds and good works." Their children: Crawford C.; William; Richard; John; George; Mrs. Cook; Mrs. Ayers; Mrs. Davis; Mary.—* **Smith, Geo.,** son of the above; went away; returned; was not a member at the time of his death, about 1874; bur. in "Greenwood." —SMITH, GEO. A.—**Smith, Hannah,** (1st) d. about 1819, probably the same person whose name is on the record, 1798.— **Smith, Hannah,** (2d,) d. "in the faith," 1845.—SMITH, HENRY ARTHUR.—**Smith, Henry R.,** rem., 1847.— SMITH, JAS.—SMITH, JENNIE M.—*Smith, Jeremiah, member in 1798.—**Smith, Jerusha,** rem.—**Smith, John,** (1st.) cl. ldr. and trus. He was a son of Geo.; bro. of C. C.; d. in 1849, age 59; last words, "All is right." [J. B. Hagany, in Ch. Ad.] He is bur. in "Greenwood." A mural tablet in commemoration of this good man may be seen in the old church. He was a carman at the ferry; in later years retired from business; a useful member of Sands-st. ch. over 50 yrs.: none more sincerely loved. D. S. Quimby says: "His example was a great help to me."—*Smith, John, (2d,) son of Geo.; rem. about 1835. He is deceased.—**Smith, John G.,** son of John (1st,) S.S. lib'n; d. June 2, 1873, age 56; bur. in "Greenwood," He was a clerk in B'klyn. Left a w. and 2 children.—**Smith,**

33

Julia, rem. by c., 1865.—*Smith, Leanah; see Valentine.—
Smith, Lewis, rem. by c., 1871; member of this ch. 5 yrs.—
Smith, Margaret, rem.—SMITH, MISS MARY G.—Smith,
Mary M., dau. of Geo. and Mary G.; unmarried; rem. to Texas,
to live with her sister d. April, 1884, in Galveston, Texas.—
SMITH, MOSES.—SMITH, PHŒBE.—*Smith, Richard,
son of Geo.; bro. of C. C. ldr of a colored class in 1826; rem. to
Southold, L. I.; d. in 1874 did not retain his membership in the
ch.—Smith, Mrs. Sarah, rem. by c., 1872.—Smith, Sarah F.,
rem. by c., 1868.—**Smith, Sarah M., d. 1870.—Smith, Sidney rem.—Smith, Wm., S.S.t. and loc. pr., 1833; rem. He mar.
Sarah Jane M'Keon; she was a S. S. t. in 1852.—**Smith, Wm.,
son of Geo., d. about 1850.—*Ann, his w., was formerly Mrs. Ann
Remsen. She died about 1880.—Snedden, Mrs. Margaret,
rem. by c., 1866.—Snediker, Martha, rem. without c., 1848.—
*Snethen, Nicholas, the 1st (known or recorded) cl. ldr. in
the Sands-st ch., was b., Nov. 15, 1769, at Fresh Pond, (Glen
Cove,) L. I. His family came originally from the foot of Mt. Snawthen, Snethen, or Snowdown, in Wales. His father was an officer in the British colonial army at the capture of Montreal, in 1760. Later he engaged in the flour trade, and resided on L. I. Nicholas passed his boyhood and youth partly on a farm and partly on a freighting schooner, and acquired what knowledge he could. "Shortly after he became of age he went with his father to reside on Staten Island, where he professed religion" among the Episcopalians. In 1791 the
family removed to Belleville, N. J., and while employed there in
tending a mill, he was converted under the preaching of the

Methodists. These dates given by his son we accept, although they are slightly at variance with a statement quoted by Abel Stevens to the effect that Snethen was conv. in his 20th yr. [See sketch of N. S. by his son, Worthington G. Snethen, in Sprague, vii, 244. See, also, Boehm's Reminiscences, p. 232, and Stevens', Hist. M. E. Ch., iii, 260.] Neither Boehm nor the writer in Sprague's Annals makes any mention of Mr. Snethen's connection with the Brooklyn ch. The Rev. N. Levings, in Meth. Quar., 1831, p. 261, writing of the Brooklyn Meth. class when John Garrison j., in 1793, says: "The ldr. was Mr. Nicholas Snethen, subsequently a zealous, useful, and popular preacher," etc. The writer does not state that there was no cl. ldr. previous to 1793, or that Mr. Snethen had no predecessor. Dr. Levings was conversant with some of the original members, and obtained his information directly from them. Dr. Wakeley, having consulted this authority, carelessly and inaccurately states that Snethen was appointed cl. ldr. by Woolman Hickson. [Lost Chapters, p. 312.] That means that he was made cl. ldr. before Sept., 1788. But Levings, Wakeley's authority, does not say that Hickson appointed Snethen cl. ldr.; and, furthermore, as Snethen was then only 18 yrs. of age, *living miles away from B'klyn, and unconverted*, the absurdity of that statement is apparent. Stevens [Hist. M. E. Ch., ii, p. 110] copies this anachronism. From a careful reading of Dr. Levings' historic sketch of B'klyn Methodism, written in 1831, and taken from the lips of the earliest members, we infer that there may have been really no leader of the class, except the preachers, until about 1793, when Mr. Snethen was app'd. He entered the itinerancy (from Brooklyn, probably) in 1794, in the 25th yr. of his age. *Appointments in the M. E. Ch.:* 1794, Fairfield cir., Conn., with Zebulon Kankey; 1795, Tolland cir., with Christopher Spry; 1796, ord. deacon,—Vershire cir., Vt.; 1797, Portland cir., Me., with J. Finnegan; 1798, no app't recorded; 1799, Charleston cir., S. C., with Jno. Harper; 1800, ord. elder, —Balt. and Fell's Point, Md., with T. Morrell, G. Roberts and P. Bruce; 1801–2, with Asbury; 1803, Balt. city, with J. Wells and S. Coate; 1804, N. York, with M. Coate, S. Merwin, (E. Cooper and J. Wilson, ed's and book stewards;) 1805, ditto, with F. Garrettson, A. Hunt, and J. Wilson; 1806–8, located; 1809, (Balt. Conf.,) Fell's Point; 1810, Balt. city, with Asa Schinn and Robert Burch; 1811, Georgetown, D. C.; 1812, Alexandria, Va.; 1813, Frederick cir., Md., with James Smith; 1814, located. His son writes concerning his entrance upon his itinerant work: "When he left home he was spare in flesh, his eye was sunken, his face wan, and a hectic glow sat on his cheek. Four yrs. of toil and hardship, being most of the time in his saddle, reversed the picture, and he brought back with him a well-developed person and elastic step, and the bloom of health was upon him." His Vershire cir. was the "1st projected in the State of Vt." He had yellow fever by which his life was greatly imperiled in 1800. The 1st camp-meeting ever held in Md., in 1803, was under his direction, and during that meeting, as he records of himself, he "fell twice in the pulpit beneath the overwhelming power of saving grace." He was active in introducing camp-meetings into the northern States. [See p. 159 of this work.] He was popular and useful while traveling with Asbury. As an active member he was present at the Gen. Confs. of 1800, 1804, and 1812. In 1800 he was sec. of the conf. His marriage, in 1804, to Susanna H. Worthington, brought him into the possession of a number of slaves. It is evident that he was opposed to the system of slavery. His views on that subject a short time previous to his marriage may be inferred from the following extract from the Journal of the Gen. Conf. of 1800: "Bro. Snethen moved that this Gen. Conf. do resolve that from this time no slave-holder shall be admitted to the Meth. Epis. Ch.—Negatived." His son justifies his holding slaves on the ground that the laws of the State forbade their manumission. The People's Cyclopedia states—on what authority we know not—that he did set them free. The cause of his location in 1806 is thus stated: "Bp. Asbury, who had very strong feelings against preachers being married, now told him that if the Fell's Point station, in Balt., would take a married preacher, he might go there. But Mr. Snethen would not consent even to consider a proposition so conditioned, and located himself forthwith, and returned to his Linganore farm." [W. J. Snethen, in Sprague's Annals.] It will be noticed that he was app'd to Fell's Point three yrs. later. His son informs us that during his location he declined an invitation to become ass't rector of Christ Ch., N. York, and that on the death of Asbury, the "Silver Trumpet," (for such the bishop called Mr. S.,) which had long been silent, resounded in ringing tones the praises of Asbury in a funeral oration which was published in pamphlet form. He engaged somewhat in politics; was a Federalist in 1816. As candidate for M. C. from Md. he was defeated, and soon afterward retired from political strife. His camp-meeting sermons were often attended with great spiritual power. "It came to his ears that some one had attributed the result to animal excitement. He stated from the pulpit that he would repeat that sermon the next day as nearly as he could, word for word, and leave it with God to vindicate his word in the production of a similar result. Immense crowds of people came to hear him, and the result was even more signal than it had been on the first occasion." [W. G. Snethen, in Sprague.] The story of his able defense of the ch. in the time of O'Kelly's revolt, and his subsequent strange acceptance of the championship of a greater schism, resulting in the formation of the Meth.

Prot. Ch., is too long to be narrated here. (For an adequate account, see Stevens' Hist. M. E. Ch., vol. iii, pp. 34, 261.) His son has given a statement of some of Mr. Snethen's own peculiar notions. He says that he proposed a Federal ch. gov't, bounded by state lines, the Annual Conf's sustaining a relation to the Gen. Conf. similar to that which the States sustain to the Federal gov't. "Sad indeed," says Dr. Stevens, "to see a man so good and great, after a useful ministry of 30 yrs. or more, spend the remainder of his weary and declining life amid the anxieties and reactions of an impracticable experiment, and in conflict with the sympathies and endeared memories of his earlier and better years." In 1829 pecuniary troubles compelled him to sell his farm in Md. and remove to Indiana. In the fall of that yr. he bur. his w. and one of his dau., which broke up his family and forced him into the itinerancy of the new ch.; but he was as busy as ever with his pen. In 1834 he was called to be one of the eds. of the Meth. Prot., and that yr. wrote for the paper about 120 articles on about as many subjects. "On his return to the West, in 1837, he was called to the head of a manual labor ministerial college. This institution soon failed for lack of funds. From 1830 to the close of his life he labored as the regularly stationed minister at different times in Louisville, Cincinnati, and Zanesville. He presided over the Gen. Conf. of the Meth. Prot. Ch. assembled in Alexandria, Va., in 1838. Some 2 yrs. before his death he was elected pres't of the Snethen Sem., in Iowa City. He d. "praising God," at the res. of his son-in-law, Dr. Pennington, in Princeton, Ind., May 30, 1845, age 76, and was bur. in the village cem., by the side of his w. and 3 of his children. The grave is marked by a marble shaft, the top carved in the shape of an open Bible. A personal friend thus describes Mr. Snethen: "He was large and of commanding appearance, with a most benignant expression of countenance; and his countenance was a true index of his character. . . . In his manners he was a perfect gentleman. . . . His intellect was comprehensive, energetic, versatile. . . . His presence was always felt to be an element of power." It is still further said that he was "eminently conscientious" and "bold" in the defense of truth or duty; "exceedingly well-informed," and "as a writer, concise, luminous, and powerful." "While preaching at a camp-meeting in a strain of wonderful eloquence, he came suddenly to a dead pause, and taking up the Bible, and pressing it to his bosom, he exclaimed, 'My Book and heart shall never part!' and then holding it out to the men, [sitting on one side in the olden fashion,] he exclaimed at the top of his voice, 'Brethren, it is *your* Bible!' and then turning to the female part of his audience, he said, 'Sisters, this is *your* Bible!' and then wheeling around to the colored people who were behind the stand, he said, 'Colored people, ye sable sons of Africa, it is *your* Bible!' There was an electric power in the appeal that nobody could resist—the whole of that immense cong. seemed completely dissolved." [Hon. P. B. Hopper, in Sprague's Annals.]—**Snow, Rob't,** the best-remembered man in the early annals of B'klyn, was b. in Ireland in 1760, and arrived in N. York (so says Miss Denmead) on the day of the "Evacuation," and saw the ships with the British soldiers going out of the harbor. He married Susanna (Meir), wid. of a Mr. Smith. He mended shoes and she took in washing, whereby they earned

ROBERT SNOW,
First Sunday School Superintendent in Brooklyn.

a capital sufficient to enable them to open a small grocery. The sale of rum and gin, a supposed indispensable part of the grocery business, was so abhorrent to his principles, that he gave up the store. He soon found employment in what proved to be a permanent position as inspector of potash in the city of N. York. His integrity was unquestioned, and it was said at his funeral that his marks on potash were always taken in Eng. as a satisfactory guarantee of its good quality. He rem. to B'klyn; became a member of Sands-st. ch., chief founder and supt. of the

1st S. S. in B'klyn, in 1816, and 1st pres't of the Apprentices' Library Assoc'n. A great lover of children, he had a happy talent for addressing them. When LaFayette laid the cor.-stone of the Apprentices' Library building, in 1825, the S. S. children being present in a body, Mr. Snow, as pres't of the assoc'n, was called out to address them, and he responded admirably. He always remembered the little ones with gifts on the New-Year's anniversary. The Rev. T. W. Chadwick writes: "I well remember Rob't Snow and his power over the children. When he said, 'Be a good boy, or Father Snow wont love you,' I determined to be good." He was S. S. supt. till his death, and "when a lingering illness confined him to his house, next door to the ch., the scholars always looked for him at the door as they passed on their way to school. A week before his death he asked to have the children march before his window." From the S. S. building on Prospect-st., bet. Wash'gt'n and Adams sts., the school marched in double file, up Prospect-st. to Fulton, and up Fulton to Sands-st., so as to pass the residence of Mr. Snow, which was on the Fulton-st. side of the ch. Thus they marched past the window behind which he sat, each boy doffing his cap, and each girl "dropping a courtesy," "while the good man returned bow for bow and blessing for blessing, as the tears rolled down his cheeks and dimmed his aged eyes." [Stiles' Hist. B'klyn, vol. ii, p. 23.] In later yrs. he was universally known as "Poppy Snow." Fortune did not always smile upon him. He met with heavy financial losses. Dan'l DeVinne says: "He bought very valuable property in Wm.-st., N. York, but lost it through defective titles; repurchased it and lost it again in the same manner. In those days there were no public records by which titles could be known. Mr. Snow was childless, yet he and his admirable wife fostered children and severally adopted them as their own, giving them a settlement or outfit in life, amounting sometimes to thousands of dollars. These children were not ungrateful to him; when he was old and paralytic, and had lost all his property, so tender were these adopted children toward him, that they not only took the best care of him, but would not let him know the loss of his property, and even indulged him in the gratification of bequeathing property which had already passed into other hands." [MS. Journal.] His w., from rheumatism, was completely helpless for nearly 17 yrs. All this time he enjoyed uninterrupted health and spirits, and "waited upon her with all the gayety and assiduity of a suitor." A few hours after her burial he was seized with partial paralysis, which rendered him, likewise, helpless and dependent till his death: yet he was remarkably cheerful in the midst of trials which would have bowed others to the earth. His old friend, DeVinne, says: "In person he was of small stature, with an open, pleasant, and animated countenance; polite, affable, and gentlemanly in manners; dressed very neatly in the old costume of small clothes, and always carried a small umbrella for sun or rain. He possessed in an eminent degree the ardor and eloquence peculiar to his countrymen." He loved to sing, and had a habit of standing on tiptoe when singing the high notes. He d. in B'klyn, March 30, 1833, age 73, [L. I. Star, Apr. 3, 1833,] and left an enduring name, which will grow brighter as the fruits of his work increase. He seems to have had no memorial in the Ch. Ad. His grave in the old ch.-yard was never marked by a headstone; and now, after all these yrs. of neglect, the Sands-st. ch. and S.S. ought to identify his remains, if possible, and build a monument to his memory.—**Susanna,** his w., d. in B'klyn Feb. 11, 1831, age 69. [See L. I. Star, Feb'y 16, 1831.] Miss Susanna Snow Denmead, a child of one of their adopted dau's, now deceased, said to the author: " Susanna Snow was handsome, intelligent, and generous, like her husband; a great sufferer for years; and yet she had a great deal of company, and even in her helplessness had the oversight of her household affairs.—SODEN, WM. H.—SOMERVILLE, LOWERY, S.S. t. and std.; b. in N. of Ireland; brought up in Ch. of Eng. till 16 yrs. of age; confirmed; afterward j. the Wesleyan Meth. Came to B'klyn in 1859, and j. Sands-st. ch, by c., (Dr. Hagany, pastor.) Dry-goods merchant, 1863-83, N. E. cor. Sands and Fulton; rem. when the property was purchased by the Bridge Co.—SONONBLOOM, J.—Southard, Marietta, rem. by c., 1867.—**Sowden, Jas. B.,** d. of cancer.—**Sperry, Henrietta C.,** S. S. t.; rem., 1848, to Newark, N. J.; mar Rev. Dr. R. S. Maclay, miss'y to China and Japan.—**Spingsteel, Anna** and **Polly,** " charter members" of Yellow Hook (Bay Ridge) class, 1822.—**Stagg, Mrs.** and **Miss Ellen,** rem. by c., 1874.—*Stanley, Dan'l, S. S. t.; b. in Peekskill; came to B'klyn while young; d. in Rochester, N. Y., 1844, age 41; bur. in Mt. Hope cem.; left 3 children, viz., David, Edward, and Clarence. Edward d. at 14.—**Rachel,** 1st w. of the above, dau. of John and Mary Garrison; d. Oct. 9, 1832, age 32. [Gravestone in old ch.-yard.]—STANLEY, CECELIA, 2d w. of Dan'l, was S. S. t. in 1829.—**Stanley, Clarence,** youngest son of Dan'l and Cecelia; b. in B'klyn, 1844; S. S. t. and lib'n in Sands-st., rem. to Nostrand ave. ch., 1871.—**Stanley, Mrs.,** rem. by c., 1871.—**Stanley, David,** son of Dan'l, b. in B'klyn, was S.S. t., off. Miss'y Soc'y; and std in Sands-st. ch.; rem. by c., 1873 to N. York ave. ch.; std and S. S. t. there. Connected with the Fulton Bank, N. York.—**Josephine,** w. of the above; rem. by c., 1873.—*Stansbury, Lorenzo, cl. ldr.; conv. at a camp-meeting in Croton, N. Y.; j. Sands-st. ch. by c., 1826, aged about 18. Rem. by c. to Carlton ave. (now Simpson) ch., 1846, where he continued to be cl. ldr.; received the fullness of the love of God at a camp-meeting in Northport in 1851. He was known in business circles as a man of industry and integrity, at home as a kind Xn. husband and father, in the ch. as a useful and powerful exh., wonderfully gifted in prayer. After a few months of painless illness, he d. Dec. 6, 1852, age about 44. He gave dying counsels to his class, his family, and his unconverted friends; last words, "I want to rest." [S. A. Seaman, in Ch. Ad.]— *Sarah, his w.; rem. by c., 1846; d. of pneumonia 1882, age 82; a Meth. 66 yrs. A son of the above is the Rev. J. H. Stansbury, of the N. York East Conf.—**Stawson, Rufus,** rem.— *Stearns, Chas., loc. pr. and cl. ldr.; b. in Pittstown, N. Y., Nov. 11, 1810. His parents attended "Friends' Meeting." The father, a farmer, moved with his family to Rahway, N. J., in 1816; the boy attended dist. school, and was conv. at 16, in a great revival, (Thos. Sargent, pastor.) After using an exhorter's license for a time he rec'd his 1st license to preach, dated Rahway cir., July 16, 1832, signed Chas. Pitman, P. E. He learned the printer's trade; mar. Miss Susan M. Martin at 21; moved with his young w. to B'klyn; worked at his trade in a newspaper office; received from the Sands-st. quar. conf. a recommendation to the traveling connection. *Appointments:* 1834, (N. York Conf.,) Stamford cir., Conn., with O. V. Amerman; 1835, New Milford cir., with J. P. Ellsworth; 1836, ditto, with F. Donnelly; 1837, Canaan cir., with A. Rogers; 1838, ditto, with A. V. Shears; 1838, ord. deacon by Bp. Morris; 1839-40, Granby cir., with A. Ackerly; 1839, ord. elder by Bp. Soule; 1841, Clinton, Westbrook, Essex, and Saybrook cir., with C. R. Adams; 1843-44, Hamden; 1845-46, Ridgefield; 1847, Derby; 1848, (N. York East Conf.,) Derby, "Humphreyville;" 1849-50, Easton; 1851-52, Wilton, with W. A. Hill; 1852, Zion's Hill, Bald Hill, and Georgetown; 1853, Sag Harbor, N. Y.; 1854-55, Huntington South cir.; 1856-57, Huntington and Lloyd's Neck; 1858-59, Patchogue and Sayville; 1860-61, Rockville Center; 1862-63, Northport and Centerport; 1864-65, Cold Spring, Woodbury, and West Hills; 1866-67, Roslyn, Searington, and Port Washington; 1868-70, Norwich and Oyster Bay; 1871-73, Smithtown; 1874, Norwich; 1875, Locust Valley and Bayville; 1876-78, Centerport and Dix Hills; 1879, Smithtown Branch, Comac, and Landing. The foregoing is a record of forty yrs. in the active ministry without a break. Allowance, 1854, Huntington South cir.: "Brother Stearns' quarterage, $100; wife, $100; one child $16; 3 children, $24 each=$72; house rent, $50; table expenses, $114; moving bills, $20; total, $472. [Quar. conf. record.] In his conf. memorial [Min. 1880, p. 49] his brethren greatly commend his remarkable fortitude, meekness, humility, and modesty, and his uncomplaining acceptance of laborious and undesirable app'ts. The same testimonial adds: "As a preacher, Bro. Stearns was endowed with a full average ability and culture; as a pastor, he was diligent, sympathetic, and conscientious. The religious element was ever with him, and permeated his entire spirit, and character, and work." His fatal illness lasted 11 weeks. Pneumonia, attended with hemorrhage, erysipelas, and paralysis, battered down the clay tenement. For the most part his mind was clear; his faith always firm. In his farewell message to the conf. he said : " Tell the brethren that I thank them for their kindness and forbearance during the 46 yrs. of my ministry." He d. in Smithtown, L. I., Dec. 20, 1879, age 69. His funeral serm. was preached by Dr. J. W. Beach, P. E., and his remains were bur. beside those of a son and a dau. in E. Norwich, where memorial services were conducted by the Meth. pastor, W. E. Tomkinson. The devoted and faithful w. of Bro. S. survives him—residence, E. Norwich, L. I., N. Y.—**Stearns, Jno. C.**, withdrew.—**Stebbins, Artemas,** loc. pr., in Sands-st ch. in 1818; withdrew about 1820, under Alex. M'Caine's ministry. He may have been the same man of whom the Conf. Min. give the following *Pastoral Record:* 1810, (N. E. Conf.,) N. London cir., with Joel Winch and E. Marble; 1811, Easton and Mansfield cir. ; 1812, ord. deacon,—Somerset and Warren, R. I.; 1813, Somerset; 1814, ord. elder,—Ashburnham cir., Conn., with B. Shaw ; 1815, New Bedford, Mass. ; 1816, located.—**Stephenson, F. R.**, rem.—**Stephenson, Thos.**, was in Sands-st. ch. as a loc. pr., and recom. to the Annual Conf. in 1854. He was b. in Market Rasen, Lincolnshire, Eng., June 9, 1830; was c onv. at 17 ; united with the Wesleyan Meth. Ch., preached his 1st sermon when 19 yrs. of age ; came to this country in 1853, and j. Sands-st. ch., (H. J. Fox, pastor.) *Conf. Record:* 1854, (New York East Conf.,) Southold, Cutchogue, and Mattituck cir., L. I,, with E. Oldrin ; 1855, Southampton; 1856, ord. deacon,—Southold; 1857–58, Seymour and Gt. Hill, Conn.; 1859, ord. elder,—Bloomfield ; 1860–61, B'klyn, Johnson-st. ; 1862–66, sup'd ; 1867–69, B'klyn, Embury Miss'n, (1867–68, he was sup'y ;) 1870–72, Greenport, L. I.; 1873–75, Glen Cove; 1876–78, Bridgeport, Wash'gt'n Park, Conn.; 1879–81, Jamaica, L. I.; 1882–84, B'klyn, Pacific-st. On the 2d of March, 1857, he was mar. to Miss Frances R. Holmes, of Orient, L. I. [Ch. Ad.] In 1862, suffering from a disease of the throat, he asked to be placed on the retired list, and visited his native land ; and while there he received from Pres. Lincoln a consular app'tment to Huddersfield, which he held for 4 yrs. The Ch. Ad. states that he declined a call to a wealthy Indep. Meth. ch. in Huddersfield, preferring to remain a member of the N. York East. Conf. Mr. S. is an able preacher; his rhetoric is well-nigh faultless ; and his fine social qualities make him a favorite every-where. To him belongs the honor of having taken the initiative in the establishing of the " B'klyn Meth. Home for the Aged and Infirm," from the " Manual " of which, (1883) we quote the following : " In the autumn of 1882 the

Rev. Thos. Stephenson, being called upon as pastor of the Pacific-st. ch. to seek a home in some charitable institution for one of the aged of his flock, was awakened to this need by his failure to obtain such a privilege. He was repeatedly met by the question, 'Why don't you Methodists provide a home for your own people?' These experiences aroused him to immediate and effective activity. He was first encouraged through the cordial indorsement of his project by some of his parishioners. He was further encouraged by the hearty sympathy and practical assistance and suggestions of Mr. W. I. Preston.... The incorporators met and joined with them many others of the worthy women of our chs. as managers. Some of these ladies, with becoming recognition of the efforts of the Rev. Thomas Stephenson, made him a life-patron of the society, and thus contributed the 1st $500 to the cause."—**Sterrit, John** and **Martha,** rem. by c., 1864; members 1 yr.—STEVENS, ELIZABETH.—**Stevens, Jennie,** mar.; see Varnum.—**Stevens, Wm.,** cl. ldr. and loc. pr. His father, Wm. Stevens, was a loc. pr., std., cl. ldr., and trus. in Eng. His mother, Elizabeth, was likewise a devoted Meth. This Wm. Stevens was b. in Burslem, Staffordshire, Eng., Oct. 18, 1818; j. the Wesleyan Meth. Ch. at 18 yrs. of age; loc. pr. on a "plan" in Eng. in 1836, age 18; came to N. York in 1843, j. John-st. ch., (Valentine Buck, pastor;) rem. to B'klyn in 1845, and j. Sands-st. ch., (H. F. Pease, pr. in charge;) mar. Mary Dealing, of N. York city, in 1852. Mr. Stevens, by request, furnishes the following incident: "When I came from Eng. I brought with me my certificate as a loc. pr. In proper time it was renewed. But when Dr. Bangs was stationed at Sands-st., the year of my license expired, and the Dr. forgot to get it renewed. After the quar. conf., when I found out the error, I wrote to J. J. Matthias, the P. E., asking him if he would consent to my preaching until the next quar. conf., and explaining that Dr. Bangs had overlooked my wish for renewal. He answered me, 'No.' (The officers of Sands-st. had asked me to preach to fill a gap.) Dr. Bangs had made arrangement for an exchange from N. York city the following Sunday ev'g; a large congregation gathered, but the exchange did not appear. After waiting until after time, J. W. Harper, Alderman M'Donald, and others, came over to where I sat and asked me to preach. I told them about my license having run out, and the P. E.'s objection to my preaching. They stated that if I would preach for them, they would give their honor to stand between me and all harm. On that assurance I preached. At the next quar. conf., when the ques. was asked, 'Any licenses to be renewed?' Dr. Bangs said, 'Yes; Bro. Stevens' license.' Bro. Matthias said some time had elapsed since it had run out. Had the preliminary steps been taken—was there a recommendation from the leaders' meeting? 'No.' 'Let us pass on then,' said the P. E. At that Bro. J. W. Harper took the floor, and state; that they could not go to any other business until Bro. Stevens license was renewed. Bro. Matthias was for some time obsti nate, but the brethren would not move; so I got my license *Conference Record:* 1853-54, (N. York Conf.,) Cortland cir., N Y., with W. R. Keeler, A. K. Sanford, and A. B. Mead; 1855 ord. deacon,—Bedford cir., with S. M. Knapp; 1856, Bedford 1857, ord. elder,—Catskill; 1858-59, Franklin; 1860-61, Mo dena; 1862, E. Fishkill; 1863-64, Lake Mahopac; 1865-67 Sharon, Conn.; 1868, Stockport, N. Y.; 1869-70, Lee, Mass. 1871-73, Red Hook; 1874-75, Lakeville, Conn.; 1876-77, Chat ham 4 Cor., N. Y.; 1878-79, Hyde Park; 1880, N. Highlands 1881-82, Fishkill Village and Glenham; 1883-84, West Stock bridge and Richmond, Mass.—**Stevens, Sam'l,** rem.—**Stev· enson, Dolly,** rem.—****Stewart, Alex. J.,** d. trusting in Christ in Feb., 1881.—**Stewart, Betsy,** rem.—**Stewart, Catherine J.,** mar.; see Austin.—STEWART, DAVID.— **Stewart, Mrs. Jane,** rem. by c., 1872.—STEWART, MRS. JANE E.—**Stewart, Janette,** mar.; see Gritman.—****Stew· art, Margaret,** (or **Peggy,**) unmarried; b. in B'klyn, of Irish parents, Methodists. She was poor, but the ch. did not permit her to lack for the comforts of life. She lived with a Rom. Cath. sister, who opened her house for the donation parties which the Sands-st. ch. people held frequently for their much-loved and needy sister. She always offered the prayer at the close of these donation visits. She d. 1880, about 80 yrs. of age.— ****Stewart, Mrs. Mary,** came with her husband from Ireland; d. in peace, 1849, age 84.—**Stibbs, Christopher,** cl. ldr. about 1829; rem. without c.—***Stibbs, Wm. O.,** S. S. t., rem. by c.; said to be deceased.—STILES, HENRY L.—STILES, VIR- GINIA.—**Stillwell, Anna,** one of the 1st members of Yellow Hook (Bay Ridge) class, 1822.—****Stillwell, Mrs. Charlotte,** d.—**Stillwell, Chas. H.** and Sarah W., rem., 1850, to For- syth-st. ch., N. York.—**Stillwell, Emma,** rem.—**Stillwell, Henry,** charter member Yellow Hook (Bay Ridge) class, 1822. —**Stillwell, Sarah A.,** mar. Chas. Davis.—STILLWELL, MISS SARAH E.—****Stillwell, Mrs. Sylvanus,** d. in 1875; quite advanced in yrs.—**Stillwell, Rob't,** rem. by c.—STOCK, MRS. HATTIE.—STODDARD, HATTIE W.—**Stokes, Elizabeth,** rem. by c.—**Stokes, Mary,** mar.; see Garrison. —**Stothoff, Sarah,** rem. by c., 1849, to E. B'klyn.—**Stratton, David G.,** loc. pr., 1856.—**Stringham, Emeline,** mar.; see M'Kay.—**Stringham, John,** rem.—St. **John, Kate,** mar. Mr. Powell.—**Strong, Emma,** rem.—**Strong, King I.,** rem. by c. — STRONG, LEWIS B.— STRONG, LIZZIE.— STRONG, STEPHEN J.—STRYKER, MRS. AGNES.— ***Stryker, Burdet,** trus.—one of the 1st; tallow chandler and butcher; at one time ferryman, plying his vocation between

N. York and B'klyn. [Stiles' Hist. of B'klyn, ii, 532.] He was for some yrs. commander of a village militia co., called The Republican Rifles, on duty for a time in the War of 1812. He was influential as a politician, and came over from the Jeffersonians to the side of DeWitt Clinton, with whom he was on terms of intimacy. He had charge of the old liberty pole that stood near his market, and took great delight in flinging the stars and stripes to the breeze on all appropriate occasions. To illustrate his shrewdness it is related that when for safety it was deemed necessary to replace this pole with a new and stronger one, he obtained subscriptions from the Quakers, who were opposed to liberty poles, *to pay for taking the old one down*, and from persons in favor of liberty poles he obtained subscriptions toward *putting up a new one*. [Stiles.] His self-sacrificing acts of kindness to the dying and the dead during several seasons of epidemic; will not soon be forgotten. Stiles describes him as "erect, alert in movement, plain in manner and address, honest of purpose, fluent in conversation; in short, a sort of rough diamond." He d. in 1825, age 55; bur. originally in the old Sands-st. ch.-yard, afterward in "Greenwood," where he has a monument. It is not certain that he was a Meth. at the time of his death.—****Hannah**, his w., d. Aug. 1, 1787. Tradition says she was a Meth., and the 1st of the little band to pass into the heavenly glory. None were more holy, none better prepared to represent the little company in the ch. above. Burdett and Hannah Stryker are commemorated by a double headstone in the old ch.-yard.—***Susan**, his 2d w., formerly the wid. of Isaac Remsen, d. Dec. 9, 1848, a member of Wash'gt'n-st ch., age 79; maiden name, Susan Roberts; j. Sands-st. when C. W. Carpenter was pastor; mother of 7 children, namely: Isaac R.; Hannah M.; Phœbe Ann; Harriet; Wm. Henry; Burdett; Francis B. Her youngest son became mayor of B'klyn.— **Stryker, Frances**, rem. to N. York, 1850.—**Stryker, Hannah M.**, unmarried dau. of Burdett and Susan; b. 1801; j. Sands-st. ch. in 1825, (Wm. Ross, pastor;) transferred to Wash-'gt'n-st. ch.; 1831.—STRYKER, HETTIE.—****Stryker, John J.**, d.—****Stryker, John Morrell**, son of John S.; same occupation; d. in 1871; comparatively young; unmarried; bur. in Evergreen cem.—****Stryker, John Seawood**, a butcher; d. in 1874, age 62; bur. in Evergreen cem.; an excellent man. —****Hetty**, his w., d. suddenly, sitting in her chair, in Dec., 1880, age 64. She was ready; a true and devoted Meth. from her youth. Two sons of the above, Frank and John, reside in B'klyn. A dau., Margaret, is deceased; see Reast.—**Stryker, Julia**, rem.—****Stryker, Mary**, w. of John, mother of John S., "d. in the Lord," 1842, age 65; bur. in Concord-st. yard, afterward in Evergreen cem.—****Studwell, John Jay**, was cl. ldr., std., and trus. in Sands-st. ch. He was born in Medford, Westchester Co., N. Y., in 1813. He was an active and industrious youth, and had acquired a good knowledge of the carpenter's trade at 18 yrs of age. At 23 he was a house-builder on his own account, employing a large number of men. He engaged in the lumber trade in Harlem; afterward (about 1840) in B'klyn, as successor to Benj. R. Prince; succeeded remarkably in business; retired after 5 yrs.; was supervisor in the ward in which he resided, 12 yrs.; became one of the founders and directors of the Mechanics' Bank; 1st pres't of the Montauk Fire Ins. Co.; for 22 yrs. pres't of the National City Bank, which position he held at the time of his death. He was also director in the B'klyn City Gas Light Co., the Atlantic Ave. R. R. Co., and the Montauk Ins. Co., and was a trus. of the B'klyn Hospital, also trus. and treas. of the City Dispensary. He became a millionaire, as was remarked at his funeral, not by accident, nor good fortune, nor indefatigable industry and sagacity alone. " A few familiar well-tried maxims afforded him the theory on which his business operations were based. That theory was short and simple, but so thoroughly was he imbued with it that his mental processes of generalizing were easy, uniform, and direct, and always suggestive to those who knew him best of the maxims from which it was wrought. The action of this theory upon his mind from time to time he called 'intuition;' hence he repeatedly stated that when he followed his intuition, he rarely made a mistake. . . . He was actuated by the noble purpose of rewarding those who had rewarded him with their confidence, by making them sharers in the fruits of his economy, perseverance, and sagacity." [Rev. L. R. Streeter—Funeral Address.] In 1844, under the ministry of L. M. Vincent, he j. the Sands-st. ch., and was made a member of the building committee with much older men in 1848. He remarked to the author that the old members considered him cool-headed and conservative, and put him forward notwithstanding his comparative youth and inexperience in church affairs. Mr. Streeter adds: " Not a few of his characteristics were exceedingly striking. . . . His habits were plain, but morally correct. . . . From certain common indulgences which he thought to be hurtful and useless he entirely abstained. He hated profanity, and the habit generally known by the word 'intemperance' he intensely deplored. He was scarcely less prompt than the sun; not a single obligation was allowed to pass the time set for its performance. He was naturally kind, tender-hearted, gentle, approachable, easily made despondent, but his normal condition was one of cheerfulness. He was conservative and wise in his counsels; his religious profession was genuine, based as it was on the purest integrity; his faith consisted in the simplest trust in the merits of the Saviour of men." [Funeral Address.] The writer, in conversation with him a few weeks before his death, heard him say that he was well assured that the Sands-st. people had missed their golden opportunity in not selling the property to the B'klyn City R. R. Co.; that he informed the official board that the officers of the company would pay $125,000, and that he would have urged its acceptance at the time, but for an apprehension that his brethren might suspect his motives, as he was largely interested in the financial affairs of the company. He was mar. in 1835, and with his companion " spent 49 yrs. of unbroken happiness." When Mr. Studwell, in 1847, was app'd trus. with Haynes, Connor, Gascoigne, Snedcker, and Chadwick, of the then new Dean-st. miss'n, Mrs. Studwell was a conspicuously active member of the Ladies' Home Mission, the society that supported the preachers who were trying to build up the new enterprise. John French, in a historic sketch, writes as follows concerning the Power-st. and Dean-st miss'n, out of which grew the Hanson Pl. ch. : " John J. Studwell and his excellent w., and, doubtless, others of this little band, would go from door to door, inviting the people to attend the services held in the second story of the sbrick tore on Powers-st. The result of their work will only be known when the Master rewards the faithful workers." [Hanson Pl. Quar., Apr., 1883.] An only child of J. J. Studwell, Mrs. Geo. W. Mead, resides in B'klyn. Mr. S. d., after a very brief illness, Dec. 12, 1884, age 71.—STUDWELL, ELIZABETH, wid. of John J.—**Sturgis, Ebenezer,** rem. by c., 1841.—**Sullivan, Mary,** mar. Mr. Johnson ; rem. by c., 1850.—**Summerfield, Mrs. Anna,** rem. by c., 1868.—***Summerfield, Wm.,** loc. pr. in this ch. ; father of the Rev. John Summerfield; b. in Devonshire, Eng., Apr. 12, 1770, eldest of 6 children ; possessed of mechanical and inventive genius; millwright near Wakefield, in Yorkshire; mar. Miss Amelia Depledge; rem. to Manchester; foreman in a factory; began to attend Meth. preaching; conv. under the labors of Jos. Benson at 21. "At once the current of his thoughts was turned. A strong yearning for the salvation of souls took possession of him. It was too late to prepare for the ministry. His business relations and the necessities of his rising family prevented that. Happily the Wesleyan Society presented an alternative. He became a loc. pr. and a cl. ldr. In these relations he found scope, somewhat, for his enthusiastic temperament, and for the singularly persuasive power for which he was always noted. Still he desired something more. If he only had a son !—*he* might do the work denied to him. So he prayed that his desire might be granted him, ' that he might have a son ; that his son might preach the gospel ; and that his name should be called John.' . . . The birth of this child, under such auspices, was an event in the household, in which none would share more tenderly and sweetly than the sisters, who were now old enough to enter into the desire and expectation of their parents. From all these sources, but chiefly from the sweet-spirited mother, who in her turn was thrown upon her boy in the months of her last sickness for companionship and sympathy, did our [John] Summerfield derive those natural gifts, which grace afterward so greatly magnified." [Rev. Dr Bottome, in Ch. Ad., Apr. 3, 1879.] John was b. while the family resided in Preston, Eng. Wm. Summerfield was a man of sanguine temperament, made unwise ventures in business, trusted partners by whom he was outwitted, and lost all his wealth. His financial troubles are referred to more than once by his son's biographer. He says: "Wm. Summerfield's sanguine temperament led him to miscalculate the results of his own upright intentions, when they failed to accord with that worldly prudence which is so generally, and in most cases so justly, the parent of success in temporal affairs. But that his moral integrity or his religious sincerity were justly impeachable, I have yet to learn." [Holland's Life of Summerfield, p. 342.] After his failure in Preston, Eng., he was for a time in Liverpool, where his w. d. in 1812, leaving 3 daughters and 1 son. It is said that John, then in his 14th yr., was the only child with her during the last 4 months of her life, and that her departure made such an impression upon his mind "that he never afterward spoke of the glorified throng to which she had ascended without mentioning her name." Mr. S. went to Ireland that yr., held positions of trust in Dublin and Cork, and after a few yrs., (1821,) emigrated with his family to N. York, where his eldest dau., Eleanor, had been some time settled with her husband, James Blackstock, Esq., a respectable cotton merchant. Mr. S. was a loc. pr. in Sands-st. ch. in 1822. He died of dysentery, Sept. 19, 1825, a few weeks after the death of his son John, age 55. The following touching letter was written by the father while confined by severe illness at Bloomingdale (now N. York city) to the son lying very low at the house of Dr. Beekman in Courtlandt-st., 4 m. away: "*Friday ev'g, May* 20, 1825. MY DEAR JOHN: The mysterious providence of our being separated by severe affliction, I sincerely feel, and were I not supported by the assurances that all things shall work together for our good my spirit would fail; but here I rest. My dear John, you are surrounded by friendly physicians who are deeply concerned for your bodily health, and probably so much as to prohibit the access of God's people. But remember, my dear, they cannot stand for you before God; therefore, any of God's people you may wish for, send for them. I know not how this our affliction will end; but it will be our highest wisdom to lay hold of God as he is revealed in his word. Your afflicted and affectionate father WM. SUMMERFIELD." When a messenger came, on the 13th of June, to inform Mr. S. of the death of his son, the sick man raised his head from his pillow, and without waiting for the message, said: "So, Mr. Sands, I perceive you are the bearer of melancholy tidings; my dear John is no more!" "After a solemn pause he raised his eyes heavenward and, with pious resignation, exclaimed, 'The Lord gave, and the Lord hath taken away,'—deeply agitated—then added, 'Blessed be the name of the Lord.'" [See Holland's Life of John Summerfield.] He wrote in his diary: "*June* 17, 1825. For the last 10 days my mind has been kept in hourly suspense. My dear John departed this life on Mon., the 13th of June, and was interred the next day beside his friend, the Rev. Wm. Ross. From the accounts I have received I have reason to thank God for his safe arrival in heaven, where I hope to meet him soon, and all my dear children that are left behind. I thank God for giving me such a son; may his death speak louder than all his preaching! Lord, prepare me to follow him to thy kingdom!" His remains were buried close by those of his son in the rear of the old white ch., and when the new ch. was built, their position was under the altar, as indicated by the tablet on the wall of the church, a fac-simile of which is here given. His grave-stone may now be seen (1885) leaning against the church. The inscription is probably inaccurate as to the date of his birth and his age at the time of his conversion. It is as follows: *William Summerfield, b. in Eng., 1771, conv. under Jos. Benson, and j. Meth. Soc'y at the age of 20; d. strong in faith praising God, Sept.* 19, 1825. *He was a man of unassuming manners and of almost unexampled self-denial. Like a faithful soldier he endured a great fight of afflictions. Well might* he be numbered among those of whom it is said, "*These are they which came up out of great tribulation.*" "*Happy sire, thy days are ended, all thy sufferings are o'er.*" *God has given him a title, through grace, to a kingdom which cannot be moved. He is arrived, thanks be to God! where not a wave of trouble rolls across his peaceful breast.* The Rev. Alex. M'Lean writes: "Wm. Summerfield was my wife's grandfather, and in the family he has the reputation of being a very holy man. I was present at the exhumation of his bones, and those of his son, the Rev. John Summerfield, from beneath the altar of the Sands-st. ch., and of their re-interment in the family plot at Woodlawn [in Oct., 1873.] Bp. Janes, Dr. Wakeley, Dr. Bottome, Dr. Roche, and others were present, and participated in the impressive services at Woodlawn. A fine marble shaft, erected by Wm. Summerfield's dau., Mrs. Eleanor Blackstock, marks the spot where the re-

mains of the noble father and the gifted son will rest until t
morning of the resurrection." [Letter to the author.] To]
Bottome we are indebted for the following interesting facts cc
cerning the less-distinguished members of this remarkable fa
ily. "Three sisters survived the father and bro. until only a f
weeks ago, [March, 1878,] when the younger one, (Anne,) M
Warner, and the elder one, (Eleanor,) Mrs. Blackstock, pass
away as they had lived, in great peace and joyful expectatio
leaving the 2d sister, Miss Amelia Summerfield, in advanc
age and partial blindness, to fill up the measure of her days, a
then to join the whole family in heaven. . . . Shortly after t
departure of the father and the son to the better land, M
Blackstock, with her husband, who had been greatly prosper
in business, retired to their beautiful mansion, near Port Chest
N. Y., known as 'Summerfield House,' where during that lo
period they both remained a beautiful exemplification of fam
piety and conjugal affection. In this hospitable home, whe
competence and refinement of a rare order had made the
dwelling, ministers of all denominations, and friends of learnir
found a charming retreat. Nor was it difficult to see in t
company of these estimable ladies how the multitudes hung
the lips of their remarkable bro. A peculiar sweetness of voic
elegance of diction, and fascination of manner, to which cultu
had given rich variety and substance, and to which the grace
God had added its completing beauty, gave to their convers
tion a rare attractiveness. Life, however, seemed to them aft
their bro.'s death but the brief supplement of a completed vo
So while still maintaining active Xn. charities, yet these we
done so silently and unobserved, that no one suspected the
devoted sisters of ever after moving from under the shadow
their brother's grave. The singular halo which rested on h
name, and perhaps more than all the hallowed memories of h
triumphal departure, gave a chastened quietness to every thir
they did, but cast no gloom on any. Whatever the convers
tion, whatever the employment, the presence of John was a
ways felt, and in the most natural and easy manner he would l
spoken of, not as one who was dead, but as one who, while l
was separated from them, yet filled so large a place in the
thoughts and affections, that they were still in compar
with him, and would share with him the ineffable glory in
which he had been only a short time before translated. It w;
beautiful to see how this thought grew upon them, and ho
while it pervaded every thing they did, yet hindered nothing
all their plans of devotion to his Master and theirs. In the fan
ily of Mrs. Warner, (the younger sister, Anne,) these tender qua
ities were specially illustrated in the careful training of he
children. Her ideal was always at hand; and had this advar
tage, that, being inwrought in her, it was an ever fresh and liv

ing one in her own beautiful life. Throwing into the domestic circle all the charm that personal grace and culture could give, she made piety attractive to her children, and her habits of religious life sat so easily in the household that to conform was but the natural bent of its members. Left motherless before she was 2 yrs. old, her bro. had always expressed a tender regard for her, and used to speak of her as 'a child of my own rearing.' Speaking afterward of, perhaps the most popular effort of his pulpit labors, his sermon in behalf of orphans, he says himself: 'Never did I speak with so much effect. I spoke from nature. Amelia and Anne were before my eyes.' His last message was to these two sisters, both of whom were at the time attending at the sick-bed of their father: 'Well—tell Amelia—tell Anne—tell them—all's perfection.' Perhaps more largely than either of these others, this sister Anne drank into the spirit of her sainted bro. And though after his death her education was directed chiefly by her elder sister, yet in the quick vivacity of intelligence, and easy acquirement of studies, specially in the accomplishment of voice and music, and all that pertained to polite literature, as well as in personal expression and manner, the hand of John left its most indelible pressure. In her younger days she was regarded as the finest private singer in the city, but resisted all offers of a public character, however flattering, and resolutely refused to sing but for the glory of God, either in the sanctuary or the culture of the home. She was mar. to E. H. Warner, Esq., a descendant of an old Knickerbocker family, whose grandfather, Geo. Warner, owned the famous 'old sail-loft' in Wm.-st., N.York, and in which the 'British' pressed him to make sails for the Eng. ships during the War of the Revo. After surviving her husband several yrs., Mrs. W. was suddenly taken ill of pneumonia while visiting her dau., Mrs. Rev. A. M'Lean, in Sing Sing, and after only a few days of quiet waiting she went, where her heart had ever been, to the home of the loved ones above. She d. on March 12, 1878, age 68. Meantime, at her home in Port Chester, Mrs. Blackstock was daily expecting her departure, but knew nothing of the death of her beloved Anne—the family deeming it imprudent to announce the event in her prostrated condition. So in all the calmness of her serene life she waited the hour of her ascension. Like her dear sister, maintaining to the last all the vigor and vivacity of her mental faculties, constantly engaging in conversation about heaven and its society until 'the weary wheels of life stood still,' she entered through the gates into the city, where among the first surprises that greeted her would be to find her youngest sister in heaven before her. Mrs. B. d. on March 24, 1878, in the 80th yr. of her age." [Article entitled "The Summerfields," in the Ch. Ad., Apr. 3, 1879.] Amelia, the only surviving child of Wm. Summerfield, still occupies the dear old homestead, where she communes with her friends " with that calm repose and assurance that is known only to those who are accustomed to sit together in heavenly places in Christ Jesus." From the " Summerfield House," on the 14th of Oct., 1884, she wrote to the author as follows : " I regret to say that no likeness of my father was ever taken. It would give me great pleasure to send one, were it in my power to do so. As to myself there is but little to say. I am the last surviving member of the family; and, having lost the sight of my left eye, am unable to be of much use in gathering information which would avail you in your laudable work, in which I most heartily wish you God-speed."—**Sutherland,** ——, rem. by c., 1870.—**Sutherland, Theo.,** rem.—*****Sutliff, Anna,** member in 1798.— **Sutton, Jno. R.** and **Leonora,** rem. by c., 1871.—**Sutton, Mary A.,** mar. Mr. Chambers ; rem. by c.—**Suydam, Henry,** rem.—**Swales, Thos. S.,** rem. by c., 1867 ; member 2 yrs.— **Swallow, Sarah,** rem.—**Swan, Margaret,** rem.— *****Sweeney, Jas.,** cl. ldr., 1831 ; b. in Phila.; left an orphan when a child ; conv. at about 19 yrs. of age, under the ministry of Martin Ruter; j. St. George's M. E. ch., Phila.; mar., 1825, Miss Margaret Connover. He was a rope-maker by trade. In B'klyn he was ldr. of the Red Hook Lane class of Sands-st. ch.; one of the 1st cl. ldrs. in Franklin ave. (now DeKalb ave.) ch., and a cl. ldr. in York-st. ch. ; ord. deacon in B'klyn, 1839, by Bp. Hedding; supply with E. Osborn, Hempstead Harbor cir., L. I., 1844; left that place for St. Louis, Mo., and became one of the founders of the Ebenezer ch., out of wh. grew the Union ch. of that city. He was 1 of the 7 loc. pr. in St. Louis who declared, in 1844, that they would not be identified with the Southern Ch. He was a man of pronounced antislavery principles. He deemed it his business to be always fighting the devil. " His ardor," says Jos. Tabor, in the Central Ch. Ad., " sometimes subjected him to the charge of imprudence, but his piety, we presume, was never questioned." J. L. Gilder, his pastor, said : " He was an earnest man—his piety glowed like a furnace." E. Osborn, his colleague in 1844, described him as " a good and useful man." He preached statedly in the Co. jail in St. Louis, standing in the lobby, while the prisoners were locked up in their cells, out of sight; then he was accustomed to go around and deliver to each prisoner, through a hole in the wall, a word of exhortation. He died of typhoid fever, in St. Louis, in 1849, age 52 ; 18 months later, his w. d. ; left 2 sons, Martin R. and James; the latter of Fleet-st. ch., B'klyn ; also 2 daughters, namely, Catharine, (Mrs. Gilbert H. Denyke,) member of York-st. ch. 40 yrs., and Emma, who d. in 1882, a member of Fleet-st. ch., unmarried.—**Sweezey, Elizabeth,** j. Cong. Meth. ch. (J. C. Green, pastor) in 1848.—******Sweezey, Janette,** d. in June, 1872.—**Swift, Amelia,** rem.—**Swift Caroline E.** ; see

Inslee.—**Swift, J. E.** and **Mrs. Mary J.**, rem. by c., 1867.—
*****Swift, Orrin,** of precious memory; S. S. t., cl. ldr., and S. S. sup't. His class in S. S. was an adult Bible class, largely attended. When succeeded in the charge of the S. S. by C. C. Leigh, a younger man, he asked the new sup't to assign him to any work in the school for wh. he might be desired—exhibiting an excellent spirit. He was rem. by c. in 1872; resided some time in Warwick, N. Y.; returned, and d. in B'klyn, in 1874, age 75, a member of the 7th ave M. E. ch.; bur. in "Greenwood"—same plot with Jos. Herbert.—****Julia A.,** his w., dau. of Jos. Herbert; S. S. t., and a true Xn.; d. 1859, age 50; bur. in "Greenwood." Two daughters: Elizabeth, and Caroline E.; see Inslee.—****Swim, Miss Sarah,** a co-laborer with Rob't Snow as the 1st female sup't.; held that position to the end of life, nearly 25 yrs.; lived in M. F. Odell's family; deformed from an injury received in childhood; very pious and intelligent; d. Feb. 9, 1852. Sec'y Cheetham penned an appreciative note in the S. S. record.—**Swithenbank, Mary,** rem. by c., 1873.

Taber, Albert P., rem. by c.—****Tabor, David,** d. about 1829.—****Talmage, Catharine,** d. "in triumph," 1837.—**Talmage, Frances,** mar.; see Harrison.—**Talmage, Hanford E.,** rem., 1846.—TALMAGE, MRS. VIRGINIA.—**Tarbell, D. T.,** cl. ldr., 1832; a physician; went to Newburgh.—**Tarbull, John T.,** cl. ldr., 1834.—**Tate, Mary J.,** dau. of Wm.; rem. by c., 1871; now Mrs. Heywood; resides in Phila.—**Tate, Sarah,** rem. by c., 1866.—*****Tate, Wm.,** b. in Belfast, Ireland; came to N. York in 1836; and was at different times connected with Willett-st., Forsyth-st., and 18th-st. M. E. chs. in that city. In B'klyn, a member of Sands-st. ch.; rem. by c. in 1866, and again in 1871 to 7th-ave. (now Grace) ch.; d. 1875, age 64; bur. in "Greenwood." His father is said to have been one of the 1st cl. ldrs. in Ireland under Mr. Wesley.—**Sarah E.,** his w.; rem. by c., 1866, and again in 1871; still living; resides with her children. A son, Major Augustus C., j. Hanson Pl. ch. during the revival in 1882.—**Tate, Wm. J.,** son of Wm.; S.S.t.; j. Sands-st. ch., 1865; rem. by c. to 7th-ave. (Grace) ch. 1871.—**Mary E.,** his w., is a dau. of Wm. M'Donald; was S.S.t. in Sands-st.; rem. by c., 1871.—**Tayleur, Jennie,** w of Wm.; j. the Episcopalians in 1877.—TAYLOR, HARRIET.—TAYLOR, MARY E.—**Taylor, Miss Mary E.,** rem. by c., 1879.—**Taylor, Mrs. Phœbe,** rem. by c., 1872.—TAYLOR, SAM'L.—**Taylor, Susan,** w. of Rev. George Taylor; also daughters of the same, **Josephine, Jennie L.,** and **Susie H.,** rem. by c., 1877.—**Taylor, Thos.,** rem. by c., 1839.—TAWS, MISS ADELINE.—TAWS, MRS. HARRIET.—**Taws, Hattie,** mar.; see Slade.—TEARE, MRS. MARY E.—**Tennant, Miss Lettie L.,** rem. by c., 1883.—**Thomas, Benj. F.,** rem. by c.—**Thomas, Edward,** S. S. t.; rem. to Wash'gt'n in 1849.—**Thomas,**

Edward and **Martha**, rem. by c., 1867.—**Thomas, Emma A.**, rem. by c., 1873.—**Thomas, Henrietta**, rem. by c., 1871.—**Thomas, Jas.**, rem. by c., 1866.—**Thomas, John E.**, rem. by c., 1871; member 6 yrs.—**Thomas, John M.**, rem. by c. to Phila.—**Thomas, Martha**, rem.—THOMAS, MARY.—THOMPSON, MISS LOUISA A.—**Thompson, Miss Mary**, rem. by c., 1868.—**Thompson, Minnie**, withdrew.—**Thompson, Thos.** and **Mrs. Eliza**, also **Miss Maggie E.** and **Miss Maria**, rem. by c., 1869.—THOMPSON, WM. C.—**Thompson, Wm. M.**, rem. by c., 1869.—THORNE, ABIA B., S. S. t., trus., and off. miss'y soc'y; b. in N. York; father a Quaker; mother a Meth., now of Sum'f'd ch., B'klyn. Mr. T. j. Greene-st. ch., N. York, in 1850; came to B'klyn in 1851, and j. Sands-st. ch.; has been sec'y of the board of trus. many yrs., and useful as a ldr. of singing in the S. S.—**Thorn, Britton**, S. S. t., 1876; rem. by c. to Sum'f'd ch., 1878.—**Thorn, Elizabeth**, rem. by c. to Sum'f'd ch., 1878.—**Thorn, Elizabeth S.**, rem, by c. to Sum'f'd ch., 1878.—**Thorn, Lavinia**, S. S. t.; see Gascoigne.—**Thorn, Mary T.**; see Fay.—**Thorp, Margaret**, rem. to N. York, 1821.—****Thorpe, Sarah**, w. of Thos.; native of Eng.; d. 1849, age 75. Her last words indicated her confidence in Christ. [W. H. Norris, in Ch. Ad.]—****Thorpe, Thos.**, cl. ldr. and S. S. t.; d. about 1843.—**Tieman, Elizabeth**, rem., 1848.—**Tilton, R. S.** and **Catharine**, rem. by c., 1866.—**Tindale, Lizzie**, rem. by c.—**Titus, Miss Amelia**, rem. by c., 1870.—***Titus, Ancel**, b. in Huntington, L. I., 1790; j. Sands-st. ch. in his youth; soldier in the War of 1812; about that time a dealer in crockery in B'klyn; delivered his goods in a basket; knew every man in B'klyn by name. (This statement he made to J. W. Barnhart, his pastor, many yrs. afterward.) He and his w. were among the original members of the Wesley ch., B'klyn, in wh. ch. he was std. and trus. for several yrs. He was more than 40 yrs. a faithful S. S. t.; excelled as a financier; used this talent in the interest of the ch. Mr. Barnhart says that during his term of 3 yrs. Ancel Titus gave $1,000 to the Wesley ch. The prayer-meeting and class-meeting he rarely missed. He was patient during his protracted sickness; repeatedly said to his pastor that all was well; d. Feb'y. 26, 1874, age 83.—**Titus, Jas.**, (colored,) exh., 1814.—**Titus, Martha K.**, 33 yrs. in Sands-st. ch.; 4 vrs. in Johnson-st. ch.; 7 or 8 yrs. in Wash'gt'n-st. ch.—**Titus, Sarah**, rem. by c. to E. B'klyn, 1848.—***Todd, Alfred**, rem.; finally became a member of Bedford ave. Bap. ch., B'klyn; d. 1883.—**Sarah A.**, his w., (it is said,) resides in B'klyn.—**Todd, Rebecca**, rem. by c., 1866.—**Tombs, Henrietta**, mar. Mr. Thomas.—**Tomlinson, Wm.**, rem. by c., 1869.—****Tomlinson, Wm.**, d. 1874.—**Tompkins, Catharine**, mar. Mr. Beekman.—**Tompkins, Hetty**, rem. by c., 1870.—**Tony, Alfred**, rem. by c., 1870.—

Towner, Martha, rem. by c., 1866.—****Traman, Elizabeth,** d. about 1818.—**Tricker, John,** rem. by c., 1872.—***Trim, John,** member in 1798.—TRIMBLE, LIZZIE M.—**Trimble, Wm.,** rem. to Forsyth-st., 1850; came from Primitive Meth.; at one time a loc. pr. in York-st. ch.—**Troop, Isabella J.,** mar. Mr. Arthur.—****Turner, Mrs. Deborah,** rem. to Balt., 1850; returned; d. 1871.—TURNER, M. M.—**Turner, Mary T.,** rem., 1847.—TURNER, MRS. MARY ANN.—**Turner, Rachel,** rem. by c., 1867.—**Turner, Rob't,** rem., 1849.—**Tuthill, Angeline,** rem. by c., 1866.—**Tuthill, Ann,** rem., 1846. —**Tuthill, David,** S. S. t. and loc. pr. in Sands-st. ch.; son of Sam'l B.; b. in B'klyn, Oct. 31, 1829; 2 yrs. in Wes. Univ.; was graduated, 1854, from the Univ. of the city of N. York; received the degree of A.M. in 1857; recommended to the traveling connection by the Sands-st q. conf. *Conf. Record:* 1858, (N. York East Conf.,) Clintonville, (Whitestone,) L. I.; 1859, ord. deacon,—(Cal. Conf.,) Los Angeles and El Monte, Cal.; 1860, Centerville; 1861, ord. elder,—Yreka; 1862, Auburn; 1863-68, pres't Female Collegiate Inst., Santa Clara; 1869, located. He was for 3 yrs. (1876-78) a member of the city council of Santa Cruz, Cal.; some yrs. previous to 1882 pres't of gas companies in Cal. and Oreg. He mar. C. Van Wyck Taylor, of San Francisco, Cal. Child: Jos. Thomas. Residence, (1884,) Santa Cruz, Cal. The trustees of the Whitestone ch., on his departure for Cal., passed highly commendatory resolutions. [Ch. Ad.] ****Tuthill, John B.,** son of Sam'l B.; d. Aug. 15, 1859, age 34. —**Tuthill, Maria,** rem. by c., 1868.—****Tuthill, Sam'l B.,** cl. ldr.; was conv. in Sands-st. ch. in 1830, (N. Levings, pastor.) For several yrs., until it ceased to exist, he was ldr. of the class of colored people in this ch., the last meeting of the class being held at his house. He was a generous man, and pious— the priest of his own household. [Ch. Ad.] He d. 1863, age 68.—****Ruth,** wid. of the above; d. Oct. 20, 1864, age 62; bur. in "Greenwood."—**Tweedle, Wm.,** rem. by c., 1873.

Ulrich, Henry, rem.—UTTER, SAM S., (name sometimes written Sam'l S.,) only son of Sam'l; S. S. t., S. S. sec., off. S. S. miss'y soc., S. S. sup't, and std.; b. in Albany, 1829; j. Sands-st. S. S. when a lad; has held office therein for more than 30 yrs. There is no one more actively enlisted in the work of the S. S., or better known among the little folks, than "Grandpa Utter." —UTTER, SARAH JANE, w. of the above; S. S. t.—**Utter, Sam'l,** S. S. t. and cl. ldr.; b. in Albany; conv. there, and j. M. E. ch.; rem. by c. to Allen-st. ch., N. York; thence to Sands-st., B'klyn, before 1843. His class was the young people's. He rem. by c. to Milford, Pa., where he d. in 1879, age 76. In person, slender; occupation, manufacturer of stoves.—**Thalia,** his wid.; S. S. t.; rem. by c., 1848. She is step-mother to Sam S. Utter.

Vail, Phœbe, w. of Sam'l, dau. of Jonas and Agaba Weeks, of Southold, L. I., and grandmother of Mrs. Thos. L. Rushmore and Mrs. Geo. I. Seney. After her father's death she moved with her mother to B'klyn. The death of her little bro. was the means of leading her to seek Christ when 11 yrs. of age. She d. in peace, 1830, age 44. [N. Levings, in Ch. Ad.]—VALENTINE, ABRAHAM.—Valentine, Annie W.,** j. Talmage's ch., 1878.—****Valentine, Ella,** d. 1882.—**Valentine, Emma,** rem., 1848.—**Valentine, Geo. W.,** S. S. t.; rem. to Cold Spring Harbor, L. I., 1848.—***Valentine, Israel,** rem. by c., 1839. One Israel Valentine was cl. ldr. in Woodbury, L. I., 1835; rem., 1837; his name is among the cl. ldrs. in Cold Spring Harbor, L. I., 1847; a carpenter by trade; built the Cold Sp. Harb. ch. in 1842; went to Cal.; returned; if report be true, he is dead.—****Valentine, Mrs. Lanie,** member of this ch. in 1796, and continued to be a faithful Meth. till her death in Aug., 1863, age 81. Maiden name, Lanie Ackerman; appears on Sands-st. membership roll, in 1798, as "Mrs. Leanah Smith." Her husband, John Smith, not a Meth., owned a rope-walk in B'klyn. He d. in 1807, age 30. [Headstone in old ch.-yd.] Their dau., Mrs. John W. DeGrauw, d. in B'klyn, 1884, at a very advanced age. Mrs. Smith was mar. to a 2d husband, Smith Valentine by name, who d. 1820. She was thenceforward a wid. 43 yrs.; blessed, however, with uninterrupted health and uniform buoyancy of spirit; much attached to her friends, of whom she had many; and to the last taking great delight in little "tea parties" at her home. She d. at the residence of her son-in-law, in B'klyn; bur. in "Greenwood." While living in N. York she was a member of Forsythst. ch. for a time; nevertheless, her connection with the Sandsst. ch. covered a period of nearly 60 yrs. She outlived all her early associates in the ch. L. S. Weed wrote a brief obituary for the Ch. Ad.—****Valentine, Mary J., (Stryker,)** w. of Sam'l; d. 1867, age 31.—**Valentine, Rebecca,** mar; see Schenck.—**Van Cott, Cornelius,** is a son of Gabrael Van Cott, who was a prominent member at different times of the Allen-st. and Forsyth-st. chs. in N. York, and of the York-st. ch. in B'klyn. His mother d. when he was a child. He was b. in N. York; rem by c. from Sands-st. ch.; was cl. ldr. some time in York-st. ch.; resides in B'klyn, E. D.; business in N. Y. P. O.—**Van Cott, Joshua Marsden,** S. S. t., and one of the founders of the Young Men's Miss'y Soc'y. [See page 24 of this work.] He is bro. of Cornelius; b. in N. York city; was a member of Sandsst. ch. several yrs.; then of Pacific-st.; thence rem. to Ch. of the Pilgrims, (Cong'l,)—Dr. R. S. Storrs, pastor. He mar. ***Mary E.,** dau. of the Rev. Thos. Burch, who, with her husband, rem. by c. to Pacific-st. ch. After her death, some years ago, he mar. Jane S., sister to his first w. Mr. Van Cott is a prominent lawyer, actively engaged in public affairs; nominated several years ago for comptroller of the State of N. Y. He performed a most excellent work as pioneer and principal mover in the formation of the L. I. Histor. Soc'y, of which he is now an active and efficient v.-pres't.—**Vandeveer, Elizabeth**, dau. of Abraham; S. S. t. and S. S. supt.; rem. by c. to Sum'f'd ch., 1880.—**Vanderveer, Elizabeth F.**, S. S. t.; d. about 1829. —**Vanderveer, Henry**, and **Adeline**, his w.; withdrew.— *Vanderveer, Jane, is well-remembered as the wid. of Abraham Vanderveer, who, though a member of a Dutch Ref. ch., was for yrs. prominently identified with the Sands-st. S. S. She j. Sands st. ch. in 1819, and after being a member 60 yrs., having changed her residence, rem. by c., 1880, to Sum'f'd ch. She d. 1883, in the 94th yr. of her age. She was a faithful and devout Xn. It was the author's privilege to converse with her about the Sands-st. ch. of olden time, and many missing links in the chain of facts were supplied by her excellent memory. She was mother-in-law to M. F. and S. U. F. Odell.—**Vanderveer, Rich'd F.**, S. S. t., 1864; d. 1867.—**Van Duzer, Sarah**, mar. Mr. Creed.—**Van Dyke, Josephine**, rem. by c. —**Van Every, Jane**, rem.—**Van Horne, Mrs. Bethia**; see Dunkinson.—**Vanier, Margaret**, member Yellow Hook (Bay Ridge) class, 1822.—**Vaningen, Sarah**, went to the Baptists.— **Van Keuren, Margaret**, d.—**Van Ness, John**, b. in Fulton Co., N. Y., in 1819; left fatherless at 10; came to B'klyn in his 17th yr. He was at first employed in a store kept by a Mr. Jacobs. Through the influence of Mr. Powell, (who was at one time mayor of B'klyn,) he secured a position in the dry-goods house of Mercein & Carpenter, on Fulton-st. When about 19 he opened a private school; followed teaching 10 yrs., and some of his pupils are now respected citizens of B'klyn. He studied medicine while teaching, and entered at length upon the practice of his profession. He joined Sands-st. ch. when a youth; was commissioned by Supts. Herbert and Swift to go out to Cross Roads as a S. S. miss'y; walked 6 m. each Sabbath; conducted S. S. in the A.M.; the loc. prs., Ducker, Leigh, and others, preached in the P.M. This pioneer work laid the foundation of the Cook-st. ch. He transferred his membership to Wash'gt'n-st. ch.; thence to Franklin ave. (DeKalb ave.) ch.; thence (1882) to Nostrand ave. ch. An active helper in building the Wesley and the Greene ave. M. E. chs.—**Van Note, Mary**, d. about 1832.—**Van Pelt, Elizabeth**, was, in 1822, a member of the Yellow Hook (Bay Ridge) class of the Sands-st. ch.—**Van Pelt, Jas.**, a member of Yellow Hook (Bay Ridge) class in 1822.—*Van Pelt, Thos., 1st treas. of the original board of trustees, (1794.)—*Sarah, his w.; early member, perhaps the same as the Sarah Van Pelt below. Peter Rickhow, son of Thos. and Sarah Van Pelt, was bap. in 1797 by Jos. Totten. [Records.]—**Van Pelt, Walter**, in 1822 a member of

Yellow Hook (Bay Ridge) class.—**VanVoorhis, Rich'd,** trus. and cl. ldr.; went to York-st. ch., where he was cl. ldr., in 1838. —*****Van Voorhis, Uriah,** b. in E. Norwich, L. I.; j. Sands-st. ch. and rem.; d., it is said, about 1880; did not retain his membership in the ch.—******Phœbe,** his 1st w., sister to Mrs. J. Rossell, was a native of N. J.; became a member of the Prot. Meth. Ch.; coming to B'klyn, j. Sands-st. ch.; d. 1841, age 23; funeral serm. by J. A. Edmonds—2 Sam. xiv, 14; bur. in E. Norwich, L. I. [P. C. Oakley, in Ch. Ad.]—**Van Zant, Ann Eliza,** withdrew.—**Van Zant, Jennie L.,** rem. by c. to Embury ch., 1880.—VARNUM, MRS. JENNIE.—VEERLAND, TILLIE.—**Vernam, Adeline,** mar.; see Vanderveer.—VERNAM, REMINGTON.—VERNAM, ELIZABETH.—******Vey, Honora,** a native of Newfoundland, where her husband, Geo. Vey, was one of the earliest loc. pr. T. Watson Smith [Methodism in the Eastern British Provinces, p. 283] states that Geo. Vey, a young man of piety and zeal, was the founder of Meth. in Port de Grave, N. F., in 1791. Mrs. Vey's church membership in St. John's, in N. York, and in Sands-st., B'klyn, extended over a period of 60 yrs. Her memory was well stored with Scripture truths. She d. June 3, 1850, age 87, and was bur. in "Greenwood." [R. C., in Ch. Ad.]—*****Vining, Geo. J.,** trus.

George J. Vining

in Sands-st. ch.; was b. in Simsbury, Conn., Aug. 31, 1801; came to B'klyn at 19 to seek employment, $5 being the sum total of his cash capital. He was engaged as a tinsmith, and was diligent, honest, and prosperous. His early identification with the Sands-st. people was a help to him in every way, and he was truly a blessing to the ch. "Few men," says his memorial, "have been more thoroughly in sympathy with aggressive ch. work. His benevolent spirit was manifested in the liberal bestowment of his means upon chs. of B'klyn and elsewhere. The Sands-st., Wash'gt'n-st., and York-st. chs., he largely aided. Highly complimentary resolutions were passed by the Sands-st. official board on Bro. Vining's departure from B'klyn." The following note, written by him and found among his papers after his death, is valuable as a matter of history, and serves to commemorate his ever-active interest in the ch. "On Sept. 12, 1843, the cor.-stone of the Sands-st. brick ch. was laid by Rev. Dr. Levings. I made the box that contains the records, and sealed it up, and helped lay the cor.-stone. . . . In 1863, in making some alterations to the building in Prospect-st., cor Adams, by those who owned it, the cor-stone of the S. S. building was taken out. I obtained it and placed it in the wall of the lecture-room of the S. S. building on High-st., and I think it is there still." He rem. by c., in 1868, to Mt. Kisco, N. Y., and immediately upon his arrival gave $500 to the ch. in that place. When his faculties failed, his Xn. ardor suffered no decline. "He often wandered," says his pastor, "to the house of God, and when no services were being held, sat for hours on the steps, or within the sanctuary, peaceful and happy. The story of his work done for God and Methodism had left such an impression upon his mind, that it was ever present. . . . At the last meeting he attended he repeated 'The Xn. Soldier;' all hearts were moved when with great earnestness he said: 'Our wages will be crowns of gold, and joys of heaven that can't be told.'" Through grace he manifested, in a marked degree, a patient, tranquil spirit. He fell asleep Aug. 28, 1882, almost 81 yrs. of age.—***Delinda (Fuller),** his w., was b. in Simsbury, Conn.; mar. May 14, 1828; a faithful w., a fond mother, an active Xn.; d. of heart disease on the 47th anniversary of her marriage, May 14, 1875, age 69. Husband and wife are bur. in Oakdale cem., Mt. Kisco, N. Y.; a granite monument marks their resting place. Three children survive: Edward A. Vining; Mrs. Sam'l Raymond; Mrs. G. N. Fisher. One grandson, Fred. Vining Fisher, is a loc. pr., a student in Drew Sem., preparing for the itinerant ministry.—**Vining, Georgiana,** mar.; see Fisher.—**Vining, Lucy,** rem.

Waddle, Margaret, rem. by c., 1850.—**Wadsworth, C.,** rem., 1847. One Chas. D. Wadsworth was a S. S. t., 1841.—**Wadsworth, Harriet,** rem. by c., 1848, to N. York.—**Wadsworth, Mary,** rem. to N. York, 1848.—**Wadsworth, Sarah,** mar., 1848; see Stillwell.—**Wales, Chas. T.,** S. S. t., and **Maria Ann,** rem. to Cleveland, O., 1849.—****Wales, Phœbe,** d. Aug. 9, 1882.—WALES, SADIE.—WALKER, HELEN.—WALKER, M. J.—**Walker, Sarah,** rem. by c., 1850, to Cen-

tenary ch.—Walker, W. A. and Sarah, rem. by c., 1869.—
Wall, Edward, d. 1873.—Wall, Elizabeth, mar. and d.;
see Compton.—WALL, MRS. JANE.—Wall, Wm., cl. ldr.,
1846.—**Wallace, Peter C., from Eng.; a butcher; d. "in the
Lord."—**Margaret, his w.; d. 1881.—Wallace, Wm., rem.
—Walling, Holmes, rem.—WALLING, MRS. MARY E.—
*Ward, Eleanor, member in 1798.—WARD, ELIZABETH.—
Ward, Sarah, rem. by c., 1849.—WARDWELL, MRS. FRANCES.—Ware, Maria, rem. by c., 1848.—Warner, Chauncey,
rem. to Cal., 1849.—**Warner, Deborah, d. 1838.—**Warrington, John A., partially deranged from sickness; d. in
Phila., 1849.—WASSON, A.—Waterbury, Silleck E. and
Mary E., rem. by c., 1879.—Waterman, Mrs. Rebecca,
rem. by c., 1869.—WATERS, LA FAYETTE.—WATERS,
SOPHRONIA.—Waters, Margaret, rem. by c. to Nashville,
Tenn., 1848.—**Waters, Martha J., d. 1865.—Waters,
Mary A., rem. by c., 1872.—Waters, Philip, Sr., a std.;
Mrs. Eliza, Philip, Jr., Jennie, and Carrie, all rem. by c.,
1880.—Watson, Sarah G., went to the Baptists.—Way,
Jos. H., S. S. t. and off. S. S. miss. soc.; rem. by c., 1852.—
Mary Augusta (Bonnell), w. of the above; rem. by c.—
WEAVER, GEO. B.—WEAVER, CLARA A.—Webb, Ebenezer, T., cl. ldr., 1833.—Webb, Frances, rem., 1849.—Webb,
Jas. and Mary Ann, rem.—*Webb, Jos., member in 1798.—
Weck, Jacob, S. S. t., 1849. He became loc. pr., entered the
itinerant ministry, and served several German chs. *Conf. Record:*
1854, (N. York Conf.,) N. York, Bloomingdale, (now 40th-st.;)
1855, L. I. German cir.; 1856, ord. deacon; 1856–57, Elizabeth,
N. J.; 1858, ord. elder,—West Balt.; 1859–60, Scranton, Pa.;
1861–62, Melrose; 1863, excluded from the ch.—Weed,
Eliza, rem. by c., 1865.—Weed, Roxanna, mar.; see Cozine.
—WEEKS, CHARLOTTE, w. of Isaac.—Weeks, Eliza, rem.
by c., 1865; member a short time.—WEEKS, ISABEL.—
Weeks, Mathilda, d. 1882.—Weeks, Washington,
d. 1882.—Weeks, Wm., rem.—WELLINGTON, ADLICA
G.—**Wells, Ann, "d. in the Lord," 1822.—Wells, Dan'l
T., S. S. t., 1833; cl. ldr., 1835.—WELLS, DEBORAH.—
**Wells, Mrs. Elizabeth, d. of cholera, 1849. Three of her
children d. at the same time.—WELLS, EMMA.—**Wells,
Jeremiah, b. on the east end of L. I.; a Meth. nearly 70 yrs.;
cl. ldr. in Sands-st. ch. about 1806; trus., 1825; at that time a
carpenter; some time chief engineer of the fire dept. [Stiles'
Hist. B'klyn, vol. ii, p. 277.] He was one of the founders of
Johnson-st. ch. in 1839, but seems to have returned to old
Sands-st. ch., within whose fold he d., beloved and honored, in
the yr. 1877, age 84. He is bur. in "Greenwood."—Mary, his
wid., is a dau. of Burdet Stryker, and half sister to Hannah and
Burdet Stryker. She is with her dau., Mrs. Montgomery Whit-

lock, the only dau. who grew to maturity.—WELLS, LIBBIE M. —**Wells, Maria,** rem.—*****Wells, Parshall,** (1st,) b. in Southold, L. I.; moved when a child to a farm-house on what is now Nostrand ave., B'klyn; conv. young; had a sweet voice, and sang in the choir. He was retiring, modest, and highly esteemed; d. of cholera in 1832, age 42; bur. in Sands-st. ch.-yard.—*****Cornelia,** his wid., was dau. of Gen. Seely, who was aid to Geo. Washington. She finished her course with joy in 1872, age 84. —WELLS, PARSHALL, (2d.)—WELLS, SARAH.—WELLWOOD, JANE.—WENGOROVIUS, GRACE.—WENGOROVIUS, NELLIE.—WENGOROVIUS, WM. R., S. S. t.— WESTERBAND, SUSAN.—WHEATLEY, FRANCIS, Jr.— **Wheatley, Francis, Sr.,** rem. by c.—**Wheaton, Danielina,** rem.—**Wheeler, Harvey** and **Phœbe,** rem. by c., 1869. —**White, James Duncan,** rem. by c., 1883.—**White, Mary,** rem. by c. to Centenary ch., 1849.—WHITEFORD, MARIA. —**Whitley, Frances,** rem. by c.—WHITLOCK, ANDREW. —WHITLOCK, ANN ELIZA.—WHITLOCK, SAM'L M.— WHITNEY, DAN'L D., off. S. S. miss. soc., cl. ldr., std., and trus.; b. in Woodbury, L. I.; came to N. York in 1837; to B'klyn in 1839; entered the grocery store of Thos. J. Gerald as clerk; succeeded him in the business in 1843, and has continued in the same more than 40 yrs. He has been for some time pres't of the Hamilton Fire Ins. Co., in New York. Mrs. Whitney is a dau. of Jas. Titus, of Glen Cove, L. I.—**Whitney, Elizabeth,** rem. by c., 1849.—WHITNEY, GERALD.—WHITNEY, MARY E.—WIDINGTON, MARY.—**Wiggins, Alice,** rem. by c., 1833.—**Wiggins, Guy C.,** rem.—**Wiggins, Sarah,** mar. Mr. Morley, and rem.—**Wightman, Isabella,** rem.—WILKINS, SARAH.—**Wilkinson, John,** rem. by c. to N. York, 1848.—** **Wilkinson, Nancy,** d.—**Wilkinson, Wm.** and **Nancy,** rem. by c., 1867.—****Willersdorf, Israel,** cl. ldr. about 1852. Said to have d. a Meth., in Orange Co., N. Y. [F. G. Reast.]—**Williams, Deborah C.,** rem. by c., 1871.—**Williams, Edward,** member Yellow Hook (Bay Ridge) class, 1822.—WILLIAMS, HARRIET.—**Williams, John,** rem. by c., 1848.—**Williams, John S.,** rem. by c., 1880. —****Williamson, Susanna,** d. 1865.—WILSON, ANNA. —****Wilson, Catharine,** d. in joyful hope, 1807.—****Wilson, Fanny,** d.—WINNER, ADAM S.—WINNER, ANNA N., w. of the above.—WINNER, REBECCA.—**Winters, Mrs. Hannah Maria,** wid. of John G.; rem. to Hanson Pl.; d. in May. 1881, age 61; bur. in "Cypress Hills."—**Winters, Sarah J.,** mar.; see Palmer.—**Winters, Josephine V.,** received into Sands-st. ch. by J. Miley; rem. by c. to Fleet-st. ch.; thence to Hanson Pl.; thence to Nostrand ave. ch.; mar. A. Perinchief.—**Wintres, Dan'l H.,** rem.—**Wintringham, Thos.,** rem. by c. to Cal., 1877.—WINSLOW, JOHN.—

WOLFF, MISS ESTHER.—**Wood, Chas.** and **Eliza**, rem. by c., 1875.—WOOD, HENRY CLAY.—**Wood, Henry C.**, rem. by c., 1875; member a short time.—**Wood, Jane**, mar. Mr. Compton.—**Wood, Mary C.**, rem. by c., 1875.—**Wood, Mary S.**, rem., 1848.—**Wood, Thos. W.**, withdrew.—WOODHOUSE, MISS.—**Woodward, Harriet**, rem. by c., 1866.— ****Woolsey, Electa**, d. Feb. 14, 1808. (See sketch of the Rev. Elijah Woolsey in this vol., pp. 179–183.)—****Worman, Mary Ann**, d. 1826.—WORTHMAN, REBECCA.—**Woodward, Harriet**, rem. by c., 1865.—**Wright, Adam**, rem. about 1819. —**Wright, Amelia**, rem. by c. to Johnson-st. ch., 1850.— **Wright, C.**, rem.—**Wright, Dan'l**, father-in-law of J. E. and Solomon H. Hanford; d. 1858, age 73.—****Sarah (Farrington)**, his w.; d. about 1834.—****Wright, John**, S. S. t.; "d. in peace," 1849, age 24; bur. in "Greenwood." [W. H. Norris, in Ch. Ad.]—***Wright, Jno. F.**, son of Dan'l; j. Sands-st. ch. when a lad. At the time of his death he was S. S. sup't. in John-st. ch., N. York.—****Wylie, Mary**, d.—**Wyman, D and L.**, rem. by c., 1867.

Yates, Ellen S., mar.; see Power.—YOUNG, GERTRUDE A.—****Young, Jane**, d. 1852.—**Young, Margaret**, mar. Mr. Waddle.—YOUNG, MARIA E.—YOUNG, WALTER.—****Young, Wm.**, d. 1849.—**Youngs, Benj.**, rem.

This volume from the
Cornell University Library's
print collections was scanned on an
APT BookScan and converted
to JPEG 2000 format
by Kirtas Technologies, Inc.,
Victor, New York.
Color images scanned as 300 dpi
(uninterpolated), 24 bit image capture
and grayscale/bitonal scanned
at 300 dpi 24 bit color images
and converted to 300 dpi
(uninterpolated), 8 bit image capture.
All titles scanned cover to
cover and pages may include
marks, notations and other
marginalia present in the
original volume.

The original volume was digitized
with the generous support of the
Microsoft Corporation
in cooperation with the
Cornell University Library.

Cover design by Lou Robinson,
Nightwood Design.

Made in the USA
Middletown, DE
27 August 2017